FUNDAMENTALS OF MARKETING

Fundamentals of Marketing provides a sound appreciation of the fundamentals of the theory and practice of marketing. It critically evaluates the effectiveness of different marketing strategies and approaches using case studies drawn from a cross section of sectors.

Case studies include:

- Coke's distinct image in Trinidad
- Role of *guanxi* in Chinese buying negotiations
- Technology development: Apple Mac to iMac and iPod
- Brand personality: image of FCUK
- Virgin's use of direct sales in financial services
- New product global success of dumpy bottles
- Rebranding New Zealand merino wool
- Online retail pricing
- Changing image of Dyson cleaner
- Dyno-Rod franchising
- Charity shop achievements
- Introducing Stoats Porridge Bars
- Internet competition with traditional channels: Amazon.com versus Barnes & Noble

Featuring a website to run alongside the text providing student and lecturer resources, this text conveys the main principles of marketing in a challenging yet accessible manner and provides the reader with insights into the workings of marketing today.

Marilyn A. Stone is Senior Lecturer and Director of the International Management degree at Heriot-Watt University, Edinburgh.

John Desmond is Reader in Management at St Andrews University, Scotland.

D0185302

FUNDAMENTALS OF
MARKETING

Marilyn A. Stone

and

John Desmond

With a contribution by
J.B. (Ian) McCall

Routledge
Taylor & Francis Group

LONDON AND NEW YORK

First published 2007 by Routledge
2 Park Square, Milton Park, Abingdon, Oxon OX14 4RN

Simultaneously published in the USA and Canada
by Routledge
270 Madison Ave, New York, NY 10016

Routledge is an imprint of the Taylor & Francis Group, an informa business

Typeset in Times New Roman and Helvetica by
Florence Production Ltd, Stoodleigh, Devon
Printed and bound in Great Britain by
MPG Books Ltd, Bodmin, Cornwall

British Library Cataloguing in Publication Data
A catalogue record for this book is available from the British Library

Library of Congress Cataloging in Publication Data
Stone, Marilyn A.
    Fundamentals of marketing/Marilyn A. Stone and John Desmond.
        p. cm.
    Includes bibliographical references and index.
    1. Marketing.   I. Desmond, John, 1952–.   II. Title.
    HF5415.S872 2006
    658.8–dc22   2006015003

ISBN10: 0–415–37096–5 (hbk)
ISBN10: 0–415–37097–3 (pbk)
ISBN10: 0–203–03078–8 (ebk)

ISBN13: 978–0–415–37096–7 (hbk)
ISBN13: 978–0–415–37097–4 (pbk)
ISBN13: 978–0–203–03078–3 (ebk)

Marilyn Stone dedicates her contribution of this work to her family, Phil, Juliette and Anthony, and to her parents, Nuala and Robert, in recognition of all the support that they have given to her in pursuit of an appreciation of international marketing. She also wishes to acknowledge gratefully all those at the Western General Hospital, Edinburgh whose efforts enabled the book to be completed.

John Desmond dedicates his contribution to his wife, Fiona, to thank her for her patience and encouragement.

CONTENTS

ILLUSTRATIONS

TABLES

CASE STUDIES

PREFACE

This book aims to provide a comprehensive introduction to the subject of marketing. While it covers most of the topics found in other texts it also provides a solid theoretical background which can act as a springboard to discuss contemporary issues and controversies within marketing theory and practice.

The text is focused on the mainstream functionalist account based on psychological theory, rather than alternative sociological and anthropological texts on offer. As psychology acts as the bedrock of most explanations of consumer behaviour, a range of psychological theories have been examined, with limited discussion of the associated controversies. In this respect Freudian theory, behaviourism and cognitive learning theory are detailed in an early chapter. This preliminary exposition informs the subsequent coverage of involvement and brand loyalty, where different theoretical explanations, such as cognitive and behaviourist theories, are discussed alongside synthetic accounts. The overall aim is to disabuse students of the belief that there is only one way of understanding marketing activities and to enable them to compare and contrast different accounts.

While the text is written from a European perspective, reflecting the point of origin of its contributors, it is intended for use by students from any country or background.

The text has been developed and written by Marilyn Stone, Heriot-Watt University and John Desmond, St Andrews University, ably supported by J.B. (Ian) McCall and by Sarah Dougan. Although all the others have discussed at length the text, particular responsibility for the individual chapters has been as follows. John Desmond: Chapter 1, 'Marketing: development and scope of the subject', Chapter 2, 'Strategic marketing and the planning process', Chapter 3, 'Consumer buyer behaviour', Chapter 4, 'Industrial buyer behaviour' (supported by Marilyn Stone), Chapter 5, 'Segmentation, targeting and positioning (supported by Sarah Dougan)', Chapter 6, 'Branding', Chapter 7, 'Product' (supported by Sarah Dougan and Marilyn Stone), Chapter 9, 'Promotion' (supported by Marilyn Stone), and Chapter 11, 'Virtual Marketing'. Marilyn Stone: Chapter 5, 'Marketing research' (supported by John Desmond), Chapter 10, 'Place: channels of distribution', and Chapter 13, 'Marketing planning and implementation'. J.B. (Ian) McCall and Marilyn Stone: Chapter 8, 'Pricing'. Once the draft chapters were prepared, the authors read each other's contribution to link the chapters of the text. Examples have been drawn from a range of countries and situations, which it is hoped will help students to relate to the issues being discussed. Marilyn Stone undertook the overall editing of the text.

ACKNOWLEDGEMENTS

Much appreciation is given to others who have supported the preparation of the marketing text, including Professor Chris Eynon, Managing Director of TNS (System Three), and Professor John Fernie, Director of Heriot-Watt University, School of Management and Languages. Thanks are due to all the others who encouraged the authors to complete the book. In particular, thanks are due to Francesca Heslop and Emma Joyes for their encouraging editing support. Hazel Loeb gave useful research assistance in the preparation of the initial draft of the distributed learning material. Thanks should also go to our students over the years who, with their enthusiasm, have encouraged and stimulated our interest in teaching marketing in its various guises. Finally, thanks go to our families and friends, who have supported the process of getting the text to press. Despite all the support and effort made to prepare a fair assessment of the topic of marketing as opined by myself, John Desmond and J.B. (Ian) McCall, the ultimate responsibility for what has been written rests with the authors. While it is intended that this should be as accurate as possible, any mistakes or omissions that may have been made are of our own making and not of those others who have supported us in the task.

Marilyn A. Stone
John Desmond

ABBREVIATIONS

A&R	artists and repertoire
ABC	Audits Bureau of Circulation
ABMRC	Association of British Market Research Companies
ACORN	A Classification of Residential Neighbourhoods
ACS	Association of Charity Shops
AGB	Audits of Great Britain
AIDA	Awareness, Interest, Desire and Action model
AMSO	Association of Market Survey Organizations
ARG	Argos Retail Group
ARS	Audience Reaction Service (British Broadcasting Corporation)
ATM	Automatic teller machines (cash machine)
ATR	Awareness, Trial and Reinforcement
BBC	British Broadcasting Corporation
BEUC	European Consumer Organization
BMRA	British Market Research Association
BMRB	British Marketing Research Bureau (market research agency)
BRAD	British Rate and Data
BSA	British Sandwich Association
BSE	bovine spongiform encephalophy
CAPI	computer-assisted personal interviewing
CASI	Computer-assisted self-interviewing
CATI	Computer-assisted telephone interviewing
CAWI	Computer-assisted Web interviewing
CD	compact disc
CEE	Central and Eastern Europe
CIM	Chartered Institute of Marketing
CIP	cognitive information processing
CIS	Commonwealth of Independent States
CJMR	Carrick James Market Research (market research agency)
CME	computer-mediated environment
CS	conditioned stimulus
CSD	carbonated soft drinks
DAGMAR	Designing Advertising Goals; Measuring Advertising Response model

DJ	disc jockey
DVD	digital video disc
DVR	digital video recorder
ECR	effective consumer response
EDI	electronic data interchange
EDP	electronic data processing
EFAMRO	European Federation of Associations of Market Research Organizations
EFTPOS	electronic funds transfer point of sale
EPOS	electronic point of sale
ESOMAR	European Society for Opinion and Market Research
EST	Erhard Seminar Training
EU	European Union
FCB	Foote, Cone & Belding (advertising agency)
FMCG	fast-moving consumer goods
FRUGGING	Funding under the guise of marketing research (for charities)
FTC	Federal Trade Commission
FTP	file transfer protocol.
GB	Great Britain (England, Scotland and Wales)
GCC	Gulf Co-operation Council
GDP	gross domestic product
GELS	General Electric Lighting Division
GI	glycemic index (diet)
GRP	gross rating points (of US television)
GUS	Great Universal Stores
H&M	Hennes & Mauritz (Swedish youth fashion clothes retailer)
HBA	Health and Beauty Audit
HBOS	Halifax and Bank of Scotland
HERO	health experience research online (YouGov panel)
HOG	Harley-Davidson Owners' Group
HTML	hyper-text markup language
HTTP	hypertext transfer protocol
IMRG	Interactive Media in Retail Group
INTV	international television research group
IPA	Institute of Practitioners in Advertising
ISP	internet service provider
ITCA	Independent Television Companies' Association
JICNARS	Joint Industry Committee for National Readership Surveys
JICREG	Joint Industry Committee for Regional Press Readership
JIT	just-in-time
JND	just noticeable difference
KFC	Kentucky Fried Chicken
LP	long-playing (record)

M&S	Marks & Spencer
MEAL	Media Expenditure Analysis
MCIF	marketing customer information files
MIS	marketing information system
MNC	multinational corporation
m.p.h.	miles per hour
MRP I	materials requirements planning
MRP II	manufacturing resource planning
MRS	Market Research Society
MUD	multi-user domain
NFS	network file system
NHS	National Health Service
NOP	National Opinion Poll (market research agency)
NRS	National Readership Survey
OECD	Organization of Economic Co-operation and Development
OFT	Office of Fair Trading
P&G	Procter & Gamble
PBG	Pepsi Bottling Group
PCB	printed circuit board
PDA	personal digital assistant
PETV	Pan-European Television Research (consortium of cable and satellite operators) replaced by INTV
POS	point of sale
POSTAR	Poster Audience Research body
PR	public relations
PSP	PlayStationPortable
PSYBT	Prince's Scottish Youth Business Trust
R&D	research and development
RAJAR	Radio Audience Joint Advertising Research
RBS	Royal Bank of Scotland
RDU	remote detection unit
ROI	return on investment
SAFE	Sustainable Agriculture Food and Environment
SEU	subjected expected utility
SIC	Standard Industrial Classification
SMR	Sender–Messenger–Receiver model (communications)
SOS	Scottish Omnibus Survey (TNS)
SRI	Stanford Research Institute
STAMP	Satellite Television Audience Measurement Partnership
sUGGING	selling under the guise of marketing research
SWOT	strength and weaknesses/opportunities and threats (analysis model)
TARIS	Television Audience Research and Information System
TNS	Taylor Nelson Sofres (market research agency)

TNS SOS	TNS Scottish Opinion Survey
TVR	television response rate
UCS	unconditioned stimulus
UN	United Nations
URL	uniform resource locator
US	United States (of America)
USP	unique selling proposition
VALS	Values and Lifestyles
VAT	value added tax
VF	Vanity Fair
VOIP	voice over Internet protocol.
VSS	Veronis Suhker Stevenson (US private equity firm)
WAN	wide area network

INTRODUCTION

A functionalist approach
to marketing

Bell (1966) discusses marketing's debt to systems theory, in particular to cybernetics, 'the science of control and communication in the animal and in the machine', first developed by Norbert Wiener. This focuses attention on marketing as part of a social system. Generally, the approach used in this text is managerialist, focused on the perspective of the firm rather than that of the customer. Both firms and customers are considered in relation to the environment in which they seek to survive. The view is that firms can best survive when they seek to ensure the survival and satisfaction of the customers on whom they depend. This approach enables the following concepts to be explored:

■ The role played by marketing in helping firms control and successfully adapt to the environment by means of a focus on customer needs. Customer orientation plays a key role in the satisfaction of organizational goals, usually profit.
■ The behaviour of firms when competition is intense and survival is the goal. A focus on competitors including the destruction of a competitor may best ensure the continued existence of the organism (Bell, 1966: 65).
■ The role of marketing in its wider social and environmental context.

This functionalist approach follows the managerialist focus of the marketing 'mainstream' orientation. It helps to understand why marketing has a paradoxical orientation both to the customer and to warfare; however, it also enables looking outside of the relatively narrow context to those wider issues which are the concerns of macro-marketing, social marketing and 'new' approaches such as relationship marketing. The approach taken in the text is to focus on traditional marketing while incorporating aspects of relationship marketing and internal marketing. Figure 1.1 summarizes some of the relationships between these with respect to the different types of relationships that can exist between marketers, other organization members and customers.

This book concentrates on the traditional marketing activities summarized in side 1 of the triangle in Figure 1.

Theme: introduction to marketing theory and practice:
■ Chapter 1: Marketing development and scope of the subject.
■ Chapter 2: Strategic marketing and the planning process.

Figure 1
The structure
of the book.
1 traditional
marketing,
2 relationship
marketing,
3 internal
marketing

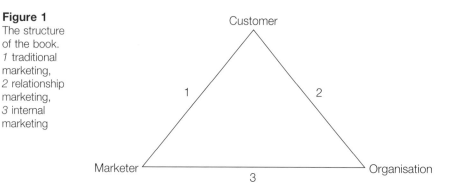

Theme: understanding and analysing customers:

■   Chapter 3: Consumer buyer behaviour.
■   Chapter 4: Industrial buyer behaviour.
■   Chapter 5: Marketing research.

Theme: constructing the offer:

■   Chapter 6: Segmentation, targeting and positioning.
■   Chapter 7: Branding.

Following this there are four key chapters, each of which is devoted to one item of the '4 Ps', otherwise known as the marketing mix:

■   Chapter 8: Product.
■   Chapter 9: Pricing.
■   Chapter 10: Promotion.
■   Chapter 11: Place.

Then there is a chapter on virtual marketing discussing contemporary developments:

■   Chapter 12: Virtual marketing.

The text concludes with a chapter bringing together the material covered throughout the text as it relates to marketing planning:

■   Chapter 13: Marketing planning and implementation

1 MARKETING: DEVELOPMENT AND SCOPE OF THE SUBJECT

LEARNING OBJECTIVES

By the end of this chapter you should be able to:

■ have a feel for the diversity of the subject of marketing and its historical development;

■ distinguish between different schools of thought in marketing;

■ know what the marketing concept is;

■ understand what is meant by the 'functionalist' approach by which this text is organized;

■ have a grasp of the major contemporary environmental trends in marketing;

■ appreciate the adaptive role of marketing strategy.

INTRODUCTION

The greatest difficulty in writing an academic book about marketing is that people already know much about the subject. The rather dry academic text can seem a poor substitute for the excitement of shopping, or working out what a particular advertisement is saying, telling friends about the latest new product you have bought. Even complaining about the poor level of service received from a shop, the local transport company or perhaps the bank can seem more relevant. Typically, people associate marketing with advertising or selling but while there is no doubt that marketing practice definitely encompasses both, there is much more to the subject than a narrow focus on either advertising or selling might suggest. The true scope of the subject is astonishing and a central aim of this book is to provide a flavour of the diverse nature of marketing. Another key aim is to ensure that your knowledge of marketing is built on solid foundations. For this reason, the approach generally follows the traditional managerialist focus on the '4 Ps' (product, price, promotion and place). Additionally, there is an overview of other perspectives, including social marketing, green marketing and relationship marketing.

THE STUDY OF MARKETING

There are many different approaches to the study of the marketing subject. Sheth *et al.* (1988) suggests that there are no less than twelve schools of marketing thought. While the variety of approaches contributes to the dynamism of marketing scholarship, the same diversity may confuse readers who expect marketing to be a unified subject. Readers may think that marketers are being contradictory when actually they represent different approaches to the subject. To discuss this diversity it is useful to outline key issues in the historical development of the study of marketing. To begin with it is important to distinguish the practice of marketing from its academic study. From earliest recorded history markets have existed as a means of bringing producer and consumer together. Likewise individuals have sought to influence the perceptions of others in favour of the goods that they offer. One might also point to medieval courtiers as being early consumers (McCracken, 1990). On the other hand, it can be argued that it is wrong to reach back into history in order to label practices that had a particular meaning and function in earlier times as being 'marketing' practices. According to American academics, the study of marketing first began in the US in the late nineteenth century. The following is a simplified account of some of the major developments in the academic study of marketing during the course of the twentieth and twenty-first centuries.

Product-centred approaches

As the study of marketing developed during the early 1900s, academics focused on understanding and classifying the profusion of products that were coming on to the market.

Much effort was expended on building a product classification which in a revised form is still used today and is reflected in the division between convenience, shopping and speciality goods. The idea is that consumers behave in different ways when purchasing convenience products, relatively inexpensive and frequently purchased goods, compared with shopping products, e.g. consumer durables such as stereos, bicycles and furniture. Speciality products possess a single unique characteristic which buyers are willing to expend a considerable amount of effort to obtain, e.g. a Cartier watch. In our text this work is integrated into the section on Product, one of the '4 Ps' of marketing. You should also be able to detect its influence in the discussion of consumer involvement in Chapter 3.

Another group of academics focused on what marketers do. This research yielded up a classification of marketing activities, e.g. in assembling goods and storing them, assuming risk, rearranging commodities by sorting, grading and breaking up large quantities into smaller units, selling and transporting. This work is integrated into the discussion of place or distribution (Chapter 11), which is another of the '4 Ps'.

In the 1930s researchers turned to explore another kind of problem; the spatial separation between producer and consumer – especially the distances consumers might be prepared to travel and the role played by distance in consumer decision to patronize one store rather than another. This work is integrated into the marketing links with logistics, physical distribution and retail location, again as part of the 'place' element of the '4 Ps'.

Functionalism

The functionalist approach was a major development in marketing and is the approach which has been used for the design of this book. The functionalist approach differs from the functional approach mentioned earlier in that it develops a systems approach to marketing, whereby behaviour is considered to be systemic and goal-driven. The functionalist approach derives in large part from the theories of the biologist Charles Darwin. Within this view the goal of marketing is to effectively match firms' supply with household demand. Functionalism is important because it views firms and households as organisms which must find some point of equilibrium (*homeostasis*) in relation to each other and the environment on which they both depend. This ecological view forms the basis of several approaches to the study of marketing, including the managerialist approach, which considers those activities which are best suited to ensuring the successful adaptation of the firm to its environment: macro-marketing, which focuses on the macro environmental impact of marketing, and green marketing, which seeks to bring the activities of firms into a new and more harmonious relation with the environment.

A MANAGERIAL APPROACH

This book takes a traditional managerial orientation to the study of marketing. This began at Harvard University in the US in the late nineteenth century but did not really become significant until the 1950s. According to Sheth *et al.* (1988) this was because there was excess capacity in the US after World War II when it was becoming harder to sell what was being produced. The development of the managerial approach is important in that it is partisan. Other schools of thought do not take sides between households and firms but study each in its own right. By contrast, as its name suggests, the managerial perspective views the subject from a manager's point of view, which influences the sorts of questions which marketers ask. A major concern to managers is to understand consumer behaviour. In order to gain the necessary insights into such behaviour marketing research techniques were developed. Following from this Chapter 3 on consumer buyer behaviour is central to the text.

Marketing orientation and the marketing concept

The appropriate orientation of the firm to the household is an important issue for those who take the management perspective. Prior to the 1950s the idea that marketers needed to create customers for mass-produced products was the norm (Drucker, 1955: 52). However, during this period this notion began to be supplanted by a new idea, that of customer orientation. This deceptively simple formulation warns the marketer that to be successful in 'competing successfully in the quicksilver of modern markets' they should 'not so much be skilful in making the customer do what suits the interests of the business as to be skilful in conceiving and then making the business do what suits the interest of the customer' (McKitterick, 1957: 78). In some respects this formulation is paradoxical as, given consumer sovereignty, the firm should ideally have no long-term interest other than that of acting in the customer's interests. This paradox may be answered by Levitt's famous 'marketing myopia' (1960). In Levitt's view managers in firms confuse false (short-term) desires with their real (long-term) interests through being blinded by a belief in the power of their product, technology or production process, or through the perceived need to get rid of 'product'. Levitt argues that such thinking can only ever hold true in the short term as in the long run consumer sovereignty would prevail. McKitterick's formulation of customer orientation has clear political and moral implications. The political implication is that if business attended to its long-run interests there would be little need for state regulation. This is tied to the moral dimension whereby managers are told that by acting selfishly they ultimately damage the long-run survival potential of the firm. In this way the marketing orientation seeks the internal regulation of the firm on the justification that managers will seek to come to believe that it is in the firm's interests to adopt a marketing orientation.

Over the years the idea of the marketing orientation has been subject to elaboration, e.g. by the creation of a range of definitions of the marketing concept. The current definition of the marketing concept offered by the British Chartered Institute of Marketing (CIM) defines marketing as 'the management process responsible for identifying, anticipating and satisfying customer requirements profitably.' This definition could be described as wanting in that it fails to focus on the long-run interests of the firm. It can be contrasted with Kotler's more completed definition: 'The marketing concept calls for a customer orientation backed by integrated marketing aimed at generating long-run customer satisfaction as the key to attaining long-run profitable volume' (Kotler, 1972b: 54).

In focusing on the long-run interest of the firm, and in calling for an integrated marketing programme, Kotler recognizes that a key problem for marketing, which is the external face of the organization, is the motivation, co-ordination and control of internal resources. Davidson, writing on marketing warfare, adopts a much blunter tone:

> The practice of marketing is almost as old as civilization, and its validity has been proved over and over again. The oldest profession in the world used classic marketing techniques: it identified and satisfied a need; it created a market where buyer and seller could meet, in the form of a brothel; and it turned a handsome profit on the operation.
>
> (Davidson, 1987: 29)

The warfare approach is reflected in Kohli and Jaworski's definition of the marketing concept which focuses on the notion of marketing intelligence and information gathering in discussing a consumer orientation:

> Market orientation is the organization-wide generation of market intelligence pertaining to current and future customer needs, dissemination of the intelligence across departments, and organizational responsiveness to it.
>
> (Kohli and Jaworski, 1990: 6)

Ries and Trout (1981, 1986), who have made the marketing warfare orientation approach their own, place the competition and not the customer as the central problem of the marketer. Within this view, the key aim is to position the product in the mind of the customer and to knock the competitor's out. Marketing warfare theorists are sceptical about those who might argue that marketers should be the lapdogs of customers. For example, Davidson (1987) describes 'consumer worshippers' as one of the 'marketing perverts'.

Levitt (1962: 8) strikes a balance by suggesting that marketing is no 'do-gooder' treatise but a 'tough-minded explanation, outline and example of how to serve yourself by serving the customer better'.[1] While the above definitions are diverse, taking either the customer or the competition as the central focus of marketing, they share the fundamental idea that the interest of the firm, as represented by the need to make a profit, is primary. The ultimate satisfaction of this interest is based on the need to satisfy customer requirements.

Table 1.1 summarizes the key distinctions between economic and marketing orientation and also between marketing orientation and production, costs and sales orientations. Levitt (1960) warns against the 'self-deceiving cycle' whereby producers can become lured into the illusory belief that the demand for their product will be eternal, or that their success is due to the technical quality of their product, or the efficiency of their operations. As an

Table 1.1 Marketing orientation

Type of orientation	Orientation details	Comment	How the moral issue is resolved	Political implications
Economic orientation	Firm should seek to maximize its self-interest in the market place	But seeking to maximize short-run desires can damage long-run interests	Through the operations of the 'invisible hand' in the market place. Firms which fail to take consumers' needs into account will ultimately disappear	Minimal regulation – the operations of the market will sort out any inequities that arise in the short run
Marketing orientation	The key to maximizing self-interest lies in understanding and meeting changing customer needs	Focuses on the adaptive potential of the individual organization to adjust to environmental change	By managers seeking to implement the marketing concept. Firms which embrace this ultimately will be more profitable	Minimal regulation – so long as most firms embrace the concept
Production orientation	Blind belief in technical excellence as route to long-run success	Levitt (1960) – this is a form of myopia that will lead ultimately to destruction	As above	As above
Cost/efficiency orientation	Blind belief that focus on cost reduction to exclusion of customer wants leads to long-run success	Levitt (1960) – this is a form of myopia that will lead ultimately to destruction	As above	As above
Sales orientation	Blind belief in the view that selling is the only way of providing long-run success	Levitt (1960) – this is a form of myopia that will lead ultimately to destruction	As above	As above
Reformist critique of marketing	Business dominates consumers	Argues that reality is the other way round to the way marketers describe this	One should not rely either on the market or on the marketing concept	Need for government regulation
Radical critique of marketing	Business and government dominate citizens and consumers	The marketing concept is a dangerous ideology	One must seek to remove the scales from the eyes of citizens	Need for a fundamental change in the system

Table 1.2 Relations between efficiency and effectiveness

Level of efficiency	Ineffective	Effective
Inefficient	Die quickly	Survive
Efficient	Die slowly	Thrive

example of the former he cites the early twentieth-century millionaire who insisted that his vast inheritance be invested solely in electric streetcars! In relation to technical quality it can be understood how easily an engineer can be lured into thinking that her or his idea of quality is consonant with that ascribed by the consumer. In a personal discussion with some MBA students who worked in the Scottish knitwear industry they heatedly supported their view that UK consumers would prefer the superior technical quality of their product to the inferior quality provided by Benetton. They were motivated by the discussion to conduct research to prove their point. Unfortunately for them, they found that consumers preferred the technically inferior product, especially when they knew the price difference.

Levitt (1960) focuses attention on to the double-edged relations between efficiency and effectiveness. While efficiency is good, one should be careful not to under or over-engineer a product, as in the knitwear example described above, but instead to give the customer what she or he wants. Related to this is the orientation to technology. Technology, too, undoubtedly can be a good thing, but it may be tempting for managers to implement technological solutions that do not take into account user requirements. Levitt's insight has been developed into a two-by-two matrix which is illustrated in Table 1.2. A company that is inefficient and ineffective will fail to survive because it produces goods that are relatively expensive, that consumers do not particularly want. Even though a company is efficient and produces goods at a low relative cost, still it will go out of business if it does not produce goods that customers want. Marketers argue that it is only when firms act effectively by making things that people want that the firm stands any chance of surviving into the long term.

Implementing a marketing orientation

Do marketing managers agree with the academics about what a marketing orientation is? In studying this Kohli and Jaworski (1990: 3) first had to construct a composite definition to describe the academic view. They found that academic definitions of marketing orientation are organized according to three core 'pillars' which underpin them all. These comprise customer focus, co-ordinated marketing and profitability. The authors asked marketing managers what they thought of the categories that the academics had decided upon by conducting a field study. Marketing managers agreed that the marketing concept is about a customer focus; however, they also mentioned something that the academics had not taken account of, which was that they took actions on the basis of market intelligence. In hindsight it seems obvious that a marketing manager will not simply be concerned with the task of ascertaining the current and future needs of customers, but will be doing so within an environment which is regulated and subject to competition. Co-ordinated marketing was not mentioned by many marketing managers, although the co-ordination of market intelligence was seen to play an important role. Finally, managers perceived profitability to be an outcome of market intelligence and customer focus.

Are marketing-oriented firms more successful?

Over the years marketing academics have sought to ascertain whether firms which are marketing-oriented are more successful than those which are not. Another focus for enquiry has been the overall extent to which firms have embraced the marketing concept.

Hooley and Lynch (1985) studied the marketing characteristics of high and low-performing companies based on a basket of indicators including profitability, market share and return on equity. They found that a number of marketing-related activities differentiated high-performance companies from their counterparts. Higher-performing companies were more likely to be found in growth markets; to be proactive in planning; to work more closely with other departments, including the finance department, and to spend more on market research.

Narver and Slater (1990) took strategic business units (SBUs) in the US as the focus of their study. They sought not only to understand the links, if any, between market orientation and profitability but, furthermore, to see if there were any differences between commodity (raw materials) businesses, such as water and minerals extraction, and non-commodity businesses. Market orientation was operationalized in terms of three components: customer orientation, competitor orientation and degree of inter-functional orientation. The authors found that for commodity businesses those with the highest marketing orientation showed higher profitability than the businesses in the mid-range. Interestingly, they found that those SBUs that were lowest in marketing orientation were also more profitable than the mid-range businesses. The authors sought to explain this by arguing that the low marketing orientation companies were highly cost-focused and, consequently, were likely to be more profitable on that basis. For non-commodity companies the authors found that businesses with the highest level of market orientation achieved the highest levels of profitability and those with the lowest orientation the lowest profitability.

DEVELOPMENTS IN MARKETING THEORY

While the above seems to indicate that those firms that embrace the marketing concept are more successful than others, to what extent has this been embraced by business? At the dawn of the 1960s there was a lot of satisfaction if not smugness among marketing academics amid a general feeling that most firms were identifying and satisfying people's needs and not merely selling things to them. It was felt that marketing had at last come of age, having moved through a series of 'phases' from a 'mass distribution' or 'production era' to 'aggressive selling' and now to a genuine 'marketing orientation', such that by the 1960s it was considered *unAmerican* for a company *not* to practise the marketing concept (Lipson and Paling, 1974; Stidsen and Schutte, 1972). Imagine then the shock, horror and disappointment of marketing academics to what happened later in the 1960s. It is difficult now to comprehend the scope of the change and, in particular, the widespread disaffection of the young with respect to much that concerned business and marketing in particular. In one year only 8 per cent of Harvard graduates decided to elect for business careers (Gartner and Riessman, 1974). Marketing, especially selling and advertising, was singled out as the most controversial and most criticized single zone of business (Bauer and Greyser, 1967: 2). In addition to this criticism, in the US business (and marketing in particular) attracted considerable attention from state regulatory agencies and by the end of the decade claims were made that industry was being tied up by the amount of consumer legislation passed.[2] Additionally, a large number of consumer affairs offices were opened to investigate consumer complaints.[3] The publication of *The Hidden Persuaders* (1957) and *The Waste Makers* (1960) by Vance Packard, *Silent Spring* by Rachel Carson (1962) and work by Ralph Nader casting doubt on the safety record of General Motors, contributed to the establishment of the consumer movement.

The response of marketing academics to the furore of the 1960s was varied. Innovators like George Fisk opened up new avenues for research by exploring macro-marketing processes, the role played by marketing activities in the wider social system. However, the general response of 'mainstream' US marketing academics to the wave of protest in the 1960s was much more defensive. Some suggested that the reason for the spate of government legislation was poor communications between government and marketers. Others felt that marketers had been targeted unfairly particularly, with claims about product obsolescence which were really the responsibility of production personnel. Management guru Peter Drucker felt that the growth of consumerism was the shame of marketing, that basically consumers saw manufacturers as people who were not bothered to find out what they wanted. He felt that there was a need to get back down to basics, or the fundamentals of marketing, and look at things from the consumer's point of view (Drucker, 1969: 61). Philip Kotler suggested that the problem was that while the business community had grasped the spirit of the marketing concept, and, while top management professed the concept, line managers did not practise it faithfully (Kotler, 1972a). Charles Ames (1970) sought to explain why marketing practices were so slow to develop in industrial marketing contexts. His general argument is that while management had adopted the superficial trappings of market orientation through the establishment of marketing departments and advertising budgets, they had not attended to its substance, a matter which required real commitment from the top and continuous effort from all managers.

Marketing academics initially viewed the consumer movement with suspicion, fear and sometimes downright hostility. Kotler poured some water on the flames by suggesting that consumerism was not a danger to marketing and could even be viewed as being pro-marketing because it helped balance the power of the seller by acting in the interests of buyers. Kotler considered that the consumer backlash was mainly due to marketing managers misinterpreting the marketing concept by equating customer satisfaction with consumer desire. He argued that managers mistakenly had catered to consumer desires for products which while they were pleasing were also harmful to consumers' long-term satisfaction, e.g. by offering products such as cigarettes and alcohol for sale. For this reason, Kotler suggested that the marketing concept should be modified to add the view that marketers should also generate long-run consumer welfare as the key to attaining long-run profitable volume. This means that marketers should pay attention to ways of reformulating *pleasing* products such as tobacco (which give high immediate satisfaction but ultimately hurt consumers' interests) so that they become more socially desirable (Kotler, 1972a).

Relationship marketing

The long-running battle over the marketing concept became the focus of a new major orientation in marketing which was to gather pace during the late 1970s and into the 1980s. This approach has come to be known as *relationship marketing*. Christian Grönroos (1996) provided the keynote address for the first online relationship marketing conference. Grönroos attacked the idea of the marketing mix, or '4 Ps' as it is more widely known, which he argues is formulaic and therefore bound to set marketing off track because it is competition and production-oriented. Rather than being in the consumer's interests, i.e. somebody for whom something is done, the '4 Ps' approach implies that the customer is somebody to whom something is done.

Grönroos suggests that the '4 Ps' approach has distanced marketers from the marketing concept and that as a result marketing has become the province of specialists. In this sense he argues that specialization of marketing has resulted in a double alienation (1996: 4).

■ This has had the effect of alienating the rest of the organization from Marketing and with this alienation it is difficult, if not impossible, for Marketing to become the truly integrative function that it should be.

■ The specialists organized within the marketing department may become alienated from customers, because managing the marketing mix means relying on mass marketing. Customers become numbers for the marketing specialists, whose actions typically are based on surface information obtained from market research reports and market share statistics. Frequently such marketers act without ever having encountered a real customer. Grönroos's concerns echo many of those which have been expressed earlier in this chapter with respect to the creation of distance by marketing processes.

Grönroos suggests that these contradictions can be resolved by means of a dynamic and fluid relationship marketing approach which alone can counter the straitjacket of the clinical transaction-based, mass-market approach of the '4 Ps'. The aim of relationship marketing is to establish, maintain and enhance relation with customers and other partners, at a profit, so that the objectives of all the parties are met. This is achieved by the mutual exchange and fulfilment of promises. Such promises are usually, but not exclusively, long-term. The establishment of a relationship can be divided into two parts: to attract the customer and to build the relationship with that customer so that the economic goals of that relationship can be achieved. This shifts the ground towards the 'part-time' marketer; the recognition that, within organizations, many non-marketing specialists actually are practising marketing functions. Internal marketing is needed to gain the support of these people. Both internally and externally, relationships have to be regulated by means of the exchange of promises to establish trust through the formation of relationships and dialogue with both internal and external customers. While the ultimate objective is to build a loyal customer base, there is no doubt that this refocusing of marketing to emphasize qualities of connectedness, dialogue and trust represents an attempt to uplift the process of marketing.

Grönroos's aspiration that marketing in the twenty-first century would be the era of a new relationship marketing based on the mutual exchange and fulfilment of promises has not so far come to fruition, nor, one might suggest is it likely to. Why? One reason is that, as it has evolved in practice, the umbrella term 'relationship marketing' subsumes a number of disparate, even contradictory discourses associated with areas such as services marketing and one-to-one marketing. In services marketing it is quite conceivable to envisage a service provider who seeks to develop more meaningful relations with customers. However, the rhetoric of direct marketing and database marketing has a quite different focus (Peppers *et al.*, 1999). Through customer databases and mass customization the marketer plans the offers and communications on the basis of customer profile and feedback and can focus on the development of an individual 'relationship' with each of a large number of customers. The term 'relationship' is used advisedly and in a technical sense to point to two features which are required of the technology: its ability to address an individual and the ability to gather and 'remember' the response of that individual by means of a cookie. It is then possible to address the individual once more in a way that takes into account his or her unique response. In retrospect there seems little to suggest that this is any less formulaic and subject to the supervision of specialists than the '4 Ps' approach that Grönroos attacked a decade earlier. The reality of database marketing in the real world to date is that it fails to live up to the ideal mentioned above (cf. Fournier *et al.,* 1998). Rather it summons to mind the myopia that Levitt (1960) mentioned all those years ago. The technologies may be new, e.g. the crude use of databases, contact techniques such as the use of remote diallers, sPAM emails, coupled with the development of remote 'customer service' centres. But the underlying motive seems to be depressingly similar to that which Levitt warned against all those years ago: the pursuit of efficiency over effectiveness.

Social marketing and societal marketing

As if the story of the development of marketing management were not enough Philip Kotler and Sydney Levy (Kotler and Levy, 1969; Kotler, 1972a) argued for an extension of marketing into non-economic areas such as public services, the arts and religion. They argued that these areas could benefit from the marketing concept too and felt that social marketing should become part of the marketer's repertoire. Seymour Fine (1981) produced the first comprehensive text on the subject where he discussed the marketing of energy conservation and road safety campaigns. Kotler *et al.* (2002) have defined it as:

> Social marketing is the use of marketing principles and techniques to influence a target audience to voluntarily accept, reject, modify or abandon a behaviour for the benefit of individuals, groups or society as a whole.

Kotler and his colleagues argue that social marketing is similar to the marketing of products and services in that what is being sold is behaviour change. Thus social marketers appeal to a target audience to accept a new behaviour, e.g. to modify current behaviour by recycling goods; to reject a potential behaviour, e.g. through anti-smoking and drug campaigns aimed at children and to encourage people to place chewing gum in wastebins rather than spitting it on to the street; or to abandon a behaviour, such as forgoing smoking in restaurants. Since the mid-1990s there has been an explosion of social marketing in the UK, with government funding a range of health promotion, drink–driving, anti-drug, anti-racism and anti-domestic abuse campaigns among others.

The legacy of 1960s America had a profound impact on definitions of the marketing concept. Reading between the lines, it seems as if Kotler (1972) believed that one of the reasons behind the turmoil in the US in that decade was because marketing principles had not permeated sufficiently into society. In this view even social marketing was not enough to cure society's ills; what was needed was societal marketing. By this Kotler meant that the marketing concept should be extended to all organizations. The conventional wisdom was that if someone does not pay for something, i.e. if it is not an economic transaction, then it is not really the province of marketing. By contrast to this, Kotler contended that not only should marketing be applicable to all organizations, economic or not: it should reflect the organization's attempt to relate to all its stakeholders, not just customers. Through the development of the generic marketing concept, by reorienting the marketing concept to recognize societal needs, it was argued that marketing could recover its worth to society. These concerns are reflected in Kotler's more recent formulations where marketing is defined as:

> A social and managerial process by which individuals and groups get what they need and want by creating and exchanging products of value with others.
>
> (Kotler, 1991)

In addition to the focus on social aspects it should be noticed that the above definition is more neutrally framed than those earlier formulations of marketing discussed earlier in this chapter, which implicitly assumed a managerial perspective. Now consider the following definition which accentuates the societal dimension where marketing is conceived of as being:

> A societal process by which individuals and groups obtain what they need and want through creating, offering and freely exchanging products and services of value with others.
>
> (Kotler, 2000)

The development of 'social' marketing by Kotler caused a stir in the marketing academy. However, a decade later much of the anger had gone out of the debate, with Kotler winning the day (see Hirschman, 1983). This did not mean that all controversy had died down. Laczniak *et al.* (1979) were prescient in noting that, while the notion of social marketing was fascinating, it could open a Pandora's box, releasing ethical and social problems reflecting the concerns of those outside the discourse of marketing;

> For example is it in the best interests of society for politicians increasingly to rely upon individuals skilled in advertising and marketing to tailor their campaigns? Is it proper that marketing research methods are used to determine which issues appeal to various constituencies and how these often conflicting views can be optimally incorporated in to the party platform without alienating many voters? Is it beneficial that image studies shape the candidates external appearance? – that copywriters and public relations people stage appealing television speeches and appearances for the candidates? – that politicians are sold like soap?
>
> (Laczniak *et al.,* 1979: 32)

Critical and postmodern approaches to marketing

Over the years marketing has not been without its critics. Some of these are within the discipline of marketing and some are outside. From within, Hayes and Abernathy (1980) can challenge the view that the adoption of the marketing concept can improve the competitiveness of organizations. On the basis of empirical evidence, they have suggested that the implementation actually has undermined competitiveness.

Critics of marketing from outside the discipline include the influential economist J.K. Galbraith (1967), who argued that the marketing concept is nothing more than propaganda because its central argument, that business is responsive to the expressed needs and wants of customers, is patently false. Instead Galbraith argued for what he called the revised sequence, the idea that big business creates and manipulates demand. In this view the 'accepted sequence' encapsulates consumer sovereignty and the marketing concept; that all needs start with consumers; that the expression of such needs sends signals to producers

MARKETING WITHIN THE SEX INDUSTRY

According to the *Economist* (1998), the sex industry is worth at least US$20bn (£11bn) a year and probably many times that figure. There are different categories of what may be called services, e.g. prostitution, striptease and telephone sex. There are also products which include pornography and sex aids. Currently the international sex business is being transformed from a largely amateurish approach associated with small business to more professional and imaginative offerings which offer products such as up-market escort agencies through the Internet or which exploit niches in the market. Globalization is a major factor, with hundreds and thousands of women from poor countries imported to wealthy countries where they work longer hours for less money and less concern for safety than their Western counterparts. A second trend is commoditisation, with prices being ratcheted downwards in a buyers' market. The same trend is happening with products, where sex videos feature more and more Central and Eastern European (CEE) actors who 'cost less and do more'. The article discusses various options for the sex entrepreneur; for the ruthless, workers are treated abominably, smuggled and sold as sex slaves. However, in the long term the prospects for this form of cut-price prostitution look bleak.

One response (the more intelligent one) to global competition and price pressure is to go up market. Prostitutes in hotel bars and nightclubs charge five or six times as much as their sisters on the street. Upscale prostitution is safer; customers may be nicer, hotels offer more protection than a pimp. The same applies to pornography where the bottom end of the market is hopelessly oversupplied and most videos are boring, 'barely distinguishable with feeble plots and dialogue'. It is argued that what really makes money is building a brand or finding a familiar face, like Tina Orlowske, the Hanover-based porn star who now runs one of Germany's largest sex video businesses. Differentiation by offering customers something new or different works too, catering to fetishes. In the US the San Fernando valley on the north side of Los Angeles's Santa Monica mountains has become home to the US adult film business. This is beginning to imitate the mainstream Hollywood industry, with its own Oscar ceremonies and studio system. Another fast-growing part of the US porn business is the home video industry, which has even lower costs. However, it is the Internet which offers the greatest prospects for growth.

Source: adapted from 'The sex industry: giving the customer what he wants', *Economist*, 14 February 1998, pp. 23–5.

who respond to this message of the market and the instructions of the consumer. The revised sequence in contrast refers to the reality asserted by Galbraith, whereby producers condition the creation and satisfaction ofneeds and wants in the interests of the managerial elite. Advertising is especially important to the managerial elite as there is a need to create a ready market for the goods on offer. In response to the riposte that much advertising is informational Galbraith sardonically replies, 'Only a gravely retarded person would need to be told that the American Tobacco Company has cigarettes for sale.' In Galbraith's view the very idea of *homo economicus* acts as a powerful protection for the technostructure which hides behind the rhetoric of the sovereign individual as a cover for its wholesale manipulation of the market place. Others have built on this argument to argue that marketing plays an ideological role in society by suggesting that everyone is equally free to buy goods, marketing masks the lack of freedom and existence of gross inequalities in society (cf. Marcuse, 1964). Similar views have been expressed by academics working inside the marketing discipline (cf. Brownlie and Saren, 1992).

Postmodern academics argue that there is no one true or authentic marketing approach but rather a range of different but equally valid perspectives. Postmodernism developed as a tendency in the arts, and more recently in the social sciences, which reflects upon, attacks and ironizes modernist thought. Modernism is that set of ideas which developed during the European Enlightenment and which came to be embodied in concepts such as 'progress' and 'scientific rationality'. Postmodernism is a reaction against modernism to the extent that postmodernists do not believe that society gets progressively better through history, nor do they believe that science will provide such progress. They argue that modernist tendencies to believe that science can uncover deep structures of meaning are subverted by appearances and so they lend great credence to appearances. Postmodernists also attack the dualisms implicit in Enlightenment thinking, for instance between 'mind' and 'body' or 'male' and 'female' which traditionally elevate one term (the 'mind' over the 'body' or 'male' over 'female') over the other. Postmodernism is concerned with deconstructing or dismantling such stable binary schemes of meaning and substituting a whole plethora of differences in their place. Put simply, postmodernism is concerned with challenging and undermining oppositions which many people take to be 'natural' and in demonstrating that these are cultural artefacts.

Postmodern marketing comes in a whole range of guises usually involving the use of irony, 'playfulness', critique and pastiche often rolled together into a seamless web. It is difficult to discuss postmodern marketing, not least because some of those who are labelled 'postmodern' do not subscribe to that view themselves. Brown (1995, 1998) adopts a joyful and ironic posture in criticizing gurus such as Ansoff, Kotler and Levitt, who are held high in the marketing pantheon. In chapter 2 entitled 'I coulda been a contender!' Brown attacks the totalizing tendencies of the subject and some of the 'mainstream's' most cherished assumptions. Brown (1998) continues this theme.

WHO HELD BACK THE STONE?

In coining the phrase 'marketing myopia' Levitt (1960) ensured his place in the marketing pantheon. By myopia he meant the short-sightedness that is characteristic of managers who become blinded by their belief in their product; their technology or their ways of doing business. While a pride in one's product, technology or formula for success is in right measure a good thing, if this is misplaced it can be seen to be the only thing that matters. This can miss that business relies on customers and customers' tastes changing. While Levitt chastized engineers, accountants and technologists, he did not mention that often marketers themselves can be blind to the emerging realities of the market place.

During the 1960s executives at Columbia Records met weekly to discuss what singles to shortlist for release. At one meeting in June 1965 the single 'Like a Rolling Stone' by a then relatively unknown singer called Bob Dylan came up for discussion. Most of those present, from among the artists and repertoire (A&R) to those working in promotions loved the fresh, raw feel of the work. Only Sales and Marketing had a different opinion. Considine (2004) remarked '[unfortunately] their opinion mattered, for Sales and Marketing was the engine behind the label's success'. The main overt objection that they raised at the meeting was that the song's length, at just under six minutes, was well over the average length of three minutes for singles played on national radio. The solution they suggested was to cut it in half. Dylan refused to change it. Already, in 1963, he had failed to persuade Columbia to release 'Talkin' John Birch Society blues'.

Lieberson, president of Columbia, had things other than Dylan on his mind at the time, not least the move to Columbia's parent's, CBS's, Sixth Avenue address. In any event Columbia's vice-president of marketing had never expressed any great fondness for Dylan, who had, according to Considine, performed at one of their mammoth sales conventions but had never 'mingled'. Considine notes that the Sales and Marketing people had other reasons for not wanting Dylan. They had fashioned Columbia's success by marketing pop, country, jazz and musicals to the mainstream market and Dylan's style was regarded as being too close to rock 'n' roll and too raucous. This attitude had led Columbia to turn down Elvis Presley in 1955 as well as the first US album by the Beatles in 1963. In the debacle surrounding the move to the new building Dylan's single was dealt with by memo; it was to be moved from an 'immediate special' to an 'unassigned release'. Considine interprets the situation as being that the single's launch had been deferred and was likely to be consigned to the dustbin of history.

Columbia executives were caught up in the move to the new building, with all the hassle and heartache that entailed, including the decision as to what to retain of the memorabilia that had been collected over the years and what was not. A 'welcoming' notice from Columbia's parent CBS had said that clutter would not be allowed in the building. Considine recalls how, during his last trek through the old A&R department, he was invited to sort through a stack of records and demos that were to be junked. In the collection he found a studio-cut acetate of 'Like a Rolling Stone'. Carefully he packaged this in an empty long-playing (LP) jacket, carried it home and played it in his apartment. He recalls how he felt exhilaration, 'Heart pounding. Body rolling – followed by the neighbours banging on the walls in protest'.

Considine brought the acetate to Arthur's, the hottest disco in town, where ironically Dylan, dressed in 'beer-spattered Army-Navy store couture', and his rowdy friends previously had been refused admission. Considine was a club member and handed the acetate to the disc jockey (DJ) while deliberately omitting to mention the name of the artist. The DJ played 'Like a Rolling Stone' at around 11.00 p.m., and, as Considine remembers, the effect was seismic as people stopped talking, jumped to their feet and danced the entire six minutes. 'Who is it?' the DJ yelled. 'Bob Dylan,' replied Considine. There were two important people in Arthur's that night. One was a DJ at WABC, the premier Top 40 radio station in Manhattan. The other was a music programmer at WMCA. Next morning both called Columbia Records and demanded to know where their copy of the new Dylan record was.

Within days, by 15 July, Dylan's single was scheduled for release. DJs were alerted that the promotional copy of 'Like a Rolling Stone' was to be pressed on red vinyl. On side 1 of the disc the label read 'Like a Rolling Stone (Part 1). Timing 3.02.' Side 2 said, 'Part 2. Timing 3.02.' Considine notes, 'The song had been cut down the middle. Sales and Marketing had struck again.' But DJs simply recorded both sides of the disc on tape and spliced the whole thing together, so that by the following week 'Like a Rolling Stone' was released in its full version. From there on the record became the subject of legend, being nominated some forty years later by *Rolling Stone* magazine as the greatest rock 'n' roll song of all time. Such was the power of the song that it propelled Columbia into the era of rock. Considine recalls that the previously omnipotent vice-president of sales and marketing did not lead the new era. Instead Goddard gave a lawyer with no A&R training and no ear for music the responsibility. His first task was to renew Bob Dylan's contract with Columbia. Dylan's demands exceeded those of top stars such as Andy Williams and Barbara Streisand, yet as Considine noted Dylan's demands were met.

Source: adapted from Considine (2004).

CASE QUESTIONS

1   Describe, using examples drawn from the case, how Columbia's sales and marketing department could be described as being myopic in Levitt's sense of the word.
2   What deep seated problems underlie these instances of myopia?
3   List each problem and discuss the possibilities of addressing it.
4   How relevant is the case to the way in which the record industry operates today?

CONCLUSION

As a result of working through this chapter you should now appreciate:

- the development of marketing thought over the past hundred years, noting the different phases of development of the topic;
- what is meant by the marketing concept;
- how a marketing orientation is different from a production or sales orientation;
- the orientation of this book, which is centred around a functionalist approach to marketing;
- how to conduct a strategic marketing analysis.

REVIEW QUESTIONS

1. Is it morally right that marketing principles and techniques should be applied to the 'sex industry'?
2. What was the primary concern of the Wisconsin school?
3. What are the differences between the functional school and functionalism?
4. What is meant by the marketing concept?
5. What reasons did Philip Kotler provide to explain the consumer backlash to marketing in the US?
6. Explain what is meant by the terms *social marketing* and *societal marketing*.
7. What are the key elements of relationship marketing?

RECOMMENDED FURTHER READING

Baker, M.J. (1996) *Marketing theory: an introductory text,* 6th edn, London: Thomson Business Press.

Baker, M.J. (ed.) (1999) *The marketing book,* 4th edn, Oxford: Butterworth Heinemann.

Baker, M.J. (2000) *Marketing theory: a student text,* London: Thomson Business Press.

Blythe, J. (2006) *Principles and practice of marketing,* London: Thomson Business Press.

Davidson, H. (1997) *Even more offensive marketing,* Harmondsworth: Penguin.

Donaldson, B. and O'Toole, T. (2002) *Strategic market relationships: from strategy to implementation,* Chichester: Wiley.

Enis, B.M., Cox, K.K. and Mokwa, M.P. (1995) *Marketing classics,* 8th edn, Englewood Cliffs NJ: Prentice Hall.

Groucutt, J. (2005) *Foundations of marketing,* Basingstoke: Palgrave Macmillan.

Guiltinan, J.P. and Paul, G.W. (1994) *Marketing management: strategies and programs,* 5th edn, Maidenhead: McGraw-Hill.

Jobber, D. (2001) *Principles and practice of marketing,* Maidenhead: McGraw-Hill.

Kitchen, P.J. (2003) *The future of marketing,* Basingstoke: Palgrave Macmillan.

McDonald, M. and Wilson, H. (2002) *The new marketing: transforming the corporate future,* Oxford: Butterworth Heinemann.

Ranchhod, A. (2004) *Marketing strategies: a twenty-first-century approach*, Harlow: Pearson.

Weitz, B. and Wensley, R. (eds) 2002) *Handbook of marketing*, London: Sage.

2 STRATEGIC MARKETING AND THE PLANNING PROCESS

LEARNING OBJECTIVES

By the end of this chapter you should be able to:

- appreciate more fully that a functionalist explanation seeks to adapt an organism's behaviour to environmental change;

- recognize the importance of understanding the changes and potential changes in the marketing environment;

- have an understanding of the major contemporary environmental trends in marketing;

- have a good knowledge of the marketing planning process.

INTRODUCTION

The analysis of the consumer environment is a keystone of the functionalist approach to marketing. On this view the marketer who fails to adapt to changing environmental trends will fail to ensure the company's survival. The discussion starts by reflecting on the difficulties of determining what may happen in the future. Bearing this in mind, aspects of the current marketing environment are considered, focusing in particular on time–space compression, the body and globalization and fragmentation. Then the business organization in relation to the marketing environment is considered. This closely adheres to the cognitive explanation which is outlined and discussed in more detail in Chapter 3. This frames organizational decision making as a form of problem solving. In simple terms it involves devising a goal state, an initial state and operators of how to get to the goal state from the initial state. In management jargon the goal state is discussed with reference to concepts such as the mission and objectives; initial state by marketing audit; and operators by strategies.

THE MARKETING ENVIRONMENT

As Figure 2.1 shows, one of the key aspects of developing a functionalist explanation is to relate the organism to its environment. In this section environmental trends are examined together with the relationship of organizations and the environment.

In the simplified illustration provided in Figure 2.1, all three firms are prospering in the prevailing environment at T1. However, an environmental change leads to firm A adapting rapidly to the new conditions, with firm B some way behind. Firm C does not adapt quickly enough and disappears.

General environmental trends

Some important aspects of the environment are considered. It is useful to point out that the environment is not simply 'seen', it is 'perceived'. This means what is happening 'out there' is seen through the cultural spectacles. It is difficult to see these 'cultural spectacles', but if looking at the past and, in particular, at the assumptions about what environmental changes were, it becomes more apparent. For example, during the 1960s people looked forward to the 1970s and 1980s as a time of leisure. Many articles appeared in the popular press to speculate about what people might do with this leisure time. It was only in the 1970s

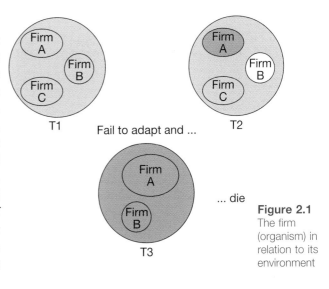

Figure 2.1
The firm (organism) in relation to its environment

when the grim truth dawned: unemployment was certainly a form of 'leisure time' but not the sort that people had expected or found tolerable. The list in Table 2.1 has been selected from a forecast of 100 technical innovations likely in the thirty-three years to 1990 as reported by Kahn and Wiener (1967). This should be examined to appreciate their success in spotting what actually happened.

It is noted that, ignoring the bad mistakes, e.g. nuclear energy, hibernation, etc., the authors were close in their predictions. Some of the predictions are so general that they were almost bound to have happened in some shape or form. In hindsight, it seems clear that Kahn and Wiener's view of the future was influenced by the prevailing social attitude of their time, especially by science fiction. This featured people in individual flying machines, which usually looked like smart sports cars that zoomed across highways in space; helpful robots which cleaned up around the home where almost all energy was provided by means of some form of fission or fusion. So, while the authors managed to get a glimpse of what actually happened, their views were distorted by the context of the times in which they were living. On the other hand, although the seeds of the Internet and bioengineering had been planted at that time, there is no mention of these innovations. That society is condemned to be trapped in a web consisting of the assumptions of the time and place is obvious. But what sort of environmental changes seem to be occurring at the present time? What effects may these changes have for consumption for organizations and households?

Consumer society and the physical environment

One fragile certainty is that capitalism has triumphed across the world. Nowadays consumer societies are taking root in even the poorest African and South American countries. Just as the East Germans exchanged the 'Trabant' for the dream of a 'Mercedes' society, so Chinese consumers are facing their government with an expectation that they have a right to the same level of prosperity (indexed by access to consumer goods) as everyone else on the globe.

At the same time there is a growing awareness, reflected in the Earth Summit and its successors, that the consumer society has major environmental implications provoking a need to see limits to growth. The problem is that this is taken to mean that for each major country that 'everyone else' should be responsible and not develop too far but that 'we' should maintain 'our' level of development.

The other major contemporary trends will now be considered.

Time–space compression

Time–space compression, perhaps the most pervasive trend in contemporary society, refers to the idea that the logic of capitalism results in a speed-up of time and a reduction in the effects of distance to the extent that they are compressed into a smaller space than ever before. Harvey (1989) refers to the constantly accelerating turnover time of capital which is the time of production together with the time of the circulation of exchange. The logic is that the faster the capital launched into circulation can be recuperated the greater the profit

Table 2.1 One hundred technical innovations likely in the next thirty years

Rank	Technical innovations predicted for the next thirty years (to 1990)
10	New sources of power for ground transport (storage battery, fuel-cell propulsion or support by electromagnetic fields, jet engine, turbine)
11	Extensive and intensive global use of high-altitude cameras for mapping, prospecting, census, land use and geological investigation
13	Major reduction in hereditary and congenital defects
16	Relatively effective appetite and weight control
25	Automated or more mechanized housekeeping and maintenance
26	Widespread use of nuclear reactors for power
27	Use of nuclear explosives for excavation and mining
33	New and more reliable 'educational' and propaganda techniques for affecting public and private human behaviour
35	Human hibernation for relatively extensive periods (months to years)
36	New kinds of very cheap, convenient and reliable birth control techniques
44	General and substantial increase in life expectancy, postponement of ageing and limited rejuvenation
45	Generally acceptable and competitive synthetic foods and beverages (carbohydrates, fats, enzymes, vitamins, coffee, tea, liquor)
48	'Non-harmful' methods of 'over-indulging'
51	Permanent manned satellite and lunar installations interplanetary travel
54	Automated grocery and department stores
57	Automated universal (real-time) credit, audit and banking systems
59	Greater use of underground buildings
66	New techniques for keeping physically fit or acquiring physical skills
69	Individual flying platforms
75	Shared time (public and interconnected) computers generally available to home and business on a metered basis
84	Home computers to 'run' the household and communicate with the outside world

Source: adapted from Kahn and Wiener (1967)
Note: Numbers on left-hand side show actual rank position out of 100 in list.

will be. Capitalists, spurred on by the threat of competition and the demand to open up new markets and raw material sources, make continuous efforts to shorten turnover times. At the same time the 'friction of distance' is condensing. The effects of this speed-up are that goods travel faster, new spaces for distribution and consumption are created (in aviation, rail transport, the World Wide Web). As a result there is a paradox, with simultaneous trends towards globalization and fragmentation.

A truly global economy?

Speed is linked to centralization and the emergence of a truly global economy. For example, in UK supermarkets one can buy not only French-grown Golden Delicious apples but also *pak choi* flown fresh from Thailand and *mange tout* and roses from Kenya. By the mid-1990s production of luxury vegetables and flowers has overtaken coffee to become the second most important export after tea, with produce going to thirty countries, with 40 per cent going to the UK (Paxton, 1994). Increased industrial concentration has led to the closure of many UK apple and flower producers while debate rages about the ethics of growing 'luxury' products for Western consumption in countries which can barely afford to feed themselves but which must meet the demands of foreign debt repayments.

In *The Marketing Imagination* Levitt (1986) argues that the modernizing power of technology is the major driving force in the development of a truly global, as opposed to international, economy. He contends that the technological imperative is driving markets and products towards a centralizing 'single converging commonality' which has 'proletarianized' communication, transport and travel, making them easily and cheaply available to the world's most isolated places. The end result is the emergence of global markets and standardized products. Levitt suggests that some part of world debt may be explained away by the demand for countries like Brazil, Romania, Togo and Malawi 'greedily wanting the modernity to which they are so constantly exposed'. He considers that all parts of the world want the most advanced things; they also wantthem in their most advanced states of functionality, quality, reliability, service levels and price competitiveness. National and regional preferences are disappearing. Linked with this is the rise of the global corporation that operates with 'resolute constancy' and at low relative costs as if the entire world were a single and largely identifiable entity. Levitt cites the global expansion of companies such as McDonald's, Coca-Cola, Pepsi as well as Greek salad and Hollywood movies as examples of this homogenizing trend.

Levitt's main argument for companies' drive towards standardization is based on a mix of preference and cost factors. He suggests that while product preferences, e.g. for washing machines, are different across countries, the costs to a company such as Hoover or Bosch in catering to these different preferences puts the company into a poor price-competitive position in those countries. More contentiously, he argues that there is a high degree of trade-off between preferences and price.

Tendencies towards globalization and centralization are ingrained into systems of production and distribution. One trend towards centralization that is inexorable unless some major environmental hazard intervenes is the projected growth in the percentage of those living in urban areas, illustrated in Figure 2.2. Another trend that is evident in Europe and can be seen in every region around the world is that towards an ageing population. This is shown in Figure 2.3 below.

Another aspect of globalization is the extent of global interdependence in production and distribution which applies to simple products, e.g. yoghurt, as well as to complex products, e.g. computers and cars. Paxton (1994) quotes a study which states that to produce strawberry yoghurt and to get it to a distribution outlet in south Germany, strawberries were

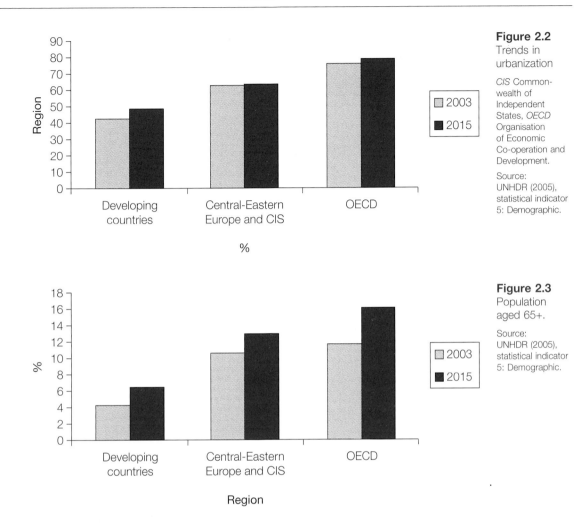

Figure 2.2
Trends in
urbanization

CIS Common-
wealth of
Independent
States, *OECD*
Organisation
of Economic
Co-operation and
Development.

Source:
UNHDR (2005),
statistical indicator
5: Demographic.

Figure 2.3
Population
aged 65+.

Source:
UNHDR (2005),
statistical indicator
5: Demographic.

transported from Poland, yoghurt from north Germany, corn and wheatflour from the Netherlands, jam from West Germany and sugar beet from the east of the country. The aluminium
cover for the strawberry jar was manufactured 300 km away from the yoghurt producer.
Only the milk and glass were produced locally. In the UK the trend towards centralization
particularly is apparent in retail distribution, rising from 40 per cent to 60 per cent in 1986
to between 70 per cent and 100 per cent for major retail stores in 1998 (Sheldon, 1998).
Over 70 per cent of fast-moving grocery product lead times in UK distribution are less than
twenty-four hours (1998: table 1.11). Evidence from the Sustainable Agriculture Food and
Environment (SAFE) report is that the same amount of food is being hauled over longer
distances, e.g. the distance food is being transported has increased by 50 per cent between
1978 and 1993 (Paxton, 1994: 18–19).

One major question posed by the preceding section is 'Is there a global consumer?'
True, there may be people around the world who drink Coke, smoke Marlboro cigarettes
and revel in the rush of feeling American for a moment. But is this enough to say that there

C
A
S
E

S
T
U
D
Y

DRINKING COKE IN TRINIDAD

According to Levitt (1986) Coca-Cola is one of the major global brands. Coke is 'The Real Thing', straight from the good ol' US of A. A key aspect of Coke identity is that it should look the same and taste the same no matter where you are. It can be assumed that Coke is proof of the existence of the global consumer. Miller (1998) is an anthropologist who decided to ignore the hype about Coca-Cola and to confront the 'free-floating' symbol which is Coke: to bring it down to earth as a glass bottle containing a sweet fizzy drink. He considered that the only way in which the relation of Coke to issues such as globalization and Trinidadian identity could be understood was to study the way in which Coke was signified and used in Trinidad. Miller found that in Trinidad Coke is identified with 'blackness' and its chief competitor, red cola (which is produced by Indians), with 'redness'. Within Trinidadian culture cola has become a vehicle for signifying identity (who you are) to others. Miller discovered that both Coke and red cola signify different aspects of black and Indian identity in Trinidad. This is not to suggest that black people drink only Coke and Indians drink only red cola. Many Indians like to drink Coke in order to identify with the values associated with it, while many blacks drink Red Cola.

The implications of Miller's study for the understanding of globalization suggest that global brands carry with them the values of their country of origin. In this case the argument would be that, in drinking Coke, Trinidadians would be 'swallowing' US culture. This is not confirmed. The 'global' brand Coke was incorporated into the construction of Trinidadian identity in a unique way which reflected the customs and signifying practices of those living on the island.

Source: adapted from Miller (1998).

is a growing homogenization of consumers at the level which Levitt is suggesting? In *The End of History and the Last Man* Fukuyama (1992) provides support for this view. In the era of the global triumph of capitalism, consumer goods begin to play a key role in satisfying the human desire for recognition. It is fair to say that consumerism is at least a global aspiration and if consumers around the world progressively become more affluent they will have further means of realizing this. Not only is this the era of global capitalism; it is the era of the global consumer. However, the question remains as to what extent is the globalization of consumption occurring? Levitt himself does not go so far as to argue that all consumer preferences are homogenized, just that it makes good sense for firms to ignore some of the differences and focus on the mainstream.

Globalization/fragmentation

From the Coke case, it seems that while it is true that globalization is happening in terms of the proliferation of global brands, these brands are being incorporated in different ways in the various contexts in which they are used. The trend is towards globalization at one level and differentiation at another. There is a growing weight of evidence to suggest that differentiation and, indeed, fragmentation are key aspects of existence in consumer societies.

In Europe, as lifetime employment largely has become a thing of the past, it no longer confers identity in the same way that it used to do. For example, being a miner, a shipbuilder or an engineering worker in the UK used to give a sense of pride and identity on the individual. The holders of these occupations were men. They felt a sense of pride and community in their work where they laboured alongside thousands of others; they also felt a sense of pride in their class identity, of being a member of the working class. The role of women in these men's lives was clear and unambiguous. The key role for a woman was to act as a wife and mother, to nurture and provide for the family. Consumption (shopping) was regarded as being women's work and was beneath the dignity of men. The tradition was that working-class men worked six days a week, took two weeks' annual holiday with their family, going usually to a British coastal resort like Blackpool or Skegness, and worked until they were 65.

In the twenty-first century, in the UK all this has been swept away on the tides of change. Employment in 'traditional' working-class occupations such as mining, steel, shipbuilding and engineering has been decimated. The proportion of women working has increased substantially. The roles played by men and women are no longer so rigid and while the idea that 'new men' have replaced the traditional male role is a myth, there is no doubt that new roles for men and women have been created. The traditional 'cornflake packet' family consisting of two parents and two children is in a minority. The fragmentation of work, class and gender identities has led to the creation of a 'mix 'n' match' culture and the creation of new 'tribal' identities. The shifting social patterns have made life much more difficult for marketers who use traditional tools for segmenting markets on the basis of family, age, gender and social class.

As social class has become less useful as a means of segmenting markets, so marketers have turned to lifestyle, to the values which people share in common and the sorts of activities they like to engage in as a new basis for segmentation. Advances in technology have enabled marketers to build massive databases containing all sorts of marketing information regarding the purchase behaviour of individuals. Another major force for fragmentation is the coming of the digital age. When people have little in common in terms of their real-life experiences they can share in a discussion of a mythical experience such as what happened in last night's television soap opera, *Neighbours* or *EastEnders*. There is a worry that the massive channel choice which will accompany the digital age will remove even that topic of conversation.

Yet another force for fragmentation is the effect of time/space compression on workers and consumers. Schor (1991) discusses the paradox that while US production doubled between 1948 and 1990, American workers were working longer hours than they were forty years before and so they simply do not have the time to enjoy their hard-won rewards. Schor suggests that:

- ■ Americans spend more time shopping than anyone else.
- ■ Americans spend the highest fraction of what they earn.
- ■ Americans' homes are more luxurious than those elsewhere.
- ■ American average income is 65 times the average of half the world's population.

Schor feels that the consumer society itself and, in particular, the economic assumption that more goods equate with more satisfaction is at the heart of the problem. It is hard to imagine how having more of something might make people worse off. But what if satisfaction depends on relative, as opposed to absolute, consumption? Schor argues that a focus on absolute consumption can lead to an insidious cycle of work–spend–credit–debt. More than anything, the American worker experiences life as a series of packets or episodes filled with time pressure. The need to escape such pressure is evident in the rebirth of movements such as Voluntary Simplicity and Downshifting.

So far discussion has concentrated on Europe and the US. However, forces for fragmentation in the developing world markets suggest that the greatest number of new consumers will come from India and China. The 'one child' policy in China has resulted in female infanticide to the extent that in 1992 it was estimated there were 20m fewer women than men. Consequently, China's 'little (male) emperors' stand at the centre of attention for their grandparents and parents. In 1996 it was estimated that in China there were 250m young men aged between 5 and 14, and following from the lack of women in society it is anticipated that these will be lonely young men, with high expectations (Henley Centre, 1998).

The body

Around the world there seems to be a growing fascination with the body. Strange things are happening in economically developed nations, with some young women and increasing numbers of men reputed to be starving themselves, while at the same time morbid obesity is regarded as a problem of potentially epidemic proportions. Starvation is a consumption issue, which causes concerns related to the ideal images of beauty portrayed by mass media. Consumers are bombarded daily with media images that zone in on and separate out parts of the body, e.g. face, eyes, nose, hair, teeth, legs and nails, constantly inviting comparison between the idealized airbrushed images and the reality of their bodies as they are. The task of such images, including advertising images, is to persuade individuals that they cannot live with their bodies as they are but only as they might be if the products which are on offer were to be purchased. These images have a powerful effect when they are brought to life in the conversation and action of the peer group, where everyone is on show and being scrutinized by others.

Given that the vast majority of media images are of young, beautiful people, one might imagine that they can hardly be blamed for the recent rise in the rate of morbid obesity. This is a complex issue whose roots lie in a web of lifestyle-related and environmental conditions. One factor is the decline in regular family meals by some groups and the concomitant increase in the purchase of ready meals and take-away meals which can contain large amounts of 'hidden' fat, salt and sugar. Another relates to the decline in exercise. The impact of other 'softer' factors is more difficult to measure, and here, paradoxically the portrayal of beautiful and slim images may have a role to play. A person who is obese is likely to be low in self-esteem. The constant reminder of their condition provided by advertising images of perception may act to lower their esteem further, thereby motivating them to engage in mood repair, by eating.

The media focus on models of perfection which are slim, hard and machine-like encourages us to think of our body as a project, something which must be endlessly worked on and improved. There is evidence that cosmetic plastic surgery, which ten years ago was not considered to be socially acceptable, is now being actively considered by more people. As European populations grow older and as bio-technologies for working on and improving the body are developed to new heights of possibility, so there should be a major focus on the body as a continuing preoccupation for individuals and a major source of corporate income. Already the focus on the body is apparent in the demand for human and animal body parts which is being fuelled by two different sources: Chinese traditional medicine and the development of Western technologies for replacing body parts. At present demand for human body parts, e.g. kidneys, retinae, etc., is fuelled by means of a transfer from poor countries to rich countries. However, as the power of technology increases so the medical profession is trying to find new sources of body parts to replace the gruesome trade www.bearwatch.org/poaching.htm Regarding Chinese traditional medicine, global trade in bear parts for use in traditional Chinese medicine is estimated to be £2bn (US$3.6bn). Bear bile, paws and gall bladders are the most sought-after parts. In Asia concern about the body is reflected in a subtly different way from that expressed in Europe. Where Europeans desire a tanned body, the Asian market for skin lighteners has grown over the years.

Developments in technology seem to ensure that our relation to the body will continue to change dramatically in the future. It is thought that within the next seventy-five years drugs will exist to restore or strengthen memory and to inhibit sleep and fear. Custom-grown replacement body parts will be available to those who can afford them and medical records for all should include their complete genome. The likelihood that 'we will see the creation of human beings which are growing yet technically dead because they have no brain' is a probability that raises important ethical issues. It is also feasible that nano-machines will be able to seek out and destroy cancer cells with no collateral damage, providing a 'natural' replacement for eyes.

With respect to the use of human body parts there is growing evidence of a trade in human organs for cash. 'We will see the creation of human beings which are growing yet technically dead because they have no brain.' (Source: adapted from Dixon, 1997.)

THE THIRD WORLD AND *LE QUART MONDE*

There is a trend towards a polarization of society based on income and wealth both within states (*le Quart Monde*) and on a global basis (the Third World). On a global basis problems caused by Third World war, debt and increasing consumption are increasingly on the agenda. The Third World not only forms a convenient source of body parts for Western markets, it also forms a convenient dumping ground for the vast surpluses created in more 'developed' military and agricultural markets.

There are startling differences on a range of indicators between countries in terms of development. In most developed countries it is expected that the majority of the popula-tion will live to beyond the age of 40. However, in a number of countries, including some well known holiday destinations, the future is bleak. According to the United Nations (UN)

Figure 2.4
Gross domestic
product *per
capita* (US$)

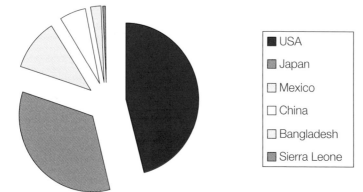

- USA
- Japan
- Mexico
- China
- Bangladesh
- Sierra Leone

GDP *per capita*
makes the
assumption that
wealth is
distributed equally
across the
population. Other
data point to
massive disparities
in income and
wealth within
countries. For
example, it is
estimated that in
Nigeria, which has
an abundance of
resources, 70 per
cent of the
population live on
an income of less
than US$1 per day.

Source:
UNHDR (2005),
statistical indicator
14: Economic
performance.

Human Development Report, in Barbados just over 6 per cent are not expected to live beyond the age of 40. In the Bahamas the figure is just over 13 per cent. In Guyana it is 18 per cent. Endemic poverty is one thing, AIDS another. In those countries most directly affected by AIDS the figures are truly staggering. In South Africa the likelihood that a person born in 2006 will not live to forty is 43 per cent; in Zimbabwe this rises to 65.9 per cent, in Lesotho to 67.6 per cent and in Botswana 69 per cent and Swaziland to over 74 per cent.

Global warming is perceived as a major potential threat in about twenty years. There are two disturbing points to comment upon in Figure 2.5.

- The fall-off in emissions that occurred in Eastern Europe following the fall of the Soviet Union, which is slowly recovering.
- The member countries of the Organization for Economic Co-operation and Development (OECD) had stabilized but not reduced emissions.

The main question is the extent to which rapidly developing countries such as India, China and Brazil will be able to develop in a sustainable manner.

LE QUART MONDE

This term refers to marginalized groups who live within the Western developed world. The economist Galbraith (1992) and the sociologist Bauman (1995) have described a trend towards polarization within the nation states of the 'developed' world with the creation of two categories. These are the 'contented' majority who count so far as 'mainstream' marketers are concerned and the 'underclass' composed of those who survive on the margins of society. For those who live a comfortable life in an industrialized country it is tempting to believe that exploitation is confined to the Third World economies. This is far from the truth, as is attested, in 2004, by the deaths of dozens of Chinese cockle pickers in Morecambe Bay, England, as well as the continuing existence of sweatshops and even slave conditions for some workers. Simmering discontent among the underclass occasionally manifests itself in rioting, as occurred in France in 2005.

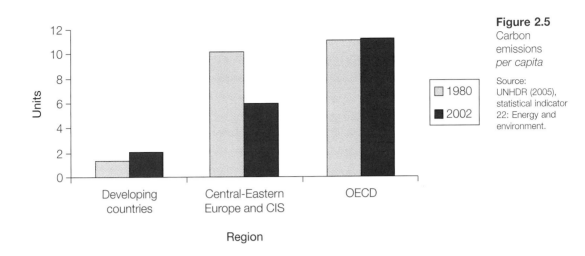

Figure 2.5
Carbon
emissions
per capita

Source:
UNHDR (2005),
statistical indicator
22: Energy and
environment.

Organization and the marketing environment

This section returns to the functionalist approach to the role of marketing. It assumes that the firm is an organism whose main goal is to survive by taking advantage of the opportunities and by avoiding the threats that are present in the environment, including responding to competitor actions. The organization is purposive. In order to survive, decision makers seek to attend rationally to environmental problems and opportunities. The problem-solving process involves analysing the current situation, developing goals and strategies to achieve those goals and, finally, providing feedback to gauge whether goals have been successfully achieved. The organizational problem-solving process is analogous to the individual problem-solving process. For example, any individual who wishes to solve any problem must consider where they are, where they want to be and how to get there. The individual questions and related organizational terms are shown in Table 2.2.

LEVELS OF PLANNING: FROM CORPORATE TO BUSINESS PLANS

It may be useful to consider firms as organisms for the sake of analysis, but it must be recognized that these are extremely complex organisms. For example, Wal-Mart has a turnover of hundreds of billions of dollars and employs hundreds of thousands of workers. Such complex entities can be organized in different ways, including functional, divisional and matrix forms of organization. A common procedure is that those at the top level of the organization conduct a corporate-level strategic analysis that, in turn, will inform analysis at the business level. Functional plans, including the marketing plan will be drafted at each level. For example, it can make sense for a vehicle manufacturer to divide its businesses into cars and trucks as it could be argued that these face quite different market places and challenges. For such a business the top team will devise a corporate plan which will set out the vision and mission of the organization in addition to spelling out the goals for executives in the Strategic Business Units (SBUs) comprising trucks and cars. The executives in each

Table 2.2 Marketing strategy process: problem-solving process

Questions to be asked	Analyses to be undertaken
Where are we now?	Situation analysis
	Gap analysis
Where do we want to be?	Mission and objectives
How do we get there?	Strategy formation
	Strategy evaluation
	Strategy implementation '4 Ps'
	Co-ordination and control
How did we do?	Feedback

SBU will then work within the constraints established by the corporate plan in setting more precise objectives and in devising strategies of how to achieve these objectives. The corporate marketing plan will be a subset of the main plan focusing on providing the long-term direction of the organization regarding the markets and needs that will be served and will set goals for the SBUs. Managers within each SBU will devise more specific marketing objectives and programmes in the light of this plan. A schematic map of the planning process is shown in Figure 2.6.

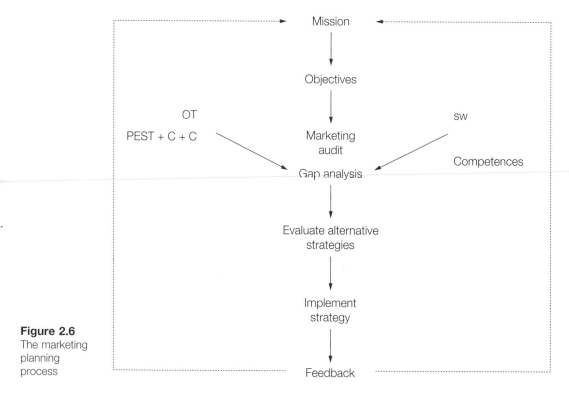

Figure 2.6
The marketing planning process

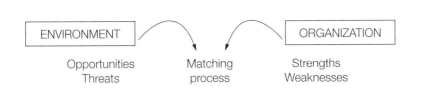

Figure 2.7
SWOT: creating a fit between organization and environment

MARKETING AUDIT: EXTERNAL AND INTERNAL ANALYSES

The marketing audit involves a systematic and comprehensive analysis of the business marketing environment. Why begin with the environment? If a systems approach is used as a starting point, it is possible to view the organization as an organism which must adapt to changing environmental conditions or die. Organizations are engaged in a battle for survival, which has a dual imperative to meet the needs of customers (Hooley and Lynch, 1985: Kohli and Jaworski 1990: 6; Narver and Slater 1990) and to fend off the competition. The logic is simple. How otherwise could a firm know where it wants to be and compute how it wants to get there if it does not know where it is now and how it got there?

Taking the perspective of the organization, if it is to survive in the long run, managers must continually scan the environment to obtain early warning of opportunities that can be taken advantage of, as well as of potential threats to survival. The process of matching is summed up in the simple acronym Strengths, Weakness, Opportunities and Threats (SWOT) analysis. Managers seek to identify the most relevant opportunities and threats that are present in the external environment and to match these with perceived internal strengths and weaknesses. The process of matching is illustrated in Figure 2.7.

AUDITING THE EXTERNAL ENVIRONMENT

Consider a brewery that is considering investing in the Chinese market. How are its managers to decide which environmental issues are relevant? There is an acronym available which can help in summarizing the key elements of the environment that are of importance to the marketer. Managers should analyse:

PEST + C + C

The task is to examine the likely impact of the:

- **P**olitical environment.
- **E**conomic environment.
- **S**ocial environment.
- **T**echnological environment.

In addition to:

- **C**onsumer environment.
- **C**ompetitive environment.

This list is not comprehensive. For example, one glaring omission is the physical environment. However rudimentary it is, it is still useful. Before proceeding to look at these different aspects of the environment in detail, it is appropriate to consider some general environmental trends.

CHINESE BEER MARKET: A CASE FOR EXPANSION?

Consider this case from the point of view of a major brewing company which is wishing to establish an operation in China. PEST + C + C are used below to identify the different factors which can influence the decision to invest market development.

Analysing the P: political and legal environment

Government regulation and legislation are major aspects of the contemporary business scene and must be paid due attention to by any organization. No corporation is beyond the law, as Microsoft has found out in being brought before the US courts to explain alleged anti-trust violations involving its Windows Web browser. Countries differ in the extent that they bind their nationals in webs of legislation. In the US the Federal Trade Commission (FTC) is the main body which regulates restraint of trade and enforces rules against unfair methods of competition and deceptive business practices. The FTC had many of its powers removed during the Reagan administration. However, in addition to the huge amount of federal legislation, organizations must also cope with state legislation. By comparison with the US, the tendency in the UK is for voluntary codes of practice for the regulation of the media and advertising.

It is obviously in the organization's interests to be mindful of government actions that may have an effect on its operations. Within the European Union (EU) there is a huge range of national and supranational legislation which may be directly relevant, on issues ranging from government budgetary policies to legislation on packaging and labelling and on deceptive advertising. Larger companies have legal departments which can be consulted on a wide range of issues. Smaller companies may seek to actively exert an influence on government policy but may lack the resources to so do. In the UK this can be achieved by banding together under an umbrella such as the Association of Independent Companies or the Forum for Private Businesses which lobby government in the collective interests of their members.

In the discussion of the Chinese beer market, the potential investor should become familiar with the national and regional laws which regulate the brewing industry in China. Investors might also wish to consider the effects which political changes might have on the regulatory framework in the medium term.

Analysing the E: economic environment

The economic environment is of key importance to marketers. Aggregate consumer expenditure on goods and services is a major indicator, as is growth in personal disposable income. One major development since the 1960s has been the growth in the electronic circulation of capital. The evidence so far is that this development has contributed to the destabilization of international markets, which have seen massive swings in the fortunes of stocks and currencies as electronic cash pours in and out of stocks and currencies at the press of a button.

Since the end of the 1960s governments have perceived the rate of inflation as the major economic indicator to control. Increasingly, observers have become worried about the prospect for the return of deflation, a phenomenon which has not been witnessed since the 1930s. Marketers are keen to track market indicators such as growth in aggregate demand, consumer spending and changes in consumer demographics.

With respect to the investor which is considering opening a brewery in China information would be sought on inflation, interest rates, employment trends and wage rates, particularly within those areas that might effect production and the market place.

Analysing the T: technological environment

The global technological environment has witnessed major change, and this change is set to continue. Even the most remote parts of the globe can be reached via satellite visual and aural communications, by phone, television and spy satellites. In 'developed' countries the installation of fibre optics networks has led to the development of video-conferencing. Changes in technology have had a profound effect on organizational structure, leading to the creation of more distributed forms of organization. With the advent of various 'loyalty' cards, retailers and others are able to observe and track consumer purchase behaviour and react to each consumer and are almost in a position to treat each consumer as an individual. Technological know-how is a major barrier to entry in many mass-market operations.

With respect to the brewing company seeking an investment opportunity in China, one would need to analyse the technologies currently used by potential competitors in China. Is the technology more advanced? Do consumer tastes demand particular technological solutions? On the other hand, one might enquire as to whether the technological infrastructure could support planned operations.

Analysing the socio-cultural environment

Aspects of change in the socio-cultural environment are of major importance to marketers, especially, those aspects which impinge on an individual's sense of identity. These include changes in social class which are considered in Chapter 3 in addition to changes in the cultural mix and the creation of new subcultures. For example, in Europe already the ageing population known as the 'grey market' is having a marked impact on the marketing strategies of producers and retailers.

One important demographic change in China has been the reduction in the population of those under 20 – the 'little emperors' who have resulted from the governmental one-child policy. Some of the demographic changes which have been taking place in China have been discussed above, most notably that related to the 'little emperors'. However, other social factors are highlighted in the brewing case. For example, *baijiu* fulfils an important social function which the government hopes to replace with beer. Other important social factors to take into account are *guanxi, guo quing* and *houmen* which collectively signify how business is done in practice in China.

Guanxi refers to the importance of networking and relationships and is a means of getting round the formidable obstacles presented by red tape. The right *guanxi* with distributors is a key to market success. *Guanxi* is linked to the concept of '*houmen*' or the 'back door' as a means of smoothing relations with state bodies. *Guo qing* is a blanket term for distinctively Chinese characteristics of which a foreigner should be aware. For example, they should be aware of the 'one-child' policy and of the Chinese preference for prosperous sounding brand names (Mak, 1998).

Analysing the competitive environment

While the direct competition must be analyzed, it is also important to assess any competition that may come from substitutes and alternatives. In analysing the competitive environment the degree of industry concentration is important to know. In the Chinese beer case, the industry still tends to be relatively fragmented, with a large number of breweries. The top ten brewers still account for less than 20 per cent of all output. Added to this is the knowledge that the idea of competition is new to producers in this sector, but that the competition is learning quickly. Indirect competition comes from substitutes for beer, e.g. other alcoholic and non-alcoholic drinks.

Analysing the customer environment

From a marketer's point of view the customer environment is the most important one to consider. The rise of the global market may be regarded as a major opportunity for marketers. One simple calculation involves estimating potential demand for products by obtaining data about relative consumption patterns around the world. Two factors are important, *per capita* consumption and overall consumption. While the former provides information on the individual use rate, which may aid decision makers in estimating the scope for market development, decision makers are also interested in the overall market size.

For example estimates of *per capita* consumption of beer in China range between 14 litres(l) and 19 l, which is low when compared with Western Europe, where it is of the order of 70 l per head. Consumption in those countries where beer and not wine is the traditional choice is even higher, e.g. in the Czech Republic around 160 l per person! Despite the relatively low levels of *per capita* beer consumption, the Chinese market, at 25bn l (Plato Logic, 2005), has overtaken the US market to become the largest beer market in the world. Importantly, given the size of the Chinese population, this indicates strong potential for further sustained growth in this market. However, marketers need to know a lot more than patterns of aggregate demand. It is also very important to have sufficient knowledge of the market so as to be able to segment the market place. Just as in Europe, geographical variation between different regions must be taken into account, as these reflect wide differences in

THE ROLE OF *GUANXI* IN CHINESE BUYING NEGOTIATIONS

In Chinese-based economies *guanxi* plays a critical role in developing interpersonal relationships that underpin negotiations within business. It is defined as being 'a concept of drawing on connections in order to secure favours in personal relations. It is an intricate and pervasive relational network which Chinese cultivate energetically, subtly, and imaginatively. It contains implicit mutual obligation, assurance and understanding, and governs Chinese attitudes toward long-term social and business relationships' (Luo, 1997).

Guanxi is a cultural phenomenon in relationships that involves:

- Tight, close-knit networks (Yeung and Tung, 1996: 54);
- Interpersonal connections (Xin and Pearce, 1996: 1641);
- Provision of a 'gate or pass' entry (Yeung and Tung, 1996: 54).

Guanxi occurs between people who share a group status or are related to a common person. It is also apparent among the frequent contacts between people as well as contacts between persons with little direct interaction (Dunfee and Warren, 2001). It involves 'factions in Chinese politics . . . groups aggregated by chains of ties in which members of the groups are bound by a combination of group ideology, institutional interests, loyalty toward charismatic leaders based on the traditional principle of rectification of names and the leaders' personal ties.' . . . 'Although networking and building relationships are important to political or business success everywhere in the world, the Chinese have much more intensive preoccupation with relationship building and deem it one of the most important principles of success than elsewhere' (Guo, 2001: 1–2).

There are four major dimensions of *guanxi* which complement and reinforce one another, namely:

- *Instrumental*, i.e. involving self-interested motivation, based on the desire for abundant repayment and achieving personal advantage.
- *Etiquette*, i.e. using social rituals to establish and maintain harmonious human relations with one's acquaintances such as co-workers, colleagues, superiors or subordinates.
- *Moral*, i.e. rules that follow a traditional system of ethics that obligates oneself to those within one's *guanxi* network.
- *Emotional* i.e. whereby friendship plays a central role in regulating interpersonal relationships.

They coexist harmoniously, but they undermine and weaken one another when they coexist in tension.

Consider the situation where two salesmen are negotiating with a buyer regarding the purchase of paper supplies for the office. The first salesperson represents a major multinational corporation (MNC) but has not previously sold to the potential buyer. The second salesperson works for a local Chinese business. The former, while Chinese, has built up few or no links with the potential buyer: the latter, living in the local community and having been to school with the buyer, has considerable *guanxi* over the negotiation situation. The pull, or obligation, to repay earlier family agreements, together with the moral and ethical elements involved, will encourage the buyer to place the order with the local Chinese business no matter what other benefits may be offered by the MNC's salesperson. Lower prices, quicker delivery and higher quality may be attractive but the power of *guanxi* is likely to override economic logic.

Source: adapted from Dunfee and Warren (2001), Guo (2001, Luo (1997) and Yeung and Tung (1997).

APPLE COMPUTER: FROM MAC TO IMAC AND IPOD

In 1998 Steve Jobs rejoined Apple Computer at a nominal salary of $1 per annum to try to rescue the company which he had created. Twenty years earlier Jobs with his buddy, Steve Wozniak, conceived the Apple I, which many believe was the world's first personal computer (PC). The Apple II followed and Apple went public as a result of sharply increased sales. Growth took off in 1984 with the launch of the Macintosh which was considered to be the most easy to use and best loved computer ever designed. The 'Mac', as it is affectionately known by enthusiasts, was launched with much publicity which has been considered to be the greatest advertising ever made. The best feature of the Mac was its ease of use and, ten years later, 13m Macs had been shipped. However, Apple itself was in trouble. In 1995 the company experienced declining share and profitability and seemed puny against the giant Microsoft Corporation. Where did Apple go wrong? Has it managed to claw its way back since?

Several answers suggest themselves. Apple spent many years pursuing a series of law suits against other companies, including Microsoft, in a bid to protect its unique operating system.

Apple took Microsoft through the US court system and right to the Supreme Court over the claim that Microsoft Windows illegally copied parts of the Macintosh user interface (anon., 1995). At the same time major anti-trust actions were being taken against Microsoft. However, Apple lost its copyright action against Microsoft in 1992. The legal action is itself taken as symptomatic of a fundamental mistake which some analysts believe Apple made in the early 1980s, in that it did not allow others to license its operating system. This was when the then mighty IBM launched its (much inferior) PC which quickly entrenched itself in the corporate market where 'Big Blue' had an unrivalled reputation. By comparison with IBM Apple was considered to be a renegade company by the men in suits.

The attractiveness of the PC and its relatively cumbersome operating system Windows designed by Bill Gates of Microsoft increased. In the late 1980s IBM's share of the PC market slipped as clone manufacturers gained a greater hold of the market, offering very competitive prices and good-quality products (Day-Copeland, 1988). By comparison, Apple discouraged clones and sought to protect its operating system (anon., 1997). For IBM the PC was a sideline, a diversion from its core business of churning out larger, more powerful mainframe computers. But it sold in millions. Unfortunately, IBM failed to secure exclusive rights to either Intel's chip or Microsoft's operating software, which led to hundreds of 'clones' of its new PC coming on to the market. All were based on the same Intel chips and Microsoft operating software, which together rapidly became the industry standard. The clones sold in even more millions than IBM's original. IBM's share of what was to become by far the largest sector of the computer industry collapsed: from close to 100 per cent in the early 1980s to well below 10 per cent in the late 1990s. The revolution introduced by the PC was both swift and brutal. From a standing start in the early 1980s, sales of PCs soared to around 50m a year globally. This market is worth $74bn (£41bn) annually, according to Dataquest, a market research company based in San Jose, California, and compares with global sales of 35m passenger cars and 100m colour television sets.

As PCs became more popular so software developers began to focus more on providing material for the mainstream PC–Windows market first and later for the Mac. This led to users who prized the user-friendliness of the Mac becoming more disillusioned with Apple, as they witnessed the growing prestige and available pool of software applications for the PC. Apple was perceived as being second best.

In 1997 Steve Jobs went back to Apple after a thirteen-year exile. Jobs had been banished from Apple by John Sculley, who had been brought in from Pepsi to strengthen Apple's marketing as market share and profits fell. Sculley was himself dismissed in 1993 after a period that saw Apple's market share drop from 20 per cent to 8 per cent. His replacement Michael Spindler lasted until 1996 when market share had fallen to 5 per cent and, with losses mounting, it was feared that Apple would go into liquidation. Even diehard Apple loyalists who had held on to their beloved Mac's against the steady advance of the PC began to defect. Spindler was in turn replaced by Dr Gil Amelio, who wrote about his traumatic 500 days when Apple's market share declined further to 4 per cent. Amelio invited Jobs back, but was then subsequently deposed by Jobs.

Once again in command, Jobs set about the task of inspiring Apple employees to develop a series of new products. Informing this was a simple vision: 'There's a very strong DNA within Apple, and that's about taking state-of-the-art technology and making it easy for people.' Apple is in the business of making complex technology accessible to those who lead busy lives and who don't want to spend their days reading manuals. Jobs disputes the conventional wisdom that suggests that the television set and the computer are going to merge so that emailing and Internet surfing can be done in the living room when not watching television, or with the television occupying only a part of the screen. His belief is that when people surf the Net they do so in active mode with their brains switched on; when they go to a television set they are passive and go to turn their brain off.

In 1998 the first of the new products off the line, the iMac, was launched, a product which prompted Keegan (1998:2) to gush that it was:

Sleekly designed in translucent blue tones, and much easier to operate, it makes most other computers – almost statutorily beige in colour – look like something from a science museum. It is the nearest thing to Jobs's vision of 'the computer for the rest of us.'

Sales of iMac exceeded expectations at 278,000 units in the first six weeks making it what *Fortune* magazine described as 'one of the hottest computer launches ever'. The iMac was the embodiment of Jobs's dream of a well designed eye-catching computer that was simple to operate. Then came the EMAC and then the powerful up-market G5 which appealed to professionals. In 2004 the iMac and G5 were married in a startling new format, the Imac G5, which integrated the processing hard drive into the screen assembly.

Alongside these developments in the computer field came a product that would have been inconceivable before schoolboy Shawn Fanning developed Napster to challenge the global music industry. Apple quickly identified an opportunity, launching IPOD in 2001 to capitalize on the Napster phenomenon. In 2001 this allowed the consumer to bypass the rather tiresome task of visiting a store and buying an overpriced CD by simply searching for the music they wanted on a central website and then downloading the mp3 files direct to disc. What Apple did was to provide a virtually unlimited space for consumers to store not only music that could be played on the equivalent of a Walkman, but also photos and indeed anything that could be stored digitally.

Source: adapted from anon. (1984); anon. (1995); anon. (1997); anon. (1998); Day-Copeland (1994); Keegan (1998: 2); McGuire (1994); Morgenstern (1996); Vinzant (1998).

CASE QUESTIONS

1   Why did Apple consistently lose market share despite the Mac being the most user friendly computer ever made?
2   What alternative strategies might Apple have followed?
3   In your view will the iMac be successful? Why?
4   Do you think that Steve Jobs is right when he says that the activities of watching television and using a computer are fundamentally incompatible?
5   Identify some current opportunities and threats that Jobs should be aware of.

wealth, consumption patterns and tastes. In particular there is likely to be a marked difference in consumption between urban and rural areas; beer consumption in urban centres such as Shanghai and Beijing is reported to be three to four times the national average.

While geography provides a basic means of segmenting the market place, this could be greatly enhanced if marketers could combine this knowledge with that about the demographics of consumers, constituting age and gender differences in consumption of beer, and socio-economics, or income. The brewery would also wish to know more about the way in which beer is consumed in China. For example, is it an everyday drink or something which is reserved for special occasions? Other questions might include:

■   Who drinks beer (and who does not) and why?
■   Who are heavy users and why?
■   Why do people drink beer (as opposed to some other drink)?
■   When do people drink beer (in bars, at home?).

It is only by asking such questions that an understanding of the behaviour of consumers in this market place can be obtained. This is why the study of consumer behaviour and marketing research are given such prominence in this book.

Implementing strategies

In terms of implementing strategies the marketer must fashion a unique marketing mix which is aimed at the market place. The basic ingredients of the marketing mix (or the '4 Ps') are:

■   **P**roduct.
■   **P**rice.
■   **P**romotion.
■   **P**lace.

In the Chinese beer example, the brewer may wish to concentrate on serving the needs for beer of 20–30 year old single male A/B's, living in urban areas (these terms will be considered later in Chapter 5).

The product is not only the beer itself, although it would be a good idea for the product development team to conduct some marketing research blind taste tests to see how favourably the market responded to the beer. Additionally, the team should consider important elements such as the packaging, e.g. should this beer be in a can or a bottle? If this was to be a premium beer and if the market perception was that premium beers only come in bottles, then it may be a mistake for the team to consider launching its beer packaged in a can. The product is not only the physical product; image also matters.

Price conveys much information about the perceived quality of the product. If this beer is to be perceived as a prestige product then it is important to find out what the market expectation for the likely price potential customers would expect such a prestige product to be. This can be difficult, as setting a price which is below expectation can have just as damaging an effect as too high a price for prestige products.

Promotion, or marketing communication, will include advertising, public relations and sales promotions. Once the beer is in a position to be launched, it may be a good idea to invite journalists who work for newspapers and broadcast media and, in particular, those who are favourites of the target market to inspect the beer being marketed. This could involve a tour of the production facility and tasting demonstrations showing the superiority of the brand over others. It could generate some useful publicity for the new brand, although care needs to be taken to minimize unwanted effects which could achieve much higher publicity. For example, it would be a major blow if the journalists thought that the beer was inferior to others. Hopefully, that would not be the case, provided sound research had been undertaken beforehand.

Place, or channels of distribution of the beer, is vitally important. If it is to be a premium beer then should it be widely distributed or sold only through exclusive outlets? If it is to be sold through exclusive outlets then there would need to be a built-in extra margin on price to secure the additional premium demanded by such outlets. A good system of physical distribution would need to be in place.

CONCLUSION

As a result of working through this chapter you should appreciate:

- **the development of marketing thought over the past hundred years, noting the different phases of development of the topic;**
- **what is meant by the marketing concept;**
- **how a marketing orientation is different from a production or sales orientation;**
- **the orientation of this book, which is centred around a functionalist approach to marketing;**
- **how to conduct a strategic marketing analysis.**

REVIEW QUESTIONS

1   Why is environmental scanning consistent with a functionalist approach to marketing?
2   What factors should the marketer take into account in scanning the marketing environment?
3   Name three important trends in today's marketing environment.
4   What factors should the marketer take into account in implementing marketing strategy?

RECOMMENDED FURTHER READING

Aaker, D.A. (1998) *Strategic market management*, 5th edn, Chichester: Wiley.

Buttery, E.A. and Wong, Y.H. (1999) 'The development of a Guanxi framework', *Marketing Intelligence and Planning,* 17 (3), pp. 14–15 (2).

Donaldson, B. and O'Toole, T. (2002) *Strategic market relationships: from strategy to implementation,* Chichester: Wiley.

Galbraith, J.K. (1975) *Economics and the public purpose,* London: André Deutsch.

Hooley, G.J., Sanders, J.A. and Piercy, N.F. (1998) *Marketing strategy and competitive positioning,* 2nd edn, Harlow: *Financial Times*/Prentice Hall.

Jain, S.C. (1981) *Marketing planning and strategy,* Cincinnati OH: South Western.

Johnson, G., Scholes, K. and Whittington, R. (2005) *Exploring corporate strategy: text and cases,* 7th edn, Harlow: Pearson.

Luck, D.J., Ferrell, O.C. and Lucas, G.H. (1989) *Marketing strategy and plans*, 3rd edn, Englewood Cliffs NJ: Prentice Hall.

Merrilees, B. and Miller, D. (1999) 'Direct selling in the west and east: the relative roles of product and relationship (Guanxi) drivers', *Journal of Business Research,* 45 (3), pp. 17–18.

Wilson, R.M.S. and Gilligan, C. (1997) *Strategic marketing management,* 2nd edn, Oxford: Butterworth Heinemann.

Useful web addresses

Poaching and the bear parts trade: http://www.bearwatch.org/poaching.htm.

3 CONSUMER BUYER BEHAVIOUR

LEARNING OBJECTIVES

After studying this chapter you should appreciate:

■ the differences between the rational economic, psychoanalytic behaviourist and cognitive explanations of consumption;

■ the lexicon associated with each of the above explanations, for example the meaning of terms such as 'the unconscious', 'displacement' and 'sublimation' within psychoanalytic theory;

■ the linkages and differences between Freudian theory and behavioural theories of motivation;

■ the relation between Freudian theory, changing social characters and the emergence of lifestyle as a construct;

■ the importance of identity in consumer behaviour, particularly related to gender, family, social class, ethnicity and religion;

■ why behaviourist and cognitive information processing explanations of involvement are different.

INTRODUCTION

As was mentioned in Chapter 1, the study of consumer behaviour is an important part of the managerialist approach to marketing. Underpinning this notion is the belief that if academics and industrialists can come to a better understanding of why people behave as they do, it should be possible to develop products which have a better chance of success in the market place. Over and above the interests of firms, there is a societal interest in seeking to understand consumer behaviour. For the first time many consumers live in societies where the impact of consumption has much wider implications than those of the transaction between buyer and seller. Many people in the world live in consumer societies where goods and services play much more than a simple economic role. In this chapter the economic explanation is briefly explained. The three powerful psychological explanations based on psychoanalytic theory, behaviourism and cognitive learning theory, are discussed. Table 3.1 summarizes some of the key aspects relating to each explanation (Kotler, 1965).

ECONOMIC THEORY

There is a fable: There once was a man who lived in Scarcity.
After many adventures and a long voyage in the Science of Economics,
he encountered the Society of Affluence. They were married and had
many needs.

(Baudrillard, 1988)

The abstraction of *homo economicus*, 'rational economic man', is the point at which the theory of consumer behaviour begins. This account considers human behaviour over the course of about 100 years. Since the 1970s, with the rise of behavioural economics, many of the following assumptions have been modified. Nevertheless, this forms a useful point of departure for understanding different accounts of consumer behaviour. In classical economic terms *homo economicus* is a rational actor who is aware of the scope of the choices available and who acts alone to evaluate each potential choice of action on the basis of perfect information to maximize his or her utility, or satisfaction. When economists say that consumers act 'rationally' they mean that they act rationally from their point of view. This

Table 3.1 Key relations between different explanations

Consumer type	Individual	Period	Discipline
Rational consumer	Marshall	Late 1800s	Economics
Unconscious consumer	Freud	Early 1900s	Psychology
Conditioned consumer	Watson/Skinner	Early 1990s	Psychology
Problem-solving consumer	Simon	Mid 1990s	Psychology

may seem to be irrational to others but is intelligible once the circumstances of the person are known. For example, Leavitt (1958) suggested the following:

> Man is an irrational animal, if by irrational we mean that he does not always do what we think is best for him, but though irrational there is an internal logic to his behaviour. So we can understand it if we look at it from the inside rather than the outside and if we try to deal with it all at once instead of in pieces.

It is the idea of the 'inside' rationality that is the basis of economic rationality. Some of the other assumptions underpinning the idea of rational economic man are that:

- The principle of pure competition where each agent acts as an autonomous individual and where the market place is composed of many small buyers and sellers.
- Consumers have complete information and foresight about economic conditions including the future about which there exists no uncertainty.
- Consumers have fixed preferences and can effectively signal these to producers.
- Consumers act to maximize their utility.
- Firms are able to satisfy every need expressed as a want for a particular product.
- Consumers act rationally and comprehensively to evaluate every choice alternative prior to action.

It is true that in contemporary consumer societies many people operate alone in conducting transactions. However, Leavitt (1958) felt that consumers can best be viewed as inter-dependent, arguing that if consumers are treated as if they act solely by themselves 'our predictions about him will go pretty far wrong'. It can be asked how often individuals really act alone. Often goods are purchased with the direct and indirect help of others. It could be argued that consumption is paradoxical. Individuals partake in the mass market with millions of others buying mass produced-goods while also combining these mass-produced goods into 'unique' combinations which provide individuals with a sense of distinctiveness from other people. In a way all consumption is social to the extent that the goods that are purchased are bought for the consumption of others, those others who look at us and judge us in terms of what we have bought. Consumers often act mimetically through vicarious learning by imitating the choices of others.

Economists also assume that individuals consciously are aware of their needs. A 'need' for this purpose is a loss of equilibrium, a change in state which indicates a lack. It is assumed that there is conscious awareness of this lack and of the means of filling it. While cognitive theorists by and large share this view, this is contested by Freudians, who would argue that instead needs often emerge as a result of unconscious conflicts and that they represent a sublimation of such conflict. Behaviourists protest that too much emphasis is placed on the importance of internal mental states in determining choice processes. They would argue for the importance of considering the environmental setting in which behaviour occurs.

The economic assumption that preferences are fixed holds some truth. For example, one of the authors' liking for sweet things appears so. However, there is a growing belief also that preferences are constructed rather than revealed. The idea of constructed preferences denies that consumers simply refer to a master list of preferences in memory when making a choice. Cognitive theorists (cf. Bettman *et al.*, 1998) are busy researching how preferences are generated. They suggest that sometimes consumers may use the forms of weighting assumed by economists, although more often than not they will use a much simpler method.

Following from the above, the traditional economic view suggests that individuals evaluate goods and services in relation to their needs. They consider these in the light of key attributes to which are attached utilities; those goods which maximize their return in terms of subjective expected utility are the ones which individuals will choose. This presupposes that it makes sense to break down personal beliefs and evaluations in a systematic manner. Cognitive learning theorists do not simply assume that this is the case but actively explore the conditions in which it occurs and when it fails to occur. In any event the reality of everyday behaviour is that most purchase behaviour is relatively routine and habitual. Cognitive psychologists argue that when managers and consumers do engage in problem-solving behaviour they do not exhaustively analyze every alternative but instead use simple heuristics or rules of thumb.

That a world of perfect information does not exist means firms must actively seek to anticipate the needs and wants of consumers. Firms do not respond to every perceived need and want. They are constrained by the environment in which they operate and must make some form of return which covers their outgoings. In any event one might also choose to question the extent to which people act rationally and comprehensively in evaluating different offerings. Cognitive theorists argue that the idea of rational comprehensiveness is not compatible with actual human information processing capability. Given limited attention span and a myriad of decisions to make, they argue that the use of means–end analysis is a more likely strategy in human decision-making behaviour.

One may summarize the discussion with respect to the economic model of the consumer. It presents an over-rationalized and over-individualized view of the consumer. It does not provide an understanding of what things mean to people and how they come to have that meaning. It is poor at recognizing or explaining the intrinsic value of things to people.

Next three different alternatives to the economic explanation are discussed, namely:

- The Freudian tradition which held sway from the 1930s to the early 1960s and which remains influential in some quarters to this day.
- The behaviourist tradition which was also influential in the 1930s but which had its heyday in the 1960s.
- The cognitive tradition which remains the mainstream explanation of consumer behaviour today.

FREUD AND PSYCHOANALYSIS

Freud's chosen topic was the human condition; how the individual comes to 'be' someone, a subject of immense scope and one which provides formidable obstacles to full appreciation.

During the twentieth century Freud's theories had an immense impact on the study of psychology, linguistics and social theory that continues to this day.

Freud's relevance to the understanding of consumer behaviour is diverse. His early writings put forward a psychodynamic notion of selfhood that relates to a conception of the human organism as comprising a storehouse of energy that develops and grows through the investment of energy into objects (people and things) and its return to the self that it nourishes. Problems can arise when the energy that has been invested is cut off. Freud's concept of the activity of the unconscious raises the question of consumer motivation. If desire is an unconscious process, then consumers are often not aware of their real motives for desiring things. In his later writings Freud developed a complex explanation for the topography of the human mind. In this explanation the self is a complex and conflicted entity which is comprised of three agencies. The *id* represents the demands of biology for immediate gratification. Pitted against the id, the *superego* represents the internalized demand of society for civilized conduct. In the middle is the *ego* that must constantly seek to reconcile the demands of the powerful forces of biology and society in attending to the survival and gratification of the person.

The extended self

Freud was an acute observer and one of the things he noticed which intrigued him was that infants and those who are ill or disappointed in love tend to be almost totally self-absorbed. In his earlier work on infant development (Freud, 1911) he had reasoned the existence of two principles; the pleasure principle and the reality principle. From birth infants are governed by the pleasure–unpleasure principle to the extent that they will strive towards those people and things that provide them with pleasure and will avoid those that do not. If satisfaction is not immediately forthcoming, the infant will hallucinate it and will, as in a dream, imagine that the source of satisfaction is actually there. Such hallucination of pleasure is not viable in the long run and the infant must learn slowly and painfully to accommodate herself to the demands of reality, for example by learning to defer gratification. Even so the lure of the pleasure principle is ever present, particularly for those adults who find that reality is so unbearable that they turn away from it to live instead in a fantasy world.

In a later paper Freud (1914) argued the same point in a different way by highlighting the role played by sexual energy or libido in the process. From the start the infant invests all her libido or sexual energy into her 'self'. This self-absorbed or narcissistic self is an amorphous concept that includes the objects (by objects Freud means people and things) that provide her with satisfaction. As she grows older she must learn not only to defer gratification but to repress those instinctual impulses that come into conflict with the requirements of society. In order to do so she sets up an ideal inside herself, the ego-ideal, which is modelled on a parent or another caregiver. The energy that was previously invested into the narcissistic ego is now invested into the ego-ideal, which constitutes an image of perfection that the child then strives to become. Development of a healthy ego consists in a departure from narcissism brought about by displacement of libido on to an ego-ideal imposed from without and satisfaction comes from fulfilling this ideal. Linked with the *ego* ideal is the superego, a censoring agency that constantly watches the ego and measures it by the standards of the ego-ideal. Freud then had to consider what happened to the sexual instinct at this point. Overt expression of sexual desire is forbidden by most if not all societies and so societal pressure makes itself felt through increased superego control, leaving the ego the possibility of making one of two choices. Either desire is repressed from consciousness, in which case it retains the potential to be severely disruptive in later life; or the desire can be sublimated, i.e. the energy is directed towards an aim other than, and remote from, sexual satisfaction. Freud argues that some of society's greatest achievements; including all the great works of human culture, are the product of sublimation.

If one conceives of the 'self' as being constituted through investment of energy then being in love represents a flowing over of ego-libido on to the object (a person or a thing). We invest energy into those people and things that we love, i.e. those things that bring us satisfaction. When a person dies we do not simply mourn their passing but also our own diminution, because we are also mourning the loss of our own life force that we had invested in that person. This can be true of any object that is important to us: the pet that dies; the coat that is lost or stolen. If death is tragic then Freud marks out the melancholia that arises when one is slighted by another in love as being even worse.

Freud's explanation is challenging in that it affirms that the self is not confined in a container but is distributed amongst a range of people and objects. In this view the notion of a healthy self is associated with a diverse range of investments in other people and things. From Freud's explanation that narcissism or self-absorption is the normal state for very young children it is assumed that only gradually will one learn to invest in others. This point is illustrated by Csikszentmihalyi and Rochberg-Halton (1981: 98), who cite the different ways in which children of different ages in their study related to a refrigerator. The authors interviewed a 12 year old girl and her 15 year old brother. Each of the children had independently mentioned the refrigerator as being special. The young girl would go to the refrigerator when she was unhappy and said she would feel better already at the thought of being able to fix herself a snack. The boy, on the other hand, said that the refrigerator gave him a good feeling because when his friends came over to visit he could open it and treat them to food and drink. Thus even at the age of 12 the younger girl is still relatively narcissistic in being primarily self-oriented, by viewing the refrigerator as a means of satisfying her own individual needs. By contrast her older brother expands the self outwards in considering how the refrigerator can create social bonds. The authors found that as adolescents mature so the relation with commodities changes. Youth tends to value objects which are associated with action and experience, for example musical instruments, sports equipment, pets and vehicles. Gradually the boundaries of the self extend or expand outwards as energy is invested in friendships and partnerships such as marriage, so that others (husband, wife, children) become assimilated into the self-concept (Csikszentmihalyi and Rochberg-Halton, 1981: 101). Whereas children focus very much on experiencing objects in relation to their individual self, older people cherish objects which link them to others and which recall memories. Objects such as paintings and photographs are particularly valued as vehicles for contemplation.

If possessions can be regarded as part of the self then an unintentional loss of possessions should be regarded as a loss or lessening of self. Goffman (1961) discusses how institutions such as mental hospitals, homes for the aged and prisons seek to strip away a person's identity by systematically depriving them of all personal possessions such as clothing and money. Csikszentmihalyi and Rochberg-Halton view that our 'selves' are constructed in proportion to the amount of psychic energy which we invest. We should mourn for treasured objects which are taken away from us in a similar manner to the way that we mourn for our loved ones who die. The theory is that we are 'mourning' our own loss of self, that bit of us which we have invested so much energy into and which has now been taken away from us. Belk (1988: 142) reports that in a small-scale test which he carried out with burglary victims they not only felt anger but also reported feelings of invasion and violation. It can be imagined that in contemporary society, which is becoming progressively individualized, where possessions take the role of people and vice versa, that the investment of psychic energy into things is greater than ever before.

The preconscious and the unconscious

In *The Ego and the Id* (1923), Freud made the distinction between the 'preconscious', ideas which an individual can bring to consciousness almost at will and 'unconscious' thought which because of its disturbing nature is not easily made conscious although it still may indirectly influence behaviour. Freud posited that people may consciously censor and repress, displace or project such threatening ideas. As an instance of 'repression' Freud offers the case history of 'Anna O'. Despite the summer heat, Anna refused to drink water. She often raised the glass to her lips only to repel it with an air of disgust. No one, including Anna herself, knew the source of this sudden malady. It was only several days later when under hypnosis that Anna revealed that she had gone into someone else's room and had seen a dog drinking out of a glass. She had felt revulsion and disgust at the sight. Once she had described this situation Anna felt better and was able to drink. Freud's explanation of Anna's predicament was that this image had so revolted Anna's sensibilities that she had unconsciously repressed all knowledge of the scene and had converted this repressed disgust into a phobia concerning drinking.

'Repression' is a form of ego defence whereby images which are thought of as being disturbing are shut out of consciousness. Such disturbing images may be related to the outward expression of desires that are considered abnormal by society. By contrast to repression, 'displacement' occurs when an unconscious impulse is redirected towards a more acceptable target.

Displacement can take many forms, but that which is of most interest for consumer behaviour assessment is 'sublimation'. Sublimation involves the displacement of sexual energy, known as 'libido', to non-sexual ends in a manner which not only avoids conflict. It actively promotes a person's adjustment to his or her social context. Oriented towards the reality principle, the ego plays a key role in sublimating id demands by channelling id energy away from the pure investment in immediate gratification demanded by the pleasure principle towards a more socially acceptable response. A Freudian explanation would suggest that within Western European culture, consumer goods play an ever increasing role in sublimating those desires expressed by Eros. Freud's idea of 'sexuality' is different from that used generally. For Freud libido is essentially a drive whose object is the stimulation of various bodily areas or 'erotogenic zones'. In order to understand what Freud means by sexual energy and the developmental process by which this is attained, there needs to be further discussion.

Researching consumer motivation

The Institute for Motivation Research, started by Dichter around 1940, employed Freudian concepts to understand consumer desire better. Dichter (1960) argued that the key to desire lies in an understanding of the unconscious motives that often lie behind it. He considered that the desire for freedom and discovery can be expressed through the glamour of a new car. Dichter pioneered a number of forms of research, including the focus group. He recalls the institute's first study, on Ivory soap. By means of detailed observation researchers learned what others had ignored, that when buying soap people do not simply look at it but often sniff it and hold it; that consequently the smell, feel and shape of the soap bar are important. Researchers carried out 100 non-directive interviews in the US enquiring why people take a bath or shower. They found that taking a bath or shower before a romantic date had more significance; interviewees bathed more carefully and took longer. People made the choice to buy based not on attributes such as price, appearance, lather and colour, but on a combination of these factors, plus an 'intangible' element which Dichter labelled the personality of the soap. The researchers found that Ivory soap had a sombre, utilitarian, thoroughly cleansing character. Dichter linked brand identity to personal identity by arguing that individuals project themselves on to products. In buying a car they actually buy an extension of their own personality (Dichter, 1964: 86–7). Likewise when they are 'loyal' to a commercial brand they are 'loyal' to themselves. In discussing areas such as brand personality and social marketing he was well ahead of his time. Dichter (1964) later published a handbook of consumer motivations that contained findings from 2,500 studies of motivation carried out by the Institute.

Later Freud: id–ego–superego

It was mentioned above that Freud's theory is hydraulic to the extent that energy plays a vital part in his explanation and provides a key role in understanding motivation. In his later work he associated this energy with the powerful instinctual forces that are produced within the id, which Freud likens to a huge reservoir of psychic energy. The id is:

> [A] cauldron full of seething excitations . . . it is filled with energy reaching it from the instincts, but it has no organization, produces no collective will, but only a striving to bring about the satisfaction of instinctual needs subject to the observance of the pleasure principle.

> (Freud, 1933 pp. 73–4)

According to Freud biological instincts drive the production of energy according to two main principles over the life of the human subject, the life drive, Eros, and the death drive, Thanatos. Eros 'naturally' should prevail over the birth and growth phases of life, to be replaced as a person grows older by the equally pervasive power of Thanatos (see Figure 3.1). During the period of the predominance of Eros the instinctual drives push all behaviour in the direction of immediate gratification of biological life-

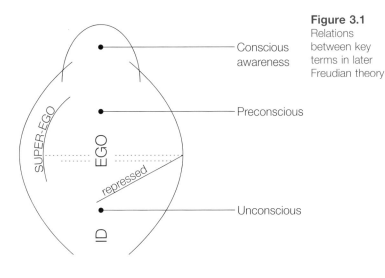

Figure 3.1
Relations between key terms in later Freudian theory

giving needs, the instinctual drives of hunger and sex. Freud's definition of 'sex' differs from the common view, a point which will be expanded upon later. The biological forces of the id are especially powerful during infancy and into early childhood.

The powerful demand of the id for immediate satisfaction is progressively countered by an equally powerful force that only becomes internalized following the resolution of the Oedipus complex at adolescence. This internalized image of society is known as the superego, which in the early years consists of parental control. Parents pass on their language, customs and cultural values to their children which subsequently are internalized by the child following a period of struggle in adolescence. The third important aspect of the self is the ego, which stands between the id and the superego. The ego has a fragile existence as it plays the role of arbitrator and mediator between the demands of biology and society by seeking to bring the influence of the external world to bear on the id. The ego aims to substitute the reality principle for the pleasure principle which governs the id.

The above relates to consumer behaviour by providing an explanation of the dynamics underlying selfhood. Psychoanalytic theory can help explain the role played by goods and services in the make-up of our selves. Freud's theory offers an explanation which focuses on the investment of psychic energy (motive force) into consumer goods. Why is such energy invested into consumer goods? It relates to the contradictory nature of the demands of biology and society and how these are partly resolved by means of consumption. Psychoanalytic theory suggests that often individuals are unaware of the motives which govern their decisions, as these are largely unconscious. This means that the importance of the unconscious in directing thoughts and behaviour should be explored.

Sexuality and development

Freud theorized that Eros is composed of ego and sexual instincts. While survival depends on fairly immediate gratification of ego instincts, libido or sexual drive is infinitely more malleable. His theory is developmental to the extent that he explains how the needs of children change as they grow older. According to this theory, children pass through a number of stages of development on their passage towards adulthood and at each stage a different erotogenic zone becomes the focus for sexual energy. Either excessive gratification or frustration of this desire will have major consequences for the individual in later life. They will help to determine not only the style of the child's sexual satisfaction in later life but also their personality and emotional character. If the child receives too much, or too little, gratification during a particular stage this creates anxiety that may result in a fixation on this zone; in adulthood they may even regress to this stage of development as the result of some trauma.

ORAL STAGE

In the first year of life the mouth of the child is the zone of interest and the breast of the mother (or its substitute) is the object of interest. The child obtains most gratification from sucking and when teeth develop, pleasure comes from biting. If the mother responds by either over or under-gratifying the demands of the child, then the child may develop great tension and anxiety about feeding. This anxiety may reach intolerable levels, at which stage the ego may act to repress the impulses which are responsible for this tension. The ego must expend large amounts of energy in repressing this anxiety, which may lead it to develop as a fragile and weak entity. When the child develops into an adult it is likely that the oral zone will be a source of fascination and of anxiety. In focusing on the mouth the adult may experience pleasure and guilt in engaging in oral activities such as smoking, drinking or perhaps a preoccupation with the preparation and consumption of food. However, a severe trauma such as the death of a relative may so stretch the resources of the ego that it can no longer contain the repressed anxieties of childhood which return in full force. This can result in a neurotic disorder where the adult regresses back to the oral stage and may exhibit a range of disorders associated with eating.

ANAL STAGE

The next phase, which lasts from around one year old to the age of 3 is the anal phase. By this time the child's sphincter control has reached the point where s/he can take pleasure in holding on to or letting go of bodily wastes. Freud's theory suggests that children who are fixated at the anal stage may well develop as adults the character traits which reflect his or her difficulties in resolving this stage. Such adults may develop an obsessive regard for order and cleanliness, value hoarding and saving and have a stubborn nature.

PHALLIC STAGE

The phallic stage, which lasts from between 3 and 5 years of age culminates in the emotional crisis known as the 'Oedipus complex'. Prior to the Oedipus complex (named after the famous Greek myth), both boys and girls identify with their mother. Boys see their father as a rival for the mother's affections but come to fear the power of the father. Their terror of the father becomes so great that eventually the boy splits his affections away from the mother and identifies himself with the father. It is by means of such an identification that the boy child achieves a male identity. In identifying with the father and 'introjecting', or internalizing, the father's values the boy develops a new structure, the superego, or conscience, which replaces the external control his parents exercised over him.

The transition for girls is not so simple. Girls seek to identify with the father and come to see the mother as a rival for his affections. However, the girl's physical resemblance to the mother means that she cannot physically identify with the father or with his power. As a result, Freud thought, the development of the female superego was a more difficult process. Those who become fixated at the phallic stage become obsessed with power and those things which symbolize power. For example, this may be expressed through the purchase of products which are recognized as signifying prestige and power, i.e. anything from powerful sports cars to expensive watches or the latest technological toys. In recent years women executives who mimic male dress codes in businesses, e.g. by wearing suits which have jackets with wide shoulders, and sometimes even shirts and ties, have acquired the label 'power dressers'.

Following the phallic stage there is a period of quiescence known as 'latency' which may last between 5 years of age and puberty. The beginnings of adult sexuality are observed in the 'genital period' when the individual's self-love or 'narcissism' becomes channelled into the love of others.

What can be learnt from Freud in terms of the role which goods play in people's lives? Firstly the id is the source of all true needs, providing the energy and motive force for the demand for need satisfaction. The id demands satisfaction in line with the requirements of Eros, the life drive. Individuals are motivated to satisfy directly those needs for hunger and thirst and safety which are directly linked with survival. The sex drive is another major motive force which demands satisfaction. However, within Freud's explanation this comes into conflict with the restraining force of the superego which in its capacity as a proxy for 'civilized' society reins in the desire for direct sexual satisfaction and replaces such actions with others which are more socially acceptable. In a consumer society, one outlet for the sublimation of sexual desire is through the purchase of consumer goods and services.

FREUD'S LEGACY: CHANGING SOCIAL CHARACTERS

Freudian theory alerts us to the importance of identity and difference in consumer behaviour. Identity can be a difficult subject to grasp because it has a dual aspect. A simple way of understanding this is to recall how Freudian theory describes two powerful forces for conditioning the emergence of the self, namely society and biology. The concept of identity reflects this duality in that it contains two forces, one of which relates to the person, the other to society. From a personal point of view identity is everything which I call 'mine'. It is the sum total of the objects (including people) with which I identify and is what marks 'me' out as being different from other people. On the other hand, individuals and groups in society treat me as if I have a particular identity.

Relating psychogenesis to sociogenesis

Central to Freudian theory is the idea of the interaction between biology and environment in the formation of the self. This has led a number of authors to speculate on the changing nature of social character through time. Authors in this tradition share in common the belief that the self is not immutable but rather that the structure of the psyche (psychogenesis), is formed in relation to the society in which it develops (sociogenesis). For example, in his epic study of the development of civilization in Europe from the period known as the Dark Ages at the end of the Roman Empire, Norbert Elias (1994) explores how psychogenetic processes (involving the structure of personality, including how the relations between id, ego, and superego are formed over time) changed within the context of a sociogenetic explanation (involving changes to the structure of society over time). Elias charts the very gradual process of development from the disorder and constant warfare of pre-modern Europe, where the expression of id desires found little resistance, to the orderly nation state where the societal expectation that individuals comport themselves in a civilized manner is realised in self-control due to the strengthening of the superego, or what some might call the policeman inside the head.

From traditional to inner-directed and other-directed characters

David Riesman and his colleagues who published their research in *The Lonely Crowd* (1950) argued that the prevailing social character in European and American societies had changed through the years. They posited that this change in character had occurred as people moved from traditional communities to work in mass-production industries in large urban areas. They argued that a person who is born in and lives in a traditional community has little need of what we might call an identity. This is because they are immersed within the community, which provides them with security. Following the industrial and consumer revolutions of the late eighteenth and early nineteenth centuries, huge numbers of people were torn from the bonds of traditional rural communities and moved to urban centres in search of employment in the new factories, mills and shipyards. While they had been reared in a traditional setting they now had to live and work among strangers who came from different traditions and who shared different values. Riesman and his colleagues describe these migrants to the cities as 'inner-directed' characters. The inner-directed character was different from the person who lived in a traditional community because they were removed from its protective embrace. These people coped with the loss of community by developing a strong internal sense of who they were, which was based on their early upbringing within the traditional community. In Riesman's explanation inner-directed individuals developed a gyroscopic sense of control, through having a clear sense of what their goal in life was coupled to a belief in self-reliance. Fulfilment came largely by following a career in the sphere of work. Pleasure and consumption were of minor importance to them, except in-so-far as the display of goods might signify their prowess.

Riesman *et al.* (1961) argue that many years later there developed another character, which they called the other-directed character. This character first appeared in twentieth-century urban America and worked in a service industry rather than in traditional industries such as shipbuilding or milling. The authors cite travellers' accounts of the time which noted that the other-directed character seemed to be shallower, more profligate with his money, friendlier, more uncertain of himself and his values and more demanding of approval than the inner-directeds. The other-directed character seemed to arise within the new middle classes who worked in the emerging service industries. Riesman and his colleagues suggest a number of reasons for the emergence of this character.

First, a new generation had grown up that lacked the solid foundation provided by traditional community. They lacked the gyroscope that had so surely guided their forebears. Popularity and the need to fit in were seen to be important by parents. Consequently the role of the superego changed as parents made their children feel guilty not so much about the violation of inner standards but about failure to be popular or to manage their relations with other children. In any event the peer group became more important and parental authority waned in the progressively permissive society that was developing. The other-directed character not only offered a more promising opportunity for marketers but was arguably partly the product of marketing activity. For years mass advertising had cultivated anxieties and insecurities among the population so as to offer solutions to these through the products of mass production. What better object for advertising than a character who felt constantly anxious and who craved social approval (Riesman *et al.* 1950: 21)?

One can see parallels with Riesman's other-directed character in the marketing character described by the psychoanalyst and social commentator Erich Fromm. In *To Have or to Be?* (1978), Fromm argued that modern society embodied a deep-seated change in values, from Being – literally, being centred on other people and social relations – to Having, which he associated with the lifeless world of machines and products, which he saw as being destructive. Fromm argues that the destructive 'having' mode is deeply etched into the customs, practices and language of Western society. One means of having is incorporation, which was a widespread practice in early societies, e.g. it was thought that by eating the heart of a brave warrior one could incorporate the symbol of this bravery. The modern consumer takes the idea of incorporation to new heights as he/she seeks to swallow the whole world. Fromm describes the modern consumer as 'the eternal suckling crying for the bottle. This is obvious in pathological phenomena such as alcoholism and drug addiction' (Fromm, 1978: 27).

Fromm saw this 'having' mode as exemplified by the emergence of a new personality, the 'marketing character'. To Fromm the emergence of this new character signalled a shift from the anal retentive 'hoarding' character to a new form:

> The aim of the marketing character is complete adaptation so as to be desirable under all conditions of the personality market. The marketing character personalities do not even have egos (as people in the nineteenth century did) to hold on to, that belong to them, that do not change. For they constantly change their egos according to the principle: 'I am as you desire me'.
>
> (Fromm, 1978: 148)

Values and lifestyles (VALS)™

Twenty years or more after Reisman wrote his book, in 1978, Mitchell and others at the Stanford Research Institute (SRI), now SRI International, conducted a series of studies in the US that culminated in the construction of the Values and Lifestyles (VALS) consumer segmentation system. From the analysis of data Mitchell devised three orientations: needs-driven, inner-directedness and outer-directedness, two of which are very similar to the terms developed by Riesman. Needs-directed refers to those who are limited by resources, i.e. poor. The VALS concept of outer-directedness is similar to that described by Riesman and signifies a person who is primarily motivated by the opinions of others. The VALS study found that this character was the prevailing social type, accounting for 68 per cent of the population. The VALS study found that another character, inner-directeds, comprised 21 per cent of their sample. However, it is important to differentiate between Riesman and Mitchell's definitions of 'inner-directedness' as this potentially is confusing. Although they share the same label, Mitchell's concept of inner-directedness is different from that described by Riesman. The most obvious reason is that US society had changed fundamentally between the 1950s when Riesman wrote his book and the 1970s when the VALS research was conducted. By the 1960s the seeds of the permissive society noted by Riesman in his study had grown into a diverse coalition of interests that sought to challenge authority and free people from all forms of repression. In Freudian terms this amounted to an attack by these theorists on the concept of the superego, which, they argued, was not so much a civilizing influence as authoritarian. Alongside Fromm, whose argument was briefly mentioned above, others trained in the psychoanalytic tradition, including Reich and Marcuse, challenged the role played by the superego in society, arguing that it had reduced the ego to a bland, inauthentic conformist caricature. To the dismay of many orthodox Freudians, Reich in particular argued for the destruction of the superego, the 'policeman in the head' that in his view gave rise to this false and inauthentic self. Instead id forces should be liberated to restore the self to a sense of authenticity. These were joined by others, including Werber Erhard, who developed a training programme, Erhard Seminar Training (EST), so that people could through self-expression come into contact with their 'true' selves. The ideas of the expressive self and the 'me' generation were widely publicized during the 1960s. Consequently the 'inner-directeds' that constituted 21 per cent of the VALS findings shared little in common with those described twenty years previously by Riesman. The idea of the expressive individual is different from Riesman's gyroscopically controlled self-made man. The new inner-directeds purchased goods to meet their own internal wants and used consumption as a vehicle for self-expression.

In 1988 SRI introduced a new measure of values also called VALS. For example, as two out of three Americans were identified as being outer-directed consumers, this category was found to be too large to be a meaningful differentiator. The original framework segmented people by their social values, attitudes towards gun control or military spending, for example. The new framework was, and continues to be, based on psychological characteristics that are correlated with consumer purchase behaviour. While social values shift over time, human psychological characteristics such as information-seeking are more stable over time. Initially this new formulation bore a strong relation to Maslow's (1958) hierarchy, in creating new categories based on esteem and actualization. For example, Weinstein (1998) utilizes Maslow by reporting that Actualizers on a base of 100 were more likely than average to own a small car (133) and a bicycle (154). They were much more likely to own a foreign luxury car (363) or sports car (330), but less likely to own a pickup truck (72). On the other hand, the Strugglers' ownership of these items was well below that of the Actualizer, with bicycle (43), foreign luxury car (3), small car and sports car (5). The only transport items which strugglers seemed to own in any numbers include small to medium cars (54) and pickup trucks (52) (Weinstein, 1998). In introducing Maslow to the scene VALS researchers had theoretically moved a long way from Freud. Maslow's core belief was fundamentally different from that of Freud. Where the latter argued that civilization must tame the beast within us, Maslow (1970), in common with the prevailing spirit of the 1960s, argued that it was civilization that was at fault and that one should cultivate a person's 'natural' need for self-expression. More recent formulations of VALS such as that discussed in Chapter 6, Figure 6.1, have somewhat moved away from Maslow's categories.

GENDER IDENTITY

While Freud provides a base for the study of identity he never actually used the term himself. Gender identity is only one form of identity. At birth individuals are identified with those forms of signification which are associated with our parents and which mark their identities, e.g. with their class position, religion or ethnicity, which are transferred to individuals. While undoubtedly identity is given to us by society, it is true that a stable identity is something which individuals strive for, as it provides a sense of belongingness, of 'home'. However, feelings about identity tend to be ambivalent. Individuals simultaneously want to be at home and to be free. Yet while being 'at home' offers comfort and security, it can also tend to be claustrophobic, even like a prison. Sometimes we long to break free from the chains of identity, particularly when these have been fashioned for us by others so that we can experience the terrors and delights of freedom. To sum up, identity is built on a characteristic or set of characteristics that makes us identical in some respect to some people and at the same time marks individuals out as being different from others. Identity is not naturally conferred, but is marked out by culture.

Strangely, perceptions of what is 'masculine' and what is 'feminine' are not given biologically but are mediated through culture. It is important to realize that while the sex categories 'male', 'female' and 'androgynous' are given to us by nature, a range of gender identities is available in different cultures. In contemporary European societies traditional rigid divisions between the sexes have been eroded with the growth in acceptability of the expression of a range of 'gay', identities. Gender is an extremely important focus for identity. A person who identifies primarily with 'feminine' traits in a society is 'feminine', with masculine traits is 'masculine' and with both sets of traits is 'androgynous'. When 'men' and 'women' are discussed, activities are identified which are enabled or proscribed by society. For example, until recently the conventional wisdom was that a man's identity was to be found in the world of work and that, by contrast, a woman's identity was to be found in the home, where she nurtured and cared for the man and their children. There is an important point that relates to consumption. As the domestic situation was the centre of family consumption and also defined as a woman's place, so consumption came to be associated with women's work. For example, it is expected that in Europe and the US women would be more involved in grocery shopping and in Christmas shopping than men. The latter provided the focus for a study by Fischer and Arnold (1990) who sought to explore the role played by sex differences and gender role orientations in Christmas gift shopping behaviours. Gender role attitude refers to an individual's level of agreement with traditional views regarding the roles and behaviours stereotypically associated with each sex. Fischer and Arnold thought that if Christmas shopping is regarded as women's work then it would be likely that women with traditional gender role attitudes would be more involved and women with more egalitarian attitudes might be less involved. Among men those with more egalitarian attitudes are likely to be more involved.

Q & A

QUESTION

In your view what reasons lie behind such hypotheses?

ANSWER

Egalitarian attitudes signify a degree of freedom from traditional role stereotypes. For a woman such disagreement may lead her to avoid 'female' stereotypical roles such as shopping for gifts; for a man it may mean the opposite, with egalitarian men more involved in shopping than traditional men because they disagree with traditional assumptions that shopping is a 'female' preserve.

Fischer and Arnold's study of Christmas shopping behaviour found that men and women differed significantly; women gave more gifts than men, started shopping earlier, spent longer shopping and were more successful in selecting gifts. On the other hand, men spent more per person and had more gifts returned or exchanged. The authors found that similar gender role attitudes have different implications for men and women. More egalitarian men were slightly more involved than traditional men, in that they bought more gifts for more recipients and spent more time shopping per recipient that either traditional men or equally egalitarian women. The hypothesis concerning egalitarian women was confirmed as more egalitarian women were found to be slightly less involved than traditional women or equally egalitarian men.

Fischer and Arnold concluded that gender identity had some of the predicted effects on involvement. More communally oriented men and women started shopping much earlier than less communally oriented men and women. Moreover, men with more communal orientations spent considerably more time shopping per recipient than other men. Overall, it was found that those (both men and women) with more feminine gender identities are more involved in Christmas gift shopping.

Family identity

Outside our own skins, the family is where we are likely to feel (at least initially) most at home.

In Western Europe the nuclear family, two adults living together in the same household with one or more children, known also as the 'cornflake packet' family, is considered to be the norm. This is the stereotypical family of 'Happy Families', of Mr Bun the Baker, Mrs Bun the Baker's Wife, Master Bun and Miss Bun. The nuclear family is itself of comparatively recent origin in Europe, where there are still strong pockets of an earlier form of family organization, the extended family (three generations living under one roof). The nuclear family emerged largely as a response to the eighteenth-century division of labour which occurred in Europe at the time of the industrial revolution. The development of the factory as a new form of work unit led to more and more men becoming separated from the household as 'breadwinners'. During this period greater pressure was brought to bear on women to become 'providers' as being responsible for cooking, housework and other 'domestic' jobs which were seen as an inferior occupation, if indeed they were thought of as being work at all. The woman as provider for the needs of the household was also associated with gathering its provisions. She became the centrepiece of the 'cornflake packet' family that emerged as the focus of advertising attention for a vast range of 'domestic' products and services.

Yet the dominance of the stereotypical nuclear family is a myth, or at least it is in the UK. In 1971 nuclear families accounted for 35 per cent of all households; by 1978 they constituted 32 per cent, and in 1996 23 per cent of all households were nuclear families. By contrast 62 per cent of the population either lived alone or were living together without dependent children, reflecting the gradual ageing of the population. Another trend has been towards lone parent families; for example, of the 36 per cent of households with children, 10 per cent were made up of lone parents in 1996. The proportion of female lone parents increased from 1 per cent of households in 1971 to 7 per cent in 1996. The dynamic shift away from the cornflake packet family has been paralleled by a growing complexity in family relationships. For example, in 1996, 8 per cent of families included more then one stepchild. Other changes which are not reflected in the figures reflect the growing incidence of stable relationships between 'gays'.

There has been much change within nuclear families which reflects changing patterns of work and leisure. Put simply more women go to work, fewer men have stable full-time employment and the home itself has become more like a nest of cells than one single unit. The Henley Centre discusses this latter point as a shift towards cellular living. This reflects the growing individualization of life in family homes and a corresponding decrease in collective ritual activities like joint family meals or entertainment. Microwaves and a thriving take-out food industry allow members of the family to have it their way; many children own their own personal stereos, television sets and even computers.

This means that, generally, the trends indicate that the cornflake packet family, while constituting a relatively large group within society, is continuing to fragment and decline. This has many implications for consumer behaviour. For example, food companies and those producing hygiene products offer less 'family' style products and more products that cater to the individual. A second and more important observation is that the cornflake packet family does not provide the stable home for the construction of identity as previously.

Social class

For many years the social class of a person has been seen to be an important determinant of their purchase behaviour, e.g. a social classification section is almost always to be found in any questionnaire survey. While social class is a complex phenomenon researchers have operationalized this, i.e. rendered it capable of measurement, e.g. in terms of the occupation of the head of household. In the UK this means that the researcher will ask who the head of household is. This used to be the 'man of the house'. However, nowadays it is based on the person who earns the most and so may be a man or a woman. The occupation of this person is then noted and forms the basis of the social classification.

Social class varies in importance. In the UK it used to be a powerful explanatory factor in purchase behaviour. It is suggested that social class dictated not only the work environment but what stores a person patronized for shopping as well as attitudes towards education, leisure and holidays. It is not possible to discuss all the fine distinctions between classes. For example, the middle classes were supposed to be knowledgeable about and were expected to drink wine (but not beer because that was 'working-class'); certainly middle-class women were not expected to be seen in public houses (pubs) because that is where working class men went to drink. On the other hand, working-class people did not go on holidays abroad and could be accused as traitors to their class if they went to university. As a result, in a major way *who you were*, i.e. what class you belonged to, determined *what you could do*. Social class position dictated a whole range of 'appropriate' behaviours which were summed up in the expression 'People like us don't . . . drink beer, go to Blackpool for our holidays, wear flat caps, train to be lawyers, or read the *Times* newspaper.' However, owing to the influence of the mass media, particularly 'fly on the wall' documentaries and soap operas, people have shown how the 'other half' live, e.g. most of the world has access to the inner workings of the British royal household. Television programmes 'educate' middle-class women about 'appropriate' forms of behaviour in 'working-class' preserves such as public houses; working-class men can learn to be wine snobs through the same channel. In a nutshell, the suggestion is that social class no longer provides the pillar for identity that it used to do. The views expressed above have been influenced by the work of Bob Tyrell while he was associated with the UK think tank, the Henley Centre.

If this is right the implications are enormous. People who feel strongly bound by class in terms of what they could and could not do are faced with an unprecedented freedom. But how powerful is social class in contemporary Britain? One question in the British Panel Household Survey 1996 asks 'Do you think of yourself as belonging to any particular social class?' In answer to this question only 38 per cent of respondents said 'yes'. However, when asked if they had to choose, 44 per cent said that they would be working-class and just under 40 per cent indicated that they would be middle-class. Asked the question 'In Britain today, how much do you think a person's opportunities are affected by the class into which they are born?', 28 per cent said 'a great deal', 40 per cent 'quite a lot', 23 per cent 'not very much' and just over 6 per cent 'not at all'. Methods of assessing social class are discussed further in Chapter 4 and in Chapter 6, especially the development of ACORN.

SECTION SUMMARY

In this section the following have been discussed:

■   the idea of the self as energy linked to the extended self;
■   the role played by the unconscious as the basis for motivation;
■   the concepts developed by Freud in later life – the *id, ego* and *superego*;
■   the development of sexuality and the consumption-related issues that can arise at each stage;
■   the study of identity, including social characters; VALS; gender identity.

BEHAVIOURISM

In 1913 Watson began the movement known as classical behaviourism and in 1938 Skinner proposed a different version known as radical behaviourism. Together with their Russian predecessors, Sechenov, Bekhterev and Pavlov, they introduced a commitment to the study of overt behaviour as opposed to internal states and coined a vocabulary of conditioned reflexes, including processes of reinforcement, extinction and generalization. Although initially Watson was well disposed towards Freud's theories, he later described it and other forms of analysis based on introspection as voodooism. In establishing the behaviourist platform Watson sought to establish psychology as a natural science, asking:

> why don't we make what we can observe the real field of psychology? Let us limit ourselves to things that can be observed and formulate laws about only those things. Now what can we observe? Well we can observe behaviour – *what the organism does or says*.
>
> (Watson, 1931: 6)

While Skinner's (1938) concept of operant conditioning is different to the classical account, he nevertheless shares with Watson a focus on the need to explain behaviour solely with respect to its environmental consequences. Both explanations thus deny any importance to the consumer's internal state of mind.

Classical conditioning

As an academic Watson was primarily interested in the development of emotions, in posing basic questions such as 'Where does fear come from?' Watson had observed the differences between very young infants, who positively engaged with external objects, and 3 year olds, who seemed to be afraid of many things which were often harmless. How did such bizarre fears arise? Watson based his explanation of the development of emotions on Pavlov's theory of conditioned response. Pavlov had found that if one repeatedly paired the sound of a bell with the taste of food, eventually the sound of the bell alone would elicit salivation from

Figure 3.2
Summary of
(a) classical,
(b) operant and
(c) cognitive
learning
processes

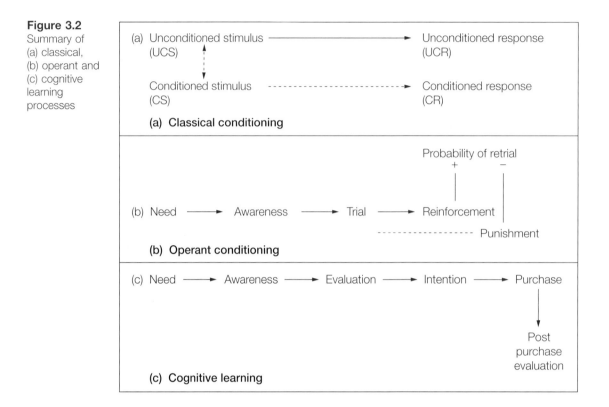

(a) Unconditioned stimulus ⟶ Unconditioned response
(UCS) (UCR)

Conditioned stimulus - - - - - - - - - - - - - -▶ Conditioned response
(CS) (CR)

(a) Classical conditioning

Probability of retrial
+ −

(b) Need ⟶ Awareness ⟶ Trial ⟶ Reinforcement

- - - - - - - - - - - - - - Punishment

(b) Operant conditioning

(c) Need ⟶ Awareness ⟶ Evaluation ⟶ Intention ⟶ Purchase

Post
purchase
evaluation

(c) Cognitive learning

a dog. Watson reports that coloured discs and geometrical forms were equally effective in eliciting the same response.

Unconditioned and conditioned stimuli

Food is an unconditioned stimulus; a hungry animal does not need to learn to salivate at the presentation of food but will do so automatically. A bell does not naturally stimulate salivation. However, this response can be learned due the contiguity, or close association between the presentation of the food (unconditioned stimulus (UCS) and the bell (conditioned stimulus (CS)). Eventually the secondary stimulus presented by the bell alone is sufficient to elicit the same reaction.

Watson extended Pavlov's work by moving away from the study of simple conditioned reflexes to the study of complex emotional responses. He reasoned that such complex responses could be derived from three innate or primary emotional responses of fear, rage and love, all of which could be observed in infants. Fear could be stimulated by loss of support or a loud bang; rage was produced by restricting the infant's movements; finally love occurred as the consequence of fondling and stroking the infant's skin, especially in sensitive areas. Additionally, Watson theorized that the infant could learn emotional responses to new, previously neutral objects.

Watson offers the example of Albert B., a 'good' baby, aged 11 months and 4 days on the day of the experiment, to demonstrate how fear arises in infancy. Albert had played happily with a white rat for weeks. On one occasion it was presented to him and a steel bar was struck by a hammer just behind his head just as he reached forward to stroke the rat. Albert jumped and whimpered and Watson reported that due to his disturbed condition no further tests were carried out that day. Subsequently, Albert would whimper and withdraw when the rat was presented to him. Not only did Albert learn to fear the rat; this fear transferred to other objects that had the white furriness of the laboratory rat; to rabbits, a fur coat and even cotton wool!

STIMULUS GENERALIZATION AND DISCRIMINATION

The reaction of Albert to rabbits and cotton wool described above reveals that the CS does not have to be identical to the stimulus associated with the behaviour during the learning process. Albert generalized the fear response from the white rat to objects that shared just one characteristic with the rat, a sense of 'furriness'. Formally the propensity to generalize one characteristic of the conditioned stimulus to other stimuli is known as stimulus generalization. In marketing one can explain the use of 'family' or 'umbrella' branding, where a company puts the same brand name on a variety of often unrelated products as an example of stimulus generalization. Given a positive brand name, each of the products carrying that name should equally be evaluated positively. On the other hand, competitors to a primary brand may copy stimuli that are associated with the primary brand, for example the pack design or colouring, to capitalize on the same associations. This occurred in the UK when supermarkets launched their own brands in competition with Coca-Cola. The packaging of Sainsbury's cola was reputedly almost identical to that used by the 'real thing'. While stimulus generalization may be of benefit in generalizing the reputation of a brand to a whole family of brands, brand managers spend a considerable amount of time in building stimulus discrimination, where they seek to associate their brand with some unique differentiating characteristic.

Advertising

When Watson joined advertising agency J. Walter Thompson he used similar techniques to those described above to promote products. Coon (1994: 42) explains the general switch to using emotional appeals at the time as being linked to the reduction in 'reason why' copy, which sought to explain to the consumer why they should use one product rather than another, thereby appealing to the customer's reasoning powers (see Figure 3.2). One problem with this was that some advertisers dishonestly made false claims, a fact that the US legislature started to take seriously by prosecuting offenders from 1912 onwards. Another problem was how to persuade someone to buy your product rather than that of a competitor, given the sheer number of products of comparable quality that vied for the consumer's attention. The temptation was to appeal less to the reader's reason and to address instead their emotions. While earlier accounts tend to overplay Watson's influence on the advertising industry, there

Figure 3.3
Example of
'reason why'
copy

Source: *Woman* 3,
3 December 1938

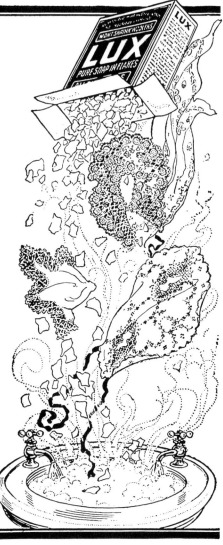

Flakes as delicate as the rarest laces you have!

The fine old laces you have kept so carefully, have grown—if you are *quite* truthful!—very, very dirty! You are afraid to trust them to soap and water, lest the fragile threads break, or the lace thicken.

The why and how of keeping laces lovely

It is rubbing—and putting soap directly on laces that ruin them.

With Lux, you can wash them often.

The dainty flakes dissolve instantly. Even the slightest rubbing is unnecessary. The rich Lux lather dissolves the dirt in a few minutes, while you are gently moving the laces about in the suds.

There are no bits of soap to stick to the fabric through all the rinsings.

Use Lux on anything that you would trust to pure water alone.

Order Lux today from your grocer or from any department store. Lever Bros. Co., Cambridge, Mass.

How to wash lace

Throw a handful of Lux into boiling hot water. Whisk into a thick lather. When cool enough for the hands to bear, put the lace in and let it stand in the suds. Do not rub. The lace may be gently squeezed or dipped up and down unless very tender. In this case let it stand in the suds. Rinse in water the same temperature. Do not starch.

If the lace is frail, before washing, it should be basted on a piece of shrunken cheesecloth which may be pulled taut and pinned for drying. Otherwise, it should be carefully pulled, every point pinned into shape and left until dry. This leaves the lace flat and makes ironing unnecessary.

LUX 10¢
For all fine laundering

is no doubt that this focus on emotions coincided exactly with his own specialist interest. At J. Walter Thompson Watson worked on Johnson & Johnson Baby Powder, Pebeco toothpaste and Pond's Skin Cream and Cleansing Tissues (see Figure 3.3).

Watson formed part of the group which used the 'fear–sex–emulation' formula in advertising. Rather than simply publicizing the product Watson used symbols to stimulate basic emotions such as fear, rage and love responses in his audience:

- For example, fear could be linked with anxiety, especially in the vulnerable, as a powerful inducement to buy. The advertisements which he developed for Johnson's

Baby Powder targeted relatively affluent white young mothers who were expecting their first child. In constructing the advertising appeal the aim was to highlight the 'purity' and 'cleanliness' of Johnson's powder, with the implication that those who did not use it would be impure and unclean. Advertising also highlighted the dangers of infection to infants and the desirability of using baby powder frequently. Should the young mother be tempted to ask advice from her own mother traditional methods of child care were disparaged as being inadequate and unscientific. Most important, the advertisements did not simply create associations of anxiety and fear but offered the solution backed by the testimonials of 'scientific experts': buy Johnson's!

■ Buckley argues that Watson used sexuality as a means of selling Pebeco toothpaste. In this case the advertisement depicted a seductively dressed young woman smoking a cigarette, encouraging women to smoke so long as Pebeco toothpaste was used regularly. In an age when the idea of a woman smoking in public was frowned upon the use of a woman smoking a cigarette carried associations of independence and assertiveness. The advertisement aimed to stimulate anxiety in the target market as it raised fears that the effects of smoking on the breath and the teeth might diminish attractiveness. In this way, toothpaste was promoted not as a contribution to health and hygiene but as a means of heightening the sexual attraction of the user; as Buckley notes, 'Consumers were buying not merely toothpaste, they were buying sex appeal' (Buckley, 1982: 216). (See Figure 3.4).

Classical conditioning is also employed by advertisers to link a product with a stimulus that evokes a positive feeling. For example, Assael (1995: 113) cites the example of the Marlboro cowboy which signifies an image of strength, masculinity and security. When linked with the cigarettes in advertising the cowboy acts as the primary or unconditioned stimulus that evokes an unconditioned response of strength, masculinity and security. Over time, as the result of repetitive advertising and contiguity, the product becomes a secondary or conditioned stimulus that comes to evoke the same positive feeling as does the cowboy. Consequently, the cowboy acts as a means of influencing smokers to buy Marlboro and reminds them to repurchase. The brand thus comes to be a conditioned response.

Important considerations when using classical conditioning

From a classical conditioning perspective, advertisers should be mindful of the following in seeking to utilize classical conditioning in order to influence consumers:

■ *Overshadowing*. The UCS should clearly stand out against other stimuli used in the advertisement and should not be overshadowed. In the Marlboro advertisement, e.g. the cowboy is often portrayed sitting astride a white horse. Given that the intention of the advertising is to link the Marlboro (CS) with the cowboy (UCS), the advertisement would not have worked if people had simply associated the brand with the horse that the cowboy was riding.

Figure 3.4
Example of
anxiety appeal

Source: *Woman* 5,
1 July 1939

- *Blocking*. Generally, unconditioned stimuli should not have previous associations to other brands, e.g. if a beer company were to use a cowboy in its advertising then it would be unlikely to work for them, given the existing link between cowboys and Marlboro. Similarly where in the example, H&M (CS1) is associated with Linda Evangelista (US) then if Esprit (CS2) subsequently employs Linda consumers may be blocked from making the connection as she is already linked with H&M. If two brands use the same advertising themes then brand confusion may result. For example, if the creative teams for Pampers and Peaudouce develop creative themes that focus on babies walking and playing, neither brand (CS) will be uniquely associated with walking and playing babies.
- *Pre-exposure effect*. This is partly linked with the blocking effect discussed above. It refers to the situation where the unconditioned stimulus becomes so familiar that it fails to work. For example, the basketball player Michael Jordan in the US and UK footballer David Beckham became associated with such an array of products that arguably their influence became diluted.

Operant conditioning

Twenty years of development of behaviourist thinking was crystallized into a new form by B.F. Skinner. Skinner's development of operant conditioning has more general explanatory power than Watson's because it is concerned with the ways in which behaviour is determined by the environment in which it is emitted. Where Watson's explanation focuses on the antecedents to behaviour, Skinner considers its consequences, e.g. some things in the environment are directly linked to our survival value, including food, water, sexual contact and escape from harm. Skinner argues that any behaviour which leads to these consequences becomes more likely to occur. Like classical conditioning, operant conditioning requires the development of a link between a stimulus and a response but the person determines the response that provides the greatest satisfaction. Suppose Pavlov had provided the dog with a choice which was to press one of two levers. When one lever was pressed the dog got an electric shock; when it pressed the other it obtained the meat powder. The dog would learn quickly to avoid the lever that provided the shock and to press the one that delivered the meat powder. In Skinner's explanation learning occurs because the same act is repeatedly rewarded or reinforced. Given that Skinner allows his subject the ability to act in a number of ways, the consequences of any action, such as the degree of satisfaction or dissatisfaction arising from it, will influence future behaviour.

The process of operant conditioning is where behaviour which has survival value is more likely to occur. The behaviour is strengthened by its consequences, or reinforcers (Skinner, 1974: 39). Reinforcers should not be confused with rewards. One rewards a person, whereas one reinforces a response (Foxall, 1990: 42). Whereas marketers provide many kinds of rewards for consumers, including store loyalty cards, two-for-one offers and even, occasionally, enjoyable advertising, these do not necessarily act to reinforce consumer behaviour by increasing its frequency. This is because the extent to which they result in satisfaction is likely to vary from one situation to another.

Positive and negative reinforcement

Perhaps the only concept that Skinner shares with Freud is the idea that humans are hedonists; that is, we are inclined towards those things that offer us survival value and pleasure and to avoid those things that are destructive of our survival and that cause pain. In this respect reinforcement can work in one of two directions:

■ It can work in a positive sense in enhancing survival and thus providing pleasure, e.g. when a hungry person exhibits behaviour that produces food, the behaviour is reinforced by that consequence and is more likely to recur.

■ Alternatively, where survival is threatened reinforcement can work in a negative sense to reduce a potentially damaging condition, e.g. moving into the shade to avoid the effects of extreme heat from the sun is reinforced by that consequence and tends to recur on similar occasions.

In *Walden Two,* Skinner's (1948) account of a fictional utopia, Frazier, the founder of the community, explains how scientific behavioural engineering is used to create a schedule of positive reinforcement. Child care is free and parents are not the sole carers of the young, whose environment is closely managed. Members do not need to travel far to work; their food is communally produced, stored, prepared and served. There is no need for retail outlets, because all clothing needs are cared for; no need to pay insurance, because the community looks after its own as well as in providing education. Members are required to work only four hours per day and are thus able to spend the rest of the time engaging in creative work as well as playing and resting. With respect to negative reinforcement, Frazier explains that the community has no need to indoctrinate its members. Rather it is sufficient for them to compare the Walden life with that experienced by those who live outside. They are encouraged to visit the outside world. In so doing they experience not only its cultural pleasures but the down side: the vast disparities in wealth between rich and poor, the miserable lives of the poor, the use of advertising to create a false illusion of the good life, the harried look of the citizens, the waste. These experiences negatively reinforce their decision to be in Walden where such problems are unknown.

HEDONIC AND INFORMATIONAL REINFORCEMENT

Products and services are replete with examples of positive and negative reinforcement. With respect to positive reinforcement products provide hedonic or utilitarian reinforcement. They are enjoyed because they nourish and sustain us. Through time the process involved in searching for these reinforcement products is found enjoy-able. Products also provide informational reinforcement, which reflects feedback on consumer performance (Foxall, 1996: 13, 283). This may take the form of a better understanding of how well consumers are doing, which may relate to the level of achievement or social status achieved by purchasing certain products and services. Many product offerings are constructed around negative reinforcement, e.g. in Chapter 7, early brand appeals identified a problem that the brand could cure. In their earliest formulation Coca-Cola, Aspirin and Kellogg's offered negative reinforcement, and it is arguably only in recent years that such brands have moved away from focusing on a deficit or lack in the consumer towards a more positive grounding (Falk, 1997)

Reinforcement schedules

Skinner points out that it is not the reinforcement itself that is important, but rather the pattern or schedule of reinforcement that makes all the difference. He divides reinforcement into a number of types.

■ *Continuous reinforcement.* This is when there is a one-to-one relationship between the response and the reinforcement, as in the cold that one feels when one puts an ice cube into one's hand. Skinner argues that when an act is reinforced then a person has a feeling of confidence. A golfer practises a particular shot until she feels 'confident', i.e. until she is good at it. Frequent reinforcement builds and maintains an interest in what the person is doing (Skinner, 1974: 58). Purchase behaviours tend to be reinforced similarly on each occasion in the case of FMCG, where product availability, quality and high levels of customer service are apparent. Skinner notes a drawback with continuous reinforcement, which is that if it fails to materialize the behaviour can quickly extinguish.

On the other hand, with intermittent reinforcement the schedule of reinforcement can either be fixed interval or variable ratio.

■ *Interval schedules*. Fixed-interval schedules require that the interval is constant from one reinforcement to reinforcement. By contrast with variable interval reinforcement the time varies from one reinforcement to the next. For example, a person might spend quite a long time reading a book or Internet surfing prior to the behaviour being reinforced. Frustratingly, the very delay in receiving satisfaction when surfing or reading seems to harden the resolve not to give up until some is obtained! Marketers are well aware of this and creatively use delay in a number of ways, e.g. through 'teaser' advertising campaigns and the organization of large entertainment events such as concerts.

■ *Ratio schedules*. Fixed-ratio reinforcement requires that the number of responses that must be made before reinforcement occurs is constant from one situation to the next. Some products cost more or less the same from one time period to the next, e.g. a can of beans. In variable-ratio reinforcement by contrast, one cannot predict the number of responses that must be made before reinforcement is made. All gambling systems are based on variable-ratio reinforcement. The gambler has been exposed to a programme through which a highly unfavourable ratio is made effective. Foxall (1996: 229) comments that pre-purchase search for luxury or status products follows a variable ratio schedule. For example, in searching for a new coat or car – items that can provide utility and enjoyment as well as conferring status – precisely how many stores/showrooms to visit and how many coats/cars to see and try cannot be readily determined.

Research indicates that intermittent reinforcers are the most effective. It has been found that when reinforcement is intermittent, occurring less than every time the response is emitted, the level of extinction is very slow. Also the reinforcement effect can be very powerful. Skinner cites examples that have little else in common, such as gambling and scientific research, where massive effort is spent for an uncertain return. He also notes how society tells the gambler that she is 'addicted' while the scientist is regarded as being 'dedicated'. He dismisses such attributions arguing that the consequence is not a matter of will power or lack of it (dedication, addiction) but of a particular reinforcement schedule. In the case of gambling, scientific discovery, and even perhaps in the search for some new products which share the characteristic of intermittent reinforcement, behaviour may be sustained over long periods of time with little return.

Punishment

It can be difficult to distinguish negative reinforcement from punishment. The difference between the two is that where negative reinforcement is used to strengthen a behaviour, as in the previous example, punishment is designed to remove behaviour from a repertoire. Much social advertising seeks to punish harmful behaviours such as smoking and alcohol and drug abuse. For example, the 'Know the Score' campaign in Scotland aims to provide unbiased information to users about the potential dangers associated with the ingestion of drugs, including cocaine. Skinner argues that punishment may lead a person to express feelings of shame or embarrassment. If the person changes her behaviour so as to avoid further punishment, she will not feel so guilty or ashamed. Skinner emphasizes that it is important to recognize in the behavioural explanation that the person does not act because of her feelings, or because her feelings are changed, but because of the punishing contingencies to which she has been exposed.

HABITUAL BEHAVIOUR

If one assumes that the consumer has a degree of choice in consumption behaviour then continuous reinforcement (repeated satisfaction) resulting in product use increases the probability that the consumer will buy the same brand. Initially the consumer has a decision to make, but with continuous reinforcement the probability of buying the same brand increases until the consumer establishes a habit.

Q & A

QUESTION

How would you then describe the following in operant conditioning terms?

- Jean is shopping for a suit for work. She says that she does not like store A. Although they have nice clothes, the last time she visited it staff were pushy and intrusive. She avoids the store.
- Jean says that she likes store B. When she visited the store looking for a suit staff were unobtrusive and allowed her to browse without pressuring her. She eventually found a suit that pleased her but in the wrong size. When she mentioned this to a member of staff they checked with the warehouse and found that a suit in the correct size was in stock – and at a discount of 10 per cent.

ANSWER

Jean's first experience is an example of negative reinforcement. Her second experience is an example of positive reinforcement.

EXTINCTION AND FORGETTING

Instrumental conditioning helps to understand how a consumer may come to cease buying a product. If the person is no longer satisfied with the product then the link between the stimulus and the expected reward is broken. Extinction leads to a rapid decrease in the probability that the consumer will repurchase the same brand. For example, anti-smoking advertisements seek to break the link between smoking cigarettes and the pleasure that they bring.

Forgetting is different from extinction and occurs when the stimulus is no longer repeated or perceived. Where the advertising for a product is discontinued, for example, consumers may forget the product. Marketers counter forgetting by repetition and seeking to maintain high awareness levels.

Behaviourists do not use words that signify internal states to describe behaviour. In this respect to say 'I *like* chocolate, or the Rolling Stones, or Perrier' is not permissible. Instead one would observe the effect that eating chocolate or listening to the Rolling Stones or drinking Perrier has on the person, and if this is pleasant then one would describe these as being positively reinforcing.

Stimulus control

The idea of stimulus control relates to the idea that the environment affects an organism after, as well as before, it responds. Stimuli, responses and consequences become linked together so that a stimulus that is present when a response is reinforced acquires some control over the response. A response reinforced on one occasion is very likely to occur on a very similar occasion. One can use both concepts to explain marketing behaviour, e.g. copy-cat brands seek to benefit by mimicking one or more of the characteristics of successful brands. However, when behaviour is reinforced only when a particular property is present, that property acquires exclusive control through a process called discrimination (Skinner, 1974: 74). For example, a store logo can act as a discriminative stimulus for pleasant shopping experience and good service – this reinforcer being contingent on entering a shop and speaking to an assistant.

Shaping

Shaping is the gradual forming of behaviour using operant conditioning. Behaviourists believe that complex new behaviours do not usually appear spontaneously. More often apparently radical changes in behaviour are underscored by a number of small incremental steps. For example, a person may seem to engage in a radical change by switching from store A to store B for his weekly shop. On closer examination it is likely that the person had overheard a conversation about how good store B was, had read something positive about store B in the newspaper and when passing store B had been favourably impressed with its attractive window display. They had then visited the store and browsed without buying anything, although they were impressed by the bright, clean, well lit store, the variety of goods on display, the competitive prices, the reward scheme and the helpful staff. They had done a proportion of shopping there, gaining a high level of reinforcement on each occasion relative to their usual store until the switch was made. In order to get the customer to try the store marketers had to experiment with different designs, etc., to find out which aspects of the store environment act to maximize feelings of satisfaction and also how to minimize those aspects that detract from this.

Chaining

Chaining explains how secondary reinforcers can be linked with primary reinforcers as part of an extended learning process. For example, a store visit may involve a chain of secondary activities that ultimately lead to the possession of food and other primary reinforcers. This can extend from writing a list to driving to the supermarket, entering the store, searching for products and selecting items taking them to the checkout and paying for them. Only the last is obviously reinforced by receiving the food and other primary reinforcers purchased. Driving, searching and queuing activities are not likely to be reinforcing in that they are not pleasurable in their own right. However, because each response is paired with a conditioned reinforcer, it can become a reinforcer in its own right.

Operant model of the consumer buying process

The radical behaviourist model of the consumer buying process developed by Foxall (1996) is shown in Figure 3.5. It can be seen that that the model focuses entirely on external observable factors.

The behavioural setting is important for understanding the context in which the behaviour takes placed. Behavioural settings can range from being almost entirely closed, as in the controlled laboratory experiment, to the relatively open settings found in traditional markets. The setting may refer to the physical environment experienced by the consumer or it may refer to the situational aspect of the decision, e.g. whether the purchase is for oneself or a gift for another. Belk (1975) wrote a most informative paper on the subject of

Figure 3.5
Foxall's
behavioural
perspective
model

Source:
Foxall (1996),
figure 10.1, p. 264.
Reproduced by
kind permission of
the author.

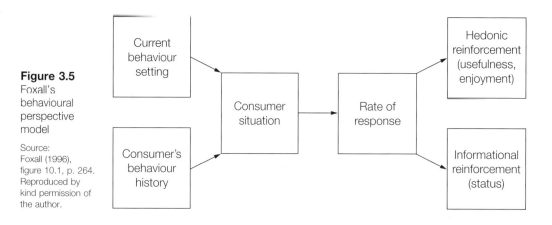

the settings. In his view settings are not simply bounded in time and space but also comprise an action pattern. Different settings require different forms of behaviour regardless of who is present: a wedding; a football match; a funeral; a birthday party; a work context. In seeking to explore this notion of the setting further, Belk came up with the following taxonomy:

■ *Physical*: surrounding, geographical and institutional location, décor, sounds, aromas, lighting and weather.
■ *Temporal*: time since last purchase, meals, payday, seasons and time of day.
■ *Task definition*: Shopping for small item or large. Shopping for self or gift? Eating at home, going to a party, eating at an hotel.
■ *Antecedent states*: e.g. moods.

Taking each in turn and thinking about it, you can see that the setting plays a major role in the purchase process. Managers in modern consumption contexts often seek to close the setting as much as possible in order to encourage consumers to conform to the behaviour programme that they have devised. In modern supermarkets every aspect of the setting has been subjected to careful scrutiny in seeking to ensure that each shopping visit has the potential to yield as great a return as possible – from the exterior look of the building to the lighting, arrangement of produce, staff appearance and arrangement of checkouts. Have you ever been tempted to barter in a supermarket setting? If no, then why not? Has this got anything to do with the way the setting has been arranged? In relatively open settings the consumer is relatively free to follow her own rules. For example, in browsing for luxury goods, one can choose which stores to visit, whether or not to invite staff to help.

As we grow older the world seems to expand around us as we learn about different kinds of products, consumption rituals and the various settings in which these are to be found. Often there are interesting interactions between the setting and a person's consumption history. Foxall (1996: 285) cites the rather extreme example about an elderly Dutch lady who visited a hypermarket on her first trip to Utrecht and spent three days in the store before being rescued by the police, because she could not find the exit. She later explained that she had been afraid to ask others how to get out. Foxall responds sympathetically. He does not find her situation funny; store designers often make way-finding difficult. Try to remember what it is like, for example, when a large store relocates its product lines to new locations. Behaviour is the outcome of the coincidence of a specific learning history and of the consumption setting. Depending on the nature of the experience, the behaviour may yield a mix of hedonic and informational reinforcement, unless of course an aversive situation occurs such as that which happened to the lady in Utrecht.

Foxall combines a variety of settings and of patterns of reinforcement to describe four different kinds of buying behaviour as shown in Figure 3.6:

■ *Maintenance*. In a comparatively open setting this describes the routine food shopping which provides relatively low levels of reinforcement compared with other categories. Foxall (1996: 266) also places hairdressing in this category, as it is a routine purchase of a necessity. It could be argued that this is much more important to people than that,

Figure 3.6
Contingencies
of consumer
choice

Source: adapted
from Foxall (1996),
figure 12.2, p. 310.
Reproduced by
kind permission of
the author.

Closed setting ◄────────────────────► Open setting		
High hedonic reinforcement	Accomplishment	High informational reinforcement
	Pleasure	Low informational reinforcement
Low hedonic reinforcement	Accumulation	High informational reinforcement
	Maintenance	Low informational reinforcement

particularly when it goes wrong! In a closed setting this includes restricted behaviours such as completing tax returns or obtaining a passport.

■ *Accumulation*. This describes the state where a consumer obtains high levels of feedback from purchasing but the item itself does not yield a great amount of pleasure. It could be the situation where purchases are rewarded with tokens or points of some kind. In an open setting this would include collecting behaviour where a person is collecting tokens or coupons. In a closed setting this could include air miles.

■ *Pleasure*. This describes activities such as watching television in an open setting, which often provides a high level of enjoyment and relaxation. In a closed setting, this might entail watching a video display while queuing or an inflight film.

■ *Accomplishment*. In open settings this will include pre-purchase search and evaluation of goods that confer status and high informational reinforcement. Or again it might include reading literature.

Influencing buyer behaviour

How can marketers influence consumer behaviour? Ehrenberg and Goodhart (2000) describe a simple sequence known as Awareness, Trial and Reinforcement (ATR) in line with the shaping of behaviour described above.

■ *Awareness*. In this respect advertising and other communications may be used to build and maintain a high level of brand awareness and to provoke sufficient interest in a proportion of consumers that will lead them to try the product. Advertising may involve vicarious learning by depicting people who look similar to those from the target group enjoying and benefiting from using the product. The idea behind vicarious learning is that it is cost-free to the extent that one can observe and copy the behaviour of others if that is seen to be successfully reinforced – or alternatively one can avoid what they do if one observes negative consequences (Bandura, 1972). Advertisers often promote vicarious learning by showing the negative results that arise if people do not use their products and social approval for those who do. Interest in trial may be further enhanced by means of an introductory trial offer coupled to eye-catching signage and a prominent placement position.

- *Trial.* Perhaps the most obvious means of encouraging trial is to ensure that there is a sufficient stock of the brand available to ensure that every customer can find the shape and size that they require. Here close attention should be paid to the setting and in particular towards estimating the extent to which the setting can be controlled or closed.
- *Reinforcement.* As can be seen, in contrast to cognitive learning theory where attitude is an important pre-behavioural state that is predictive of behaviour, the radical behaviourist sees no role for a concept which mediates between intention and overt behaviour. Choice is not the outcome of internal mental deliberation but is simply a behaviour.

SECTION SUMMARY

In this section the ideas of Watson and Skinner are discussed. It is important to remember:

- Behaviourists have no time for mentalistic or 'within the skin' concepts such as attitudes, but seek to explain behaviour by external observable events.
- In classical conditioning the most interesting events are those that occur when the presentation of a CS is contiguous with an UCS. Over time the response associated with the UCS transfers to the CS. Classical conditioning can explain how products, which at first have meaning, can gain the meaning associated with other stimuli. In this explanation more complex behaviours are made up of the simpler behaviours that constitute them.
- Operant conditioning focuses on the consequences of behaviour and specifically on the extent to which this is reinforced. This may be reinforced positively by means of incentives or negatively by means of avoidance. Marketers use both forms of reinforcement in advertising and in devising behavioural settings by which they seek to control important aspects of behaviour. Social marketing often uses punishment in a bid to cut the link between behaviour and its reinforcement. Models of consumer decision making focus purely on a behavioural explanation. Behaviourists argue that the feelings that are experienced at the same time as behaviour may seem to be their causes precisely because they occur simultaneously. But in behavioural explanation they are little more than collateral products of the contingencies of reinforcement that occasion and strengthen the purchase response (Skinner, 1974: 47).

COGNITIVE INFORMATION PROCESSING (CIP)

It is considered the cognitive revolution took place in 1956 when Simon developed a computer program called the General Problem Solver. Unlike previous attempts this was not based on the abstract rules of logic but was an effort to simulate human thinking processes; something called 'artifical intelligence' was in the process of being born (Bruner in Miller, 1983: 36).

Simon made much of the distinction between his outlook and that adopted by theories based on the principle of *homo economicus*, in particular, the Subjective Expected Utility (SEU) theory. It was the prevailing mode of theorizing human decision-making processes, being based on much contemporary economics, theoretical statistics and operational research. He was critical of the assumptions made by SEU theory as being ill fitted to an understanding of human decision making, e.g. in dealing with uncertainty one should assume that knowledge about the future values of one or more variables is given in the form of a probability distribution. Simon thought it highly unlikely that this was the way in which humans formulate estimates of an uncertain future. He offered the following example to illustrate his point:

> If you were to ask a sales representative to provide an answer to the question 'What do you think your sales will be for the next twelve months?' then the chances are that although the answer may not be reliable, the question will be meaningful to them. If, on the other hand, you asked them the question 'Please estimate the joint probability distribution of sales over the next twelve months', then, as Simon says, 'I have tried this out a couple of times; fortunately my behaviour was interpreted as attemptedly humorous rather than insane.'
>
> (Simon, 1957: 204)

Simon introduces his theory suggesting that a house thermostat is confronted with the same problem as a sales manager. He explains this superficially odd connection by saying that for both to perform optimally (according to SEU theory), the latter would have to predict sales correctly and the former to predict the weather accurately. However, in reality a house thermostat does not attempt to do this. It regulates temperature not by predicting but by relatively prompt corrective action to eliminate deviations between the actual temperature and the desired temperature. In the same way the sales manager who knows what his desired level of sales is can monitor it against actual sales, which knowledge enables him to make good the deficit should one arise. Put another way then both the thermostat and the sales manager formulate the problem as follows:

- What is the initial state, the current position?
- What is the desired state?
- What is the difference between initial state and goal state?
- What alternatives exist for reducing the difference?
- Which alternative is best?

Finally there is execution, or implementing the best alternative. The above is an example of a rule of thumb or heuristic that Simon argued is prevalent in human problem solving known as means–ends analysis. This requires some explanation. Where Freud conceived of human attention as a vehicle for the transmission of psychic energy, Simon was drawn to its limitations. In perceiving the world, everything around is not perceived but rather selective attention is made to those aspects that are salient, while others are blocked out. When a decision has to be made, precious time is not wasted in considering every possibility, assigning a probability to it, projecting this towards a number of potential future states and selecting the optimum. Indeed, this could not be done even if it were desirable because of lack of the processing capacity; the working memory is limited. Instead, Simon argues, heuristics, or rules of thumb, are used in selecting operators. Frequently, means–end analysis is used heuristically by people faced with complex situations. Means–end analysis works by determining differences between a current state of a problem and a goal state; differences between where we are now and where we want to be – and selecting operators known to be useful in reducing such differences. The basic idea is that people have knowledge about the means (operators) at their disposal for achieving certain ends or goals. For example, on arrival at Heathrow airport and wanting to go to Harrods store in central London the goal is to get from Heathrow airport to Harrods. The goal is to transform 'you at Heathrow' to 'you at Harrods'. The first task is to compare the two states and to find the difference between them. The difference is one of location. The means of reducing differences in location are operators such as 'walk', 'go by underground', 'go by taxi' and 'go by bus'. Some operators are not feasible. The individual may be a particularly lazy one who will not walk the sixteen miles involved. It is decided to go by airport coach (bus) because this is the cheapest. The new sub-goal is made to reduce the difference between 'you at Heathrow airport baggage collection' and 'you at coach stop for Victoria coach station'. When the coach arrives at Victoria the problem is transformed once more, and so on until arrival at Harrods. Means–end analysis is used extensively in managerial decision making. In Chapter 2 it is encountered under Initial state (situation analysis); Goal state (mission, objectives) and Operators (strategies; tactics).

Marketing and CIP

From the above, cognitive learning theorists view human decision making as a form of problem solving. Researchers employ the analogy of a computer to investigate the working of the mind, which is taken to be an information processing unit. In contrast to behaviourists, cognitive theorists seek to understand internal mental states. Consumers are conceived of as being motivated by goals and researchers seek to learn more about the operators that people use in order to seek to move from initial states to goal states. Some salient aspects of the CIP approach are that it is:

■   *Adaptive*. Problem-solving involves a fit between the problem solver and the situation.

■   *Selective*. Perception does not simply mirror the world, it works selectively to organize it.

THE USE OF HEURISTICS IN MARKETING

Often behaviour as consumers is far from optimal, e.g. prospect theorists have found that people are willing to take more risks to avoid losses than to realize gains. Tversky and Kahneman (1974) identified three simple heuristics, or rules of thumb, that lead to predictable errors in many cases allowing the reduction of cognitive effort.

Availability The frequency of an event is estimated by the ease with which it can be summoned as an example from memory. Economically, this is important because the performance of different products has often to be evaluated. The most effective consumers are those who do not place too much weight on recent performance.

Representatives Patterns in random sequences are noted, e.g. people often judge probabilities by the degree to which A is representative of B or A resembles B, even when there are major differences between A and B. For example, in 1993 more than half the stock price of Dell computers, amounting to $2.3 billion (£1.3 billion), was wiped off the company's balance sheet because the company had been categorized in a group with IBM and Digital Equipment. The latter was faring much worse at the time.

Another example is regression to the mean. A group scores high on one test, gaining 80–100 per cent. On retest usually the score is much lower. This is not due to any change in the innate intelligence of the group, but to a certain randomness in performance. Usually, good performance is followed by lesser, and bad performance is followed by better. Often this is not recognized, which has implications for perceived customer service and brand loyalty.

Anchoring and adjustment The first choice is an estimate and then the estimate is maintained. For example, on being asked how many countries belong to the UN a person sticks with the number twenty-five, even though this was generated by spinning a wheel. In like manner, a person believes that a discount computer store is more likely to sell computers cheap than a department store, although they may be surprised if they actually check the difference. The view that the best deals are available on the Internet has been discounted.

■ *Bounded*. Processing is limited primarily due to constraints in working memory. Often heuristics are relied upon to make up for lack of processing capacity. Only in the simplest situations will consumers reach a decision in one giant step. It is much more likely that they will use the heuristic of means–end analysis by splitting large problems into more manageable sub-problems. Examples of other heuristics commonly used in marketing contexts are described in the box.

Although the CIP approach stresses that it is important to understand the fit between the problem solver and the situation, much research focuses on aspects of internal processing

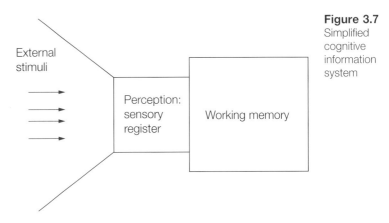

Figure 3.7
Simplified cognitive information system

and tends to ignore the situational aspect. According to Foxall (2005), it almost entirely ignores the environment in which the behaviour takes place. The ideas of selectivity and boundedness focus attention on the problem-solving process. A simple representation of a CIP system is shown in Figure 3.7.

The funnel shown in Figure 3.7 indicates that information processing deals with relatively few stimuli present in the external world. For example, when sitting in class, students are exposed to a number of different sounds, smells and draughts in addition to the visual stimuli. Thankfully, the perceptual process linked to the sensory register directs attention towards those stimuli that are salient and relevant to the situation. Perception is a complex process which ranges from exposure to attention, comprehension and retention of information from the environment. Consider personal exposure to a communication advertising a new product. If perceived to be relevant then this may enter the sensory store, and if it goes no further this may last for micro-seconds. Within that time it may be admitted into working memory, where its visual and auditory components might persist for up to fifteen or twenty seconds. If the information is considered important enough to repeat or rehearse, it may last for around twenty minutes and will have a chance of entering long-term memory. It is clear that only a minority of stimuli such as advertisements will be attended to, comprehended and retained in memory.

Working memory is considered to be similar to computer RAM. The term 'working' implies that the system is active and split into a number of sub-routines whereby a central executive assigns inputs to visual and auditory stores (Baddeley and Hitch, 1974). Working memory capacity is limited to the ability to process five units of information at a time, plus or minus two with an average of four (Cowan, 2001). Manipulation of longer lists is possible by categorization, chunking and by linking new information with existing knowledge. Chunking is the process of grouping several pieces of information and treating them as a single unit – for example 'a', 'c', and 'r' to make 'car' – or by grouping individual numbers into a composite phone number. Novel stimuli must be processed serially, i.e. one at a time. Those stimuli that are important are selected, and precious attention is directed to them in order to figure out those aspects that are relevant. Information that is found to be useful is retained.

Long-term memory contains a huge amount of declarative 'this is' knowledge in addition to procedural or 'how to' knowledge. Declarative knowledge may be gained by learning what a bicycle is and what its components are by reading a book. Procedural knowledge like learning how to ride a bicycle or to drive a car is gained initially by slow, incremental and serial action. However, once the novelty has worn off this is routinized. Long-term memory contains episodic memories that reflect on how previous life experiences have been remembered and connect to the sense of who we are and our past. Semantic memories relate to meaning and learning.

Levels of processing. Some authors disagree with the separation of short-term and long-term memory (cf. Cowan, 2005). Craik and Lockhart (1972) suggested that it would be more useful to conceive of different levels of processing where stimuli can be processed at a range of different levels depending on the character of the information. Stimuli can be processed in a shallow manner, e.g. by attending to the colours, or the brightness of a visual stimulus such as an advertisement, but with no processing of meaning. On the other hand, stimuli that are considered to be important because they are relevant to life experience and identity can be subjected to deeper semantic processing. Petty and Cacciopo (1986) adopted a similar line of reasoning in seeking to understand how individuals might process a persuasive advertising message. They suggested two routes to persuasion, central and peripheral, with the differences between being accounted for by contextual and personality factors. Where there was a degree of complexity in choice, and where the perception that a person's identity was important, a person would be likely to elaborate the message by means of conscious information processing. This active processing by the central route involves a sequential process that moves from pre-attention to focal attention, comprehension and elaboration to the reception of information in memory and then further processing to produce attitudes. By contrast processing by the peripheral route moves straight from pre-attention directly into memory, avoiding costly expenditure of time and effort. The idea of levels of processing is central to the cognitive explanation of involvement.

Do men and women process advertisements differently?

The levels of processing theory outlined above has been used to explore the ways in which men and women process advertising stimuli. In the early 1900s there was a belief that men and women differed both in their approach to advertising and in the manner in which they purchased goods. One commonly held view has been that menare more analytical and logical in their approach to information processing whereas women are more subjective and intuitive. This thinking was prevalent among advertising creatives, who targeted women using emotional appeals. More recent research indicates that such stereotypical thinking is some way from the truth. Meyers-Levy (1986; Meyers-Levy and Maheswaran, 1991) developed the selectivity model to explain the different ways in which men and women process advertising messages. She suggests that men and women differ not because of some subjective/objective divide, but to the extent to which they process information. Generally, the selectivity model suggests that men use heuristics or simple rules of thumb in processing advertising messages. Men tend to process advertisements in a shallow manner by attending to colours and images but do not process them in a way that relates to their deeper meaning or relevance to self. The researchers found that, in contrast to men, women tend to employ comprehensive processing of all information prior to making a judgement based on an advertising message. Women as comprehensive processors attend to both subjective and objective aspects of the message. This claim is supported by Darley and Smith (1995), who found that, when risk is low, women are equally favourable to objective and subjective claims and, when risk is moderate, that objective claims produce a more favourable response. This finding has important implications for copywriters and advertisement managers who still follow traditional reasoning and highlight the subjective aspect of purchase and use when females are the target market. It suggests that advertisers should be more flexible in choosing attributes to emphasize and the copywriter more flexible in choosing writing styles.

QUESTION

Is that the end of the story?

ANSWER

No, definitely it is not the end of the story. While the Darley and Smith (1995) study has made a useful contribution towards our understanding, it suffers from several limitations:

■ It treats men and women as homogeneous groups and it tests for differences between these groups. This ignores the often substantial variation in styles within sex (male and female) categories and the overlap between them. The manner in which they lumped together 'men' and 'women' on the basis of sex (physical characteristics) rather than gender orientation tends to assume a rigid linkage between sex and gender which may not exist.

■ The researchers used an experimental design which has benefits and disadvantages. The benefits are that the researchers could carefully control the presentation of stimuli and the general context in which respondents processed the advertisements. On the downside, however, there is the problem of ecological validity, or the manner to which the experiment corresponds to how people process advertisements in real life. In real life individuals are not told to attend to advertisements, nor is the advertising stimulus controlled. The test situation is artificial and this itself may play a role in our processing strategies. Another factor is that only 120 people formed the basis of the experiment. So there is enough room for disagreement to allow academics to debate this issue for some time to come.

Q
&
A

Another area for research is the stereotype of whether men are more emotional than women. Fisher and Dubé (2005) explored attitudes to advertising, finding that males tend to adjust their emotional displays towards what they believe is appropriate or socially desirable expression. The authors link the behaviour of males to social approval; in private they can express themselves freely but are much more constrained in the public situation, where they feel they are on show and so must seek to ensure that their emotional expressions fit with the context.

Changing gender orientations are apparent in the development of the 'gay' market in the UK. In a 1995 readership survey conducted by *Gay Times*, it was found that average income among gays was £17,000 (US$30,500) a year, while the average gay household brought in £36,000 (US$84,600). This is considerably more than the typical 'straight' family unit. The *Gay Times* survey found that 77 per cent of its readers are ABC1s, against a 43 per cent proportion of the general population (Fry, 1997). It must be remembered that while marketers may zero in on the market because of its value to them, the 'gay' market presents a formidable marketing challenge, as it constitutes a diversity not only of gender orientations but also of age, social class and ethnicity.

Attitude

Attitude is an important concept to understand because it divides cognitive from behaviourist explanations of consumer behaviour. Behaviourists such as Foxall eschew 'within the skin' concepts such as attitude. On the other hand, although the concept of attitude pre-dates Simon's cognitive revolution, cognitive theorists insist that it plays a key role in 'central' processing (cf. Petty *et al.*, 1983). The battle between cognitive and behaviourist explanations, where the former celebrates the importance of attitude and the latter contests it, features in differences about explanations of involvement, of branding and brand loyalty and in the role of advertising.

An attitude is a predisposition to behave towards an attitude object in a consistently favourable or unfavourable way. The notion that attitude is a predisposition to behave is interesting to marketers because, if the situation is right, then a positive attitude towards a product or service should lead to an intention to buy it. Attitudes are considered to be closely linked with self-protection and self-expression. For example, if Jane feels anxious about success then she may well develop positive attitudes towards products that allow her to aspire to it: a fountain pen, designer briefcase, fine restaurants, fashion-brand clothes. Marketers seek to influence personal feelings across a spectrum of products and services, from cars to financial services products to social marketing issues such as drinking and driving, smoking, racism and domestic abuse.

Attitudes are consistent, but most important they are evaluative, summing up what is believed and felt about attitude objects. The underlying theory is known as expectancy value theory. An 'expectancy' is another term for a belief or a probabilistic expectation about the future and 'value' refers to a feeling or evaluation. This means that when a person has to choose between alternatives which involve the formation of an attitude, she is likely to process these alternatives in a deep manner. She will seek to choose that option which she expects

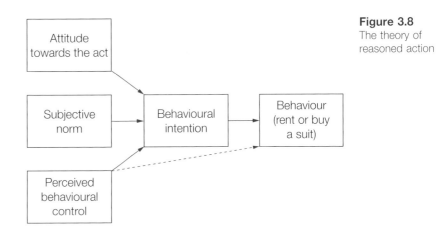

Figure 3.8
The theory of
reasoned action

will lead to the most favourable outcomes, i.e. the option with the highest subjective expected utility (which is the person's subjective judgement of use or value). Consumers do not always seek to maximize subjective value but may satisfice it (see Figure 3.8).

In the cognitive explanation a key aspect of attitude lies in its ability to predict behaviour. Fishbein and Ajzen (1975; Azjen, 1991) have sought to investigate the links between attitude and behaviour. As shown in Figure 3.8, this has grown more complex as the authors have incorporated new elements that improve their predictions. One addition has been the concept of a subjective norm. This was included because it was found that, although a person might personally be in favour of a particular course of action, this was not shared by important people in their peer group and, consequently, the person might not behave as predicted. By including a subjective norm, which measures two aspects: (1) beliefs about others' norms for the behaviour, (2) person's motivation to comply with the norm, they found that prediction could be improved. For example, Jane would like to buy a Skoda car because she believes that they are good value and of good quality. However, her friends think that Skodas have a cheap image and are for old people. Consequently, Jane does not buy the Skoda!

Some time later Azjen (1991) introduced the idea of perceived behavioural control to describe that a person may feel favourable to doing something and their significant others may also be positive about this, but they may feel lacking in confidence about their ability to do it. For example, Jane's friends think that a Citroën car would be a good choice. She has visited some car dealers and has developed a favourable attitude to the car. She would like to buy one online because she can save 10 per cent and money is critical. However, she lacks the confidence to buy online as she has not done so before. Additionally, she has heard that it is not trustworthy. In this respect the perceived behavioural control is lacking and Jane may not buy online. What factors do you think might encourage Jane to buy online in future?

The main objection that behaviourists such as Foxall (2005) have to the above explanation is that these additional variables, such as subjective norms and behavioural control are situational variables that are encompassed by the behaviourist explanation.

Cognitive consumer decision process

The cognitive information processing approach described above has been grafted on to a much older scheme. For example, Strong (1925) developed a scheme known as the hierarchy of effects that sought to measure the effectiveness of marketing communications. The hierarchy of effects provided marketers with a set of sequential objectives, namely to:

■   Build awareness of the product in the mind of the target group.
■   Ensure that a good proportion would become interested in trying the product.
■   Create a desire for the product that would then lead to the fourth term, action.

Consider how these relate to the CIP approach to explaining the consumer decision process which is shown in Figure 3.9.

PROBLEM IDENTIFICATION

If the problem solving view of consumer behaviour is adopted, then the problem identification stage may be thought of as a change in people's well-being as the result of a difference between their actual state and the state which they would like to be in (their desired state). This difference creates a sense of lack, a gap, a loss of equilibrium and well-being which in turn is the propulsion engine for desire. The resultant energy is directed towards means for satisfying that desire. In a consumer society the provision of goods and services play a major role in the provision of such satisfaction. Consider the example of Joe, a final-year student who is applying for a job. A bank has notified him that he has been selected for interview for a job in its computer department.

INFORMATION SEARCH

Usually Joe has no real interest in clothes and had not thought about what he might wear until his friend Jane pointed this out. He looks in his wardrobe and then conducts a 'fashion show' for Jane and some other friends in his flat. Jane and the others are horrified that Joe thought that it would be appropriate to wear his favourite combination of slash jeans and Killers T-shirt to the interview.

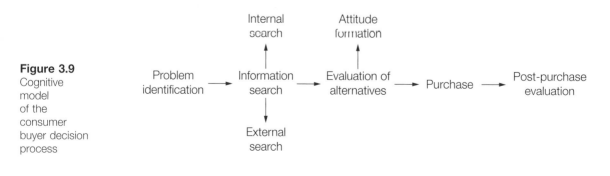

Figure 3.9
Cognitive model of the consumer buyer decision process

EVALUATION OF ALTERNATIVES: ATTITUDE

No wonder Joe has a headache! He has already had one attitude changed by his friends and he is finding that he is forming new attitudes. Attitudes are hard work. Joe finds himself spending precious attention on what different suits of clothes say about him as a person. Jane reminds him that he should consider the kind of suit that bank staff might consider appropriate, so that he will improve his chances of getting the job. Consequently he begins to form some beliefs about the kind of suit he is after. It should be stylish and upbeat to reflect his personality, but restrained in its colouring. (Jane had insisted that the purple suit he fancied initially might not impress bank staff.) It should be durable and of good quality. Joe has developed attitudes about which stores offer the kind of attributes he is after. Joe forms attitudes regarding the suitability of various retail stores for this purchase. He decides not to go to the discount store where he usually purchases his jeans but rather to visit a long-established and exclusive men's outfitter a friend has mentioned. While traditional economists argue that Joe would evaluate different suits on all available criteria, cognitive psychologists (cf. Bettman *et al.*, 1998) are well aware of processing constraints.

QUESTION

From the above what is Joe's attitude towards what to wear? What is his subjective norm?

ANSWER

The answer is that Joe has a positive attitude to wearing his favourite clothes, but that his friends think he would be crazy to do so. The key thing in changing his behaviour is the other part of the subjective norm, which is his motivation to comply with what his friends tell him. They manage to convince him that, to get the job, he is going to have to buy a suit. Joe's granny had given him £100 for his last birthday to 'buy something nice'. Originally, he had thought of contributing this towards a new mp3 player but reluctantly he decides that he will have to buy the suit instead.

At 9.00 a.m. the next day Jane takes Joe shopping. Initially he thinks it is going to be easy: they will walk into the shop, look at a few suits that cost less than £100 (US$179), try one on that fits, pay for it and leave – fifteen minutes maximum! But it turns out to be not quite so simple. As he browses various suits he begins to realize that he has beliefs that some stores are better than others because they offer better value for money and have a good returns policy. He also begins to discriminate between suits; some are more stylish than others but also much more expensive. Others are good-quality and affordable but are rather boring. Joe starts to get a headache. It is 4.00 p.m. and they decide to go home and think about it.

Joe will try to work out the relative importance of these attributes or the minimum acceptable performance of each. The set of attributes used by Joe and the relative importance of each represent Joe's choice criteria. For example, Joe may decide that the kind of suit he is seeking is 'blue', 'sober', 'clean-cut', 'single-breasted' with a 'high wool mix' at a price of no more than £75 (US$135). He is concerned that the trousers are the right length, as he does not want to have the problem of having them taken up. He would like to be reassured that he can change the suit if for some reason it seems to be unsatisfactory when he takes it home. All these factors contribute to the beliefs and attitudes which Joe has developed towards the different brands which he evaluates. A worked example of what Joe does when he goes on holiday is included at the end of Chapter 5.

PURCHASE

Finally, Joe reduces his options to a 'short list' of two suits in two different shops. As it is an important decision he takes a friend with him who is knowledgeable about clothes. In the first shop Joe takes a dislike to the assistant and they leave. As the result of this situational factor Joe and his friend visit the second shop. Joe tries on a suit; his friend thinks that it looks good, it is a good price and Joe decides to buy the suit.

POST-PURCHASE EVALUATION

In terms of post-purchase evaluation, Joe is worried about whether or not he made the correct choice. His friend likes to be at the forefront of fashion and Joe's interview is with a bank where people like to dress soberly. This creates anxiety for Joe. He had second thoughts and went back to the shop to see if he could return the suit. Joe's doubts are known more formally as cognitive dissonance. Doubts about whether the best possible choice has been made produce an uncomfortable psychological tension that consumers can reduce in two ways.

- They can simply withdraw from the situation. Joe could simply take the suit back and ask for a refund.
- Consumers really believe that they did make the correct choice to reduce cognitive dissonance. Many people continue to seek information about the chosen brand after a purchase. Marketers can play a major role in helping to reduce dissonance. On the one hand, some major retailers like Marks & Spencer (M&S) have built a reputation on their readiness to change goods or refund money with no questions asked. Many car manufacturers send follow-up letters and even company magazines to customers who have recently purchased one of their products. In Joe's case, Joe goes back to the shop with the suit and asks the salesperson for a final opinion. The salesperson asks him to try the suit on once more and assures him that he has made a good choice for an interview with a bank. Joe is reassured and prepares for his interview with renewed confidence.

The good news is that Joe got the job! He realizes how important it is to look good in today's high-pressure environment. He buys a magazine which contains information about all the latest styles and goes shopping more regularly. Joe is now involved on an enduring basis.

SECTION SUMMARY

In this section the cognitive explanation of consumer behaviour is discussed. This considers:

■ **the consumer to be a computer or information processor;**
■ **the extent to which capacity limitations lead consumers to use heuristics in problem solving;**
■ **the important distinction between central processing, which includes attitude formation and peripheral processing which uses rough heuristics;**
■ **consumer involvement linked with levels of processing, high involvement is through the central route and low involvement using the peripheral route.**

CONSUMER INVOLVEMENT

Given the discussion on the basics of psychoanalysis, behaviourism and cognitive information processing, the composite and rather controversial theory of involvement can be appreciated. Involvement is a composite in that it incorporates aspects of Freudian theory, behaviourism and cognitive theory. While this seems to yield an explanation that is useful, it must be appreciated that each explanation provides a fundamentally different account. Mainstream involvement and the alternative behaviourist will be discussed below.

Mainstream explanation of involvement

The mainstream explanation of involvement borrows from all three of the psychological theories discussed in Chapter 2. It fully deserves its description by Lastovicka and Gardner (1979; cf. O'Donohoe and Tynan, 1997) as 'a bag of worms'. From Freud comes the view that involvement represents the amount of psychic energy that a person invests in goods and services. Involvement is linked intimately with consumer identity, e.g. Assael (1995: 72) asks when a consumer is most likely to be involved with a product? His answer is when the product:

■ Relates to the consumer's self-image as an expression of his or her personal style.
■ Is of continual interest to the consumer.
■ Entails significant risks, e.g. the social risk of buying the 'wrong' suit of clothes, or the financial risk of buying a new house.
■ Is involved in emotional appeal.
■ Has badge or 'sign' value (when it has a mark of status).

Involvement is a relationship between a person and a product which reflects the amount of psychic energy which that person invests in that product. In this respect it is not appropriate to speak of products as being intrinsically 'involving' or 'uninvolving'. However, marketers are not interested in everybody but in people in general or the mean estimate. It is possible to find marketers talking about some products, e.g. cars, as being high-involvement and others, e.g. socks, being low-involvement. Kapferer and Laurent (1985/6) obtained mean involvement profiles for a range of goods with respect to female French consumers. Table 3.2 shows the scores for a range of these.

Kapferer and Laurent use a different measure of involvement from that discussed by Assael. *Interest* refers to the ego-importance of the product class; *pleasure* to the rewarding value of the product; *sign*, the 'badge' value of the product; *risk importance* relates to the perceived importance of the negative consequences of a mispurchase; and *risk probability* the subjective probability of making a mis-purchase. From the above, it can be seen that a washing machine is regarded as a high-involvement purchase, as almost all scores are over 100. The risk of buying a washing machine is highest, possibly because of the economic risk involved in its cost. Risk probability is lower as washing machines are much more reliable nowadays than they used to be. On the other hand, the only item which comes anywhere near involving people for batteries is their risk probability.

Involvement and consumer decision making

A high-involvement decision process may be followed for one of two reasons. A person may be involved because of the situation which they find themselves in or they may have an enduring involvement in a particular type of goods or services.

SITUATIONAL INVOLVEMENT AND ENDURING INVOLVEMENT

Think back to the example of Joe, who required a new suit of clothes for a job interview, that was used to illustrate the cognitive decision process. Joe originally had little interest in clothes and so his interest in buying a suit was due to the situation he was in, that is, because

Table 3.2 Mean involvement profile

Goods	Interest	Pleasure	Sign	Risk importance	Risk probability
Washing machine	130	111	104	136	102
Perfume	120	154	164	116	97
Chocolate	94	130	86	76	91
Hose	71	83	102	75	94
Champagne	75	128	123	123	119
Batteries	3	39	59	65	98

Source: adapted from Kapferer and Laurent (1985/6).

his friends persuaded him to buy a suit. Joe developed attitudes about the kind of suit for which he was looking. With the job he finds that he judges people on their appearance and style. He is more sensitive to the way that others look at him and to comments that are made. He goes to the mall more often in search of appropriate clothes that will express his sense of style to others. Enduring involvement describes a person who has a continual interest in a particular type of product. This could be literally anything from clothes to music, stamps, sports, theatre or the opera. The relationship between involvement and complexity of purchase is of great interest to marketers.

DISTINGUISHING HIGH FROM LOW INVOLVEMENT

In contrast to the above, low-involvement decisions characterize the vast majority of the purchases that are made. These reflect more or less opposite tendencies to the high-involvement profile and include examples of products that are considered to be mundane and unimportant to our self-image and which involve little risk if a mistake is made in purchasing them. Traditionally, marketers have ignored this area as being beneath their concern; however, recently low-involvement purchasing behaviour has attracted considerable interest. Low-involvement behaviour is reminiscent of Freud's theory in that many of the decision processes are unconscious. The differences in styles between high and low-involvement purchasing are shown in Table 3.3.

From Table 3.3 it is clear that, according to the mainstream explanation, different modes of involvement give rise to different approaches to learning and information processing.

Table 3.3 Differences between low and high-involvement styles

	Low involvement: passive consumer		High involvement: active consumer
1	Consumers learn information at random.	1	Consumers are information processors.
2	Consumers are information gathers.	2	Consumers are information seekers.
3	Consumers represent a passive audience for advertising.	3	Consumers represent as active audience for advertising resulting in the effect of advertising being weak.
4	Consumers buy first; if they do evaluate brands, it is done after purchase.	4	Consumers evaluate brands before buying.
5	Consumers seek an acceptable level of satisfaction, resulting in their buying the brand least likely to give them problems with their buying on a few attributes.	5	Consumers seek to maximize expected satisfaction resulting in their comparing brands to see which provides the most benefits.
6	Personality and lifestyle characteristics play little if any role in the purchase decision.	6	Personality and lifestyle characteristics are related to consumer behaviour because brands are tied to the person's identify and belief system.
7	Reference groups exert little influence on product choice because products are unlikely to be related to group norms and values.	7	Reference groups influence behaviour as the product is important to group norms and values.

Source: adapted from Assael (1995) p. 156.

In the high-involvement condition consumers act purposively according to the central route (Petty *et al.*, 1983) as problem solvers who seek and evaluate information prior to purchase. The product is important to the person either because it plays a critical role in the way in which they present their identity. It may reflect in terms of what other people might think about them (known as 'badge value'), or in terms of economic risk (expensive purchase) or social risk, where the social cost of making a mistake might be high. In the high-involvement mode the consumer passes through the stages of awareness to comprehension and retention.

There are differences between the high and low-involvement buying situation with respect to the sequence known as the hierarchy of effects. This means that consumers form beliefs (what they think) about the brand, which influence their attitudes (what they feel) towards the brand, which in turn influence their intention to buy (their actions). The details relating to the hierarchy of effects will be discussed later in this section when examining beliefs and attitudes. In the high-involvement condition it would be expected that people will actively evaluate brands to form beliefs, attitudes and finally to form an intention to buy the brand. This is important for marketers, who can conduct research to find out consumers' current beliefs, attitudes and behavioural intentions, which may in turn provide some evidence about consumers' current state. The example in Chapter 5 on p.149 onwards concerns methods of measuring Joe's beliefs, attitudes and intentions with respect to taking holidays abroad.

By contrast in the low-involvement mode consumers are not acting as active problem solvers but respond passively to stimuli such as advertising. Learning does not occur through active problem solving but more on the basis of association, by seeing or hearing advertisements, usually when in a relaxed state and then recalling these at a later date, perhaps when in the buying situation. The low-involvement mode favours passive learning, a different mode from the active learning which takes place when the consumer is highly involved. Advertising is likely to be more effective in the low-involvement mode, as consumers will not actively evaluate the advertisements or check out the claims which are made in the advertising by discussing them with friends or checking through consumer publications and other sources. By definition low-involvement products are not considered to be important to the self, or to the image that one might have with others. As a result such purchases are not considered important and often are routinized to the extent that they become programmed and automatic unconscious responses. In the low-involvement situation the consumer is unlikely to follow a stepwise progression through the hierarchy of effects but may well buy first and evaluate later, particularly if the product is considered inexpensive and the risk involved to be low.

The differences between low and high involvement can be of considerable benefit for marketing planners. For example, while advertisers would need to pay careful attention to the construction of advertising messages for high-involvement consumers who process messages centrally, less involved consumers are likely to be influenced more by peripheral features. These could be the use of colour in the advertisement, the nature of the background or the use of an expert spokesperson. Low-involvement purchasers are passive information gatherers, encouraging advertising to focus on a few key points to make it as easy as possible for them to gain familiarity and positive associations with the brand. If the budget allows,

Extent of decision making	Extent of involvement		
Extended	High Complex decision making Therory: CIP	Low Limited decision making
Habitual	Brand loyalty Therory: operant condition	Inertia Therory: classical conditioning

Figure 3.10
The relationship between involvement and complexity

Source: adapted from Assael (1995), p. 153.

then television should be the primary medium, as it allows passive learning. Print media are much more important in high-involvement decision making where consumers are actively seeking information. Usually price is of keen interest to consumers in the low-involvement mode, as they frequently buy products on price alone. As a result, special offers or promotions featuring free trial or coupon offers can be effective in gaining a trial of such products. If no problems are experienced in using the product then consumers may continue to repurchase the product through inertia until a more attractive alternative appears. Generally, those products which consumers feel are low-involvement products should be distributed widely, as consumers are not really prepared to search for these. Such products may be purchased on impulse, so often they are positioned at waist height or at supermarket service tills to be within easy reach. This approach has been so successful, particularly with respect to small children who may grab a bag of sweets while sitting on their parents' trolley, that some supermarkets have created special checkouts which have no promotional displays attached to them in response to parents' complaints.

Assael (1995) summarizes the mainstream view in Figure 3.10.

The purchasing process: high-involvement, complex decisions

Beginning by examining the decision-making process for the top left-hand quadrant of Figure 3.10 when purchasing high-involvement products or services, theory suggests that consumers actively go through a number of processing stages. These are shown in Figure 3.11.

The hierarchy of effects for brand loyalty (high-involvement routine decision making)

According to Assael, those high in involvement and who are in a complex buying situation, for example where the purchase is novel, will use a CIP approach to purchasing. They are likely to actively search for information and to evaluate a number of alternatives, forming attitudes prior to purchase and evaluating the decision afterwards.

Figure 3.11
The purchase decision process: high involvement

Problem identification

↓

Information search

↓

Evaluation of alternatives

↓

Purchase

↓

Post-purchase

What if a person has already bought the product, is satisfied with their purchase and intends to buy it the next time because it has provided them with satisfaction? The decision sequence is different for consumers who are brand-loyal, as they have already tried the product and like it. As a result they know that they really only have to recognize the need, do an internal memory search, retrieve the name of the brand and purchase it. The decision process for brand loyalty will resemble that presented in Figure 3.12.

Brand loyalty is based on a degree of repeat purchase. People repurchase goods on the basis of the continuous satisfaction or rewards that they receive from purchasing them. A 'brand' is a product which has been effectively differentiated from others and which has been provided with a form of personality which resonates with its target customers. Classic brands include Kellogg's, Heinz, Coke and Harley-Davidson. According to this argument customers are fiercely loyal to the brands that they are attached to, so that some brands such as the Apple Macintosh and Harley-Davidson motor cycles have attracted fanatically loyal fans who are almost religious in their fervour.

Assael argues that operant conditioning processes of awareness trial and reinforcement can best explain brand loyalty. Brand loyalty should persist so long as the brand continues to provide reinforcement by means of continual satisfaction. Because the brand already contributes repeated satisfaction, the consumer has little need to search for information or to evaluate alternatives, which is why these are shown in brackets in Figure 3.12.

Low-involvement routine decision making

This situation, which is sometimes known as inertia, can be confused with brand loyalty. The general decision process is similar: I have bought the product before and so do not need to carry out an intensive external search. As this purchase is low-involvement I do not really want to spend much time on the decision in any case. How is the decision confused with brand loyalty? Brownlie and his colleagues discuss the case of Ever-Ready batteries in the UK. During the 1970s Ever-Ready was the market leader and enjoyed a dominant share of the UK battery market. When a rival called Duracell came which based its appeal on the promise that its batteries simply lasted longer, Ever-Ready managers dismissed this as they felt that their customers were brand-loyal. However, the 'Duracell bunny' advertisements were particularly effective in pointing out to consumers the key competitive advantage they had over Ever-Ready and many began to switch to the competitor brand. The moral of the story is that while Ever-Ready managers thought that their

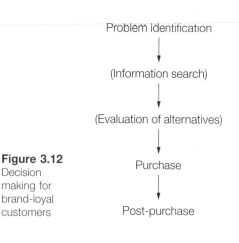

Figure 3.12
Decision making for brand-loyal customers

Problem identification

↓

(Information search)

↓

(Evaluation of alternatives)

↓

Purchase

↓

Post-purchase

customers were brand-loyal, the reality was that they were in inertia, buying the least worst batteries on offer, so that when a new offering came along, the customers switched to it.

Assael argues that because low-involvement purchases follow the peripheral route of processing, where people use heuristics that focus on superficial aspects of the advertising that classical conditioning is the best explanation.

The hierarchy of effects for limited decision making (low-involvement extended decision making)

This situation is also sometimes known as variety seeking. The product is not of much particular interest, but owing to boredom with existing products a decision might be made to try out new products when they appear. The external information search in this instance is not comparable with that which characterizes high-involvement decision making. Information is not actively sought but rather it is received passively. For example, an individual may have been watching television when he/she saw an advertisement for the new sandwich. On visiting the shop the product was 'recognized' on the shelves and so it was decided to try it out. Information has not been seriously sought: alternatives have not been evaluated as the purchase risk is low.

Variations in the level of involvement

One of the benefits of the concept of involvement (and arguably a weakness) is that it is based on the average number of people who believe a product to be involving to them. For example, most people in Europe would consider socks (hose) to be a low-involvement product. Yet there may be some people who have an enduring interest in socks, perhaps because they have sore and itchy feet, or for some aesthetic reason. Involvement researchers ignore such people and focus instead on the mass of consumers. Some researchers have asked whether products which are perceived to be low-involvement in Europe will be perceived to be low-involvement in other countries. For example, Samuel *et al.* (1996) found that many goods which would be considered low-involvement in Europe such as processed food and beverage products may have the status of high-involvement goods in China. They found that Chinese consumers tend to travel long distances (23 per cent travelled over 10 km) to purchase relatively few items (three to five), usually weighing less than 2 kg.

Increasing the level of involvement

Sometimes firms may seek to make products more involving to customers for a number of reasons. The most important reason is that if people are purchasing primary through inertia they are not brand-loyal and are only purchasing the product out of habit. In attempting to create brand loyalty marketers may resort to a number of tactics.

■ *Link the product with identity or risk.* As might be expected there can be links between the product and a person's sense of self or identity, e.g. 'the Pepsi generation'. Other associations are badge value (will your friends like your new deodorant?) or economic or social risk (what if something goes wrong? I ought to be sure). In addition, marketers may try to link the product with an involving issue, e.g. paper towels could be made more involving by linking their use with the effective prevention of salmonella or *E-coli* through the use of medicated towels in the kitchen. Cereal manufacturers have sought to link their products with health by emphasizing their use in a high-fibre diet. It is possible to change the importance of product benefits. This was true of some cooking oils which based their appeal on their being 'low in cholesterol'. However, this proved to be an unacceptable claim, as the advertisers did not reveal that these products still had a high fat content.

- *Link to an involving situation.* Another alternative is to try to link the product with a personally involving situation, e.g. by advertising car cleaning or maintenance products during the rush hour.
- *Create involving advertising.* Alternatively, the product may be linked with advertising which relates closely to the consumer's ego or values. In the academic literature often this is referred to as 'attitude to the ad'. This will be discussed further in Chapter 10.

THE BEHAVIOURIST EXPLANATION OF INVOLVEMENT

Recapping on the behaviourist explanation of consumer behaviour, this seeks to explain behaviour solely with respect to its environmental consequences. It denies any importance to the consumer's internal state and so dismisses 'within the skin' events as being, at best, epiphenomenal. In other words, even though they might agree that internal events such as dreams, memories and attitudes exist and are important, they regard them as being non-causative. The feelings that arise in the course of behaviour may seem to be its causes precisely because they occur simultaneously. But the behavioural explanation insists that they are little more than by-products of the contingencies of reinforcement that occasion and strengthen the purchase response (Skinner, 1974: 47).

Regarding the conflation of different theories summarized by Assael in Figure 3.10, Foxall (1990) argues that the postulates of behaviourism are opposed to the cognitive paradigm and so would protest that these should not be conflated in this manner. He argues that it is because the explanations are so different they provide an active clash of explan-ations, which can be useful from a learning point of view. Following from this it could be argued that by creating a composite explanation this dynamic tension is erased.

Radical behaviourists would disagree with the explanation of high involvement and complex behaviour that is figured in the top left-hand box of Assael's model in Figure 3.10. This is because radical behaviourists find the idea problematic that attitude, when framed as a mental predisposition, feeds into behavioural intentions which are predictive of behaviour. They argue that the predictive ability of 'pure' attitude, i.e. conceived of as the summation of beliefs and feelings, is poor. It is only when 'situational' factors such as social pressure and behavioural control are factored into the equation that the predictive ability of the model increases (Foxall, 2005: 62–5). Where cognitive explanations stress the consumer's intention, radical behaviourism stresses context. In this respect behaviourists would not be too surprised that the form of verbal behaviour expressed as an attitude is not particularly good at predicting overt behaviour. Radical behaviourists would assert that the important factor is that expressing an attitude about buying a car and actually buying a car are different classes of behaviour, each of which is influenced by different response contingencies. Radical behaviourists might seek to explain complex consumer behaviour such as buying a new product, which seems to be novel, as being the outcome of an extensive incremental learning process involving observation, trial and reinforcement. In this respect behaviourists would argue that there is no need to impute the existence of some underlying mental predisposition.

Another criticism of the model is the assumption that large numbers of people will be fiercely brand-loyal. Ehrenberg (1972) has shown repeatedly that comparatively few purchasers of a product, at around 11 per cent on average in one study (Ehrenberg and Uncles, 1999), are 100 per cent loyal to a particular brand. Usually, when consumer behaviour is tracked over a sequence of shopping trips, they are shown to buy a number of brands within a small repertoire of available brands. Ehrenberg argues that this is because brands are similar in terms of their physical characteristics and in task efficacy and are more or less directly substitutable for one another.

Fishbein *et al.*'s theory of reasoned action suggests that, for high-involvement products, individuals will take time to formulate attitudes towards a new product prior to purchasing it. In contradistinction to this, Ehrenberg and Goodhart (2000) found, based on a study of twenty-three newly launched brands, that loyalty to a brand occurred almost instantly right from launch. However, it could be claimed that Ehrenberg's study included many brands that normally would not be considered high-involvement. Regarding personal purchases, which of the following are high-involvement and which are low in involvement for you? The study included brands drawn from product categories such as anti-depressants, cereal bars, chocolate biscuits, coffee, detergents, fruit drinks, shampoos, tea and toothpaste.

Given that radical behaviourism ignores the existence of 'within the skin' concepts like investment of energy, 'attitude', 'identity' and 'badge value' then can one retain a meaningful concept of involvement? Foxall (1990) explains that a radical behaviourist understanding of involvement stresses the environmental determinants of the activities. Situational involvement refers to the immediate consequences of a particular set of purchase behaviours. Involvement is taken to be an instrumental behaviour which is maintained by means of those pleasurable and satisfying reinforcers that are encountered either during the consumer's reinforcement history or in the immediate situation. Enduring involvement results from the person's reinforcement history with the product, the stimulus control and consequences of pre-purchase, purchase and post-purchase responses. Behaviour maintained by high levels of both hedonic and informational reinforcements would be most involving. Behaviour maintained principally by situational factors would be described as being least involving.

CONCLUSION

As the result of reading this chapter and answering the questions you should understand:

- The differences between economic and psychological approaches to explaining consumer behaviour.
- How psychoanalysis, behaviourism and cognitive learning theory highlight different aspects of consumer behaviour as being important.
- The terminology associated with different explanations.
- Different accounts of the buying process contributed by behaviourism and cognitive learning theory.
- How the concept of involvement was constructed as a composite from different theoretical underpinnings.
- Two different explanations of involvement.

This chapter has been wide-ranging covering economic; psychoanalytic, behaviourist and cognitive approaches to understanding consumer buyer behaviour. Each of these approaches has different consequences for the explanation of behaviour. For example, Freudian views, which were especially popular in the 1950s, stress the role of unconscious desire in motivating buyer behaviour. While there are still many researchers who are inspired by Freudian theory, and who are working to uncover the underlying unconscious motives of buyer behaviour, the cognitive problem solving approach, as exemplified by the complex, high-involvement decision-making process, is currently dominant. This approach has much to offer, in that it explains both extended and routine behaviours in addition to the conditions of high and low involvement. It allows for many purchasing decisions to be largely subconscious, but for a different reason from that advanced by Freudians. While Freudians place the unconscious motivation of desire as the central motivation for behaviour, cognitivists emphasize the idea that complex behaviour becomes gradually routinized and subconscious over time, freeing up valuable attention for other activities. There is no doubt that the cognitive approach to consumer buyer behaviour is most useful, as it incorporates concepts such as beliefs, attitudes and intentions. However, this model can be criticized by behaviourists, who argue that their explanation is simpler and more effective.

REVIEW QUESTIONS

1   Discuss the benefits and potential drawbacks of an economist's view of consumer behaviour.
2   Discuss the benefits and potential drawbacks of relying on a Freudian explanation of consumer behaviour.

3   Do people know what they want? (And if they do will they tell you?)

4   What are the key distinctions between 'inner-directed' and 'outer-directed' characters?

5   Discuss the main areas of agreement and disagreement between Abraham Maslow and Sigmund Freud.

6   Which factors influence consumer identity?

7   Describe the consumer buying process as described by (a) behaviourists, (b) cognitive learning theorists.

8   What is meant by the 'Hierarchy of effects'?

9   What are the differences between high and low-involvement decision styles?

RECOMMENDED FURTHER READING

Ahmed, P.K. and Rafiq, M. (2002) *Internal marketing: tools and concepts for customer-focused management*, Oxford: Butterworth Heinemann.

Blackwell, R.D., Miniard, P.W. and Engel, J.F. (2001) *Consumer behavior,* 9th edn, Fort Worth: Harcourt.

Britt, S.H. (1966) *Consumer behavior and the behavioral sciences*, New York: Wiley.

Bruhn, M. (2003) *Relationship marketing: management of customer relationships*, Harlow: Pearson.

Christopher, M., Payne, A. and Ballantyne, D. (2002) *Relationship marketing: creating stakeholder value,* Oxford: Butterworth Heinemann.

Egan, J. (2004) *Relationship marketing: exploring relational strategies in marketing*, 2nd edn, Harlow: Pearson.

Evans, M.J., Moutinho, L. and van Raaij, W.F. (1996) *Applied consumer behaviour*, Harlow: Addison Wesley.

Horton, R.I. (1984) *Buyer behavior: a decision-making approach*, Columbus OH: Merrill.

Little, E. and Marandi, E. (2003) *Relationship marketing management,* London: Thomson.

Loudon, D. and Della Bitta, A.J. (1988) *Consumer behavior: concepts and applications,* 3rd edn, Maidenhead: McGraw-Hill.

Robertson, T.S. and Kassarjan, H.H. (1991) *Handbook of consumer behavior*, Englewood Cliffs NJ: Prentice Hall.

Sheth, J.D., Mittal, B. and Newman, B.I. (1999) *Customer behavior: consumer behavior and beyond,* Fort Worth TX: Dryden.

Solomon, M., Bamossy, G. and Askegaard, S. (2002) *Consumer behaviour: a European perspective*, 2nd edn, Harlow: Pearson.

Useful web addresses

National Food Survey: www.maff.gov.uk/esg/nfs/pressnfs.htm.

British Panel Household Survey 1996: www.irc.essex.ac.uk/bhps/doc/wave1/aindresp6.htm.

Competition in the Dutch flower market: http://kambil.stern.nyu.edu/teaching/cases/auction/flowers.html.

4 INDUSTRIAL BUYER BEHAVIOUR

LEARNING OBJECTIVES

Having read this chapter, students should be in a position to:

- understand the various types of Business-to-Business (B-to-B) market and their influence on industrial buyer behaviour;

- understand the differences between consumer and industrial buyer behaviour;

- evaluate traditional models of industrial buyer behaviour and be able to critique these;

- appreciate the relevance of new approaches to studying B-to-B buyer behaviour;

- use appropriate terminology.

INTRODUCTION

In this chapter the key aspects of industrial buyer behaviour are introduced. The different types of organizational markets, government, institutional, producer and reseller markets are outlined. The role of the organizational buying centre is described and discussed. The B-to-B buying process is described first with reference to early models of buyer behaviour. This approach is critiqued and then contrasted with more recent views which stress the significance of flexibility, open communications and relationships. Finally, B-to-B buyer behaviour is compared with consumer buyer behaviour.

TYPES OF ORGANIZATIONAL MARKETS

Organizational purchases span a wide realm including everything between that of a power station to paperclips. It makes sense to try to organize the types of purchase decision made according to the type of organizational market. These may be divided into four types: government, institutional, producer and reseller markets.

Government

Government is a major purchaser in any country, spending billions of pounds across the range of government expenditure, e.g. on health, defence, social security, transport, communications and education. Theoretically the UK government is accountable to the public as government agencies spend public funds to buy the products which they require.

This accountability has resulted in a complex set of buying procedures, which suppliers must conform to if they are to meet with government requirements. Usually governments make their purchases through bids. Generally, government cannot protect its industry by limiting bids to national firms but, as within the EU, bidders can come from across the Union. Initially, suppliers apply and are vetted to join a list of qualified bidders. Government agencies wishing to purchase equipment send out detailed specifications to qualified bidders and those that feel they are in a position to meet the specifications submit a bid. Usually the government unit accepts the lowest bid. Where the purchase is unusually large or complex, government agencies may use a negotiated contract whereby the agency selects some companies and negotiates with each until a satisfactory outcome has been arranged.

Institutional markets: organizations with non-business goals

These include organizations with educational, charitable and other non-business goals. Universities are numbered among this group. An organization wishing to sell to a university must first identify where the buying decision is to be made. This can be difficult, as some large universities employ thousands of staff in hundreds of academic departments. Purchases of computing equipment are a good example. Senior administrators at one university decided to replace the existing variety of computing systems with a standard system which was approved and chosen by its central computer services and then installed in several departments. At another university central computing services evaluated several types of computer network before approving one and then approved several types of hardware to run on it. Staff within departments were allowed to make its own choice so long as the cost fell within the guidelines set by the university finance department. From this, it should be noted that computer companies dedicate sales staff to particular institutions who familiarize themselves with the way in which decision making is organized within that institution. In particular, the staff who have the authority to make different decisions and who influence the buying decision in each case are monitored carefully.

Producer markets, including buyers of raw materials, semi-finished and finished items

Producer markets range across the spectrum of industries, including public utilities, mining, forestry, fisheries and construction, transport, retailing and manufacturing. Such purchases include buyers of raw materials and semi-finished items used to produce other products. For example, farmers may require animal feed, a range of machinery from milking machines to tractors, seeds for planting and fertilizer. Supermarkets may form producer markets for some items such as carrier bags, scanning equipment and store maintenance products.

Manufacturers buy raw materials and components in order to manufacture products to satisfy consumer needs. The demand for industrial products derives from that for consumer products and is called derived demand. For example, the demand for denim cloth derives from the demand for denim jeans. When in 1998 demand for denim jeans fell in the UK and the US, it had a major 'knock on' effect for jeans manufacturers. The nature of events 'downstream' in the consumer market place results in a chain reaction as effects are experienced by manufacturers and their suppliers who are 'upstream'. For example, in 1998 British Airways shifted its purchasing policy strongly in favour of Airbus for the first time and as a result over 40,000 jobs were lost during the year at Boeing, Airbus's major rival. However, this was only a fraction of the jobs actually lost, as it did not include losses incurred by the thousands of suppliers to Boeing. Another example is that demand for eggs in the UK rose by over 1m per week as the result of a widely televized cookery programme by a famous cook called Delia Smith. Egg producers found it difficult to respond to such a quick change in demand as their hens already were working to capacity to produce eggs for existing markets.

The demand for many industrial products is relatively inelastic, i.e. a price increase or decrease will not alter greatly the demand for the item. The price elasticity of demand is covered in Chapter 9. Price increases that affect only one or two parts of the product will yield only a slightly higher per-unit production cost because many industrial products contain a number of parts. This is considered to be relatively inelastic, as a component accounts for a large percentage of overall cost, which can have a major effect on costs. For example, when engine manufacturers raised the prices of aircraft engines, Boeing was forced to raise the overall price of its planes.

Manufacturers are often clustered together in locations such as the Ruhr valley in Germany. Since the late 1970s manufacturing has been in decline in the UK although it remains significant in other European countries such as Germany. As global capital has shifted to find lower costs elsewhere, so manufacturing industry has shifted to the Pacific rim and more recently to India, Sri Lanka and Morocco as well as to China. Increased global competition means that costs, quality, throughput and flexibility are major issues for those who wish to supply manufacturers.

Reseller markets

Reseller markets are composed of those intermediaries between manufacturer and the consumer which are known as wholesalers and retailers. Wholesalers purchase products for direct sale to retailers, other wholesalers, producers and government. On the other hand, retailers purchase products and resell them to final customers. There has been a general decline in wholesaler numbers in the UK over the past thirty years while retailer power has grown substantially (see Chapter 11).

THE ORGANIZATIONAL BUYING CENTRE

Most high-value purchases in B-to-B markets involve people from different departments and functions within the organization. People play different roles with respect to the buying decision. Several roles are listed below:

■ *Users* In the case of the purchase of a new university computer network system, discussed earlier, users are the people who will use the network. They will probably know much about hardware and software but little about the various network standards and configurations available. Despite this, users should be involved in the buying process so that they can feel included and can contribute usefully their experience of the present system. It would be worth while knowing any defects in the present system to ensure that the new system does not replicate them.

■ *Influencers* provide information for evaluating alternative products and suppliers. With respect to the computer network example, the university central computing services personnel should have the expertise to evaluate different standards and platforms. They should be able to help in drawing up a technical specification for the network system and to advise on the performance and reliability of different options. Other influencers would include computing officers within departments who could communicate the specific requirements of each department.

■ *Gatekeepers* control the flow of information to other people in the purchasing process. Primarily, they involve the organization's purchasing agents and the suppliers' sales people. Within the university example, staff within the computing services section and departmental computing officers would act as gatekeepers and would be able to slant the information flow with respect to the options which they thought were most feasible.

■ *Buyers* are usually referred to as the purchasing agents within the role of purchasing manager. In most organizations buyers have the authority to contact suppliers and negotiate the purchase transaction. In the university computer network example, this may be carried out by a person nominated by the university IT committee, who would report back to the committee.

■ *Deciders* are the persons with the authority to make a final purchase decision. In the university computing network example it would probably be the university IT committee. This would include personnel from the central university administration and persons representing departments directly involved.

B-to-B decision making can be much more complex than consumer decision making, although sometimes family decision making approximates to it.

THE B-TO-B BUYING PROCESS

The questions of what is the nature of the B-to-B buying process and how different is this from consumer buying behaviour are addressed in this section. Research in this area splits into two periods. During the first period of about six years Robinson *et al.* (1967), Sheth (1973) and Webster and Wind (1972) developed the first deductively based theoretical models dedicated to B-to-B buyer behaviour. More recently, there has been a shift in research focus from studying buyers and sellers in isolation to studying the relationship between firms. The whole area of relationship marketing is one that has received much attention, including a special issue of the *Journal of the Academy of Marketing Science* (1995).

Early models

Robinson *et al.* (1967) specified a model of the organizational decision process. It involved recognition of need, determination of characteristics and the quality of the needed item; specification of the characteristics and quality of the needed item; search for and qualification of potential suppliers; acquisition and analysis of proposals; evaluation of proposals and supplier selection; selection of order routine; performance evaluation and feedback. While the model shares certain similarities with the consumer buying decision process mentioned earlier, there are some differences. A more simplified version might follow the process as shown in Figure 4.1.

Figure 4.1
The decision process for choice of supplier

RECOGNITION OF NEED

The organizational purchasing process begins with the recognition of the need for a product or service. For example, computer manufacturers have a need for printed circuit boards (PCBs). Some firms will make PCBs internally; for others it is more convenient to outsource this to a subcontractor who will deliver PCBs to a predefined routine. This routine will depend on how work in progress is sequenced through the shop floor. For example, many manufacturers use Materials Requirements Planning (MRP I) in conjunction with Manufacturing Resource Planning (MRP II) systems which if used effectively can alert suppliers to the firm's requirements for the next month (or specified time period). Many suppliers have 'visibility' of their customers' real-time stock situation through Electronic Data Interchange (EDI). In these cases, the 'recognition' of a need is almost automatic as when the computerized inventory control system reports that an item has fallen below the reorder level. However, where changes to products and new products are concerned, people become more involved in the process.

DETERMINATION OF PRODUCT SPECIFICATIONS

In industrial marketing situations it is important to specify exactly what is required in terms of the product specification. For example, the computer company which is buying PCBs will specify the type of board required and will make specifications for those specific components which are to be mounted on to the board. Unlike consumers, for whom much of the joy of shopping comes from elements of surprise and experimentation, the business buyer must specify the physical characteristics of the product in some detail, detailing its function, design, expected quality and performance levels as well as its relationship and compatibility with related components.

While a level of fine detail is appropriate for an engineering context this does not apply across all contexts, e.g. the 'creative brief' is a form of specification issued by a client to an advertising agency which forms the basis of an advertising campaign. In this case, it is important that the brief is not specified in detail as that might stifle creativity.

EVALUATION AND SELECTION OF SUPPLIERS

The next stage involves the search for a suitable supplier who can best meet all the specified criteria. This is similar to the process which was outlined in Chapter 3, where 'Joe's' choice of a suit was described. Theorists suggest that B-to-B marketers evaluate potential suppliers according to a list of attributes which reflect desired benefits. The criteria used and the relative importance of each attribute vary according to the goods and services being purchased and the buyers' needs. Usually price is a critical factor, although product quality is very important. Of even more importance nowadays is flexibility of response.

Researchers have found that just as the steps in the consumer decision-making process can vary with respect to the level of involvement, the B-to-B decision-making process can vary with respect to the type of buying situation. Three important and interrelated factors determine the buying task faced by the organization and these can influence choice of supplier:

■   The newness of the problem and the relevant buying experience of decision makers in the buying centre.
■   The information needs of the people in the buying centre.

- The number of new alternative approaches and/or suppliers to consider in making the purchase decision.

There are three kinds of buying tasks or situations: the straight rebuy, the modified rebuy and new task buying.

- *Straight rebuy*. Here the buyer orders something without any modification which, usually, is handled on a routine basis by the purchasing department. The buyer simply chooses from the various suppliers on his/her list. In order to gain an edge, some suppliers will suggest automatic reordering and will be keen to maintain product and service quality, e.g. the situation where computer reordering takes place. In this case, where there is low perceived risk associated with a frequent purchase and a satisfactory supplier, the existing supplier might simply be asked to tender a price for resupply.
- *Modified rebuy*. This happens when the organization's needs remain unchanged but when buying centre members are not satisfied either with the product or with the supplier. They may wish to have a better-quality product, better service or are looking for a keener price. In this case, the buyer requires information about the different products and suppliers. This opens up an opportunity for new suppliers to gain entry. The modified rebuy may end with renegotiation of the contract with an existing supplier or with the choice of a new supplier.
- *Newtask buying*. A firm that is buying a product or service for the first time faces a new task situation. The size of the buying centre rises in proportion to the cost and complexity of the decision. In this case, the procedure for supplier selection will be more complex and lengthy, involving negotiations at a high level with a number of potential suppliers before a decision is made.

One factor which can influence selection of supplier is reciprocity whereby the organization favours a supplier that is a customer, or potential customer, for the firm's own products or services. While this offers a number of advantages, it can operate to restrict the available options and may lead to a situation where the best supplier is not selected.

COMMITMENT

The process does not end once the decision has been finalized. The supply situation is monitored as it unfolds and the supplier performance is measured to determine whether or not it is suitable. For example, frequently a sample of goods supplied is tested to ensure that it has been produced according to specification. If the sample is not deemed to satisfy specifications which have been set, the whole batch may be returned to the supplier. In other situations where the customer uses Just-In-Time (JIT) systems to schedule work in progress the result of a late supply order can be very serious, resulting in the closure of a production line for hours, days or perhaps even weeks. It has been known for customers to invoice suppliers for the entire plant overhead as a form of penalty for late supply, a drastic move which can put small suppliers out of business.

There are several ways of handling supply relationships. The customer may keep suppliers under constant threat and may change suppliers if a product falls below specification on quality or delivery. On the other hand, the company may decide to build and maintain a relationship with the supplier to allow close co-operation and relationships to develop. This does not mean that the customer does not levy penalties on the supplier in the case of poor quality or late delivery, just that these instances will be investigated with a view to ensuring that they do not happen again.

EVALUATION OF THE MODEL

While the model described in Figure 4.1 highlights certain features of the buying process, it hides others. The model charts the process as a linear development whereby the organizational buyer follows a sequence of steps in selecting the most appropriate purchase. The model illustrates the importance of developing specifications as to precisely what is required, leaving nothing to chance. For example, if one wishes to purchase a machine component in a manufacturing bill of materials, the physical characteristics of the component must be specified in terms of function, design, expected quality and performance levels. Additional specifications may be drawn up with respect to delivery and price. The establishment of specifications will bring a number of different personnel together; e.g. a machine component may involve a design engineer and a production engineer and a quality manager as well as personnel from Procurement and Marketing. Conflicts can and do arise between these personnel and the means of coping with them are often evolved but not directly managed. For example, the current author was engaged on a research project with a company which manufactured oscilloscopes and where design engineers held considerable power because most senior management were drawn from this group. Consequently, design engineers felt that it was their right to order components which would be incorporated into production. Marketing and Quality personnel were not happy with this procedure because although the components ordered were of a high standard they were not as reliable as less sophisticated components which had been tried and tested. Products tended to fail and be returned, which led to dissatisfaction on the part of Quality and Marketing personnel. Procurement personnel were unhappy because of the number of different makes of the same component which were ordered; each engineer had his own favourite make. The company could have saved time and money by standardizing. It was only when a new managing director was appointed who recognized this problem that a team was formed to explore the issues, leading to the recognition of other people's concerns.

One difficulty with the traditional buying model is that organizational buying/purchasing is not viewed as a value-adding function. Buying activity is perceived to be a largely clerical operation, with purchasing agents being evaluated on their negotiation skills. The levels of price discounts obtained from suppliers typically measure purchasing performance. This reward system fosters an adversarial climate between buyers and sellers because these goals are in direct competition. In addition, the approach characterized by Figure 4.1 is:

a short-term business orientation, buying based on lowest price, inspection of incoming shipments, large inventories, and very little interaction with suppliers other than the initial negotiations and to express post-purchase dissatisfaction when performance was poor.

(Wilson, 1994: 55)

COMPARISON BETWEEN B-TO-B AND CONSUMER BUYER BEHAVIOUR

Business-to-Business and consumer buyer behaviour may be compared on several dimensions including demand characteristics, the market demographic profile and buyer-seller relationships.

Taking demand characteristics first, as has been discussed above, while consumers buy for their own use and consumption, the demand for B-to-B goods and services is derived from consumer demand. B-to-B demand tends to be relatively price-inelastic, in that an increase or decrease in the price of one or two components of the thousands that might constitute a computer, for example, will not have a great effect on the overall price. Changes in consumer demand can lead to erratic developments in industrial markets, as even small increases in consumer demand can have a major effect.

The market demographic profile is also different for B-to-B markets. There are fewer B-to-B buyers than there are consumer purchasers; the former are larger and usually more geographically concentrated.

When one considers the buying process there are some broad similarities between the steps of the process followed by consumers and B-to-B buyers. There are some similarities between the concepts of 'involvement' which relate to consumer buyer behaviour and the 'buy' class which relates to industrial buyer behaviour. Both models range from simple, routine decisions to more complex and conscious decisions which may involve a number of people. A certain similarity in terms of the structure of the 'high involvement' consumer buying decision and the 'new task' organizational buying decision can be noted. However, the similarity ends there; the key element of involvement is that it relates to the consumer's ego involvement in relation to the product, while the new task purchase decision is related to lack of experience with the product or service.

While consumers generally buy for themselves and for their families, most consumer purchases are relatively low-risk, low-involvement purchases. Organizational buyers are always buying on behalf of others. This can mean that the organizational buying process is much more complex than that for consumer goods. For this reason, organizations are likely to have formed clear purchasing policies and guidelines which may be summarized in a purchasing manual. Organizational buyers are more apt to buy on specification. B-to-B purchases usually are dealt with by professionals because of the complexity of the decision. With respect to complex purchases the buying centre can be expected to be large. Of course, there are group influences in consumer buying behaviour, most notably in family decision making, e.g. when choosing a holiday or a new car. However, the family decision making structure is structured more formally than that which is to be found in the organization.

NEW APPROACHES TO B-TO-B BUYING BEHAVIOUR

A number of researchers have commented on the dramatic changes which have taken place in B-to-B purchasing over the past thirty years. For example, Wilson (1996) discusses environmental changes which in her opinion led to profound changes in the business environment affecting buying behaviour.

Under the new approach, organizations must work more efficiently in order to stay competitive and survive. Costs must be lowered on all fronts, from operations/production, buying and inventory management, supplier development and management to customer service. Buyers and sellers take a more long-term view of their business activities and the satisfaction of joint goals (a 'win–win' approach) is the desired outcome. For example, to achieve efficiencies in operations, many customers are using fewer suppliers than in the past. Xerox went from 2,000 suppliers of copier parts to 350 in its desire to build vendor loyalty/supplier partnerships. Each supplier gets a larger share of Xerox's orders and in return must provide high-quality parts and service to this increasingly important customer.

Other elements of the new model are increased communication and information sharing. 'Open communication also increases the speed and flexibility of new product development for the buying firm when the supplier can help solve potential problems before they arise' (Wilson, 1994: 55). Changes in competition have driven firms to operate more efficiently and effectively. More co-operative and mutually beneficial relationships between buyers and sellers are one result. Lewin and Johnston (1996) noted the following responses to environmental changes which they felt were having a major effect on buyer behaviour:

■ Move from high volume to high value.
■ Experimentation with novel organization structures and processes in order to accommodate the process of change.
■ Knowledge-based economy move from large hierarchical organizations to small flexible structures.

The aim in the emerging 'knowledge'-based businesses of the twenty-first century is to add value by thinking smarter than the competition. Within manufacturing industry, where prices are moving inexorably downwards, value can be created by re-engineering the production processes to remove bottlenecks and maximize throughput and flexibility. This has led to experimentation with new 'flatter' forms of organization which place an emphasis on team working. Senior management needs to take care to ensure that it retains the knowledge base at the same time as it reduces organizational complexity. In the short term cost savings may be effected by reducing the need for several layers of middle management (Bahrami, 1992), further enhancing organizational competitiveness by providing additional reductions in overall operating costs. However, it is possible to go too far and to lose a valuable store of knowledge and experience. Beyond the anticipated cost savings, 'flatter' organizations are expected to be more flexible and responsive to market and competitive dynamics by reducing the time lag between decision and action (Bahrami and Evans, 1987).

Another way in which firms are trying to increase 'flexibility' and generate 'high value' is through outsourcing (Gupta and Zhender, 1994). Firms which successfully manage to stick to their core competences, and which form relationships for supply with others for other work are more flexible and responsive to fluctuations in demand.

Technology is initiating major changes within retailing. In this sector the advent of loyalty initiatives has generated a wealth of customer information. The successful retailers of the next few years will be those which make full use of these data by using IT effectively to understand and serve their customers' needs better. The benefits will be in reduced costs and increased customer satisfaction. One means of achieving this goal will be through Effective Consumer Response (ECR) and effective supply chain management, involving close collaboration between retailers, suppliers and service companies. Many differences can be observed in the development of this concept across Europe. In the UK and the Netherlands suppliers and retailers are making great efforts to become partners, with joint programmes in logistics, sales and product development. By contrast, France and Spain exhibit a much less co-operative approach, with less evidence of collaboration.

STRATEGIC USE OF TECHNOLOGY IN BUYING: INTRANETS AND EXTRANETS

Internet communications are of key importance to marketers. Two innovations have been organizational intranets and extranets. The creation of an intranet, using Windows XP or another platform such as Lotus Notes, allows authorized personnel to gain access to database records which are stored on a central server from their desktop computer. The creation of an extranet involves hooking up authorized suppliers and distributors to the intranet to allow them access to data. The creation of intranets and extranets is an important strategic choice for a firm as this often involves changes in organizational culture and procedures for the different partners in addition to the resolution of issues concerned with network and data access.

The appeal of extranets lies in their ability to provide cheaper, more effective and, most important, faster means of communicating with others. The pressure for increased effectiveness and speed is due to increasing competition in many markets, decreasing product development times and lucrative rewards for those who get to the market first. Sometimes a matter of weeks can make the difference between achieving this.

Some organizations use extranets for ordering. For example, PC wholesaler Merisel has found that it is 70 per cent cheaper to process a customer order through its extranet than to have one of its telesales personnel handle it over the phone. Another example concerns computer chip manufacturer LSI, which was looking for an efficient way to transmit design information among its design team, its subcontractors and its customers. Since 1996 LSI has been working with twelve of its top 100 customers over the extranet. The time to get a new product to market was the main motivating force behind the move to establish the extranet. LSI is better known as the company which designed the chip used in the Sony Playstation, a 32 bit game machine from Sony Computer Entertainment America that hit the market for Christmas 1994, six weeks before its competitors. Time is of the essence in providing competitive advantage.

However, one should not underestimate the difficulties involved in implementing extranet systems. As it takes two or more organizations to make up an extranet, each must seek to achieve the same high standard of quality of network addressing systems. Difficulties can arise with accusations that 'It's not my network problem, it's yours.' This means that the implementation must be handled sensitively and should involve all the parties concerned.

General Electric uses its extranet for bids for parts ordering for its Lighting Division (GELS). This is a highly complex process costing millions of dollars per year. In order to implement the extranet which would enable potential suppliers to access information through the Web. GELS first worked with a cross-section of suppliers on work flow and technical issues, then it held focus groups. GELS helped those suppliers that bought new PCs to support the extranet system by configuring Windows for them. It assisted others with posting purchasing information electronically and pulling that data into their costing systems. GELS also held a four-hour training session for its fifty-five suppliers. Despite all this hard effort, not everyone was happy with the system. One supplier claimed that the extranet had created more work because now he had to pull a GELS engineering drawing off the extranet, print it, analyse it and reply with a quote. He claimed that it took him three hours to extract, analyse and respond to thirteen drawings from GELS's extranet – an hour longer than it used to take him using the fax. As this example demonstrates, bringing business partners together online can take considerable effort.

Another difficulty of extranets is that whereas other 'sharing' technologies such as EDI use a set of standards between companies and their customers or suppliers to facilitate B-to-B transactions, uniform technologies are not guaranteed in electronic commerce. Often this extends beyond ordering and fulfilment processes. In addition, with a company's mission-critical databases a needed part of almost any extranet, access privileges and security become mammoth concerns.

Despite this there can be advantages, particularly for smaller organizations which may wish to create strong electronic bonds to confront large competitors. One such supplier in the US called Monitor Medical found that in confronting huge equipment companies like Baxter International it needed every source of competitive advantage available. Monitor developed an extranet which may provide that advantage by enabling customers to check inventories online, helping sales representatives to respond more quickly to activity in their accounts. One day it might enable customers to check inventories online, helping sales representatives to respond more quickly to activity in their accounts and develop a national distribution network of other small suppliers. Ideally, if the extranet works out, large hospital chains might place orders with Monitor Medical rather than with one of the big chains, if it is successful at establishing a network of local distributors.

BUYING A COMPUTER SYSTEM FOR A HOSPITAL

In early 1992 four hospitals in East Anglia, England, collaborated to buy a new information system from McDonnell Douglas. The group comprised Addenbrooke's in Cambridge, Norwich Acute Unit, West Suffolk and James Paget of Great Yarmouth. Their £8.3m system was the largest joint proposal so far for the taxpayer-funded National Health Service (NHS) which spent approximately £250m on computer equipment that year.

Within the NHS rising costs have become a matter of public concern and are the subject of frequent newspaper headlines and radio talk shows. Hospital managers faced stark choices with respect to IT spending: should they upgrade the mainframe or buy a kidney dialysis machine? While dialysis machines were considered to be urgent requirements, nevertheless it was recognized that computers were urgently needed to streamline hospital administration to link the increasingly broad range of hi-tech equipment.

The goal of the consortium was to create a unified system within each hospital which would hold all the patient data centrally. Traditionally, each department collected and stored its own data such as the names and addresses of the general practitioners (doctors who work in the community) of its patients. This meant that patients who needed to visit several different departments had to repeat the same information each time so that computer staff could rekey the data into a separate computer system. The new computer system would put an end to this time-wasting repetition of patient details and it would make complete patient histories available at the touch of a button throughout the hospital. However, implementing the system would be a major task, as the average medical records department holds around 3.5bn pieces of information relating to current patients.

In the past such a major decision would not have been made at hospital level but by the local health authority. While legislation had passed decision making to the hospitals themselves, it meant that hospitals had to compete with each other for patients. Despite this, the idea of a collaborative bid was considered to be common sense. One advantage was that by pooling resources the hospitals were able to exert pressure to secure cost savings which were well in advance of anything that could have been achieved if they had acted individually. Technical expertise was also shared between the sites. This, in turn, had effects for problem solving, which was shared. If one hospital encountered a difficulty with respect to system implementation everyone became involved and once it was solved everyone benefited.

Despite this there were some drawbacks. As has already been mentioned, the hospitals had to compete for patients. However, the technology itself was not thought to be an essential competitive issue. Instead competition was based on price and on perceived quality of service which would flow in part from better use of the system. In any case the hospitals had different competences and addressed different needs: two provided general health care and two were specialist. Another problem was that the weakest member dictated the speed of progress. Finally, the project required a great degree of collaboration between people from different sites. Despite these drawbacks the benefits were seen to outweigh the disadvantages.

To ensure that nothing was missed out in defining the original requirements, lengthy consultations were held with all categories of hospital staff, from radiographers and pathologists to administrative, catering and clinical staff. At least 150 people were involved in the discussions, so that everyone knew what was going on. A document outlining 250 individual requirements was published in August 1992. This led to thirty-nine requests for copies from computer suppliers and was followed by sixteen serious responses. Then the process of selection began. NHS procurement is governed by European Commision/World Trade Organization (EC/WTO) regulations intended to ensure fair competition. They oblige customers to debrief all would-be suppliers on the reasons why they were not selected. Although decision makers found this process to be tedious, it was a valuable exercise that forced them to examine their selection criteria. In particular, one decision maker stated that he thought that while often decisions are influenced by a mixture of subjective and objective views, people are not always honest with themselves about the subjective component. By being forced to debrief potential suppliers, decision makers had to face up to the reasons why they were making certain decisions.

To aid the selection process, the East Anglia consortium laid down specific requirements for every stage. In particular, the winning candidate would have to prove that it had the ability to pull together the existing islands of information in each hospital. For example, one supplier who offered to put together the best software on the market for each individual application was rejected while others who offered a common core took precedence, even though their separate modules might not have been quite as good.

This screening process reduced the contenders to eight. Users were then invited to test the systems. 'User feedback is essential,' said the co-ordinator, 'because suppliers will always try to disguise the weak points of their systems.' For example, a system might require doctors to order pathology tests individually, whereas the doctors might want tests grouped so that a request for one automatically triggers several others. Such problems do not come to light until users are experimenting with the system.

The trials reduced the number of suppliers to four possible alternatives. Final judgement was based on technical capabilities, applications and customer support. The same two companies came out on top in all three areas. Since both suppliers could clearly meet the requirements, the final decision was made on price, with adjustments to allow for the time that would need to be spent on training. Once the winner had been selected the twelve-month selection process was over.

Source: adapted from Bird (1997).

BAXI LOOKS TO EUROPE FOR EXPANSION

In 1866 Richard Baxendale, iron moulder, founded the Baxendale company in northern England. In 1935 the company launched the first product with the Baxi name; it built up a reputation for marketing Baxi boilers. Then, in 1983, the firm was sold as a management buy-out to its employees. This was followed by a series of acquisitions in the 1990s and into the 2000s. In 2004 it was bought by Kidde, the engineering company, and then it was transferred to BC Partners and other investors for nearly £600m (US$1,076m). The company continues with its main UK plant in Preston and factories in Italy, France, Denmark, Germany and Turkey. About half of Baxi's sales (€1bn in 2004: £1.5bn) come from the UK and the remainder are predominantly from continental Europe. In Britain, Baxi is market leader in the boiler business in volume terms.

In 2005, as part of Baxi's strategic expansion, Baxi bought Roca, a leading Spanish boiler maker, for £135.8m (€200m, US$244m) to gain a higher share of the European gas-fired boiler market, valued at about (€5.6bn, £8.2bn). The deal increased Baxi's share of European boiler business to 11 per cent in volume, behind the German companies Vaillant and Bosch, which remain leaders with 18 per cent and 16 per cent respectively. Boilers have a relatively stable market with revenues increasing only slowly in most countries. However, the major makers see growth opportunities through equipping their products with new techniques that reduce energy consumption, so fitting in with the global drive to reduce carbon dioxide emissions. They are keen to switch more households, particularly in poorer countries such as Turkey or in the CEE away from solid fuels and towards 'cleaner' natural gases.

Steady growth is expected in the next few years across most of Baxi's markets, although a downturn from 2005 was predicted in the UK due to government regulations requiring plumbers to install new energy-saving boilers. Consumers were expected to be dissuaded from specifying the new systems, which are more expensive to buy although they offer lower running costs, and instead consumers may choose to repair their older systems.

Source: adapted from Marsh (2005).

CASE QUESTION

1   When government is encouraging industry to move towards 'equipping their products with new technologies to reduce carbon dioxide emissions' why might industrial buyers have different approaches to consumers regarding buying such products?

CONCLUSION

By the end of this chapter you should be familiar with:

- different types of B-to-B buyer behaviour;
- key differences between consumer and B-to-B buyer behaviour;
- two different models for understanding B-to-B buyer behaviour;
- the appropriate terminology, including concepts such as the buying centre and Buygrid, intranets and extranets.

REVIEW QUESTIONS

1   Compare and contrast the key differences between industrial and consumer buyer behaviour.
2   What are the deficiencies of the 'old' model which purports to explain B-to-B buyer behaviour?
3   Why is the concept of the buying centre useful to B-to-B marketers?
4   How can technology such as intranets and extranets aid B-to-B buyer behaviour?
5   What are the difficulties involved in implementing extranets?
6   What sort of decision is this: government; institutional, producer or re-seller?
7   How useful are the models of the buying process described in this chapter in seeking to understand the process followed in this case?

RECOMMENDED FURTHER READING

Ford, D. (1990) *Understanding business markets: interaction, relationships, networks*, London: Academic Press.

Kerrigan, F., Fraser, P. and Özbilgin, M. (eds) (2004) *Arts marketing*, Oxford: Butterworth Heinemann.

McNeil, R. (2005) *Business to business market research: understanding and measuring business markets*, London: Kogan Page.

Michel, D., Naudé, P., Salle, R. and Valla, J.P. (2003) *Business-to-business marketing: strategies and implementation*, Basingstoke: Palgrave Macmillan.

Timmers, P. (2000) *Electronic commerce: strategies and models for business-to-business trading*, Chichester: Wiley.

5 MARKETING RESEARCH

LEARNING OBJECTIVES

When you have completed this unit you should be able to:

■ know the definition of marketing research;

■ understand the role of the Marketing Information System (MIS) within the Management Information System;

■ distinguish between the nature and role of qualitative and quantitative research methods;

■ use marketing research, including test marketing, to determine appropriate marketing mix, i.e.:
 – product;
 – pricing;
 – promotion;
 – place: channels of distribution;

■ construct a basic instrument to measure attitudes;

■ appreciate the resource implications associated with using marketing research, i.e.:
 – financial;
 – staff;
 – time;

■ be aware of the controls used to manage the ethical issues related to marketing research practice.

INTRODUCTION

Marketing research is the activity whereby market information is gathered and analysed to help management reduce the risk associated with decision making and, as such, marketing research plays an important role within Management Information Systems.

Management Information Systems

Within every organization management is required to bring together the information gathered through its functional activities and to analyse that information to help management decision making. The information obtained can come from a range of sources. The Marketing Information System (MIS) concentrates on the provision of the data related to the market being targeted. These marketing data contribute to the overall Management Information System for the organization. A MIS has been defined as being:

> people, equipment and procedures to gather, sort, analyze, evaluate and distribute needed, timely and accurate information to marketing decision makers.
>
> (Kotler, 1997)

Persons operating within the marketing and marketing research functions undertake the MIS. Internal staff within the Marketing Services function (or department), usually located at, or within close proximity to, the organization's central head office, are expected to manage the MIS. The marketing information is gathered through a combination of informal and formal communication routes using internal and external sources within the organization. It can come from any, or all, of the functional areas, including Accounting and Finance, Research and Development, Production and Personnel. Informal communication routes can cover the networks used by the sales staff to reach potential and actual buyers; formal routes could include the functional reporting systems feeding their progress reports to management. Formal internal sources of information are likely to involve sales monitoring and sales force reports; while informal sources could be intelligence gathered through meetings with colleagues and associates. Formal external sources of information can come from sources including statistics produced by international bodies such as the United Nations, the World Health Organization and the World Bank, national governments, trade associations, and so on. More informal external sources of data might be gathered from experts attending trade exhibitions and seminars, as well as from industry marketing research agencies, advertising agencies and management consultancies.

A MIS is developed from the inter-linkage and analysis of data collected from three types of information gathering (Figure 5.1). These are internal reporting, marketing intelligence and marketing research. The three information-gathering sources should interact on a continuous basis. In this way, internal reporting sources covering information obtained from within the organization can be used in the preparation of marketing research studies. Similarly, marketing intelligence environmental scanning may be used in conjunction with the internal reporting process which, in turn, can feed into the marketing research function.

Figure 5.1
Marketing
information
system

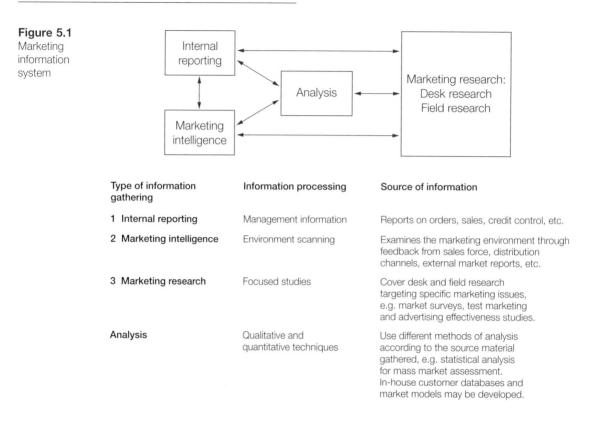

Type of information gathering	Information processing	Source of information
1 Internal reporting	Management information	Reports on orders, sales, credit control, etc.
2 Marketing intelligence	Environment scanning	Examines the marketing environment through feedback from sales force, distribution channels, external market reports, etc.
3 Marketing research	Focused studies	Cover desk and field research targeting specific marketing issues, e.g. market surveys, test marketing and advertising effectiveness studies.
Analysis	Qualitative and quantitative techniques	Use different methods of analysis according to the source material gathered, e.g. statistical analysis for mass market assessment. In-house customer databases and market models may be developed.

All the data gathered from the internal reporting process, from marketing intelligence and from marketing research should be analysed and assessed to determine market trends. These, in turn, may be used to develop databases for the organization which are likely to comprise listings of actual and potential customers. They may be used as a management tool to monitor market activity and to ascertain the organization's performance within the market. For example, a list of present customers might detail customer locations, their purchasing patterns and the payment methods that they use. This information could enable the marketing department to decide on the most appropriate marketing mix to use to reach the customer, i.e. it could be used to make targeting and product positioning decisions related to the product's pricing, promotion and its channels of distribution.

Within the organization, the information gathered from the MIS should be analysed and assessed. The findings should be passed upwards from the marketing services function/department through to corporate or strategic planners to help strategic decision making. The strategic planners should, in the same way, feed information back into the MIS to direct, or target, marketing interests within the marketing services department. This information should also be communicated to, and should be received from, the other functional sections of the organization, including Production, Research and Development, Finance and Sales. Within the organization, individual functional departments, company subsidiaries and Strategic Business Units (SBUs) should provide marketing information related to their own particular product, or service, to include within the MIS. The system should take this information, assimilate it with the data from all the other sources, inside and outside the organization, analyse the data and feed back the findings to the various functional departments for management decision making.

The information obtained for the MIS will be of varying quality and may require careful interpretation in the light of its source. Information gained from SBUs within an organization may be delayed or adjusted before being passed to the central marketing services for processing within the MIS. For example, sales may be provided in an incomplete manner in an attempt to avoid highlighting a down-turn in sales that might lead to reductions in resources for the SBU concerned. Consequently, close control is required in the collection of data for the MIS to ensure that accurate market assessments are made.

While the specific objectives of the MIS will differ from organization to organization, generally, such systems monitor the marketing environment and the performance of the organization within that market. The MIS should provide information that will bring together the different functions, or departments, within the organization. It should identify the needs of customers, competitor performance and indicate how well the organization is performing within the market. It should help to decide on production levels, the most appropriate marketing mix and sales effort as well as product stocking policies, transport and distribution within logistics to enable customer service needs to be addressed in a cost-effective manner. The MIS should be an effective and reliable decision-making tool to help management satisfy consumer demand.

Definition of marketing research

Marketing research has been variously defined but, essentially, it relates to the collection of information regarding actual and potential customers in the market place together with the analysis and interpretation of these market data for use in management marketing decision making. Usually such decisions relate to the elements of the marketing mix, i.e. to product, pricing, promotion and channels of distribution decisions. The following are examples of marketing research definitions:

> the systematic and continuing study and evaluation of all factors bearing on any business operation which involves the transfer of goods from a producer to a consumer.
>
> (Delens, 1950)

> the objective gathering, recording and analysing of all facts about problems relating to the transfer and sales of goods and services from producer to consumer.
>
> (British Institute of Management, 1962)

> the gathering and analysis of information to assist management in making marketing decisions. These decisions involve the manipulation of the firm's pricing, promotion, distribution and product variables.
>
> (Wentz, 1972)

the systematic design, collection, analysis and reporting of data and findings relevant to a specific marketing situation facing the company.

(Kotler, 1997)

Thus, marketing research systematically collects market data about a product or service which are then analysed to help management decision making.

Definitions of marketing research have been developed further:

any research activity which provides information relating to marketing operations. Whilst the term embraces conventional market research, motivation studies, advertisement attention value, packaging effectiveness, logistics and media research are also included, as well as analysis of internal and external statistics of relevance.

(Hart and Stapleton, 1981)

the process of generating information around given problems or areas of interest, using either secondary or published data sources or the undertaking of primary research to generate new data at the market place level.

(Piercy and Evans, 1983)

the collection, processing and analysis of information on topics relevant to marketing. It begins with problem definition and ends with a report and action recommendations.

(Lehmann, 1985)

links the organization with its market environment. It involves the specification, gathering, analysing and interpretation of information to help management understand the environment, identify problems and opportunities and develop and evaluate areas of marketing action.

(Cravens and Woodruff, 1986)

a set of techniques and principles for systematically collecting, recording, analysing and interpreting data that can aid decision makers who are involved with marketing goods, services or ideas.

(Parasuramun, 1991:5)

the function which links the consumer, customer and public to the market through information   used to identify and define marketing opportunities and problems; generate, refine and evaluate marketing actions; monitor marketing performance; and improve understanding of marketing as a process. Marketing research specifies the information required to address these issues; designs the method for collecting information; manages and implements the data collection process; analyses the results; and communicates the findings and their implications.

(American Marketing Association, 1987)

the means used by those who provide goods and services to keep themselves in touch with the needs and wants of those who buy those goods and services.

(Market Research Society (MRS), 1989)

a formalized means of obtaining information to be used in making marketing decisions. It has a single purpose – that of providing information to assist marketing managers to make better decision. The function of marketing research is to provide information that will assist marketing managers in recognizing and reacting to marketing opportunities and problems.

(Tull and Hawkins, 1990)

a specialized function of marketing: it is by no means restricted to profit-motivated business activities. It adopts an objective approach when investigating marketing problems and opportunities; it is motivated by the principles of scientific enquiry.

(Chisnall, 2005)

The nature of marketing research

Marketing research provides a mechanism for identifying and anticipating customer requirements, producing products and services that consider customer demand and for measuring customer satisfaction with the product (or service) offerings. It aims to provide market assessments, often in the form of a research report. The report should discuss the research methodology used, the analysis of research findings, the forecasts of future demand and the recommendations for future action.

Marketing research can determine the most appropriate marketing mix components in helping to define strategy and policy for:

■ *Products*, e.g. product range and quality.
■ *Pricing*, e.g. base price and discounts.
■ *Promotion*, e.g. communications through advertising, sales promotion, public relations and personal selling.
■ '*Place*' or channels of distribution used within logistics and the supply chain.

It examines actual and potential demand for products and services using quantitative and qualitative research methods.

As marketing research becomes integrated within an organization's operational functions, it contributes to management decision making in marketing strategy as well as providing effective tactical decision support to marketing management. It may also have the role of sharing responsibility for decisions with management as in the case of high-risk new product decisions for the fast-moving consumer goods (FMCG) sector, e.g. confectionery. Marketing research endeavours to develop closer relationships between product and service providers and their customers, using databases to build customer profiles that match customer life cycles which, in turn, help management to meet demand. Nevertheless, the costs of undertaking marketing research, which may appear relatively high, may prevent its being used as effectively as might be recommended.

THE STRUCTURE OF THE MARKETING RESEARCH INDUSTRY

During the 1980s, both internationally and within the UK, there was spectacular growth in the advertising and marketing research agency industries resulting in considerable acquisition activity and even the flotation of some of the larger agencies on the stock market. By the end of the 1980s the large marketing research agencies had become larger and increasingly dominant.

The middle-sized agencies with turnovers of under £5m (US$9m) found their activities and profits were curtailed. Many reacted by setting up small specialist operations concentrating on specific market sectors, while others, especially the smaller agencies, concentrated on providing qualitative research services. In the early 1990s weak agencies failed and those that remained were left to fight in a market where clients' budgets were squeezed in real terms. There was an increase in international marketing research but, while turnover increased, profit margins dropped, making tough operating conditions for the marketing research industry.

The larger marketing research agencies concentrated on providing marketing research services for the mass, consumer markets, e.g. the A.C. Nielsen group (owned by VNU) has focused on the consumer product and services industries. It has dominated the global market, using its strength in the US market to expand internationally by supporting US-based multinational corporations (MNCs). It provides marketing research services in about eighty countries. It has strengths in the provision of market information that monitors consumer behaviour over time, including television audiences in the US. In the UK it has concentrated on continuous panel research using retail auditing techniques.

Marketing research is also provided by national marketing research agencies within individual countries, which may themselves have international activities, e.g. UK-based Taylor Nelson Sofres (TNS). Clients use marketing research agencies that concentrate on national coverage or, if appropriate they use an agency with coverage of a range of countries.

Global marketing research industry

In 2003 the top twenty-five organizations had total revenues of US$11.7bn (£6.5bn) and controlled about 62 per cent of global spend by commercial firms on marketing, advertising and public opinion research services (see Table 5.1). They expanded their dominance during 2003 by acquiring seventeen other research firms, which had a combined revenue of US$675m (£376m) at the time of their acquisitions (Honomichl, 2004). In particular, a major change in ownership for the 2003 top twenty-five listing was the acquisition of NFO World Group, based in Greenwich CT, by TNS in London whereby TNS moved up to second place. The percentage of the combined global research revenues of the top twenty-five companies for each firm's country is US (30 per cent), UK (29 per cent), the Netherlands (26 per cent), Germany (6 per cent), France (6 per cent), Japan (3 per cent) and Italy (1 per cent) (Honomichl, 2004).

For 2004 the top twenty-five companies had combined revenues of $13.3bn (£7.4bn) which was a 4.8 per cent growth on 2003 revenues. Net growth, growth minus inflation, was 2.5 per cent, a healthy improvement on 2003's net growth of minus 0.6 per cent (Honomichl, 2005).

As a group the top twenty-five firms had annual revenue growth of 1.4 per cent in 2003 with growth in the US, Japan and Europe being closer to 2 per cent. The impact of the drive towards increased efficiency involved the move for US and foreign-owned research firms to outsource back-room work such as Electronic Data Processing (EDP), software development and interviewing to low-cost countries such as India and the Philippines has had debatable consequences. While the amount of work done for clients has increased that work provides little revenue growth as the efficiencies only reflect the drive toward increased competition.

Increasingly, firms on the top twenty-five list are truly international in nature. In 2003 only one, US-based Westat, did not report any revenues from outside its home country. In the case of the market leader, VNU, based in the Netherlands, only 1 per cent of research revenues came from operations within its home country, the balance came from operations in eighty other countries. In 2003 VNU, by far the largest research conglomerate in the world, alone accounted for 30 per cent of the top twenty-five companies' total revenue, due to its ownership of A.C. Nielsen, Nielsen Media Research and several other firms in the US and outside the Netherlands. By 2004 VNU had a global revenue of US$3,429m (UK£1,191m) accounting for 26 per cent of the top twenty-five companies' total revenue (see Table 5.1).

Further consolidation is continuing within the marketing research industry. In 2005 the German market research group GfK bought NOP World's European operations for £383m ($687m) and announced closer integration of its two US businesses. In October 2005 Aegis had a take-over approach, valuing its subsidiary, the media and market research group Synovate, at around £1.5bn ($2.7bn). Analysts speculated a likely bidding war between rival advertising groups Omnicom, WPP and Havas, whose chairman bought a 6 per cent stake in Aegis in August 2005 (Tarran, 2005). At the same time, in 2005, the French Ipsos group acquired UK MORI with its expertise in opinion polling.

In 2002 world value for marketing research was US$16,610m (£9,259m) with Europe leading with 41 per cent and the US following with 38 per cent, compared with Asia-Pacific having 13 per cent, Central and South America 6 per cent and the Middle East and Africa 1 per cent (see Table 5.2).

In 2002 the top ten markets had marketing research agency expenditures in Europe of US$6,116m (£3,409m); in Asia Pacific of US$2,057 (£1,147m) and in Latin America of US$599m (£334m) (see Table 5.3). The UK, Japan and Mexico lead the respective markets. Within the three markets Europe dominates, with the UK, Germany and France much larger than the other markets. The US market is the largest individual country market.

Table 5.1 Top global research organizations, 2003–2004

Rank	Organization	Parent country	Global research revenue (US$million), 2004	Global research revenue (US$million), 2003	Research full-time employees, 2003	No. of countries with subsidiaries/ branch offices, 2003
1	VNU[a]	Netherlands	3,429	3,048	33,073	81
2	Taylor Nelson Sofres (TNS)	UK	1,721	1,565	13,150	70
3	IMS Health	US	1,569	1,382	6,300	75
4	Kantar Group	UK	1,136	1,002	6,000	61
5	GfK Group	Germany	836	674	5,065	48
6	Ipsos Group	France	753	644	4,181	36
7	Information Resources	US	573	554	3,400	18
8	Synovate	UK	499	358	3,446	46
9	NOP World	UK	407	336	1,473	6
10	Westat	US	398	382	1,700	1
	Total top 10		11,321	9,945	77,782	
	Total top 25		13,320	11,651	85,471	

Source: adapted from Honomichl (2004, 2005).

Note: a VNU owns A. C. Nielsen and Nielsen Media Research.

Table 5.2 World marketing research expenditure, 2002

Region/country	US$ million	UK£ million	% of total
Europe	6,820	3,801	41.1
EU nations (15)	6,280	3,500	37.8
North America	6,756	3,766	40.7
US	6,307	3,516	38.0
Asia Pacific	2,165	1,207	13.0
Japan	1,037	578	6.3
Central and South America	661	369	4.0
Middle East and Africa	208	116	1.2
Total world	16,610	9,259	100

Sources: adapted from *Marketing News*, 15 July 2004, p. 13, and European Society for Opinion and Marketing Research (ESOMAR).

Note: applies to marketing research expenditure by marketing research companies, excluding work conducted in-house or by advertising agencies, universities, government departments or non-profit institutions.

Table 5.3 Top 10 marketing research markets in Europe, Asia Pacific and Latin America,* 2002

Europe	US$ million	Asia Pacific	US$ million	Latin America	US$ million
UK	1,755	Japan	1,037	Mexico	243
Germany	1,490	China	302	Brazil	188
France	1,260	Australia	272	Colombia	47
Italy	461	Korea	120	Chile	40
Spain	303	Taiwan	82	Venezuela	26
Netherlands	267	New Zealand	65	Peru	18
Sweden	223	Hong Kong	60	Argentina	18
Belgium	135	India	50	Costa Rica	7
Switzerland	133	Singapore	37	Guatemala	7
Denmark	89	Thailand	32	Panama and Uruguay	5
Total	6,116	**Total**	2,057	**Total**	599

Sources: adapted from Marketing News, 15 July 2004, p. 12, and ESOMAR.

Note: applies to marketing research expenditure by marketing research companies, excluding work conducted in-house or by advertising agencies, universities, government departments or non-profit institutions

UK marketing research industry

The UK marketing research industry turnover comprises commercially available research undertaken through marketing research agencies that are members of the British Market Research Association (BMRA). In 2003 BMRA found that overall UK marketing research industry revenue reached an estimated £1.22bn (US$2.2bn), growing by 2.2 per cent on the previous year (see Table 5.4). However, these estimates exclude the contribution made by market leaders A.C. Nielsen and WPP. The domestic sector has 79 per cent of the market and grew by 5.4 per cent. The international sector experienced a decline because of the strong value of the pound and diminished investor confidence owing to uneasiness about global security and speculation about the US presidential election taking place in November 2004 (Mackenzie, 2004).

Moreover, other non-members undertake marketing research, including related management consultancy firms and some firms undertake their own marketing research using their own internal staff rather than marketing research agencies. The overall UK marketing research expenditure is estimated to be in excess of £1.5bn (US$2.7bn) p.a.

The largest marketing research group in the UK (and the world's second largest market information company) is TNS. It has grown from Taylor Nelson's acquisitions including Audits of Great Britain (AGB) in the UK in 1992 and the French Sofres agency in 1998. It has considerable international expertise especially European consumer research.

As noted above, further consolidation has taken place within the industry, in particular in 2005, when NOP was taken over by the German group, GfK and the French IpSOS took over MORI.

Table 5.4 UK marketing research agency turnover, 2003

Marketing research agency	UK turnover £ billion	Change between 2003 and 2002 (%)
TNS	159.5	–0.4
NOP World	76.4	–0.8
Ipsos (UK)	47.0	6.7
MORI	39.4	10.1
Information Resources	33.6	–3.1
Maritz/TRBI	26.7	6.2
Incepta Marketing Intelligence	19.6	15.6
Martin Hamblin	17.4	–9.7
Synovate	16.2	3.8
ORC International	12.5	–0.8
Total	1,222.0	–0.8

Sources: adapted from estimates by Mackenzie (2004) and BMRA

Marketing research agency methods

The existing well tried and tested marketing research methods continue to be used, although often in a repackaged form, using IT to improve efficiency. Personal interviewing, more especially face-to-face interviewing, is the more commonly used method of collecting field research data. Interviewing involves 'contact with a respondent, or group of respondents, in order to obtain information for a research project' (MRS, 2006: 42). In 2002 personal face-to-face interviews (mostly in-home interviewing) accounted for 27 per cent of marketing research agency turnover and telephone interviews for 22 per cent (see Table 5.5). Audit/panel interviewing accounted for a further 11 per cent and group discussion for 10 per cent. Other methods of marketing research undertaken by marketing research agencies, while important, individually had less that 10 per cent of turnover. They included hall test, self-completion/postal questionnaire survey, depth interview, street interview, mystery shopping and Web/Internet interviewing.

Within the marketing research industry methods of determining market demand are always being examined and developed to improve operational efficiency. Alternative methods and investment in IT together with related equipment are considered. Investment in IT has influenced the methods used in marketing research. In particular, IT has developed the methods for collection of data, for analysis and interpretation of the research findings as well as for the development of customer databases.

One development is the use of the Internet, which not only provides access to global databases for desk research, but also is used as a tool for collecting primary market data with global access at low cost. It is used for conducting questionnaire surveys, although this is still in the development stages, with challenges being to obtain representative sample frames.

The Internet can only target those persons with computer linkage to the system which makes it unlikely to replace traditional marketing research methods related to mass consumer markets. But it is possible to use it to target specialist markets, and/or to use it in conjunction with other methods (see Chapter 12.)

THE MARKETING RESEARCH PROCESS

Figure 5.2 outlines the market-ing research process. It demonstrates setting the research objectives and determining a brief that should be followed by the persons under-taking the research. The brief should summarize the objectives of the research. It should describe the nature of the research that is to be con-ducted and indicate whether it should be undertaken internally within the organization or, as is more common, by a market research agency. The brief is used as the base for putting the contract out to tender and is likely to become part of the contract that ultimately is agreed as a base for the research. It should provide a framework of questions to be used, together with the research methodology to be employed to gather the information required. It will indicate the desk and field research expected to be undertaken. Frequently, desk research will be carried out within the organization using internal staff, while the field research is contracted out to a market research agency. The brief should detail the proposed research methodology to be used for the field research covering decisions on the nature of qualitative and/or quantitative techniques, sampling methods, including the sample size, and other related issues. There will also be specifications of resource constraints, in particular the budget, labour and time scale for completion of the research. The brief should also cover the nature of the anticipated analysis of the research findings and the style of the final report that is to be prepared and presented.

Table 5.5 Research methods used by UK marketing research agencies, 2002

Research method	% of turnover
Personal (face-to-face) interview	27
Telephone interview	22
Audit/panel	11
Discussion group	10
Hall test	8
Self-completion/post	7
Depth interview	3
Mystery shopping	3
Street interview	2
Web/Internet interview	1
Other	6

Sources: adapted from Advertising Association Marketing Pocket Book 2005, p. 125, and BMRA (2003)

Note: estimates are based on returns by BMRA members accounting for about half the Association's total sales turnover, representing about one-third of UK industry turnover

MARKETING RESEARCH METHODOLOGY

When undertaking any form of research, including marketing research, the first area to consider concerns the objectives, or the goals, of the research. For marketing research this is likely to concentrate on defining the information that is required to answer a managerial question, e.g. information may be required to decide whether or not to pursue a new product

Figure 5.2
The
marketing
research
process

concept. In this case, market information might be sought concerning customer demand to the potential new product. Further information may be needed to decide on the most appropriate approach to promoting the product, as well as data to determine the appropriate pricing and distribution policies. At this stage of the study it is critical to decide what type of information is required, how detailed that information should be, how it might be obtained and who might provide the market data. The target for market opinion could be potential customers (individuals or companies) as well as other influential decision persons within the product's value chain, including wholesalers, agents, distributors and retailers. It is appropriate to consider the questions that might be asked and how answers to these questions might be obtained. This information should be summarized in a research brief which is agreed by all persons involved in the research, especially the client and the marketing research agency. The possible methods of obtaining the desired information will be discussed below.

Once the research objectives have been determined, marketing research may use a combination of desk and field research. Desk research is the 'collation of existing research results and data from published secondary sources for a specific, often unrelated, project' (MRS, 2006: 42). It refers to the collection and analysis of data that have been obtained from earlier research. It is called desk research because usually it can be acquired while sitting at a desk.

By contrast, field research involves undertaking studies using primary sources which are specific to the investigation in question. 'Field research relates to fieldwork, the live collection of primary data from external sources by means of surveys, observation and experiment' (MRS, 2006: 42). Field research, sometimes termed fieldwork, can be 'made to measure' or 'off the peg'. 'Made to measure' research is commissioned, designed and produced specifically to meet the requirements of a client by a marketing research agency. Normally this type of survey and its findings are guaranteed confidential to the organization commissioning the survey. 'Off the peg' research uses data collected by a marketing research agency which would be too expensive for the clients to collect individually. These market data are accessible to any client that needs the information and can pay for it. Generally, such arrangements are termed syndicated research.

The role of marketing researchers is varied. It may involve desk or field research. Most commonly the client using internal staff undertakes desk research, while field research is contracted to marketing research agencies. The popular stereotype of the marketing researcher is that of a lady with a clipboard asking questions in a street interview but, in reality, the marketing researcher can undertake a variety of roles involving both men and women. These include designing the marketing research project, undertaking desk and field research to collect the market data, analysing the findings, often using computer statistical analysis and presenting the market information to the client. Clearly, the nature of marketing research jobs varies considerably.

Research methods used may be quantitative or qualitative in nature. Quantitative research 'seeks to make measurements as distinct from qualitative research' (MRS, 2006: 43); i.e. it attempts to measure what is done in the market using analytical research methods. On the other hand, qualitative research methods seek 'insights through loosely structured mainly verbal data. Analysis is interpretative, subjective, impressionistic and diagnostic' (MRS, 2006: 43); i.e. qualitative research tries to explain why the results occur. For example, quantitative research can measure how much washing powder is bought, where it is bought, which brands and in what quantities the brands are bought. However, quantitative research does not necessarily explain why the washing powder is bought. Qualitative research sets out to establish the reasons why consumer behaviour is as it is, e.g. it might examine the influences on consumer purchasing of, say, washing powder, using descriptive methods to assess that behaviour.

Often, it may be appropriate to use both quantitative and qualitative research methods in the same marketing research study. For example, qualitative methods may be used in an exploratory manner at the beginning of the study to gain insight into opinion regarding a concept for a new product; quantitative methods may be used to measure the likely demand for the proposed product, or service. Qualitative research is also used to identify issues which can then be built into the questionnaire design for validation on a larger, numerically robust sample. Usually data obtained through quantitative research are quantified in terms of numbers, proportions, statistical significance, etc. Frequently, subsequent to the quantitative research, more qualitative research is undertaken to explain unexpected quantitative findings.

Desk research

Sources of desk research may be internal or external to the organization: internal information is that which is obtained from within the organization while external comes from outside the organization. Examples of qualitative sources of data might include feedback from attendance at research seminars in the form of general impressions regarding the progress of competitor research and development as well as information gathered from group discussions held for earlier product development. Examples of quantitative sources that could be available from within the organization include sales statistics, sales force reports, production levels and research and development reports. Internal sources are inexpensive to use, but they relate to the market experience from within the organization and, consequently, can be subject to bias. Furthermore, access to the desirable data may be influenced by internal political group dynamics within the organization, e.g. departmental managers may prevent full disclosure of sales to protect the sales force. This may encourage the researcher to use external sources rather than internal sources, despite the information being available within the organization, resulting in higher associated costs.

Field research

Field research (or fieldwork) involves the live collection of primary data from external sources by using methods that provide qualitative data, e.g. personal in-depth, focus interviews and group discussions or quantitative data, e.g. surveys, observation and experiment. This research may be undertaken on an *ad hoc* or continuous basis. *Ad hoc* research is conducted on one particular occasion, e.g. to assess market demand for a new product. Continuous research is defined as being 'a survey conducted on a regular and frequent basis among parallel samples with the same population, or in which the interviews are spread over a long time period' (MRS, 2006: 42). It may be used to monitor changes in customer demand over the period in question.

Qualitative research methods

Qualitative research methods may be used to investigate issues in marketing research, including to:

- Define areas for investigation.
- Obtain background market information.
- Identify and explore concepts.
- Develop creative ideas for advertising.
- Study sensitive, personal or embarrassing issues.
- Identify relevant behaviour patterns.
- Undertake preliminary screening process.
- Conduct post-research investigations.
- Pilot questionnaires.

The methods used can include: in-depth focus interview, sometimes termed intensive interview; group discussion (focus group); brainstorming, sometimes termed 'synectics'; observation; accompanied shopping; mystery shopping.

IN-DEPTH FOCUS INTERVIEW

Depth interviews cover 'a variety of data collection techniques, but mainly for qualitative research undertaken with individual respondents rather than groups' (MRS, 2006: 42). Such an interview is a face-to-face meeting between an interviewer and an interviewee (or respondent) where the topic in question is explored in depth. Usually it takes at least one hour and may be extended to cover half a day or more; it may take place on one occasion or on several occasions with the same individuals. Focused interviewing may be either unstructured using a topic list as a guide for the interview process, or it may be semi-structured using a questionnaire covering relevant themes. The former are more frequently used; the latter usually require larger samples. The interview may be used alongside other forms of interview, e.g. accompanied shopping (see below). The interview may be recorded using a voice tape and/or video-recorder (Greenbaum, 1998).

GROUP DISCUSSION (OR FOCUS GROUP)

Group discussion involves 'a number of respondents gathered together to generate ideas through the discussion of, and reaction to, specific stimuli. Under the steerage of a moderator, focus groups are often used in exploratory work or when the subject matter involves social activities, habits and status' (MRS, 2006: 42). These groups involve persons who have not previously met who discuss issues related to the topic being investigated. Usually, nine persons are recruited to attend the group discussion but, typically, seven or eight persons actually turn up to participate in the session. With any more than eight persons attending there is a danger of the group becoming unmanageable, as respondents break off into side discussions with neighbours when they cannot get in to make their point in the main discussion. The group discussions are held in congenial places such as a hotel meeting room or in the sitting room in the home of the recruiter, or in custom-built viewing facilities. The person controlling the group discussion, termed a moderator, leads the discussion, focusing on issues of interest to the marketing research. Usually these groups meet for between one and two hours on a single occasion. Such group interviews may be recorded using tape and/or videos. The room used for the group discussion may have an observation suite, sometimes termed 'viewing facility', with a one-way mirror window or by a video link so that the group discussion proceedings can be observed without disrupting the group process. Always the participants should be told that they are being observed. These viewing suites provide the marketing researchers' clients with exposure to their customers and their opinions (Greenbaum, 1998).

BRAINSTORMING (SOMETIMES TERMED 'SYNECTICS')

This is the monitoring of the behaviour of a group of persons while involved in problem solving and creative thinking tasks. It can be useful for marketing research when considering potential new product concepts and designs and may be used in conjunction with group discussions.

OBSERVATION

Actual and potential customers can be observed using cameras and tape recordings to establish patterns of behaviour. Such observation takes place in many situations, including in a retail outlet when the individual is shopping, when he/she is reading a magazine to examine attention to advertising, and, if appropriate, when the individual is passing a poster site. Such observation methods may use both qualitative and quantitative techniques and can be supplemented by other research methods including accompanied shopping (see below).

The observation method can be combined with interviewing techniques to examine how the respondent makes decisions, termed the decision protocol interview. In particular within a shopping situation, behaviour is monitored using recording cameras and in-store interviews at the time of undertaking the purchasing behaviour. These methods give useful insights into how shopping decisions are made.

ACCOMPANIED SHOPPING

In the consumer market, when assessing a customer's approach to food purchasing, marketing researchers accompany the participant in the act of shopping. In this situation the interviewer asks questions to determine why the individual shops in particular ways at the time of purchase.

The accompanied shopping technique was used by the British Market Research Bureau (BMRB) market research agency when examining the market for mayonnaise and salad cream in the UK. The research showed that the customer buying decision process was influenced by a number of factors, including the household taste preferences and the nature of the container for the salad dressing. The findings were used to determine the preferred container for Hellmann's mayonnaise and to develop a theme for the promotional campaign for a revamped product presentation of the mayonnaise.

MYSTERY SHOPPING

Mystery shopping is the 'collection of information from retail outlets, showrooms, etc., by people posing as ordinary members of the public' (MRS, 2006: 42) which in the UK has been estimated to be worth about £37m (US$66m). Specialist interviewers (or shoppers) act as possible customers using both telephone and physical customer interface. Usually telephone calls are taped, with copies of the tapes supplied to local management. The video can be used in the same way to record the interview process. The findings are used to monitor customer service provision, e.g. banks assessing the quality of teller advice to customers concerning the availability of banking servicesor car manufacturers assessing the performance of their distributors' salesmen. It is also used as part of sales incentive schemes, supplementing sales achieved, as in the situation where the quality of service is assessed for the 'best pub of the month' award.

It should be appreciated that there are ethical problems associated with using mystery shopping related to the rights of the staff being interviewed. The MRS code of conduct (discussed at p. 167) ensures the data collected through mystery shopping are used fairly (MRS, 2006: 17–23).

USE OF PROJECTIVE METHODS

Qualitative research uses a 'body of research techniques which seeks insights through loosely structured, mainly verbal data rather than measurements. Analysis is interpretative, subjective, impressionistic and diagnostic' (MRS, 2006: 43). It uses unstructured stimuli, objects or situations to elicit the individual's characteristic way of perceiving the world. Examples of such methods include:

- *Sentence completion tests.* Sentences may be partially formed and left to be completed by the respondent, e.g. 'The person who uses instant powdered milk is . . .'
- *Word association tests.* Certain words are introduced and the respondent is asked to link them with the product, service or brand being investigated. Opposite meaning

words may be considered, e.g. 'hot and cold'; 'sweet and sour'; 'black and white' and the association of the words to give a profile for the subject being investigated. Such information is used to determine product images which may need to be adjusted by promotional campaigns.

■ *Cartoon completion exercises.* A cartoon picture with an empty 'bubble' is presented to the respondent for caption completion. Frequently such methods are used for studies of children's demand.

■ *Third-person tests.* Sometimes respondents are more willing to discuss their personal behaviour pattern when they can dissociate, or distance, themselves personally from their behaviour. By discussing the behaviour of a third person the respondent may describe behaviour characteristics which, in reality, relate to his/her own behaviour. For example, when discussing the consumption of chocolate, the respondent may be more likely to highlight the idiosyncrasies of the eating habits of a third person than when describing his/her personal habits. Typically, this type of research presents a number of buying situations to the respondent, e.g. different people buying in different places. The respondent is asked to comment on the behaviour. Such tests can provide information related to sensitive matters that the individual might otherwise decline to discuss.

■ *Personification.* Since consumers tend not to think in terms of brand images, a means of 'projecting' this image is through descriptions which are easier to understand, e.g. what type of person would a particular newspaper be? Does it feel male or female; old or young? What type of job would it do? Such personification projecting also can be done with reference to types of cars which are easy to interpret, e.g. the character of a Rolls-Royce compared with that of a Ford Focus.

Frequently, consumer opinions are assessed through the respondent preparing a collage to express views about a particular product or brand. An assortment of words, pictures and images are taken from magazines and the respondent is asked to select those which most closely relate to the product or brand in question. With personification, or collage, as with most projective methods, exploring the reasons why respondents come up with their particular answers on images is probably more important than the answer itself.

■ *Picture interpretation.* Examples include: the Thematic Apperception Test (TAT); the Rorschach inkblot test; picture drawing; fantasy situation explanation. These are a series of research methods that have been developed by psychiatry and psychology which, on occasion, have been used in marketing research. However, the interpretation of their findings has been subject to low reliability and validity so their use is uncommon in present-day marketing research. Essentially, they use prompts to encourage the respondent to discuss personal associations. Responses related to marketing research are difficult to elicit.

■ *Psychodrama situation acting.* It is difficult to use this research method within marketing research. In essence, the respondent is asked to act out the typical purchaser of a particular brand of, say, coffee and to compare that behaviour with that of the purchaser of other competing brands. This could be feasible if brand awareness and images were strong, but often the awareness attributes are subtle, showing limited differences for similar products. Moreover, usually, it takes more time to elicit the behaviour pattern using psychodrama than using other research methods such as group discussion which can obtain the assessments more readily and more quickly.

PROBLEMS ASSOCIATED WITH QUALITATIVE RESEARCH

While qualitative research provides explanation as to why particular behaviour occurs which may not be given by quantitative research methods, the use of qualitative research can be criticized. In particular, areas for concern include:

- Cost.
- Timing.
- Small sample size.
- Interpretation of results.
- Intrinsic subjectivity.

C A S E S T U D Y

DEVELOPMENTS IN QUALITATIVE RESEARCH METHODS

In the 1990s there was increasing concern regarding the lack of information on particular societal groups such as 'minority ethnic' groups both in domestic and international markets. Silverman (2005) cites the case raised by WPP's Ogilvy & Mather advertising agency in South Africa of a lack of information about black Africans. The standard marketing research tools such as focus groups were found to be inappropriate for use in the difficult conditions of black townships. Practical considerations led to improvisation whereby camera crews were sent into black areas to video-tape consumers and this yielded unexpected results. Not only was useful market information concerning potential consumers in black townships obtained, but, additionally, clients demanded videos of consumers in other places, beginning the trend towards reality television for the boardroom. By combining the ethnography technique of the study of human cultures, marketing service companies found a way to win the attention of corporate clients by showing them video-tape of consumers going about their normal lives. The rise of a more visual corporate culture in marketing research has been helped by the development of cheaper video cameras and improvements in personal computers.

The idea behind corporate reality television is that by watching people in natural situations advertisers can develop better marketing ideas. In order to address this interest, in 2000 Ogilvy created Field Brand Investigation, a subsidiary to produce video research. Its work includes more than 250 documentaries depicting a range of people from Thai auto enthusiasts to British schizophrenics. Another WPP subsidiary, Ogilvy RedCard, based in Singapore, specializes in research into the 'secret lives' of consumers. One case followed young Japanese women into the bathrooms of discos and found that the women frequented the bathroom

Undertaking qualitative research can be seen to be expensive in terms of comparable quantitative research. For example, undertaking a series of group discussions typically involves about eight group sessions, in which the reaction of four groups in one area is compared with four in another. Each group discussion would involve around eight participants, giving around sixty-four respondents in all. The group discussions cost at least £2,000 (US$3,588) each to administer, making a total of more than £16,000 (US$28,704) for the project, i.e. at least £250 (US$449) per person interviewed. Some group discussions might involve fewer than eight persons per group session, so the cost per person interviewed could be higher. These costs will be higher than the apparent costs per person interviewed using quantitative methods such as street interviewing.

However, the benefits of qualitative research often outweigh that of quantitative research. Qualitative research is expected to provide 'richer' market data. In terms of time to complete the interviews, an in-depth, focus interview will take at least an hour per person interviewed, probably longer, and more than one interview per person may be required to be interviewed. Typically, street interviews take around ten minutes to complete, but then there is the need to administer the collation and interpretation of the interview questionnaires.

C A S E   S T U D Y

a lot to reapply make-up. This result had implications for cosmetics makers operating in Japan and could be used in developing effective marketing strategies, including the direction of promotional messages. Video research is also used by pharmaceutical companies that know what their drugs can do but want to know more about the people who take them, such as schizophrenics.

However, it can be difficult to interpret the video research, as OMD, a media buying unit of Omnicom, discovered when it taped people watching television at home. While people's behaviour can be recorded, their thinking processes can be interpreted in various ways. Nevertheless, video research helps to address the growing distance between the corporate elite and the consumers. Executives in MNCs often find themselves doing business in places about which they are ill informed. For example, firms such as Ogilvy's FBI unit might undertake market development in difficult territories such as South Africa and China which are becoming tomorrow's business opportunities. Marketing research agencies are filling a void left by media companies. Journalism has been growing more local, as cuts in the foreign bureaux of television networks and newspapers demonstrate, while MNCs have been growing more global. This has created opportunities for marketing executives to play the role of foreign correspondent. Corporate reality television enables highly paid executives to cross the class and income divide and get a glimpse into the lives of targeted consumers. The corporate interest in seeing more of life may be deepening.

Source: adapted from Silverman (2005).

While a group qualitative project can be turned around within three weeks, the logistics of quantitative research, generally, take much longer. For group discussions, four group sessions will take six hours of intensive interviewing and more than another six hours will require to be spent on transcribing the interview tape recordings and the analysis of the tapes. The whole process is labour-intensive, involving a high input of senior marketing research executive time. The eight groups represent twelve hours' intensive executive interviews, as opposed to five to ten minutes with each respondent in a street interview.

Furthermore, usually the sample sizes used for qualitative research are small. Typically, four to eight group sessions are held, which might give between thirty-two and sixty-four respondents on which to base recommendations. Such a sample size is not likely to satisfy the needs of statistical analysis. Some clients express concern regarding the qualitative research process because they prefer to have quantitative data to interpret. These concerns show a lack of understanding of the process and the skill of the marketing researchers. Any attempt to assess the value of qualitative research on a cost per respondent basis should be dismissed on the grounds of lack of understanding of the process.

The intrinsic subjectivity of the research topics can lead to difficulties in understanding and interpreting the findings. Researchers can differ in their interpretation of qualitative research findings, but this very difference can provoke deeper consideration of the research theme. Increasingly, qualitative research is accepted for its ability to allow marketing researchers to delve more deeply into consumer behaviour patterns to elicit findings that could not have been found using traditional quantitative research methods.

Quantitative research methods

Usually quantitative research methods in marketing research involve some form of survey, i.e. the systematic collection, analysis and interpretation of information about some aspect of study. In marketing research the term is applied to the collection of information about actual and potential customers, often using sampling to select the individuals and organizations. The techniques used may include: postal survey; personal interview survey; observation; consumer panel; omnibus survey; opinion poll.

POSTAL SURVEY

Postal surveys involve 'the collection of primary data using a self-completion questionnaire or diary distributed or returned by post' (MRS, 2006: 43). The questionnaire is designed (see p. 147) in such a way as to encourage self-completion by the targeted respondent. Usually postal survey questionnaires have questions with pre-coded answer choices that provide quantitative information. These may be supplemented with open-ended answer questions to give additional qualitative data. Postal questionnaires can vary in length although the use of around twenty questions is favoured, as more questions can lead to a lower response rate.

The BMRB market research agency uses the postal questionnaire technique to monitor consumption of mass consumer products and services for its Target Group Index (TGI). An extensive questionnaire of over ninety pages in length is targeted at 24,000 adults aged

15 and over from across Great Britain. It collects data on respondents' lifestyles, their purchasing patterns, concerning over 4,000 brands within more than 500 product fields, and their exposure to the promotional media, especially television and the press. In this way, product use can be compared with respondents' demographics and lifestyles as well as with promotional media influence to help advertisers, advertising agencies and media owners to target marketing promotional strategies and advertising campaigns.

PERSONAL INTERVIEW SURVEY

Personal interviews can take various forms and are used for gathering both qualitative and quantitative data. Usually a questionnaire guides the interviewing process. IT is used to help manage the interviewing process and for collecting and analysing the interview data. Often face-to-face interviewing uses Computer Assisted Personal Interviewing (CAPI) with portable laptop computers. The interviewer is prompted with the question by the computer and the appropriate response codes are keyed in directly according to the respondent's answers. Routing procedures use these codes to determine which question appears next. Since the data are entered directly into the computer, analyses can be produced quickly (MRS, 2006: 42).

Increasingly, telephone interviewing is undertaken by Computer Assisted Telephone Interviewing (CATI); Computer Assisted Self Interviewing (CASI) is used to improve the monitoring of the survey process. CASI involves self-completion of a questionnaire on a laptop computer or disc sent by post (for business surveys). Self-completion on a laptop computer leads to greater accuracy in response to sensitive issues such as crime, drugs, sex, etc., due to greater confidentiality than pen-and-paper recording methods. Recent developments have led to the introduction of multimedia methods to enable personal interviewing in the home or office without the physical presence of the interviewer, but these methods are still at the development stage. Computer Assisted Web Interviewing (CAWI) is conducted over the Internet rather than by using face-to-face interviewing.

However, problems have been encountered associated with the high investment involved in the provision of laptop computers among the freelance field interviewers, who often work for a number of marketing research agencies, each of which is expected to provide the researcher with a laptop.

Face-to-face interviewing takes various forms with different completion times. The typical street (or shopping mall) interview lasts for ten minutes whereas the personal interview with a marketing director is more likely to take up to one and a half hours. Increasingly, face-to face interviews are difficult and expensive to effect. Interviewers face problems in obtaining the participation of the desired interviewees. The personal safety of both the interviewers and interviewees is a concern. While personal face-to-face interviews can provide rich data for market analysis and remain the most prevalent technique for obtaining market data, marketing researchers still look for alternative ways of collecting such data, frequently turning to telephone interviewing.

In the UK, BMRA marketing research agencies conduct about 5.7m telephone interviews, i.e. 15,500 interviews, per day. Telephone interviews can be undertaken from a call centre that monitors the interviewing process using CATI techniques. The computer is used at all stages of the interviewing:

- For selecting the sample of interviews using random selection methods, quota controls and automatic dialling for conducting the interview (when the questionnaire can be shown on a monitor screen and the interviewer inputs respondents' answers directly through the monitor for analysis).
- For analysis of findings during and after the interview.

In this way the process can be controlled through almost simultaneous interviews and results. While it is anticipated that telephone interviewing for collecting marketing research data will increase in the future as other methods become more expensive to administer, telephone interviewing is becoming more problematic. Response rates are falling as call screening through answering machines and voicemail in the case of business executives is more prevalent.

OBSERVATION

Observation techniques involve 'a non-verbal means of obtaining primary data as an alternative or complement to questioning' (MRS, 2006: 43). Data collected in this manner may be of a quantitative or qualitative nature and involve the marketing researcher observing the behaviour of targeted actual, or potential, consumers. Quantitative measures such as the number and value of purchases of products can be monitored.

CONSUMER PANEL

A panel is a form of sample survey from which comparative data from the same sampling units are taken on more than one occasion. It is 'a permanent representative sample maintained by a market research agency from which information is obtained on more than one occasion either for continuous research or for *ad hoc* projects' (MRS, 2006: 43). Panels may be made up of individuals, households or firms. They can be used to monitor market trends, e.g. national house building or food consumption, as well as to examine specific issues such as brand switching, repeat buying and media audiences. A range of tools are used to monitor behaviour, including home audits (sometimes involving dustbin checks), diary recording, television set meters and online shopping recorders. Usually, participants on consumer panels are given small rewards to encourage their involvement such as a token voucher for a national retailer or the chance to enter a prize draw.

Latterly, to address declining response rates associated with traditional panel member selection and also to identify respondent types more cost effectively than surveys, access panels have been introduced. Marketing research firms build up databases of willing panel participants from which the sample for specific panels is selected. This process saves time and effort in developing individual panel memberships and ensures that those selected are more likely to participate.

The continuous consumer purchasing panel is the most commonly used form of panel. Normally it will be set up by a marketing research agency with the information gathered sold to individual customers (or syndicates) to monitor consumer demand and client performance in the market. Examples of these panels are shown below. A.C. Nielsen and TNS dominate the world's consumer tracking services.

A.C. Nielsen

In the US A.C. Nielsen operates Homescan panel, covering 120,000 households, while in Europe its Homescan in the UK covers 14,000 households. Panel coverage is being boosted in France, Germany, Italy, Portugal and Spain.

TNS

TNS (see p. 123) runs the Superpanel, which covers 20,000 households and provides purchasing behaviour data across a range of mass consumer markets in the UK. It is used to monitor product and retailer performance, e.g. the success of a new brand of soap powder can be compared against the sales and market share of established products within an UK region. The sales achieved are shown in terms of commercial television region, type of retail outlet and social class of consumers. The Superpanel has international coverage which is being expanded to increase sample sizes of households in Malaysia, the Philippines, Portugal, Spain and Vietnam.

TNS operates other panels, including:

- Impulse panel measuring the purchasing behaviour of 5,250 individuals across a range of personal purchases such as confectionery, snacks, soft drinks and ice cream. It uses telephone interviewing methods to ascertain respondent behaviour.
- Fashiontrak panel measuring the purchasing behaviour of 15,000 individuals across the clothing and footwear markets. It provides estimates of products' market sizes and brand shares as well as information on participant store loyalty.
- Television audience measurement panels (see Broadcasters' Audience Research Board, BARB, see p.158).

Media Plus Research

This marketing research agency has the contract to run a dedicated company panel for the *Financial Times* European newspaper to help its management to select the most appropriate format for the newspaper. The panel is made up of a representative sample of readers who are asked to complete three questionnaires a year, each covering a range of topics. As with other consumer panels, membership runs for about two years and there are prize draws for each survey to encourage participation.

Problems associated with panel methods

The selection of the sample of participants, or panel members, may be open to bias. Within marketing research quota sampling is the common form of sampling which has been developed to meet the needs of the industry. However, where the quotas are difficult to achieve, interviewers may compromise the selection procedures and the data collected. Despite the quota selection procedures, the panel participants may be atypical of the general population in so far as they are prepared to be involved at all. They could comprise individuals who do not represent the typical consumer.

Moreover the reliability of the continuity of the panel reporting process may be questioned. Usually individual panel members remain on the panels for up to two years, with panel members being introduced and removed throughout the life of the panel, which may be as long as thirty years. However, panel members may not maintain their interest in participating throughout the two years, so that their effective contribution may vary. In the initial months of membership, panel members may adapt their normal behaviour to create a favourable impression. Participants may be encouraged to over- (or under-) perform the behavioural activities being assessed, making the validity and reliability of the panel findings suspect. This poses problems in the analysis and interpretation of panel data. While it is to be supposed that the continuous study of underlying patterns of consumer purchasing through consumer panels provides deeper insight into consumer behaviour, this may not prove to be true, as participants may adjust their behaviour to be favoured by those persons managing the panels.

OMNIBUS SURVEY

Omnibus surveys cover 'a number of topics, usually for different clients. The samples tend to be nationally representative and composed of types of people for which there is a general demand. Clients are charged by the market research agency by questionnaire space or number of questions required' (MRS, 2006: 43). Costs vary according to type of question (pre-coded or open-ended) and sample size. RSGB charges around £450 (US$807) per question for a pre-code on 1,000 and £900 (US$1,615) on 2,000 placed in the survey and, normally, there is an additional 'joining' fee. Most omnibus surveys operate on the basis of fresh samples of respondents, rather than panels. The survey uses a series of short questions which are presented through the questionnaire on behalf of the different clients who share the cost of collecting the data, which may be by personal face-to-face or telephone interview. Usually, samples of 1,000 or 2,000 are undertaken from the sample frame of men, women or businesses which should be nationally representative. Less frequently for niche surveys smaller samples of 500 may be used.

Omnibus surveys are run by most of the marketing research agencies that have specialist consumer behaviour panels. Some examples are shown below:

BMRB

Access omnibus panels include:

- Personal interviewing (CAPI): covers 2,000 adults and youth aged over 15 using face-to-face weekly interviewing supplemented by 1,000 7 to 19 year olds interviewed monthly.
- Telephone interviewing (CATI): covers 2000 adults aged 16 and over conducted over a weekend with results provided on Monday.
- Online survey: covers 1,000 samples of customer specified target demographics.
- Global; covers adults throughout the world.

National Opinion Poll (NOP)

NOP operates the Solutions surveys which use:

- Weekly interviewing of 1,000 adults with CAPI.
- Monthly interviewing of 1,000 7 to 16 year olds (called the Young generation).
- Weekend telephone interviewing of 1,000 adults throughout Britain.
- Monthly telephone interviewing of 500 adults in France, Germany, Italy and the UK (called the European Telebus).

It also operates a monthly Healthcare panel survey using 200 face-to-face interviews with general practitioners.

Sample surveys

The Omnicar is a specialist motoring survey which interviews a different sample of 1,000 motorists at random locations every month. It uses twenty-five standard questions to monitor motor accessory demand which can be cross-analysed against a client's additional questions.

Carrick James Market Research (CJMR)

The marketing research agency CJMR operates omnibus surveys targeted at children, youths and parents in Britain and continental Europe, the data being used by manufacturers for developing products and services for young people. In Britain it has surveys of:

- 1,200 children aged between 7 and 19 reporting bi-monthly (face-to-face).
- 800 children aged between 7 and 14 reporting monthly (face-to-face).
- 3,000 children aged between 7 and 14 reporting weekly (phone).
- 400 children aged between 0 and 6 reporting bi-monthly (face-to-face).

Its continental Europe panels cover France, Germany, Italy, Spain and Poland targeting 6–14s.

Ethnibus

It runs the ethnic omnibus, undertaking 750 face-to-face monthly interviews across the UK.

Continental Research Surveys

This operates a monthly survey of 200 managing directors and/or financial directors within mid- to large-sized companies as well as a monthly survey of 300 managing directors and/or owners of small businesses.

Some omnibus surveys concentrate on particular regions within the UK, e.g.:

■ TNS Scottish Opinion Survey (SOS) based on interviewing 1,000 adults monthly throughout Scotland in-home using CAPI methods.
■ MRUK, a fortnightly telephone survey covering 500 adults in Wales.
■ Mori Ireland uses face-to-face interviewing of 1,000 adults in Northern Ireland.

International omnibus surveys

Omnibus surveys operate in similar ways to the UK panels in most developed countries. For example, in Spain, Millward Brown conducts three omnibus surveys per annum using personal in-home interviewing to reach 3,000 adults of 15 years and over and 2,000 housewives from across Spain.

There are also omnibus surveys that operate across more than one country, enabling cross-country comparisons to be made. An example of this type of omnibus survey is the Mass-Observation monthly telephone omnibus covering France, Germany, Italy and the UK.

Use of omnibus surveys

Omnibus surveys are used to help in marketing decision making in various ways. A typical situation is the producer of a new range of products such as yoghurt, who might wish to assess the effectiveness of a television advertising campaign. The producer places a number of questions in the relevant omnibus survey. From the response, brand and advertising awareness, and possibly purchasing, can be monitored for the new product from pre- and post-campaign waves of the surveys.

The role of IT in consumer panel development

Since the late 1980s Electronic Point of Sale (EPOS) and Electronic Funds Transfer Point of Sale (EFTPOS) have provided retailers with online virtual information regarding customer demand based on scanned purchases at checkout tills. This has given retailers information on customer demand traditionally used for operations management, e.g. stock control and logistics. These data have been developed for marketing. As UK retailers, especially grocery retailers, have become ever larger and their market shares have increased so, too, have their customer databases more closely represented total demand. Together with retailer loyalty card findings, the data collected can provide information on trends in customer sales in terms of product, brand, outlet, region as well as customer names, payment method, frequency of visiting the outlet and so on. Customer addresses and postcodes are determined through linkage with customer identifiers such as membership of loyalty schemes. The data are analysed in conjunction with other marketing databases, in particular geodemographic databases such as A Classification of Residential Neighbourhoods (ACORN) and MOSAIC (see Chapter 6) and used in marketing decision making. For example, the success of a retailer's promotional television campaign could be gauged by product sales achieved in its outlets in the targeted region for the duration of the campaign which can also be compared with sales of competing brands across the region. Geodemographic analysis identifies the retailer's customer ACORN or MOSAIC groups and suggests appropriate marketing to match customer demand.

Traditionally, marketing research agencies developed consumer panels and retail auditing to produce national market databases servicing primarily FMCG producers. As retailers have developed their databases, in order to compete, marketing research agencies have had to improve theirs. Indeed, some marketing research agencies have joined forces with retailers to buy into their databases, placing ever more power in the hands of the retailers concerned. It remains to be seen how manufacturers will react to this development.

Computer model building, or the development of market simulation, has become more feasible with improvements in IT. Using the 'application of specific assumptions to a set of variable factors and the relationships which exist between them' (MRS, 2006: 42) simulations of the market situation can be made. Models of consumer markets primarily using mathematical analysis, graphical or purely verbal techniques have been used as experimental tools of strategic marketing to investigate 'what if' scenarios. With IT development different consumer databases, based on actual consumer behaviour, can be brought together. With the relevant statistical analyses, the databases can provide simulations of likely consumer behaviour which, in turn, can be used to predict market demand. Research is being undertaken to produce models of consumer behaviour from the information from the consumer databases using data fusion techniques to create simulated virtual consumers. However, as yet, the reliability of the data provided is open to question.

OPINION POLL

The opinion poll aims to measure the general public's assessment of the popularity of political parties as well as to ascertain its opinion regarding contentious political issues. Often, the findings of opinion polls are highly publicized, especially in the lead up to general elections; however, opinion polls only account for about 4 per cent of all the marketing research industry's turnover in the UK. NOP and MORI are well known specialist marketing research agencies conducting national opinion polls. Some opinion polls are targeted at the regions, e.g. TNS Scottish Omnibus Survey (SOS) sampling the Scottish population.

More recently, online polling as an approach is gaining in popularity, used not only for political and social research, but also for traditional market research such as product and concept testing, use and attitude surveys and brand tracking. For example, YouGov, founded

in 2000, has pioneered the use of the Internet and IT for market research and public consultation. It has become the leading UK provider of insight and tracking on political and
social issues for both media and private clients. Its panels include:

- POLL SE omnibus 2000, operating a twice-weekly schedule targeted at 2,000 adults
  using questions which are suitable to be asked of a nationally representative sample.
- BrandIndex, launched in 2005 to poll about 2,000 online shoppers every day. It counts
  thirty-two product and service sectors and 1,149 brands. Respondents are asked to
  identify brands within sectors that they regard positively, or negatively, based on seven
  criteria: buzz; general impression or feel for the brand, quality, value, satisfaction,
  corporate reputation and would they recommend it?
- HERO (Health Experience Research Online) has the National Health Service
  (NHS) as the major stakeholder. Its clients include a number of NHS Strategic Health
  Authorities.

In 2005 YouGov extended its operations from the UK to cover the Middle East, where,
with a base in Dubai, it operates a specialist panel of businessmen and women across the
Gulf Co-operation Council (GCC).

Further details of YouGov services can be obtained from: http://www.yougov.com/.

PROBLEMS ASSOCIATED WITH QUANTITATIVE RESEARCH

Quantitative research material will rarely suffice for answering marketing problems. While
marketing research techniques might provide quantitative data such as the size of the market,
the market segments within the market and market share analysis, this type of information
seldom answers the question of why customers purchase certain goods rather than others.
It is for this reason that qualitative research techniques are introduced to explain or, at least
to provide a better understanding of, consumer behaviour.

SAMPLING METHODS

Within marketing research, sampling plays a crucial role. Sampling involves taking 'a part
of subset or a population taken to be representative of the population as a whole for the
investigative purposes of research' (MRS, 2006: 43). Although when researching industrial
markets, total populations considered may be low, frequently no more than thirty firms or
individuals, so that the whole population can be surveyed, within the consumer market the
potential population to be considered can reach millions of individuals. For example, if a
researcher wishes to examine the market for a new food product such as a muesli bar, the
population to be investigated could be up to 30m persons, or 24m households in the UK
alone; globally it would be much larger. Few researchers would wish to consider the views
of each one of those potential customers for the muesli bar. A more practical approach is
to take a representative sample of the total population of potential customers. With care,

the response from the sample should provide the answer regarding the demand for the new product that represents the total population's likely demand.

Steps in sampling

The marketing researcher has to identify the target population to be investigated. This requires the selection of a sample frame, the selection of the method of sampling (non-probability or probability) and determining the desirable sample size.

Sample frame

The sample frame is the list of the total population that is targeted for consideration. This total population can be derived from a number of listings. For example, to target buyers in consumer markets some or all of the following listings could be used:

- The electoral roll (for adults of 18 years and above).
- Members of a particular leisure association.
- University student registration list.
- Magazine subscribers.
- Credit account customers at a particular department store.

The sample frame could be segmented to enable targeting of the sample of the total sample frame. A useful approach is to use geo-demographic segmentation, e.g. ACORN and MOSAIC listings (see Chapter 6).

For industrial markets sample frames might be derived from various sources, including:

- Company sales records.
- Members of a trade association (found through CBD *Directory of Associations*).
- *Yellow Pages* (unduplicated version).
- *Kompass Trade Directory*.
- Jordan's Top 500 private companies.

Probability sampling methods

Various methods are used, including: simple random; probability random; stratified; cluster; multi-stage; disproportional.

SIMPLE AND PROBABILITY RANDOM SAMPLING

A simple random sample occurs when the process of selection permits all items in the universe (or population) to have an equal chance of being drawn. A probability random sample is one in which every member of the population has a known, or calculable, chance of being included in the survey. The population may be the population of a country or the population of a company's customers, depending on what the marketing research sets out to investigate. Marketing researchers use random samples to represent the population so that if, for example, 40 per cent of their sample own their own houses, they will say 40 per cent of the entire population are likely to own their own houses. Based on statistical probability theory the 'limits of accuracy' of the sample can be calculated. Thus, a sample of 1,000 may be quoted as having an accuracy level of ±3–4 per cent at a 95 per cent confidence level. The most common methods of drawing a random sample are to assign a number to each name and select the required number of people by using random number tables or to use a random number generator.

A systematic sample uses a selected number which determines the position in the sample frame of the sample taken. The frequency of sampling should be decided say one out of every n members. In the first group of n numbers a random number between 1 and n is used to select the first case. Subsequently, every nth case is selected until the total sample required has been selected. The selection would proceed systematically taking every nth case, which for the sample could consist of the fifth, sixteenth, twenty-seventy, thirty-eighth . . . elements.

STRATIFIED SAMPLING

A stratified random sample occurs when a universe is divided into groups that include all the universe items and a simple random sample is taken from each group (or stratum). A stratified random sample would occur if 100 respondents were divided into strata by age and a random sample was taken from each stratum.

CLUSTER

A cluster sample occurs when the items in a universe are separated into clusters, a number of clusters are chosen at random and then a sample (even 100 per cent) is taken from each chosen cluster. For example, a cluster sample of respondents living on campus would be taken if two dormitories were selected on a random basis out of all dormitories and a sample were then drawn of students in each of the two chosen dormitories.

MULTI-STAGE

It may be appropriate to undertake sampling at various stages of the survey to achieve a representative sample of all the groups required. In this situation, the sample would be selected using random selection techniques at every stage of the survey.

DISPROPORTIONAL

It may be critical in the study to reach particular cases in the total population. In this situation, it can be necessary to over sample particular sub-sets of the population, i.e. to select more from one sub-set to ensure that coverage of this sub-set is met.

Non-probability sampling methods

Sometimes in marketing research it is critical to reach certain persons or organizations in the sample frame and it is necessary to use non-probability sampling methods. This does mean that the meaningfulness of any statistical analysis undertaken may be questioned; but it does have the advantage that the critical respondents are covered. Non-probability techniques that can be used include: judgemental; snowball; convenience; quota.

JUDGEMENTAL

The person selecting the sample uses personal judgement to decide the choice of persons or organizations. Although this procedure is likely to involve personal bias, it may have the benefit of ensuring that those selected are the persons known to fit the criteria required for the study.

SNOWBALL

In this situation, the researcher finds one person that matches the criteria for study, and then, assuming that 'birds of a feather flock together', that individual is asked to find another with similar characteristics. For example, if the study targets twins, one set of twins would be identified, say by using judgemental selection, then the twins, would be asked to find another set of twins and so on. It is more likely that twins would be selected through that procedure than by trying to find them using random sampling, or another form of probability sampling, on the total population.

CONVENIENCE

There are situations where, for convenience, particular persons or organizations might be selected. While the results of the study are likely to be biased through not using probability, there could be considerable benefits associated with the ease of reaching the sample. For example, if the study targeted physics students, it would be easier and much less expensive to select from persons attending a lecture on physics than to attempt to find such persons through probability sampling of the electoral roll.

QUOTA

While random sampling is used in marketing research, e.g. for the selection of persons to participate on the Joint Industry Committee for National Readership Surveys (JICNARS, 1981) National Readership Survey (NRS), common practice is to use quota sampling. Certainly, for personal interviewing selection, it can be difficult to achieve the desired sample using strict random sampling procedures. The administration usually of up to three calls back to the house address of the selected individual may prove expensive and time-consuming. Consequently quota sampling, which is more cost-effective, is used to ease the effort required to select individuals for marketing research studies. Generally, the organizers of a study determine quotas: the interviewers, who are usually different individuals, follow the specified quota, matching the selection of the persons to include in the study to the quota specified. Frequently quotas are set with reference to the demographics given in the census of population. For example, they could specify the number of individuals to select for interview as being x males and y females in two age groups, a and b. Theoretically, probability statistics should not be used to interpret results that have been collected by using quota sampling. However, the practice of quota sampling and the larger sample sizes that may be practical to use have evolved so that, with care, probability statistics are used in marketing research analysis.

Methods of determining sample size

While there are statistical ways of determining the appropriate sample size, using standard error measures, in practice, for most marketing research more *ad hoc* methods are frequently used. Practical considerations, which often preclude the use of statistical approaches to determine sample size, are as follows: 'rule of thumb': 100 or more cases per sub-group; budget constraints; comparable studies.

'RULE OF THUMB': 100 OR MORE CASES PER SUB-GROUP

Generally, a desirable sample size is one which would give at least 100 cases (individuals or organizations) in each sub-group, or segment, that is to be investigated. Clearly the more sub-groups that are required to be studied the larger the sample size is required to be.

BUDGET CONSTRAINTS

Most marketing research studies have financial limits which in themselves restrict the size of the study and the associated size of the sample to be investigated.

COMPARABLE STUDIES

General practice and the size of samples used for past, similar studies provide an indication of the appropriate size for the study. There are few marketing research studies undertaken by marketing research agencies with samples of more than 30,000. More typically, for consumer panels samples of between 1,000 and 4,000 are used. Face-to face personal interview surveys may use smaller samples of 500 to 1,000 individuals; telephone personal interviews may have larger samples of over the 1,000 level due to the relative ease of tracking the respondents.

The factors to consider when deciding on the appropriate sample size would be:

■ The number of groups and sub-groups to be analysed.
■ Variability within the population.

- ■ The cost of reaching the sample.
- ■ The value of information in general and degree of accuracy required of results.
- ■ The non-response situation.

These issues will be discussed in more depth in the section on quantitative methods.

QUESTIONNAIRE DESIGN

Questionnaires may use pre-coded (sometimes termed 'closed') or open-ended questions. Pre-coded questions are those for which there are a limited number of possible answers. The respondent can select from a list of possible answers on the questionnaire which may include a catch-all 'other' category to ensure that all possibilities are given. Analysis and data processing of these kinds of pre-coded answers is relatively straightforward. Computer analysis may use programmes such as SPSS.

Open-ended questions allow the respondents to decide how they will reply. These question are much less readily analysed and interpreted and their use is likely to give lower reliability and validity of the questioning process than would be the case for pre-coded questions. However, they do have the benefit of not restricting respondents' answers.

Before the actual marketing research process begins, survey questionnaires should be pre-tested to check for any ambiguities in the question used or the format of the questionnaire itself. A pilot survey should be undertaken at this stage whereby a small-scale survey is completed to test the questionnaire and the questionnaire survey procedures prior to full-scale survey. In this way the effectiveness of the questionnaire in eliciting the information required can be gauged before commitment of the resources required for the full survey. At the same time it is possible to check the administration procedures used for the survey to ensure that they work efficiently. For example, for a postal questionnaire survey that the size of the envelopes matches that needed for the questionnaire, that the postal services are prepared for the volume of mail that is being proposed and that the questionnaire format is appropriate for data input for computer analysis. Similarly, when undertaking an Internet questionnaire survey, the appropriateness of the questionnaire and the process of gaining respondent co-operation can be assessed. Within the questionnaire it may be necessary to determine customer attitudes towards particular marketing issues.

ATTITUDE, BELIEFS AND BEHAVIOUR

You will remember that in Chapter 3 we mentioned that attitude is a central aspect of the cognitive information processing approach. Although behaviourists strenuously object to the concept, attitudes are also thought to be useful by many practitioners in marketing, particularly by those involved in advertising and in social marketing. Consequently attitude research is among the most frequently used research vehicles in marketing research. The aim of this section is to to explain:

- What attitude is.
- Why attitude research is commissioned.
- Its relation to other concepts such as belief and behavioural intention.
- The limitations of the concept.

If you want to understand what attitude means, then you *must* understand all the key words of the definition below:

> An attitude is a learned predisposition to respond towards an attitude object in a consistently favourable or unfavourable way.

Four key features of attitudes are that they are:

- Stable.
- Learned.
- Represent our feelings towards things.
- Taken as an indicator of our likely behaviour.

Referring back to the above definition, attitudes are learned, we are not born with them, although we do identify with the feelings of those people to whom we are closest. Attitudes are learned from what other people or institutions such as the mass media tell us or through our own experience. Attitude is linked with affect, the feelings that we have about things. There is strong evidence to support the view that not only do feelings influence how we act; how we act may also influence how we feel.

The underlying theory is known as expectancy value theory. An 'expectancy' is another term for a belief or a probabilistic expectation about the future and 'value' refers to a feeling or evaluation. This means that when a person has to choose between alternatives s/he is likely to choose that option which s/he expects is likely to lead to the most favourable outcomes, i.e. the option with the highest subjective expected utility (which is the person's subjective judgement of use or value).

Attitudes are important to marketers for a number of reasons. A favourable attitude towards a product or service is likely to provide a motivating force for behaviour. Attitude research may help identify those benefits which consumers desire and, in particular, the key product attributes which influence their decision making. Knowledge of these attributes may be used for segmenting the market, for positioning products and for developing and evaluating promotional strategies. In the last case, the brand attitude may form the basis of the promotional campaign which seeks to change it.

Attitude research involves much more than evaluation. Usually it involves finding out what a person's beliefs about a product or service are as well as their behavioural intention with respect to using that service. However, the name 'attitude research' reinforces the importance of evaluation or affect on the process.

Consider, for example, a researcher working for Lo-Cost Holidays, a major budget travel company which is investigating attitudes among UK C1 and C2 class potential customers towards the Seychelles as a holiday destination. The task is to: ascertain and measure brand beliefs and evaluations of those beliefs; obtain overall brand evaluations; obtain an indication as to the intention to buy.

Ascertaining and measuring brand beliefs and evaluations

Taking up the case of Joe introduced in Chapter 3, Joe has bought the suit, attended the interview and finds that he has his first job. After a short time he starts to think of a holiday. As an upwardly mobile young executive Joe gains the attention of Lo-Cost, which has obtained his name and address from a mailing list into which they have bought. Lo-Cost sends a marketing researcher whose task is to establish what Joe's attitude is towards the Seychelles as a holiday destination. This in-depth interview will help in the compilation of a questionnaire which will be administered to a sample of people. During their preliminary chat the researcher finds that Joe has heard of the Seychelles but is not sure where the Seychelles are located, just that they are far away, romantic and exotic.

DECOMPOSITION OF BELIEFS

The following is the complete list of attributes elicited from Joe. The researcher's task is to elicit Joe's hierarchy of beliefs about the Seychelles and to gain a quantified indication of the strength of his beliefs. S/he then has to measure systematically Joe's feelings towards these and to obtain his overall evaluation of the Seychelles as a holiday destination together with his intentions of travelling to the Seychelles. S/he elicits the following set of beliefs from Joe:

- The Seychelles are romantic.
- The Seychelles are exotic.
- The Seychelles have clear blue sea.
- The Seychelles have crystal white beaches.
- The Seychelles are exclusive.
- The Seychelles are expensive to get to.
- The Seychelles are only for people with money.
- The Seychelles are far away.
- It is hot and humid in the Seychelles.

However, s/he does not stop there. When Joe says that he believes that the Seychelles are romantic she asks him 'Why?' He replies, 'Well, you know, they are the sort of place you want to go if you are in a couple.' This statement forms a second level in the hierarchy of Joe's belief system. When pressed on this, he answers further that he does not really believe that the destination is for 'singles' such as himself. When asked what he thinks about 'exotic' locations, Joe first says that they are 'foreign'. When asked what this implies, he replies, 'I probably won't like the food.' Second, he believes that 'exotic' places will have poor health facilities. The researcher works systematically through the implications of each belief until s/he constructs a hierarchy like that contained in Table 5.3.

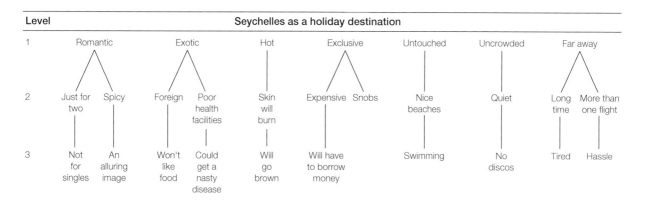

Level	Seychelles as a holiday destination							
1	Romantic	Exotic	Hot	Exclusive	Untouched	Uncrowded	Far away	
2	Just for two / Spicy	Foreign / Poor health facilities	Skin will burn	Expensive / Snobs	Nice beaches	Quiet	Long time / More than one flight	
3	Not for singles / An alluring image	Won't like food / Could get a nasty disease	Will go brown	Will have to borrow money	Swimming	No discos	Tired / Hassle	

Figure 5.3
Decomposition of Joe's hierarchy of beliefs about the Seychelles

The researcher then asks Joe to estimate the extent of his strength of belief. This involves Joe estimating the probability that each attribute he has listed really is characteristic of the Seychelles. For example, if Joe is absolutely certain that the Seychelles are romantic, he will allocate that a score of 10; on the other hand if he thinks they are definitely not romantic he allocates them 0. If he feels that they are between these two extremes, he estimates a probability somewhere between 0 and 10. Joe believes strongly that the Seychelles are a romantic spot and so allocates a score of nine points. He proceeds to allocate scores to the rest of the attributes which he has listed.

The researcher then asks Joe to give some indication of affect or feeling about each attribute. He is asked to evaluate each attribute allocating up to +5 if he strongly likes this to -5 if he strongly dislikes it. Joe allocates a maximum of five points to 'romance', indicating that he really likes the idea. The full range of values obtained for Joe's beliefs and evaluations is as illustrated in Figure 5.4. This approach to scoring beliefs was developed by Martin Fishbein, who specified that consumers will combine evaluations across multiple attributes to arrive at a single overall score. The calculations shown in Figure 5.4 use a compensatory approach, as Joe's overall attitude towards taking a holiday abroad is taken to be determined by the weighted sum of the ratings for all attributes. A poor evaluation on one attribute is compensated for by a positive evaluation on another. If Joe actually followed this process the mental processes involved in making the decision would be complex. On the other hand, Joe might feel that one attribute is absolutely essential. For example, if there is no possibility of romance he will not be interested. If this was correct then the appropriate approach would be non-compensatory, as one attribute, romance, cannot be traded for the others.

Using a compensatory approach, then Joe feels positive about travelling to the Seychelles if the score is summed only for level 1 (score = 82). However, if the levels 1 and 2 are summed, the score is negative (82 − 112 = −30). On the other hand, if this is considered from a non-compensatory point of view, then Joe might still be interested, as the score for 'romance' is positive at 45.

It can be seen from Table 5.6 that while Joe feels good about many of the 'level 1' attributes, he is much more negative about most of those at level 2. What can be inferred

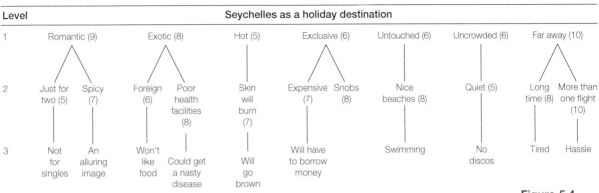

Level | Seychelles as a holiday destination

Figure 5.4
Decomposition of Joe's hierarchy of beliefs, indicating strength of belief (figures in brackets)

from the above, given that Joe has not been personally met? First, there is a good indication as to the nature of his beliefs together with the strength and evaluation of these. If the total score is summed, then, using a compensatory method, the score of 82 for level 1 is outweighed by the negative score for level 2 which is (–112). It could be surmised that Joe's overall evaluation is that he would not go on holiday to the Seychelles.

While the set of beliefs and attribute evaluations that have been elicited from Joe are possibly unique to him, it is definitely possible that his evaluations are at least in some ways related to those of other people who come from a similar point of view. They share the same social representations or ways of looking at the world that Joe does. Typically, a researcher will interview a number of people during the 'pilot' phase of a research project. Usually this will reveal large areas of overlap between different people which can form the basis for the development of a questionnaire founded on these general beliefs and evaluations to test people's responses to destinations and brands.

Table 5.6 Decomposition of Joe's hierarchy of beliefs for level 1

Attribute	Beliefs		Evaluation		Total
Romantic	9	×	+5	=	45
Exotic	8	×	+3	=	24
Hot	8	×	+2	=	16
Exclusive	5	×	–3	=	(–15)
Uncrowded	6	×	–2	=	(–12)
Untouched	6	×	+4	=	24
Far away	10	×	0	=	–
Total					82

Table 5.7 Decomposition of Joe's hierarchy of beliefs for level 2

	Beliefs		Evaluation		Total
Just for two	5	×	+4	=	20
Spicy	7	×	−3	=	(−21)
Foreign	6	×	−2	=	(−12)
Poor health facilities	8	×	−1	=	(−8)
Burn	7	×	−1	=	(−7)
Expensive	7	×	−5	=	(−35)
Nice beaches	8	×	+2	=	16
Snobs	8	×	−5	=	(−40)
Quiet	5	×	−3	=	(−15)
Long journey	10	×	−1	=	(−10)
Total					(−112)

OBTAINING OVERALL BRAND EVALUATIONS

This is relatively simple and involves rating the Seychelles overall in terms of its likeability and favourability. This could be obtained by means of a question such as

Rate the Seychelles according to the following scale:

Like them a lot	1 ☐	2 ☐	3 ☐	4 ☐	5 ☐	6 ☐	7 ☐	Don't like them at all

You will probably be familiar with the scale used, particularly if a marketing researcher has ever interviewed you.

OBTAINING INTENTION TO BUY

Once again this is straightforward to research, using a question such as:

What is the likelihood that you would visit the Seychelles the next time that you travel abroad?

1   Definitely.
2   Probably.
3   Maybe.
4   Probably not.
5   Definitely not.

PREDICTING BEHAVIOUR

It should be appreciated that measures of attitudinal components are complex; involving eliciting beliefs, attribute evaluations, overall brand evaluations and intentions to buy. The rationale for expending all this resource is that an attitude to an act will predict the act, whether it is buying a fizzy drink, voting in an election or travelling overseas. However, the relations between attitude and behaviour are by no means as straightforward as they have been described here. Attitudes can be influenced by other factors, e.g. by social norms (Fishbein and Ajzen, 1975) and by the situation in which a person finds him or herself. Even although Joe has a negative attitude towards the Seychelles he may be persuaded to go by Kirsten, his new girlfriend, who simply loves them.

Definition of an attitude

'Individual's predisposition to interpret experiences subjectively according to feelings determined by social and psychological influences'.

Attitudes contrast with opinions in so far as attitudes reflect deeply felt behaviour predisposition and, for marketing, can influence the individual's behaviour towards a product or service (see p.147). The components of attitudes include:

■ Cognitive elements related to knowledge or beliefs.
■ Affective elements related to emotional feelings.
■ Conative elements which influence the way the individual is disposed to behave.

Scaling methods for attitude measurement

Researchers have evolved different methods for measuring attitudes. Some like that developed by Thurstone during the 1930s have attempted to use ordinal scales, equivalent to those used in the sciences. However, these have proved difficult to produce and implement so that more commonly within marketing research there has been a move towards approximating the scales, using the methods introduced by Likert.

THURSTONE SCALE

This method requires:

■ The collection of as many statements as possible about the issue towards which attitudes are to be measured.
■ A large number of people sort statements into eleven piles representing the scale from extremely favourable to extremely unfavourable attitude.
■ A limited number of statements selected (possibly twenty) that show agreement among judges and whose scale values have approximately equal intervals between them.

Advantage:

■ Statements are ascribed numerical values based on social perceptions of the society in which testing occurs.

Disadvantages:

■ The scale deals with equal-appearing intervals which may not be equal.
■ The use of a continuum of eleven units is arbitrary.
■ The construction of the scale is cumbersome and time-consuming.

OSGOOD'S SEMANTIC DIFFERENTIAL SCALE

Osgood expanded on the work of Thurstone and developed a scale based on the apparent differences between opposite extremes of given adjectives, or adjectival phrases. The Osgood scale uses a number of seven-point rating scales that are bipolar, with each extreme defined by an adjective or adjectival phrase.

Advantage:

■ The scale is relatively easy to apply and interpret.

Disadvantages:

■ The semantic meanings attached to an adjective may vary for different situations and individuals, e.g. 'fast' may mean 50 miles per hour (m.p.h.) to one person and 150 m.p.h. to another.
■ The evaluation of one dimension may affect evaluation of other dimensions, i.e. the halo effect may occur.

Nevertheless, within marketing research the Osgood semantic differential scale may be used with care. When investigating a particular product, the appropriate bipolar adjectives and adjectival phrases are selected from the feedback from the group discussion sessions and then, during later stages of the research, individuals can be asked to express their attitude towards the product and its image using the framework of these adjectives.

LIKERT SCALE

The Likert scale attempts to quantify the attitude that the individual has towards the product or service. Each individual is asked not only if he agrees or disagrees with a given statement, e.g. 'Capital punishment is morally wrong' but also the extent of the agreement, by choosing one of five categories. The categories are given scores that allow quantified measures to be made, as shown in Table 5.8, e.g.:

Table 5.8 Example of Osgood scale

Level of agreement	Scoring	Scoring
Strongly agree	5	+2
Agree	4	+1
Neutral/don't know	3	0
Disagree	2	−1
Strongly agree	1	−2

The minimum and maximum scores can be calculated as can the individual's ranking along this minimum/maximum score range.

Advantages

■ The Likert scale is much easier to administer than the Thurstone scale.
■ It can be adapted readily to suit the specific characteristics of attitude being measured.

Disadvantages

■ The overall score can be obtained in many different ways, so patterns of responses are more meaningful than actual score. Such patterns are easier to obtain from the Osgood semantic differential scale than from the Likert scale.
■ The technique does not produce equal intervals along the scale. There may be some difference in the apparent scale interval between 'disagree' and 'strongly disagree' compared with that between 'neutral/don't know' and 'disagree'.

Other attitude measurement scales have been developed and may be worthy of consideration for further analysis of actual and potential customer attitudes. These include:

GUTTMAN'S SCALOGRAM ANALYSIS

This scale is useful for examining small changes in attitudes, but it uses laborious procedures which are based on the cumulative ordering of items to construct a scalogram, developing the Thurstone approach. Generally, these scales are reliable and can be repeated with different groups and on different occasions to give similar results. However, the scale does not have equal-appearing intervals and its validity depends on item content. The laborious procedures required to develop the scale have dissuaded marketing researchers from using it extensively.

KELLY'S REPERTORY GRID TECHNIQUE

This technique involves mapping individuals' personal constructs, their interrelationships and changes over time. The constructs are considered to be ways in which two things are alike and in the same way different from a third. It can be used in marketing research by asking a respondent to consider three objects, persons or products and to comment on which way two are alike, but also different from a third. Kelly's repertory grid through factor analysis can be used for brand positioning, with the grid indicating the subjective perceptions of individuals.

Thus, while Osgood's semantic differential scale and Likert's scale are the more frequently used methods of measuring attitudes for marketing research, other methods exist and can be developed, as appropriate, provided resource is available.

DEFINITION OF THE MARKETING MIX

One of the major uses of marketing research is to help management make decisions associated with defining the most appropriate marketing mix components. Various research techniques have evolved to determine the most appropriate product, pricing, promotion and place: channels of distribution strategies to use within marketing. These techniques can be used for an individual component of the marketing mix, e.g. when help is required regarding decisions for a promotional campaign, or the techniques may be used cumulatively to examine the likely effectiveness of the whole marketing mix. In the latter situation, test marketing is used.

Product research

Marketing research related to product research and development takes many forms. It will require both desk and field research using both qualitative and quantitative data from which product concepts and product prototypes will evolve. At this stage, various forms of product testing are used. Such testing may lead to full-scale test marketing being conducted with the prime objective of reducing the risk associated with new product development. Details of the test marketing process are discussed in Chapter 7.

Pricing research

Marketing research concerning pricing strategy and implementation can be undertaken using the appropriate methods discussed under desk and field research in above. Frequently, it is this element of the marketing mix that will be examined using test marketing techniques (see p. 246 for further details). The effectiveness of different pricing approaches is determined using control groups to monitor sales achieved. Conjoint or trade-off analysis may be used.

Promotional research

With more than £17bn (US$30bn) being spent on advertising through the major media (television, press, radio and cinema) in the UK alone, promotion in its various forms is considered a major expenditure (or investment) within the marketing mix. Typically, it accounts for 5 per cent or more of sales. Management is required to ensure that such expenditure is justified and uses a range of methods to assess advertising effectiveness.

METHODS OF ASSESSING ADVERTISING EFFECTIVENESS

These methods of assessing advertising's success progress from the pragmatic approach of considering how well an advertisement concept attracts attention from the targeted audience and moves on to more specific testing of the attributes of the advertising used. Initial questions concern the general level of attraction of the advertisement, e.g. 'Does this advertisement make me stop and look at it?' 'Does it attract attention?' 'Is there an original idea in the advertisement?' As the advertising is examined in more depth, questions associated with the details of the advertising campaign approach should be considered, such as 'Does the advertisement fit the advertising strategy selected?' 'Will the promotional programme work?' At this stage the specifics of the advertising campaign and its effectiveness can be ascertained.

Both quantitative and qualitative research methods can be used for advertising research. Quantitative methods centre on the analysis of sales (or market share) and the relationship between the advertising expenditure and the sales achieved. Usually the assessment starts by examining the sales achieved through earlier advertising campaigns and comparing the sales achieved for the present advertising. Sales can be monitored at various stages of the advertising campaign: before the advertising, at the beginning, during, towards the end, or after the end of the campaign. Such sales can be monitored using internal sales records which would indicate the growth that was achieved. Sales (or market share) can be assessed by using continuous tracking data such as those provided by consumer panels which show not only the sales performance of the product in question but also its performance against competing products. However, sales data may be difficult to interpret, especially where there is a time lag between advertising in the media and the consequent sales effect. While tracking sales (or market share) provides some indication of the effectiveness of an advertising campaign it may not be the complete answer, and further research may be required.

Although generally it is preferable to use quantitative data to measure the effectiveness of advertising, there are occasions when such quantitative measures may not be available, e.g. when the advertiser has to decide the nature of the advertising to be used. At this stage, research techniques that give more qualitative assessments may be appropriate. Frequently, at the early stages of advertising development, the techniques used will examine subjective issues to ascertain the favoured advertising concepts to select. Often group discussions are used to explore the potential communication and appeal of different creative approaches, e.g. 'What is the perceived message?' 'How relevant and appealing is this to the brand and its potential consumers?'

Once the advertising concept has been agreed, it is converted into advertising 'stories' which will be the base for the advertisements to be considered for the advertising campaign using common themes and 'strap lines' in the different types of media, television, press, radio and cinema. 'Mock-ups' or rough illustrations of the proposed advertisements using storyboards and, on occasion, videos are introduced to consumer juries for their comment. Using image and awareness studies, advertising effectiveness may be assessed in terms of its impact, reach and communication ability on actual or potential consumers. Measures used to assess impact can include sentence recall; potential reach can be gauged by recognition from a prompt of the advertisement, and communication is ascertained from the changes achieved in the brand image of the product being advertised. Typically, recall tests have a low level of recall, so, more commonly, recognition tests using some form of prompt are used. Attitude testing, projective association testing, as well as consumer surveys and even test marketing trials may be used, if appropriate. Advertising effectiveness assessments can be undertaken before, after or during the advertising campaign.

TELEVISION AUDIENCE RESEARCH

With about 25 per cent of advertising expenditure being spent on television, a high proportion of advertising research concentrates on the television media. Within the UK, BARB acts as an executive body on behalf of the television industry, for the provision of the television audience measurement service. BARB is a provider of information on all elements of the television industry, broadcasters, buying agencies and advertisers. It uses professional research suppliers to conduct and report on audience research (see enquiries@barb.co.uk). It commissions television audience research covering both audience measurement and audience reaction for the Independent Television Companies' Association (ITCA) and the British Broadcasting Corporation (BBC).

The system uses a combination of a PeopleMetering panel, polling and processing to measure audiences. The panel covers more than 4,700 households with online meters attached to their television sets. Each set is monitored by a Remote Detection Unit (RDU) passing information online overnight to a central processor. The television set meters record the programmes when the television is switched on and push-button handsets monitor the audience through the allocation of numbers to all household members over the age of 4 years. Electronic diaries, using light pens instead of pen and ink have been developed to support the set-meter recording. The panel indicates television audience within the selected households which can be used to estimate national audiences.

BARB audience measurements have been criticized on a number of grounds, as shown below:

■ In 1997 the charge for a tape giving the weekly audience estimates is in excess of £30,000 (US$53,820). Subscribers are liable to an annual registration fee of £5,000 (US$8,970) and there may be an additional £1,000 (US$1,794) levy for each instance of third-party use (MRS, 1997). It is expected that charges will have increased substantially for current rates and will continue to do so.

■ The sample used for the panel is small (under 5,000) compared with the potential total number of households of 14m.

■ Panel members may not be accurate in recording their watching of television programmes, and indeed, although they are within the room when the television set is turned on, actually they may not be watching the television programmes or the advertising being transmitted.

■　Video-recorders further confuse the audience measurements. Frequently, television programmes are videoed for individuals to watch the programme at another time and these recordings are likely to exclude the advertisements, presenting more difficulties in audience measurement.

Nevertheless, despite the expense and the imprecision of audience measuring tools, the BARB audience measurements continue to be used, as they provide the best information available for television advertising decisions. Furthermore, considerable investment is being made in the development of improved audience measuring tools to enhance the panel data.

In 1996 the Pan-European Television research consortium (PETV) of cable and satellite operators, including BBC World, CNN International, Discovery, NBC and TV5 was formed. In 1998 PETV launched the Satellite Television Audience Measurement Partnership (STAMP) to provide across Europe a single television audience measurement system which

DEVELOPMENTS IN TELEVISION AUDIENCE RATING MEASUREMENT

C
A
S
E

S
T
U
D
Y

Nielsen Media Research, a subsidiary of A.C. Nielsen, owned by VNU, based in the Netherlands (see Table 5.1) is the ratings company whose audience measurements have for decades served as the benchmark for advertising-supported television. In 2006, in the US, Nielsen launched a set of national television ratings that take into account programmes replayed on digital video-recorders (DVRs) such as TiVo. The technical hurdles are formidable. Nielsen once made do with devices that checked to which channel a television dial was tuned. But its systems became overwhelmed by DVRs, which allow viewers to watch programmes when they please and to skip past commercials. Time-sensitive advertisers, such as film studios, want more precise data concerning viewers. No longer is knowledge that a particular programme has been replayed sufficient. Advertisers want details as to when viewers watched as well as whether or not the viewer skipped over their commercial.

To solve the problem, Nielsen invested more than US$10m (£5.6m) in a new system to overhaul the way it collects data. The company convinced television stations to coat their signals with distinct audio and video signals at their broadcast source. Nielsen's new Active/Passive Meter picks up the code when the television is playing and then cross-checks it against a database of programming schedules. However, industry's reaction has been cautious. Some media buyers, such as Magna Global, have ignored the new DVR viewer measurements, largely out of scepticism whether DVR viewers actually watch the commercials. That has prompted the six US broadcast networks to fight back, by using Nielsen data to argue that DVRs have led to increased viewing and advertising exposure. Such debates are likely to increase as Nielsen attempts to measure video-on-demand viewing in 2006 and, eventually, tackles iPods, mobile phones and other devices.

Source: adapted from Chaffin and van Duyn (2005).

MARKETING RESEARCH'S STRATEGIC CONTRIBUTION TO THE EXPANSION OF CARBONATED SOFT DRINKS MARKETS IN EMERGING ECONOMIES

A.G. Barr, the UK's leading independent branded carbonated soft drinks (CSD) manufacturer, founded in Falkirk, Scotland, in 1875, has its headquarters in Glasgow. It has three UK plants with about 950 employees producing its Irn-Bru soft drink, introduced in 1901, which, has about 5 per cent of the UK CSD market. Despite tough domestic competition, Irn-Bru is Scotland's largest-selling single flavoured CSD with a market share value as recorded by A.C. Nielsen Scantrak in excess of 20 per cent of total CSD in Scotland in the year 2004–05. It is the third best-selling soft drink in the UK, after Coca-Cola and Pepsi, outselling high-profile brands such as Tango, Lilt, Dr Pepper, Sprite and 7-up. In the year to January 2005 Barr's turnover was £127.2m (US$228m; €186m), an increase of 3 per cent on the previous year and pre-profits of £15.6m (US$28m; €23m), an increase of 13 per cent (A.G. Barr, 2005).

International strategic market expansion

In the late 1980s Barr considered international expansion options within Europe, concentrating on France, Germany and the Benelux countries. However, marketing research showed that the MNCs Coca-Cola and Pepsi dominated these mature markets, making competition fierce and margins tight. Consequently, Barr looked to other emerging countries, in particular to Russia, which marketing research showed had a large population, with growing prosperity and a rising standard of living, driving a growing demand for consumer goods.

Barr uses different market entry strategies to match the level of perceived risk involved. In high-risk economies preference is given to exporting, with no production presence in the local economy. Orders are not actively pursued in these markets and business tends to be *ad hoc*. In other markets, a market attractiveness model is used which weighs scores for each market based on population, GNP, soft drink market size, language barriers, bureaucracy, corruption index, etc. Investment decisions are based on market score, using the model and Irn Bru's test-marketing performance in the market. Interestingly, the market attractiveness model results in many underdeveloped countries such as Russia scoring much higher than developed countries like Japan.

Barr takes no equity stake in overseas markets, preferring to operate production franchises, with revenue and profit coming solely from the price received for its exported essence. Currently, Barr's principal export markets are Russia and Spain, but it also operates in the US, Greece, Netherlands and Cyprus as well as in parts of Africa and Asia. Irn-Bru is its prime export brand.

Spain

Barr has been exporting Irn-Bru to Spain for the past thirty years predominantly selling in the tourist areas such as the Costas, the Balearic Islands and the Canary Islands. It operates through two local bottlers – one in Mallorca and one in Zaragoza. Sales of Irn-Bru have remained buoyant with British tourists and, encouragingly, research has shown that the product is also popular among Spanish consumers, so channels of distribution targeted at the local market are being developed.

Russia

In 1994 Barr began direct exports of the Irn Bru brand to Russia, using distributors providing sales of about US$500,000 (£279,000: €409,000) p.a. However, direct exporting resulted in long lead times and, consequently, in 1998, with venture capital support from the US, Barr set up a manufacturing franchise with a Russian partner to make its Irn-Bru and cream soda Vysotka brands in association with a local distributor. Unfortunately the poor local infrastructure, limited product range together with the adverse economic climate, which prevented charging premium prices, posed challenges to profitable growth. Yet Barr persevered and, in 2002, it agreed a manufacturing franchise contract with the Pepsi Bottling Group (PBG) of Russia to produce, distribute and sell Irn-Bru across Russia. Thanks to the partnership with PBG and the continued investment in marketing activity, Irn-Bru has become established as one of the leading brands in the country, with a healthy market share and very high levels of awareness showing considerable potential for the future. The Russians, like the Scots, have a 'sweet tooth' leading to high soft drink consumption. 'The place has a fantastic buzz. There are lots of street cafés, clubs, restaurants and far more designer shops than you would see in many large cities. There are 144.5m people, making it the seventh largest country in the world, so there is great potential for Scots to export in areas like construction, architecture, fashion design and so on' (A.G. Barr annual report, 2003).

Within its marketing strategy, management pursued its promotion targeted towards both the end consumer and the trade, especially retailers, cafés and nightclubs. Early in 1998, television advertising was undertaken to create awareness among consumers and the trade prior to a new Irn-Bru brand launch. However, in August 1998 the Russian economic crisis with the devaluation of the rouble and associated high inflation led to severe cash-flow problems for the trade. Most major competitors withdrew from Russia, but Barr decided to remain, and set out to support its trade suppliers. The sales force was increased and the trade was given favourable credit terms in return for volume orders. This approach positively increased Irn-Bru's brand image within the trade and with the public at a time when the competition was less visible.

Nevertheless, difficulties were encountered with the Irn-Bru brand name, which Russians found hard to pronounce. The traditional humour associated with the brand was difficult to communicate to potential consumers, e.g. the strap line 'only for adults', used as a joke to attract young customers, was misinterpreted and taken in its literal sense. A risqué advertising campaign based on the 'pregnant city' theme was misunderstood. Consequently, marketing research was undertaken directed at both consumers and the retail trade to address the situation. It was contracted to Russian-based marketing research agencies working in support of the advertising agency to develop an effective advertising campaign.

The consumer research used a combination of focus groups; in-store interviews with shoppers involved product sampling programmes and telephone interviews with consumers who responded to the telephone hot line number which was printed on the Irn-Bru labels. The findings revealed that:

- Irn-Bru was well perceived but there was a problem with the 'strange' foreign name.
- Consumers were willing to pay a premium price if consistent quality and taste could be ensured.
- There was an opportunity to develop the carbonated mixer drinks market.
- Consumers wanted a smaller, cheaper pack than the Irn Bru 500 ml and 2.0 l bottles.

Trade research involved face-to-face interviews and a two-day open discussion conference where clients could confer about their business needs and question Barr's management about future plans. The research showed that:

- Although Irn-Bru was selling well, clients wanted a wider range of drinks.
- Clients would pay a premium price if strong advertising were given in support.
- Large retailers would accept premium-priced products if they were given support with in-store promotion.
- Retailers lacked space for specialist promotions.
- Larger clients expected better credit terms for which they were willing to pay a premium.
- Many clients had extensive business interests in the Russian regions.

Management determined to address these issues. From the research findings a US$2m (£1.1m: €1.6m) promotional campaign was developed to relaunch the Irn-Bru brand. It was based on an amusing animated ostrich-like character, with a Russian persona dressed in boots typically worn in a winter snow setting. Irn-Bru was positioned as a truly alternative brand that did not take life too seriously and had 'fun' appeal, which related to Russian humour of all age groups to widen the target market. Throughout the campaign, telephone interviewing was conducted to gauge consumer and trade reaction which enable minor modifications to the advertising to be made.

Following this experience, Barr combines its promotional methods, sometimes using UK advertising and, as appropriate, tailoring its methods by using advertising agencies in host countries such as Russia and Poland to ensure that the campaign message is communicated in a style and manner that are readily understood.

In Russia Irn-Bru's first major 'above the line' promotional campaign started in May 1999 with a television campaign supported by commercials on the major radio stations such as Radio Maximum, outdoor posters and a 'wacky' fan club website. The commercials provided a talking point to attract attention. Instead of spoken words, the characters used a nonsensical but humorous catch phrase 'Xaba-xaba' (pronounced Habba-habba) associated with the Irn-Bru brand to minimize communication confusion. The advertising achieved a high 92 per cent prompted brand awareness level in December 1999 and, indeed, the catch phrase became popular slang.

'Below the line' promotion was targeted at both the consumer and the trade to increase trade awareness and support. Consumers were targeted through field marketing undertaken in conjunction with the Moscow-based Radio Maximum. Promotional activities included product tastings with consumer feedback sessions and competitions with merchandising goods.

The website was developed to provide corporate and brand information together with details of field promotion, merchandising offers and the Irn-Bru fan club.

In this way it can be seen that marketing research has been used to gauge customer reaction and trade opinion to help in developing the marketing mix, including a distinctive promotional approach. Using marketing research, including market tracking data, Irn Bru has continued to perform well in Russia, maintaining a market share of around 1 per cent of the CSD market (A.G. Barr, 2005).

Expansion within Central and Eastern Europe (CEE)

Following the success achieved in the Russian market, Irn-Bru began to investigate the potential of taking Irn-Bru to CEE, in particular, to Poland. In 2004 Barr undertook marketing research in Poland. It tested two 'cells' of respondents; one was exposed to the Irn-Bru UK advertising and the other to the international approach applied in Russia. The initial intention was to use the UK-style advertising, with the Russian being included as a benchmark as a precaution in case the UK tested route failed to deliver.

Both routes were tested against a Key Action Standards model which Irn-Bru has to pass to be considered seriously by any potential franchisee. Three of the Action Standards measured Irn-Bru are benchmarked against the results of other FMCGs.

Poland

Irn-Bru as a product achieved, or exceeded, all the Key Action Standards in the test marketing, although there was some concern regarding the target entry price. In the pre-trial tests the vast majority of teenagers said:

- They would 'definitely' or 'probably' buy Irn-Bru.
- Irn-Bru was one of the 'best they had ever tasted' or 'better than most soft drinks'.
- Irn-Bru was 'good' or 'excellent' in terms of taste.
- Irn-Bru was 'very refreshing' or 'refreshing'.

An even higher proportion of teenagers considered Irn Bru was:

- 'Just right' overall in terms of mouth feel.
- Of the right colour, fitting the taste 'very well' or 'quite well'.

The Polish results were sufficiently positive for the marketing research agency to recommend the launch of Irn-Bru in Poland. After extensive search for a partner, in 2005 Barr selected a well established distributor with limited experience in soft drinks distribution but an outstanding track record in marketing and bringing FMCG products to market.

As this book goes to press, Barr and its partner are preparing to launch Irn-Bru in Poland during 2006. A roll-out market entry whereby performance is monitored carefully is proposed.

Source: adapted from Stone (2005); A.G. Barr PLC annual report (2003); A.G. Barr PLC annual report (2005).

Acknowledgement: Marilyn Stone appreciates the support given by A.G. Barr (Soft Drinks) PLC in preparing this case.

CASE QUESTIONS

1   **Consider the role of marketing research in determining a successful promotional strategy for to pursue for the Irn Bru brand in emerging economies.** Marketing research is used to support marketing decision making by reducing risk. It does not replace marketing management decision making but rather provides deeper understanding of consumer and trade perceptions. Armed with marketing research findings, management should make better decisions.

2   **What are the difficulties in transposing marketing research findings from one country to another?** In the case discussed, the promotional tactics used in the UK were misunderstood when introduced in Russia. Marketing research showed it was necessary to develop a brand image and associated promotional message that related to Russian culture and humour. Marketing research was used to test the acceptability of alternative promotional concepts, with the campaign based on a bird creature wearing Russian-type boots being particularly favoured. Similar marketing research in Poland showed it preferable to use promotion that relates to local culture rather than import that used in the UK.

3   **What are the challenges of undertaking marketing research in international markets?** Decisions have to be made regarding the selection of the marketing research agency including whether to use a local agency or a subsidiary of an international marketing research agency. In the case discussed, marketing research agencies are encouraged to work closely with the advertising agency to develop the creative element of the proposed promotion.

would give credible, affordable viewing data for advertisers. This pilot, run by RSL-IPSOS, used a prompted diary approach to measure both in-home and out-of home viewing (which has a large share of cable and satellite's market); set meters were considered impracticable, as some European countries have up to seventy television channels. 250 households per country are sampled as well as 150 high-income homes.

However, as digital television grew, some global television operators like Discovery started to buy into local television audience measurement services, a trend that is expected to continue. PETV has been replaced by INTV, which has a different objective. It is an informal group of research managers that occasionally commission original pan-European research. It represents the interests of international broadcasters to suppliers of industry projects. Further information can be found at the website: www.intvresearch.com/members. html. This form of panel adds to the national television panels such as that for BARB in the UK (discussed above).

In the UK, the quantitative television audience panel data are supplemented by audience research undertaken by the television producers to determine reaction to the programmes broadcast on air. The BBC research department conducts the Audience Reaction Service (ARS). It has a daily survey of radio listening whereby a sample of 1,000 persons over the age of 12 is interviewed daily concerning radio listening habits and some of these respondents are asked to complete a diary recording the television programmes they have watched and their appreciation of those programmes. This information is used to monitor audiences and their opinions of television programmes, which may add to the panel audience data.

PRESS READERSHIP RESEARCH

Within the UK, about 50 per cent (£8bn: US$14bn) of all advertising is spent on the press in its various forms, making it important to ascertain the reach of the different press publications, i.e. the numbers and types of people who purchase and read the publications. Press circulation figures (the number of copies sold) are provided by the Audit Bureau of Circulations (ABC) and British Rate and Data (BRAD). However, this only provides data on how many copies of each publication are sold and does not indicate the number or type of reader a publication might have.

The JICNARS representing the media, advertisers and advertising agencies provides information on readership of the major press publications. It has contracted out the NRS to the market research agency RSL. The survey covers 130 or so national publications by interviewing a random sample of 30,000 adults each year. Reports which give publication readership profiles in terms of demographics, social class, sex, regional distribution are issued twice per year, covering January to December and July to June. Details of the publication penetration achieved using the measure of the readers per copy and the number of publications read per head are also given. From these data, the readership profile and the penetration achieved for the publications can be ascertained and matched to the requirements of the target audience for the advertising. The Joint Industry Committee for Regional Press Readership (JICREG) provides details of readership of the regional press, covering 1,600 daily and weekly newspapers, and free sheets to supplement JICNARS data.

RADIO LISTENER RESEARCH

In the UK radio advertising has had a low, but increasing, share (3 per cent valued at about £582m: US$1,044bn) of total advertising expenditure, which has traditionally attracted limited marketing research interest. However, as radio advertising has become more popular for reaching targeted groups, especially the under 30 age group, so has the demand for effective audience measurement increased.

The Radio Audience Joint Advertising Research (RAJAR) industry body has responsibility for assessing radio audience levels. RAJAR has been using IPSOS-RSL to collect the data for UK radio audience measurement in a contract worth £11m (US$20m) over four years. It uses a panel of radio listeners targeted at adult individuals. Individuals use a personal repertoire diary termed a 'card sort' diary choosing from a set of cards listing all stations available in the area. Audiences for all radio stations report each quarter on a three-month rolling basis. With that contract nearing completion, in 2005 RAJAR issued an invitation to tender for its audience measurement survey. It remains to be seen who will undertake the contract in the future.

POSTER AUDIENCE RESEARCH

In the UK outdoor and transport advertising is about £900m (US$1,615m). The outdoor advertising industry's Poster Audience Research body (POSTAR) invested £4m (US$7m) in poster effectiveness research over the three years 1999 to 2002 to encourage greater use of this media.

Place: channels of distribution research

Marketing research is used to help in logistics decision making related to the selection and use of channels of distribution to enable the product or service to reach the end user. Test marketing can confirm the appropriate selection of distribution channels. The intermediaries within the channels of distribution, especially the retailer, are increasingly powerful within the value chain. These issues will be developed in Chapter 11.

MARKETING RESEARCH INDUSTRY CONTROLS

Traditionally the practices used by the UK marketing and the marketing research industry have been controlled by its professional marketing bodies.

Marketing research professional bodies

MRS

In the UK the leading professional body for marketing researchers is the MRS. It liaises with members, users of marketing research, the public and government to develop the marketing research industry and to increase awareness of its benefits to society. It has lists of marketing research agencies and member marketing researchers together with profiles of their expertise that can help in agency and/or market researcher selection.

In 2004 MRS had 8,204 members working in marketing research agencies, industry and commerce. Marketing research may also be undertaken by persons who are not members of MRS; in particular, many field interviewers undertaking both consumer and industrial marketing research are not members. It is estimated that there are around 10,000 persons directly involved in marketing research within the UK. These marketing researchers (and agencies) cover the whole of the UK but are concentrated in London and the south-east of England; some work in other countries, especially within continental Europe.

The MRS operates a Code of Conduct, revised in 2005, which all its members agree to follow in their marketing research (MRS, 2005a: codeline@mrs.org.uk and www.mrs.

org.uk/standards). The code regulates the procedures for marketing research, covering the confidentiality of market research findings, the ways in which market research interviews are obtained and conducted and the use of the data collected. MRS also has guidelines for handling databases which supplement the Data Protection Act (1984) regulation to protect confidentiality of individual's personal information.

The principles underpinning the MRS Code of Conduct are summarized as follows (MRS, 2006: 17–23):

■ Research is founded upon the willing co-operation of the public and of business organizations. It depends upon their confidence that it is conducted honestly, objectively, without unwelcome intrusion and without harm to respondents. Its purpose is to collect and analyse information, and not directly to create sales nor to influence the opinions of anyone participating in it.

■ The general public and other interested parties are entitled to complete assurance that every research project is carried out strictly in accordance with the code, and that their rights of privacy are respected. In particular, they must be assured that no information which could be used to identify them will be made available without their agreement to anyone other than the researcher responsible for conducting the research. They must also be assured that the information they supply will not be used for any purposes other than those described and that they will not be adversely affected or embarrassed as a direct result of their participation in the research project.

■ Respondents must be informed as to the purpose of the research and the likely length of time necessary for the collection of the information.

■ Finally, the research findings themselves must always be reported accurately and never used to mislead anyone, in any way.

The MRS maintains a professional educational programme leading to the MRS Diploma, which is the entry base for membership. MRS publications which provide useful guidance regarding the marketing research industry's responsibilities and practices include: 'A Basic Guide to the Data Protection Act 1998 guidelines' (February 2002); 'Research: decisions: evaluating and buying fieldwork services' (2004). Useful websites: www.mrs.org.uk, www.iqcs.org, www.bsi-global.com, www.hse.gov.uk or www.suzylamplugh.org.

BMRA

The BMRA is the trade association for companies and organizations involved in the supply of marketing research. It operates in juxtaposition with the MRS, whose membership is of individuals who work in, or have an interest in, market and social research.

In 1998 the BMRA was formed to represent the UK marketing research industry from the merger of the UK market research industry trade bodies, the Association of Market Survey Organizations (AMSO) and the Association of British Market Research Companies (ABMRC). In 2005 almost 180 companies and organizations were members of the BMRA. Their combined turnover represents about 65 per cent of all the marketing research placed in the UK, estimated at £1.22bn (US$3bn) in 2003 (MRS, 2005b: 16).

ESOMAR AND EUROPEAN FEDERATION OF ASSOCIATIONS OF MARKET RESEARCH
ORGANIZATIONS (EFAMRO)

ESOMAR is the traditional representative of the European marketing research industry, which promotes the use of opinion and market research for improving decision making in business and society globally. Founded in 1948, ESOMAR brings together 4,000 members in 100 countries. It facilitates the exchange of experiences between suppliers and users of research in order to optimize the integration of research results in the decision-making process.

However, ESOMAR is facing competition from the EFAMRO, which represents major national marketing research supplier associations for Belgium, the Czech Republic, France, Germany, Italy, the Netherlands, Poland, Portugal, Spain, Sweden, Turkey and the UK, promoting the role and value of research to European governments and the European Commission.

Both ESOMAR and EFAMRO monitor the rules, regulations and directives that have been introduced to control the marketing research industry. ESOMAR, in particular, has introduced a guideline for Internet research to show legislators ways in which the marketing research industry can regulate itself on the Web.

CHARTERED INSTITUTE OF MARKETING (CIM)

The CIM is the UK professional marketing association which encourages good practice in marketing. Some of its members may also be members of the specialist marketing research associations. The CIM maintains a professional CIM Certificate and Diploma educational programme with EU approval which is the entry base for membership.

Ethical issues in marketing research

Conventional marketing data collection methods are considered to be expensive to undertake; consequently, alternative methods are evolving which may threaten the traditional approaches of marketing researchers as well as individual privacy. In particular, householders are being asked to participate in national shopper surveys to obtain money-off coupons and samples. Respondents answer questions related to their lifestyles and the brands of products that they purchase which then provide a database that can be used for direct sales targeting.

As discussed above the MRS Code of Practice for its members precludes linkage and misleading sales practices using marketing research and sales research, i.e. selling under the guise of marketing research, or 'sugging', where companies pretend to be conducting a survey in order to identify potential sales leads. Marketing research should not identify individual respondent responses to clients, unless the respondent's permission to do so is obtained. Nevertheless, despite efforts to introduce controls, it is common practice for non-professional sales persons, or 'suggers', to use marketing research as an entry to the sales pitch. For example, double-glazing sales forces might ask questions regarding house improvements and then use the information obtained as sales leads. This is contrary to the MRS Code of Practice recommendations. Another related concern is fund raising under the guise of marketing research, or 'frugging', which is sometimes used by charities to raise donations. A postal survey is sent to potential donors directed at, say, health issues, which concludes with a request for funds to be sent to the charity concerned. The respondent is attracted to the issues through the apparent *bona fide* research before the direct question to contribute to the charity is made. Once again, the MRS Code of Practice precludes undertaking marketing research and disclosing personal details of the respondent for the purposes of charity fund raising. The data collected through marketing research should be kept separate and should not identify individual respondents from the database for fund-raising appeals.

Government regulations are being made to prevent sugging and frugging. The US in 1995 introduced a ruling against sugging which was extended to frugging through the Telemarketing Sales Rule in 2005. Within the EU, preparation of similar controls is being developed through sales promotion regulation.

The marketing research industry is concerned with other ethically related issues. In particular, the increased linkage between retailers and marketing research agencies to develop marketing databases, e.g. Boots the Chemist, the UK's leading high-street pharmacy, renewed its EPOS retail audit data with retail trackers IRI. The decision in 1994 to award Boots first contract to supply data for the health and beauty manufacturers exclusively to one agency caused protest from one competitor, A.C. Nielsen, to the Office of Fair Trading (OFT). Nielsen argued that IRI's contracts with Boots and Superdrug gave it a monopoly on data provision to the Health and Beauty Audit (HBA) market. In this case the OFT concluded that the deals were of benefit to users and would not intervene. At the same time the HBA industry watched to see how the European Commission's 1996 ruling that Nielsen's business practices were anti-competitive could affect the Boots contract. Nielsen undertook to unbundle its services and to stop demanding exclusive contracts with retailers, but the issue is one of considerable debate.

CONCLUSION

This chapter has defined the nature of marketing research and has emphasized its role in management decision making. While marketing research will not necessarily guarantee a perfect solution to marketing issues, it can help to solve many marketing problems. Marketing research is defined as a systematic research approach to determine market demand. It gathers market data from a range of sources which can be fed into a MIS linked into the organization's Management Information System. The sources may be from internal reporting, marketing intelligence and marketing research and these, in turn, can be analysed to develop appropriate marketing databases. Usually, the process of collecting, analysing and using data is continuous, with inter linkage between the source data. For example, when the use of sales reports (internal reporting) include information gained from sales force attendance at trade seminars (marketing intelligence) and both these types of information are used for marketing research studies. All three types of data are analysed and the resulting findings entered into the MIS.

Marketing research may use either qualitative or quantitative research methods, or a combination of both. Qualitative research methods include focus interviews and group discussions. Quantitative research methods cover the various types of surveys, including using personal face-to-face, telephone interviewing, the Internet as well as the post.

Marketing research is used to determine the most appropriate marketing mix components. Once the individual elements of the marketing mix have been defined, the process of test marketing can be used to reduce the risk of new product introduction to check the proposed product approach, promotional activity, pricing strategy and channels of distribution use in the marketing mix. The high costs of undertaking full-scale marketing research are encouraging the search for alternative methods of ascertaining likely new product success.

Throughout the marketing research process, the major resource constraints of finance, staff expertise and availability as well as time have to be considered. These constraints are encouraging users of marketing research to contract out their needs to marketing research agencies rather than to keep these services within the organization. The marketing research role within the organization is increasingly one of monitoring the research process rather than of actually undertaking the research.

With the growth of professionalism within the marketing research industry, especially the marketing research agency sector, there is increasing awareness of the need for industry quality controls to manage the ethical issues related to marketing research practice. Such controls are coming from the users of the marketing research, the practitioners and from the source of the marketing research data, i.e. the general consumer public. It is expected that controls will increase, adding to the professionalism of the industry to the advantage of all concerned, especially the respondents to marketing research.

REVIEW QUESTIONS

1   Using examples, compare and contrast the four types of information gathering involved in developing a MIS.

2   How can qualitative and quantitative marketing research methods be assimilated into an effective marketing research programme when assessing market demand for a consumer product?

3   Discuss the circumstances whereby personal interviewing would be likely to be favoured rather than postal survey techniques in marketing research.

4   Evaluate how useful consumer panels are in determining the most appropriate marketing mix components at the various stages of the PLC.

5   A major detergent manufacturer proposes spending £2.5 million (US$4.5 million) on a twelve-month national advertising campaign to promote an environmentally friendly washing liquid. Advise the marketing director how the effectiveness of the campaign could be monitored.

RECOMMENDED SUPPLEMENTARY READING

Aaker, D.A., Kumar, V. and Day, G.S. (2004) *Marketing research*, 8th edn, New York: Wiley.

Baines, P. and Chansarkar, B. (2002) *Introducing marketing research,* Chichester: Wiley.

Birn, R.J. (2004) '*The effective use of market research: how to drive and focus better business decisions*', 4th edn, London and Sterling VA: MRS and Kogan Page.

Burns, A.C. and Bush, R.F. (2002) *Marketing research: online research applications,* 4th edn, Englewood Cliffs NJ: Prentice Hall.

Crouch, S. and Housden, M. (2003) *Marketing research for managers*, 3rd edn, Oxford: Butterworth Heinemann.

Hague, P. (2002) *Marketing research: a guide to planning, methodology and evaluation,* 3rd edn, London: Kogan Page.

Hague, P., Hague, N. and Morgan, C.A. (2004) *Market research in practice: a guide to the basics*, London and Sterling VA, MRS and Kogan Page.

Hair, J., Bush, R. and Ortinau, D. (2006) *Marketing research: within a changing environment,* 3rd edn, New York: McGraw-Hill.

Kent, R. (1999) *Marketing research: measurement, methods and application*, London: Thomson.

Lescher, J.F. (1995) *Online market research: cost effective searching of the Internet and online databases,* Reading MA: Addison Wesley.

Malhorta, N.K. and Birks, D.F. (2006) *Marketing research: an applied approach*, 2nd edn, Harlow: Pearson FT Prentice Hall.

Malhorta, N.K. and Peterson, M. (2006) *Basic marketing research: a decision-making approach*, 2nd edn, Harlow: Pearson FT Prentice Hall.

McDaniel, C. and Gates, R. (2004) *Marketing research essentials*, 4th edn, New York: Wiley.

McGivern, Y. (2003) *The practice of market and social research: an introduction*, Harlow: Pearson FT Prentice Hall.

McNeil, R. (2005) *Business to business market research: understanding and measuring business markets,* London: Kogan Page.

Oppenheim, A.N. (1992) *Questionnaire design, interviewing and attitude measurement,* 2nd edn, London: Pinter.

Proctor, T. (2003) *Essentials of marketing research*, 3rd edn, Harlow: Pearson FT Prentice Hall.

Wright, L.T. and Crimp, M. (2000) *The marketing research process,* 5th edn, New York: Prentice Hall.

Zikmund, W.G. (2000) *Exploring marketing research*, 7th edn, Orlando FL: Dryden.

6 SEGMENTATION TARGETING AND POSITIONING

LEARNING OBJECTIVES

When you have completed this unit you should be able to:

■ describe the benefits of breaking markets down into smaller, more manageable parts or segments;

■ explain the ways in which market segments are defined in both organizational and consumer markets;

■ list the segmentation variables that can be applied when segmenting markets;

■ create criteria for selecting and evaluating target markets;

■ list the steps involved in positioning;

■ prepare a perceptual map based on marketing research data;

■ recommend a segmentation, targeting and positioning strategy for an organization.

Organizations that sell to consumer and business markets recognise that they cannot appeal to all buyers in those markets, or at least not to all buyers in the same way. Rather than trying to compete in an entire market, sometimes against superior competitors, each company must identify the parts of the market that it can serve best. This chapter explains the process of segmentation: dividing a market into distinct groups of buyers with different needs, characteristics or behaviour that might require separate products or marketing mixes.

Once the market has been segmented the marketer must determine a targeting strategy. This involves decisions about which and how many customer groups the organization is going to 'target' with its product or service. This chapter considers the targeting options that are available to the marketer.

The final stage involves establishing a positive image of the product or service in the minds of consumers. It explains what is involved in positioning and describes the positioning strategies that are available to organizations.

The chapter concludes with the opportunity to apply the technique of segmentation, targeting and positioning to the Tiberias Hotel case study.

INTRODUCTION

In the early days of motor car manufacturing Henry Ford stated that 'the customer can have any car that he wants, so long as it is black'. He was speaking at a time when the novelty value of the product enabled him to treat his customers as identical parts of a mass market.

Increasingly, marketers in both consumer and industrial markets are accepting that, because of the varying characteristics, needs, wants and interests of customers, there are few markets where a single product or service is satisfactory for all. Marketers have developed a technique, known as segmentation, that involves breaking the market down into groups of customers with similar characteristics in order to concentrate on serving the needs of one or two groups really well rather than trying to satisfy the mass market. In this section the benefits, methods and criteria of successful segmentation will be discussed.

LEARNING OBJECTIVES

After completing this section, you should be able to:

■   **Describe the benefits of segmentation.**
■   **Identify ways in which a range of different markets could be segmented.**
■   **Apply key assessment criteria to identify viable market segments.**
■   **Compare and contrast the segmentation variables that are used for consumer and organizational markets.**

MARKET SEGMENTATION

Segmentation involves an analysis of the nature and composition of a market to identify groups of potential buyers who have similar needs or characteristics, or display similar behaviour. These groups are known as market segments. Each segment seeks a unique set of benefits from the product or service purchased. Segmentation is quite different from a total market approach. For example, it used to be common for many people to use a 'family' medicated shampoo. While 'family' shampoos are still produced their share progressively has been taken away by others which have been tailored to the needs of particular groups of users. Consider the sorts of benefit desired by the following groups:

- People with a dry, itchy, flaky scalp.
- Babies.
- People with greasy hair.
- People with permed or damaged hair.
- Men.

It is relatively easy to consider the benefits desired by the first four categories, and various manufacturers' brands can be readily identified which are tailored to them. Manufacturers of hair products consider it worth while to construct specific marketing programmes to cater to the needs of these groups. The trade-off between the increased costs and the potential sales gains to be made from offering products targeted at specific segments is a fundamental managerial concern. Managers should ask themselves two important questions:

- How many segments should we define?
- On what criteria should each group be selected so that the marketing opportunity is maximized?

The example below illustrates how one company, the Vanity Fair (VF) organization, addressed these questions successfully.

Segmentation in practice: VF organization

In the 1980s the VF organization in the US overlooked important changes in consumer markets and, consequently, experienced plummeting sales in its well known brands such as Wrangler, Lee jeans and VF lingerie. The company responded by commissioning detailed marketing research into fashion changes and establishing closer relations with fashion retailers. The research found that although the company had developed specific promotions and pricing strategies for products which were aimed at different segments, it had created some confusion in the market place by selling all of its brands through a wide variety of retailers. As a result of the research VF refocused its distribution by targeting specific brand names towards the retail outlets patronized by specific segments. For example, high-involvement purchases such as the sophisticated Girbaud line were stocked only in higher-priced department stores, while mass-marketing outlets likely to be patronized by low-involvement purchasers stocked the cheaper brands of Lee jeans, Wrangler and Rustler. VF's cheapest jeans are sold through discount stores.

Segmenting consumer markets

The craft of market segmentation owes much to the study of consumer buyer behaviour. For example, many of the bases for segmenting markets are derived directly from the ways in which the consumer constructs his or her identity in terms of gender, family, social class and lifestyle. This is not surprising, as many of those factors which help confer an individual identity on individuals are also badges of group membership. Such group membership signals specific needs to which organizations respond by means of the offering which they devise.

Theoretically the marketer's choice of a segmentation base is related to consumers' needs for, uses of or behaviour towards a product or service. The main variables used as bases for segmenting consumer markets can be grouped under the four headings below:

- Geographical: e.g. region, urban/suburban/rural and population density.
- Demographic: e.g. age, sex, marital status, socio-economic status, social class, religion and education.
- Psychographic: e.g. lifestyles, personality, self-image, value perceptions and motives.
- Behavioural: e.g. use rate and volume, occasions when used, brand loyalty and benefits sought.

Each of these variables will be discussed in greater detail below.

GEOGRAPHICAL SEGMENTATION

This method defines customers according to their location. Geographical factors can play a major role in segmentation. For example, for businesses such as discount warehouses, major supermarkets and franchised restaurant operations, market density is an important factor to consider. This refers to the number of customers within a unit of land area such as a square kilometre. The different retail mixes in the central belt of Scotland where the majority of the population live and in the highlands where there are small numbers can be explained on the basis of market density.

Another important geographical consideration is that of locality. In many ways this is common sense. Experience tells that within urban and rural environments districts differ according to a number of related factors: whether communities are established or new; the number of people who own their home; levels of affluence; the geographical location, whether 'inner city', 'suburban' or 'rural'. In the UK, A Classification of Regional Neighbourhoods (ACORN) has adapted census data in order to create profiles of different areas according to forty such variables. People are then classified within a particular ACORN profile on the basis of the postcode of their home address. A copy of an ACORN summary table for the UK is shown in Table 6.1.

Table 6.1 The ACORN consumer targeting classification

Category		% population	Groups		% population
A	**Thriving**	19.8	1	Wealthy achievers, suburban areas	15.1
			2	Affluent greys, rural communities	2.3
			3	Prosperous pensioners, retirement areas	2.3
B	**Expanding**	11.6	4	Affluent executives, family areas	3.7
			5	Well-off workers, family areas	7.8
C	**Rising**	7.5	6	Affluent urbanites, family areas	2.2
			7	Prosperous professionals, metropolitan areas	2.1
			8	Better-off executives, inner-city areas	3.2
D	**Setting**	24.1	9	Comfortable middle-agers, mature home-owning areas	13.4
			10	Skilled workers, home-owning areas	10.7
E	**Aspiring**	13.7	11	New home owners, mature communities	9.8
			12	White-collar workers, better-off multi-ethnic areas	4.0
F	**Striving**	22.8	13	Older people, less prosperous areas	3.6
			14	Council estate residents, better-off homes	11.6
			15	Council estate residents, high unemployment	2.7
			16	Council estate residents, greatest hardship	2.8
			17	People in multi-ethnic, low-income areas	2.1
Unclassified		0.5			0.5

Source: CACI Ltd, 1993 (source: OPCS and GRO(S), Crown copyright 1991). All rights reserved. ACORN is a registered trade mark of CACI Ltd.

DEMOGRAPHIC SEGMENTATION

Demographic characteristics are means of describing individual consumers and households. This general label encompasses a large range of measurable criteria related to the consumers' sex and gender identification such as age, income, race, socio-economic status and family structure. For example, the manner in which gender identity is constructed means that women tend to express a much more differentiated and complex need for skin care products than men do, although there are signs that this may be changing slowly. Marketers of skin care products may use other segmentation bases to further segment this market. They may decide to target a market segment composed of women in the UK who are older (60–70), who are well educated, upper-class JICNARS classification (A/B) Succeeders. In this case the market has been segmented on the bases of geographical, demographic and lifestyle variables to yield a precise definition of the target market. This approach leads to a definition of the target market which may form the basis of research into NPD. There is a considerable amount of information available with respect to the media readership and product use of this group which may prove invaluable in designing an appropriate marketing strategy. Segmentation

Table 6.2 Mean equivalent income of age group as proportion of overall mean, selected countries, mid-1980s

Age group	<25	25–34	35–44	45–54	55–64	65–74	75+	Total population
France	0.91	1.04	1.08	1.05	1.08	1.03	0.98	1.00
UK	0.93	1.11	1.10	1.14	1.05	0.85	0.80	1.00
US	0.84	1.07	1.11	1.20	1.18	1.05	0.82	1.00

Source: estimated from LIS data files, Whiteford and Kennedy (1995), table 3.3 p. 30. Crown copyright. Adapted and reproduced with the permission of the Controller of Her Majesty's Stationery Office.

gives the marketer a profile of the customer that is incorporated in marketing strategies. Some other demographic approaches to market segmentation are discussed below.

AGE SEGMENTATION

One means of classifying marketing segments is with respect to age. In Chapter 3 Freud's two concepts, Eros and Thanatos, associated with life and death instincts are discussed. These suggest that, as on growing older, not only life circumstances but our very motivations are subject to change. For marketers the implications are simple. Often the early and middle stages of a person's life are spent in the process of acquisition of things, e.g. houses, furniture and goods for display. As death approaches so people begin to think of handing on their favoured possessions. Freud's ideas were further developed by Erikson (1965), who developed the concept of the life cycle which comprises eight developmental stages or as he calls them 'ages of man' ranging from infancy to old age. Erikson hypothesized that a specific form of ego conflict and resolution accompanied each stage. Table 6.2 shows mean incomes of particular age groups.

Table 6.2 shows that persons under the age of 25 in France on average have incomes that are 91 per cent of those for the whole population and that this rises to 104 per cent for the next age band. There are some interesting variations between countries. However, one can detect a pattern of a general growth in income followed by a decline over the path of the life cycle in each country.

Today virtually every age band from life to death is the focus of a marketing campaign. For example, there are ranges of products aimed at the youngest babies (and of course their parents) such as the television programme *Tellytubbies* with its associated merchandise. As some markets such as the teenage market become saturated so the definition of what constitutes a teenager is stretched. In the 1960s pop music promoters focused only on teens and above. As it became clear that younger children were becoming interested in this music so pop groups have been developed which are targeted specifically towards children. For example, bands such as the Spice Girls and Bewitched gain a large proportion of their audience from this age group.

THE 'GREY' MARKET

At the other end of the spectrum, there is growing interest in the 'grey' market. Within most Western economies there have been substantial swings in the birth rate since the Second World War. For example, in the US and the UK the post-war period from 1946 to 1964 is known as the Baby Boom period reflecting the increase in birth-rate during that time. At the present time, Baby Boomers represent a large proportion of the population which has been targeted by a vast number of marketing initiatives. As the Boomers have aged so a new market has come to be of significance to marketers, the 'grey' market or the 'third age' group. According to some commentators the 'grey' market is composed of those aged 50 or over. The idea that a person is 'old' at 50 will come as a surprise to those traditionalists who would define 'old' as beginning when a person retires from work.[1] It can be seen in this stretching downwards of the age barrier a parallel to the sort of stretching downwards which has just been described for the 'teen' market.

This sudden interest in 'older' people is partially for reasons already described. It constitutes a large number of people, some of whom are very affluent, as is evidenced by the data in Table 6.2.

The 'grey' market is itself split into different segments according to lifestyle and other criteria. For example, referring to the UK, those born before the Baby Boom have shared different experiences to those of the Boomers. This older group aged between 60 and 70 has memories of war and rationing. They have a cautious attitude to consumerism, like to pay in cash and prefer saving to spending. The over-70s are even more entrenched in these attitudes. On the other hand, those Baby Boomers who are aged over 50 are children of the consumer revolution for whom products and material culture play an integral role in the construction and expression of identity and expression of self.

WOOPIES, OPALS AND JOLLIES

Although there are deep pockets of poverty in this age range, it constitutes 40 per cent of the UK electorate and between 70 per cent and 80 per cent of the UK's private wealth. Perhaps more important for marketers, Third Agers are of a generation which has enjoyed house price inflation, is unmortgaged, unencumbered by children and has savings. They are ready to spend a lot of money even if they do it in a conservative manner. A range of exotic acronyms has been spawned to describe this group; 'Woopie' (Well Off Older Persons); Opals (Older People with Affluent Lifestyles) and Jollies (Jet-setting Oldies with Loads of Loot). This may be contrasted with the more traditional image of the financial circumstances of the retired which characterizes later life as a time of impoverishment. According to Falkingham and Victor (1991) Woopies in the UK are characterized by high rates of home ownership, higher than average access to consumer durables and high levels of car and phone ownership. In terms of demographic features they are disproportionately male, aged under 75 and from higher income groups. A small number (14 per cent) derive their income from employment; however, the vast majority (86 per cent) receive income from investments and from occupational pensions. Woopies are likely to be married and to live in one-person or two-person households. By comparison with other older people Woopies have access to a greater range of consumer durable goods.

Currently, the grey market is the focus of interest for a growing range of publications such as *Saga Magazine*, which has the largest circulation, estimated at between 600,000 and 800,000 in 1998, *Yours*, *Choice*, *Mature Tymes* and *Active Life*. *Active Life*, which is published bi-monthly and in 1999 had a circulation of 300,000, provides a good example of a segmentation approach, as the product has a unique marketing mix which is aimed specifically at 60–70 year olds. Most copies are distributed free at the post office. Its editorial content is typical of most magazines catering for the older market, providing information on holidays, health, finance, legal matters, competitions and how to cope with retirement. The publishers of *Active Life* know that this segment is not the wealthiest group; however, most of them have paid off their mortgages and have seen property values go up. Even if they are not on high incomes, normally they have savings. Like *Active Life*, *Mature Tymes* is a free title which has developed a tailor-made distribution system through local libraries – 64 per cent of whose users are over 50 years old – and the supermarket chain Asda. Saga is the best known of all organizations which cater to the needs of this market and offers a wide range of products from holidays to selected financial services.

On the other hand, it must be remembered that the 'grey' market is not one but many different markets. Not only is it, as usual, divided by social class, region and household (whether single household or not) it is also divided by generation, with around 16 per cent of the UK population in the 50–64 category and another 16 per cent – many of them the first group's parents – in the over-64 age group. 20 per cent could be regarded as being well-off. These are the households with an income of twice the state benefit or more. The other 80 per cent are divided: one half who are almost entirely dependent on the state for their income; the other half who are 'the property-rich income-poor' – people who may be living in a valuable asset (their home) but experience considerable difficulty in converting this into liquid cash.[2]

Returning to the discussion of trends in Chapter 2, it is important to recognise that nowadays age no longer denotes a particular type of behaviour or set of attitudes. This diversity within the market place makes the process of segmentation on the basis of age multi-faceted.

To add to the complexity, some social commentators take a different view of attempts to package old age as just another lifestyle. For example, Falkingham and Victor (1991) feel that the glossy lifestyles promoted by marketers create a picture of false affluence and ignore the demographic realities of later life. By spreading the image that older people are affluent, the researchers argue, marketers could effectively provide a rationale for government public spending cuts towards these 'affluent' consumers. While in the UK Woopies may own their own homes, this masks a considerable variation in ownership. Over 80 per cent of the highest quintile own their home outright; 65 per cent of those in the lowest quintile own their own home and are asset-rich and cash-poor. However, home ownership in the second and third quintiles is 34.6 per cent and 31 per cent respectively (Whiteford and Kennedy, 1995: table 4.9, p. 78.). There are extreme levels of poverty to be found in older age groups. For example, just over 1 per cent of older people in the UK and 15 per cent of older people in the US have to rely on incomes which are 40 per cent lower than the national average. Over 8 per cent of older UK residents and 25 per cent of US residents have incomes that are less than 50 per cent of the average (Whiteford and Kennedy, 1995: table 3.1.4, p. 49).

FAMILY STRUCTURE

Just as with age segmentation, marketers often incorporate some measure of life cycle with respect to family structure. The family life cycle concept charts the progress of family development from birth to death. For example, Lansing and Morgan (1955) put forward the scheme shown below:

- *Bachelor stage*: young single people.
- *Newly married couples*: young, no children.
- *Full nest I*: young married couples with dependent children.
- *Full nest II*: older married couples with dependent children.
- *Empty nest*: older married couples with no children living with them.
- *Solitary survivor*: older single people.

This classification can be useful in segmenting markets. For example, the needs for financial services can be different during the stages of the life cycle, with distinct implications for those offering the services. Many young single people are students and it is well known that many students spend their term of study owing money to the bank. Although many students live with others the first major change is when she or he sets up home with someone else. Usually this only happens when one of them has a job which can help them qualify for a mortgage. As children appear on the scene so the young couple moves further into the red (debt). At this stage children are encouraged to save. Astute bank staff will have provided a piggy bank and a savings account for their prospective new customers. During the first three stages it is likely that the couple will have a negative balance with the bank. However, as time moves on, with growing children moving out of the parental home to establish their own homes, the couple find themselves for once in surplus. This example has been grossly simplified and excludes many of the needs which people may have and the solutions which financial institutions may offer.

The Lansing and Morgan model may be criticized because it excludes 'non-traditional' families. For example, those who are divorced and childless or those who engage in homosexual relations are excluded. In countries such as the UK where levels of divorce, childlessness and single-parenthood are high, marketers must be sensitive to these factors.

SOCIAL CLASS

Often social class is used as a basis for market segmentation. Social class is a complex multi-faceted construct and so something is lost from it when it is objectified. Means of objectifying social class include income, occupation and location of residence. A widely used classification for socio-economic groupings in the UK is that provided by JICNARS. Table 6.3 shows the JICNARS social classifications, which are calculated on the basis of the occupation of the head of household.

Table 6.3 Socio-economic classification (JICNARS)

Social grade	Social status	Head of household's occupation	% of families
A	Upper middle	Higher managerial, administrative or professional	3
B	Middle	Intermediate, managerial, administrative or professional	10
C1	Lower middle	Supervisory of clerical and junior managerial, administrative or professional	24
C2	Skilled working	Skilled manual workers	30
D	Working	Semi-skilled and unskilled manual workers	25
E	Subsistence	State pensioners, casual or lowest-grade workers	8

Source: reprinted with kind permission of National Readership Surveys Ltd.

As discussed in Chapter 3, behaviour, social class used to be a major factor in UK consumption patterns. Social class at least to some extent determined almost everything, from the composition of family meals and the times at which they were eaten to clothes, holidays and sports. While social class has lost much of its influence in some spheres, it is still a very important factor in helping determine market segments.

The main disadvantage of demographic segmentation when used on its own is that it assumes, incorrectly, that all people in the same group have similar needs and wants. Adopting such a naive view can make an organization vulnerable to competitors who have developed products that are more closely aligned with customer profiles. It is most appropriate for products that have a clear bias towards a particular demographic group. For instance, cosmetics are segmented initially into male/female, and school fee endowment policies appeal to households within a higher income bracket at a particular stage of the family life cycle.

PSYCHOGRAPHIC SEGMENTATION

As social class has lost some of its force in providing a vehicle for identity so people have become associated with different lifestyles. In Chapter 2 David Riesman's concepts of inner-directedness and outer-directedness are discussed in relation to changes in lifestyle orientation. In the 1970s the Stanford Research Institute (SRI), now SRI International, developed Values and Lifestyles (VALS™) following research which was conducted in the US. Today Japan VALS and UKVALS are also available. VALS has been adapted to offer geo-demographic profiling through GeoVALS™ which estimates the percentages of the eight VALS groups by zip code.[3] In the first VALS programme, VALS confirmed Riesman's categories by identifying three broad consumer segments based on cultural 'values': (1) outer-directed (2) inner-directed and (3) needs-directed. The first two values have already been discussed: 'outer-directed' types tend to buy goods with an eye to their appearance and to what others may think (badge value) while consumers in the inner-directed segment buy more to meet their own inner wants than to respond to the cultural norms of others.

Figure 6.1
The VALS
segmentation
system.

Source:
SRI Consulting
Business
Intelligence (
SRIC-BI),
www.sric-
bi.com/vals;
Martha Farnworth
Riche,
'Psychographics
for the 1990s',
*American
Demographics*,
p. 26. Reprinted
with permission;
© *American
Demographics*,
July 1989

VALS™ Framework

INNOVATORS

High Resources
High Innovation

Primary Motivation

Ideals	Achievement	Self-Expression
THINKERS	ACHIEVERS	EXPERIENCERS
BELIEVERS	STRIVERS	MAKERS

Low Resources
Low Innovation

SURVIVORS

The label 'needs-driven' is a well disguised synonym for poverty: people who have very low discretionary income and who are motivated by need rather than choice.

The difficulty with the original VALS system was that almost two out of three, the vast majority of US consumers, fell into the 'outer-directed' category. A new research effort was undertaken. The research team was made up of effort from SRI, Stanford University, and University of California at Berkeley. Their research led to the identification of the eight consumer groups shown in Figure 6.1. The vertical dimension of Figure 6.1 represents resources and education, age, self-confidence, health and consumerism. On investigating the horizontal bands vestiges of 'inner' and 'outer' directedness can still be detected. These are labelled 'ideals-motivated' and 'achievement-motivated' groups. A third category represents self-expression motivation. This group seeks activity and risk taking. Maslow's work in this figure can be recognized. Within this context 'innovators' feel safe and are confident and comfortable in the company of others. They are avid consumers, travel widely and are active in a wide variety of activities. Those 'inner-directed' people who are 'ideals-motivated' split into two groups: 'Thinkers' are mature, well educated and relatively wealthy individuals who buy from a sense of their individual well-being more than from feelings of social pressure. They are interested in knowledge and learning and in maintaining good health. In contrast 'Believers' are less wealthy than Thinkers; their values reflect tradition and 'family' values. These groups may be contrasted with the status-seeking 'Strivers', who value style but who are less well off than Achievers and, in turn, from the young risk-seeking 'Experiencers' and physically active and self-sufficient 'Makers'.

Increasingly, marketers are segmenting their markets by consumer lifestyles. Lifestyle segments are either off-the-shelf methods from agencies or customized methods for individual companies. The advertising agency Young & Rubicam's Cross Cultural Consumer Characterization (4Cs) is similar in many ways to the VALS typology shown below:

- *Constrained*. People whose expenditure is limited by income. It includes the resigned poor who have accepted their poverty and the more ambitious struggling poor.
- *Middle majority*. This segment contains mainstreams, the largest group of all, aspirers and succeeders.
- *Innovators*. A segment consisting of transitionals and reformers.
- *Successors*. A group of people who like to feel in control.

American Express targeted this latter group with a series of advertisements depicting travellers who had lost their travellers' cheques. In each advertisement the traveller remained calm throughout the unfortunate situation and had his/her cheques returned within a short time. In contrast mainstreams need security. The former UK Prime Minister, Margaret Thatcher, is believed to have won elections by appealing to this segment's fear of change. Reformers are more willing to try new ideas and are at the forefront of many new trends such as ecologically friendly products and new tourist destinations.

Marketers have also used personality variables to segment markets, giving their products personalities that correspond to consumer personalities. This method is popular among producers of cigarettes, alcohol, cosmetics and insurance.

BEHAVIOURAL SEGMENTATION

Markets can be divided into discrete sub-groups according to the way people react to and interact with the product itself. Although a more difficult concept to grasp, in markets where other forms of segmentation are found to have little relevance, behavioural segmentation holds the key to effective and innovative marketing. Some of the most popular forms of behavioural segmentation criteria are discussed below.

OCCASIONS

Buyers can be grouped according to occasions when they decide to buy, make their purchase or use the purchased item. This can help firms to increase product usage. For example, when Kellogg's identified that a significant proportion of its customers ate cornflakes as a snack food later in the day, it decided to promote cornflakes as a late-night snack. Other organizations that use this segmentation base include florists, card and gift manufacturers who use Mothers' Day, Fathers' Day and Christmas to promote their products.

BENEFITS SOUGHT

Different people want products to benefit them in different ways. Consider the yellow fats market: butter is an ideal product for those who are most interested in taste; low-calorie spread is aimed at those who want to lose weight; polyunsaturated margarine will appeal to those who are health-conscious; block margarine is preferred by those who want to make good pastry and basic own-label spreads will satisfy those for whom economy is paramount. Different brands have been created to provide the benefits sought by these and many other groups in this heavily segmented market. The task of defining some of these segments can help the marketer identify some of the demographic or lifestyle characteristics of the people seeking the benefits.

Referring to the example of trains introduced on the next page, trains in the UK would be very different from what they are now if train operators paid attention to the benefits desired by different groups of customers. For example, business people like to work on trains and so require carriages which are fitted like an office with computer ports. Other people like to talk and socialize on trains; special carriages could be devised for these people which have tables and seats. Other people may be tired and wish to rest, in which case their carriage could have low lighting with quiet music and comfortable reclining seats. Other people may wish to spend their time productively, perhaps in learning a language or in other forms of study. All these could be potentially profitable ways of attracting and keeping customers; however, each needs to be considered in the light of its costs and returns to the train operator.

APPLICATIONS

Different people want to use products for different purposes. For example, cotton wool has three primary applications: baby care, child care and cosmetic use. These three uses can be subdivided into a number of further segments, e.g. in baby care and cosmetic use cotton wool is used both to apply substances such as lotions and make-up and cleansing. Consequently the market is characterized by product forms that are suited to these tasks. Flat cotton wool pads are sold in polythene tubes for convenience for make-up removal, cotton wool buds are an easy shape to use for make-up application and cotton wool balls are ideal for general cleansing.

USER STATUS

As an alternative to benefit segmentation, markets can be subdivided on the basis of what is referred to as user status. In this way, segments can be identified for non-users, first-time users and regular users. The final two categories can then be subdivided on the basis of use rate. Segmentation on the basis of user status is popular, as it forms a key component of direct marketing.

The rationale of using user status in this way is that it helps to increase purchase volumes. For example, non-users and potential users need to be persuaded to try the product, while first-time users need to be persuaded to become medium users, and medium users to become heavy users. This is the philosophy behind the 'frequent flyer' schemes that many airlines offer.

ACTIVITY

Segment the following markets according to the time that people use or consume the products or services. Indicate how this might affect the way you would promote and price them:

1 Supermarkets.
2 Train journeys.
3 Telephone services.

One way in which supermarkets might be segmented is in terms of the kinds of people who use them at different times. Table 6.4 is a list of the typical segments that might want to visit a supermarket in the UK.

Table 6.4 Typical market segments visiting a UK supermarket

Time of day/night	Market segments
Up to 11.00 p.m.	Families
11.00 p.m. to 1.00 a.m.	Young couples on their way home from a night out
2.00 a.m. to 4.00 a.m.	Partygoers and nightclubbers, media workers
4.00 p.m. to 6.00 a.m.	Shift workers, nurses and taxi drivers on their way home
6.00 a.m. onwards	Families with young children who are early risers

The market for trains can be segmented according to time. For the business traveller, time is very important. If a train enables them to reach a city-centre destination in roughly the same time as a plane, they may well be tempted to use the train, if it is known to be reliable and offers working facilities. Price is not so important a consideration for the business traveller as it is for the tourist and so prices may be higher during the times that business travellers want to make their journey. On the other hand, price is more important than time to many tourists, who would rather spend less and take more time to travel.

USER VOLUME

The relatively new approach to marketing known as direct marketing prizes the value of customer retention over that of customer acquisition. It is argued that it costs much more to seek and find new customers than it does to satisfy and nurture existing customers. Of particular importance is the Pareto effect or the '80/20' rule which applies to many instances of consumer purchase behaviour. This means that frequently only 20 per cent of valued customers contribute to 80 per cent of turnover and/or profits. If this is correct then it is important to ensure that this 20 per cent remains happy with the product or service offering. With recent developments in technology retailers have been able to track high-volume users and to reward them appropriately. In the UK many major retailers including supermarkets offer their customers 'loyalty' cards.

Segmenting industrial markets

The overall concept of segmentation applies equally to both consumer and organizational markets, but there are differences between the variables by which they are measured. There are two stages involved in segmenting industrial markets:

■ Identify sub-groups within the whole market which have common general character-istics. These are called macro segments.
■ Select target segments from within the macro segments based on differences in specific buying characteristics. These are called micro segments.

Macro segments are based on the characteristics of organizations and the broader purchasing context within which they operate. Defining a macro segment assumes that the organizations within it will exhibit similar patterns and needs which will be reflected in similar buying behaviour and responses to marketing stimuli.

The bases for macro segmentation tend to be observable or readily obtained from secondary information, i.e. published or existing sources, and can be grouped into two main categories: organizational characteristics; product or service application.

ORGANIZATIONAL CHARACTERISTICS

There are three organizational characteristics: size; location and usage rate.

■ *Size*. The size of an organization influences the way in which it views its suppliers and purchases supplies. Large companies with factories, depots or warehouses in a wide range of locations are likely to have different requirements for service from small businesses. They may have specific delivery instructions, complex invoicing procedures due to a central buying function and they may have less need for after-sales service thanks to in-house repair and installation facilities. They may prefer to deal with other large businesses and perceive small businesses as less reliable.

- *Location*. Organizations may focus their selling effort according to the geographical concentration of the industries they serve. This used to occur when the UK had thriving manufacturing industries such as shipping, mining and chemical production. This has changed with the emergence of smaller manufacturers, many of which are based in technology parks and industrial estates. Examples of geographical segmentation still exist, however, among the financial and information technology sectors.
- *Use rate*. The quantity of product purchased may be a legitimate means of categorizing potential customers. A purchasing organization defined as a heavy user may have different needs from a light user, e.g. demanding different treatment in terms of special delivery or prices. A supplier may define a threshold point, so that when a customer's use rate rises above it, its status changes. The customer's account may be handed over to a more senior manager and the supplier may become more flexible in terms of co-operation, pricing and relationship building.

PRODUCT OR SERVICE APPLICATION

This second group of segmentation bases acknowledges that the same good can be used in many different ways. This approach looks for customer groupings either within specified industries as defined by Standard Industrial Classification (SIC) codes, each with its own requirements, or by defining a specific application and grouping customers around that.

The SIC code may help to identify sectors with a greater propensity to use particular products for particular applications. For example, glass has many industrial uses, ranging from packaging or architecture to the motor industry. Each of these application sectors behaves differently in terms of price sensitivity, ease of substitution, quality and performance requirements. Similarly, cash and carry wholesalers serve three broad segments: independent grocers, caterers and pubs. Each segment will purchase different types of goods, in different quantities and for different purposes.

The macro level is a useful starting point for defining some broad boundaries to markets and segments, but it is not sufficient in itself. Further customer-oriented analysis at the micro level is necessary.

MICRO SEGMENTATION BASES

When selecting the bases of micro segmentation in organizational markets, the marketer must consider the purchasing approaches, personal characteristics and situational factors concerning the organizational buyer. The following questions can help to clarify some of these issues.

Purchasing approaches

Should we focus on:

- Companies with highly centralized or companies with decentralized purchasing organizations?

- Companies that are engineering, finance or marketing-dominated?
- Companies that prefer leasing, service contracts, systems contracts or sealed bidding?
- Companies that are seeking quality, service or price?

Personal characteristics

Should we focus on companies:

- Whose values are similar to ours?
- That are willing or unwilling to take risk?
- That show loyalty to their supplier?

Situational factors

- How urgent is the delivery for the company?
- Should we focus on certain applications of our product rather than all applications?
- Should we focus on large or small orders?

Criteria for successful segmentation

There are four requirements for any successful segmentation exercise. Unless these conditions prevail, the exercise will fail to deliver any marked advantage.

- *Distinctiveness*. The most promising segments and the easiest to target are those that are distinct from the other segments. For example, buyers of business stationery demand different sizes and styles of paper from domestic users and there is relatively little overlap between the two segments.
- *Size*. Is the segment a worthwhile target? A segment should not be so large as to be indistinct from the mass market, but it should be large enough for it to be worth while treating its members as being different from others. For example, car manufacturers are sometimes approached by very tall drivers who suffer from insufficient headroom in their cars and very short drivers who find visibility difficult. While some manufacturers attempt to meet their needs with adjustable seats,there is insufficient demand to justify launching a new range of vehicles for such small segments of the population.
- *Accessibility*. The organization must be able to find the means of delivering its goods and services to the customer. Particularly, this task is difficult when the segment is spread over a wide geographical area and the product or service is purchased infrequently. When this happens it is easier to limit the segment to customers within a defined catchment area, or those who are prepared to order from direct mail. The second aspect of access is that of communication, as each segment must be able to receive the marketing messages that have been aimed at it.

■ *Identifiable.* Which is implied if they are to be accessed through a marketing programme.

Benefits of segmentation

When the above criteria are met, the organization will benefit from the process of segmentation in several ways.

■ *Improved customer relations.* Segmentation enables customers to find products that fit more closely with their physical and, in certain cases, psychological needs. Customers are more likely to be loyal to suppliers with products that are tailored to their needs.

■ *Accurate marketing mix.* Segmentation helps to define shopping habits (in terms of place, frequency and volume), price sensitivity and required product benefits as well as laying the foundations for advertising and promotional decisions. Any decision concerning the 4 Ps is likely to be more accurate if a clear and a detailed description of the target segment is available.

■ *Resource allocation.* Segmentation can help the organization to allocate its resources more efficiently.

■ *Competitor analysis.* Any organization that wishes to compete must ask the following questions: Who are the main competitors? At which segments are they targeting their products? The answers enable the marketer to identify the most appropriate segments to target and the nature of the competitive advantage that should be sought. Companies that have overlooked the way the market is segmented risk competing head-on against larger organizations with superior resources.

■ *Strategic marketing planning.* Dividing markets up allows marketers to develop plans that give special consideration to the particular needs and requirements of customers in different segments. The time scale covered by the strategic plan can be structured to reflect those segments where change occurs more frequently than others.

SECTION SUMMARY

Having completed this section, you should be able to:

■ **Decide on the variables that can be used to segment a market.**

■ **Distinguish between the segmentation variables that are applied to consumer and B-to-B markets.**

■ **Describe the benefits of market segmentation.**

■ **Apply segmentation criteria to a market.**

SELECTING TARGET MARKETS

Having decided how best to segment the market, the next stage is to decide how many and which segments to target.

After completing this section, you should be able to:

■ **Describe the factors to consider when evaluating target markets;**
■ **Evaluate the attractiveness of potential target markets using Porter's five force model.**
■ **Describe the ways target markets can be selected.**

Evaluating market segments

In evaluating market segments a firm must look at three dimensions: the size and growth potential of each segment, segment attractiveness and company fit.

SEGMENT SIZE AND GROWTH

The company must ascertain whether the segment has the correct size and growth characteristics. In general large companies prefer segments with large sales volumes and often overlook small segments. For example, train operators may create specific services which cater to the needs of business travellers. They may not be so keen to introduce those for personal travellers which, although they may meet a need (such as spending time productively by learning a language) may not provide a profitable service. Often small companies avoid large segments because they require too many resources.

SEGMENT ATTRACTIVENESS

It is important to note that, even when a segment appears to have the desired size and growth potential, it may be unattractive in terms of profitability. The company must examine several significant structural factors that affect long-run segment attractiveness. Porter has identified the five forces that determine the intrinsic long-run attractiveness of a particular segment or the whole market. The five forces arise from:

■ Industry competitors.
■ Potential entrants.
■ Substitutes.
■ Buyers.
■ Suppliers.

These pose the following threats:

- Segment rivalry.
- Substitute products.
- Growing bargaining power of buyers.
- Growing bargaining power of suppliers.

A segment is unattractive if it:

- Contains strong competitors.
- Is stable or declining.
- Has high fixed costs.

When these characteristics exist, price wars, advertising battles and new product introductions will make it expensive for companies to compete.

New entrants threaten the target market by introducing new capacity and resources. The threat can be reduced if the cost of entering the market is high. For example, the automotive market has high barriers to entry because the cost of establishing production and marketing facilities is high, which reduces the threat of new entrants. Even for markets that require relatively low capital investment to enter, there can be high barriers to entry if the dominant competitors are well established and act swiftly against new entrants. For example, when a detergent manufacturer attempted to launch a new cold water detergent in the UK market P&G and Unilever retaliated by increasing advertising budgets and providing incentives for their distributors to stock only their products. The new detergent survived only a short time.

Markets also have exit barriers which represent the cost of divesting from a market that has become unattractive. The steel industry has experienced high exit barriers in the UK, where divestment of steel production for markets no longer considered feasible has resulted in the scrapping of high-cost capital equipment and high redundancy pay-offs for the work force. By contrast, exit barriers for a software producer are low, since the work force can be redeployed relatively easily and capital equipment can be reassigned for different tasks.

The threat of substitute products

If technology advances or competition increases in substitute industries, prices and profits in the segment are likely to fall.

The threat of the growing bargaining power of buyers

Buyers with strong bargaining power can force prices down, demand higher quality, increase competition and reduce profitability. Buyers' bargaining power grows when the following characteristics exist:

- Buyers are well organized.
- The product represents a significant proportion of the buyer's costs.
- There are alternative sources of supply.
- The buyer's switching costs are low.
- Buyers are price-sensitive because of low profits.
- Buyers find it easy to produce their own supplies if dissatisfied with their suppliers (backward integration).

BUSINESS STRENGTHS AND OBJECTIVES

Even if a segment has the right size and growth and is structurally attractive, the company must ensure that its objectives and resources are matched to that segment. A small electronics company may find a highly attractive opportunity for an innovative consumer electronics product, but may be unwise to incur the marketing costs of entering the consumer electronics market. Segments may also be a poor choice in environmental, political or ethical terms. For example, in recent years several drinks companies have been criticized for targeting teenage segments with alco-pops.

Selecting the target market

After evaluating different segments, the company must decide which and how many segments to serve. This is the problem of target market selection. The process of selecting target markets is illustrated in Figures 6.2 and 6.3.

UNDIFFERENTIATED MARKETING

The undifferentiated approach is the least demanding of the three approaches as it assumes that the market is a homogeneous unit, with no significant differences between individuals within that market. The offer will focus on what is common in the needs of consumers rather than what is different. The product and marketing mix is designed to appeal to the largest number of buyers, relying on quality, mass distribution and mass advertising to give the product a superior image in people's minds. Often undifferentiated approaches are used when the product has limited psychological appeal.

Undifferentiated marketing provides cost economies. The narrow product line limits production, inventory and transport costs. The costs associated with advertising, marketing research and planning are reduced. Many organizations avoid this strategy owing to the difficulties of producing a product that will satisfy all consumers. When firms pursue undifferentiated marketing they develop an offer aimed at the largest segments in the market. When several firms do this, there is heavy competition in the largest segments and there are neglected customers in the smaller ones. Increased competition reduces the profitability of the larger segments, forcing many firms to address smaller market segments. The mass market can be eroded by competitors who develop new products. For example, Polo mints have faced attacks from competitors aiming at different benefits segments: extra strong mints for people who want a strong taste and Clorets as breath fresheners.

DIFFERENTIATED MARKETING

A differentiated strategy involves the development of a number of individual marketing mixes, each of which serves a different segment. For example, many car manufacturers produce cars for female drivers, families, company sales fleets and status seekers.

Using this strategy, the firm can spread risk across the market, so that if one segment declines the firm still has revenue from others. The disadvantage is that it requires a high level of marketing expertise and will incur higher costs in trying to manage the marketing mixes for different products.

CONCENTRATED MARKETING

The concentrated approach involves specializing in one specific segment. This can lead to detailed knowledge of the target segment's needs and wants, with the added benefit that the organization is regarded as a specialist over its mass-market competitors. Using this strategy even small companies can realistically aim to be market leaders in their fields. The manufacturer of cereal health food, Jordan's, concentrates on health-conscious consumers and has succeeded in retaining a strong position in this segment even though other large manufacturers dominate the market as a whole.

Another advantage of concentration is that it reduces costs, as there is only one marketing mix to manage. The concentration of resources may mean that the segment is protected against competitors who are spreading their effort more thinly.

There are risks associated with concentration. It may be more difficult to diversify into other segments, whether through lack of experience or problems of acceptance arising from being identified with the original niche. The firm must consider the risk of putting all its eggs in one basket, especially if the firm fails by committing all its resources to a single segment. Finally, competitors may be tempted to enter the segment if they see a rival becoming established and successful.

When selecting a targeting strategy the firm will have to consider the additional points that are summarized below.

- *Company resources*. e.g. if the firm has limited resources then concentrated marketing may be appropriate.
- *Product variability*. Undifferentiated marketing is suitable for uniform products such as fruit or steel. Products that can vary in design, such as cameras, require differentiation or concentration.
- *Stage in the PLC*. Undifferentiated marketing is more suitable for products that are new to the market, as these products initially are aimed at a small segment.
- *Market variability*. Undifferentiated marketing is appropriate when buyers have the same tastes, buy the same amounts and react the same way to promotional messages.
- *Competitors' marketing strategies*. It is unwise to use undifferentiated marketing against competitors who have developed distinctive segments. Conversely, when competitors use undifferentiated marketing, a firm can use differentiated or concentrated marketing to its advantage.

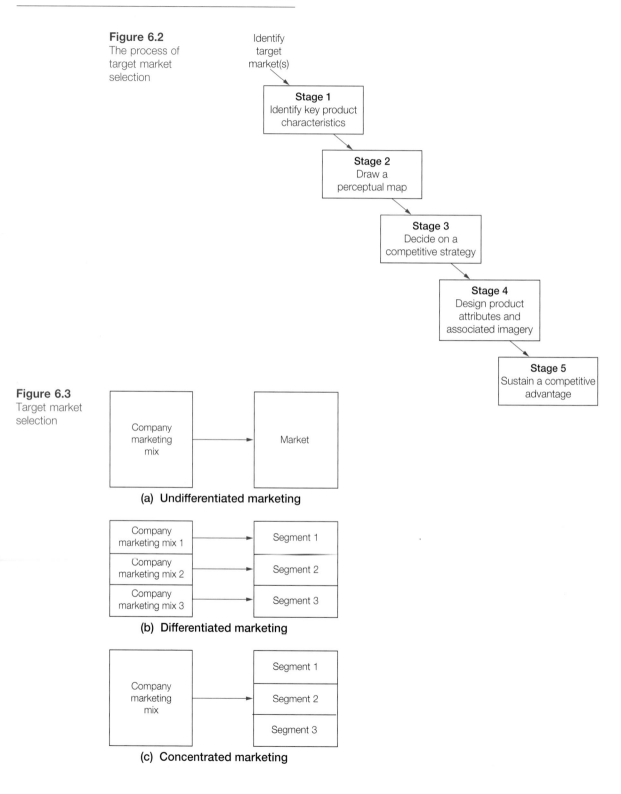

Figure 6.2
The process of target market selection

Identify target market(s)

Stage 1
Identify key product characteristics

Stage 2
Draw a perceptual map

Stage 3
Decide on a competitive strategy

Stage 4
Design product attributes and associated imagery

Stage 5
Sustain a competitive advantage

Figure 6.3
Target market selection

Company marketing mix → Market

(a) Undifferentiated marketing

Company marketing mix 1 → Segment 1
Company marketing mix 2 → Segment 2
Company marketing mix 3 → Segment 3

(b) Differentiated marketing

Company marketing mix → Segment 1 / Segment 2 / Segment 3

(c) Concentrated marketing

SECTION SUMMARY

Having completed this section, you should be able to:

■ Establish clear criteria for selecting a target market;
■ Evaluate possible target markets by considering their size and growth potential and company fit;
■ Select target markets that will yield maximum growth potential for your company;
■ Apply Porter's five force model to determine the structural attractiveness of a segment.

POSITIONING

Having segmented the market and decided on a targeting strategy, the next stage is to create and maintain a clear and appropriate positive image of the product or service in the minds of consumers. This helps to differentiate the product from current and potential competing products. For example, Porsche is positioned in the prestige segment of the car market with a differential advantage based on performance while Volvo is positioned in the family segment, where it has capitalized on its reputation for safety. In this section the stages that are involved in the positioning process will be considered.

After completing this section, you should be able to:

■ Define what is meant by positioning;
■ Describe the stages involved in positioning;
■ Draw a perceptual map.

Stages involved in market positioning

There are six stages involved in product positioning, each of which is described below.

STAGE 1 IDENTIFY KEY PRODUCT CHARACTERISTICS

Marketing research data should be studied in order to select the key product characteristics that members of the target market consider most important when making purchasing decisions. These features may be tangible, e.g. colour, size, design, or intangible, e.g. reputation or guarantees.

STAGE 2 DRAW A PERCEPTUAL MAP

This is a useful tool by which the current brands available to a market segment can be depicted visually. In its simplest form the perceptual map consists of a grid that shows the two most

Figure 6.4
Perceptual map
of financial
services

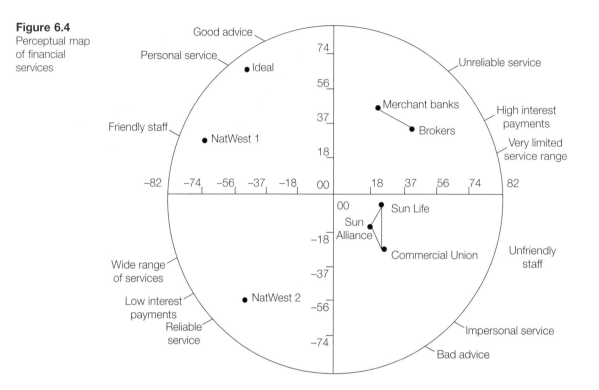

important attributes identified at Stage 1 placed at two axes on the grid. Qualitative marketing research enables consumer perceptions about the current brands to be plotted, so that the organization can see at a glance where competition is most intense and where there might be gaps in the market. Figure 6.4 shows a perceptual map for financial services in the UK and focuses on the first two dimensions. The way in which the perceptual map has been prepared is similar to the attribute scoring method which was described in Chapter 2. In this case the attributes were derived by means of the Kelly Repertory Grid, a method which was developed by the psychologist George Kelly for clinical use.

Financial institutions are evaluated with respect to constructs such as 'personal service' versus 'impersonal service', 'reliable service' versus 'unreliable service', 'friendly' versus 'clinical' attitude, etc. Figure 6.4 is based on responses for one person, although this can be aggregated to any number of people. It can be seen that this person differentiates the services offered by banks such as Natwest and Barclay's, merchantbanks and brokers and insurance companies. Such maps can be useful for repositioning services or for introducing new services.

STAGE 3 DECIDE ON A COMPETITIVE STRATEGY

Perceptual mapping provides insights into appropriate competitive actions and helps firms to decide whether they should compete head-on or position their products away from competition.

Avoiding the competition

At first glance it seems evident that a strategy to avoid the competition holds most potential. Even when a quadrant on a perceptual map may indicate an area where there is a gap in the market, it may be difficult to enter. Sometimes, firms which enter these segments may experience only short-term profitability. This leaves them with the costly task of repositioning themselves if they wish to build their profit margins as well as their sales revenue. However, in the example given, the costs involved in stocking a wide range of goods may be incompatible with sustaining a profitable low-price strategy.

Head-on competition

This may be equally, if not more, problematic. Unless the market is growing significantly, there may be no room for extra supply without the profitability of all firms suffering badly. None the less, often, large and well financed firms are reluctant to leave a segment unchallenged and sometimes are willing to challenge a leader head-on, e.g. sales growth in Cadbury's Caramel spawned 'me too' products in the form of Galaxy toffee bars and Rolo bars. Smaller firms with less financial backing may be squeezed out or will fail to find a foothold unless their product offering is demonstrably better than existing brands.

STAGE 4 DESIGN PRODUCT ATTRIBUTES AND ASSOCIATED IMAGERY

At this stage the features of the product should be designed, along with the type of imagery to help the targeted customers identify the benefits being offered to them. Features such as brand name, packaging, advertising themes, price levels and distribution outlets are all important in creating this position in the mind of the customer.

STAGE 5 SUSTAIN A COMPETITIVE ADVANTAGE

Competitive advantage is gained when the firm establishes a market position that sets its product apart from competitors in the eyes of its target market. In order for this advantage to be sustained, marketing information must be kept up to date to ensure that the needs of the target markets are being met more effectively and efficiently than by competition.

SECTION SUMMARY

Having completed this section, you should be able to:

■ Draw a perceptual map for a product or service.
■ List the stages involved in positioning.

The following text case study concerns the Tiberias Hotel.

After completing this case study, you should be able to:

- Apply the theory of segmentation, targeting and positioning to a case study.
- Analyse the problems facing the Tiberias Hotel.
- Recommend a marketing strategy for the Tiberias Hotel.

SEGMENTATION APPLIED TO THE TIBERIAS HOTEL

In May 2005 the Board of World Mission of the Church of Scotland presented a disturbing report to the General Assembly of the Church of Scotland. This showed that by the end of the year the £13m (US$22m) Tiberias resort development by the Sea of Galilee would drain the Church of a further £555,000 (US$996,000). The board admitted that the development 'inevitably has a negative impact on its work elsewhere in the world' in forcing the Church to cut back on overseas aid and on AIDS prevention work.

Dr David Watt Torrance, a young Scottish doctor, who believed in his mission to heal the people of the Holy Land, established the original medical centre in the nineteenth century. He first arrived in Tiberius in 1884, as the head of the Church of Scotland mission and, motivated by the poor health and sanitary conditions, worked day and night to serve the rapidly expanding population. In January 1894 the first Tiberias hospital was opened with the specific purpose of being available to all regardless of race or creed. During the 1950s, following Dr Torrance's death, the centre was taken over by the Church of Scotland.

As the house was located in the middle of Tiberias, only a few miles away from some of the holiest sites in Christendom, the Church decided to open a guest house for pilgrims and visitors from across the world. Although it was popular with pilgrims the new centre cost a great deal to run and maintain but did not bring in much revenue. Consequently, in 1999, Church planners decided to undertake a major refurbishment of the guest house to make the most of its beautiful location, which included a beach front site. Planners decided that it was imperative to conserve the original buildings and provide first-class service in a place of reconciliation for all people including Jews, Christians and Muslims as a tranquil multicultural, multi-racial retreat, a flourishing site of faith in a very special atmosphere.

In 1999 the hotel development project commenced and since then the Board has spent over £10m (US$18m) in converting the house. In 2004, after a number of long delays, the new centre opened for business.

Sources: adapted from http://www.scotshotels.co.il/history.html and Johnston (2005)

QUESTIONS

1   Evaluate the segmentation approach adopted by the Church of Scotland with respect to the Tiberias development.

2   Given that the Church administration spent a great deal of money on this development and that it may continue to act as a drain on Church resources, you are asked to conduct a segmentation exercise as the basis of a report to the Church authorities. Having conducted your analysis, you should come up with a list of target segments and be able to advise the Church administration on an appropriate positioning strategy.

3   At present the marketing of the centre tends to be directed towards the independent traveller. How might the hotel's marketing task differ if it targeted tourists travelling in organized groups as opposed to the independent traveller? Is the hotel wise to avoid block bookings from tour operators, as it does currently?

ANSWERS

1   The Church administration has not fully considered segmentation issues. All that is mentioned in the case study is that segmentation is aimed at people of all religious faiths requiring a first-class service in a tranquil setting. Further consideration of the issues should be made.

2   Start by going back to the basics. What kinds of people might want to come to Israel and to this site in particular? In order to prompt your analysis consider demographics, gender, life style, life cycle. Also consider combinations of these, e.g. high versus low income, older/younger, male/female, Experiencers, Actualizers, etc. In selecting target segments it is important to consider potential competitors and the potential value that each segment might represent to the Church, given its current financial situation. When considering positioning you should identify dimensions on which to target appropriate positioning strategies.

3   If the hotel's marketing task changed to target tourists travelling in organized groups, as opposed to the independent traveller, management would have to consider modifying its services to match the organized groups' requirements. For example, it might have to arrange for groups to stay for durations to match package holiday arrangements, e.g. full week stays starting and finishing on Saturdays, and special tours to local sites. Analysis would have to be made regarding the potential financial benefits of taking block bookings from tour operators. While the income per visitor might decline, it could well provide a regular income throughout the year, which would be attractive. Consideration of the effect of tour groups on individual customers should be made and a decision made as to whether it would be possible to service both types of travellers effectively or whether it would be best to concentrate on one segment only.

CONCLUSION

This chapter introduces three interrelated concepts of segmentation, targeting and positioning. Segmentation involves the identification of potential buyers on the basis of a shared similarity, such as need, a particular characteristic or similar purchase behaviour or use. Segments are most often identified by combining a number of variables, for example by segmenting according to geographical location, age, gender and lifestyle. Targeting involves an assessment of the opportunities for growth presented by each segment, coupled with an analysis of potential competitive threats. Following from this, the decision may be made to adopt an undifferentiated approach which treats the market as a homogeneous unit. On the other hand, the analysis and subsequent discussion may result in the elimination of segments that are perceived as low in growth, that cannot be adequately resourced, or where the competitive threat, or buyer power, is perceived to be too high. As a consequence it may be decided to adopt a differentiated approach to more than one segment, or a concentrated approach, to focus on just one segment. The positioning decision takes place once the market has been segmented and a targeting strategy has been decided upon. This hinges around the need to create a clear and consistent image of the product or service in the mind of the customer.

REVIEW QUESTIONS

1   How might the market for personal computers sold to organization markets be segmented?
2   Suggest appropriate ways of segmenting the markets for the following products or services: (a) rail travel; (b) banks; (c) ballpoint pens; (d) package holidays.
3   How would you go about assessing the needs of the 'grey' market?
4   What sort of promotional appeal would best be suited to the grey market?
5   Some industrial suppliers make above-average profits by offering service, selection and reliability at a premium price. How might these suppliers segment the market to locate customers who are willing to pay more for these benefits?
6   Cite examples of organizations that use each targeting strategy, i.e. undifferentiated, differentiated and concentrated. Discuss why they have chosen this strategy.
7   List the attributes that can be emphasised to differentiate a product or service and create a market position.
8   Is positioning helpful to not-for-profit organizations? If so, how should a charity select and implement a positioning strategy?

RECOMMENDED FURTHER READING

Weinstein, A. (1994) *Market segmentation*, New York: McGraw-Hill.

7 BRANDING

LEARNING OBJECTIVES

After studying this chapter you should be able to:

■ describe the advantages that are ascribed to branding;

■ understand the historical development of branding;

■ appreciate the key differences between a mainstream and a behaviourist explanation of branding.

INTRODUCTION

Perhaps the earliest instance of branding was in the branding of slaves and criminals for purposes of identification. Branding has been associated with property in its widest sense. Although a slave is undoubtedly a person, in ancient times slaves were treated as if they were socially dead. To mark this event slave owners habitually renamed their slaves with contemptuous titles such as 'irritation'. Within this context branding is associated with power, control, a sign of ownership indicated through marking a brand physically on the body and property.

In modern times the concept of branding has taken on a more positive inflection with the development of commodity brands in the early twentieth century that offer to protect and heal the self. Individuals now mark themselves with brands as a means of self-affirmation rather than negation. In Western culture the discourse about brands has travelled beyond the marketing of traditional products and services to swamp every aspect of life. From Chapter 1, it can be recalled that this was what Kotler called for (or did he?) back in 1972, when he asked that the marketing concept be applied to all institutions. Someone must have been listening because from birth the infant is wrapped in a branded cocoon of 'absorbent' nappies, 'trustworthy' bottle-feeds and medications, 'cute' clothes, and, of course, the ubiquitous branded pram. From about that age the infant begins to learn the language of brands from the mass media and by observation of the actions of those around IT.

In this chapter the traditional world of goods and services is considered. It starts by outlining the conventional wisdom that argues why branding is important. Then themes are discussed under what is loosely referred to as the conventional wisdom about branding, i.e. brand congruity, personality, subculture and community. Consideration is given to discussion of a way by which brands gain their meaning and by which they may recirculate this back to consumers as symbolic resources for the construction of identity. Then branding is assessed from a radical behaviourist point of view and different accounts of brand loyalty are explained.

BRIEF MODERN HISTORY OF BRANDING

In Chapter 3 the work of the behaviourist J.B. Watson was examined as being one of the first who used the fear–sex–emulation model in advertising during the 1920s. The strategy appeared to be simple. Basically, the advertisement had to first identify some problem, deficit or lack in the consumer. This was achieved by inducing feelings of anxiousness or lack of confidence, e.g. with respect to the fear of underarm sweat. Early brand advertising clearly identified the deficit and the benefit in the shape of the product that could cure it (Falk, 1997). Familiar brands started life as patent medicines, e.g. Coca-Cola and Heinz Ketchup; as part of a controlled 'healthy' diet, e.g. Kellogg's Cornflakes; as an aid to the creation of a more 'hygenic' domestic environment through banishing 'invisible' germs and dirt, e.g. Sunlight soap; or in focusing on the development of 'personal hygiene', e.g. Zam-buk,

Lifebuoy carbolic soap and Odorono. The brand is offered as the means to resolve the anxiety, redress the deficit and fill the lack. This meets with Levitt's (1986) advice to marketers when seeking to define consumers' needs; that it is better to start with the deficit. For example, the market for 'six inch holes' rather than the benefit of the market for drills; a hospital may produce surgery; customers seek 'relief of pain'; and purchasers of perfume may be purchasing 'dreams', those of cosmetics 'confidence'.

Why brand?

Authors cite a plethora of benefits that arise from branding. Most of these are from the producers' perspective:

- *Protection*. The brand mark and other aspects of the brand constitute a legal sign. Anyone who uses 'Coca-Cola' in the particular font prescribed without permission is likely to end up in court. Brands are protected by copyright, trade marks and patents that are underpinned by the notion of intellectual property rights, as written into WTO standards. Such devices have been used to attack brand piracy, where, for instance, Napster featured as a high-profile case. Klein (2000) notes that there are two sides to this. Protection of the brand mark has reached the extent that authors such as ourselves, in writing this book, can be accused of 'stealing' the brand mark. Klein argues this has become a powerful new form of censorship as global brands dominate huge swathes of social and cultural space.
- *Property*. The brand mark is a shorthand device in that it readily identifies what belongs to one person, what that person has a right to which is different from what belongs to other people. The brand mark needs to be distinctive and easily recognizable if it is to fulfil its function.
- *Differentiation*. The idea of differentiation with a capital D features in most populist books on the subject. The provenance of this idea tracks back to the days of the Unique Selling Proposition (USP) developed in the US in the 1940s. The brand should offer a proposition that is unique and which signifies a benefit that will pull the customer to the brand. Put in behaviourist terms, the various stimuli associated with the brand, e.g. the brand logo and packaging, should act as a discriminative stimulus that prompts the person to associate this with some unique aspect that has provided reinforcement. In cognitive terms the idea is to create a favourable attitude about the brand based on a key set of attributes. Levitt (1968) supports this idea in arguing that the core brand should reflect the specific quality which makes the brand different from others. This is known as the 'brand property'. Once this aspect of the 'core' brand has been identified, the marketer has a basis to define the need and the plenitude or wholeness that consumption of the brand will bring. The brand itself is a positive creation which offers the promise of negating the evil of the need.
- *Added value*. The argument for differentiation would make little sense if this did not lead to the creation of added value. The thinking is that if the marketer can make an

addict of the consumer, by inducing her or him to rely upon the brand and to consistently demand it, the brand may command a price premium over those which purport to service the same core need. One way of creating added value is by ensuring that the brand consistently delivers a quality offering. One source of information about the relative performance of brands can be found in the PIMS database (Buzzell, 1987). This contains financial and strategic information collected by the Strategic Planning Institute on 2,600 SBUs that form part of 450 institutions in the US. Subsequent analyses of this database have revealed the six 'PIMS principles'. The first and most important principle relates to perceived quality, that in the long run the most important single factor affecting a SBU's performance is the quality of its products and services relative to competitors. By building in higher perceived quality, it is argued, units can charge a higher price and reflect this on the bottom line or on R&D and NPD. There is a strong positive relationship between perceived quality and profitability, which occurs as the result of customer loyalty, more repeat purchases and less vulnerability to price wars.

■ *Brand equity*. In some instances the value of a brand (not to be confused with brand values, which are discussed later) has been listed on a company's balance sheet, which is a controversial move. This is understandable given that Nestlé paid £2.5bn (US$4.5bn) for Rowntree, which was six times the value of net assets.[1]

■ *Market share*. When a company buys a brand it is buying market share. Although the data are dated, PIMS data suggests that there is a strong positive relationship between high market share and profitability. More important, brands promise the purchaser consistent profitability. PIMS findings indicate that on average brands with a market share of 40 per cent generate three times the ROI of those with a market share of 10 per cent. In supporting this view Doyle (1998) argues that strong brands generate exceptional levels of profit through a triple leverage effect. The most obvious effect is through the higher volume which provides 'experience curve' effects, involving higher asset utilization and scale economies. The second source of advantage is through the higher price that the brand commands. Sometimes this price premium holds at the final consumer level, although it is usually at the retailer or distributor level that it is most apparent. Successful brands build such loyalty that they are able to generate superior earnings. A premium brand can earn 20 per cent higher returns than discounted products. Brand leaders also have lower unit costs as they can take advantage of experience effects which may occur in development, production or marketing, depending on the industry's value chain. The larger the brand the more is spent on the total marketing effort, and the larger the brand the less is spent in unit cost terms on marketing. The end result is that the brand leader's market share advantage is magnified substantially at the profit level. Here a brand advantage of 3:1 results through leverage in a profit contribution of nearly 6:1.

■ *Functional device*. Although this is the shortest section it is also probably the most important. Brands enable consumers to identify high-quality products and services and save on search costs.

BRAND DECISIONS

Companies must make a number of decisions with respect to their brand strategy.

Choice of presentation format

The presentation format to be used is important. The following constitutes a simple menu.

- *Company brand.* In this case the company uses the corporate name as the focus for all external communications, through advertising, products and letterheads, e.g. companies such as Coca-Cola, Heinz and ICI.
- *Individual brand.* Here the company behind the brand maintains a low corporate profile with respect to customers and focuses on the creation of strong brand identities. A prime example in the market for detergents, where P&G and Unilever dominate the UK market, although this is disguised by the focus on competing brands.
- *Mixed format.* Sometimes referred to as an endorsed brand. This is where the brand identity is displayed prominently but the corporate identity also features, e.g. Kellogg's with Kellogg's Cornflakes, Kellogg's Rice Krispies, etc.

The presentation formats mentioned above may be made more complex by building in other elements. Through the cowboy, Philip Morris uses a brand user strategy to promote Marlboro. Another format is the product class or brand family, e.g. Matsushita, group families of brands under separate range names. For example, Matsushita markets its electronic products under four brand families: National, Panasonic, Technics and Star.

Companies have made use of nationality in building corporate and brand identity. For example, it is reputed that 'Sony' was developed as a name not because of what it meant (it did not mean anything), but because it was thought to be a name that might appeal in the West. Using the same logic in a reverse direction, the British chain of electronics retailers, Currys, chose the Matsui brand name, as it was felt that British consumers would identify it as being of Japanese origin (it was not).

Eight steps to building a brand

The following describes an idealized notion of what ought to be done in building a brand. Later you will be asked to compare what Midland Bank planners did with this. We further revisit these issues in Chapter 8 on product policy.

- *Identify the brand position.* What are the brand's values? Where does it stand in the mind of the customer? What differentiates it from others?
- *Gap analysis.* Following a SWOT analysis – are there opportunities for brand extensions, i.e. by adding in additional products under the brand umbrella, or might these act to dilute the brand?

- *Develop the brand property*. The brand property is that element that is 'unique, memorable and indissolubly linked to that brand and no other' (Barry Day, vice-chairman, McCann-Erickson, in Clark, 1988). The brand property does not lie in the intrinsic nature of the product, e.g. a sweet fizzy drink, a sweet fizzy drink made with apples, a mint-flavoured chocolate or a medium-alcohol aperitif. Rather it is found in the rich tapestry of available referent systems which the advertisers plunder in their search for the creation of the new, the dazzling, the exclusive, the necessity. Through such a process the fizzy drink becomes 'the real thing', Coke; Babycham turns girls into Cinderella; After Eights are 'exclusive', while the 'Martini generation' live idyllic lives in tropical bliss.
- *Test alternative propositions*. Once developed, brand propositions may be tested with small groups of customers from the target segment, their reactions noted and changes suggested and implemented.
- Make the 'go/no-go' decision.
- *Construct the implementation plan*. This involves a consideration of the 4 Ps in relation to the brand. All these decisions will defer to the notion of 'brand property' and the target market segment which has been identified for the brand.
- Implement the plan.
- *Monitor the plan*. Go back to the beginning – identify the brand position.

In the next section recent ideas about brands are discussed, including brand congruity, personality and community. This view is compared with a behaviourist explanation of brands and brand loyalty.

MAINSTREAM EXPLANATION OF BRANDING

So far the mainstream explanation of branding has been discussed. Some of the assumptions made, e.g. with relation to brand differentiation, will be challenged later in this chapter when a behaviourist account is considered. In this section a mainstream explanation of branding is constructed that reflects that peculiar mixture of Freud, cognitive theory and semiotics that is to be found in marketing accounts of branding. Concepts relating to brand congruity, brand personality and brand community are discussed. We then consider how brands gain their meaning in more depth.

Brand congruity

The idea of congruity can be linked with Cognitive Information Processing (CIP) to the extent that people seek to achieve balance or consistency between their attitudes about people and things (Heider, 1958). For instance, Joe falls in love with Jean. Subsequently he finds out that she hates golf, although Joe is madly keen on it. When Joe learns of this, he feels a sense of disorientation and loss of balance, which he tries to restore, either by altering his relationship with Jean (loving Jean less) or by lowering his involvement level with golf (loving golf less). People seek consistency by preferring products and brands that have a symbolic meaning which is consistent with their self-concept. Self-congruity theory (Sirgy, 1982) suggests that consumers prefer to use a specific brand because they see themselves as similar to the kind of people that are thought to use it. For example, you may consider yourself to be 'studious' and also think that other people who are 'studious' buy Volvos. In this explanation you may view Volvo favourably when you come to consider a car purchase. An instance is discussed of how this happened in practice in relation to Midland Bank brands (see the following case study).

Brand personality

The idea of brand personality is related to brand congruity in that it refers to 'the set of human personality characteristics associated with a brand' (Aaker, 1997). This argues that, while brands may be functionally similar in fulfilling similar needs, a brand personality allows consumers to select that brand that best expresses their own individuality. Consequently, even allowing that brands may be similar, those which express clear and effective personalities should result in higher preferences and increased market share.

Fournier pushes the idea of brand 'personality' to its limits by arguing that a brand can be seen to be an 'active contributing partner in the dyadic relationship that exists between the person and the brand' (Fournier, 1995: 393). In this view, all marketing mix activities and brand management activities, e.g. advertising and direct marketing campaigns, are construed as being 'behaviours' which are enacted on behalf of the brand 'personality'. These

Figure 7.1
Differences
in brand
personality?

behaviours then trigger attitudinal and other responses on the part of the customer. According to Fournier this allows the audience to elevate the status of the brand from that of a passive object to that of being a 'relationship partner'. Following in this line of thought Govers and Schoormans (2005) found that consumers described variants of screwdriver and coffee maker in different ways.

Figure 7.1 shows three coffee makers and three food mixers. According to Govers and Schoormans (2005) respondents used words such as 'introvert', 'outspoken', 'sociable', 'kind', 'warm', 'friendly' and 'dependable' to describe the coffee makers in their study. Taking these as cues, how then might you describe the coffee makers in Figure 7.1? In your view do the different variants of coffee maker have different personalities? Now look at the food mixers. Do these have different personalities? What words or signifiers would you use to describe them?

On the other hand, Cornelissen and Harris make the point that, as brands are not people the use of terms

SHAPING BRAND CONGRUITY: MIDLAND BANK BRANDS

Although this research was conducted some time ago by one of the authors, it describes an example of the attempt to devise a brand that fitted the contours of a target segment. In 1985 planners at the UK-based Midland Bank recognized problems stemming from the bank's external environment. The domestic market was saturated with financial institutions offering the same product, with little choice or variation. The number of players was increasing whereas market potential was not. The number of customers overdrawing was in decline (which was bad news for banks!); the bank's overall share was declining; there was a net monthly loss in accounts. Finally, the introduction of free-if-in-credit banking and interest-bearing accounts had resulted in a transfer of value to the customer. Managers at Midland decided that something had to be done quickly. In order to maintain market share a decision was made to focus on the bank's main product, the current account. This was a valuable source of income in its own right which was considered to be key to sales of other profitable products and to the relationship with the bank. However, current accounts were perceived as being generic, leading to the use of the analogy of the Model T Ford within the bank. In any case, as the smallest of the 'Big Four' UK banks, Midland Bank could not compete on price alone. Applying the 'Model T' analogy to the bank situation, there was a perceived need to offer differences in both styles and ranges of account.

Branding was seen as key to successful differentiation. But how could this be achieved? A freelance researcher was commissioned to conduct a segmentation analysis of the consumer market. Findings indicated that bank customers could be segmented along two dimensions; the degree of confidence in dealing with the bank and the attitude towards the bank relationship. Initially this yielded up four segments: Traditionalists, Opportunists, Minimalists and New Bankers:

- *Traditionalists* expected a high level of service and respect from bank staff.
- *Opportunists* were similar to traditionalists in that they were confident in their dealings with banks. However, in contrast to Traditionalists, Opportunists had very little respect for banks. Opportunists tended to borrow at will without permission, yet became annoyed when 'hassled' by the bank. They were willing to pay for the service but wanted a minimum amount of hassle and to be in control of whatever was agreed.
- *Minimalists* were accustomed to dealing with banks but were keen to ensure that they minimized costs.
- *New bankers* were people who traditionally had been paid in cash but whose salary was now paid monthly into a bank account. They were unsure how to deal with banks.

Strategists within the bank decided to target Opportunists, as they felt that the needs of this market had not been fully addressed, and for the obvious reason that it would be a lucrative segment. Attention was paid to devising a product that would be attractive to the Opportunists. The product that the team came up with initially offered a current account with interest interlinked to a savings account, a cash card, a credit card, a fixed fee per month for money overdrawn up to £250 (US$449) or up to £1,000 (US$1,794) at a special rate. One statement covered all transactions. In May 1986 image consultants Fitch were asked to research names for the new product. Following a detailed investigation the name Vector was chosen as the brand name for the product.

Next attention was devoted to developing the promotional mix. Prior to developing any advertising concepts, qualitative research was conducted amongst the target audiences. Research findings indicated that the campaign should build on the existing corporate image 'Listening Bank' (corporate) campaign, yet should be strongly differentiated from this, more serious and less frivolous. The products must not be seen as money-making gimmicks. The first advertisement was developed for Vector on the basis of qualitative research. It became clear that the final advertisement would hinge on the character of the bank manager as much as that of the customer. The team envisaged a context where an Opportunist customer was seeking a loan from a bank manager. As the bank manager reflected the brand personality it was important that he should convey the correct tone. It was decided that it would be a man, to match the image of the traditional bank manager. The manager would be in control of the situation in the advertisement but it would also show that he listened and was attentive to the customer's needs. Consequently he emerged from the advertising as a wiser, improved bank manager. The team decided that the customer should reflect the ideal profile of the Opportunist: clever, confident, with a lack of respect for banks. These features were incorporated into the research brief for the advertising agency. In 1987 Vector was launched as a 'money transmission' product aimed at Opportunists. Subsequently two other brands were launched: Orchard, a mortgage product aimed at Traditionalists, and Meridian, a savings product. However, following the launch of the brands, managers began to change their perceptions of what these brands would portray.

It was only when Vector was launched that managers began to realize its full potential as a vehicle to adapt their products more closely to customer needs. As one manager put it, 'Up until then we had thought mainly about products and then we realized that we should be focused much more on the customer'. An example of this product-based thinking related to Vector. Initially, the thinking behind this product was that it was a money transmission account, in that it was devised to help Opportunists to manage their money more efficiently. In retrospect managers thought that surely self-confident Opportunists would want other products; why restrict the Vector person to a money transmission product? Why not offer a tailored mortgage and savings and loan scheme as well? The concept of multi-service accounts was developed from this concept and, in September 1989, Vector was relaunched with its sister brands, Orchard and Meridian. However, because of the launch of a rival product by First Direct, the launch date was brought forward. The multi-media campaign which followed was the largest that the bank had ever undertaken.

The immediate effect of the campaign showed that 15 per cent of the total sample who were aware of new or improved current accounts spontaneously recalled Vector. Among Midland customers the respective level of awareness was 31 per cent. Some 6 per cent of Midland customers expressed interest in holding a Vector account. By December 1990 Vector brand awareness average, at 62 per cent, was just behind the market leader. Thus when Brian Pearse, the incoming CEO at Midland Bank, announced that he was going to shelve both Vector and Orchard in 1991, it came as a bolt out of the blue – even apparently to Kevin Gavaghan, the bank's marketing director. Seemingly, Vector had attracted only 230,000 new customers, despite high levels of awareness.

such as 'identity' and 'personality' leads to the creation of the false belief that there is some essence of corporate personality or some form of real organizational self (Cornelissen and Harris, 2001: 63). This point is so obvious that it is often missed; brands are not people but rather like puppets that dance to the puppet master's tune. The question is, who are the puppet masters? Arguably brand managers can do little to infuse a brand with life. Brand mascots like the Pillsbury doughboy, Churchill the bulldog (the face and tail of an insurance company) and the Andrex puppy may be lovable but do we form relationships with them? The way in which a brand acquires a 'personality' is mysterious and can have an end that was unanticipated by its original designers. For example, the story of how Nazi Germany's 'people's car', the Volkswagen Beetle, became transformed into Herbie, beloved emblem of 1960s 'flower power' for US and European students, had much more to it than the movie. Returning to consideration of brand personality, some authors do not go to the extreme lengths of Fournier. Allen and Olson define brand personality more impersonally as: 'the set of meanings constructed by an observer to describe the "inner" characteristics of another person' (Allen and Olson, 1995: 392).

Through the use of the scare quotes around the word 'inner' Allen and Olson imply that there are no real inner characteristics. Rather the observer imputes these. If the notion of some form of inner essence is insufficient to characterize the brand personality, then how might this be constructed? If, contrary to what Cornelissen and Harris (2001) suggest, it is possible to think of brands as being personalities, then what are the mechanisms by which people treat brands as if they really are personalities? Allen and Olsen (1995) argue that people make attributions about brands in the same way that they do about each other's behaviour. For example, if an observer sees another person kicking a dog they may well think of that person as being 'cruel'. In this view attributions about personality traits are based largely on experience, observations of behaviour which are caused by the unobserved personality trait, e.g. 'the guy kicked the dog because he was cruel'. They suggest that one can use the same logic to conceptualize brand personality. To do so the brand must seem to perform intentional behaviours; it must seem somehow to be 'alive'. Based on these observed characteristics consumers make attributions about the brand personality, its 'inner' nature. For example, Aaker considers that the personality of Levi's 501 jeans is 'American, western, ordinary, common, blue-collar, hard-working and traditional' (Aaker, 1995: 394). As a result these authors urge brand builders to stress the 'aliveness' and action potential of the brand which they are advertising.

But can it seriously be said that the 'relations' between the buyer and a brand constitute a relationship? The word 'relationship' was popularized by 'humanistic' psychologists such as Carl Rogers (1980) to describe 'meaningful' interpersonal relationships. Even within its 'proper' psychological context some people find the word to be clichéd. One could suggest that describing the 'relationship' between a person and their brands as being akin to human relations ultimately devalues the latter. In this sense Cornelissen and Harriss (2001) may be making an important point. Transferring meaning from what usually defines relations between people (identity, personality, relationships) to those relations between people and things may do more than 'humanize' what are otherwise 'impersonal' transactions. It may have the reverse effect in making 'relations' between people more thing-like.

Brands, meaning and identity

The discussion about brand congruity and brand personality raises the question of how brands attain their meaning and how this is in turn transferred to consumers? Allen and Olsen (1995), discussed above, suggest that consumers attribute meaning as well as action and purpose to brands. But what are the mechanics of how this works? In marketing the focus on meaning can be traced to Levy (1959), who argued that people do not buy products for what they do but for what they mean. While these are inseparable in practice, it makes sense analytically to divide the discussion about brand meaning and identity into two sections, one dealing with the role played by brands in our lives, the other which focuses on how brand meaning is mediated through advertising (cf. Elliott and Wattanasuwan, 2001).

In this respect brands are symbols whose meaning is used to create and define a consumer's self-concept. In Chapter 3 the Freudian view was discussed showing that possessions can come to be regarded as being part of the extended self (Csikszentmihalyi and Rochberg-Halton, 1991; Belk, 1988). Elliott and Wattanasuwan (2001) follow this line of thinking, arguing that consumers invest psychic energy into people and objects. In this view the self-concept is complex as energy may be invested in a number of people and things. Consequently a person possesses a multiplicity of identities. This account highlights the role played by narratives or stories in the formation of identity. Much of the knowledge that is gained about ourselves and our culture comes to us from the commercial process of story-telling called branding. In building up these stories meaning is constructed from two sources; our lived experience and the mass media.

LIVED EXPERIENCE OF BRANDS

Freudian theory suggests that at a certain point in our life course the issue of identity becomes important to us. In this respect Erikson (1968) argues that identity confusion is experienced by most adolescents. This is because by that stage of development the individual feels independent of the family and ventures beyond the safe confines of the family to sample other social contexts. New social contexts can be frightening and challenging to the adolescent's sense of self, particularly if they have not previously mastered the ability to take different roles. Consequently a person may react to this sense of confusion by clinging to the security provided by their peer group and may overidentify with the heroes of that group to the extent that they seem to lose their individuality. Where the adolescent fails in positively responding to the identity crisis they may attempt to create a negative identity by seeking to become everything that they have learned ought to be avoided. From the above, it is important to consider the context in which interaction takes place with products in order to gain meaning from them. As children we consume many food and beverage brands in the familiar and often secure context of the family home. This is why such brands attain such a nostalgic appeal later in life. Life in the school context brings us into contact with others, and here brands may become implicated in the struggle for esteem and status, signifying who is 'in' and who is 'out' of the group. Most children who must negotiate the changed balance between home, school and a widening circle of social contexts feel confused and some will be disaffected. This latter group are the targets for a host of branded identities, many of which are to be found on MTV or something similar, from Marilyn Manson to Pete Doherty of Babyshambles or, more extremely, the 'stars' of Death Metal. Given Erikson's comments then as children grow into adolescence a range of brands targeted at the 'anti-hero' image should become salient. Identity is lucrative for marketers; like spots it does not seem to go away. Some claim that the identity crisis is occurring at younger ages than ever and have coined the neologism 'tweenie' to describe it.

The idea of a reference group (cf. Newcomb, 1948) plays a key role in the construction of identity as one moves from the family context to the school and the ever widening social context. This divides the 'in group' that we feel comfortable with, from 'out groups', those we tend to avoid and in turn the aspirational group to which we seek to belong. In consumer societies brands can play a key role in differentiating 'in' groups from 'out' groups. For example, in the UK, the luxury Burberry brand has been identified with 'chav' culture:

> Chav is a slang term which has been in wide use throughout the United Kingdom since 2004. It refers to a subcultural stereotype of a person with fashions such as flashy 'bling' jewellery and counterfeit designer clothes or sportswear, an uneducated, uncultured, impoverished background, a tendency to congregate around places such as fast-food outlets, bus stops or other shopping areas, and a culture of antisocial behavior.
>
> (Wikipedia online)

When chavs begin to wear Burberry other groups stop wearing the brand. On the other hand, those who are proud to be chavs may react strongly against brands such as Polo, which may be perceived as being associated with 'upper-class twits'.

Mediated experience of brands

While lived experience is in the here and now, the consumption of media products involves the ability to experience events that are spatially and temporally distant from the practical context of everyday life. Elliott and Watanasuwan (1998) argue that individuals draw from mediated experience and interlace this with lived experience in constructing the self. In this view brand advertising is a major source of symbolic meaning. Mediated experience consists of what we learn from the mass media and in particular from our consumption of television, radio and films or movies. We do not simply soak up meaning from advertising but actively recreate this in group situations. We are likely to watch the same television programmes and advertisements as our 'in group' does and to swap stories about them. But how exactly is advertising meaning created? This is explained below in more detail.

ADVERTISING AND REFERENT SYSTEMS

The concept of referent systems discussed here should be distinguished from that of reference groups which were outlined above. A simple but crude way of differentiating them is to say that reference groups tend to exist in the real lived world whereas referent systems exist in the mediated world. When products are new they have no intrinsic meaning but most draw this from the general cultural context. One way of doing so is to associate the brand with a well known personality. For example, the perfume Chanel No. 5 was originally associated with its founder, Coco Chanel, who was well known as being a role model for other women, being perceived to be chic, sophisticated and glamorous. Coco was so influential that she is credited with bringing to an end the idea, prevalent in Europe at the time, that having a pale skin was attractive for women, by staying out in the sun and gaining a 'tan' while on holiday in the south of France. When Coco died the brand had to be redefined for a new generation. The 'chic' and 'sophisticated' brand values associated with Coco were retained by the company, as they defined the brand's core. Brand managers then searched for other 'chic' and 'sophisticated' women who could represent Chanel brand values. Over the years these have included the French actress Catherine Deneuve, Vanessa Paradis and, more recently, Kate Winslett (see Figure 7.2). Brands like Chanel initially gain their meaning by taking it from sources in the wider cultural context. To reiterate, a referent system consists of an entire system of meaning as it exists at one point in time. One example of a referent system is the system of models discussed above (Williamson, 1978).

There are two noteworthy aspects of referent systems:

■   Individual items gain their meaning in terms of what they are not. Margot Hemingway was used to signify a competing brand called Babe at the same time when Catherine Deneuve was employed to signify Chanel. Hemingway was the daughter of the famous author Ernest Hemingway, a kickboxer and 'new woman'. The image she gave Babe was quite different from that conveyed by Deneuve. Williamson argues that it is only when one is in the know about the referent system, in this case the meanings associated with famous models, that one has access to the full meaning of the advertisement.

■   The referent system is not concerned with real people but with their symbolic meaning as marked out within a code. Catherine Deneuve is one element which connotes 'sophistication' within the code whereas Margot Hemingway occupies another position that signifies 'new woman'.

Some more up-do-date examples of models used in perfume advertisements include Riley Keogh, Elvis's granddaughter, who at the age of 16 became the face of 'Miss Dior Cherie'. She is thought to signify mischievous fun and innocence, in addition to the halo effect provided by her dead grandfather. Chen Huilin, the famous Hong Kong singer, is the face of Dior Capture in China. By comparison Charlize Theron, who signifies passion and sexiness, became the spirit of J'adore. Other referent systems include humour, which was

Figure 7.2
Referent system for perfume products

Source: adapted from Williamson (1978), p. 29.

successfully used in promoting Hamlet cigars in the UK and nature, which often is used in promoting car brands.

Williamson argues that, over time, the product and the correlate or image which has been attached to it become linked to the extent that it appears 'natural'. The product merges with its correlate and they appear as one thing. The transfer which initially takes place, whereby the signifier 'Marlboro' is constantly juxtaposed with the signifier 'cowboy', becomes naturalized. Marlboro itself seems to signify the 'wild west.'

THE BRAND AS GENERATOR OF MEANING

Once the correlate becomes fused with the product so that it appears that the link between them is natural, the product begins to generate meaning in its own right. In this case, if we were to see a person with the product, the transfer might be from the product on to the person. For example, the owner of a Mercedes car becomes recognized as being sophisticated, because the signified 'sophistication' has transferred from the car to the person. In this case the person is seen to become sophisticated as a result of her consumption of the car. Here the product purports to become the actual referent (the real thing) for the sign (sophistication). For example, advertisements tell us that they can create the feelings which they represent (if we buy the Mercedes we will be sophisticated). Williamson describes this effect when she says that a product can be connected to an emotional referent in two different ways:

- ■ 'You can go out and buy a box of chocolates because you feel happy; or you can feel happy because you have bought a box of chocolates; and these are not the same thing. In the first case the chocolates do not pretend to be "more" than a sign; they mean something, but in terms of a feeling you had anyway. They are a sign for a feeling which is the referent. But if the product creates the feeling, it has become more than a sign: it enters the space of the referent, and becomes active in reality' (Williamson, 1978: 36/7).

- ■ The second interpretation provides an illuminating insight into how a brand can literally come to be 'the real thing'. Williamson suggests that products having been associated with particular feelings for a long time become linked to the feeling to the extent that they come to 'be' the feeling. For example, in the UK the brand Lucozade was for many years associated with images of health and energy and came to be identified with these to such an extent that people who were raised on a diet of Lucozade advertising began to think that only it (or its counterpart Ribena) could create the appropriate healthy feeling. Williamson's explanation is useful in that it shows how brands can come to be used as symbolic resources for the construction of the self. Elliott and Wattanasuwan (1997) argue that for the meaning of brands to become fully concrete the mediated meaning derived from advertising and promotion must be negotiated with the lived experience of purchase and use. In this respect it is not sufficient merely to have the brand; in real life other people expect us to be sufficiently competent to live up to its expectations, i.e. if we own a Fender guitar, to be a competent player, or a sports car, to be able to drive it well.

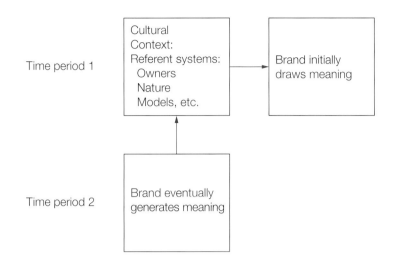

Figure 7.3
Brand from
drawer of
meaning to
brand as
signifier of
meaning

BRAND AS STABLIZER OF MEANING

Not only do brands generate meaning, it is argued that they stabilize meaning for people at a time when other cherished institutions are under threat. In modern times it sometimes seems that the only things that are familiar and unchanging are the brands we have consumed since childhood. Marketers play on such anxieties and just as in the old days of branding they offer the solution, 'If only everything in life was as reliable as a Volkswagen'. Elliott and Wattanasuwan (1997: 5) argue that nostalgia can play a key role here in that adults tend to buy brands that remind them of sensitive periods such as childhood and adolescence. In particular, they contend that adults will use brands that they have had olfactory experiences with in childhood as a means of restoring a sense of security. Brands that we have lived experience with acquire a depth of meaning during sensitive periods that are unattainable by brands at a later point in our lives. They discuss Hovis bread, Yorkshire Tea and Levi's.

Brand groupings: subcultures, communities and tribes

Above we outlined the way that reference groups form an important context for the understanding of brand consumption. We now consider how different descriptions of brand-user groups can allow new understandings of the lived and mediated experience of brands.

BRAND SUBCULTURES

The notion of a 'subculture' of consumption moves beyond cognitive psychology and into the realms of social psychology and sociology. On this view, while the brand is central, it comprises one aspect of an entire subculture of consumption. The 'sub-culture' is marked off from the mainstream through key elements in style, or the way in which a person comports himself. Dick Hebdige describes the emergence of 'Mod' and 'Rocker' subcultures in

England in the 1950s and 1960s. Each group differentiated itself from the other primarily in terms of the bike they rode: Rockers straddled heavy British Triumph or BSA motor bikes; Mods sleek, streamlined Italian Vespa scooters. The groups also differentiated themselves from each other in terms of the clothing they wore, where they liked to hang out and their choice of music and recreational drugs.

Hebdige also noticed that within each group a pecking order emerged according to how well one could handle the machine, distinguishing oneself from 'inauthentic' riders. A more recent study by Schouten and McAlexander (1995) which focuses on the Harley-Davidson user illustrates how the organization of this subculture is layered like an onion, with the 'Easy Rider' or 'Electra-glide on Blue' leather-clad, tattooed aesthete forming the centre and day trippers acting as outriders to the culture. The brand positively plays a role in establishing and maintaining a sense of separation, cohesiveness and solidarity necessary for the formation of the subculture, in addition to providing resources for the identity work of members.

BRAND COMMUNITY

McAlexander and Schouten (2002) have since revised their terms, arguing that the term 'community' is more appropriate than that of 'subculture'. Their subsequent research indicated that, in particular, the notion of subculture overplayed the role of the white male leather-clad biker and underplayed that played by others such as women and minorities who also owned and rode Harleys. Muniz and O'Guinn (2001) define community in terms of the following:

■ Consciousness of kind, refers to a shared consciousness.
■ Shared rituals and traditions.
■ Sense of moral responsibility or duty to the community as a whole.

Consciousness of kind means that, although brand users feel a strong attachment to the brand, they feel an even stronger attachment to each other. They refer to a sense of 'we-ness, whereby owners of Saabs or Apple Macs refer to themselves as 'Saabers' or 'Mac' people. Muniz and O'Guinn (2001) found that each community formed a kind of hierarchy based on the extent to which the brand was used authentically and legitimately. For example, many Saab owners disparaged 'yuppies' who bought Saabs because they were rich but who were not really committed to them. A sense of community was sustained through oppositional brand loyalty; Saab owners defined themselves as not-Volvo owners (which they associated with tractors); Mac users were definitely not PC users. The authors found evidence of the exercise of rituals and traditions in the groups which they studied, including Saab drivers flashing their lights and waving at other Saab drivers. While these rituals may at first glance seem to be insignificant, they function to create consciousness of kind. It was considered important to know the history of the brand, which often distinguished the 'true believer' from the acolyte, and to circulate stories or myths. Finally, these groups were infused with

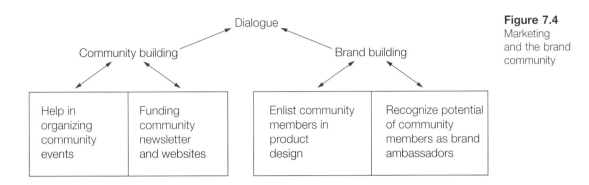

Figure 7.4
Marketing and the brand community

a sense of moral responsibility to the community as a whole. The obverse of this was indicated, e.g. when a Mac user who switched to using PCs was regarded as being 'morally reprehensible', a 'Mac turncoat'. Owners helped each other by providing assistance and advice on how to use the brand. The notion of community enables one to think of a brand as being the common property of those who work for the company and those who form the 'community'.

As Figure 7.4 shows, the idea of brand community goes beyond that of brand congruence. A person may buy a brand that is congruent with their self-concept. They may also buy brands that fit in with the values of their 'in group'. However, the notion of community is more active, suggesting management is not simply responsive to the needs of users but maintains a continual dialogue with them so as to ensure that the needs of the community and of the brand that sustains it are met. Academics and researchers such as Schouten and McAlexander can become part of that dialogue. For example, the latter recounts being recruited to advise Jeep on how to build a community around the brand. Jeep101 was the first in the Camp Jeep series that flowed from this venture.

The idea of brand community may convey a sense of warmth but also carries the whiff of saccharin to some. For example, one blogger asked, in noting Schouten's 'handsome sum' from Harley for his work on brand community, and how film maker Adam Berman had won an award for his film 'Biker Dreams', what did the bikers get out of it? She answers her own question; 'they are robbed of their bad-boy/tough-chick/Hell's-Angel image by a homogeneous, warm-and-fuzzy portrayal' (Melander, 2005). In any event some might take the ascription of the word 'community' in relation to brands to be a step too far. The traditional word 'community' can be taken to represent something much deeper by referring to those who share not only their daily food but also their ritual food in common (communion) (Falk, 1994).

BRAND TRIBES

The idea of a brand tribe is looser and has a more dangerous feel to it than that of the brand community described above; there is something here that is beyond the influence of brand

BRAND CULT: WHO NEEDS ENEMIES?

The idea of a cult has connotations of religion and even fanaticism. The creation of a fanatical band of loyal customers might seem to be the dream of every marketing executive. But there is another side to the story. First there is the bizarre. For example, Wells (2001) describes a ceremony where a priest 'marries' a group of devoted Mazda Miata owners to their cars. She follows through by suggesting: 'If a person can come to believe that they are genuinely in love with a product, then what happens when the "love" is not reciprocated?'

Brady *et al.* (2004) describe the case of a self-professed Apple junkie called Niestat who was building his film career using Apple computers and software. When he and his brother discovered that the original iPod's batteries were irreplaceable, they made a film called 'iPod's Dirty Secret' and launched a protest website that received 1.4m hits. They argued that they made the film because they believed in the brand so much. Brady makes the point that such loyalty flies in the face of conventional marketing wisdom. Customers demand love rather than simple reliability and want their brands to be a form of self-expression. The senior vice-president of strategic marketing at Samsung is quoted in the article as saying 'Consumers are empowered in a way that is almost frightening.'

Always there have been cult brands that have a set of 'true' believers. Even in the relatively homespun UK brands such as Guinness, Heinz and HP sauce have raised their heads above the pack. Brady and her colleagues argue that, alongside the iPod, such a band of believers helped Apple to rise almost 24 per cent to $6.9bn (£3.8bn). One problem with this band is that they are not necessarily easy to control. Brand fanaticism can be dangerous, as the Niesdat case described above illustrates. No doubt Steve Jobs of Apple has the occasional sleepless night when he recalls the good old days of the early 1980s when Apple announced the original MacIntosh with the most stunning advertisement ever made. Just one year later, the stock price of Apple fell to $14 (from $63 in 1983). The cult status of the brand perhaps led Jobs to believe that he could control everything from the design of the hardware to the software. In contrast IBM allowed anyone to clone their system and consequently IBM, and its Windows platform that had been developed by a fledgling company called Microsoft, rapidly took the lead over Apple. Since Jobs's return to Apple in 1997 he has been helped by the same loyal band of Apple devotees – over 85,000 annually attend the MacWorld Expo in San Fransisco. While welcoming the innovative launches of the iMac, G5, iPod and iTunes, devotees were not so welcoming of Apple's deal with Intel in 2005.

managers. A tribe does not necessarily refer to a bounded group. For example, a large enough proportion of the Coca-Cola 'tribe' were outraged when managers changed the Coke formula some years back, before telling them that they done so, that they forced the company to retract. The entire story is interesting. It is suggested that you follow it up on the Internet if you can. As described by Maffesoli (1996), the neo-tribes consist of configurations of members who are connected by loose bonds of 'common affect'. The idea of a tribe enables us to think beyond the idea of those who support the brand to those who actively identify against it. There is the possibility that, for every brand community out there, there is also likely to be an anti-community, an anti-McDonald's, anti-Nike, anti-Harley, group. The idea of tribal identities accords with the romantic vision which many anti-consumers have of themselves, as guerillas who hollow out 'temporary autonomous zones' or crevices in the monolithic space of commodity consumption, which become the sites of a never-ending guerilla war. George McKay's work (1998) provides an excellent summary. One might argue that it makes more sense to view those excluded from consumption as constituting a number of different marginalized groupings: the aged poor, immigrants and vagrants.

SECTION SUMMARY

In this section the symbolic role that brands play as projected personalities that people come to identify with is discussed. Consideration is made as to how the meaning of brands is negotiated in the context of lived and mediated experience. Particular emphasis is given to how brands gain their meaning through interaction with reference groups and referent systems. A common thread running through the entire section is that brands are important in the construction of a person's identity. Advertising is important in linking meanings to brands whose meaning is, in turn, incorporated into the self-concept of consumers. The lived experience of consumers is recycled back into advertising. This argument suggests that advertising can play an important role in the differentiation of brands. Some brands come to generate symbolic meaning, e.g. the mere possession of the brand can connote the meaning that a person is sophisticated and successful. However, this does not mean that consumers uncritically absorb the meaning of an advertisement. Rather this is negotiated within the context of reference groups and the personal situation of the receiver.

BEHAVIOURIST VIEW

If the previous discussion may have led you to believe that the key to successful branding lies in the idea that advertising creates powerful identities for brands, that endows them with symbolic meaning, which differentiates them from their rivals and enables them to attract bands of devoted brand fanatics, then this section may disabuse you.

Behaviourists would accept that some of the foregoing discussion is consistent with their principles. For example, Williamson's (1978) account of how brand meaning is created by drawing this from referent systems that exist in the wider cultural context can be read in a way that is consistent with a classical conditioning explanation. Taking the examples of Catherine Deneuve and Margot Hemingway, Catherine acts as the UCS for Chanel (CS) and Margot as the UCS for Babe (CS). The use of actresses who signify quite different properties (chic and elegant versus tomboyish) is sensible, as it avoids blocking effects. Despite this, a behaviourist explanation would not proceed to consider the role played by 'within the skin' concepts such as 'attitude' or 'identity'.

How might B.F. Skinner explain the feelings that I have with my Harley-Davidson motor cycle, my Gibson or Fender guitar, my Volkswagen Beetle or, for that matter, my Dunkin Donuts? He would argue that the effects of operant reinforcement are often represented as inner states or possessions, such as 'love' and 'identity', but that what this comes down to is that when I say that I 'love' my Harley 'community' because they give me a sense of 'identity', it is simply to say that I find Harley and the people who ride them are reinforcing. Similarly, when Elliott and Wattanasuwan (1997) link nostalgia as a powerful link with identity and brands, Skinner (1974: 59) retorts that desire or longing is closely related to a current absence of appropriate behaviour. 'Nostalgia' is literally the pain generated by a strong tendency to return to a previous state of affairs when return is impossible. In this respect nostalgia occurs when a person no longer has an appropriate occasion to engage in rewarding behaviour.

An operant conditioning explanation would argue that the mainstream account, described above, places too much emphasis on constructs such as attitude and image and in turn on the putative role played by persuasive advertising. The mainstream argument portrays advertising as moving the consumer along the hierarchy of effects from awareness to interest to desire (AIDA) and, subsequently, to purchase behaviour. Remember that in Chapter 3 discussion showed that when a person is highly involved with a purchase they will be more likely to process the advertising message content using the central route, as opposed to merely attending to the execution (Petty and Cacioppo, 1983). Consequently, consumers ought to be more attentive to the rational claims made about the product and also to links to the consumer's identity made by the advertisement. Although overall the effect of advertising will be relatively weak in this context, its role is seen to be persuasive, in seeking to change and solidify attitudes which in turn will instigate behavioural change. Linked with this idea is the belief that one can make a brand more highly involving by associating it with advertising that is involving in its own right. In contrast to the above view, which sees attitude change and image to be important components of persuasive advertising, behaviourists argue that there is little evidence to support the claim that attitudes and intentions actually predict behaviour. Additionally the finding of 'near instant' loyalty to brands suggests that, at least for the brands under review, consumers did not take a lot of time to construct an attitude prior to purchase (Ehrenberg and Goodhardt, 2000). Behaviourists would suggest to the contrary, that advertising has difficulty in raising awareness, because of the operation of selective perception by consumers and that there are no strongly persuasive techniques. Instead, they argue, the real role played by advertising lies in reinforcing satisfaction after purchase has taken place (Foxall, 1996: 42–7).

In fact the division between 'mainstream' and 'behaviourist' points of view that has been constructed here is not so clear-cut. For example, Elliott and Wattanasuwan (2000) whom we have been parcelled into the 'mainstream' viewpoint, acknowledge that the most powerful attitudes are developed after purchasing and using the product. However, these authors do acknowledge that advertising plays an important role in creating symbolic meaning for the brand. Furthermore, the mainstream view is that a brand, to be successful, must be differentiated from the competition. On this view consumers need a reason, whether it is functional or emotional, for choosing one brand over another. A behaviourist explanation would argue that competitive advantage is soon copied and so is unsustainable in the long run. Consequently it is not so important to differentiate the offering as to ensure a match with the rival. Where the mainstream argument focuses on AIDA, which is the process leading up to behaviour, the behaviourist focuses on reinforcement, or the creation of satisfaction, desire and conviction that arise after purchase.

Some of the more perceptive among you might wonder how the discussion of the importance of advertising matches with Chapter 3, where J.B. Watson's use of advertising to stimulate fear and then behaviour change is described. Like modern behaviourists he would not resort to the use of words signifying 'within the skin' factors such as 'attitude'. On the other hand, there is no doubt that, contrary to his modern counterparts, he believed firmly in the persuasive role of advertising!

The behaviourist explanation of brand choice

An operant conditioning explanation would emphasize the pattern of reinforcement associated with brand use. Foxall (2005) used TNS Superpanel data, drawn from 15,000 UK households over a sixteen-week period to seek answers to questions about brand choice. The brands selected were fruit juice, packet tea, tea bags, margarine, butter, baked beans, instant coffee, cheese, breakfast cereals and biscuits. One of the main aims of his study was to identify the actual effects of different contingencies, e.g. the effects of price and non-price elements of the marketing mix on consumer choice. In investigating the food brands Foxall measured utilitarian and informational reinforcement for the food brands. On average individuals bought 70 per cent of their goods at the same status level. When people bought at a different status level they usually bought from adjacent levels rather than from distant ones. Some people bought exclusively the cheapest brands while others bought exclusively the most expensive, indicating the unsurprising but important fact that people have different budgets. For all but one of the nine categories the majority of consumers bought 70 per cent or more of their purchases from the same utilitarian level. Foxall concluded that consumers choose their repertoire of brands on the basis of the informational and utilitarian level of reinforcement offered by the brands.

BRAND LOYALTY

Definitions of brand loyalty differ according to whether one shares a cognitive or a behaviourist outlook. Sheth (1968) provides a definition that is consistent with a behaviourist understanding, which is stochastic, focusing on relative frequency of purchase. On the other hand, Reynolds *et al.* (1975; see also Ha, 1988) are in line with a cognitive, or deterministic, explanation, which defines brand loyalty as the tendency for a person to continue over time to exhibit similar attitudes in situations similar to those he/she has previously encountered.

A strong attitude and commitment are important in the deterministic explanation. This describes the core member of the brand subculture who will refuse to buy an alternative if their favourite brand is not in stock. It links very much into the adoption process which we discuss in more detail in the chapter on communications. On the face of it the findings of stochastic research pose some problems for a deterministic understanding. For example, Ehrenberg's findings (1988, 1999) suggest that:

- Mainstream accounts emphasize the persuasive role of advertising, via the ideas of the USP and AIDA in making people desire the brand before they have bought it. This has led to the idea that the consumer will be influenced by the last advertisement seen or the weight of past advertising. In turn this has led to the use of advertising awareness and recall measures in pre-testing and monitoring advertisements. However, Ehrenberg argues that there is little evidence that advertising for established brands works like this. In its persuasive role advertising is thought to create desire or conviction or at least to add value to the brand. For this reason those advertisements that seek to create a brand image, selling a USP, or informing consumers that they need a special product to meet a particular need, e.g. special shampoo for oily hair. But there is no empirical evidence that advertising succeeds in this aim when there are no differences to sell.

- Comparatively few purchasers of a product are totally brand-loyal to a particular brand over a period of time. Ehrenberg and Uncles (1999) explored a range of FMCG categories provided by Nielsen and concluded that on average 11 per cent of customers were 100 per cent loyal. Foxall (2005) found that while multi-brand purchasing was found for all products, the proportion of sole buyers ranged from 59 per cent for butter to 14 per cent for cereals and cheese, noting that such findings are entirely consistent with ratio schedules of reinforcement (Foxall, 2005: Table 7.4, p. 136). He also noticed that some consumers switch each week, based on what the cheapest brand is.

- Most consumers are not loyal to one brand but purchase a number of brands from a small repertoire of available brands.

- Most brands within a product category are substitutable in that they are similar in terms of their formulation and functionality. Given that their benefits are directly substitutable, he suggests that it is not surprising that consumers switch brands. Foxall (2005) found that all the nine product categories analysed were close substitutes.

- Repeat purchase loyalty tends to be similar for brands that have similar market shares. Smaller brands not only attract fewer buyers but those buyers buy less of the brand, or buy it less frequently.

- The finding of 'near instant' brand loyalty (Ehrenberg and Goodhardt, 2000).

- There are no real differences in attitudes between users of different brands.

BRAND PERSONALITY: FCUKED?

The retailer French Connection was a well known brand on British high streets in the 1980s. However, in the period spanning 1988 to 1992 the company found that it was in a static market and subject to heightened competition. Management decided that something had to be done to arrest the decline and a strategy of refurbishment and development of new ranges took place between 1992 and 1996. With growing alarm management noted that this did not halt the decline and decided that there was a need to give the brand an emotional point of differentiation which would make it stand out in the high street for members of the target audience. Observation indicated that most UK advertising campaigns were similar, that there was considerable emphasis on the product and little differentiation between store brands. The French Connection strategy was to break with convention by focusing on linking the brand with its target group.

Fairly early on it was decided to cultivate an 'anti-hero' image that would involve a deliberate attempt to generate controversy to create lots of free media publicity. The slogan FCUK reflected a dual meaning that on the one hand suggested the abbreviation 'French Connection, UK'; and on the other a swearword that was perceived to be off limits to respectable people. Managers knew that the campaign would be distasteful to some but counted that this would not include the target group which would identify with the overall image generated. As with other 'anti-hero' advertisments such as the Irn-Bru campaign that was developed for A.G. Barr (see p. 162), French Connection was reputed to have tracked the success of the campaign by the number of complaints received by the Advertising Standards Authority.

Following the campaign the company reported an increase in turnover by 17 per cent, compared with 3 per cent overall for the sector. They also reported high brand awareness. Due to the success of the campaign it is perhaps inevitable that it was imitated by others. One group was the British Young Conservative Party which labelled itself CFUK. French Connection's share price increased fourfold between 1999 and 2004 as it developed a reputation as a highly fashionable high street retailer. With the rather obvious connotations of FCUK, it was inevitable that someone would seek to sue. Retired businessman Dennis Woodman felt that the logo was so blatant that it went against 'generally accepted principles of morality' in the light of how it could be misread. However, perhaps alone of all those who had seen the advertisements, the UK Trade Mark Registry read them without any trace of irony. They dismissed Woodman's complaint, citing the success of the brand that stood for French Connection United Kingdom, and opening the way for the logo to be extended to watches and jewellery.

By 2005, however, beneath all the hype, it was clear that all was not well in the FCUK stable. Analysts began to wonder whether the latest French Connection clothes were special enough to convince customers they were worth the top-end prices. In early 2005 they had projected pre-tax profits for the year ending January 2006 at £20–25m (US$36–45m). However, following a disastrous winter, the reality was closer to half that figure and to one-third of pre-tax profit for the previous year. More worryingly, this sales downturn came at a time when competitors such as John Lewis and M&S were showing signs of recovery (anon., 2005). Some blamed the 'premium positioning' of the French Connection brand for the latest disappointment. Rumours circulated that French Connection was to scale down if not discard the outdated FCUK image and that it would be axing its controversial T-shirts. No mention was made of the logo when the company announced its fightback promotional campaign based on the more 'subtle' theme of 'fashion versus style'. The first advertisement for the new 'subtle' campaign featured two women kickboxing and sharing a lingering kiss, attracting fifty complaints in the first few days (anon., 2006). Results declared in 2006 suggest that French Connection's problems have still to be addressed.

CONCLUSION

By the end of this chapter students should be:

■ familiar with relevant terminology such as brand equity, brand congruity, brand sub-culture, brand community, brand tribe, stochastic and deterministic;

■ aware of key differences between mainstream and behaviourist explanations of branding and brand loyalty;

■ able to explain relations between concepts, for example between brand congruity and brand personality;

■ able to understand the mainstream explanation of how to build a brand.

REVIEW QUESTIONS

1 Is there any relation between self-congruity and brand personality?
2 Summarize the key differences in the explanation of branding from (a) a cognitive point of view; (b) a behaviourist point of view.
3 How might Elliott and Wattanasuwan (2000) and B.F. Skinner differ with respect to what nostalgia is?
4 What are the relations between brand communities, brand subcultures and brand tribes?
5 What are the differences between reference groups and referent systems?
6 Can anything be branded?
7 How did Midland Bank management seek to establish congruity between the brand and the customer?
8 Referring back to Chapter 2 on marketing planning, how does the process entered into by Midland Bank managers fit with the ideal model described?
9 How should a brand like Apple seek to work with the cult?
10 What would a behaviourist think of this?
11 To what extent might one ascribe the success and slipping fortunes of French Connection to the FCUK personality?
12 To what extent can a brand rely solely on advertising to boost its fortunes?
13 How might a behaviourist explanation of FCUK differ from a mainstream explanation?

8 PRODUCT

LEARNING OBJECTIVES

When you have completed this unit, you should be able to:

- discuss the differences between 'product' and 'service' marketing;

- understand the bases for the classification of products;

- understand the following concepts: product mix depth and width; product line; product item;

- evaluate the usefulness of using the PLC as a planning tool;

- develop a product idea into a commercial product;

- discuss the role played by products in the marketing mix;

- evaluate the importance of branding to marketing management and key brand decisions;

- recommend appropriate marketing activity at different stages of the PLC;

- appreciate the role of test marketing in supporting marketing management decision making associated with product development.

INTRODUCTION

After this section you should understand:

▨ **Different levels of product.**

▨ **Different classifications of products.**

▨ **The anatomy of products including terms such as: product mix width, product line depth, product items.**

▨ **How these might be managed strategically by the product line manager.**

What is a product?

The product is at the heart of the marketing exchange. If the product fails to deliver to customer expectations then all has been in vain. A product is a complex entity consisting of a number of overlapping layers. The basic anatomy of a product may be represented as a series of four bands representing the core product, the tangible product, the augmented product and the potential product.

■ The *core product* represents the central meaning of the product and conveys its essence. This is centrally related to the key benefits expected by customers. For example, in considering a holiday some people like to 'get away from it all' to relax; others want to 'have a ball'. Each of these benefits could become core products for a holiday company.

■ The *tangible product* is related to the core product to the extent that it places flesh on the bones of the former. For the holiday described above, this would involve the way in which the holiday was designed to suit customer requirements; including the activities, accommodation, transport arrangements and the brochure.

■ The *augmented product* includes those add-on extras which are not an intrinsic part of the product but which may be used to enhance the product benefits. For the holiday company such extras might include the placement of a bottle of champagne and roses in the hotel room for those who seek to get away from it all.

■ While the first three layers describe how the product is now, the *potential product* constitutes a vision of what it could be in the future. By considering the potential product the marketer is trying to ensure that continuous improvement is at the heart of the process. This is embodied in the question 'How can we improve this, how can we do it even better?'

Classifications of products

Products can be sorted into a number of classifications. In the discussion in Chapter 1 of product-centred approaches to marketing that grew up in the 1920s with the development of the commodity school, the threefold classification convenience, shopping and speciality products was used. The idea is that consumers behave in different ways when purchasing convenience products (relatively inexpensive and frequently purchased goods) compared with shopping products (durables such as stereos, bicycles and furniture). Speciality products possess a single unique characteristic on which buyers are willing to expend a considerable amount of effort to obtain, e.g. a Cartier watch. This relates to a parallel with the concept of involvement which was discussed in Chapter 3.

CONVENIENCE PRODUCTS

Convenience products correspond with the routine response buying situation; the buyer puts little effort into the purchasing situation and convenience takes precedence over brand loyalty. The marketing implications for convenience products are similar to those for low-involvement products.

SHOPPING PRODUCTS

By contrast to convenience products, shopping products represent something of a risk to the purchaser and so the consumer is likely to be more active in searching out information and evaluating them. Specialist sources and friends are likely to be consulted. In a similar manner to the concept of involvement which was discussed in Chapter 3, the classification of a product into this category depends on the individual consumer's perception of the importance and complexity of the purchase; one person's convenience good could be another person's shopping good or speciality good. The implications for marketers are that they should focus on all items of the marketing mix and not just on the product. The mass distribution strategies of the convenience marketer may no longer be appropriate. So, for example, in buying a camera it is likely that the consumer will visit specialist retailers to see what they have available and may well visit more than one source to judge between different offerings. As customers are likely to consult specialist publications and ask friends who may be camera enthusiasts for their opinions on different cameras, it is important to promote the camera to specialist magazines, perhaps by sending out demonstration samples which can be evaluated by staff. The camera manufacturer would be advised to brief sales staff in retail outlets. This could be achieved by means of briefing notes to sales specialists.

SPECIALITY PRODUCTS

These products are what have come to be called 'high-involvement' and 'complex' products. While shopping products could be said to be high in involvement, this is qualitatively different in that the perceived risk is high and the product is infrequently purchased. It should be noted that the classification of which products are speciality products is in the hands of the consumer. For some consumers the camera example used above could qualify as a speciality product.

Understanding the product range

Most organizations offer a range of different products. The product mix is the total sum of all the products and variants of products which are offered by a firm. The product mix for a company such as Procter & Gamble (P&G) might consist of the following lines and items.

The product mix may be divided into a number of product lines. A product line is a group of products that are closely related to each other. For example, a clothing company might arrange its mix into shirts, coats and jeans to reflect the particular production requirements and problems for each line. On the other hand, a company might organize the product mix according to market requirements or a mixture of production and market requirements. For example, Michelin has a tripartite product organization into tyres, maps and restaurant rating services. While only a limited number of the actual lines offered by P&G is shown in Figure 8.1, this example helps to illustrate concepts such as the product mix width, length, depth and consistency.

The product mix width refers to how many different product lines the company carries. In the simple example shown above, the width of the mix is four (although other lines such as household cleaning products, disposable nappies, etc., could be added).

A product line consists of a number of product items. These are the individual products or brands, each with its own features and price.

Product line length refers to the number of items within the product line. According to Figure 8.1, Crest has a length of one item. Product line depth refers to the number of variants of each item within the product line. A deep product may have many different variants. For example, if Crest came in three sizes and two formulations (regular and mint) then Crest would have a depth of six items.

The consistency of the product mix refers to how closely related various product lines are according to the criteria devised by management. For example, P&G's lines are consistent to the extent that they go through the same distribution channels to the final consumer. The lines are not so consistent when their end use is considered.

The definitions of product mix width, depth and consistency create a common vocabulary with reference to a particular set of products which allows the marketer to analyse the mix and to take strategic actions such as to build, maintain, harvest or divest product items or lines. The product line manager needs to know the percentage of sales and profits contributed by each item in the line so that she can decide whether or not to maintain this

Detergents	Toothpaste	Bar soap	Hair care	
Dreft	Crest	Ivory	Head and Shoulders	Product line
Bold		Camay	Vidal Sassoon	
Ariel		Oil of Olay	Pantene Pro-V	
Daz				
Length product mix width				

Figure 8.1 The product mix, Procter & Gamble

Source: Heriott-Watt University estimates, cited for illustrative purposes only.

item. Another task for the product line manager is in deciding whether or not to lengthen a product line by adding products or to deepen existing products by offering more variants.

CHARACTERISTICS OF THE PRODUCT LIFE CYCLE AND THEIR MARKETING IMPLICATIONS

All products and services have a distinct life span that is measured by the chronological history of sales from the launch of the product until its withdrawal from the market. This section explains each stage of the product life cycle (PLC) and the marketing activities that accompany each stage.

After completing this section, you should be able to:

■   **discuss the characteristics of the PLC;**
■   **recommend marketing activities that are appropriate for each stage;**
■   **evaluate the usefulness of the PLC as a marketing tool;**
■   **modify the PLC to improve its effectiveness;**
■   **use the PLC to assist in case study analysis.**

PLC

After a product is launched there will be times when its sales levels will grow, times when they will be relatively static and other times when sales will decline, particularly if it is superseded by a new product that satisfies consumer needs better. Consider, for example, consumer preference for CD over vinyl records and the disappearance of launderettes in town centres following the introduction of domestic washing machines. The PLC is a model that helps describe the common levels of sales growth and decline that can be observed over the lifetime of a product (see Figure 8.2).

The model helps marketers determine the level of support that is required to secure the present and future success of the product. Figure 8.2 indicates that there are four main stages in the PLC: introduction, growth, maturity and decline. These are each discussed in greater detail along with their implications for marketing strategy.

Characteristics of the PLC

The PLC illustrates the four key stages that a product is likely to experience between its launch and disappearance from the market. These stages are discussed below.

INTRODUCTION

When a product enters the market, sales will begin slowly and profit, if any, will be small owing to the lead time required for marketing efforts to take effect. As the product is new

Figure 8.2
The product life cycle model

Source: reprinted from Hill and O'Sullivan (1996), figure 6.3, p. 154, by kind permission of Addison Wesley Longman Ltd.

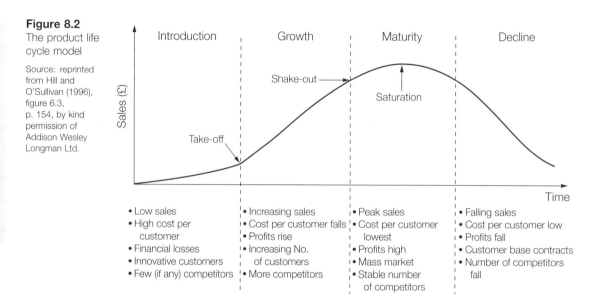

and untested, potential customers may be unwilling or reluctant to buy it. Another reason for low profitability is that the firm is unlikely to be making full use of its production capacity and will be unable to enjoy the economies of scale that are associated with higher levels of output. Low profitability is also a result of the need to recoup development and launch costs.

The marketer's main priority at this stage is to generate widespread awareness of the product among the target segment and to stimulate trial. If the product is truly innovative, the absence of competitors means that primary demand will have to be established. Firms focus their selling on those buyers who are readiest to buy: usually the higher-income groups. This behaviour was evident when the manufacturers of video-cassette recorders (VCR), electronic calculators and mobile telephones targeted business and professional users as their products were introduced to the market.

There are several marketing strategies that can be used for introducing a new product. Two pricing strategies are available, depending on the nature of the product and the competition:

■ *Price skimming* involves charging a high initial price, with a view to reducing it once the market grows.
■ *Price penetration* involves setting a lower price than is likely to be maintained over the long-term, so as to expand the market as quickly as possible.

Price skimming and penetration are discussed further in Chapter 9.

Many products fail to progress beyond the introduction stage of the PLC. Customers who are dissatisfied with their first purchase will fail to make the repeat purchases and recommendations that are essential for sales increases. It is crucial to ensure that the products offer genuine benefits to the consumer if survival and growth are to follow.

VIRGIN'S APPROACH TO DIRECT SALES IN FINANCIAL SERVICES

Virgin decided to enter the growing Personal Equity Plan (PEP) market by setting up a completely new company, Virgin Direct Personal Financial Services, in partnership with Norwich Union. An article in the *Sunday Times* describes the attraction for Richard Branson: 'I cannot walk past a fat and complacent business sector without wanting to shake it up a bit.'

Virgin broke with convention by offering direct sales to the consumer while avoiding the high-pressure selling, hidden charges and jargon that characterized traditional financial services organizations. This illustrates the way in which the PEP market accommodated a new entrant at the growth stage of the market, as there was sufficient scope to cater for a new segment of uncertain investors seeking the reassurance of a trustworthy name (Hinde, 1995).

GROWTH STAGE

If the product meets market needs or stimulates previously untapped needs, it will enter a growth stage, in which sales will start climbing quickly. Profits are generated as sales revenues increase faster than costs. Competitors will have had time to assess the product and predict its impact on the market. Some competitors may be tempted to respond with modifications or improvements to their existing products or launch a new product on to the market. As the total size of the market is growing, the new competitors can increase their sales by attracting new customers rather than undercutting each other on price. At the same time, there is likely to be an expansion in the number of distribution outlets.

MATURITY

The stage at which a product's sales growth slows down is known as maturity. During this time there is a tendency for firms to poach customers from their competitors by offering cheaper prices and increasing their promotional efforts. As competitive rivalry intensifies, the least effective competitors are forced out of the market (known as the shake-out point), leaving only the strongest players to dominate a more stable market. The maturity stage lasts longer than the previous stages and poses the strongest challenges to marketing management.

At this stage there is likely to be heavy price competition and increased marketing expenditure from all competitors in order to retain brand loyalty.

Some famous brands are still in the maturity stage after thirty years or more, e.g. Mars' Maltesers and Mars bars, Cadbury's Dairy Milk, Oxo, Coca-Cola and Amami (setting lotion). While these products have changed little since their launch, many other products survive by evolving to meet changing consumer needs.

During the mature stage product managers can choose between innovating in the market (market development), modifying the product (product development) and altering the marketing mix (marketing innovation).

C
A
S
E

S
T
U
D
Y

CRAYOLA CRAYONS

In 1903 Binney & Smith started making Crayola crayons in the US. Crayola has become a brand leader in the US and sixty other countries. Part of the brand's success lies in Binney & Smith's ability in making many adjustments to keep the brand in the mature stage and out of decline. For example, the number of colours has expanded from eight to 103, with similar variations in the size and shape of the crayons.

The company has added several programmes and services to help strengthen its relationship with Crayola customers. For example, in 1984 it began its Dream Makers art education programme, a national school programme designed to help students capture their dreams on paper and to use the artistic process to help make their dreams more tangible. A telephone hot line is available to provide better customer service.

Kotler and Armstrong (1996).

Market development

Here the company tries to increase the consumption of the current product. It looks either for new users or a new market for the company, as when Johnson & Johnson targeted the adult market with its baby powder and shampoo. Alternatively, it may decide to reposition the brand to appeal to a larger or faster growing segment, as Lucozade did when it targeted its new line of drinks at younger users instead of convalescents, the original target market.

Product development

The product manager can also change product characteristics, such as quality, features or style, to attract new users and to inspire more use.

■ *Quality improvement* aims at increasing product performance, e.g. durability, reliability, speed, taste. This strategy is most appropriate when buyers believe the claim of improved quality and when there is sufficient demand for higher quality.
■ A strategy of *feature improvement* adds new features that expand the product's usefulness, safety or convenience. The Japanese have used this strategy effectively in the manufacture of watches, calculators and copying machines.
■ *Style improvement* is used when the manufacturer wants to increase the attractiveness of the product. For example, car manufacturers often modify car designs to attract new buyers.

Marketing innovation

Changes to one or more of the marketing mix elements can be used during the mature phase. Price cuts can attract new users and competitors customers. Advertising campaigns, sales promotions and trade deals can sustain consumer interest. The company can move into larger

BUTLINS HOLIDAY CAMPS

In the 1950s when Butlins holiday camps opened in the UK they were highly popular among the lower socio-economic groups. However, holiday patterns changed radically in the 1970s as increasing numbers of tourists were lured to the sunnier alternatives in Spain where they enjoyed higher standards of facilities and entertainment. Butlins was unable to prevent the decline in its market and was forced to close some of its camps (Brassington and Petitt, 1997).

Competitive activity becomes even more intense at this stage as the existing firms are chasing fewer customers to make their sales. There are a number of possible options for dealing with declining products which include milking or harvesting; phased withdrawal; contracting out or selling.

market channels, as Dell Computers did with mail-order selling of personal computers. Finally, the company can offer new or improved services to buyers in order to maintain brand loyalty (Kotler and Armstrong., 1996).

DECLINE STAGE

This is the stage when sales of a product start to fall, often because substitute products offer the consumer superior benefits.

Milking or harvesting

When this strategy is used, the product is given little or no marketing support. This strategy enables the firm to maximize the life of the product, as well to generate the cash and the time to help establish new products. The slow decline of the product gives the organization time to adjust to the declining cash flow and to find other means of generating revenue.

Phased withdrawal

Unlike the milking strategy, where the product can continue indefinitely, phased withdrawal involves setting a cut-off date for the product. Prior to the cut-off date there may be interim stages at which the product is either pulled from certain channels of distribution or geographic areas.

While phased withdrawal enables the organization to plan the introduction of replacement products, it can be a source of displeasure to consumers, who can sometimes be disappointed when they discover the sudden disappearance of their favoured product, as was evident when Cadbury's Aztec chocolate bar was withdrawn.

Table 8.1 Top world's most valuable brands, 2004

Rank	Brand	Sales US$million	Country of origin
1	Coca-Cola	67,394	US
2	Microsoft	61,372	US
3	IBM	53,391	US
4	GE	44,111	US
5	Intel	33,499	US
6	Disney	27,113	US
7	McDonald's	25,001	US
8	Nokia	24,041	Finland
9	Toyota	22,673	Japan
10	Marlboro	22,128	US
11	Mercedes	21,331	Germany
12	Hewlett-Packard	20,978	US
13	Citibank	19,971	US
14	American Express	17,683	US
15	Gillette	16,723	US
16	Cisco	15,948	US
17	BMW	15,886	Germany
18	Honda	14,874	Japan
19	Ford	14,475	US
20	Sony	12,759	Japan

Sources: adapted from Advertising Association *Marketing Pocket Book 2005*, London: Advertising Association, pp. 187–8 and Interbrand Corp, J.P. Morgan Chase & Co., Citigroup and Morgan Stanley.

Normally, car manufacturers operate on a phased withdrawal basis, so that both dealers and the public are notified of product withdrawals and launches. For example, Renault phased out the Renault 25 in readiness for the launch of the Safrane in 1993 (Brassington and Petitt, 1997).

Contracting out or selling

Loyal users can be retained by selling the brand to a niche operator or by subcontracting its marketing and/or production. Many smaller firms benefit from this strategy, as they are flexible enough to offer the product's market a satisfactory return. Each party involved in this strategy benefits: the originating organization can dispose of a product it no longer wants; consumers can buy products they desire and the subcontractor or buyer can gain experience of marketing a brand they could never have built for themselves.

Table 8.2 Top ten ranked brands in the UK, 2004

Rank	Brand	Sales £million 2003	Sales £million 2004	% change	% penetration
1	Walkers	470–5	530–5	11.8	86.5
2	Bird's Eye	520–5	515–20	–1.2	82.8
3	Kellogg's	475–80	495–500	4.5	81.5
4	Cadbury's	440–445	480–485	9.1	86.7
5	Heinz	430–435	435–440	1.4	92.1
6	Coke and Diet Coke	385–390	385–390	0.1	62.0
7	Müller	370–375	375–380	0.9	73.8
8	McVitie's	340–345	340–345	–0.6	90.2
9	Mathew's	335–340	340–345	1.4	70.7
10	Stella Artois	275–280	305–310	11.4	27.9

Source: adapted from Advertising Association *Marketing Pocket Book* 2005, London: Advertising Association, p. 79.

Branding

Firms invest heavily, in promotion especially, to develop brands at both a national and international, even at the global level. In 2004 brand leaders came from the FMCG, communications, motor industry and the financial sector, as shown in Table 8.1. Brands such as Coca-Cola, Microsoft, IBM, Disney, McDonald's and Marlboro have become globally known. Interestingly, among the top twenty world brands most originate from US-based firms, with the exceptions being from Finland, Japan and Germany.

In the UK leading brands occur within the FMCG sector, with household names such as Walkers (crisps), Bird's Eye (fish and vegetables), Kellogg's (cereals) and Cadbury's chocolate (see Table 8.2). Turnovers for these brands are large in the £300mn–555mn (US$538mn–996mn) range, although some fluctuation occurs from year to year related to marketing, especially promotional activity. These dominant brands have high market shares that frequently reach 80–90 per cent market penetration.

Summary of PLC characteristics

The characteristics and strategic implications of the PLC are summarized below:

■ Products have a finite life.
■ During this life, they pass through distinct stages, each of which poses different challenges to the seller.

Table 8.3 Marketing responses to the product life cycle

Strategy	Introduction	Growth	Maturity	Decline
Marketing emphasis	Create product awareness	Establish high market share	Fight off competition	Minimize marketing expenditure
	Encourage product trial		Generate profits	
Product strategy	Introduce basic products	Improve features of basic products	Design product versions for different segments	Rationalize the product range
Pricing strategy	Price skimming or price penetration	Reduce prices enough to expand the market and establish market share	Match or beat the competition	Reduce prices further
Promotional strategy	Advertising and sales promotion to end-users and dealers	Mass media advertising establish brand image	Emphasize brand strengths to different segments	Minimal level to retain loyal customers
Distribution strategy	Build selective distribution outlets	Increase the number of outlets	Maintain intensive distribution	Rationalize outlets to minimize distribution costs

Source: reprinted from Hill and O'Sullivan (1996), figure 6.4, p. 157, by kind permission of Addison Wesley Longman Ltd

■ All elements of the organization's strategy need to change as the product moves from one stage to another.

■ The profit potential of products varies considerably from one stage to another.

■ Demands upon management and the appropriateness of managerial styles vary from stage to stage (Wilson and Gilligan, 1997).

Table 8.3 summarizes the key features of the PLC and describes the appropriate marketing responses for each stage.

FACETS OF THE PLC

While the PLC can guide managers as to the likely developments in their markets, it does not offer a definitive description of the development of all products. Some products survive no longer than the introduction stage, some survive for lengthy periods in the maturity stage and some start to decline before being revitalized after a successful repositioning campaign. The effectiveness of the PLC can be improved by considering the following additional factors.

Length of PLC

There are significant differences between the length of the PLC from market to market and from brand to brand within the same market. Some board games, e.g. Monopoly, Scrabble and Cluedo, are long-term sellers while other games such as Rubik's cubes and 'Tamagotchi' pets have a much shorter life span.

In order to anticipate and plan for key transition stages of the PLC, the pace of change in the external environment should be monitored closely. The effectiveness of promotional campaigns, the organization's support of the product in the introductory phase and its approach to defending and refreshing its products will also affect how the PLC develops.

Product level, class, form and brand

There are important distinctions between the PLC of total industries (such as the motor industry), product classes (such as petrol-driven private cars), product forms (such as hatchback cars) and individual brands (such as the Fiat Uno).

Industries and product classes are generic names for groups of products that satisfy similar customer needs, such as cars, soaps and margarine. Product classes have the longest life cycles, with long maturity phases, even though individual brands come and go. For example, in the motor industry the hatchback is probably a mature product form, while the people carrier is still in its growth stage. Usually the decline phase occurs when there is a change in the macro-environment. In this way, UK car manufacturers may be concerned about the possibility of a decline in sales following the announcement about government plans to limit the number of cars allowed to enter cities and the introduction of tolls to ease traffic congestion and pollution.

Product forms are sub-sectors of product classes that deliver the benefits offered within a product class in different ways. Even if a product class has an extended maturity period, the different product forms may not survive for that length of time, or may experience growth at different rates and at different times. For example, video-cassettes are common household products at the mature stage of the PLC, but only the VHS product has survived into the maturity, with the Sony Betamax form having failed to survive the shake-out.

The life cycle of a brand is the most unpredictable of all, as firms attempt to create growth for their own brands by tempting customers away from competitors. The life cycle of many branded products such as chocolate bars is usually scallop-shaped, to reflect the ways in which the individual products lose market share, only to regain it when the firms retaliate with marketing campaigns (see Figure 8.3).

Fads may be product classes, forms or brands that have very short life cycles. Children's toys often fall into this category, as their novelty value wears off quickly (see Figure 8.4).

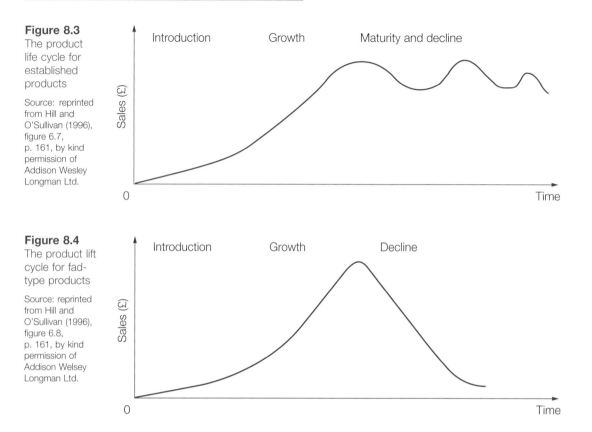

Figure 8.3
The product life cycle for established products

Source: reprinted from Hill and O'Sullivan (1996), figure 6.7, p. 161, by kind permission of Addison Wesley Longman Ltd.

Figure 8.4
The product lift cycle for fad-type products

Source: reprinted from Hill and O'Sullivan (1996), figure 6.8, p. 161, by kind permission of Addison Welsey Longman Ltd.

SECTION SUMMARY

Having completed this section, you should be able to:

■ describe each stage of the PLC and recommend appropriate marketing strategies for each stage;

■ modify the PLC concept to improve its effectiveness as a marketing planning tool;

■ explain the differences in the characteristics of PLCs for specific product forms, classes, brands and fads,

■ apply the PLC to a case study.

NEW PRODUCT DEVELOPMENT (NPD)

Given the rapid changes in taste, technology and competition, existing products are insufficient to sustain growth or to maintain profitability for a company. Organizations need a flow of new products to keep their portfolios fresh, their customers interested and their sales growing. This section will outline the stages of New Product Development (NPD). It considers the rationale for pursuing an active programme of planned new product launches, and warns of the dangers facing organizations that ignore the importance of NPD.

After completing this section, you should be able to:

■   **distinguish between the different types of new product;**

■   **understand why organizations choose to become innovators;**

■   **identify sources of new product ideas and use structured techniques for idea generation;**

■   **develop criteria for the evaluation of new product ideas;**

■   **explain how buyer behaviour influences the rate at which markets adopt new products.**

What is a new product?

There are four categories of new product:

■   Major innovations.
■   Product improvements.
■   Product additions.
■   Repositioned products.

Major innovations present radically new user benefits to customers, often through the development of new technologies. Compact discs, the home video-recorder, microwave ovens and mobile telephones are all examples of new products that created new markets rather than entered old ones. One problem with this category of product is that potential buyers may be sceptical about its reliability and usefulness. The firm must tackle the problem of convincing customers that they actually need the product, especially if they have existed quite happily without it. Despite the risks and marketing problems associated with this category, the firm's pioneering success can enhance its reputation among customers, shareholders, potential investors and employees.

Product improvements are innovations within existing markets that are aimed at taking market share from competitors rather than building extensive new primary demand. This tactic is popular among detergent manufacturers, who frequently use the adage of 'new, improved formula' to retain the existing customers and lure those of competitors. It is also used within the crisps snacks market, e.g. Quaker Oats introduced Snack-a-Jacks rice and corn snacks 'with 10 per cent less fat' and 'suitable for coeliacs' (an allergic condition associated with wheat and related products).

Product additions cover imitative products that are based on the competitor's approach and technology. Product additions may offer new product features to a market, but offer limited new benefits to customers. This approach is popular among smaller companies that prefer to enter the market with cheaper imitations after their larger competitors have invested the time and resources with the initial launch. Sony discovered this to its cost when it invested considerable resources into the research, development and launch of the Walkman, only to be faced with stiff competition from a wide range of imitative products. Newcomers who try to enter the market with product additions or product improvements must overcome the difficulty of gaining distribution in an established market that is dominated by competitors who will use marketing counter-measures to prevent the successful entry of a new product.

Repositioned products are normally thought of as product adaptations rather than new products. Instead of offering features that are tangibly different, they create a new image for the product through a change of promotional emphasis. The manufacturer of Lucozade used this technique when it changed the image of Lucozade as a drink for convalescents to an energy-boosting drink for sports enthusiasts (Hill and O'Sullivan, 1996).

Key stages in the process of innovation

Most successful new products result from a conscious search for opportunities and a systematic attempt to remove the uncertainty surrounding them. This process needs to pass through eight stages if mistakes are to be avoided. These stages are illustrated in Figure 8.5.

Idea generation
↓
Idea screening
↓
Concept testing
↓
Business analysis
↓
Product development
↓
Test marketing
↓
Commercialization
↓
Monitoring and evaluation

Figure 8.5
Stages in new
product
development

STAGE 1 IDEA GENERATION

A company typically has to generate many ideas to find a few good ones. Sources that can supply the flow of ideas include employees, customers, competitors, distributors, suppliers and others.

Many new ideas originate from employees. While ideas can come from all parts of the firm, those employees who are involved in making the products and selling them to customers, such as Research & Development (R&D), production and marketing staff are particularly valuable, as they are knowledgeable about the technology and the needs of the market. Some large companies such as 3M, M&S and Toyota have tapped this potential to great effect. For example, Toyota receives over 2m ideas a year from employees and claims to implement about 85 per cent of them.

In order to use this source of information to full potential, senior management should create a culture in which employees are encouraged to put forward ideas. Many companies do this by setting targets for each department, e.g. five ideas per employee, and provide rewards for ideas that are implemented.

There are several creativity techniques that have been developed by psychologists and marketing researchers to help individuals and groups generate creative ideas. Among the more popular techniques are brainstorming, morphological analysis and forced relationships.

- *Brainstorming* involves a group of six to ten people in an intensive session focusing on a specific problem. The purpose is to generate as many ideas as possible no matter how wild they are. An important requirement of brainstorming is that no negative comments should be made about the suggestions during the idea generation stage in order to maximize the number of ideas.
- *Morphological analysis* means looking at a problem and its components and then finding connections and solutions. For example, a firm researching the construction of an electronic car would consider aspects relating to fuel source, power transmission, body shape and surface contact.

Customers

Almost 28 per cent of new product ideas come from watching and listening to customers. These ideas can be obtained from analysing customer surveys, complaints or simply observing customers. General Electric's Video Products Division, Sony, Toyota and many other effective innovators are known to have their design engineers talk to final consumers to get ideas for new products.

One company to benefit greatly from customer observation was Boeing, that sent a team of engineers to study the problems facing pilots in Third World countries. When the engineers discovered that runways were too short for planes they redesigned the wings on its 737, added lower-pressure tyres to prevent bouncing on short landings and redesigned the engine for quicker take-off. As a result the Boeing became the best-selling commercial jet in history (Czinkota and Kotabe, 1990; Rees, 1992).

Competitors

Companies such as Canon, Xerox, Hewlett-Packard and Ford use competitor benchmarking whereby they systematically compare their products with the best competitor to look for potential advances.

Distributors, suppliers and others

Resellers and suppliers are close to the market and can pass along information about consumer problems and new product ideas. Other idea sources include trade magazines, seminars, government agencies, advertising agencies, university research laboratories and science parks.

Table 8.4 Idea-screening criteria

Criterion	Weighting	Idea 1		Idea 2		Idea 3	
		Raw score	Weighted score	Raw score	Weighted score	Raw score	Weighted score
Fit with corporate strategic goals	15	8	1.20	3	0.45	5	0.75
Fit with marketing strategic goals	15	7	1.05	3	0.45	5	0.75
Market growth	5	9	0.45	9	0.45	3	0.15
Size of targe market	10	6	0.60	8	0.80	9	0.9
Access to market	10	4	0.40	9	0.90	7	0.7
Differential advantage offered	10	9	0.90	5	0.50	7	0.7
Profitability potential	10	7	0.70	7	0.70	4	0.4
Timing	5	8	0.40	7	0.35	9	0.45
Synergy with existing products	5	7	0.35	3	0.15	6	0.3
Synergy with existing technology	5	7	0.35	3	0.15	2	0.1
Synergy with existing distribution channels	5	3	0.15	8	0.40	8	0.4
Synergy with existing skills and assets	5	6	0.30	4	0.20	5	0.25
Total	100	81	6.85	69	5.50	70	5.85

Source: reprinted from Brassington and Pettitt (1977), table 9.1, p. 344, by kind permission of Pitman Publishing Ltd.

Note: raw score = market of 10; weighted score = (raw score × weighting)/100.

STAGE 2 SCREENING IDEAS

The second stage involves scanning ideas to eliminate those that are unlikely to prove appropriate or successful. Potential success depends upon three factors: namely, the idea's compatibility with the firm's corporate strategy, the potential demand for the product and the firm's capability to exploit the product opportunity.

Many organizations use a semi-formal weighting procedure to establish the relative importance of screening criteria. This produces a score for each idea, allowing them to be compared with one another. Table 8.4 contains criteria that might be applied for screening assessment purposes. In this case idea No. 1 scores better than the other two.

Given that numerical scores are based on management judgements, a great deal of care is required when assessing ideas, particularly those ideas that lie on the borderline between accept and reject.

STAGE 3 CONCEPT TESTING

Ideas that make it past the screening stage need to be tested out on their potential market. This can be achieved only if the product features and benefits can be explained to potential customers. It is important to distinguish between a product idea and its positioning concept. The product idea is the new physical good or functional service that is being considered by the company. The positioning concept is the choice of target market segment and benefit proposition. The distinction is crucial because most new products can have very different positioning strategies. For example, when lasers were invented they were positioned for military use. However, far greater opportunities lay in positioning the laser as a key component in technologies as diverse as compact disc players, communication and medical surgery. Even a simple product idea such as a new brand of aspirin could have multiple positioning concepts, e.g. adults or children, cold or headache sufferers. The reason to buy might be that, compared with competitors, it is more efficient, faster, longer-acting, easier to swallow or has fewer side effects (Doyle, 1994).

Testing alternative positioning concepts for the product is essential in the NPD process. It involves presenting alternative benefit propositions to different potential target markets. Managers then research the following:

■　*Communicability*. Do consumers understand the benefit being offered?
■　*Believability*. Do they believe that the product has the benefits claimed?
■　*Need*. Do they need the benefit being offered?
■　*Need gap*. If a need exists, is it perceived as being satisfied by existing providers?
■　*Perceived value*. Do customers perceive the new product as offering value for money?
■　*Usage*. How would the customers use the product and how often? (Doyle, 1994)

STAGE 4 BUSINESS ANALYSIS

The fourth stage of NPD requires the product concept to be specified in greater detail so that production, marketing and finance projections can be made. A marketing assessment will be the starting point. This will include:

■　Description of target markets.
■　Forecast of sales volume.
■　Indication of product positioning.
■　Judgement of likely competitor reactions.
■　Calculation of potential sales losses from existing products as customers switch to the new product (known as cannibalization).
■　Specification of the new product features, including quality levels.
■　Assessment of achievable price levels.
■　The distribution strategy.
■　Statement of promotional requirements.

A financial statement will follow. Based on the marketing assessment, calculations can be made to project:

- Sales value.
- Variable costs of production.
- Incremental fixed costs.
- The contribution and profitability of the new product.

STAGE 5 PRODUCT DEVELOPMENT

At this stage the R&D and/or engineering department develops the product concept into a physical product. So far the product has existed only as a word description, a drawing or a crude mock-up. A large sum of investment is required to ascertain whether the idea can be turned into a workable product.

The length of this stage varies according to the degree of innovation required and the complexity of the product. The process will be more straightforward if the product uses known technology. For example, a firm launching a new shape of potato crisp will face greater problems in creating a successful brand image and maintaining consistent quality than in developing the production process.

This stage requires close co-operation between the different functional areas of the firm. The development experts will be leading the design of the product; manufacturing will be seeking to achieve low-cost production; marketing and distribution will be aiming to achieve the correct marketing mix, sales and logistics. Tests with potential consumers should evaluate functional performance, efficiency, safety and apparent benefit. For consumer goods, pack tests should check ease of use, performance and product image. Research can be conducted to test advertising effectiveness and consumer attitudes towards projected pricing levels.

STAGE 6 TEST MARKETING

Consideration of product development and associated test marketing has been referred to in Chapter 5. Their critical role within NPD is reinforced at this point in the text and detailed at pp. 246–251. This test marketing stage provides information on the likelihood of the target market buying the product, trade response to the product and product performance compared with competition. Such information enables the firm to modify the product where necessary.

A standard test market is commonly used for testing FMCGs. It should correspond, as far as possible, to a scaled-down version of an intended national market, in terms of distribution structure, media availability, competitor activity and the target market profile.

However, there are a number of disadvantages with test markets. They can take up to three years to complete, at the end of which the firm may lose substantial sums of money if it is unsuccessful. Test markets provide competitors with a chance to study the new product and, perhaps, even to launch a retaliatory product before the new product is launched nationally. For example, prior to its launch in the UK, Carnation Coffee-Mate, a coffee whitener, was test-marketed over a period of six years. This gave a rival firm, Cadbury, ample warning and the opportunity to develop and introduce its own product, Marvel, to compete head-on with Coffee-Mate.

Competitors can cause further disruptions in the test market by cutting their prices in test cities, increasing their promotion and buying the product being tested. They are likely to use their best sales forces, which may bias sales results, making them poor predictors of likely total market sales.

Test-marketing industrial goods

Test marketing may be inappropriate for industrial products owing to the following characteristics:

■ *Market structure*. As the total number of potential customers may be small, a test market may be tantamount to a full launch.

■ *Buyer–seller relationships and customization*. Product development in organizational markets is often the result of close collaboration between the buyer and seller. The buyer's involvement at the prototype stage and his or her agreement in discussions about price and availability during the development stage mean that test marketing is unnecessary.

■ *The product's life-span and purchase frequency* may be long for many industrial products, such as capital equipment, so that purchases are made infrequently. Consequently, many of the potential purchasers are unwilling to test the new product, as their existing products may have several years before a replacement is required.

While it may be possible to use some industrial goods in standard test markets, trade shows and distributor/dealer display rooms and product clinics (discussed below) may be more appropriate for others.

STAGE 7 COMMERCIALIZATION

Assuming that no significant changes are required to the product, once the test-marketing results have been analysed, the product is ready to be launched into the market. There are two alternatives:

■ An immediate *national* launch can be used if the company has sufficient resources. This allows the advertising campaign to achieve maximum impact and can prevent competitors from disrupting the launch with rival products or publicity campaigns. The risk of a national campaign is that some organizations experience teething problems, especially if they have failed to invest sufficient time and resources in ensuring that their production, quality and supply systems are operating at maximum efficiency.

- A *rolling* launch is the other alternative to the national launch. Few companies have the confidence, capital and capacity to launch new products into full national or international distribution. This method is popular among small firms which prefer to select an attractive city and conduct a campaign to enter the market. They may then enter other cities one at a time.

STAGE 8 MONITORING AND EVALUATION

After the product is launched it is important to evaluate the process of the launch and the product performance after the launch. When reviewing the process the firm will have to address questions such as:

- Were the correct people involved in the launch?
- Was sufficient time and resources allocated to the launch?
- Was the marketing research information adequate for the launch?

The answer to these questions will help the firm improve future NPD initiatives.

Before the product launch takes place the firm will set performance criteria such as sales targets, market share relative to competition and promotion objectives. By setting such criteria, the firm can measure the actual product performance. Any mismatch between the two needs to be analysed to determine whether it was caused by poor decision making, lack of information or unforeseen market conditions.

Definition of test marketing

Test marketing involves selecting a limited sector of the market for a trial to test the effectiveness of the marketing mix that is to be used for full-scale introduction of the product, or service to the market. Test marketing:

> is a controlled experiment, done in a limited but carefully selected part of the market place, whose aim is to predict the sales or profit consequences, either in absolute or relative terms, of one or more proposed marketing actions.
>
> (Achembaum, 1974)

> is a procedure by which a company attempts to test on a small basis the commercial viability of the marketing plan for a new or modified product or package.
>
> (Boyd *et al.,* 1989: 711)

> is the process in which the product is actually introduced into selected geographical markets where developers can observe how consumers and dealers react to the handling, use and promotion of the product.
>
> (Bennett, 1988)

is a controlled experiment conducted in one or more limited, but carefully selected, parts of the market. These are chosen to be representative microcosms of the total market. The aim is to use the test to predict and explore the consequences of one or more proposed marketing actions, notably new product introductions.

(Cannon, 1992)

For many products test marketing is essentially a preliminary skirmish into the marketing battlefield, designed to iron out the problems before the final product 'roll-out' . . . Test marketing is the final and most complex of a series of marketing research techniques used to reduce the tremendous risks inherent in new product development.

(Lancaster and Massingham, 1999: 144–5, 2001: 196–7)

is the stage of a new product development when the product and marketing programs are tested in more realistic market settings. . . . A good test market can provide a wealth of information about the potential success of the product and marketing programme.

(Kotler and Armstrong, 1996)

has the goal of helping marketing managers make better decisions about new products.

(Proctor, 1997)

allows marketers to experiment with variations in advertising, price and packaging in different test areas and to measure the extent of brand awareness, brand switching and repeat purchases that results from alternatives in the marketing mix.

The limited introduction of a product into certain geographic areas chosen to represent the intended market.

(Dibb *et al.*, 1997, 2001)

The stage of new-product development in which the product and marketing program are tested in more realistic market settings.

(Kotler and Armstrong, 2001, p. G–10)

Objectives of test marketing

The main objectives of test marketing are to:

■ *Test the market*, i.e. the test is used to establish whether the product will sell within the targeted market at the levels that are viable for its success. At the same time, the test can indicate whether all the components of the marketing mix, the product characteristics, the pricing approach, the promotional communications campaign and, for place, the channels of distribution, used are appropriate to achieve the desired success.

■ *Pilot launch*, i.e. the test may be used as part of full roll-out national market coverage. The decision to attempt to introduce the product to the full market at one and the same time may be too challenging so that instead the product is introduced in a test market area and then extended to national coverage as experience in the test area is gained. Theoretically, the test market should allow unbiased decisions to be made based on the test results as to whether or not to proceed to the national market. However, often firms have invested so much in the new product that by the test marketing stage, it is only fine-tuning of the marketing mix components that would be viable; major decisions to stop the further introduction of the product are difficult to take.

■   *Predict brand performance*, i.e. the test results may be used to undertake brand launch analysis whereby, through continuous monitoring of the market using consumer panel data, the market share achieved by the new product is compared with the established competitors. In this case, the test market area should match the area covered by the consumer panel data; frequently it would be a commercial television region. Predictions can then be made as to likely market shares that the product can be expected to achieve across the country.

Test marketing attempts to determine factors that influence sales. These can include:

■   *Trial rates*, i.e. the number of persons who test the product out of the total potential population.
■   *Repeat purchase rates*, i.e. the number of persons who purchase the new product on more than one occasion within a given period.
■   *Adoption rates*, i.e. the number of persons who change to purchase the product on all occasions.
■   *Purchase frequency*, i.e. the number of occasions that purchases of the product are made within a given period.
■   *Volume buying rate*, i.e. how much is bought on each purchasing occasion.

Factors that management has to consider when undertaking test marketing include:

■   The cost of test marketing.
■   The time taken to undertake market testing.
■   The likelihood of warning competitors of new product development.
■   The reliability of the final test marketing results.

Use of test marketing

It should be appreciated that while test marketing is used to reduce the risk of failure in NPD, it does not guarantee success. It is expensive to undertake and care must be taken in interpreting the results of such tests. While there are numerous examples of firms that have made costly mistakes in new product introduction through not test marketing, there are examples of test marketing with inconclusive findings which have been revoked in the full market situation. Examples of failures in new product introduction include Ford losing over $350m on its Edsel model, RCA $580m on its SelectaVision and Texas Instruments

$660m on home computers (Kotler and Armstrong, 1996). An instant mashed potato product failed when it was first introduced due to culture tastes not suiting consumer practices at the time of introduction. McDonald's introduced a McPloughman's Lunch and fried chicken products which were failures (Dibb *et al.*, 1997). Green Giant brought in Oven Crock baked beans but found that 'Our beans were terrific, but they were a solution to no known problem' (John M. Stafford, vice-president of Pillsbury). On the other hand, test marketing of After Eight mints in Scotland suggested that they would fail in the market. Nevertheless, management decided to proceed with the product, which has become an international success. More recently, the traditional dark chocolate After Eight mints line has been extended to white chocolate cover.

Steps in test marketing

■ *Define objectives, including criteria for success.* The importance of having well defined objectives for the test marketing should be emphasized. Awareness of these objectives by all involved in the test marketing will help to ensure that the test is conducted efficiently.

■ *Integrate test marketing operations.* Throughout test marketing it is critical for management to maintain close control of the operations to simulate a miniature market situation that does truly represents the national market in which ultimately the product will be sold.

■ *Establish controls.* The ideal controls may be difficult to implement to achieve the desired experimental design. There may not be the resource to have sufficient test areas, or to run the test for sufficient time to establish likely long-term buying behaviour. Nevertheless, the appropriate controls should be used to enable reliable evaluations to be made.

■ *Select representative test areas.* Test areas are required to reflect in miniature the national market. In Britain the favoured test towns include Bristol, Leeds and Derby: favoured test areas for confectionery products are Tyne-Tees and the central valley of Scotland, where consumption *per capita* of confectionery is high. Test areas selected on the basis of commercial television coverage are Bristol and the south-west of England; Grampian and the north-east of Scotland. Unfortunately, media availability within test towns and areas does not always match the requirements of the experimental design or that available for a national market. Furthermore, some test towns and areas have been overused for test marketing so that they may be liable to give atypical results.

Test shops within particular test areas may be used. These can be 'flagship' shops where new products are introduced and their sales performance compared with established sales. Multiple retailers such as M&S and Laura Ashley to test new designs of clothing use such testing. Sometimes media representatives join with multiple retailers to offer a test marketing package, e.g. a television company and a superstore might combine to offer a service whereby television advertising and sales achieved could be tracked within the test area.

- *Decide on the number and duration of test markets to conduct.* Resources and time factors will influence the level of test marketing to be undertaken. It is likely that the longer the duration of the test the more successful it will be in predicting the product's success. However, other factors, especially the need to achieve product secrecy and to prevent competitors becoming aware of the new product proposals, may preclude full-scale marketing research.
- *Evaluate the results.*

Other difficulties to overcome can be the following:

- *Sales force.* It may be that the best sales teams are used for the test and they may gain better results than would be possible on a national scale.
- *Retailer influence.* They may discourage the test from taking place at all by not giving shelf space in their outlets for the test product.
- *Competitor influence.* Competitors may introduce activities such as increased promotions in the test area to distort the test results and make interpretation of the test outcomes difficult to assess.

Test marketing methods

Test marketing aims to establish whether or not a new product (or service) is likely to be successful prior to full commitment to introduce the product to the national (or international) market. Full-scale test marketing involves testing the product in a 'miniature' market, i.e. in a representative sample of the total market, using the equivalent methods that would be used for a national product introduction. The marketing mix should be the same as, or very closely similar to, that to be used in the national market. Such tests may be conducted for between six months and a full year until it is considered that the targeted customer has settled into a steady buying behaviour that would allow market size estimates to be made.

Full-scale test marketing is expensive to undertake. While it provides management with help in deciding the most appropriate marketing mix to use for successful introduction of new products, it has some disadvantages. The high cost of undertaking test marketing and the sometimes inconclusive results of such testing have led to the use of alternative ways of introducing new products to the market. Frequently the test has become, in reality, a form of roll-out national launch whereby the product is introduced on a small scale in a particular area (or shop) and this is extended over time to national coverage. At the introductory stage, close monitoring of the product's performance can enable lessons to be learnt and appropriate adaptations made to the marketing mix to ensure that the product is successful in the national, or international, market. The introduction of the product becomes part of the product development process, rather than merely a testing exercise.

Sometimes, management uses alternative tests that are less comprehensive in the information given, but may provide adequate data with less resource requirement than full-scale test marketing. Firms that wish to reduce costs or to avoid the risks associated with standard test markets can use alternative tests, including simulated test marketing, mini-markets, hall tests and product clinics, which are discussed below.

SIMULATED TEST MARKETING

Involves the introduction of a brand to a number of selected stores or in a simulated shopping environment in a form of shopping panel test. Mobile shops, or vans, can be used to simulate the conventional retail outlet. These are used to monitor purchasing behaviour for some consumer panels and to undertake small-scale test marketing of consumer reaction to new products. The panel members conduct their regular shopping through the mobile shop and their reactions to new products are tested at the same time. Up to forty new products may be introduced alongside the usual food products and the reaction of the panel respondents assessed. Customer reaction is ascertained more quickly, often within six weeks, than with full-scale test marketing and can be less expensive to obtain than conventional test marketing methods. Such shopping panel testing provides more confidentiality than conventional full-scale test marketing.

The market data obtained from market testing are used to fine-tune marketing management decisions concerning the marketing mix. Often, one component of the marketing mix, rather than all the components, is tested through panel assessments, e.g. pricing strategy. A firm wishing to consider the most appropriate pricing approach could introduce the new test product, say a type of chocolate biscuit, to members of the panel, using different prices for those living in different areas. The sales made to panel members in each area could be assessed and the favoured price ascertained.

Free samples might be distributed and consumers questioned about their buying habits and brand preferences. Using sophisticated computer models, the researchers then project national sales from the results of the simulated test market.

MINI-MARKETS

For controlled distribution several research firms keep controlled panels of stores that have agreed to carry new products for a fee. The company with the new product specifies the desired number of stores and geographical locations to be used for the test. Similar control is exercised over the shelf location, amount of shelf space, displays, point-of-sale material and price. Sales results are then tracked to determine the impact of the new product. Controlled distribution mini-market testing has become less popular owing the relatively high costs involved and the possibility of divulging NPD secrets to the competition in advance of full market entry.

HALL TESTS

Involve recruiting a group of respondents 'to attend at a fixed location, often a large room or hall, where they respond, usually as individuals, to a set of stimuli' (MRS, 2005: 36) e.g. samples of food or beverage. The individual participates in various product tests and gives an opinion of the product in question. These may include taste trials and sip tests, whereby the individual is given samples of the food or drink product and asked to comment about the likelihood of purchasing the product. Sometimes, where it is considered that the household

C
A
S
E

S
T
U
D
Y

TEST MARKETING CHOCOLATE

In 2003 the UK confectionery market was valued at £4.88bn (US$8.8bn) with chocolate contributing £3.36bn (US$6.0bn) (69 per cent) and sugar-based sweets £1.52bn (US$2.7bn) (31 per cent) (Cadbury, 2004). Cadbury Trebor Bassett is market leader in the UK. Its holding company, Cadbury Schweppes, is a major international company that manufactures, markets and sells confectionery and soft drink beverages, with a turnover of £6,738m (US$12,088m) and operating profits of £849m (US$1,523m) in 2004. It employs over 55,000 people and has manufacturing operations in more than thirty-five countries (Cadbury Schweppes, 2005).

Spira

In the 1980s Cadbury (the predecessor of Cadbury Trebor Bassett) developed a new production process which could extrude chocolate into different shapes and textures without the use of moulds which was used to manufacture a new impulse 'countline' snack product. Countline is the name given to chocolate bars originally sold by number in units rather than by weight. In 2006 the overall countline market was worth around £850m (Cadbury promotional literature, 2006). The new product brief was to develop a product that would 'build on Cadbury's Dairy Milk heritage in a pure chocolate countline format, exploring all possible textures, configurations and resultant "eats"' (Cadbury, 1991).

Three products were chosen from the many research and development concepts which were developed for consumer research. Concept boards presenting the product idea, positioning and target were produced together with pack designs. Reactions to these concepts researched the issues of product appeal, the relationship of the new product concept to other brands, imagery and the distinctiveness of the concept. Qualitative research was undertaken using informal group discussions of about eight persons, lasting around two hours. The group reactions were analysed and from these, the development team evolved 'Rollers', a twisted-shape bar with a cartwheel interior that was easy to eat, a convenient 'one-handed eat' and different from other products already on the market.

The product concept and its image were reconsidered in the light of the findings obtained from the group discussions. The new product targeted younger people (15–24 year olds), especially the teenage sector. It was to have an image of convenience to suit the young, active, trendy individual with a change in its brand name from 'Rollers' to 'Spira' (Cadbury, 1991).

A £1m investment in a test market plant was made to enable test marketing to start in 1987. The product was test-marketed in the north-east of England covered by the Tyne-Tees commercial television region. The region covered 12 per cent of the GB population and had a demographic profile that matched the younger age group targeted for the product. Major promotional support was allocated during the test, including television advertising and promotional literature. Over the period of the test, Spira achieved a 6.3 per cent share of the targeted market and reached No. 2 chocolate position, despite supply problems. However, such was the success of Spira that it had to be temporarily withdrawn, as supply from the test market plant could not keep up with demand! Further investment in plant capacity was made and the test marketing was extended to a second area in the south-west of England covered by South

West television, which represents under 4 per cent of the GB population. The product performed successfully in the second test. The product was taken to full-scale national coverage in 1990 and has continued to be a success. In 2006 Cadbury Spira had a turnover of around £15m (US$27m) (Cadbury, 1991, and Cadbury promotional literature, 2006).

Wispa

Wispa is 'a textured milk chocolate bar that tastes completely different', with a turnover of over £40m (US$72m) per annum in 2006. Wispa was targeted at young people aged 16–24 with an image of showing its purchaser to be adult, light-hearted and modern. It was test-marketed during 1981 and launched on to the UK market in 1983. Like Spira, the north-east of England in the Tyne-Tees area was used for test marketing and, again, demand exceeded production capacity. Wispa sales rose to achieve first place in the north-east market sector within sixteen weeks. Consumers bought boxes of forty-eight bars at a time and one shop sold 36,000 bars in the first two days of the test market. The product had to be withdrawn after four months until a new production plant could be built to match demand (Cadbury, 1991).

The product continued to be successful during the 1980s. However, in 1991 a relaunch of the product was undertaken whereby modifications were made to the product and its wrapper. A promotional campaign costing £7.5m (US$13.5m) was used with the theme 'Try a new Wispa' and television advertisements saying 'Cadbury's Wispa . . . bite it and believe it.' Posters, the regional press, money-off coupons, samples and sponsorship of local events were also used.

Wispa Gold was launched in 1995 when a new piece of manufacturing equipment was purchased to allow a layer of soft caramel to be deposited into the shell along with the Wispa chocolate. In 1997 Wispa Mint, together with Wispa Orange and Wispaccino, coffee-flavoured caramel, were added to the Wispa range. By 1997 Cadbury sold over 160m Wispa bars (Cadbury, 2004).

Wispa has been advertised consistently over the years. The most famous campaign, for the brand was the original launch campaign which featured contemporary personalities. Following this were a couple of different campaigns, which were less memorable, including the 'Whisperer' campaign, the 'frothy block of choc' advertisement and the 'We do it' campaign. These campaigns were not as successful as the original ones and as a result Cadbury returned to the tried and tested 'duos' campaigns when they launched Wispa Gold. Grif Rhys Jones and Windsor Davies were used in a cutdown which superimposed the new Grif and Windsor on to the original 1980 advertisements to make humorous new advertisements. In 1998, with the launch of Mint Wispa, a series of advertisements using Grif Rhys Jones as the brand spokesman alongside Lloyd Grossman of *Through the keyhole* and *Masterchef* as well as with Louise Lombard, star of the television series *House of Elliot* and *Bodyguards* (Cadbury's promotional material, 2006).

Heroes

For sixty years two brands, Cadbury's Roses (launched in 1938) and Nestlé's Quality Street had dominated the 'twist wrap' market (i.e for individually wrapped sweets where the wrappers are twisted at each end). In 1999 Heroes was launched by Cadbury to compete in this market.

Cadbury Trebor Bassett decided that it would capitalize on its Roses 'thank you' brand, by introducing Heroes, a boxed chocolate assortment of eight of Cadbury's most popular chocolate brands in miniature, Cadbury Dairy Milk, Caramel, Twirl, Time Out, Fuse, Crunchie, Picnic and Fudge. The new Heroes brand was to be positioned as having an informal appeal targeted at the younger consumer with higher levels of disposable income and a lifestyle involving more informal home entertaining. It would be suitable for purchasing for a range of occasions such as the cinema, watching a video or hanging out with family and friends.

The launch of Heroes was challenging, involving a multi-million investment and taking less than two years to complete. Over 15,000 sample units were hand-made by the product developers for concepts, wrapping and storage tests, trade shows and market research. Between 200 and 300 recipes were developed from which the eight products were selected.

Making the bars smaller was difficult. In the case of Crunchie it was not possible to cut the honeycomb into small chunks, so crunchie pieces were used. As uncovered Crunchie goes soft quickly, it was critical that none was left exposed, so extra chocolate was needed on the bottom of the unit. New moulds were required for the Caramel and Cadbury Dairy Milk miniatures. These were tried and tested to make sure that they worked on the manufacturing plant and that the Caramel unit had the correct amount of caramel and chocolate. New ingredients were needed for the Picnic and Fuse units. Smaller raisins had to be used and different flavours developed to give an authentic peanut taste.

The launch was backed by a multi-million-pound support package, including television advertising, sponsorship of the popular soap opera *Coronation Street*, a direct marketing programme and development of a new website. The brand had to deliver a sense of 'Cadburyness' in a fun and original way, so an innovative, contemporary tub was designed with a tamper-proof seal and a plastic resealable lid. The tub featured the light-hearted 'chocotoon' characters, which had an edgy adult appeal and brought the bite-size chocolates to life. Each of the 'chocotoons' reflected the individual brand personalities, e.g. Caramel was relaxation, Fudge was quirky and cute.

In order to maintain the momentum generated at the product launch, a series of special edition packs was developed. These included the addition of a ninth miniature bar, Nuts about Caramel, under the banner of a 'new hero in town', a limited edition Euro 2000 football pack and an XXL 1.5 kg tin tub. In 2002 a white chocolate Dream unit was added which, in 2003, was followed by a Wholenut unit. By 2004 the mix featured ten miniature bars (Cadbury, 2004).

Changes in packaging have taken place. In 2003 the tall tub shape was replaced by a 1.5 kg round tin as used by Roses, helping the consumer to associate with gifting and sharing.

Dream

In 2002 Cadbury Trebor Bassett launched Cadbury 'Dream', a creamy white chocolate targeted at women aged 16–34. Extensive research and development, combined with consumer testing, were undertaken to ensure the product was preferred to other products in the market over two weeks or so. The initial format for the brand was a moulded block, as it helped to differentiate the product from key competitors and was the preferred choice for adult chocolate consumers (Cadbury, 2004).

A number of different brand names and pack designs were researched to determine the favoured Dream pack with blue and white packaging. The 2002 product range comprised a number of products which service consumer needs, e.g. 45 g moulded, 200 g moulded and a 46 g multi-pack format. A Dream filled egg and shell egg were developed for the Easter market, whilst Dream Snowbites were launched for Christmas. A Dream unit was introduced into Cadbury Heroes for Christmas 2002 and a white chocolate Dream ice cream stick was launched in the summer of 2002 by Cadbury's ice cream licensee. In 2003 a thin tablet 20 g bar was launched.

The launch was supported by marketing activities including:

■ £3m (US$5.4m) television campaign, comprising advertising and *Coronation Street* television soap opera sponsorship.
■ Direct mailings to 250,000 targeted consumers.
■ Visual point of sale (POS).
■ Campaign using over 3.5m product samples.
■ Special packs of Roses for Easter 2002 with free Dream samples.
■ Promotional support.

By the end of 2002, less than twelve months after its launch, Dream sold £24.7m (US$44.3m) in retail sales, beating the forecasts (Cadbury, 2004). Sales have continued to grow steadily, reinforcing Dream's success.

Source: adapted from Cadbury (1991), Cadbury (2004) and Cadbury promotional literature (2006).

rather than an individual makes the buying decision, home trials are undertaken. The product is delivered to the selected houses and the household members are asked to comment on its performance. For example, a new range of detergent or soya-based food products might be tested, or placed, within households rather than by using a hall test.

PRODUCT CLINIC

It may not be feasible to use full-scale test marketing for certain industrial and consumer durable goods products such as fork-lift trucks, leisure cruisers and cars. The time required to achieve repeat buying of the product may be too long. Consequently, potential customers are asked to meet at central locations, such as an exhibition hall in a large city, where the product (or at least the product prototype) is presented for their comment. Representatives of the persons who are influential in the purchasing decision are invited to assess the proposed product. Such persons will be the end users or purchasers and may also include purchasing influencers such as retailers, distributors and others in the supply chain. The participants are questioned concerning their opinion of the product proposals and may be asked to make

SUCCESSFUL INNOVATION IN THE FLOAT GLASS PROCESS

The case history described illustrates characteristics of successful innovations. Although the manufacture of glass dates back to the ancient Egyptians, centuries elapsed without any innovation in the method of production. The float glass process, which is used by all the major manufacturers of plate glass, was new concept developed by Pilkington in 1954 whereby molten glass is fed continuously on to the surface of a bath of molten tin on which it floats. The production method eliminated waste and reduced the production costs of previous methods.

The breakthrough would not have taken place without Dr L. Pilkington, who was able to transmit his enthusiasm and optimism for the project to his fellow workers. Additionally, he received the support of the company's top management even when costs began to escalate during the development phase. At one time it looked as though the project was destined to fail. Pilkington wrote,

> On our first production plant we made unusable glass for one year and two months. I had to report regularly to the board and every month put in a requisition to justify another month's expenditure of £100,000 [US$179,400]. It was a tremendous credit that they gave unwavering support throughout.

Even though their existing product was under no threat from a competitive innovation, the Pilkington board was willing to encourage innovation for its own sake. Dr Pilkington played a major role in maintaining this support through his relentless optimism. His membership of the Pilkington family was an obvious advantage, as he had immediate access to many of the board members.

In this case, as in many others, it is common to experience difficulties in moving from pilot plant to full-scale production. When the first production plant was constructed, Pilkington notes, 'We were woefully unaware of the magnitude of the problems we were going to face when we reached a mass production scale.'

Twiss (1992) makes the following observation about Pilkington: 'It is interesting to note that many of the difficulties experienced arose from the absence of a theoretical understanding of the process involved, which followed rather than preceded development.' Twiss contradicts the sequential process outlined above which describes innovation as a process that begins with research followed by applied research before development is commenced. He continues, the higher-risk approach where development is commenced before the theoretical base is established often leads to the most successful innovations as well as some of the most notable failures'.

The Pilkington case illustrates the deficiencies of a project selection system based on a cost–benefit analysis. The difficulties with float glass development occurred at a late stage in development. A more cautious approach might have delayed the construction of a production plant until the firm had gathered more information about the technology. This might have had the effect of reducing the production costs and delaying the commercial launch.

History has shown that the project that took seven years to develop and cost £4m (US$7.9m) before the first glass was available for sale. However, it was an outstanding success that reduced production costs by one quarter and plant size by over a third.

comparisons between the new product and other competing products. Interviewees spend two to three hours evaluating the product designs through a combination of completing lengthy self-completion questionnaires, participating in group discussions and individual unstructured interviews.

Usually product clinics are held in a number of areas with different types of potential purchasing decision makers, e.g. clinics for cars take place at various locations within a country and within different countries. They could target decision influencers such as car dealers, older, married car and house owners, two-car house owners and so on. Industrial goods may also be tested through product use tests at trade shows, or in distributor and dealer display rooms.

The customer adoption process

Consumers and organizational buyers approach the decision to buy a new product using a process known as the adoption process. This is a sequential process consisting of five stages, each of which takes them closer to a decision to buy a new product. The stages outlined below were discussed in Chapter 2 with reference to the concept of the hierarchy of effects.

- *Awareness*. The potential buyer knows of the existence of the product but lacks information about it. Digital television is at this stage in the adoption process for many households in the UK.
- *Knowledge*. Potential buyers seek information about the product to determine whether they need it. Some of this information is available through word of mouth from those already using the product. Marketers can influence this stage by providing informative advertising. For example, with digital television consumers require information about what it can do, how easy it is to operate and the likely cost.
- *Evaluation*. The potential buyer considers whether the product will meet his/her particular needs.
- *Trial*. With some products the customer will try the product for a limited period before deciding to make a financial commitment to buy it. For example, with digital television the consumer may go along to a television showroom to view the product or they may be able to sample one of the systems on a trial bases. Sometimes FMCGs are given away in sales promotions and food products can be sampled in in-store promotions. Car showrooms allow potential buyers to go for a test drive in a demonstration vehicle.
- *Adoption* occurs if the consumer decides to make full and regular use of the product.

A number of important points emerge from this second case study:

- Innovation transformed the entire glass manufacturing industry.
- Successful innovation offered an economic advantage through a reduction in manufacturing costs.
- The new idea came to fruition through the efforts of Dr Pilkington, the project champion, whose efforts were supported by his senior managers.

- The risks were high and the financial difficulties could not have been anticipated.
- The technical problems were resolved in the absence of theoretical knowledge.

THE MARKET DIFFUSION PROCESS

The adoption process describes the way in which an individual customer learns about an innovation. The diffusion process describes how an innovation spreads through a market and provides information that enables management to identify target markets. During this process the marketer must recognize that people differ greatly in their readiness to adopt new products. There are five market segments that are distinguished by the time consumers take to adopt a new product are discussed below:

- *Innovators* are the first to adopt the new product and usually are no more than 2.5 per cent of the population. They are venturesome in nature and are prepared to run the risk of buying a product that ultimately proves disappointing rather than miss the chance to try something new. For the marketer this group is important as the initial target because they influence later adopters. A new product that fails to win the esteem of this group is unlikely to penetrate the mass market.
- *Early adopters* represent the next 13.5 per cent of the population to adopt a new product. They are respected members of the community and are likely to be opinion leaders for others who will only buy the product when it has been given the seal of approval by the early adopters.
- *The early majority* represent 34 per cent of the population. They are more cautious of new products than the early adopters. If they are exposed to sufficient information, they will follow the example of the early adopters. This group is an important target for firms who wish to take their products from the introduction to the growth stage of the PLC.
- *The late majority* are the 34 per cent of the population who are more sceptical about new products and harder to persuade. They place greater importance on word of mouth recommendations than the media for product information.
- *Laggards* are the last 16 per cent of the population who are the most reluctant to try new products. Often they are forced to adopt new products when their favoured items have been discontinued. Members of this group are often older and or from lower socio-economic groups.

Marketing implications of diffusion process

The diffusion of innovation is closely related to the PLC and can be used both as a means of segmenting a market and for suggesting appropriate marketing activities. Promoting to the 'average' consumer will be ineffective unless the innovators and early adopters have experienced the product and are willing to recommend it. The marketing mix will need to change radically as the product moves through the segments. For example, innovators

Table 8.5 Approaches to new product development

Approach	Advantages	Disadvantages
Brand managers	Close to the market	Preoccupation with existing brands, a short-term perspective, lack of specialist NPD skills
New product managers	Provide a strong focus for NPD, add professionalism	Sometimes lack authority, preference for quick fixes instead of long-term solutions
New product committees	Add credibility to process, as members are often senior employees	Bureaucratic, can overlook detail, often slow and cumbersome, prone to political conflict, sometimes concentrate on pet projects and ignore others
New product departments	Strong focus, suited to large organizations with large portfolios	Strong guidelines required; sometimes fail to communicate with other departments
Venture teams	Encourage entrepreneurial development	Expensive if the results are not significant; staff can experience problems when returning to original posts

normally use different distribution channels and read different media from later adopters, e.g. a manufacturer of a new hi-fi product may decide to reach the innovators and early adopters through specialist magazines and hi-fi centres in the premium priced sector of the market. In order to attract the late majority and the laggards, different media and retail outlets will have to be used to promote the product.

ORGANIZING FOR NEW PRODUCT DEVELOPMENT

The success of NPD depends on two principal factors: the structure and effectiveness of the NPD process and the nature of the organizational structure and culture. Having discussed the first factor in some detail, the final part of this section will consider the importance of organizational structure and culture.

A variety of approaches for NPD have been suggested, ranging from the responsibility resting with brand managers through to new product venture teams. The advantages and disadvantages of each of these approaches are listed in Table 8.5.

A venture team consists of staff brought together from different departments and given the specific responsibility for developing a new product or business. Members are taken away from their normal duties and relocated. Emphasis is placed upon informal relations and getting the job done. Among those who have used venture teams with some success are Olivetti, 3M and Dow (Wilson and Gilligan, 1997).

FEEDING THE FURBY FAD

Once upon a time a middle-aged computer programmer called David Hampton quit the city rat race and moved to a log cabin in an American national park. In the cabin he began to think and one day he remembered the day when he visited a toy trade fair and recalls how dull the computerized toys were. 'I can do better than that!' he thought.

Encouraged by his two young sons, he began to design what is effectively a pet, but a pet that would not die; similar to the ubiquitous Tamagotchi in some respects, but otherwise quite different. For one thing the face and body of his original designs resembled the owls which he saw swooping through the forest. However, the key to the new design is the complex system of electronics contained within the furry creature.

Some months later Hampton approached Tiger Toys, a dynamic young Midwest company, known to take calculated risks with new products. Hampton found a warm reception at Tiger and passed over his invention, the 'Furby' to the development team at Tiger Toys in return for a lucrative contract. While Tiger was a small company, the giant Hasbro, one of the two biggest toy companies in the world, owned it.

The strategy for marketing Furbies was developed soon after Hampton's visit to Tiger Toys. In February 1998 the Furby was first unveiled at the prestigious New York Toy Fair, where toy buyers gather for a preview of what manufacturers will be offering for the high-selling products of the next twelve months. At that time the Furby was available only in a non-working form, as the company had not had the time fully to develop the complex electronics that made the toy work and which made it 'cute'. Despite this, buyers were impressed by what they saw, and on the basis of their initial orders Tiger worked out how many to make at its factories in China to supply the US, Canada and the UK. By March 1998 it decided that the UK market would be covered adequately by 350,000 Furbies. During the summer months, while schoolchildren in the UK played with the latest 'cool' toy, the yo-yo, engineers were working hard at perfecting the electronics of the Furby. It was absolutely essential that the electronics of each and every Furby sold should work perfectly, or there would have been serious consequences for the image of the company which made it. Toys reaching the top sales rankings often remain in that position only while the craze lasts, which may only be for a year or two (see Table 8.6).

It was not until August 1998 that the Furby went into production, because of the time taken to ensure that the electronics were up to standard. By September production was stepped up, with more factories being commissioned to cope with the escalating number of orders. By October the company closed its order books for the US and the UK, as orders far exceeded production capacity.

The consumer advertising campaign for the Furby started in the UK on 19 October 1998. A series of thirty-second commercials were run on breakfast-time television shows, particularly on channels popular with young children, such as the cartoon network.

Additionally, a full media relations campaign was planned, with a range of celebrity stunts and product placements on high-rating shows such as soap operas and product reviews on

Table 8.6 Top ten toys, 1988–1997

1988	Ghostbusters
1989	Sylvanian Families
1990	Teenage Mutant Ninja Tutles
1991	Nintendo Game Boy
1992	Tracy Island (Thunderbirds)
1993	Tracy Island (Thunderbirds)
1994	Power Rangers
1995	Power Rangers
1996	Buzz Lightyear
1997	Teletubbies

television, radio and in newspapers. The company also gave away some Furbies to television and radio stations to be used as prizes in competitions. The intention was to obtain maximum exposure for the Furby on shows with high children and parent appeal.

By this time, shops throughout the UK began to receive their first deliveries of the first half of the 350,000 Furbies that had been allocated. Most were sold out within a few hours. Then calls began to flood in from parents who were desperate to find a Furby for their child. Argos, one major retailer, reported receiving over 25,000 telephone calls requesting information about the next batch of Furbies, by late November 1998. The situation for smaller toyshops became nightmarish, as parents flooded them with requests for information about the toys. When the second batch of Furbies arrived, parents queued for hours to obtain one so that they could proudly give it to their child as a present for Christmas.

Meanwhile, somewhere else, frantic preparations were being made to prepare the next toy sensation associated with the new *Star Wars* epic, episode 1, *The Phantom Menace*.

Follow-on to Furby

While Furby continues to be sold and as at December was being sold in toy sections of prestigious department stores such as Jenner's, Edinburgh, its inventors have been developing the precursor to a range of robotic dinosaurs. In February 2006 Ugobe, based in San Francisco Bay and the co-inventor of Furby, together with its partner Sony, introduced its latest new toy, Pleo, at the Demo 2006 exhibition in Arizona. It will go on sale to the public in autumn 2006 for around $200 (£112). Pleo is a lifelike dinosaur robot that has fluid movement and sensors to stop it walking into walls and falling off edges. It has been developed by co-creator Caleb Chun and a team of biologists, animators, robotics experts and programmers, and is the first of a range of 'designer life forms'. According to Bob Christopher, Ugobe chief executive, sophisticated software and artificial intelligence have been used to enable Pleo to 'walk fluidly and balance itself and not just walk like a tin man, while at the same time being able to make emotive gestures'. The intention is that these designer robots will interact with one another and be the base of a new kind of game between light sabre-wielding robots on the tabletop rather than the traditional computer-based games. It will be interesting to see whether this range of robotics will be as successful as the Furby fad, which has lasted longer than might have been expected when ten years on it is reaching its mature stage of the NPD cycle.

Source: adapted from Watson (1998) and Nuttall (2006)

C
A
S
E

S
T
U
D
Y

DUMPY BOTTLES FOR BABY PROVE A WORLD BEATER

In June 2005 Edward Atkin sold his family business Cannon Avent for £225m (US$404m). It had become one the largest producers of babies' feeding products, including bottles, sterilizing equipment and breast pumps. In particular, Atkin invented the first babies' bottles that were squat rather than long and thin. Cannon Avent, which was renamed Avent after the sell-out, does all its manufacturing in the UK, mainly at a high-technology plan in Suffolk, exporting 80 per cent of its products on the feeding side, total sales of which have risen nearly twenty-fold since 1989. It sells in sixty countries. Its strong exporting is managed through its fifty-strong head office in London that accommodates people from twenty-two countries, capable of speaking many languages and able to sell products around the world.

Total global sales of feeding products are estimated at about £600m (US$1,076m). Avent has about a sixth of the market, with 80 per cent of its sales coming from outside the UK. The US produces about 40 per cent of revenue. Total sales in 2004 were £109m (US$196m), of which about 85 per cent was accounted for by baby products and the rest from automotive parts. In 2004 Cannon Avent made pre-tax profits of £18.5 m (US$33m), a high ratio for a UK manufacturer.

The new management at Avent is continuing to follow a strategy of developing innovative baby feeding products. Following this objective, it is expanding into new types of breast pumps that are easier for women to use, including novel electronic systems to express a given amount of milk in as short a time as possible. It is investigating entering areas such as skin care lotions for mothers and babies and equipment to hold nappies and other baby-related items. It wants to expand in emerging economies such as Brazil and China, where the business of baby products is relatively undeveloped.

Source: adapted from Marsh (2005a).

C
A
S
E

S
T
U
D
Y

PRODUCT REBRANDING RELATED TO MERINO WOOL IN NEW ZEALAND

Over the 1990s entrepreneurs in New Zealand created a new niche export industry by remarketing the wool of the merino sheep flocks, a traditional product that had been in decline. 'There has been a radical shift, in a relatively short time, from merino being a raw material export into it developing high-value markets,' according to Cheryll Sotheran, director of creative industries at New Zealand Trade and Enterprise, a government agency (Marsh, 2005b).

Just ten years earlier the merino segment had no strategic direction, little knowledge of its customers, limited new product or market development and suffered from a perception that all New Zealand wool was coarse. In the mid-1990s there was dissatisfaction with the generic, global approach to marketing wool as well as rising concern at the shrinking relevance of wool as the popularity of fleece-based and other synthetic clothing grew. Both the broader New

Zealand industry, and merino farmers in particular, decided to break away to form their own marketing organization. The approach has created a separate identity and niche for merino and engineered a better commercial outcome for farmers.

When the organization was formed, sales were conducted through auctions with volatile prices. Currently, they are grouped into supplier clubs, with about 70 per cent of local merino sold through contracts arranged by NZ Merino. The company, which is owned by farmers and Wrightson, a local agriculture group, has introduced a rigorous wool grading system that enables it to match buyers with the most appropriate suppliers. The most favoured market segment is outdoor clothing, the niche occupied by Icebreaker, which is growing fast. In 2005 it consumed about 25 per cent of local merino production, up from just 5 per cent in 2000.

After being repositioned as a distinct fibre, it has become highly prized by international luxury labels such as John Smedley, the British knitwear group, and Loro Piana, the Italian suit and clothing company, which developed its range of fabrics based on it. In New Zealand it has been intrinsic to the success of new companies such as Icebreaker, which produces only merino clothing.

Source: adapted from Marsh (2005b).

CONCLUSION

Having completed this section, you should be able to:

■   **Describe each stage of the NPD process.**

■   **Cite examples of successful NPD campaigns.**

■   **Evaluate each method of organizing for NPD.**

■   **Analyse a case study based on an organization that is involved in NPD.**

■   **Appreciate the contribution that test marketing can make to support marketing management decision making.**

REVIEW QUESTIONS

1   Evidence suggests that consuming a high-fibre diet may be helpful in reducing cholesterol levels. What impact might this health benefit have on the life cycle of high-fibre, e.g. oatmeal and oat-based, food products?

2   Consider a major FMCG manufacturer that wishes to add to its range of savoury crisps by introducing a new health food crisp that has added vitamins and minerals. Discuss the nature of the test marketing that should be undertaken to minimize the risks associated with introducing such a new product.

3   Compare the development process of the Furby with the model of NPD shown in this chapter.

4 Which parts of the NPD process are given most prominence in the above account?

5 Put yourself in the role of brand manager for the Furby. How many different people will you have to liaise with during the course of the development of this product?

6 Consider the positive and negative consequences of fads such as the Furby for manufacturers, retailers and consumers.

RECOMMENDED FURTHER READING

Andreasen, M.M. and Hein, L. (1987) *Integrated product development,* Bedford: IFS (Publications), Berlin: Springer-Verlag.

Barclay, I., Dann, Z. and Holroyd, P. (2000) *New product development,* Oxford: Butterworth Heinemann.

Bradbury, J.A.A. (1989) *Product innovation: idea to exploitation,* Chichester: Wiley.

Cooper, R.G. (1993) *Winning at new products: accelerating the process from idea to launch,* 2nd edn, Reading MA: Perseus.

Crawford, C.M. and Benedetto, C.A. (2000) *New products management,* 6th edn, Boston MA: Irwin McGraw-Hill.

Hartley, J. (1992) *New product design to successful innovation,* Dunstable: Department of Trade and Industry.

Hartley, R.F. (1992) *Marketing mistakes,* 6th edn, New York: Wiley.

Kotler, P. and Trias de Bes, F. (2003) *Lateral marketing: new techniques for finding breakthrough ideas,* Hoboken NJ: Wiley.

Kotler, P., Armstrong, G., Saunders, J. and Wong, V. (1999) *Principles of marketing,* 2nd European edn, Englewood Cliffs NJ: Prentice Hall.

Trott, P. (2005) *Innovation management and new product development,* 3rd edn, Harlow: Pearson.

9 PRICING

LEARNING OBJECTIVES

When you have completed this unit, you should be able to:

- identify the links between economic, accounting and marketing orientations to pricing;

- evaluate the importance of relating pricing decisions to other elements of the marketing mix;

- list the factors which influence price;

- discuss the ways in which firms set prices for the first time;

- appreciate how firms respond to price changes by others;

- understand the increasing importance of IT and the contribution of the Internet to pricing decisions related to online shopping;

- distinguish the differences between pricing for industrial and consumer markets.

INTRODUCTION

The price of a product or service will determine how consumers perceive it, reflect on its brand positioning, influence the choice of marketing channel, affect how it is promoted and have an impact on the level of customer service expected by target customers. The price ingredient of the marketing mix will also affect the viability of the supplying organization. The concept of pricing is complex and of fundamental importance to the successful implementation of a marketing strategy.

Pricing is one of the most important elements of the marketing mix, as it affects profit, volume and share of the market and consumer perceptions. Just as pricing plays a crucial role in determining brand image, increasingly companies are being judged on the transparency and equity with which they treat price as a marketing variable.

Generally, it is acknowledged that pricing decisions are the most difficult to make because of the complexity of the interaction between three groups involved in the marketing process: consumers, the trade and competitors. In addition pricing decisions often have to be made quickly and with limited, or even no, test marketing. They almost invariably have a direct effect on profit.

Among consumers, price is the principal determinant of choice. Its significance is further emphasized by price being the only element among the four marketing mix components that generates revenue – the others produce costs.

Frequently, a series of mistakes are associated with pricing, the most common of which are:

- Being too cost-oriented, i.e. biasing prices towards costs and overlooking competitor or customer probable response patterns.
- Setting prices in isolation from other elements of the marketing mix.
- Ignoring opportunities for differentiation.
- Setting standard prices across different market segments.
- Setting prices as a defensive response rather than an offensive approach to market conditions.
- Holding prices nominally consistent for too long, i.e. not reviewing pricing in line with market changes

Taken together, these points suggest that pricing decisions run the risk of emerging largely as a result of habit rather than of detailed strategic thinking. The haphazard approach to pricing is compounded by the ways in which responsibility for setting prices is allocated within many firms. It is standard practice for pricing decisions to be made by senior management rather than sales and marketing staff who are likely to be closer to the end consumer. This chapter considers why pricing should be the responsibility of the marketing department. It also covers the merits of the various approaches to pricing and the influence of environmental factors on the pricing process.

PRICE AND THE MARKETING MIX

In the past twenty years, pricing has become an increasingly important element in the marketing mix because consumers have a much higher awareness of price owing to:

■ Increased inflation and a reduction in real income.

■ Increased competition in global markets.

■ Recessions which have led to seller markets becoming buyer markets.

■ Better opportunities for customers to compare and consider prices, e.g. by skim-reading consumer magazines before purchasing them or, most significantly, by finding out comparable prices on the Internet. Many studies (e.g. McCall and Warrington, 1989) have shown that price in relation to value has been an important factor for product success or failure for a number of reasons:

■ While other variables in the marketing mix can take time to affect sales, a change in price can affect sales relatively quickly.

■ Price change can be achieved without too much preparatory work compared to changes in other marketing mix components, e.g. deciding upon a new advertising campaign would take comparatively much longer to implement.

■ Owing to price elasticity, a small change in price can have a significant effect on sales.

Each element within the marketing mix must be consistent with the others. For example, it is unacceptable to set a low price on a premium product or to distribute a premium product through a low-quality retailer. Generally, premium products are perceived as having high quality, are priced higher relative to competition and are selectively distributed through high-quality channel outlets. Conversely, products that are less than premium have less quality with lower prices and are usually mass-produced.

Each element within the marketing mix must also be integrated with the others. For example, extensive advertising may be used with a high selling price because the added margin permits the extensive advertising which in turn creates the product positioning to justify a higher price. Ralph Lauren, Perrier and Stella Artois are national brands employing integration in this form. Integration of price is also found with promotional pricing, where lower prices are combined with advertising and merchandising. Leverage in the marketing mix is obtained by using each element to the best advantage in support of the total marketing mix. For example, if promotion pricing in the form of rebates is more effective at building market share than either heavy advertising or improved distribution, then it would be advisable to invest in price discounts through rebates. If discounts result in diminishing returns, however, it would be better to shift the emphasis to another element that will bring greater returns per unit of investment. Beer and soft drinks are examples of products where the price element leverage is in the form of lower promotional prices.

PRICING OBJECTIVES

Prices should relate to the objectives of the firm. The price needs to be weighed against the impact on the firm's other products, the need for short-term profits against longer-term market position, and 'skimming' as opposed to 'penetration' objectives. For example, in launching a new product, a company may decide that, as it is the first to market, there will be little competition and so it will be able to 'skim' the market by charging a relatively high price. Alternatively, it may decide to enter the market at a relatively low price so as to gain a high market share before competitors enter. This, in turn, will allow the firm to benefit from experience curve effects. Each decision rests on different sets of assumptions made by planners. On the other hand, pricing may be geared towards earning a particular rate of return on funds invested or, indeed, on making a profit on the product range as a whole. In the latter case a strategy involving 'loss leaders' may be used whereby products are sold below their cost of production to encourage purchases of other more profitable products.

Setting pricing objectives

As with objectives in any area of management, pricing objectives must be clearly defined, time-specific and consistent with each other. The four types of objectives that pricing decisions can help achieve are:

- Income-related. How much money can be made?
- Volume-related. How many units can be sold?
- Competition-related. What share of the available business is wanted?
- Societal. What are the responsibilities to customers and society as a whole?

Income related objectives

Price adjustments are an obvious way of increasing the flow of money coming into an organization. This method of income generation depends on the resilience of consumer demand to an increase in price. In other words, how many customers will go elsewhere or stop buying altogether if the price increases beyond a certain point? This question is what economists call *price elasticity*.

Some firms have calculated that they can afford to lose some customers because those customers who remain loyal are willing to pay the higher prices. Japanese car manufacturers took this decision in the 1980s when they increased the price of cars in their European markets. While this resulted in fewer customers overall, those who remained generated higher income for the companies concerned.

Another reason why companies decide to focus on income rather than volume is when they are the first into the market with an innovation and want to recoup their research and development costs before competitors enter the market with similar products. This is known as price 'skimming' because the firm is aiming high at a limited number of customers whose need for the product is high enough to justify a high price. The practice is common among high-tech and pharmaceutical companies. Additional examples of price skimming can be found among high-priced products such as colour televisions, pocket calculators, digital watches and cameras, all of which have been characterized by skimming prices when they were introduced.

Firms may decide to concentrate on maximizing the short-term money gains from price skimming when the company finds it is threatened by acquisition. In order to convince shareholders of the financial health of the organization, managers may increase prices to bolster profits. Prices often return to their former level once the threat of take-over has receded.

Volume-related objectives

Volume-related objectives are approached by what is known as penetration pricing. As the name implies, this pricing policy aims at penetrating the market as extensively as possible with the aim of recruiting the maximum number of customers. Often penetration pricing is found in manufacturing industries when production capacity needs to be fully utilized. Unless the firm has a large enough production capacity to cope with anticipated demand and can reduce costs, penetration is unlikely to succeed.

The success of penetration will vary according to market conditions. In a mature market where expansion has slowed, there may be little point in buying market share. A penetration policy is more suitable in a growing market such as health drinks.

Societal objectives

Competition between firms battling for market share has the effect of driving prices down. But in some markets competition is limited by the sheer size of the enterprises concerned and it can be seen to be against the public interest. Statutory controls are brought to bear to prevent such situations from developing – such as antitrust law in the US or the activities of the Monopolies and Mergers Commission in the UK. Certain industries such as broadcasting, transport and public utilities are subject to watchdog bodies with advisory or regulatory powers. For example, companies within the privatized UK power industry are required to keep to the prices agreed with the independent regulator.

FACTORS AFFECTING PRICING DECISIONS

From the above, it can be seen how marketing objectives affect pricing decisions. Factors which also influence pricing decisions are: the nature and structure of the competition; the product life cycle (PLC); the legal considerations. Each of these will be discussed in greater detail. A marketer needs to know competitors' prices so that the firm can adjust its own prices accordingly. This does not mean that a company will necessarily match competitors' prices; it may set its prices above or below theirs.

The nature and structure of competition

When adjusting prices, marketers must anticipate how competitors might respond. Organizations operating in an unregulated monopoly can set whatever prices the market will bear. However, the company may avoid pricing the product at the highest possible level for fear of inviting government regulation or because it wants to penetrate the market by using a lower price. If the monopoly is regulated it normally has less pricing flexibility; the regulatory body lets it set prices that generate a reasonable, but not excessive, return. A government-owned monopoly may price products below cost to make them accessible to people who otherwise could not afford them.

Oligopoly takes place when only a few sellers operate and there are high barriers to competitive entry. The motor, mainframe computer, telecommunications and steel industries are examples of oligopolies. A firm in such an industry can raise its price, hoping that competitors can do the same. When an organization cuts its price to gain a competitive edge, other firms are likely to follow suit. In this way, very little is gained through price cuts in an oligopolistic market structure.

A market structure characterised by monopolistic competition means numerous sellers with differentiated product offerings. The products are differentiated by physical characteristics, features, quality and brand images. The distinguishing characteristics of its product may allow a company to set a different price from its competitors. Sellers try to develop differentiated offers for different customer segments and, in addition to price, freely use branding, advertising and personal selling to set their prices apart.

PLC

The implications of the PLC for pricing are illustrated in Table 9.1.

Legal considerations

In many markets the pricing policies of large companies and particularly those of MNCs are a controversial issue, with some governments, especially those in the Third World, viewing MNC strategies as unduly manipulative and against consumer interest. This has resulted in various forms of price legislation, often in the form of anti-monopoly rules in an attempt to protect small companies, domestic manufacturers and consumers from large firms.

A second area of concern for governments which has also led to the emergence of legislation is that of price dumping whereby an international firm uses its revenues from one market to subsidise abnormally low prices in another. Often the consequences of dumping have proved disastrous for indigenous manufacturers. At one time or another dumping has affected the steel industry, textile manufacturers, electronics companies and agricultural machinery manufacturers. It has also occurred in the agricultural industry as when the EU has been accused by Brazil, in particular, of dumping sugar on the international market, although this issue is being addressed with the proposed reduction in subsidies given to EU producers. In transnational institutions like the EU, actions affecting trade between member countries are subject to EU laws that take precedence over domestic laws.

Table 9.1 Stages of the product life cycle

Stage	Nature of price decisions
Pre-launch	Set price objectives. Analyse influences on potential sales that might affect sales, e.g. anticipated demand, costs, competitor pricing, supply factors and product characteristics
Introduction	Select penetration or skimming prices. Determine nature of trade discounts. Develop special offers to encourage product trial
Growth	Consider pricing approach to combat competition. Exploit economies of scale to introduce lower prices. Strengthen dealer ties with pricing concessions and improve consumer product price/value perceptions
Maturity	Price to protect market position. Identify opportunities for differentiation. Consider introducing a low price-fighting brand. Identify alternative distribution channels offering scope for higher prices to increase profits
Decline	Price to maximize profits, even at the expense of market share. Consider viability of using price reductions in short-life product segments

SETTING A PRICE

The various pricing approaches that are available to the marketer include: cost-based pricing; demand-based pricing; competition oriented pricing; target return on investment pricing.

Cost-based pricing

In setting a price normally it is advisable to cover all relevant costs. Costs for this purpose may be divided into two categories, fixed and variable costs. Taken together with price, these may be used to calculate the break-even quantity (fixed costs divided by price less variable cost per unit).

The four most important cost concepts are fixed costs, variable costs, marginal cost and total cost. These are defined as follows:

- *Fixed costs* are those which do not vary with output in the short term. This category includes management salaries, insurance, rent, buildings and machine maintenance, etc. Once output passes a certain threshold, however, extra production facilities might have to be brought on stream and so fixed costs will show a step-like increase.
- *Variable costs* are those which vary according to the quantity produced. These costs are incurred through raw materials, components and direct labour used for assembly or manufacture. Variable costs can be expressed as a total or on a per-unit basis.
- *Marginal costs* involve the change that occurs to total cost if one more unit is added to the production total.

■ *Total cost* is all the cost incurred by an organization in manufacturing, marketing, administering and delivering the product to the customer. Total costs are obtained by adding the fixed costs and the variable costs.

Cost-oriented pricing is the most elementary pricing method. It involves the calculation of all the costs that can be attributed to a product, whether variable or fixed, and then adding to this figure a desirable mark-up, as determined by management.

The simplicity of this method is that it requires no other effort beyond consulting the accounting or financial records of the firm. There is no necessity to study market demand, consider competition, or look in to other factors that may have a bearing on price. Cost is considered the most important determinant in the firm's pricing effort, which is then directed towards covering these costs and realizing the desired profitability.

Cost-plus pricing is popular among many retailers and wholesalers. For example, in the case of retailers, the purchase price of the product is added to the product's share of the operating expenses and a desirable margin, determined by the type of product under consideration, is then added to determine the selling price.

In the construction and defence industries, the public utilities and some service industries, the use of cost-oriented methods is widespread. Provided an astute accountant or financial analyst can calculate the necessary cost figures, this method can deliver the desired results in a short time.

Marginal cost pricing

In cost-plus pricing, the margin set reflects all the costs and overheads attributed to a particular product or service. In marginal cost pricing (often called marginal pricing) only a proportion of the costs (those directly attributable to the production of the item under consideration) is included in the price. The fixed costs of production, e.g. the rent of the building, are discounted and only the variable costs, e.g. direct materials, direct labour, etc., are included. This means that the cost is less than might otherwise be expected and a more competitive price can be charged. Marginal pricing is useful when a company has short-term excess capacity. In the long term it is inappropriate because all costs must be covered otherwise the company will

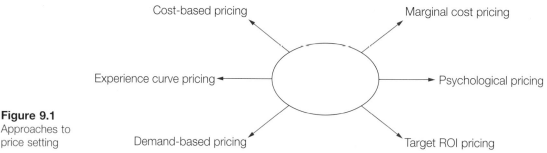

Figure 9.1
Approaches to price setting

go out of business. Another disadvantage of marginal pricing is that existing customers may be antagonized to learn that a competitor, or another group of customers, has been offered a reduced price.

Despite its simplicity, there are a number of weaknesses in the cost-plus pricing approach that limits its practicality. The price an individual is willing to pay for a product may bear little relation to the cost of its manufacture. Studies of consumer behaviour have produced considerable evidence that contradicts the assumptions of classical economists, in that the consumer as a wholly rational buyer may knowingly select a product or service at a higher price, even though substitutes may be available. This is particularly true with status items such as designer clothes, sports cars and first-class travel. An investor in diamonds, art or stamps does not value the object in question in terms of its costs of production or extraction, but rather in terms of its value to him/her.

Power of suppliers

Although usually price increases are explained to consumers as the result of more expensive raw materials, successful organizations will have enough of a buffer in their pricing structures to enable some control over the timing of such increases with an eye to their possible effect on demand.

Target return on investment pricing

This is similar to cost-plus pricing as it assumes that costs can be known or estimated with enough accuracy to feature in the calculation of price. Target pricing, which looks for long-run average rates of return, is one method of cost pricing, used especially when fixed costs at launch are high. Among those who have used this in the past have been the privatized utilities and, in the US, General Electric and General Motors. The calculation is straightforward:

$$\text{Price to meet target return on investment (ROI)} = \text{Unit cost} + \frac{\text{Target percentage return} \times \text{Capital invested}}{\text{Unit sales}}$$

This approach to pricing is prone to the same difficulties as any cost-based approach, but it has the advantage of forcing consideration of whether a proposed price is feasible from a purely commercial point of view.

Experience curve pricing

As organizations produce more units, experience and learning lead to greater efficiency. The sources of the experience effect are varied and include such factors as labour efficiency, as the assigned tasks are repeated over and over again, and work specialization, as the worker becomes more proficient in performing a single-facet operation as opposed to a multi-faceted

PRICING OF FORD MUSTANG

In the early 1960s the Ford car company launched a plan to compete with General Motors and European car manufacturers in the sports car market. Ford's approach to this task was unique in the sports car industry.

Under the traditional systems, management would have begun the process by sending a memo to the design department, instructing it to develop a sports car that would top the competition. Each designer would then have drawn on individual preconceptions of what makes a good sports car to design bodies, suspensions and engines that would be better. Next, management would have turned those designs over to the marketing research department. Its researchers would have asked potential customers which design they preferred and how they compared with competing cars. This information would have been used to produce cars with prices that would cover their costs and yield the desired rate of return. Ultimately, the best choice would have been built. It would have shared with competitors the adoration of many but be purchased by only the few customers who could afford it.

Fortunately, Ford's general manager, Lee Iacocca, was a marketer, unlike many of the top executives in the US car industry. When he began to research the new car, he began with the customer rather than the design department. Iacocca found that a large and growing share of the market longed for a sports car and that most people could not afford one. He sought to understand his customers more deeply and discovered what they wanted. The challenge for Ford was to design a car that looked sufficiently sporty to satisfy most buyers, but without the usual mechanical elements of a sports car that drove its price out of reach. To meet that challenge, Ford built its sports car with the mechanical workings of an existing economy car, the Falcon. Many sports car enthusiasts were appalled.

In 1964 Ford introduced the Mustang sports car at a base price of $2,368. More Mustangs were sold in the first year of sales than any other car Ford ever built. Ford's new product strategy for the Mustang reversed the traditional, product-driven focus related to cost-based pricing. The product-based price assumes that the attributes of the product are given and cannot be readily changed. The price is determined by estimating the product's costs and calculating the price that would cover cost plus a given yield (or profit). Only then does the marketer consider whether customers can and will pay the price. In the case of the Mustang, Ford began to consider the favoured price by asking customers what they wanted and what they were willing to pay for it. Their response determined the car's selling price. Only then did Ford attempt to develop a product that could satisfy potential customers at a price they could afford, that still permitted a substantial profit. This reflects a customer-orientated marketing approach to pricing.

one. Unlike cost reductions from capacity utilization, cost reductions resulting from experience are a result of concerted effort by management. For example, the relative prices of fax machines and mobile phones are falling, partly because of the experience curve effect.

Demand-based pricing

Demand-based pricing looks outwards from the production line and focuses on customers and their responsiveness to different price levels. Even this approach may be insufficient on its own, but when it is linked with competition-based pricing (see below), it provides a powerful market-oriented perspective that cost-based methods ignore.

Demand-based pricing allows the price to go up when demand is strong and, vice versa, for the price to go down when demand is weak. Examples of demand-based pricing can be found within the package holiday industry where prices are highest during the school summer holidays and in the travel industry where prices vary according to the level of demand, e.g. highest during the morning rush hour and cheapest during off-peak times.

This method requires decision makers to make volume forecasts for different price levels and calculations of production and marketing costs at different levels to cover overheads. In setting a price information has to be obtained about demand factors, e.g. the price elasticity of demand. This is calculated by estimating the percentage change in quantity demanded over the percentage change in price. By gaining knowledge of demand factors the marketer helps avoid the potentially disastrous mistake of focusing too much on costs. Typically, this involves estimating likely demand at different prices; estimating what happens to cost as demand rises; estimating the likely effects of raising or lowering price. How is this done?

Example. One means of estimating the importance of price is to consider how customers rate this attribute in terms of the buying decision. Competitive products are ranked in terms of key customer buying factors and customer response to price may be tested by field experiment, direct attitude survey (buyer response curves) and, for new products, value analysis of customer cost saving benefits, e.g. energy or labour saving costs.

However, problems with the above approach should not be minimized. Perceptual mapping of prices is notoriously difficult to research; the process is highly subjective and the marketing environment is highly dynamic.

There are a number of more sophisticated forms of demand-based pricing, as shown below.

PSYCHOLOGICAL PRICING

In using psychological pricing, sellers consider the psychology of prices as well as the economics. When consumers can judge the quality of a product by examining it, or by calling on past experience, they use price less to judge quality. When consumers cannot judge quality because they lack the information or skill, price becomes an important quality signal, as the following case study illustrates.

C A S E   S T U D Y

THE PRICE OF VODKA

A few years ago the producer of Smirnoff vodka, Heublein, was concerned when a competitor, Wolschmidt, entered the market with a competitor product priced at $1 less than a bottle of Smirnoff. There were a number of counter-strategies available to Smirnoff. It could lower its prices by $1 to retain market share; it could hold Smirnoff's prices by increasing advertising and promotional expenditure; or it could hold Smirnoff's price by allowing its market share to fall. None of the three strategies appeared attractive; each would lead to lower profits.

Heublein's response to the competitor attack was highly innovative. The price of a bottle of Smirnoff was raised by $1! The company then introduced a new brand, Relska, to compete with Wolschmidt. Moreover, it introduced yet another brand, Popov, priced even lower than Wolschmidt. This product line-pricing strategy positioned Smirnoff as the elite brand and Wolschmidt as an ordinary brand and won extra profit for Heublein.

Despite Heublein's three brands being the same in terms of taste and manufacturing cost, they were perceived differently by their consumers. Using price as a signal, Heublein sells roughly the same product at three different quality positions. This method relies on the consumer's emotive responses and feelings towards purchases.

The following are examples of psychological pricing:

- *High-level pricing*, usually maintained throughout the entire PLC: prestige items such as fine jewellery and designer clothing use high pricing together with associated advertising that lends an aura of prestige and quality to the item. For example, Mercedes cars gained on Cadillac in the US by offering a car of higher quality and higher price.
- *Odd–even pricing*, i.e. the practice of ending a price with certain numbers. Odd number price endings like £999.99 for a computer system are seen by customers as a price in the under £1,000 range rather than in the next higher category. If a company wants a high-price image rather than a low-price one, then it should avoid the odd-ending tactic.
- *Bundle-pricing*, where two or more products or services are offered at a particular price, usually gives a lower price than the total price of all the items sold separately. For example, a fly-drive arrangement for one price, a hotel arrangement including sightseeing tours at a special price or a book of theatre tickets for the season at a cheaper price than if they had been bought singly. The opposite process of unbundling involves breaking up the bundle when conditions indicate it is no longer useful.

Competition oriented pricing

This method involves setting prices on the basis of what competitors are charging. Once the firm identifies its competitors, it conducts a competitive evaluation of its product. Competitive factors that must be considered include:

- The 'market price' charged by the market leader.
- Price sensitivity.
- Market position.
- Product differentiation.
- The type of competition, i.e. whether this is monopoly or oligopoly.

In assuming how a competitor might react to a price move, several factors need to be considered. These include:

- The competitor's cost structure.
- Past price behaviour.
- Market demand.
- The relationship of the product to others in the competitor's line.
- Plant utilization.

If the cost-oriented approach to pricing is considered to be forward in nature, the competition-oriented method can be thought to be a backward exercise in pricing. Under the cost-oriented approach, prices are determined on the basis of total cost calculation to which a reasonable profit margin is added. In other words, the pricing process proceeds forward with the calculations of variable and fixed costs, to which a desirable return is added to reach a price. Under the competition-oriented approach, price is the starting point in the calculation process. Obviously, this price is only an indication of the appropriate price to charge in view of the competition in the market place, but it has no necessary relation to cost. In this way, the manager works 'backwards' from this given price to see if the designated price is sufficient to cover costs and desired profitability. When the price does not cover costs plus the firm's profit objectives, management has to decide whether to:

- Bear the losses or reduced returns for a period of time until the product is strong enough to be profitable.
- Adjust the choice of materials, equipment and manpower to produce the product at a lower cost sufficient to make it profitable.
- Drop the proposed product entirely, as a last resort.

EXAMPLE OF COMPETITION PRICING

It has been noted that there are products, e.g. an industrial boiler installation (mainly 'one-off') and markets, e.g. the defence market (mainly those with monopoly buyers) where price elasticity of demand does not exist. Equally, there are modest products like bread and some luxury products like malt whisky where price elasticity is so limited that minor variations in price have little effect on sales and profits. But usually concern is with products where there is some choice in relation to such elasticity. It is necessary to determine the combination of price and volume that will best suit, given what is being paid for competitors' products. An obvious answer might be the alternative that gives the maximum profit, assuming given knowledge of fixed and variable costs. It can be assumed a high-tech product with an estimated volume of 475,000 units in a given period at a proposed selling price of $100 with variable manufacturing and marketing costs $50 per unit and distributor's margin of 20 per cent and retailer's mark-up of 50 per cent.

Retail price per unit	$100.00
less retail mark-up 50% (one-third on sales)	33.33
Distributor's selling price	66.67
less distributor's margin of 20%	13.33
Price to distributor	53.35
less variable manufacturing and marketing costs	50.00
Contribution per unit	$3.34

The anticipated volume of sales is 500,000 units. The total contribution is therefore 500,000 × 3.34 = $1,670,000. If the allocated fixed costs are $500,000, then there is a projected profit of $1,170,000.

But there is a problem in that any allocation of fixed costs is arbitrary. Fortunately, the calculations do not need to be based on an arbitrary division of overheads although accountants often insist on so doing. Rather, instead, the total contribution to overheads and profit of different combinations of price and volume where fixed costs have already been incurred can be used. That is, the combination of unit contribution × the number of units sold which gives the alternative that offers the highest profit or lowest loss. If it is assumed, in addition to the combination in the above example, marketing research volume projections of 475,000, 450,000, 250,000 and 100,000 at prices of $110, $125, $150 and $175 respectively, it is possible to compute the contribution for each combination, as shown in Table 9.2.

It will be seen, if working out the unit contribution for each of the alternatives as in the above example, that the highest unit contribution is at a price of $175 but that the combination that gives the greatest total contribution is at a price of $125. This is the optimum price, all things being equal, which is not always the case. Data can be made out of date by inaccurate information, changes in consumer preferences, innovative offerings by other companies, unexpected price reductions by competitors and volatile economic conditions, among other reasons. As a result, they may need to be reviewed from time to time and

Table 9.2 Computation for each projection combination

Retail price (US$)	100	110	125	150	175
Unit sales (000)	500	475	450	250	100
Sales revenue ($000)	50,000	52,250	56,250	37,500	17,500
Total variable costs ($000)	48,330	48,127	44,244	30,000	13,166
Total contribution ($000)	1,670	4,123	12,006	7,500	4,334

updated. This method endeavours to construct a 'going rate' of price and perceived quality for each market segment. Also, different combinations may be chosen, depending on the strategy to be adopted. For example, a skimming price strategy or a market penetration price strategy might involve the selection of a high price or a low price combination respectively. This illustrates that an economic concept, the notion of price elasticity of demand, is given commercial relevance by the financial concept of contribution which in its application may have to be adjusted to take marketing concepts into account or changes in the marketing environment.

OTHER PRICING ISSUES RELATED TO COMPETITORS

When a firm considers introducing a price change it has to consider carefully the reactions of its customers and those of its competitors. A price cut in a consumer durable might be interpreted as a signal of the introduction of a new model. It might induce the customer to wait. Alternatively, it might be seen as an indication that the product is flawed and not selling well, or the company is in financial trouble and may not be able to honour its guarantees. The messages conveyed by price changes in these circumstances have to be carefully considered. If the price is increased, a practice normally expected to reduce sales, that may well be viewed as evidence that the product is going to be in short supply or the customer is being 'ripped off'. Similarly, competitors may react in ways that reflect their self-interest. A company aiming for increased market share is likely to match a price reduction if it is looking to maximize its short-term profits. In other circumstances it may react differently, e.g. by improving the product quality or increasing its advertising budget. The challenge is to anticipate what the competitor will do by using as many sources of information as possible.

The firm facing a price change by a competitor needs to understand the competitor's reasons for the change and how long it is likely to last. It could be to gain market share, take up spare manufacturing capacity, or respond to changes in the cost of raw materials or labour, among many possible reasons. The firm needs to know the likely effect on its profitability if it does not respond, and if adversely affected, the proposed action to counter it. The response varies with the particular situation. For example, a market leader attacked by a price reduction aimed at increasing the competitor's market share might respond by introducing a lower-priced brand. This is necessary if market share is being lost in a segment that is price-sensitive, since it will not respond to arguments of higher quality.

PRICING INDUSTRIAL GOODS

Industrial markets consist of individuals and organizations that purchase products for resale, for use in their own operations or for producing other products. Establishing prices for this category of B-to-B buyers is sometimes different from setting prices for consumers. Industrial marketers have experienced much change because of economic uncertainty, sporadic supply shortages and an increasing interest in service. Differences in the size of purchases, geographical factors and transport considerations require sellers to adjust prices.

Marketers may use special pricing incentives to encourage sales. These can include the following unique to the pricing of industrial products and B-to-B markets: cash discounts; seasonal discounts; allowances; geographical pricing.

Cash discounts

A cash discount, or simple price reduction, is given to a buyer for prompt payment or payment in cash. Accounts receivable are an expense and a collection problem for many organizations. A policy to encourage prompt payment is a popular practice and can be a major concern in setting prices.

Discounts are based on cash payments or cash paid within a stated time. For example, '2/10 net 30' means that a 2 per cent discount will be allowed if the account is paid within ten days. However, if the buyer does not pay within the ten-day period, the entire balance is due within thirty days without a discount. If the account is not paid within thirty days, interest may be charged.

Seasonal discounts

A seasonal discount is a price reduction given to buyers who purchase goods or services out of season. These discounts let the seller maintain steadier production during the year. For example, car hire companies offer seasonal discounts in winter and early spring to encourage firms to use cars during the industry's slow sales months.

Allowances

Another type of reduction from the list price is an allowance which is a price concession given to achieve desired sales. Trade-in allowances are price reductions granted for turning in a used item when purchasing a new one. For example, $50 for an old washing machine is credited against the purchase of a new machine. Allowances help to give the buyer the ability to make the new purchase. This type of discount is popular in the aircraft industry. Another example is promotional allowances, which are price reductions granted to dealers for participating in advertising and sales support programmes intended to increase sales of a particular item.

Geographical pricing

There is a choice of two approaches to geographical pricing. The first is to give a price for delivery from factory or warehouse and leave the buyer to make his own arrangements. Designated 'ex works' or 'ex warehouse' or 'free carrier', this approach is seen by its advocates as the most equitable way to allocate freight charges because all the customers pick up their own costs. The US term is 'free on board (f.o.b.) factory but it should be noted that this can be confusing in an international context, as under the International Chamber of Commerce definition adopted by most of the world, f.o.b. means free on board a ship. An alternative within this approach is the 'delivered price' to the customer's premises or, in US terms, 'f.o.b. destination'. A delivered price implies that the manufacturer takes responsibility for the actual cost of shipping the merchandise to the customer. It involves the seller in overheads to provide the facility either through the use of the company's own transport or through contact with transport firms.

The second approach, uniform geographical pricing, avoids the problems inherent in 'free carrier' or 'delivered price' to the customer whereby different prices can be charged to different customers. Uniform geographical pricing, sometimes called postage stamp pricing, is based on average shipping costs. Customers are charged the same price regardless of location, with the price being based on average transport costs for all customers. Petrol, paper and office equipment are often priced on a uniform basis. There are variations within this approach whereby certain zones are created in larger land areas and different charges apply depending on the distance.

In this way, a f.o.b. factory price indicates the price of the merchandise at the factory, before it is loaded on to the carrier vehicle. It excludes transport costs. The buyer must pay for carriage. An f.o.b. destination price means that the producer absorbs the costs of shipping the merchandise to the customer. This policy may be used to attract distant customers. Although f.o.b. pricing is an easy way to price products, it can be difficult for marketers to administer, especially when a firm has a wide product mix or when customers are widely dispersed. It requires the seller to keep abreast of transport costs to inform customers regarding the most economical method of consignment.

PRICING AND INFORMATION TECHNOLOGY

The Internet is a natural medium for international buying and selling. People can bid at electronic auctions and prices in many sales transactions may be negotiated over it often in association with a face-to-face element. Driven by the World Wide Web, the practice of the 'name your own price' system has turned commercial logic on its head. It proves that, for the right price, people will buy something without knowing the brand or, in the case of airline tickets, without knowing when the flight takes off. In the world of priceline.com, the buyer writes the price tag. There is a competing group of sellers whose prices are matched against it by the company. NexTag.com is a company that has come up with an even better way of setting prices. To all appearances it is another online auction house, albeit a large one, featuring more than 150,000 items. But the firm does not let buyers compete by bidding the prices up. It offers the opposite; multiple sellers bid prices down to win a buyer's business. The attraction for sellers is that they can discount products without having to lower prices at their own outlets. NexTag.com provides sellers with free software to automate their responses to bids, and capture data about potential buyers, which is equally enticing. However, if the idea catches on with buyers, the sellers may change their minds. The medium remains in a state of flux.

As is shown in the following case study on online retailing, retailers have different approaches to pricing. Some retailers try to have the same price online and in stores, others find a saving on Internet selling which they pass on to customers.

ONLINE RETAILING PRICING

It is well appreciated the Internet has become a good first source for obtaining information on pricing approaches for goods and services in both the consumer and industrial markets. In particular, the Internet is the place to find price bargains, for books, compact discs (CDs) and even electrical goods, although electronics manufacturers have been threatening to refuse to give discounts to online stores to protect their traditional retailers. Even so, some electronics goods can be bought nearly 20 per cent cheaper over the Internet, although for many items price differences are rapidly closing. A small survey of shopping list items by the *Financial Times* showed a mixed picture (Palmer, 2005). For the newest electronics devices, such as Apple's video iPod and Sony's PlayStationPortable (PSP) hand-held games console, the online and high-street price difference is small. However, for other items, such as digital video data (DVD) recorders and digital radios, considerable saving can be found through online shopping.

> There is some flattening out of prices, but there is no cohesive picture [according to Glen Drury, Managing Director of Kelkoo.com, the price comparison website] Every retailer is still trying to feel their way through this. Some feel it is very important to have exactly the same prices online and in stores. Others are finding there is still a saving from selling over the Internet, which they are passing on to customers.
>
> (Palmer, 2005)

Interestingly, in the US, unlike the UK, there is little difference between online and store prices. Large US retailers such as Wal-Mart are so powerful in driving down manufacturers' prices that small independent online retailers find it difficult to undercut these any further. It remains to be seen if a similar trend occurs in the UK in due course.

In the UK the most obvious online discounts are for books and CDs. The immense power of Amazon.com, the largest online bookstore, is keeping the price of books extremely competitive, while many online music retailers are benefiting from a tax loophole which allows them to avoid Value Added Tax (VAT) if their goods are sold through Jersey, in the Channel Islands, which is outside the EU. European law allows goods that are less than £18 (US$32) in value to be imported without VAT, which enables online music stores, whose goods mostly fall into this price range, to undercut high-street rivals and even supermarkets, which are often the most aggressive discounters of CDs. There are plans to limit the number of new companies setting up in Jersey to curtail this practice. However, according to the Interactive Media in Retail Group (IMRG), the industry body for online retailers, other tax-liberal countries such as Luxembourg and Switzerland could readily replace Jersey as the new base for distribution (Palmer, 2005).

For clothing, online price bargains are less clear. According to the IMRG, online sales are growing rapidly, especially for branded sports clothing. But, from the *FT*'s survey evidence, the price difference is small, suggesting that convenience rather than cost attract shoppers. With food and alcohol, the Internet appears to be at a disadvantage, where prices for drinks

C
A
S
E

S
T
U
D
Y

often are comparable for basic costs but heavy delivery charges make Internet purchasing much pricier. Nevertheless, despite the apparent hidden extra costs that can be associated with online shopping, its use is steadily increasing as customers have become accustomed to its convenience and flexibility, especially at peak purchasing times such as the lead-up to festive shopping.

Of course, there are still other restrictions imposed, often for the convenience of retailers, in particular, that have to be considered with online shopping. Geographical coverage for online shopping may only apply to a particular country or currency using a given language. But, even in these cases, where appropriate, arrangements can be made for stores to adapt their websites for use in countries other than that of the originator. Language can be translated and selection of goods for sale targeted to country needs and acceptance of international credit and debit cards for payments can be made. There may also be specific consideration for delivery charges, together with any other export/import documentation expenses that come within the remit of international marketing.

Source: adapted from Palmer (2005).

THE DUST IS SETTLING ON THE DYSON MARKET CLEAN-UP

C
A
S
E

S
T
U
D
Y

In 1993 James Dyson set up the domestic appliance business manufacturing in the UK. The 56 year old designer shot to prominence through his invention of a new 'high suction' machine that revolutionized the world of vacuum cleaners by dispensing with the need for bags. The company gained favour with the British public, thanks to its image as being a home-grown newcomer taking on industry giants. Indeed, Dyson became one of Tony Blair's favourite businessmen, participating in a small group reviewing innovation and productivity in the UK for the Department of Trade and Industry.

However, in 2001, to achieve production cost savings it became necessary to transfer manufacturing from the UK to Malaysia, which caused considerable adverse publicity among the British public. Iayn Clark, director of International Strategic Management, a London-based consultancy, commented that this sent out a 'disastrous' message both to the public and to the business world. 'It put off many consumers from buying Dyson's product and also said to businesses that outsourcing [to low-cost countries] can be a panacea' (Marsh, 2003).

By 2003, while Dyson remained the UK market leader in vacuum cleaners with pre-tax profits of about £40m (US$70m), twice that of 2002, he faced challenges. Within the vacuum cleaner business worth £530m (US$951m) in the retail market, Dyson was losing market share related to the emergence of low-cost competitors, many selling look-alike versions of the Dyson machines. Dyson's share of British vacuum cleaner sales fell to 15 per cent by volume in the year to October 2003, well below the 40 per cent the company claimed in the late 1990s. His premium pricing meant that the market by volume, equivalent to 38 per cent by value, was down from 44 per cent in 2002.

Dyson was affected by the backlash against its decision to cut 600 manufacturing jobs in Britain and move to a cheaper location as a way to cut its production costs by a quarter. Furthermore, sales of the company's upmarket washing machine, launched in 2000, considered to be among the most innovative technology advances in washing in 100 years, were disappointing. They accounted for only about 0.5 per cent by volume of the British market, worth nearly £800m at retail prices. In 2003 Dyson sales were about £275m (US$493m), with about 35 per cent coming from outside Britain. More than 90 per cent of the company's revenues came from vacuum cleaners, with washing machines accounting for the remainder.

Electrolux of Sweden and Glen Dimplex of Ireland (owner of the Morphy Richards brand) led the assault on Dyson's dominance of the British vacuum cleaner market together with low-price rivals such as LG and Samsung of South Korea. Frequently, such competing products sold for less than £100 (US$179), compared with £200 (US$358) or so for a Dyson. According to the marketing research agency GfK, research showed that only 35 per cent of owners of a Dyson vacuum cleaner would repeat-buy from the company, as against more than 50 per cent five years earlier. Replacement levels were low.

Nevertheless, Dyson justified the high-price strategy as relating to the innovative features of the products. For the vacuum cleaners, these include the original 'dual cyclone' system that pushes air through the machine and maintains an unusually high suction power, enabling the product to be bagless. He considered it arrogant to assume the expense would deter buyers. The machines competed at the high end of the premium market with competitors such as BSH (jointly owned by Bosch and Siemens) and Miele, both of Germany. However, despite Dyson's insistence that it was not reviewing its pricing strategy, new strategies leading to price cuts for some models were introduced. Premium pricing can be difficult to justify in the face of severe competition from lower-cost producers, especially if the prestige of the premium product cannot be maintained. Premium products have to be fully supported by targeting and positioning all the marketing mix elements, especially product quality and promotion, to ensure the desirable image. By changing the manufacturing location, Dyson lost much of the kudos associated with the vacuum cleaner product range, obliging a discreet change in pricing strategy to be introduced.

Source: adapted from Marsh (2003).

CAR PRICE WAR LOOMS IN CHINA AS SHANGHAI VOLKSWAGEN CUTS PRICES

Volkswagen (VW) operates two joint ventures, FAW and Shanghai, in China. It is market leader but, with increasing competition from a growing number of MNCs, VW's market share in China fell from about 50 per cent in 2003 to 15.7 per cent in the first seven months of 2005. Indeed, in the first half of 2005 VW made an operating loss of €23m (US$28.4m) compared with a profit of €251m in 2004. For the full year of 2005 losses were expected. The joint ventures with FAW and Shanghai sales fell 31 per cent and 49 per cent respectively, according to Automotive Resources Asia.

In response to this situation, VW's strategy was to improve efficiency by merging the retail operation of the two joint venture partners, cutting costs and changing sourcing strategies. The Chinese expansion plans were postponed during the restructuring.

In what could be the beginning of a new price war, and as an attempt to maintain its position as the brand leader in China, in August 2005 Shanghai VW's made substantial price cuts of between 6 per cent and 14 per cent on its best-selling models such as the Santana and the Gol. This move could have encouraged other car makers to follow suit and reduce prices, given VW's important position in the market, although some price cutting had already been undertaken. Certainly, the price cuts emphasized the slump in margins that car makers were facing in China.

General Motors' joint venture also saw sales slip. The main gainers have been foreign rivals such as Hyundai and Honda and domestic car markers, including Dongfeng and Chery.

Zhu Junyi, analyst at the Shanghai Information Centre, a government-backed consultancy, felt the move by VW was inevitable, as, compared with cars of the same category, VW's prices were fairly high because its labour costs were high. But another industry consultant in China considered VW needed to do something more radical than price cutting. It did not have enough new models. Its two joint ventures did not always work well together and they did not have a competitive cost structure.

It remains to be seen how and whether VW will be able to maintain its leadership in the potentially enormous Chinese market. Clearly, a change in its pricing strategy to cut prices sent mixed messages to customers as well as other competitors in the market for the market leader. Great care to assimilate the other elements of the marketing mix will have to be taken if the leader is not going to lose face in the apparent price downgrade.

Source: adapted from Dyer (2005).

ROVER DRIVERS AND DEALERS FACE SUBSTANTIAL LOSSES IN THE VALUE OF THEIR CARS AND RELATED FINANCING

In the UK, MG Rover dumped an extra 3,000 to 4,000 unordered cars on to its dealer network in the final months before it collapsed in April 2005. The issue was the focus of meeting between dealers and Capital Bank, part of Halifax Bank of Scotland (HBOS), which financed the cars through a triangular deal that released cash to Rover when cars were ordered but left the dealer liable to repay the debt after 180 days.

Alan Pulham, of the National Franchise Dealers' Association of the Retail Motor Industry Federation, commented that during the last month (March) in particular, but over the last six months to a year, Rover had been transferring financial responsibility for cars to dealers without the cars having been requested. It was commercially naughty but not fraud. What Rover claimed was that they did not think dealers were ordering enough cars and they were helping them (Mackintosh, 2005). The failure of the company left dealers in dispute with the bankers about liability for the debt on the cars, which could be more than £40m (US$72m). Dealers were considered to be within their rights to refuse to pay, although it was a complex situation with no recent legal precedents.

Rover used other methods to boost its cash flow in its last days, including a bonus scheme whereby £1,000 (US$1,794) per car sold was promised to dealers on certain types of car. This is standard practice in the industry, but was especially apparent at the end of March and early April. However, dealers who sold cars under the scheme lost out and had to queue up with other creditors in the hope of being paid part of the money they were owed.

Rover also used its own dealerships, branded as Phoenix Venture Motors, which was in administration, to raise much-needed cash through cut-price deals of up to 28 per cent on new cars in March, when the company was on the verge of failure.

While dealers lost out on the financing of Rover car sales that did not materialize, so too did the owners of 100,000 Rovers and MGs bought since the beginning of 2004 who faced a sharp drop in the value of their cars as a result of the Rover collapse. This fall may not necessarily be catastrophic or unexpected. Depreciation on Rovers had long been among the most severe in the industry, with a 2002 model 45 being worth only 24 per cent of its original list price in 2005 compared with 33 per cent for an equivalent age and price Vauxhall Astra (Mackintosh, 2005).

The trouble is, the cars were mostly old; with so many good new cars around, why buy a Rover? The fleet people had already taken them right off their lists. So far, there had been a viable dealer network keeping residuals up. But after this experience the dealers were expected to quit and move to other franchises. Growing difficulties in getting parts and service would make things worse, but the cars will always have value. For example, CAP, the motor trade pricing analysis group, projected that a just-purchased Rover 75 would retain about 25 per cent of its value in 2008. Residual values of MGs have been higher, with the MG version of the Rover 45 retaining well over 30 per cent of its value after three years, marginally better than the volume car industry norm. 'The MG is a brand that still counts for a lot; it's the Rover brand that has dragged everything down' according to Martin Ward, CAP's manufacturer relations manager (Griffiths, 2005).

Clearly, a great deal of financial suffering was incurred by the demise of the Rover group. While appearing to operate a premium pricing strategy, Rover had to introduce numerous incentives and price-cutting approaches through its intermediary dealerships to encourage sales and cash flow. Ultimately, these could not be justified and many made substantial losses.

Source: adapted from Griffiths (2005) and Mackintosh (2005): www.ft.com/rover.

THE ROLE OF PRICING IN THE CASHMERE KNITWEAR INDUSTRY

Cashmere traditionally comes from the soft underhair beneath the thick coats of goats from China and Mongolia and is the main source of supply for the Scottish cashmere knitwear industry. It takes the underhair of at least three goats to make one sweater. The Scottish cashmere business, which originated in the 1870s, employs 4,000 people, mainly in the Borders, and has annual sales in excess of £100m (US$179m), 70 per cent of which is exported. However, it is facing increasing competition from low-cost producers, so much so that the Scottish textile industry's work force has halved over the past ten years as former customers such as M&S have increasingly sourced their products from low-cost countries such as Turkey. It is fighting back by investing heavily in improving its production methods to meet competition, e.g. by introducing expensive whole-garment machines that eliminate side, shoulder and underarm seams to ensure its goods are of the highest quality and design. The industry has to face the challenge of producing new designs within a tight time frame.

> Chinese companies will buy our latest designs and can copy them within three to six months, so we have a maximum of a year's lead. But we have a palette of colours that is world-beating. Partly it's because of the softness and cleanness of the water . . . In China, colours don't have that sparkle. Most of our customers know what they are buying and appreciate such differences, they are not [low-price] Tesco customers.
>
> (Bolger, 2005)

Regarding price competition, since 2003, Tesco, the supermarket chain, has been selling cashmere sweaters for £25 to £30 (US$45 to US$ 54), challenging to Scotland's traditional cashmere knitwear manufacturers, who produce *haute couture* garments that retail for ten or twenty times that price. According to James Sugden, chairman of the Scottish Textile Manufacturers' Association, 'It has polarized the industry. We cannot compete at that level and would not want to' (Bolger, 2005). Instead the Scottish industry has consolidated and focused on brand quality design to defend its niche as a supplier to the world's best–known fashion houses and luxury goods groups.

Tesco's sales of cashmere sweaters for men and women have proved popular, so much so that it has been difficult to meet demand. According to a Tesco's representative, 'It is similar to what we've done with champagne, where we introduced our own brand. Traditionally, champagne was seen as a very aspirational product, out of the range of a lot of customers. However, they quickly took it up, and we have grown the market' (Bolger, 2005).

Tesco makes little or no profit on the cashmere sales, which are being used as a loss-leader to encourage customers into its stores. Tesco has benefited from the easing of restrictions on Chinese imports through the ending of the Multi-Fibre Agreement at the beginning of 2005. Tesco said, 'We would defend our quality. Our supplier has been manufacturing cashmere for twenty-five years and uses the same process for other customers it supplies, such as Whistles, Karen Millen and Next' (Bolger, 2005).

It remains to be seen whether demand will allow the wide divergence in price and quality for cashmere products and whether it will be possible to maintain distinctive branding with market segmentation targeting and positioning to meet the needs of the luxury and mass markets.

Source: adapted from Bolger (2005).

BAE SYSTEMS SELLS DEFENCE SUBSIDIARY AT KNOCK-DOWN PRICE DUE TO NATIONAL SECURITY

In 2005 BAE Systems, Britain's largest defence company, was forced to sell a German-based electronics business, Atlas Elektronik, to Thyssen-Krupp, the German steelmaker, and EADS, the Franco-German defence group, at a knock-down price. The German government blocked a more lucrative sale to a French company on grounds of national security (Boxell, 2005). Thyssen and EADS paid €145m (£100m) in cash for the naval electronics business and picked up the pension liabilities of €72m (£49m) well below a rival offer of €300m (£205m) from Thales, the French defence group. The original expectation was of a bid of around €250m and €280m (£171m–£191m).

The deal highlights the fraught nature of cross-border deal making in the defence sector because of political interference. Increasingly, German government officials have become protectionist towards their defence industry. In 2004 to address fears that French companies would acquire German assets a law was passed whereby the German government can veto transactions that would involve a foreign company buying 25 per cent or more of any domestic defence business on the grounds of national security.

After a series of deals, Thyssen has emerged as Europe's largest naval shipbuilder and is the first to fully consolidate its domestic naval sector. The company, which also owns shipyards in Sweden and Greece, has said Europe could do with fewer yards and it is poised to play a lead role in the wider consolidation of the European shipbuilding industry.

However, there remains some unease and ill feeling at the outcome as far as the French group, Thales, is concerned. It is considered a 'missed opportunity' to have created a European champion in naval electronics.

Source: adapted from Boxell (2005).

CONCLUSION

Pricing cannot be divorced from the other elements of the marketing mix. It should relate to the overall objectives of the firm, its place in the structure of the industry of which it is a constituent part, the stage in the PLC of the product/service concerned and the applicability of the law, whether domestic or transnational. The different approaches to pricing show that, while each of these approaches is useful, companies tend to take an eclectic approach, using whichever techniques are the most helpful in a given situation. They use economic, accounting and marketing concepts as well as tactical moves and responses to help in making their pricing decisions. The chapter considers the pricing of industrial goods as well as the pricing issues and practices within B-to-B operations. It addresses the increasing importance of the use of the Internet for online shopping and the effect on pricing.

Finally, it introduces case studies showing the critical messages that are communicated through changes in pricing strategy. In particular, with premium priced products and services price cutting in any form should be most carefully considered.

REVIEW QUESTIONS

1   Explain what you understand by price elasticity of demand. Give examples of inelastic and elastic products or services, discussing how the concept might be used in marketing situations.
2   What is cost-plus pricing? Consider the advantages and disadvantages of the system.
3   How would you decide whether or not to drop the free telephone consultation service provided by your company's brand of computer software?
4   Determine the price and services contribution to a new business-class air service aimed to create a competitive advantage.

RECOMMENDED FURTHER READING

Ford, D. (1990) *Understanding business markets: interaction, relationships, networks*, London: Academic Press.
Gabor, A. (1977) *Pricing: principles and practices,* London: Heinemann.
Galbraith, J.K. (1975) *Economics and the public purse,* London: André Deutsch.
Hague, D.C. (1971) *Pricing in business*, London: Allen & Unwin.
Kotler, P. and Armstrong, G. (2001) *Principles of marketing*, 9th edn, NJ, Prentice Hall, ch. 10, pp. 369–427.
Livesey, F. (1976) *Pricing,* London and Basingstoke: Macmillan.
Marshall, A. (1979) *More profitable pricing,* London: McGraw-Hill.
Sonkodi, L. (1969) *Business and prices*, London: Routledge.
Taylor, B. and Wills, G. (1969) *Pricing strategy*, London: Staples.
Winkler, J. (1983) *Pricing for results*, Oxford: Heinemann.

10 PROMOTION

LEARNING OBJECTIVES

On completion of this chapter you should be able to:

- understand the strengths and weaknesses of the basic 'hypodermic' model of communications used in the study of promotions;

- feel confident in using the language of communications, including concepts like noise, redundancy and codes;

- understand how the 'hypodermic' model can contribute to appreciating marketing communications;

- know how to plan Integrated Marketing Communications (IMC), including analysis, objectives, strategy, contact, response, follow-up and evaluation;

- differentiate between different contact techniques, such as advertising, direct marketing, personal selling, sales promotions, publicity and sponsorship;

- apply these techniques to a marketing communications problem.

INTRODUCTION

This chapter provides an introduction to communications theory developing a basic communications model. The chapter covers the planning of an IMC campaign and deals with some of its components, notably advertising, direct marketing and personal selling.

The scope of marketing communications is immense, including all advertising, sales promotions, personal selling, Internet marketing and media relations. Any form of paid-for communication may be viewed as a marketing communication. When the scope of marketing is extended to those non-financial transactions including social marketing the field becomes enormous, as it encompasses any form of communications process linked to a transaction. In practice, usually discussion of marketing communications refers to organizational communications which are based on either one-off advertising campaigns or, more generally, campaigns which seek to build brand equity. An example of the former is the AIDS awareness campaign that ran in the UK in the early 1990s. The latter includes the majority of campaigns which seek to create awareness of new brands or to reinforce the value of existing brands.

In this chapter we develop the arguments that were first outlined in Chapter 3 with respect to cognitive and behaviourist explanations of consumer behaviour. In reading this chapter you will gather that, despite the arguments of behaviourists such as Ehrenberg and Goodhart (2000) and others, the mainstream explanation of marketing communications adheres to a cognitive view linked with the hierarchy of effects. It is beyond the scope of this book to discuss in detail why this is so.

RELATIONS BETWEEN CORPORATE AND MARKETING COMMUNICATIONS

There is a degree of overlap between marketing communications and corporate communications. Corporate communications has a wider scope than marketing communications as it deals with the management of relations with a whole range of stakeholder publics, including employees, shareholders, members of local communities and shareholders. Marketing communications is a sub-species of corporate communications which focuses specifically on one stakeholder group, i.e. customers. The next section introduces some important general concepts in communications theory.

THE COMMUNICATIONS PROCESS

The simple model shown in Figure 10.1 introduces the subject of marketing communications. Reading the model from left to right, the communication chain assumes a source that, through a transmitter, emits a signal via a channel. At the end of the channel the signal is transformed through a receiver into the message for the addressee. This model helps to

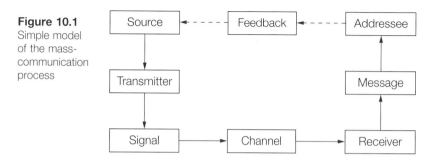

Figure 10.1
Simple model
of the mass-
communication
process

explain many forms of communication, both human and non-human. For example, Umberto Eco (1976) describes the scenario whereby the inhabitants of a town develop an early warning system to enable them to take action when a reservoir high in the mountains above is in danger of bursting its banks and flooding the town. To do so they place a transmitter on a buoy on the lake which sends two forms of signal 'A' indicates that the situation is normal; on the other hand '−A' indicates that the lake is threatening to flood the town. Signals are transmitted through a cable to a receiver in the town where they are converted into messages for the local flood alert personnel, who can act quickly to open the floodgates or if necessary evacuate the population.

Noise and redundancy and codes

Eco then makes his example more complex. Interference on the channel may sometimes lead to A being received as −A and vice versa. This interference, or noise, is of great concern to the town dwellers, as on some occasions they have opened the floodgates or evacuated the town when they need not have; whereas on others the town has flooded when the message received indicated otherwise. In order to get round this difficulty they must devise a code which can provide messages which are unlikely to occur as a result of noise on the line. They decide to opt for a more complex code which is made up of combinations of the letters ABCD.

AA	BA	CA	DA
AB	BB	CB	DB
AC	*BC*	CC	DC
AD	*BD*	*CD*	DD

The flood control personnel reduce the possibility of error by removing those combinations which are repetitious and which are the reverse of others. They are then left with six possible combinations which are marked above in italics. They choose four of these to get the options shown in Table 10.1.

Table 10.1 Denotation and Connotation

Expression	Content	Content
Signifier	Signified, Level 1	Signified, Level 2
AB =	Danger	Evacuate village
BC =	Alarm	Be on guard
CD =	Rest	No action
AD =	Insufficient water	Need to fill the reservoir

Within the context of the code which has been devised (based on variations of the letters ABCD), the expression 'AB' signifies the content or meaning 'danger' and this, in turn, signifies the meaning and associated action 'evacuate village'. As long as both the source and the addressee are aware of these conventions and share this code, then messages ought to be comprehensible in the absence of noise. The new set of messages is more complex than the last and more costly to produce. However, it achieves two things:

■ The chance of making a mistake is considerably reduced, as the chances of noise on the line producing 'AB' by mistake are slight. By complicating the code the chance that the wrong message will be received has been reduced. This redundancy is a means of overcoming channel noise.

■ The new code allows more flexibility in that a greater number of messages can be sent and these in turn allow for a wider range of responses.

DENOTATION AND CONNOTATION

The 'message' in the example has two levels given the technical names *denotation* and *connotation*. Denotations refer to the first levels of association between expressions and their content (between signifiers and signifieds, to use the technical terms). The first level in the example is 'AB = danger'. Based on this denotation is the second-level connotation 'danger = evacuate the village'. The first level of signification is straightforward: 'AB = danger' and when the water level rises to a certain level such as to trigger the signal 'AB' there can be no doubt that, in the absence of noise, the situation is dangerous for the villagers. There are few other interpretations which can be made. However, the range of possible interpretations at the level of connotation is much greater. For example, rather than evacuating the village any one of a range of different alternative interpretations and actions could have been coded, e.g. 'danger = ring bell', 'danger = blow whistle', 'danger = wave flag'.

The concepts of coding, noise and redundancy are built into a revised model of the process shown in Figure 10.2. These concepts are described in more detail. When redundancy is built into a message it ensures that noise is kept to a minimum. Noise can literally be 'noise', e.g. the noise made by a washing machine in the same room where one is trying

Figure 10.2
Development
of the model
of the mass-
communication
process

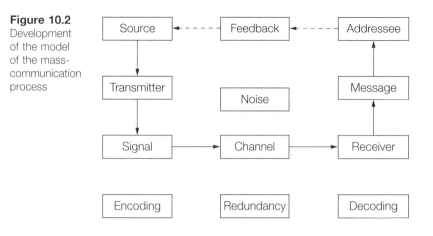

to listen to a radio programme. Often verbal communications are a major source of noise. For example, the author's name is frequently decoded as 'Devlin' rather than 'Desmond' by people whom he contacts by telephone, which means that he must spell each letter. To be sure that the message is being received correctly he may use the phonetic language 'Delta', 'Echo', 'Sierra', 'Mike', 'Oscar', 'November', 'Delta' and then ask the other person to provide feedback by repeating the message.

The code is the set of communicative conventions which the source and the addressee share. In the previous example the code consisted of combinations of ABCD. Without a shared knowledge of this code major difficulties could ensue. For example, if the source decided to change the code so that 'CD' = 'danger' and 'AB' = 'rest' and did not inform the receiver of this change there could well be a major panic in the town. Eco (1986) offers a more humorous example to illustrate this point. A woman and her lover come to an agreement that if she places a light in her bedroom window it means that her husband has gone out. However, the woman tires of this and on one occasion uses Morse code to transmit the message 'my husband is at home'. The man continues to refer to the previously established code whereby 'light' means 'husband absent' and on entering her room receives a major shock.

The relations between the referent, denotation and connotation are important with respect to the understanding of communications. The referent is the actual state of affairs which in the example is the actual level of water in the lake. It is important to note that the denotative relation with the referent is arbitrary; that 'AB' should equal 'danger' has been agreed as a form of convention between the source and the addressee. 'Danger' could equally well be represented by any sign. The connotation that if 'danger' then 'evacuate the village' is a sub-code, as it relies on the primary code that 'AB' = 'danger'. The relation between denotation and connotation is most interesting, as it shows that the same signifier, e.g. 'AB', can mean different things to different people. Consider the meanings of the colour red (Table 10.2).

According to the conventions used in the English language, when the letters r, e and d are combined to form the expression 'red' they signify the colour red. This is the first

Table 10.2 Meanings of the colour red

Expression	Content	Content
Signifier	Signified, level 1	Signified, level 2
'Red'	The colour red	Romance
		Anger
		Anger
		Embarrassment

level of signification, the denotation. The connotations or further interpretations which are likely to be made on the basis of reading the word 'red' or seeing the colour red will depend on the context. It is possible to identify several different sub-codes, including romance, anger, embarrassment and even political orientation from the context. For example, if a man were to present a woman with a red rose, the denotation 'red' in this context probably would be associated with the connotation 'passion' (if the couple were French) or 'romance' (if the couple were English). The denotative meaning of the red rose is that it is a 'flower'. The denotation stays the same (red roses); however, the connotations made by people from the different countries are slightly different to 'romance'/'passion'. Whereas often denotations are stable between cultures (people from most cultures would agree that a red rose is a 'flower') connotations may vary. It could well be that in some cultures 'red' roses signify neither romance nor passion. One such example is found in the city of Glasgow in Scotland where some people share the connotation that 'red and white flowers = blood and bandages'. This is because there is a local tradition that red and white flowers together signify 'blood and bandages'. It is considered unlucky in Glasgow to bring a bunch of mixed red and white flowers as a present for a relative or friend who is sick in hospital. However, in London, where red and white flowers do not have this connotation, it is perfectly acceptable to send people red and white flowers. Imagine the difficulties which could arise as a result of a London advertising agency using red and white flowers as part of a hospital advertising campaign aimed at building positive images of hospitals in the Glasgow area! To avoid making potentially damaging mistakes, marketers should be sensitive to the fact that people from different areas and from different socio-cultural backgrounds can form different connotations on the basis of the same denotations. As a final example, Eco (1986) discusses the connotations of the denotation 'no more':

> For example if I write the phrase 'no more', you who use the English language code will read it in the sense that is most obvious to you. Read by an Italian, the same words would mean 'no blackberries'. Further if, instead of a botanical frame of reference, the Italian reader used a legal one, he would take the words to mean 'no respites' or, in an erotic frame of reference, as a reply: 'No, brunettes' to the question 'Do gentlemen prefer blondes?'

Signs can deceive

In considering the relations between the referent, denotation and connotation it has been mentioned that the relation between these is arbitrary to the extent that 'AB' does not naturally represent danger. This relation is conventional in that it has been agreed by the source and the addressee. It is true that it would be possible for someone to lie about the state of the referent (the level of water in the reservoir). In a curious way this is not important to the way in which the system works. If I tampered with the system and lied so that 'AB' was sent when everything was normal, still the message would be read by the addressee as indicating 'danger' and then 'evacuate the town'.

The study of how signs can be used to deceive is most interesting. One intriguing non-verbal interaction between source and addressee comes under the remit of pupillometry, the psychology of the pupillary response. Early travellers to China noticed that the detection of changes in pupil dilation constituted a key element in the Chinese negotiators' 'bag of tricks' in spotting when a client was ripe for plucking. One story, for example, recounts how a jade buyer in pre-revolutionary China learned from an experienced fellow businessman named Mr Newell the subtler aspects of the pursuit of jade objects from oriental merchants. The Chinese were aware that the pupils of the eyes dilated when one's interest was aroused and acted accordingly. Newell had solved this problem by wearing dark glasses. Middle Eastern rug merchants were likewise aware of the response of their prospective customers, as were professional card players (the poker face). Belladonna (deadly nightshade) played an important role for the women of antiquity as it dilated the pupils making the women seem more attractive to the unwitting suitor.

Marketers can seek to control the spaces that constitute the behavioural setting in order to maximize the chance of a sale. Attention is paid to controlling all aspects of the setting in retail contexts: to lighting, colours, product display, location of product categories, smell and pack design. What goes on the pack is particularly important. For example, when one sees the word 'Lite' scrolled in large letters on the pot one might assume the yoghurt to be low in fat. Such may well be the case. However, if one looks at the much smaller writing on the back of the pot one finds that the yoghurt contains up to 15 per cent sugar! On another product the slogan 'Ninety per cent fat-free' is only a clever way of informing us that a product contains 10 per cent fat. Another trick is to use packaging bigger than the product, thus signifying value – until the pack is opened. A new trend is towards foods that have medicinal properties – for example, yoghurts that are 'clinically proven' to aid digestion, spreads that reduce cholesterol or milk that enhances brain function.[1] These products are often badged with 'cod' Latin names, just as a medicine would be. Not only are these products expensive – from twice to thirteen times the price of alternatives – their supposed benefits are contested.

Summary and implications for marketing

So far discussion has concerned the role which the source plays in sending messages through channels to the addressee. This process may be complicated by the message having to be made redundant and both parties having to share the same code if communication is to take place. In considering the code the source must be aware of the sub-codes or connotations which the receiver uses in decoding the message. The implications for marketers are clear. For effective marketing communications to take place then the source must try to minimize noise. This unplanned distortion of the message can occur as the result of errors in the encoding of the message or distortions of the signal or distractions at the point of reception. For example, taking noise at the point of reception, one research study found that 38 per cent of people watch only television when they are 'watching' television. Often they are simultaneously engaged in other activities such as reading, eating, ironing, sleeping, playing with children or pets, playing games or talking on the phone. They may even be out of the room making a cup of tea or coffee during the commercial break. Of those who are actually watching the television, many will use the 'zapper' to switch channels between programmes and during commercial breaks. Research evidence indicates that when people pre-record programmes on video they tend to 'zip' through the commercials. Zipping and zapping are sources of 'noise' at the point of reception. Physical sources of noise might be a poor reception, or perhaps a radio is on in the same room or a person is talking. Another type of noise is 'psychological' noise when I may be 'watching' television but my mind is totally preoccupied with problems at work.

Marketers must pay attention to the codes and sub-codes, the denotations and connotations used by the addressee. This is not just to ensure that the addressee can understand the message; failure to encode the message properly indicates that the source is not 'with it' and so the source may lose a significant amount of credibility. For example, those who devised the 'Scotland against Drugs' campaign which was run in 1997 first had the idea that they would make an advertisement to alert children aged between 12 and 15 to the dangers of glue sniffing. Luckily they researched this proposition before developing it. Research showed that children as young as 8 years old were involved and that children had moved on to 'buzzing gas'. If the advertisement had been designed on the basis of alerting the 12–15 age group to the dangers of glue sniffing, immediately children would have been made aware that those involved were not 'tuned in' to what was actually happening.

Finally, there is the implication that signs can be manipulated and used to deceive. This is a highly controversial area of marketing where practitioners deny strenuously involvement in overt manipulation.

The usefulness of applying the communications model for studying marketing communications processes is apparent. However, this simple model suffers from limitations.

■ As it is a linear model it fails to reflect the truly interactive nature of many communications. The source is treated as active and the addressee, characterized as passive, which has given rise to the 'hypodermic needle' notion that the media somehow 'inject' people with views of their choosing.
■ The model treats both source and addressee as individuals. In particular, with respect to the addressee, there is a tendency to downplay the essentially social nature of

communication. The model recognizes social influences to the extent that groups of people share codes and sub-codes (languages) which constitute the cultural and subcultural groups to which they belong.

In the next section more attention is placed on the social milieu of the addressee.

The two step model of communication

The simplest model, referred to as the 'hypodermic needle hypothesis', or the Sender–Messenger–Receiver (SMR) model, has been challenged by laboratory research and field research. It is clear that the addressee is active in evaluating messages from the point of view of her own existing attitudes and in relation to her own social group and interpersonal relationships. An early version of this view became known as the 'two-step flow of information' (Katz and Lazarsfield, 1955), which has had a major influence on the way that mass communications has been perceived (Katz, 1957, 1987). The model developed from studies of how American voter opinion changed during the 1940 election and of women's buying behaviour. While the hypodermic model maintains that the media tend to influence the individual directly and as isolated individuals, the two-step model suggests that information reaches the public indirectly through opinion leaders. These are people who are viewed by others as experts, people who consume and discuss more media output than the others around them. Opinion leaders play an important role in translating the media output into a form which is comprehensible to those around them, who often are referred to as 'followers'.

One of the benefits of the two-step model is that it combines mass and interpersonal modes of communication. It provides an important route for media planners who may wish to design strategies which encompass both methods of communication. It highlights the importance of combining different channels of communication. Most important, it demonstrates that while mass communication may play a role in the provision of information, much of the work related to persuasion takes place at the interpersonal level (Rogers, 1983). The focus on opinion leaders highlights another difficulty in the communication process. Opinion leaders are strong-minded by definition; as such they can actively negotiate and change the message of a communication programme to reflect their own ends. The usefulness of the model depends on the ease of identification of the opinion leader. For example, sports stars may be useful opinion leaders for those who are active in sports although they may not work for those outside the sports networks.

Network approaches

The idea that people live in clusters, or networks, represents a further development of the two-step flow model which has been developed by theorists such as Rogers and Kincaid (1981). These researchers consider the hypodermic needle model cannot describe adequately what happens in dynamic and complex situations and claim that interaction is beyond its scope. One variable to which this approach contributes is the notion of network support. This has proved useful in understanding some of the communication problems associated with AIDS campaigns. For example, often people who have been tested for HIV antibodies are reluctant, because of the stigma of the disease, to share that information with others in their communication networks, effectively neutralizing the worth of the campaign.

Within communications networks the notions embodied in 'hypodermic needle'-type communications are not valid. Instead theories refer to participants and to shared understanding. They focus on the properties of the communication network, on areas such as connectedness, integration, diversity and openness. Connectedness measures to what extent the members of a certain network are linked to the network. A highly connected network offers greater potential for the dissemination of information than one which is loosely connected, since there are fewer isolated individuals. Integration measures the degree to which members of the network are linked to each other. Knowledge about the degree of diversity may be important. Greater diversity indicates that ideas may enter the system relatively easily through weak ties. Openness affects decisions based on how well a certain group, system or network communicates with its environment. A closed group will be harder for the planner to reach from the outside.

Windahl *et al.* (1992) provide an example of how network analysis operates:

> In a health communication campaign, the planner focuses on relaying information about good eating habits to upper-level high school students. As a follow up, students in some classes are interviewed about what they think of the message, whom they talk to about it, what consequences talking with others has in terms of their own and joint behaviours, and so on. The picture the planner forms includes information about the salience of the theme of good eating habits: does the topic encourage discussions with others? If so, who are these others and did they also receive the initial campaign messages? Do those who hear the message from others in the network pass it on in some form? Do the students discuss the topic with their families, thereby helping the topic to find its way into new networks? If so does this lead to any kind of action by the family? And do families serve as bridges into other networks? Is individual action more common than collective action? Are any cliques in the network more active than others in responding to messages? Does influence in the network travel through the network only in one direction or in several?
>
> (Windahl *et al.*, 1992: 77)

Different network roles have been specified by Monge (1987). The membership roles in groups and clusters of the networks are:

- *Liaison role*, individuals who link clusters together within the network.
- *Star role,* held by individuals who are linked to large numbers of other individuals.
- *Isolate role*, comprising individuals to whom few others are linked.
- *Boundary-spanning role*, which links the network to the environment.
- *Bridge role,* which links one or two groups together.

Through an understanding of these roles, together with the structural aspects of the network (such as how closed it is), the communications planner can predict how and to what extent information will move within a network. For example, in organizations, people who work alone or on night shifts who are isolated tend to be less well informed. In health care it has been found that unhealthy people have smaller communication networks than healthy people.

Diffusion of innovations theory

Following from the discussion of the hierarchy of effects in Chapter 2, another factor which may have an influence on the communications process is the relation between the message which is being communicated and the audience. For example, if the message is concerned with a novel behaviour this will have a selectively different impact on the audience than if it was related to a well known behaviour. Diffusion of innovations theory is dominated by the work of Rogers (1983). It is an attempt to explain the various stages which must be passed through before an innovation is adopted. As such it is important in aiding those who are seeking to persuade the consumer to adopt a particular product or service. It has been used for a wide number of innovations, from the adoption of 'safe' practices for drinking water in the Third World to the diffusion of advice on AIDS. Largely diffusion research is based on empirical observations of various forms of planned communication.

The adoption process is divided into five different stages, each with its own characteristics. These stages are the knowledge, persuasion, decision, implementation and confirmation stages. The *knowledge* stage occurs as a person becomes aware of the innovation. The theory differentiates between two types of people, active seekers who turn to a variety of sources to seek a solution to a problem and a passive group. Media planners must come to understand the media and channel preferences of the latter group if they are to communicate effectively with it. Usually awareness information is conveyed through the mass media.

In the *persuasion* stage people form an opinion or an attitude concerning the innovation. Interpersonal channels are important, as people are making a decision which personally is relevant. Important factors are source credibility and media credibility.

As the title suggests, the *decision* stage involves the individual making a positive or negative decision on whether to adopt. The individual may be aware of the innovation and feel strongly positive towards it. However, she may still reject the innovation, e.g. because she wishes to conform to the largely negative opinions and behaviours of her peers. Factors which may help adoption at this stage are suggestions on how to use the innovation and free samples. Consider some of the more frightening examples of exotic fruit which have been gracing supermarket shelves over the past few years. Supermarket owners have been offering 'money off' coupons and have placed accompanying 'menu planners' next to these to provide the relevant consumer information. It is easier for potential adopters to adopt if there are role models available. This is difficult in the case of AIDS campaigns, as adopters of 'safe sex' tend not to talk about it to others. An approach developed by the Stanford Heart Disease Prevention Program was successful. The organizers selected 500 people in two Californian communities. These people had taken steps towards lowering their heart disease-related risk through quitting smoking and changing diets. Each was recruited as a promoter of the health awareness programme and put into contact with ten high-risk followers, creating a pool of 5,000 people who would pass on preventative information to the remaining 95 per cent of the population.

Individuals begin using the innovation during the *implementation* stage when innovators know how to get hold of the innovation. It helps if the innovation is available. This point may seem somewhat trite. However, it is easy for a communications programme to proceed when the actual development of the innovation has been delayed for some reason. For example, Swedish people were encouraged to take an AIDS test as part of a wider campaign. Unfortunately, hospitals were not in a position to process the number of requests which they received and asked people to contact them several weeks later.

In the *confirmation* stage, people need to be told that they made the right decision. This is to reduce the dissonance which may result from negative communications from competing sources.

Another important aspect of innovations is the form of medium used at each stage of the process. Generally, it is agreed that mass media are more useful in the earlier stages while interpersonal sources are more important in the later stages. An important aspect of the interpersonal sources concerns the degree of innovativeness of the individual.

According to Rogers (1962, 1971, 1983), innovators constitute a small minority of around 3 per cent of the total population. They tend to be more cosmopolitan than those of other categories. Early adopters, who constitute about 14 per cent of the population, are respected locals and are those to whom others turn to for advice, forming the second step in the two-step flow model described earlier. The early majority tend to be deliberate in their decision making, while the late majority tend to be sceptical. Between them these groups account for around 70 per cent of the total. Later adopters are laggards. Percentages are based on Rogers (1983) and should not be taken to be definitive.[1] For example, in Chapter 6 it was outlined that 1 per cent of older people in the UK and 15 per cent of older people in the US have to rely on an income which is 40 per cent lower than the national average. This would lead to widely differing estimates of the number of potential 'laggards' in the grey market in each country.

An important role in the diffusion of innovations is that played by the *change agent*. Change agents point out the need for change and help facilitate the adoption process. The principle of homophily is important with respect to change agents. It suggests that people are more likely to be influenced by people who are like them than by those who are different, e.g. in social status or in cultural origin.

Further implications for marketers

The implications of the above for those involved in marketing communications are clear: the communicator must obtain a good knowledge of the social context of the addressee. This will involve a knowledge of:

- Relevant codes and sub-codes; the language used by the addressee.
- Relevant opinion leaders.

- The network structure of the addressee community. How open is the network? Who are the stars and the isolates?
- Whether the communication relates to an innovation.

All of these have implications for research, suggesting that the active involvement of members of the addressee community can play an important role in helping design communication campaigns.

THE MARKETING COMMUNICATIONS PROCESS

So far discussion of communications has been general. The aim of this section is to relate this to the context of marketing communications.

Organization source

In marketing communications the organizational source is much more complex than the simple hypodermic model implies. Only a minority of organizations deals with all their marketing communications in-house and even then often these functions are found scattered in various parts of the organization. Marketing communications bring together a range of marketing functions, including marketing strategists, category and brand management, market analysts and researchers, information managers, media relations specialists, media buyers and creatives. In practice, many of these roles are contracted out, with people in the organization acting as clients for those agencies who provide the service. It is common to contract out marketing research, advertising, public relations and direct marketing services, as these are expensive services to build and maintain in-house and as there is a fiercely competitive market place for them. The organizational source is composed of a complex web of relations between a number of parties. This is illustrated in Figure 10.3. Many of the lines representing possible relationships have been omitted from Figure 10.3. For example, many advertising agencies contract out marketing research, design and direct marketing to others.

The industry structure has evolved in a particular way whereby each specialism is contained within a particular type of agency structure. Historically, advertising has developed separately from other functions such as public relations. Public relations has a wider scope than advertising as it is concerned with the maintenance of good relations with a number of different organizational stakeholders. Traditionally, the advertising agency has been considered the hub of the process. Advertising is a paid form of non-personal communication which usually is delivered through mass media by an identified sponsor. Mass media include broadcast (television, radio and cinema): published (press magazines and directories) and outdoor (posters, taxicabs) media. For most commercial organizations the key role of advertising is in building powerful brands by advertising through the mass media. Often advertising agencies have major links with design, marketing research, public relations and more recently Internet agencies, if these functions are not carried out within the advertising agency itself.

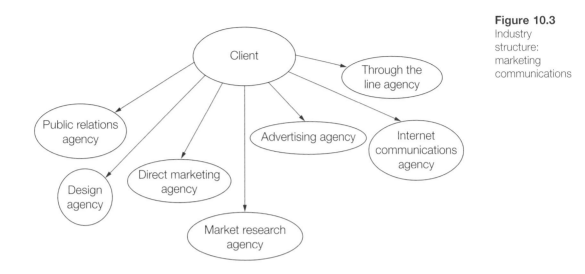

Figure 10.3
Industry
structure:
marketing
communications

Since the 1980s the development of network computing systems and powerful database management techniques has led to the rise of direct marketing agencies in the UK. These agencies specialize by using the power of technology to address the customer personally. Direct marketing is interactive to the extent that it involves establishing contact with the customer and then managing the customer response to that contact. Usually, contact is made through direct mail, telephone or email. Historically, advertising and direct marketing have evolved along different routes in the UK. Advertising was there first and their 'grand' cousins looked down upon the rather humble direct mail operations. More recently, with direct marketing's success, there are three trends towards:

1   Blurring of the lines between the advertising and direct marketing, e.g. it is not unusual for an advertisement to have a coupon response slip included.
2   Growing animosity between the two in some quarters with direct marketers referring disparagingly to advertising as 'image' marketing.
3   Calls for integration of the two through the creation of 'through the line' (TTL) agencies which handle all aspects of marketing communications. From a client's point of view the TTL agency appears to be the best solution, as it enables consistent delivery of core brand values through the most appropriate media enabling the same creative idea to be reflected throughout the entire breadth of the campaign. All advertising, design, direct marketing, sales promotions and sponsorship activities are co-ordinated through the same agency, e.g. Saatchi & Saatchi and Leo Burnett.

However, integration is hard to achieve, as:

1   Clients may have bureaucratic departmental structures.
2   Communications are difficult across traditionally warring divides.

So, while theoretically integration may be desirable, in practice it is rarely seen to be the norm.

Marketing channels

ABOVE AND BELOW-THE-LINE COMMUNICATIONS

Marketing channels represent the range of media available to move the message from source to addressee. It is difficult to measure the volume of many of these channels, e.g. production of 'Guinness' T-shirts will be known only to Guinness and to the company which manufactures them. Similarly, promotional literature including brochures, handbooks, leaflets and 'give-aways' must be regarded as being 'below the line' in that there is no public record or measurement of the cost of the medium.

On the other hand, detailed records are maintained of all television, press and cinema and poster advertising, which because it is measurable is known as 'above the line' communication.

In general, national and regional newspapers and consumer and business magazines have experienced a relative decline in the UK during the 1990s and into the 2000s. By contrast television increased its share of the total expenditure and outdoor advertising and radio advertising also increased from a low initial base. In the 2000s the relative share of television advertising has declined as advertisers have looked to most cost-effective promotional expenditure (see p. 327).

FRAGMENTATION OF THE MEDIA

One factor which is of major concern to marketers is the continuing fragmentation of broadcast media, usually related to radio and television. There has been a substantial increase in the number of channels offered as the result of satellite, cable and digital technology. For example, in the UK, consumers up to the late 1990s had access to five main television channels, which with digital television are estimated to rise to several hundred channels. According to some commentators this means that the audience is much more widely dispersed, which makes life trickier for advertisers. However, if 'broadcast media' is taken to mean the entire range of media, it is almost impossible to find anything which is not a medium, e.g. T-shirts, cars, billboards, carpets and walls are all used as media. In sporting activities marketing communications are found not only on the conventional advertising hoardings but on the products (footballs, tennis rackets), the players and their apparel, the fans and even on the pitch.

DUAL ROLE OF THE MEDIA

The media are not just passive receivers of marketing communications. The media play a dual role. They promote messages on behalf of others at a price and they investigate and uncover stories that media owners, editors and reporters think will be in the public interest or of general interest to their readers. Below are some extracts of press reports on two of the UK clearing banks, Midland Bank and Barclays Bank. While this relates to research conducted some time ago, it provides a flavour of the way in which the media create a different view of the organization from that which it wishes to create itself:

All clearing banks are the same; one bank manager is indistinguishable from another; that's the cynics view of the clearers. But its not borne out by the boardroom facts. For instance, Lloyds is the academic board, Midland is the meritocratic board . . . if you're kind Barclays is the professional board, if you're unkind it's the oligarchic board. Natwest is the huntin' shootin' fishin' board.

(Anon., 1980)

Consider how the Midland Bank was characterized in press reports:

If Crocker were a used car, Midland would now be sputtering back to the previous owner with a few scores to settle.

(Anon., 1984)

Current indications are that Midland is blushing to the tips of its corporate ears'.
(*Mail on Sunday*, 7 August 1983)

With further reference to the Midland:

Today the sluggard of the Big Four banks.
(*Evening Standard*, 15 August 1980)

Midland the poor relation.
(*Financial Weekly*, 19 November 1982)

Midland the problem child of the Big Four.
(*Investors' Chronicle*, 21 January 1983)

Midland the Cinderella of the Big Four.
(*Financial Weekly*, 4 March 1983; *Evening Standard*, 10 March, 1983)

Midland the Ugly Duckling of the Big Four.
(*Daily Express*, 11 March 1983)

Midland the duffer of the Big Four has every reason to be delighted.
(*Guardian*, 11 March 1983)

For more than a year it has been the black sheep.
(*Financial Times*, 12 March 1983)

Contrast the above with the following references to Barclays Bank.

A bank in many ways different from the rest of the pack.

(*Financial Times*, 4 August 1980)

The largest bank in the world.

(*Financial Times*, 4 August 1980)

True Blue Barclays.

(*Financial Times*, 22 August 1980)

Barclays the most aggressive in the big bank invasion.

Big and ugly Barclays has the sneaking admiration of the rest . . . it's prepared to stick to its principles.

Barclays likes to think of itself as a bit more sporting, innovative, daring.

From these reports it is clear that it is important for marketers to build and sustain good media relations. Often the media publish publicity that is released by organizations; however, there can be a price to be paid if good media relations are not developed.

The addressee: the active audience

From the earlier discussion of the two step flow model of communication and other more complex models of the communications process, it is clear that it is a grave mistake to think of consumers as passive dupes of communications campaigns. Unfortunately, this is a feature of the hypodermic model, which treats the consumer as a target and which has given rise to a number of models which reinforce this view (see Colley, 1961; Lavidge and Steiner, 1961). The Awareness, Interest, Desire and Action (AIDA) model of activities is linked with the 'hierarchy of effects' discussed in Chapter 3 and relates to the sequence of raising attention–interest–desire and action in the addressee; the Designing Advertising Goals, Measuring Advertising Response (DAGMAR) model refers to designing advertising goals and measuring advertising response. Both of these will be discussed in more detail below under marketing communications planning. While these are useful tools there is a danger of oversimplification, as the addressee is treated as a target, as someone to whom something is done. For many years authors have cautioned that the reality of communication models is much more complex (Franzen, 1994: 6).

Marketing communications do not just 'work'; they are actively 'worked on' by the audience. For example, Stephanie O'Donohoe (O'Donohoe and Tynan, 1997) conducted qualitative research with young adults in Scotland in a bid to step out of the narrow experimental context shared by most studies of advertising involvement. Participants were encouraged to describe their experiences of advertising in their own words. O'Donohoe found evidence to support an Elaboration Likelihood (cf. Petty and Cacioppo, 1983) explanation of involvement. However, this did not work exactlyin the way predicted by the model in that elaboration did not go hand in hand with the desire for information, nor was it necessarily linked to brand attitudes. Consistent with a behaviourist explanation, a person sometimes saw an ad, tried the product and then stayed with it. While brand attitudes were sometimes antecedents of advertising involvement, O'Donohoe found that in general these were bound up in the personal life histories, life themes and projects of the informants, a finding which offers tentative support to a behaviourist explanation that emphasizes the person's situation. Given that mainstream views of the consumer are dominated by a cognitive account of 'involvement', this suggests that more attention should be paid to behaviourist accounts (cf. Foxall, 1990, 1996) which focus on social and cultural contexts. For example, Davidson (1992) discusses how drug dealers have used anti-drug advertising to good effect in promoting drugs. Some time ago a UK-based anti-heroin advertising campaign featured wasted images of victims coupled with the strap line 'Heroin screws you up.' Reputedly this anit-heroin theme was used by dealers to promote heroin – the exact opposite of what was intended. One explanation is that for rebellious young adults the promise that heroin can screw you up is taken as an incentive to buy it.

McDonald (1992: 99/100) supports the view that addressees are actively in control and pick and choose what they will attend to. He makes the following points:

- An advertisement has no value at all unless the respondent chooses to give it one.
- Following from this, it is noted that most advertisements are of no interest to most people.
- To sort out those few advertisements that are interesting, people use their power of selective perception.
- Intrusive advertising tries to get beyond the barrier by devising advertisements that stand out.

REFERENT SYSTEMS

For advertising to 'work', the message must fit in closely with the codes and sub-codes which constitute referent systems for the audience. The idea of referent systems was discussed in Chapter 7 on branding. To recap briefly, a referent system relates to a code which makes sense to the audience at which it is directed. Frequently, marketers refer to referent systems in attaching meaning to products. This was first pointed out by Judith Williamson, who used the product category of perfume and the referent system 'the model' system. It must be remembered that a product when it is first developed has no intrinsic meaning: a perfume is merely a smelly clear liquid. By placing this liquid in a bottle it is provided with some context although as yet it still has little meaning. According to Williamson (1978) this happens as the result of transferring meaning from one system which is imbued with meaning to the system of products to which we wish to attach meaning. She uses the example of two perfumes, Babe and Chanel No. 5. Babe was a new perfume and its marketers wished to convey the meaning that 'Babe' was youthful, impetuous, a 'tomboy' personality; on the other hand, those who marketed Chanel wished to retain its image as 'sophisticated'.

Advertisers have become sophisticated in terms of the referent systems they draw upon in order to seduce consumers. For example, it can be difficult, if not impossible, to reach some elements of the youth audience with traditional forms of advertising. Many males in the 18–34 age range are sophisticated and highly advertising-literate; they pride themselves on not being drawn in by hype. This group forms a crucial part of the target audience for Red Stripe lager. In the late 1980s the key question for the marketers of Red Stripe was how to position the lager in such a way as to encourage young male drinkers to identify positively with the brand. Since its launch in the late 1970s Red Stripe sales had grown steadily. The brand mission was to develop a 'cult' brand, not one that would be 'here today and gone tomorrow'. As part of this strategy the company developed advertisements using a well known US 'alternative' comedian who represented a macho, tough, adventurous, strong and different image among the target audience. Research found that the advertisement was regarded as intrusive and memorable – in other words, wholly appropriate to the brand.

REFERENT SYSTEMS AND REFERENCE GROUPS

It is important to differentiate between reference groups and referent systems, which, although they sound similar, are actually quite different concepts. Reference groups refer to those groups of people in society that to which we consider we belong (affiliation groups) and those to which we aspire to (aspirational groups). At the time of the making of the Chanel advertisement, Catherine Deneuve, as a successful actress and model, may have been aspirational for many women. Regarding a referent system, reference is not made to the people but to their symbolic meaning as marked out within a code. Within this system, what matters is what people mean or signify; e.g. Catherine Deneuve is one element in a referent system which signifies 'sophistication.

PLANNING MARKETING COMMUNICATIONS CAMPAIGNS

In this section an overview is provided of the marketing communications planning process, sketching out how an integrated communications campaign might be pieced together.

Integrated Marketing Communications (IMC) campaign

According to Shimp (1997) IMC shares five key aspects. (1) the goal is ultimately to affect behaviour; (2) it should use all forms of communication and all forms of contact as potential message delivery systems in seeking to influence a prospect's behaviour; (3) start from the perspective of the prospect and work backwards; (4) all elements of the promotional campaign should speak with one voice; (5) build a relationship with the customer.

COMMUNICATIONS AFFECT BEHAVIOUR

To the uninitiated it seems like stating the obvious to suggest that the goal of marketing communications is to affect behaviour. But you will already know from the discussion in

Chapter 7 on branding that cognitive theorists and behaviourists differ about its role. Cognitive theory emphasizes the pre-behavioural process described by the hierarchy of effects. Cognitive theorists contend that advertising is persuasive. People do not simply buy a product or service: they first form beliefs about the brand which influence their attitude to it, which in turn influences the intention to buy or not to buy.

Strong (1925) developed the AIDA model to describe the hierarchy of advertising effects. According to the model a campaign should focus initially on awareness raising and building positive beliefs about the product. The next step is to create favourable attitudes to the product. Then a campaign can work to precipate action. On the other hand, behaviourists question the cognitive explanation, arguing that there is sparse evidence to support the view that attitudes influence and predetermine behaviour. Instead, behaviourists argue, marketing communications play a role in creating awareness, in stimulating trial and then acting as reinforcers of purchase behaviour. A person may be made aware of a product by advertising and then try it – provided, of course, that other situational factors are favourable: the product must be in stock, the sales assistants friendly, etc. Even so, having tried the product they may not like it and may never buy it again.

Ehrenberg (2002: 41) challenges Strong's (1925) AIDA model, arguing that there is little evidence to suggest that advertising can lead to a favourable response to brand choice or to the creation of desire through the use of a unique selling proposition (USP). On this view, if advertising is so powerful, then how is it that small and medium-size brands with relatively tiny budgets can maintain a stable share against competitors? Alternatively, if advertising is so powerful, then how is it that when advertising budgets are cut there is often no catastrophic fall in sales?

Despite Ehrenberg's critique, most commercial marketers are advocates of Strong's (1925) AIDA model. They believe that the ultimate aim of all marketing communications is to effect a change in consumer behaviour. Consequently they can be scathing about ads which may be aesthetically pleasing and win awards but ultimately fail to attract customers. Bird (1997) is highly critical of an 'image' advertisement for the Nissan Infiniti which:

> consisted of a few million dollars' worth of ads with no car in them, but lots of moody shots of Japanese gardens and such. Maybe it sold some rocks and sand, but the great-looking car didn't take off nearly as well as the Lexus – whose agency, lacking all imagination, showed pictures of cars.

CONSIDER ALL FORMS OF COMMUNICATIONS

Contact refers to any message channel that is capable of reaching target customers; the range is vast and contacts include television commercials, magazine ads, messages on football fields, T-shirts, vehicles, the Internet or in-store displays. The most appropriate forms of contact that fit should be used:

- The objectives of the campaign.
- The characteristics of the target market.

- The characteristics of the product.
- The resources actually available.

In practice, all these are linked and in a real situation often the options are glaringly obvious. However, from an analytical point of view it is useful to separate them. The objectives of the campaign must be specific, measurable and accountable and usually relate to achieving some change in the hierarchy of effects. For example, if the campaign objectives are to raise awareness of a new consumer durable, then this calls for a different contact mix than if sales of more units of an existing durable are required. Probably the first case will call for a substantial commitment to advertising, or targeted communications towards known innovators, while the second could well involve more promotions at the point of sale, direct mail to selected households and personal selling through stores.

The nature of the target market influences the contact mix. For example, B-to-B markets often involve a different approach from consumer markets. In the former advertising may be in the trade press to inform potential customers, sales force briefings and visits to push the product, together with sales promotions in the form of bulk discounts. In some marketing communications campaigns the target market for the communications campaign is not the user but maybe a buyer or an important opinion leader or decision maker. For example, often advertising is focused on children, who in turn bring pressure to bear on their parents to purchase products. Another example relates to anti-drug campaigns. Some youths are considered to be so knowing and cynical with respect to anti-drug advertising that they are thought to be impervious to it. In this case the strategy of the advertisers has been to target their friends who in turn can exert influence on them. If one has a good knowledge of the target group network this can be used to create an effective campaign.

The characteristics of the product are important. For example, the communication campaign based around the marketing of power stations will be different from that based around savoury snacks. High-price products afford more risk to the customer and so are rarely sold in purely self-service contexts with no sales support. However, there are exceptions. Warehouse-style discounters such as Cost Co offer high-ticket items such as refrigerators, television sets and PCs costing several hundred pounds.

The stage in the PLC is an important factor to consider. During the introductory stage a good deal of advertising may be undertaken and in the case of non-durables this commitment to advertising may extend into the growth and maturity phases. On the other hand, often industrial products include personal selling and promotions during these phases.

Although in the ideal situation how best to achieve the campaign objectives would be worked out and then how much this might cost in terms of time and effort; in practice, this means fitting the campaign to the available resources. Where one has limited money, it is surprising how many ways there can be to attract attention. For example, the entrepreneur Richard Branson has gained publicity worth millions of pounds for his Virgin group through his exploits with power boats and even hot air ballooning. The key to all of this is to be aware that there is no formula and that one must be creative in using the best tools available.

ONE VOICE

A key element of an IMC strategy is synergy, the need for all the elements of the communications campaign, from point-of-sale promotions to television advertising and sponsorship to speak with one voice. This is a major benefit for IMC over more traditional approaches that may appear to be more haphazard and piecemeal. Given that the amount of communications clutter is growing year on year, it is important to ensure that unity of voice allows for clear recognition of the message even though this is transmitted through a variety of media. Franzen (1994) discusses instances of research which suggest that consumers are bombarded with cumulatively more clutter from advertising and other sources year on year.

BUILD RELATIONSHIPS

Where communication is on a continuous basis, e.g. in seeking to build a brand, care must be taken to manage the relationship with the customer over time. Marketers are acutely sensitive of the worth of seeking to retain customers. In devising a campaign it is important to think of the total impact on the addressee and how this might affect the relationship in the long run.

Planning for IMC

In the first instance the sort of planning process for the 'ideal type' of IMC will be considered. The bare bones of the process are sketched out in Figure 10.4.

MARKET ANALYSIS

This is vitally important and requires a commitment to research. For consumer markets it is important to understand the decision making process. In Chapter 3 it was emphasized that the level of involvement with respect to consumer markets is useful. The high and low involvement purchase decisions indicate different decision modes. Involvement theory suggests that advertising has a major impact on low-involvement decisions but only a limited impact on high-involvement decisions. This is because the person who is highly involved actively seeks out information from a variety of sources, including advertising, relevant media reports and friends. This is where the two-step flow model of communication which was discussed earlier in this chapter comes into its own. People actively discuss the merits and

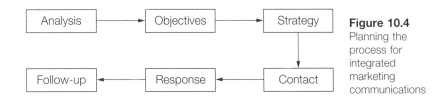

Figure 10.4
Planning the process for integrated marketing communications

disadvantages of products and services with people who are considered to be knowledgeable and take care to ensure that the product fits in with their desired self-image and that of reference groups.

It is important that involvement is a characteristic not of a product but rather a relation between a person and a product. Marketing communicators should not make assumptions about high and low involvement without first checking with the target group. For example, while it is thought that a product such as toothpaste is a relatively low-involvement purchase, this may not be the case for teenagers, for whom appearance may be everything. Involvement is a tool, and while it may help provide some clues for action, it does not replace careful thought about a particular communications context.

For consumer markets, an analysis of the target group should focus on the level of involvement and should consider the various segments which constitute the market place. For example, Widgery *et al.* (1997) found that car manufacturers treat married women as one homogeneous group while their research indicated that this in reality was comprised of two to three groups. Marketers should seek to understand the codes and sub-codes which constitute the referent systems of the target audience. The concept 'reference group' refers to those people that a person identifies with; the concept 'referent system' is similar but refers not to the people as people but to what they signify within a particular code.

For industrial markets the focus of the analysis is on the buying centre. With large and important customers it is important to determine who the users, influencers, gatekeepers and budget holders are and what relative power they have. The analysis phase can enable the marketing communicator to assemble a 'clean' contact database (reliable, accurate and up-to-date) which may form the basis for future direct marketing or personal selling operations. This is particularly the case for large organizations.

OBJECTIVES

Objectives relate to what the campaign intends to achieve. Objectives must be clearly stated and should specify what is to be achieved in measurable terms, over what time period and who is responsible. Consider the following question. 'How do we persuade owners of private cars which are less than three years of age to buy our latest model?'

The first question to ask is 'Is this a communications problem?' The answer is a qualified 'no'; we cannot get people to buy the car. However, their awareness that the car exists can be raised. It can influence how they perceive the car, their attitudes, evaluations and even their purchase intentions. Communications can help by influencing those stages of the hierarchy of effects which precede behaviour, notably perceptions, attitudes and intentions. In 1961 Russell Colley developed a model for setting advertising objectives which can be broadened to encompass all marketing communications. This model was entitled DAGMAR (see below). The main thesis of the DAGMAR model is that communications effects are the logical basis for advertising goals and objectives against which success or failure should be measured. Colley suggested that the communications task is based on a hierarchical model of the communications process, with four stages:

- *Awareness*: making the consumer aware of the existence of a brand or company.
- *Comprehension*: developing an understanding of what the product is and what it will do for the customer.
- *Conviction*: developing a mental disposition in the customer to buy the product.
- *Action*: getting the customer to buy the product.

There are strong links between DAGMAR and Strong's (1925) AIDA model which was described above.

Returning to the car example, the stated objective is not really enough to form the basis for action and needs to be operationalized or rendered as being capable of measurement before it can be treated as realistic. Objectives should state clearly which levels of the hierarchy of effects are to be influenced, with which specific and measurable target group, over which period of time. For example, it may be to raise the general public's level of awareness of the new car to 80 per cent and 95 per cent for the key target group (which is composed of 30–50 year old ABs with a car less than three years old). It is hoped that 40 per cent of the target group would be interested enough to try the car out and that 15 per cent might actually try it. Overall the sales objective might be 5 per cent. Once objectives have been stated, how are these to be achieved?

STRATEGY

Strategy addresses the question of how to achieve objectives. The marketing communicator can choose from a range of alternatives in constructing the strategy. The key questions which must be asked are:

- What mixture of 'push' and 'pull' should be used?
- What sort of message should be constructed?
- Which form or mix of contact approaches should be used to communicate this message?

'Push' and 'pull' strategies

Before acting, there must be understanding. The objectives which have been drawn up partially reflect this understanding. Effective strategy development relies on a good knowledge of the customer and how she or he will react. However, the final customer is not the only party to consider. Often marketing textbooks differentiate between push and pull strategies, although in practice many campaigns contain elements of each (see Chapter 11).

From Figure 10.5, using a 'pull' strategy, the marketer appeals direct to the target group through some form of mass or personalized communication. Once informed, members of this group actively demand the product from retailers. A problem exists where the product is not in stock. Often retailers must be convinced that products will sell and contribute to their own bottom line. This is true with the sophisticated scanning equipment that can be used to calculate and compare the precise returns offered by alternative products.

Figure 10.5
'Push' and
'pull' strategies

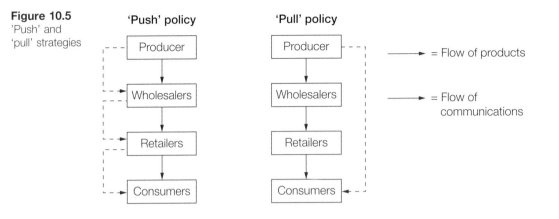

While advertising may help persuade retailers and other intermediaries to stock products often it is necessary to supplement advertising 'pull' with trade 'push'. This involves the manufacturer pushing the product through the various levels of intermediary, using a variety of means, ranging from personal selling to discounts in a bid to ensure that the product is available on the shelves.

With respect to the car example, it is most likely that the campaign will combine a mixture of push and pull factors. Probably pull factors will include mass advertising to raise general awareness and interest in the product coupled with more specific direct marketing to a group of prospects. As this is a high-involvement purchase advertising would focus on that which stresses the benefits of the product. Direct marketing could involve the issue of personalized communications to people whose existing cars were three years old or less to come and try out the new model at a local dealership. As car manufacturers in the UK bind nominally independent dealers in tight franchise agreements, they will not have the difficulty of having to persuade dealers to stock the new model. However, they ought to ensure that all personnel, and in particular sales personnel, are briefed as to the benefits of the new model over the old one and over competitor models. This will involve the preparation of briefing notes and of point-of-sale literature. At this point there is no idea of how the objectives are to be achieved. What platform or 'tone of voice' should the communications campaign strive for?

Constructing the message

Before preparing a specific message the marketing communicator should be aware of the communications platform which forms the basis for the campaign. The communications platform is vitally important, as it is through this that the message, a 'tone of voice' to the consumer, is created. If a brand is involved then the communications platform is the means by which brand values are related to customer values. Brand values are not static but must move with the times. For example, American Express used to base its communications on a platform based on exclusivity, how the brand fitted into the customer's self-image as someone who had status. In the early 1990s research indicated that consumer attitudes to exclusivity had changed and that this was now seen to be a '1980s' thing associated with 'yuppie' values. Research indicated that the target group no longer placed value on the American Express card as something which expressed their identity; rather they were more concerned with pragmatic concerns of what the card could do for them. The new platform developed by American Express emphasized the functionality of the card and how it fitted in with the demands of the user's lifestyle. The communications platform plays a key role in the construction of the creative brief, which is discussed later in the section devoted to advertising.

Obviously, marketing research is an important means of helping establishing a platform for a brand. However, use can be made of what is already known about involvement to form some hunches about the kind of platform that might be appropriate. Richard Vaughn and his associates at the US advertising agency Foote Cone & Belding (FCB) developed a grid to account for the primacy of feelings in involvement behaviour. Particularly, this is important with respect to high involvement, as Assael's model, which is discussed in Chapter 3, suggests; a rational informative appeal is the only appropriate appeal with respect to high-involvement purchases. The FCB grid (see Figure 10.6) provides a corrective to this view, as high-involvement appeals may be based on either rational or emotional approaches. The grid outlines four potential strategies.

You'll remember from the cognitive explanations of high involvement discussed in Chapter 3 that purchases are split into two types:

■ Those which involve us rationally, because they entail substantial economic risk in that they are expensive complex products.

■ Those which are primarily involving substantial psychological and social risks because of high ego involvement and badge value.

Addressees actively scan marketing communications relating to high-involvement products and use these in conjunction with cues from other media and opinion leaders in making a purchase decision. Vaughn suggests that the informative strategy is best suited to those high-involvement products where rational thinking and economic considerations prevail and the consumer moves through a standard hierarchy of effects. It has been suggested that this

Figure 10.6
The Foote Cone & Belding grid

Sources: adapted from Brian T. Ratchford, 'New insights about the FCB grid', *Journal of Advertising Research* 27 (August–September 1987): 24–38, and Henry Assael *Consumer Behaviour and Marketing Action*, 5th edn (1994), figure 5–3, pp. 169, by courtesy of South-Western College Publishing, International Thomson Publishing.

	Think	Feel
High involvement	Informative (thinker) Learn–Feel–Do	Affective (feeler) Feel–Learn–Do
Low involvement	Habit formation (doer) Do–Feel–Learn	Self-satisfaction (reactor) Do–Feel–Learn

model is most appropriate for standard cars, houses and furnishings. On the other hand, an affective strategy is thought to be more appropriate for products such as jewellery, fashion apparel and cosmetics. In this instance the appeal should stress emotional motives, focusing on ego appeals. The habit formation strategy is for those products with such routinized behaviour patterns that learning occurs most often after a trial purchase. The key here is to reinforce behaviour by means of repetition. A self-satisfaction strategy is built around low-involvement products which appeal to sensory pleasures and where social motives are important, e.g. relationships with cigarettes, alcohol and chocolate.

Returning to the car example, it is debatable whether an informative or affective strategy would be the most appropriate. Involvement theory would suggest that this type of high-involvement product would best be positioned by means of an informative strategy, unless the car was closely identified with the buyer's self-image, as might be the case with a sports car. This is supported by Hirsh *et al.* (2003), who found that car buyers tend to focus principally on cost and performance. Despite such findings the platforms developed by advertisers in the UK and US are often based on emotional appeals. The use of emotional appeals may be more attractive to managers, given that most cars tend to look and perform much the same as others in their class. Given this state of affairs, an emotional appeal may improve the salience of the brand in the mind of the customer against competing brands. However, in evaluating the car the consumer may then use rational criteria in evaluating the brand against others. The important lesson to be learned is that the development of a platform cannot simply be read off an involvement chart and applied in the market place. Rather the development of a successful platform emerges as a result of careful research and clearheaded thought.

The 'tone of voice' which is developed as part of the communications campaign should be closely linked into the form of appeal which is likely to be most influential with the customer. In the previous example managers thought that a mixture of rational and emotional appeals should be used in communicating about cars. Marketers draw on a range of appeals in constructing messages. Often fear appeals are used to persuade consumers to use a product, e.g. life insurance, or not to use a product, e.g. cigarettes. In constructing a fear appeal the marketer must be careful not to create too much anxiety, as the receiver group may construe the message as being simply too threatening to process and perceptual defences may come into play to screen it out. The marketing communicator may draw on several different types of appeal. Humour is used to gain attention and to generate positive feelings about a product, as are puzzles. Some specific appeals are discussed in the later section on advertising.

Choice of contact mix

Contact refers to the manner in which the addressees are to be approached and the kind of message which will be used to appeal to them. Often contact is referred to as a sort of menu including advertising, direct marketing, personal selling, sales promotions, publicity and sponsorship. In many ways this is a mistake, as it reinforces the view that communications planning is mechanistic and formulaic and does not involve the creative intelligence of the planner. Nothing could be further from the truth! Here are some thumbnail descriptions of the various methods, some of which are developed in more detail later.

Advertising. Advertising refers to a paid form of non-personal communication about an organization and its products that is transmitted to a target population through a mass medium. Traditional mass media include television, newspapers, radio, posters, transport and outdoor displays. In the UK precise estimates of expenditure on advertising by brand are calculated by Media Expenditure Analysis (MEAL). The creation of a media plan is central to managing contact in advertising. This is discussed in more detail in the section devoted to advertising.

Direct marketing. Direct marketing has evolved out of the direct mail industry and incorporates telephone selling and email. Often direct marketing is used as a pre-sell technique prior to a sales call, to qualify prospects for a sales call, to generate orders and to follow up a sale. Direct marketing requires good database management techniques, as errors can create much bad feeling, e.g. the mispelling of a name or the inclusion of the name of someone who is deceased. In the UK, direct marketing is still used as a crude weapon to engineer sales by double-glazing companies, financial institutions and charities.

Sales promotion. Sales promotion offers some form of incentive to purchase a product. Marketers devise sales promotions to produce immediate sales increases, e.g. by means of 'two for one' offers and competitions. Supermarkets have used loyalty cards to award extra points to products which they are promoting.

Personal selling. Personal selling is the process of informing customers and persuading them to purchase products through personal communication. Millions of people are involved in a wide variety of selling roles in retailing, trade, technical support and field operations among others. The cost of training and maintaining a sales force depends on the type of sales operation. However, it is far from inexpensive. Personal selling is considered to be more appropriate to B-to-B marketing, where there are fewer customers and there is a higher volume of transactions than in consumer markets.

Sponsorship. Sponsorship is an indirect form of communication as it involves financing or supporting an activity which usually is unrelated to the business environment, such as sports or the arts, which are regarded as worthy by the target group. For some, such as cigarette companies, sponsorship has provided a convenient means for working around the UK ban on television advertising. The benefits accrue by means of association. For example, if one pairs images of cigarettes with images of various sporting events a link may be created between cigarettes and sport. Sponsorship has gone beyond its traditional boundaries; well known television programmes and even educational institutions are sponsored.

Publicity. Publicity refers to the link between marketing and public relations. Where marketing and public relations are integrated within a company then public relations personnel will ensure that journalists are briefed and may even be invited to the launch of a new car. For products such as cars, personal computers and digital cameras the opinions of panels of 'experts' in specialist magazines are of great importance and so a large amount of effort is expended in seeking to ensure that they pass a favourable verdict on the product. Many people describe publicity as if it were free. It is not free to the extent that people must be employed to create the publicity. Furthermore, publicity can be a double-edged sword, which can work in favour of or against the product.

REACHING THE AUDIENCE

The Television Response Rate (TVR) represents the number of the target population that communicators feel should be exposed to the communication if objectives relating to awareness and interest are to be achieved. This can be calculated by considering the reach and frequency of a given communication. *Reach* may be defined as the unduplicated proportion of a population that is exposed to the advertising message at least once during the designated time period (usually four weeks). *Frequency* refers to the number of times within the period that a prospect is exposed to the message. Frequency may be expressed as an average. If it is expressed as an average of 3.0, for example, the average prospect is exposed to the message three times during the period. But certainly not all prospects are exposed three times; some people may be exposed five or six times during the period, while others may not receive the message at all. There is no guarantee that people actually saw the advertisement. Often people are not really 'watching' television at all. For example, if the aim is to raise awareness of 80 per cent of A/Bs about the new brand, it may be decided to commission three one-page or half-page advertisements in all of the broadsheets over a week-long period.

Example. Imagine a new mineral water-based herbal drink is being sold and it is hoped to achieve a 15 per cent share of the 40m case market which is expected to grow by 10m cases per year over the next few years. The target of 6m cases is to be obtained by attracting first-time drinkers of herbal drinks and by persuading existing herbal drinkers to switch brands. If it is assumed that there are 10m herbal drinkers and a net addition of 2.5m drinkers each year, then to gain a 15 per cent share 2m drinkers must be reached.

Next it is necessary to determine the percentage of the target audience that should be made aware of the brand to induce a trial and repeat use rate (three or more bottles that will attract 2m consumers). The advertising agency estimates that 40 per cent of those who try a bottle of the new brand will become long-term users. This means that 5m people must try the product. The agency further assumes that 75 per cent of those who become aware of the product will try it. This translates into a need to make 6.67m or 53 per cent of the 12.5m total present and prospective buyers aware of the brand.

Next the number of advertising impressions needed to obtain an awareness level of 53 per cent followed by trial and repeat buying needs to be evaluated. The agency estimates that thirty-five impressions on average will be needed for each of 12.5m individuals in the target audience to bring this about (less than one per week). Thus the total number of impressions needed is $35 \times 12.5m = 437.5m$.

Media planners calculate the overall weight of the campaign using Television Ratings (Gross Rating Points (GRPs) in the USA). TVRs indicate the gross coverage delivered by a particular advertising schedule. One TVR is one percent of a given audience (usually comprising a specific demographic) seeing an ad once. At time of writing in Scotland the value of a TVR for daytime viewing is between £180 and £200. If one is targeting the UK as a whole, the figure is likely to be 20 times that (between £3,600 and £4,000) because this yields the much larger audience of 20 million households. At the UK level, one TVR is equal to 1%, or 0.2 million households.

Returning to the example, we require 437.5 million impressions. As a TVR is 0.2 million people then, dividing 233.45 by 0.2 results in 2187.5 TVRs. If we assume a high figure of £4,000 per TVR, then the overall budget for the campaign would be £8,750,000. Planners then select programmes which are most likely to be tuned into by the target audience. Television programmes such as ER might achieve a TVR of 10, indicating that it is watched by 2 million adults, while radio programmes may reach smaller but more precisely targeted audiences. Such specific information is used by media planners in seeking to tailor their choice to those media vehicles which are geared heavily towards the target market.

BUDGET

If an objective and task approach to setting the budget for a marketing communications campaign is followed, then the cost implications will be clarified once the communications planner knows which contact mix to implement to achieve the campaign objectives. In real-life situations it is not at all unusual that the budget has been predetermined. In some cases this is based on a percentage-of-sales approach, which has one major flaw in that it is based on the incorrect assumption that sales create marketing communications and not vice versa. The implications are that at a time when sales are in decline the marketer will find that the budget has been sharply reduced when it ought to be increased. Another common approach to setting budgets is to follow the competition. In several industries one dominant company acts as market leader in establishing the 'going' rate for pricing and advertising and others follow.

RESPONSE

While all marketing communications should seek to elicit some form of response, some are more immediate than others. Direct response advertising such as advertisements which have response coupons obviously invites an immediate response from the customer, as does television shopping and free-phone using 0800 numbers. On the other hand, some advertising which seeks to create awareness or interest cannot be expected to elicit an overt response. Instead the marketer must take care to ensure that objectives linked with the hierarchy of effects such as awareness, interest and intention to purchase are tracked as the campaign unfolds.

Response and follow-up are important in direct marketing. Organizations must be ready to handle the expected response from a campaign. This is not easy to calculate and it is not at all unusual for estimates to fall wide of reality. For example, management at the UK direct banking operation First Direct had to cancel a television advertising campaign in early 1993 because staff could not cope with the demand created by press advertising and a mail shot, which was three times greater than that anticipated. First Direct did not return to promotions until 1995. In retrospect the campaign had been well researched and the conclusions had reinforced the view that most customers prefer relationships and that the uptake of the new brand would be small. However, managers had to conclude that in this instance customers said one thing but did another. First Direct claimed to have learned from the experience. Amanda Richards (1994) noted that 'In most sectors poor projections such as these have caused many a senior marketer to lose his or her job'. But not at First Direct. 'We got it wrong. Maybe we could have projected it better. But we have learned', said First Direct CEO Kevin Newman.[2]

FOLLOW-UP

Follow-up relates to the organization's reaction to customer response. Where the response is in terms of some form of enquiry, often organizations are poor at following these up. As director of an MBA degree the author had to devise a system which could deal with response and follow-up from the despatch of brochures to individuals. Once an enquiry came in by telephone, fax, email or in person the person's name was registered on a database together with their preferences (how they liked to be called, e.g. 'Mrs' or 'Ms') and other details such as address and telephone number. If an application form was received within sixty days, then this triggered a further response from the unit; if no application form was received within sixty days this triggered a letter which asked the person if they were still considering applying, if they had applied elsewhere or if they had decided not to apply anywhere. Replies to this mailing were entered into the database. It is easy to underestimate the amount of work and discipline involved in establishing such procedures and ensuring that they work smoothly.

EVALUATION

The campaign evaluation should be carried out in terms of the objectives which have been set. The hierarchy of effects which has been discussed in this and in other chapters often plays a key part in evaluation. Frequently, measures of awareness, interest and intention to buy are used to measure the effectiveness of communications campaigns.

When measuring awareness, recall or recognition should be measured. Recall is when the researcher asks the respondent 'Have you recently seen or heard any marketing communications for cars?' and then, if the reply is 'Yes,' says, 'Which ones?' and records the answers. This is a difficult test, as the person must conduct an internal memory search to find the name of the brand and then retrieve it. An easier measure is a recognition test whereby if the answer is 'yes' the interviewer asks the respondent to scan through a list of the names of various brands and to tick the brands which s/he has seen.

If respondents indicate that they are aware of the brand, the researcher can establish their degree of interest in and propensity to try the brand. Responses to these questions are tallied and compared with the objectives defined in TVR. Market research agencies such as Millward Brown are specialists in conducting advertising tracking studies which involve

MADAME TUSSAUD'S SEEKS STAR PARTNERS

In 2003 Charterhouse put its leisure group, including Thorpe Park, Alton Towers and Madame Tussaud's in London, New York, Las Vegas, Amsterdam and Hong Kong up for sale. However, when offers only reached £800m (US$1,435m), it retracted its offer. Madame Tussaud's, the London waxwork attraction, suffered from falling tourist volumes after 11 September 2001, but visitor numbers began to rise. In 2003 it had some 2m visitors, up from 1.8m in 2002. Domestic visitors make up half the visitors, whereas in the past 70 per cent of visitors were tourists.

Madame Tussaud's has become an interactive experience, seeking to capitalize on its status as 'the oldest celebrity brand in the world'. Visitors can dance alongside models of Beyoncé and Britney Spears in the Diva area, or 'do a Johnny' (taking a kick at the rugby posts in the style of Johnny Wilkinson). Visitors can mingle with the models, experiencing Kylie whispering that she 'can't get you out of my head' or even squeezing the bottom of the Brad Pitt model.

New management at Madame Tussaud's has sought to increase revenue through sponsorship deals associated with linkage to the wax models. Madame Tussaud's is putting a price on fame by selling the right to be associated with its renowned brand. In 2004 Managing Director James Bradbury began looking for a commercial partner for the forty-year old Planetarium, operating within the Madame Tussaud's complex, when it reopened after a £2.6m (US$4.7m) overhaul. The partner would buy the right to combine its brand name with that of the Planetarium and maintain visibility throughout the attraction. Bradbury, a former retailer, was inspired by Selfridge's store in Oxford Street, London, which raised about £35,000 per month by renting out its window displays and concession areas to brands such as Sky television and Carylon Bay property development in Cornwall, south-west England. Bradbury considered 'the currency of celebrity is one of the most lucrative. Brands are constantly looking for ways to associate with it' (Murphy, 2004). Unfortunately, in 2006, the Planetarium was closed down due to its failure to attract sufficient audiences.

Bradbury is working with Heavenly Marketing, an agency that arranges sponsorship deals, to develop a newspaper-style rate card valuing various parts of the Madame Tussaud's venue. The World Stage area is considered to be the most valuable, with visitors spending an average eighteen minutes there looking at wax models of famous figures, including George Bush and Adolf Hitler. Branding on these figures' information plaques, on souvenir guides and on the Madame Tussaud's website has been valued at £70,000 for six months' visibility. The Premiere Night area hosts models of Hollywood stars. Visitors spend an average of eight and a half minutes in this area, giving a projected rate card value of £40,000 (US$71,760) for six months.

Tussaud's has relationships with third-party brands, such as HMV, which sponsors the Diva area. In 2004 Kimberly-Clark paid the attraction to create a wax model of its Andrex puppy, the first brand character to feature in Madame Tussaud's.

Interest from film companies prompted consideration of prices to be put on the various parts of the attraction by creating a rate card. When Universal suggested that the attraction could create a wax figure of the Incredible Hulk to coincide with the film release, Tussaud's produced a game area as well as a 20 ft Hulk model to increase the interactive options on offer. The deal with Universal did not involve payment for promoting the film but licensing fees for selling Hulk-related merchandise were waived, which for a Hollywood blockbuster can exceed £200,000 (US$358,880). A similar deal was agreed with Sony Pictures for the Spider-Man attraction. In this way, Tussaud's has learned to generate revenue with third parties to increase brand awareness by using brand association with its wax models to reach FMCG customers.

Adapted from Murphy (2005).

conducting quantitative market research through the course of a campaign and measuring this against TVR.

While measures such as recall and recognition are useful and are of great comfort to marketers their limitations must be recognized. Earlier discussion in this chapter highlighted the complexity of the consumer's response to marketing communications. While it is not possible to go into detail here in outlining more complex means of tracking marketing communications the creativity of the consumer should always be borne in mind.

COMMUNICATIONS CONTACT TECHNIQUES

Advertising

Advertising is so ubiquitous in our society that it is taken for granted as a seamless part of everyday life. Advertising as it is known developed as a form of mass communication to 'educate' new consumers into the ways of the market place. As it developed so advertising has come to be associated with the creation of brand properties, that element of a brand that is considered unique to that brand and to no other. For example, over the years Coca-Cola has tried to educate us into linking the signifier 'Coke' (the denotation) with (the connotation) 'the real thing' as the catalyst that can bring people together through its association with global events, from the World Cup to Christmas. As advertising has placed itself into the fabric of society so its tendrils have reached into new areas. For example, government advertises a range of 'products' from drink driving to health promotions, anti-drugs and anti-AIDS campaigns; charities constantly vie for attention and political parties engage advertising agencies as a weapon in their increasingly complex armoury.

PLANNING ADVERTISING CAMPAIGNS

In theory the advertising process should follow the broad outlines of the IMC process described above. Precise objectives should be specified for the campaign, a platform should be developed, a budget should be allocated, a message created and specific forms of contact identified before the campaign is executed (implemented). The campaign should be evaluated. It is easy to think that advertising is uniquely for large organizations. However, most people spend money on advertising at some point in their lives, perhaps in advertising an item for sale in a local newspaper or when selling a property or in the personal section of a newspaper or magazine or on the Internet through E-bay. When something personally is advertised much the same process is used as for organizations. Objectives are developed (ultimately to sell the item); budgets are determined; the best available medium for contact is selected, and afterwards an evaluation as to whether the campaign was worth the money or not is made. Sometimes the advertising is entrusted to an agent, e.g. an estate agent.

ADVERTISING AGENCIES

Organizations and individuals are confronted with the same set of advertising decisions: they can do it themselves, or they can work jointly with an agency in devising an advertising campaign. For most organizations the latter alternative has advantages: to build and maintain an advertising section can be expensive requiring specialist skills. Over the years agencies have developed effective arrangements for working with clients and as agency staff do not belong to the organizational culture of the client they can breathe some fresh air into the campaign through the introduction of new ideas.

AGENCY STRUCTURE

Over the years advertising agencies have evolved a structure which facilitates the development of effective relation between client and agency. Usually, it is composed of an account director, a creative director (linked with the creative team), a media director and a planner. The account handler works on what must be achieved, the planner works on how it may be achieved, the media planner is involved in the where?/when? issue; the creative director and her team must assemble the final message.

Account handler

The account handler is responsible for maintaining continuity in the relationship with the client, essentially providing the role of liaison and co-ordination. One key skill is the ability to recognize who has the power in the client organization. The client's advertising people may be involved: however, the sales director, who may have considerable power, may not be. Unless the account handler can address the needs of the sales director and the sales force the campaign may not have the desired impact. Often the account handler is jointly responsible with the client for developing the creative brief which forms the basis for the work of the creative team.

Creative team

The creative brief (see Figure 10.7) forms the basis for the work of the creative team. For many this is the most important function of any agency, as it effectively creates the essential difference that is being offered to the target group. As one creative director told the author, this is undoubtedly a challenging prospect. 'On the face of it there might only seem to be one or two ways of telling people that your tyres are cheaper and better than anyone else's.'

The creative team is responsible for translating the creative brief into the advertising message. The message is itself composed of copy and artwork or visuals. In many agencies the 'creatives' work in teams of two, the copywriter who writes the message and the art director who works on the visuals. Copy includes all headlines, sub-headlines, body copy and signature.

Together the creative team must devise the appeal of the advertisement. This is the 'hook' which is used to snare the addressee's attention. This issue has already been referred to in connection with the FCB grid (see Figure 10.6). When constructing the message advertisers use rational appeals when they are trying to engage a person's cognitions and emotional appeals to influence affect. It is useful to combine the skills of both copywriter and art director, as the appeal of the advertisement should be reflected in both the words and the images used. Over the years creatives have developed a range of appeals on which to base the creative platform. In addition to the use of fear and sex appeals, Williamson (1978) mentions a number of different ways of attracting the addressee's attention, including:

■ Advertisements which do not feature a person, a product or both.
■ Humour.
■ Puzzles.

CREATIVE BRIEF

Client: Job title:

Date of issue: Job No:

Internal review date: Account Handler:

Client presentation date: Author:

On air/insert date:

1. WHY ARE WE ADVERTISING?

2. WHO ARE WE TALKING TO?

3. WHAT DO THEY THINK AND FEEL ABOUT THE PRODUCT?

4. WHAT IS THE SINGLE MOST IMPORTANT POINT WE WANT TO MAKE?

5. WHY SHOULD THE CONSUMER BELIEVE IT?
   RATIONAL
   EMOTIONAL

6. TONE OF VOICE (ONE WORD)

7. PRACTICAL CONSIDERATIONS

Budget guidelines:

Total: £ [   ]   Media: £ [   ]   Production: £ [   ]   Cost to client: £ [   ]

Proposed media: [   ]

Approved by: CD [   ]   PD [   ]   AD [   ]   Client [   ]

Figure 10.7
The creative
brief

Some modern cigarette advertising is so sophisticated that it contains no mention whatsoever of the product, the user of the product or the company which makes the product. The only way one can 'recognize' that this is a cigarette advertisement is by means of associating the colours used in the advertisement with a particular brand or by recognizing the 'Government Health Warning' on the pack.

The creative team is responsible for the design process. Roughs are literally the creative team's portfolio of rough drawings. Sometimes these are shown to clients to impress them about the amount of work that has gone into the creative process. However, it is more likely that the client only gets to see the scamps or visuals. For television advertising creatives may produce a storyboard, which is a sequence of frames or panels that depict the commercial in still form. These may contain one or two basic propositions, e.g. for a print advertisement or a brochure. Many visuals at this stage will be comprised of library shots, may include headers and cross-headers, although the body copy will be 'greeked' in *lorem ipsem*. At this stage different propositions are researched. If the client is content with the visuals and signs off on these, copywriters and artworkers are involved in producing the actual visuals and copy. Once the visuals have been finished at the colour proof stage, it becomes expensive to change anything. The work is then sent to a repro (reproduction) house where the work can be reproduced in a variety of formats: matched print, Cromolin or wet proof, which is the most accurate (Ozalid for black-and-white). Following some final checks the job then goes to printing.

Planner

The role of the planner in an advertising agency is to stand between the client and the creative as the representative of the customer. As the planner needs to be an expert in the consumers' relationship with brands s/he must use research and not just do it. Planners may use a whole range of research in their jobs, from secondary research reports which map trends in the relationship of a brand to the competition to specific research based on the brand itself. Through the use of research, planners have encouraged their clients to adopt a more sophisticated view of their customers than might otherwise be the case.

As planners have been associated with the view of the customer, so they have quickly become involved in issues relating to evaluation, in particular the pretesting of advertisements. For example, one or two different formats, including scamps, visuals, storyboards and copy, may be pre-tested to check that the intended message is being received by members of the target group. Pre-testing may include some measure of reception, comprehension or response, for example:

- *Reception*. Did the message get through? Was it remembered? Did it catch his or her eye or ear?
- *Comprehension*. Was the advertising understood? Did the person get the message? Was the message identified with the brand?
- *Response*. Did the customer accept the proposition? Did the advertising affect attitudes to the brand? Did the person think or feel differently following the exposure?

Measures of reception include the recall and recognition tests mentioned earlier. However, while one may recall or recognize a brand this is no guarantee that the message is actually understood. It is important to check the linkage with the brand: does the person associate the advertisement with the brand advertised? Finally, just because a person recognizes an advertisement and links it with the correct brand does not mean that they accept the proposition. Pre-testing seeks to measure some features of response. The role of the planner in pre-testing and in measuring response is to be wary of clients' perceived need to rely on simplistic measures which may provide them with reassurance (a crutch, as one said). These are unlikely to reflect the complexities of the true response, or to result in effective communications.

Media director

The role of the media director is to devise the media strategy and to buy media time, a job which has become more complex as media have proliferated. The choice of media has a major effect on the content and form of the message. For example, the notorious Benetton campaign which featured dying AIDS victims, kissing clerics and blood-spattered newborn babies achieved an enormous hard-hitting impact because these images were displayed prominently on posters. Media departments purchase large amounts of time and space on television for which they receive discounts.

STRUCTURE OF THE WORLD ADVERTISING INDUSTRY

The world's leading advertising agencies have their headquarters in Japan, the US and France and include Dentsu, McCann-Erickson, Walter Thompson, Publicis, Leo Burnett and Ogilvy & Mather, as shown in Table 10.3. Turnovers for the top ten agencies range from nearly US$2bn (£1.1bn) for the dominant leader, Dentsu, to US$0.7bn (£0.4bn). From their bases these agencies operate through a network of subsidiaries and associates, bringing together national and regional operations for global coverage, matching the needs of their global MNC clients.

While globally the advertising industry is huge, it is perhaps easier to envisage it as a consolidation of national and regional advertising agencies' operations, with similar media available but distinct differences in application according to the regulation and culture of each country. Typically, for the UK, advertising expenditure is approaching £17.5bn (US$9.8bn) which is spent on press (49 per cent), television (25 per cent), direct mail (14 per cent), outdoor and transport (5 per cent), cinema (1 per cent), radio (3 per cent) and the Internet (2 per cent) (see Table 10.4).

In the UK major advertisers predominantly come from the FMCG, communications and motor industries, with Procter & Gamble ranked top, spending £192bn (US$107bn) in 2003, followed by COI Communications (£143bn, US$80 bn) and BT (£97bn, US$54) (see Table 10.5). The distribution of advertising expenditure across the various media varies. While most advertisers concentrate their spending on television, FMCG producers such as Procter & Gamble and L'Oreal Golden spending the higher shares (76 per cent and 72 per

Table 10.3 The world's top ten core advertising agency brands, 2002

Rank	Agency	Headquarters	US$ million	£ million
1	Dentsu	Tokyo	1,864	1,039
2	BBDO Worldwide	New York	1,238	690
3	McCann Erickson Worldwide	New York	1,220	680
4	J. Walter Thompson	New York	1,179	650
5	Publicis Worldwide	Paris	1,022	570
6	DOB Worldwide Communications	New York	943	526
7	Leo Burnett Worldwide	Chicago	887	494
8	TBWA Worldwide	New York	771	430
9	Euro RSCG Worldwide	New York	756	421
10	Ogilvy & Mather	New York	706	394

Sources: adapted from Advertising Association *European Marketing Pocket Book 2005*, p. 22, and *Advertising Age*, April 2004.

Table 10.4 UK total advertising expenditure by medium, 2003

Medium	£ million	US$ million	% of total
Press			
National newspapers	1,902	3,412	11.0
Regional newspapers	2,986	5,357	17.3
Consumer magazines	784	1,407	4.3
Business and professional magazines	1,048	1,880	6.1
Directories	1,029	1,846	6.0
Press production cost	634	1,137	3.7
Total press	8,382	15,037	48.7
Television	4,374	7,847	25.4
of which production costs	656	1,177	3.8
Direct mail	2,431	4,361	14.1
Outdoor and transport	901	1,616	5.2
Cinema	180	323	1.0
Radio	582	1,044	3.4
Internet	376	675	2.2
Total	17,227	30,905	100.0

Source: adapted from Advertising Association Marketing Pocket Book 2005, p. 116.

Table 10.5 Top ten advertisers in the UK, 2003

Rank	Advertiser	Total £000s	Advertising expenditure			
			TV	Radio	Press	Other
1	Procter & Gamble	192	76	6	13	5
2	COI Communications	143	51	17	24	8
3	BT	97	54	6	31	9
4	L'Oreal Golden	93	72	1	21	6
5	Ford Motor Co.	79	49	7	29	16
6	Lever Fabergé	71	67	2	13	18
7	Nestlé	70	69	3	10	18
8	Masterfoods	64	63	3	15	19
9	Orange	62	32	9	20	39
10	DFS Furniture	62	45	5	46	4

Sources: adapted from Advertising Association *Marketing Pocket Book 2005*, p. 122, and Nielsen Media Research.

cent respectively), other advertisers spend relatively more of their expenditure on press, radio and other media. There will be differences in the relative shares of the different media related to the advertising strategy selected, the targeted audience and the PLC position of the product being promoted. The FMCG producers will be targeting the mass market through television whereas the communications and motor industries while using television will target audiences more generally across the media, especially the press. In other countries the relative proportions of the various media used will vary according to cultural and regulatory conditions. In this way, television and radio, in particular, may have higher shares of advertising expenditure than generally is used in the UK (see Table 10.6). While television accounts only for 21 per cent in Sweden, it has 42 per cent in Spain (39 per cent in the US). On the other hand press has 64 per cent in Sweden and only 40 per cent for Spain (41 per cent for the US, not much different from television).

Direct marketing

What is direct marketing? This is a complex question, as this is referred to by various marketing authors not only as 'direct marketing' but also as 'database marketing' and 'relationship marketing'. The objective of this section is to provide some linkage for these concepts. A management information system with a database at its heart is the hub around which all direct marketing activities turn. The difference between effective and ineffectual direct marketing campaigns rests on the manner in which this system is managed.

The purposes of having a database are to build a list of prospects or customers, which can form the basis of direct marketing initiatives, which can in turn be managed in such a

Table 10.6 Advertising expenditure by medium in selected European countries, 2003, as percentage of total

Medium	France	Germany	Netherlands	Spain	Sweden	US
Total advertising expenditure (US$ million)	11,042	18,250	3,907	6,169	2,074	137,181
Press	45	62	66	40	64	41
Television	31	26	22	42	21	39
Radio	8	4	7	9	3	13
Cinema	–	1	–	1	–	–
Outdoor	11	5	4	7	5	3
Internet	5	2	1	1	7	4
Total	100	100	100	100	100	100

Sources: adapted from Advertising Association *Marketing Pocket Book 2005*, Advertising Association: London, pp. 184–5 and European Advertising and Media Forecast.

Note: US shown for purposes of comparison.

manner as to maximize the potential value of the relationship to both the customer and the organization.

The links between database marketing, direct marketing and relationship marketing become clear. At the heart of all direct marketing is a database. The database is used to identify and contact key groups of customers; it allows one to track all marketing communications and consumer responses to enable the marketer to ensure that customer retention is maximized. Direct marketing promotions are specifically targeted and addressed to individual customers. It should be noted that there is a major difference between marketers who merely use a list of prospect names to blanket-market their products and those who have established a fully functional direct marketing database which contains demographic, psychographic and behavioural data. Only the latter is a full instance of direct marketing.

The rapid growth of direct marketing has been influenced by a number of factors which include:

■ Dilution of the effectiveness of mass marketing efforts as a result of the profileration of channels.
■ Major increases in the power and decreases in the cost of technology, coupled with the development of distributed systems.
■ Realization of the value of existing customers to the organization.

Some of the key processes and steps involved in direct marketing are discussed below.

BUILD A LIST

The construction of databases known in the trade as Marketing Customer Information Files (MCIF), containing a list of prospects or customers, is a key aspect of all direct marketing activities. The quality of information provided in the MCIF is critical. It should be complete, timely, accurate and sufficient. Customer information should be as complete as possible in that it contains the maximum number of identifiable prospects within the target group. It should be timely, in that it is up to date and accurate in correctly identifying the preferences stated by existing or prospective customers (known as prospects). Failure to attend to such mundane factors as a person's name can have a major effect on the prospect. For example, many women are upset if they are addressed as 'Mrs' when they prefer 'Ms' and vice versa. The required information for an MCIF will come from internal and external sources. Internally there are numerous types of data to compile, including customer names, addresses, phone, fax and email numbers, key demographic variables, past purchasing history, including Recency, Frequency and Monetary (R, F & M) value of purchases and payment history.

In the B-to-B database internal data could include SIC codes, the number of employees, purchasing preferences and names of key members of the buying centre. Some authors argue that for a database marketing system to be really effective it should contain real behavioural data. Krzyston (1996) suggests that it is only by building a dynamic database that marketers can successfully judge the value of promotions. A database allows marketers to decide what information to send to customers based on their value and then enables comparisons between the purchase behaviour of those who received the promotion and those who did not.

CUSTOMER LOYALTY SCHEMES

One currently successful means of establishing a customer list is based on 'loyalty' schemes (see p. 360). Loyalty schemes have a long history. In the UK this device can be traced back to the beginnings of the co-operative movement when the Rochdale Pioneers set up their first stores and gave every customer a 'dividend' which was based on the amount which they purchased. Since then similar forms of promotion have involved forms of promotions based on trading stamps, tokens and more recently Air Miles. Air Miles, run by British Airways, was first set up in 1988 and had 3.6m collectors in 1997 according to Wall (1997). The crucial aspect of modern loyalty schemes is not so much the incentive offered as the value of the resulting list of prospects which can form the basis of targeted marketing communications.

In the UK supermarkets have developed loyalty cards as a means of promotion. In February 1995 Tesco launched its Clubcard. The incentive for customers to join the scheme is that they receive one point for every pound spent and the 'opportunity' to earn extra points on selected items. Every quarter the customer receives a statement telling how many points have been collected. If this is 150 or more then they receive money-off vouchers for Tesco. The first mailing of vouchers took place in 1995 with a distribution of £12m (US$21,528m) vouchers. Clubcard Plus, which offers a savings account linked with a debit card, was launched in the spring of 1996 in partnership with the Royal Bank of Scotland. By 1997 it was estimated that Tesco had 9.5m cardholders, Sainsbury's 10m and Safeway 6.5m.

The Pareto effect discussed in Chapter 6 comes into play in analysing the customer list. Effective use of customer databases focuses on identifying the 20 per cent of households that contribute 80 per cent or perhaps more to the organization's bottom line, or profitability. This is not as simple as it seems. For example, Gerson (1998) describes how database systems can find those best households that erroneously appear at the bottom of prospect lists.

> For example, Dr. Jones is at the top of the list. She has a US$585,000 (£326,816) mortgage and US$30,000 (£16,722) in car loans with your institution. She also keeps US$50,000 (£27,870) in her money market account and has an average US$12,000 (£6,703) balance in her checking account. She is one of your most profitable customers. On the other hand, database research has also identified one Dr. Johnson. With only a $300 (£167) passbook savings account with your institution, it's not surprising that he occupies a spot at the bottom of your prospect list. However, the crucial extra information that the MCIF system offers about Dr. Johnson is that he's got a US$700,000 (£390,189) mortgage with another bank, US$50,000 (£27,870) in a money market account with a brokerage house and two car loans totalling US$40,000 (£22,297) through the Mercedes-Benz Credit Corporation. Clearly, Dr. Johnson is one of your community's most profitable bank customers.

As Gerson notes, the critical issue is that the potential value of Dr Johnson to the bank was hidden and he would have remained at the bottom of the bank's list until his value was revealed by the MCIF analysis. In the trade such analyses are known as data mining. Once Dr Johnson has been recognized as an important prospect, the bank can proceed to court his favour through a personalized contact strategy.

Analysis of the database allows marketers to identify their current best clients and to study their behaviour and demographics including income, home ownership status, home value, number and ages of children, kinds of cars driven, credit cards used and marital status. Using an MCIF system, an organization has the opportunity to examine whole customer profiles and juxtapose them with the products and services being used. This may form the basis of direct promotions. For example, if a retail marketer finds that loyal customers are trying other stores s/he may target this group with special promotions. They could be invited to a special evening which features selected products at special discount rates with snacks and drinks provided. This forms part of the contact strategy which is described next.

CONTACT STRATEGY

Database research becomes database marketing when an MCIF is used not only to identify potential profitable customers but also to craft the specific messages sent to them. This strategy addresses the discovery that all current customers should not receive the same level of attention; that more effort should be spent in retaining existing valuable customers than on attracting new ones. This does not rule out attempts to recruit new customers. In the example described by Gerson (1998) the bank could devise a highly personalized direct mail piece which offers Dr Johnson substantial savings if he transfers his mortgage and other transactions to the bank. The direct mailing could be supplemented by a follow-up telephone call perhaps a week later.

PROBLEMS WITH IMPLEMENTING DIRECT MARKETING

The compilation of an effective list can pose a major difficulty for organizations because information may be stored in different databases within the organization. MacMillan (1996) quotes a Henley Centre survey which suggested that over one third of businesses have multiple databases in a competitive departmentalized structure with the result that there is little integration between them. Technology lies at the heart of compiling a database. Where companies had multiple databases, only 13 per cent claimed that there was any kind of integration; there are many databases but there is little crossover between them. This fragmentation was also found within the marketing department, where traditionally separate functions such as Sales, Marketing and Customer Service have different databases.

Another problem is the antipathy between marketing and IT personnel. MacMillan says that the Henley study found that few companies have a database manager. Denny (1995) reported that in a study carried out that year 54 per cent of marketing departments had IT people in them compared with 40 per cent the previous year. Denny considers that this was a sign that the traditional antipathy between marketing and IT staff was being addressed.

Another difficulty is that current attempts to promote goods and services through direct marketing can be crude and may work from a prospect list which is not used to monitor and respond to subsequent behavioural information. For the author, writing in 2006, this is particularly true of financial institutions, which send the same 'personalized' letter which urges me to buy a credit card once every three months. Such junk mail is a instant turn-off!

The traditional structure of the marketing communications industry with its division between advertising and direct marketing must be considered. While the issue of integration is being addressed through the development of TTL agencies which deal with all aspects of the communications mix, there is a long way to go.

IT INFLUENCE ON ADVERTISING MEDIA

In 2005 the Bellwether Report prepared by the Institute of Practitioners in Advertising (IPA) showed that UK companies are shifting their marketing expenditure to activities with a more easily measurable impact (Silverman, 2005). The study found that the UK marketing business, in general, is still adversely affected by the collapse of technology stocks in 2000. Corporate marketing budgets in the UK were being increased, but there is a distinct change in emphasis. Budgets for advertising in traditional media, such as television, print and radio, are being cut back, while spending on direct marketing and Internet advertising increased substantially.

According to Stephen Woodford, IPA president, the changes reflect the growing corporate interest in tracking the ROI in advertising and other marketing efforts. He considers companies are embracing forms of marketing that can be monitored more precisely. In direct

SOCIAL ADVERTISING

Figure 10.8 is an example of an advertisement for a social issue. Read the text of the advertisement and then answer the questions.

A Special Home
For A
Special Girl

Sarah Louise at 5 1/2 is a chatty petite child who likes to dress up and go for runs in the car. She is fond of animals and enjoys playing outside. Sarah Louise is presently living with short term foster parents, but now needs long term care.

She will present many challenges to her new foster family and therefore needs foster parents who will have the patience, commitment, energy and an ability to be firm but loving.

Could you provide a special home for Sarah Louise? A specialist fee of £9,810, together with fostering allowances will be paid. Training and support will also be provided.

For further information please contact:

Figure 10.8 Social advertising

CASE QUESTIONS

1   What was the target market for this advertisement?
2   What sort of advertising appeal is being used here?
3   This advertisement appeared in a local newspaper. How much do you think it cost?
4   How much might this advertisement have cost if it had appeared in a national newspaper?
5   Do you think that this subject is an appropriate subject for advertising?

marketing, companies can measure exactly how many responses a sales pitch generates. Internet advertising works in much the same way when consumers click on advertisements, creating a rich up-to-the-minute data stream. There is a shift towards greater accountability with ever-increasing pressure to demonstrate a return on investment.

The Bellwether Report, produced by NTC Research for the IPA, is based on a survey of more than 200 UK companies. The basic methodology is to ask UK companies whether they are increasing or decreasing their marketing budgets. The results suggest that marketing expenditure increased in 2005, but by less than might have been expected. In particular, it found that higher oil prices were putting pressure on industrial and travel companies. Nearly a quarter of companies (23.6 per cent) had cut their budgets for media advertising in the last quarter, while 19.6 per cent increased them and 56.8 per cent kept them the same. In another sign of difficult business conditions, 18.6 per cent of the companies said they were scaling back sales promotion spending, while 17.1 per cent were increasing such efforts and 64.3 per cent were standing still. By contrast, companies were more bullish about direct marketing than in any previous survey, with 27.7 per cent increasing their budgets, 61.3 per cent keeping them the same and 10.9 per cent cutting them.

The popularity of Internet advertising grew, with 31.5 per cent of companies increasing online advertising budgets, 60.8 per cent keeping them the same and 7.7 per cent reducing them. Only 20.5 per cent of companies were not advertising on the Internet. More than an eighth of the companies devoted more than 10 per cent of their marketing spending to the Internet. However, the study probably understates the shift to using the Internet as a medium for marketing messages, because companies account for their Internet spending in different ways. Website design, which is emerging as a key weapon in marketing (see Chapter 12), is often paid for out of product development budgets. Similarly, some companies consider sales promotions to be a marketing expense, while others simply report lower sales revenues to account for discounts. (Silverman, 2005)

Another survey conducted in 2005 in the US by Veronis Suhker Stevenson (VSS), the private equity firm, confirmed the shift toward the Internet, which is pushing fundamental changes as advertising money shifts online and as consumer attention drifts from traditional media (Duyn, 2005). The report predicts that new media advertising, which includes cable and satellite television, Internet and video game advertising, will grow in the US by nearly 17 per cent p.a., reaching US$69bn (£39bn) by 2009. By then, spending on digital-based media will push average annual consumer spending on media in the US over the US$1,000bn (£557bn) level.

Traditional media companies have reacted by increasing their acquisitions in the Internet space, with News Corp spending up to US$2bn (£1.1bn) investing in the space, and others such as the *New York Times*'s parent and Dow Jones making similar purchases.

Rutherford, vice-president of VSS, considered the difference between 2005 and five years previously, when media companies also rushed to make Internet investments, most of which were written off, is the solid growth opportunities provided currently by the Internet. As in the UK, following the Internet bubble there was a substantial fall in advertising in 2000 and 2001, leading to a recession in the media and communication industries which was overcome only in 2004, when the sector grew strongly. VSS estimated US advertising would reach US$858bn (£478bn) in 2005 (6.8 per cent growth on the 2004).

The Internet is proving to be effective because advertisers can measure audience response by monitoring the number of people who click on links. This, combined with consumer complaints about advertisement clutter, has resulted in a shift from advertising-based media, such as broadcast, television, radio, newspapers and magazines. Five years earlier, these media accounted for 64 per cent of consumer time spent with media. In five years' time, VSS predicts, these will account for 54 per cent of consumer time spent, with subscription and fee-based media accounting for only 46 per cent (Duyn, 2005).

CONCLUSION

By the end of this module students should be:

- Familiar with relevant terminology such as noise, codes, redundancy, denotation, connotation and two-step flow.
- Understand the nature of the communications process.
- Able to provide a critique of the S-M-R model of communications.
- Able to plan a communications campaign.
- Appreciate the points to consider in planning and advertising or direct mail campaign.

REVIEW QUESTIONS

1 There are many examples of the role of noise in human communications. One story concerns a communication exchange which purportedly took place during the First World War. The message sent by the source was 'Send reinforcements, we're going to advance'. As the result of 'noise' in the channel the message which finally arrived was 'Send three-and-four-pence, we're going to a dance'.
   (a) What forms of noise may have contributed to this miscommunication?
   (b) State some ways in which this noise could have been reduced.

2 Considering what you now know about terms such as Source, Transmitter, Signal, Channel, Noise, Addressee and Code, what categories in your view correspond to the following?
   (a) What is the alphabet?
   (b) What is a street?
   (c) What is a suit of clothes?
   (d) What is light?
   (e) What is having to repeat the same story over the phone because of a crackly line?

3 What process should the marketing communications planner follow in constructing an advertising campaign?

4 Critically evaluate the strengths and weaknesses of using the 'hypodermic' model of mass communications to understand marketing communications.

5 Discuss the kinds of research that could be carried out as part of a marketing communications campaign, indicating when this research should be conducted.

6 What criteria should the marketing communicator take into account in selecting an appropriate communications mix for a product or service?

7 How can you frame the Red Stripe example with reference to denotation and connotation?

8 Consider the role of sponsorship within IMC campaign for a FMCG firm such as Kimberly-Clark?

9 Discuss the benefits of association with celebrity brands for film companies.

10 How can the potential value of a sponsorship agreement be ascertained?

RECOMMENDED FURTHER READING

Chernatony, L. and McDonald, M. (1998) *Creating powerful brands,* 2nd edn, Oxford: Butterworth Heinemann.

Clifton, R. and Maughan, E. (eds) (2000) *Interbrand: the future of brands*, Basingstoke: Macmillan.

Cooper, A. (ed.) (1997) *How to plan advertising*, 2nd edn, London: Cassell.

Cummins, J. (1998) *Sales promotion: how to create and implement campaigns that really work*, 2nd edn, London: Kogan Page.

Davidson, D.K. (1996) *Selling sin*, Westport CT: Quorum.

Davies, M. (1998) *Understanding marketing*, London: Prentice Hall.

Drawbaugh, K. (2001) *Brands in the balance: meeting the challenges to commercial identity*, Harlow: Pearson.

Fill, C. (2002) *Marketing communications: contexts, strategies and applications*, 3rd edn, Harlow: Pearson.

Gobé, M. (2001) *Emotional branding,* Oxford: Windsor Books.

Haig, M. (2003) *Brand failures*, London: Kogan Page.

Haig, M. (2004) *Brand loyalty*, London: Kogan Page.

Hankinson, G. and Cowking, P. (1993) *Branding in action: cases and strategies for profitable management*, Maidenhead: McGraw-Hill.

Jefkins, F. and Yadin, D. (2000) *Advertising*, 4th edn, Harlow: Pearson.

Jones, J.P. (ed.) (1999) *The advertising business: operations, creativity, media planning, integrated communications,* Thousand Oaks CA: Sage.

Lindström, M. (2005) *Brand sense*, London: Kogan Page.

Lindström, M. and Andersen, T.F. (1999) *Brand building on the Internet*, South Yarra, Victoria, Australia: Hardie Grant.

O'Shaughnessy, J. and Jackson, N. (2004) *Persuasion in advertising*, London: Routledge.

Ottesen, O. (2001) *Marketing communication management*, Copenhagen: Copenhagen Business School Press.

Pelsmacker, P., Geuens, M. and Bergh, van de, J. (2004) *Marketing communications: a European perspective*, 2nd edn, Harlow: Pearson.

11 PLACE: CHANNELS OF DISTRIBUTION

LEARNING OBJECTIVES

When you have completed this unit you should be able to:

■ know the nature of the channels of distribution available;

■ be aware of the developments taking place within the channels of distribution including:
- Vertical Marketing Systems (VMS);
- Horizontal Marketing Systems (HMS);

■ and those related to the channel intermediaries:
- sales agents;
- distributors;
- wholesalers;
- retailers;

■ understand the role of franchising within retailing;

■ be aware of the problems associated with channel conflict;

■ appreciate the role of the channels of distribution within the marketing mix;

■ realize the implications of the increasing importance of online

INTRODUCTION

Products and services have to reach their customers to be consumed. In the early stages of trade, it is possible for producers and their customers to meet face-to-face to exchange goods and services as in the situation where the farmer takes the produce to the local market. However, when trade becomes more sophisticated, the services of various intermediaries along the supply chain may need to be used to ensure that the goods or services reach the consumer in the right manner at the right place, time and price. It is the process of moving goods and services through these intermediaries to reach the end user that will be discussed in this module.

The nature of channels of distribution

The channels of distribution used within the market place have evolved to match the needs of the users of these services and they continue to be adapted to meet those needs. The objective is to move the goods or services efficiently, with the lowest possible number of intermediaries between the producer and the end user. Ideally, the producer aims to exchange the products directly with the consumer. However, as the physical distance between the two parties and the volume of goods to be exchanged increases, it becomes necessary for producers to use the help of others to complete the movement of the goods associated with the transaction. These are the intermediaries within the channels of distribution, or the 'value chain', as it is termed. This is particularly the situation for producers supplying the consumer mass market, where it becomes impracticable to exchange products directly between the producer and the consumer.

CHANNEL CONSTRAINTS

A number of factors affect the nature of the supply chain that evolves to suit the needs of the producer and to meet customer demand.

Customer characteristics

NUMBER

The number of customers that a producer targets influences the selection of the intermediaries used within the supply channel. In situations where the producer is serving the mass market there may be millions of consumers, as in the UK, with up to 60m individual customers and 24m households. Such numbers make it difficult to resource personal individual selling to each potential customer. Yet if, as in an industrial market, the producer is supplying a small number of customers, e.g. a few component suppliers within the car industry, it is feasible that the component suppliers could use their own sales and logistics teams to service customer needs.

GEOGRAPHICAL DISPERSION

As the geographical distance between the supplier and the consumer increases, the process of moving the goods within the supply chain becomes more complex. If the distance extends across geographical country boundaries, challenges related to legal, regulatory and fiscal issues as well as the obvious cultural and language difficulties complicate the movement of goods between the intermediaries within the distribution channels.

PURCHASING PATTERNS

Customer purchasing patterns of goods differ. For example, within the mass consumer market, some people buy foodstuffs on a daily, weekly, fortnightly or even monthly basis, depending on the needs and the resources of the individual. Customers vary in the frequency with which they shop and the volumes of products that they purchase, so that some customers purchase small quantities of products frequently, while others purchase larger quantities of the same products but on a less frequent schedule. Customer segmentation (see Chapter 6) can categorize key types of purchasing patterns, e.g. heavy and light consumers of a particular product. Within the industrial market purchasing patterns differ, depending on the organization concerned and its particular culture.

BUYER SUSCEPTIBILITY TO DIFFERENT SELLING METHODS

Customers may prefer one form of sales approach to another and not all customers have the same preferences. For example, older customers may prefer to purchase banking services through the branch's bank manager, but younger customers may find purchasing the same services using the Internet and telephone sales is more convenient.

Product characteristics

The product characteristics will influence the choice of the channels of distribution to be used.

PERISHABILITY

Products have differing degrees of perishability that influence the type of storage and warehousing required and the distance that such products can be moved. Highly perishable products such as fresh food require different warehousing conditions from products such as vegetable oil, lubricating oil and toilet paper. Some products need to have temperature-controlled chilled or freezing conditions; others are better stored at room temperature. Safety of dangerous products also necessitates special storage, e.g. petroleum and gaseous fuels.

BULK

Products vary in the weight and volume per unit value, e.g. toilet paper occupies a high volume for its weight and unit value whereas computer components have much smaller volumes compared with their weights and unit values. Management will endeavour to reduce the distances that high-volume products are transported, but for smaller volume products such considerations are less critical.

PRODUCT STANDARDIZATION

The degree of product standardization will influence the selection of the intermediaries within the channels of distribution. The more standardized the product the more likely it is that a standardized route through the channel intermediaries can be achieved; conversely, the more individualized the product, the more likely it is to use a wide range of intermediaries.

SERVICE SUPPORT REQUIREMENTS

The degree of service support that a product requires influences the selection of the channel intermediaries. For example, if limited support is required, as with the sale of tinned soup, where the purchaser takes the tin and determines how it will be consumed, then the selected channel has merely to ensure that the product reaches the end of the channel, the retailer's outlet, in sound condition. The retailer will be required to give minimum customer services apart from ensuring availability of the product for the consumer to purchase. However, should the consumer expect the product to be supplied with extra service provision, e.g. for a car, a dishwasher or a life assurance policy, the purchaser will expect such service support from the car dealer, electrical product retailer or assurance adviser. These intermediaries will be required to have the resource to provide such services.

UNIT VALUE

Products with higher unit values may require and justify more expensive channel support than those with lower unit values. The supplier of designer jeans such as Armani finds it is appropriate to instigate a channel system using a global network of prestigious boutiques located in high-status locations. The supplier of mass market ladies' fashion clothes will target high-street multiples such as Monsoon, Principles, Dorothy Perkins, Miss Selfridge, Wallis and Zara in the UK. The channel intermediaries required to support these two types of retail clothing outlets would differ.

Company characteristics

SIZE OF ORGANIZATION

The resources of the supplier of the product, or service, influences the selection of the channels of distribution. Such resources include finance, the number of employees and the geographical spread of the organization's operations. For example, the MNC is likely to have access to a more extensive range of channel intermediaries than the smaller firm, and the MNC could use a combination of different intermediary routes to target particular market segments.

PRODUCT MIX

The range of products that an organization supplies affects the channel selection. The organization supplying different product types to different markets, of necessity, will be likely to operate more complex channel systems than the firm supplying a more limited range of standard products.

PAST CHANNEL MIX EXPERIENCE

The channel mix used evolves over time and is influenced by the experience of past practice. If, traditionally, a product has been distributed by a supplier using wholesalers and retailers, and that system has worked effectively, then the supplier will probably continue to use the same system. It is when the system fails, or when the cost of using such channels becomes excessive, or the competition becomes intense, that suppliers consider alternative approaches. For example, within the UK until the 1980s suppliers of building materials used the wholesaler/retailer channel of builders' merchants and D-I-Y retail outlets to distribute their products. The builders' merchants obliged their suppliers to use their services. But from the mid-1980s, the distinguishing features of builders' merchants and the general public D-I-Y retailers became blurred as did their roles of servicing the trader and the general public. This led to the individual role of the wholesaler, or builders' merchant, becoming much reduced. D-I-Y retailers, such as B&Q in the UK, began to service both the trade and general public customers and grew to dominate the channel intermediaries, thereby circumventing the use of traditional builders' merchants (or wholesalers). Similar developments have occurred in many other industries, including tyre distribution for cars and commercial vehicles, not only in the UK but globally, especially in the US.

Other factors influencing channel selection

The selection of the distribution channel, and the intermediaries to use, are influenced by the characteristics of the environment in which the firm operates, the competitor approaches to distribution and the type of intermediaries that operate within the channel.

ENVIRONMENT CHARACTERISTICS

The environment will determine the range of intermediaries required to reach the customer. For example, in the case of the drinks and tobacco industries, an extensive network of retail outlets is used to ensure wide geographical coverage. These outlets include independent corner shops, petrol station forecourt shops as well as multiple food retailers. Intermediaries within the distribution channel perform a variety of roles that support such retail outlets. For the drinks and tobacco industries there are intermediaries that provide bonded warehousing services at ports of entry for the collection of excise duty for the government as well as similar bonded warehousing at production locations for goods such as tobacco and alcohol. The conventional logistical services of general warehousing, distribution and transport will also be provided. The environment and government controls play a critical part in determining the roles of the intermediaries within the channel. Moreover, while some drink and tobacco producers manage the bonded warehouses themselves, others prefer to delegate the management to a third-party intermediary. The producers can keep control themselves or they may subcontract the responsibility for the roles within the channel.

TRENDS IN LOGISTICS SUPPORT

Increasingly, there has been a move towards centralizing distribution using large hubs to service large areas reaching across national boundaries to become a global phenomenon. Retailers that once used a string of distribution hubs in any particular country are using fewer. Instead of sending goods to a dozen different points, they are more likely to drop them off at one vast warehouse, termed a 'shed', with up to 1m sq. ft capacity. From there, lorries travel further to deliver products to supermarkets and wholesalers. For example, in 2005 Dixons, now Currys, the UK electrical retailer, was cutting its number of distribution centres from seventeen to two. Indeed, some retailers are seeking single distribution hubs for the whole of Europe, with the hubs being supported by a much smaller number of urban centres in the 'hub and spokes' model (Pickard, 2005).

In 2005, to meet this demand, a new distribution industrial park on the outskirts of Paris, France, was opened at Chanteloup. The park will house up to eleven huge warehouses with about 3m sq. ft (0.3m sq. m) of space which will act as European distribution centres. Danone, the food manufacturer, was one of the first firms to use this base (Pickard, 2005).

US-based ProLogis, the world's largest provider of large industrial sheds, is hoping to benefit from this trend. As part of its expansion strategy, in 2005 it bought Catellus, the US west-coast rival, for US$4.6bn (£2.6bn) and it is also linked with the possible take-over of Gazeley, its largest UK competitor, which is owned by Wal-Mart/Asda. In France ProLogis launched a distribution shed base at Moissy-Cramayel which is the size of 350 football pitches, confirming the move towards industrial sheds getting larger and larger to satisfy global distribution (Pickard, 2005).

The challenges of the expansion of the EU and the associated rise of the CEE mean that retailers need distribution hubs closer to markets in Poland, the Czech Republic and Hungary, which may conflict with the single mega-warehouse development. Compounded with this, the adoption of the working hours directive means drivers in the UK, at least, must cut their hours from an average fifty-five per week to forty-eight per week. With a shortage of skilled drivers, the logistics industry is becoming more reliant on Polish and Czech drivers. It remains to be seen how the value chain develops to bring together the environmental and physical challenges of logistical support.

COMPETITOR CHARACTERISTICS

Within an industry the practices of the market leaders influence those of the other competitors. Frequently the practices of market leaders dominate within the channel, with followers copying the example of the leaders. Exceptionally, new entrants to the market use alternative channel routes but they are required to have sizeable resources to change the accepted industry practice. An example of such a change was the advent of telephone selling of car insurance as introduced by Direct Line and the Royal Bank of Scotland (RBS). The general practice was to operate through agents, independent financial advisers and through the bank's own branch structure. The change of approach led to circumventing traditional intermediaries in the distribution channel within the financial services sector to reduce selling costs. However, the change had to be introduced alongside the traditional routes. Only as consumers gain confidence in the new channel approach can the use of the traditional intermediary route be reduced and, ultimately, replaced.

Channel networks take various forms and may use intensive, selective or exclusive intermediaries along the value chain.

Intensive distribution

Mass-market products have to be made available in as many outlets as possible to ensure that consumers have the convenience of being able to purchase the products whenever they wish. This strategy is used for lower-priced convenience items, e.g. confectionery, snack foods, tobacco and soap. Producers of these types of goods use a range of outlets of varying status, including railway kiosks, multiple high-street shops and retail superstores. Location convenience is the priority in selecting these retail outlets.

Selective distribution

Rather than intensive distribution, producers may select their preferred outlets to match their marketing strategies by targeting particular market segments. For example, the producer of digital cameras may select electrical goods retailers that are located in prime shopping centres and in airport duty-free zones, rather than use all the available electrical goods retailers. In this way, the digital camera producer can concentrate efforts on retailers that perform best at selling the cameras.

Exclusive distribution

Should the producer have an exclusive range of products, e.g. Omega watches or Gucci fashion clothes, it is appropriate to distribute the products through exclusive retail outlets and to limit the number of intermediaries handling the company's goods or services. Exclusive distribution is used when the producer wants to maintain control over the service level offered. Frequently it involves exclusive dealer arrangements in which the retailers agree not to carry competing brands.

While, in principle, the choice of whether to use intensive, selective or exclusive distribution relates to the nature of the products or services being marketed, and the distribution methods appear to be mutually exclusive, yet there are pressures to move towards intensive intermediary coverage. Often the user of exclusive and selective distribution is under pressure to widen the outlet coverage, especially in times of falling sales. However, the greater coverage can reduce the image of exclusivity, thereby losing the advantages associated with the established outlets. The situation has to be monitored carefully to choose the most appropriate outlet coverage.

Throughout the selection of the most effective distribution network, the channel design has to consider the demands of the manufacturer, i.e. the need to move the goods or services from the location where they are produced, through the intermediaries, to the consumer. At the same time the pressures of the customer on the supplier of the goods or services must be considered. Compounding this situation, the retailer places pressures on the channel network, obliging the supplier to meet the retailer's demands. The demands of all concerned must be met.

In this way, channel design is affected by 'push' and 'pull' factors:

- *Push* from the manufacturer pushing production on to customers through the channel intermediaries.
- *Pull* from customers exerting product stocking pressure on retailers and manufacturers through the channel intermediaries.
- *Constraints* come from retailers, e.g. stock specifications on suppliers to match customer database information.

This leads to channel of distribution 'shuffle' whereby the nature and responsibilities of intermediaries within the network change to meet the pressures imposed by users of the system. Increasingly, it is the retailers within the network that have the dominant role within the channels of distribution, or the value chain. Retailer influence will be discussed further below (see p. 352).

THE STRUCTURE OF CHANNELS OF DISTRIBUTION

The channels of distribution used to move products to the consumer vary according to the nature of customers, products and manufacturers of the products or services concerned. They are influenced by the characteristics of the environment in which the marketing is taking place. Furthermore, different channel routes may be used by the same organization to target different markets or market segments. An outline of the types of channels and the intermediaries that are available is shown in Figure 11.1.

Within consumer markets manufacturers distribute their products direct to the customer using their own sales forces, sales agents, direct mail/mail order, or even the Internet, to communicate with the consumer. Firms such as Avon (cosmetics), Betterware (household goods) and Amway (domestic cleaning products) use their sales forces and sales agents to

(a) Consumer marketing channels

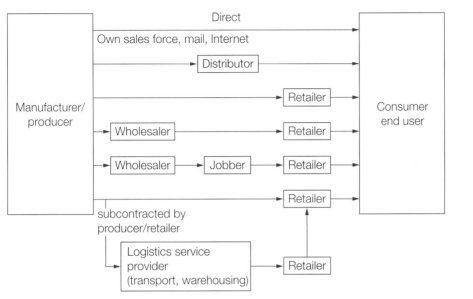

(b) Industrial marketing channels

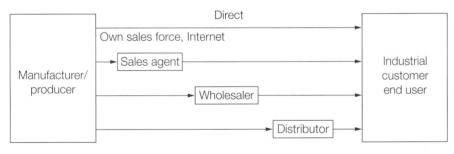

Figure 11.1
Consumer
and industrial
channels of
distribution

sell their products direct to the customer using door-to-door sales techniques. Typically, products sold in this way have relatively low prices and are infrequent purchases. Other firms use direct mail order with catalogues to communicate directly with consumers, e.g. Great Universal Stores (GUS) covering general consumer goods, Patra for silk clothes and Swim Shop for swimming gear. Many charities use mail order catalogues to sell produce for fund raising such as Oxfam, the Red Cross and the World Wildlife Fund. Typically, such channels do not provide sales services for the goods. Some goods may require service support, including expert advice, repair and maintenance services that cannot be readily provided by direct mail order. In these situations, distributors (sometimes termed dealers) dedicated to marketing a firm's product range may be used. Firms marketing consumer durable goods often use distributors as intermediaries, e.g. BMW, Ford and Nissan for cars, Mira for shower systems, Hoover for household appliances such as washing machines.

Other firms consider that their intermediary requirement is only for warehousing and storage provision and will use wholesalers to provide these services. Sometimes jobbers, or packers, are introduced to provide services not readily given by wholesalers to the final retailers. These could include break-bulk packing, e.g. of fruit, vegetables and cheese. Ultimately, within the consumer market, most products reach the consumer through retailers. The services of other intermediaries may be used to support the retailers. But it is the retailers that have become increasingly influential and powerful within the supply chain, especially in defining the nature of the services provided by intermediaries within the channels of distribution.

It should be appreciated that there can be conflicts of interests between the members of the conventional channels of distribution structure as shown in Figure 11.1. The members are likely to act individually to achieve their own particular objectives rather than work as a co-ordinated team. For example, wholesalers and retailers with different interests may not act in a cohesive manner, creating tension and inefficiencies within the value chain. Consequently, vertical marketing systems (VMS) have been introduced which, as defined by McCammon (1970), are 'professionally managed and centrally programmed networks, pre-engineered to achieve operating economies and maximum market impact'. VMSs arose to support strong channel members' attempts to control channel behaviour and to eliminate the conflict that results from independent channel members pursuing their own objectives. VMSs have brought together the channel intermediaries, the producer, wholesaler(s) and retailer(s) to act as a unified system. They can achieve economies through their size, bargaining power and elimination of duplicated services. Generally, one channel member, such as the producer, the wholesaler or the retailer, owns the other channel members, or franchises them, or has so much power over them that they all co-operate (Kotler, 1997; Kotler *et al.*, 1999).

There are three types of VMS which will be discussed below: corporate; administered; contractual.

Corporate VMS

This combines successive stages of production and distribution under single ownership. Such vertical integration is favoured by companies that wish a high level of control over their channels of distribution, e.g. Benetton.

Administered VMS

This co-ordinates successive stages of production and distribution through the size and power of one of the members within the channel. Channel captains that may be either the manufacturers or retailers control the system. In this way, members of a dominant brand can secure strong trade co-operation and support from resellers. For example, Kellogg's, Gillette, Procter & Gamble (P&G) and Heinz can command high levels of co-operation from their resellers in connection with displays, shelf space, promotion and price policies. Major retailers such as Tesco, Asda (Wal-Mart), Marks & Spencer (M&S) or Boots can demand support from their suppliers and the intermediaries within the channel.

Contractual VMS

This consists of independent firms at different levels of production and distribution within the channels of distribution integrating their programmes on a contractual basis to gain more economies of scale and associated increased sales than if the firms acted individually. Johnston and Lawrence (1988) have called contractual VMSs 'value-adding partnerships' (VAPs) suggesting the partnership linkage that is formalized within the contract agreement.

There are three types of contractual VMSs: wholesaler-sponsored voluntary chains; retailer co-operatives; franchise organizations.

WHOLESALER-SPONSORED VOLUNTARY CHAINS

These are systems whereby wholesalers organize voluntary chains of independent retailers to help them to compete with the large multiple chain retailers. The wholesaler develops a programme in which independent retailers standardize their selling practices and achieve buying economies that enable the group to compete effectively, e.g. Independent Grocers' Alliance in the US (Kotler and Armstrong, 1997, 2001).

RETAILER CO-OPERATIVES

These are systems in which retailers organize a jointly owned business to carry on wholesaling and, sometimes, production activities. Members buy most of their goods through the retailer co-operative and jointly plan their advertising. The profits made by the group are allotted to members in proportion to their purchases. Examples include Certified Grocers and Associated Grocers in the US and Spar within Europe. Through such co-operation members gain the strength to compete effectively with major retailers in the supply chain.

FRANCHISE ORGANIZATIONS

Franchise operations within the channels of distribution link stages within the production–distribution process and have become increasingly important within the supply chain. Retail franchise operations are discussed on p. 349.

Sometimes, companies lack the capital, know-how, production or marketing resources to venture alone, or they may be afraid of the risk involved in developing a marketing opportunity. In this situation, it may be appropriate to use horizontal marketing systems (HMS) whereby two or more unrelated companies put together resources or programmes to exploit an emerging marketing opportunity. The companies work with each other on a temporary or permanent basis or they may create a separate company through which to operate. HMSs are becoming increasingly important and take many forms. They are typified by the development of commercial linkages between major food retailers and some banks, e.g. to provide banking services such as automatic teller machine locations at retail outlets, credit cards and, even, pensions and mortgage provision.

INTERMEDIARIES WITHIN CHANNELS OF DISTRIBUTION

As discussed above, the main types of intermediaries used within the channels of distribution are: sales agents; distributors; wholesalers; retailers; franchising.

Sales agents

These are intermediaries who are paid by commission on the sales they achieve. Sales agents do not receive regular employee salaries and associated benefits and, consequently, their commission rates are usually higher, typically between 3 per cent and 10 per cent of sales, than commissions given to sales forces. Sales agents do not hold stock. They do not take ownership of the stock prior to its being delivered to the customer. Sales agents may operate for a number of clients and usually will cover complementary product ranges rather than competing products or services. However, manufacturers can have problems controlling the sales efforts of sales agents, who may have conflicting loyalties.

Distributors

These are sales intermediaries who share willingness to hold stock. Usually, distributors are linked to a single supplier for each line carried. For example, in the car industry, Ford has a network of distributors (or dealers) that provide showrooms (and salesmen) as well as car servicing dedicated to the Ford range of cars. The manufacturer contributes to the costs associated with the running of the dealership. However, such distributor agreements are becoming less rigorously maintained, so that some distributors are beginning to carry cars for more than one car manufacturer, which inevitably leads to conflicts of interests for all concerned.

Wholesalers

Traditionally wholesalers have been used to service the mass markets, taking manufacturers' production and breaking it down into smaller volumes ('break-bulk') to service retailers who, in turn, supplied individual consumers. Wholesalers carried large volumes of stock and supplied smaller volumes to retailers. Usually wholesalers concentrated on providing a range of competing brands of similar types of products, e.g. foodstuffs, fashion clothing and building materials. Normally wholesalers did not deal with the end customer.

However, in the UK and elsewhere, since the 1980s, the role of wholesalers has changed. Wholesalers have faced increasing pressures, especially from the major retailers that have taken over wholesaler services within their own traditional services (see discussion of VMSs above). Wholesalers, like the other intermediaries, have had to adapt their services to the changing market circumstances. Some wholesalers providing consumer goods and food-related products have become cash-and-carry organizations servicing the higher sales volume customer, e.g. Makro, the Dutch world leader, with over 130 stores operating across Europe, South America and the Far East. Usually, in such cases, the stores are large warehouses, one-storey buildings with extensive car parks; customers are mainly owners of small businesses such as restaurants and independent shops.

Retailers

Retailers undertake the final link within the channel of distribution. They effect the sale of the goods, or services, to the customer. The other intermediaries between the producer and consumer work towards supporting the retailer so that goods are available in the right place and at the right time to match consumer demand. Developments within the retailing industry will be discussed on p. 352 below.

Franchising

Franchising has been defined as being 'an arrangement whereby a supplier, or franchisor, grants a dealer, or franchisee, the right to sell products in exchange for some type of consideration, e.g. percentage of total sales in exchange for furnishing equipment, buildings management know-how, marketing assistance and branding to the franchisee' (Dibb *et al.*, 1994: 333–5). The intermediary agrees to follow certain procedures and not to buy from others, or to sell competing products or services.

Within the retail sector, franchising arrangements have become an increasingly important source of growth. In the US, franchising accounts for at least one-third of all retail sales (Kotler and Armstrong, 1997). In 1995 the UK had over 750 companies involved in franchise operations which in themselves had 24 per cent of UK retail sales volume. Growth has continued, as is shown by the extensive examples of franchise operations in 2003 within the UK (see Table 11.1).

TYPES OF RETAIL FRANCHISE AGREEMENTS

A range of franchise agreements is used within the channels of distribution to give retailer coverage. Typically, using franchise arrangements, a manufacturer can license its production processes to other producers or distributors that can sell the given product to retailers, e.g. Coca-Cola. Increasingly, franchising has been used to gain closer linkages with retailers. For example, a manufacturer may authorize a number of retail outlets to sell its brand-name items such as cars and trucks, farm equipment, earth-moving equipment and petroleum. Similarly, retailers use franchising to expand their outlets by supplying brand names, techniques or other services to franchisors, e.g. US Kentucky Fried Chicken (KFC), McDonald's, Starbucks and Subway, UK Body Shop and Wimpy. Italian Benetton, with both manufacturing and retailing activities, has franchise agreements that cover the supply of merchandise as well as retail management know-how. Spanish Zara and Mango and Swedish Hennes & Mauritz (H&M) have been more recent franchisers entering the youth fashion clothing retailing.

Many retailers have expanded both nationally and internationally using a franchise arrangement. It has the following advantages:

- *It enables business start-up with limited capital.* Firms have used franchise agreements to finance their expansion usually by the franchisee investing capital in the business

Table 11.1 UK franchise operations, 2003

Operation	Owned by company	Owned by franchisee
Food and drink		
Burger King	85	700
Domino's Pizza Group	35	240
McDonald's Restaurants	1,200	468
O'Brien's Irish Sandwich Bar	–	90
Pizza Hut	460	50
Wimpy International	5	286
Motorist services		
Autosmart International	–	109
Budget Rent-a-car International	15	123
Hertz	49	82
Business-to-Business		
Clear-a-cheque	1	650
Money Shop	140	288
Cleaning and maintenance		
Oven Clean	12	74
Wheelie Bin Cleaning Co.	1	89
Property care		
Dyno-rod	–	92
Retail and fashion		
Alldays Stores	598	30
Clark's Shoes	400	106
Thornton's	400	200
Sales and distribution		
Post Office	595	280

Sources: adapted from A.C. Nielsen and Advertising Association *Marketing Pocket Book 2005*, pp. 112–14, and British Franchise Association.

enterprise. In particular, Benetton, with its headquarters in Italy, uses franchise agreements and franchisors' personal capital to achieve global retail coverage. The benefit to the franchisor is the provision of capital for expansion; for the franchisee it is the involvement in a tested enterprise formula with less risk than the conventional new business and more guarantee of success.

■ *It uses the business experience of others.* Entrepreneurs with capital can reduce the risk of entering a new business by using franchise agreements based on the success of other entrepreneurs, e.g. Burger King, McDonald's and Wimpy fast food chains.

■ *It allows management guidance.* Many entrepreneurs with little experience in setting up a new business find that a franchise agreement provides a quick route along the learning curve of starting a business. Franchise agreements provide the framework to the procedures, both operational and for marketing, required for the business.

■ *It reduces risk.* It has been found that during the first two years of operations 5–8 per cent of franchisee retail businesses fail compared with 54 per cent of independent retail businesses (Urbanski, 1988).

■ *It allows increased support from the franchisor.* Rather than spending resources on raising capital for expansion, the franchisor can concentrate on developing the management skills appropriate to the business. The franchise agreement obliges strict adherence to the management rules throughout the organization.

However, franchise arrangements can have disadvantages, such as:

■ *The franchisor can dictate aspects of business.* While it may be advantageous to have a ready-made business, some entrepreneurs feel constrained by the rigid specifications that are required to be followed concerning decor, design of employees' uniforms, types of signs and details of business and so on. Sometimes, limited adaptations are allowed to suit particular markets, e.g. the provision of alcohol in McDonald's outlets in France, but these are closely monitored by the franchise owner.

■ *Franchisees pay to use the franchisor's name, products and assistance.* Usually there is a once only franchise fee to pay as well as continuing royalty and advertising fees that are collected as a percentage of sales. The franchisee may consider these excessive as the business becomes more successful over the years.

Thus, while franchise agreements are increasing and have helped many retailers to expand, both nationally and internationally, yet they have to be used with care.

FRANCHISING FOR DYNO-ROD

Jim Zockoll formulated the concept for Dyno-Rod, the industrial and domestic drain cleaning service, when on leave as a Pan Am pilot in London. He discovered that the Knightsbridge hotel where he was staying was due to close while the floor of the ballroom was dug up to clear a blockage in the drains at a cost of £25,000 (US$44,650). He offered to clear the drains without digging up the floor for £5,000 (US$8,970) using high-pressure jetting equipment and from that initiative founded the firm. He developed the company through eighty-nine franchises covering the UK and Ireland, as well as a network of thirteen plumbing franchises and sixty lock franchises. By 2004 Dyno-Rod had pre-tax profits of £6m (US$11m) on turnover of £13m (US$23m). In the same year, 2004, the company was sold to Centrica, the electricity and gas supplier that owns British Gas, for £57.6m (US$103.3).

Source: adapted from Tassell (2004).

C A S E S T U D Y

DEVELOPMENTS IN RETAILING

US-based retailers lead on the global market, with Wal-Mart dominating the top ten global retailers with sales of US$256bn (£143bn) in 2004 (see Table 11.2). French Carrefour ranks second, Metro from Germany ranks fourth and UK's Tesco comes in sixth place.

Within the UK, retail grocer Tesco is dominant, with sales of US$51bn (£28bn) in 2004, followed by Sainsbury's and Safeway, since taken over by Morrisons (see Table 11.3). Kingfisher Group, ranked fourth in the UK, concentrates on D-I-Y warehouse retailing operating over 600 stores in ten countries in Europe and Asia. It also has strategic alliances with Hornbach, Germany's leading D-I-Y warehouse retailer, operating 117 stores in Germany, Austria, the Netherlands, Luxembourg, Switzerland, Sweden and the Czech Republic.

Dixons (DSG International), ranked sixth, specializes in high-technology consumer electronics, personal computers, domestic appliances, photographic equipment, communication products and related financial and after-sales services. It has 1,400 stores worldwide. In the UK it operates through Currys, PC World and the Link. Its international operations include outlets in the Nordic countries, Spain, France, Italy, Sweden, Hungary and the Czech Republic as well as in Greece.

GUS, ranked seventh, covers retail and business services, operating general merchandise retailing through Argos Retail Group (ARG). It also undertakes information and customer relationship management services through Experian, concentrating on information systems for locating stores and customer credit rating scoring. It has a luxury goods interest through a 60 per cent majority shareholding in Burberry Group which it is expected to sell as part of its focusing on the core retail business.

From the 1970s onwards, within the developed economies, there has been a general move towards one-stop shopping, with retail premises becoming larger and located within

Table 11.2 Top ten global retailers, 2004

Ranking	Retailer	Country of origin	Sales turnover (US$billion)
1	Wal-Mart	US	256
2	Carrefour	France	80
3	Home Depot	US	65
4	Metro	Germany	60
5	Kroger	US	54
6	Tesco	UK	52
7	Target	US	47
8	Ahold	Netherlands	45
9	Costco	US	42
10	Aldi Enkauf	Germany	40

Source: adapted from *Retail Week*, 28 January 2005, p.16.

Table 11.3 Top ten UK retailers, 2004

Ranking	Retailer	Turnover (sales in US$billion)
1	Tesco	51.5
2	Sainsbury's	28.6
3	Safeway	15.1
4	Kingfisher	14.5
5	Marks & Spencer (M&S)	13.5
6	Dixons	10.7
7	Great Universal Stores (GUS)	9.5
8	Morrisons	8.2
9	Somerfield	7.7
10	Boots	7.7

Source: adapted from *Retail Week*, 28 January 2005, p.16.

shopping centre complexes, usually on the outskirts of town. In the UK, as in the US, these stores have become ever larger, so that, in 2005, Asda (Wal-mart) had eleven 100,000 sq. ft (9,290 sq. m) stores in the UK.

Stores have been classified in terms of their floor selling space coverage as:

- *Speciality stores* (non-food) and convenience stores (food) (less than 1,000 sq. ft: 93 sq m).
- *Variety stores* (non-food) and supermarkets (food) (less than 1,000 to 2,500 sq. ft: 93–232 sq m).
- *Discount sheds* (non-food) and superstores (food) (less than 2,500–5,000 sq. ft: 232–465 sq. m).
- *Hypermarket* (over 5,000 sq. ft: 464 sq. m).

With the increasing difficulty in obtaining UK planning permission for further retail development in the 2000s, the dominant retailers, e.g. Asda (Wal-Mart), have begun adding social amenities such as low-cost housing and flats, leisure community centres, even a football stadium, to gain favour for their expansion plans. Additionally, some stores have developed mezzanine floors of up to 33,000 sq ft to increase floor coverage as a route to gaining more floor sales space without having to proceed through the time-consuming planning process. Frequently, retailers cover the expense of introducing new road systems to accommodate the extra car traffic involved. Free and extensive car parking is provided. Usually, the shopping centres (or malls as they are termed in the US) comprise one or two major multiple retailers, often a food retailer, e.g. in the UK John Lewis, M&S, Tesco, Asda (Wal-Mart), Morrisons or Sainsbury's. These are supported by a large number of smaller multiple retailers selling mass consumer durables such as clothing, electrical goods and jewellery. The shopping centres have fast-food suppliers which frequently are franchised outlets, e.g. Burger King, McDonald's, KFC, Pizza Hut and Wimpy. Many of the larger shopping centres have become leisure complexes offering entertainment such as sport, cinemas and even educational activities, including museum displays, as well as conventional shopping.

Over time the large retail premises that were predominantly functional, warehouse-type buildings have been changed to have more pleasing designs and an ambience that is ever more conducive to encourage shopping. Grocery retailer outlets have baking smells piped to the shop entrance; music is played to encourage relaxation. Stores have become designed to ensure ergonomic convenience for the shopper and the retailing staff with the overall objective of persuading shoppers to increase their spending. For example, aisles have been widened for ease of shopping trolley access; carousels are placed at the end of aisles with promotional goods and confectionery; shopping magazines at the checkout exits to encourage impulse purchases. Bulk weekly shopping is encouraged.

Over the first five years of the century, in the UK, major grocery retailers looking for new customers have returned to town centres, targeting the daily shopper serviced by the corner-shop independents. They include Tesco Metro, Morrisons Citystore, Sainsbury's Central and smaller, convenience-sized outlets such as Tesco Express and Sainsbury's Local. Their activities are reported to have caused drops in business of 30–40 per cent for the independent shops that increasingly are being threatened. Typically, these major retailer stores have twenty-four-hour opening and stock a relatively low proportion of fresh, unprocessed food and a high proportion of fast-turnaround prepared foods.

Developments in UK retailing

Within the developed economies, increasingly, retail industry has become concentrated amongst the larger multiple groups. In the 1970s UK grocery retailers were organized within co-operatives, multiples and independents, with their share of total commodity turnover being respectively 13 per cent, 44 per cent and 43 per cent, multiples and independents having almost the same shares. Yet, by 1995, grocery multiples had doubled their share to 82 per cent of turnover compared to independents with only 10 per cent and co-operatives 8 per cent of all commodity turnover. Retail grocery multiples have grown to dominate within the retail industry, at the expense of small, independent local shops in rural villages and city centres. Critics of this trend comment that supermarket dominance is reducing consumer choice and the quality of food. Their suppliers are under increased pressure to standardize production to enable price cutting, which has become fundamental to marketing for supermarket chains (e.g. Blythman, 2004).

By 2002, in the grocery trade, there were under 5,000 multiples (see Table 11.4) with a combined turnover of £66bn (US$118bn) accounting for two-thirds (66 per cent) of total retail grocery turnover. Impulse retail trade, with nearly 80,000 stores, undertaken through co-operative grocers, convenience multiples, multiple forecourts, multiple off-licences, symbol groups and independents, had a third (34 per cent) of total grocery trade, half the turnover of the multiples, confirming the increasing concentration on a few dominant

Table 11.4 The structure of the retail grocery trade in Great Britain, 2002

Retail group	No. of stores	Turnover £million	% of turnover
Total grocery multiples	4,907	65,503	66.4
Total impulse	77,876	33,218	33.6
Co-op grocers	2,298	4,641	4.7
Convenience multiples	2,807	2,481	2.5
Multiple forecourts	4,065	2,058	2.1
Multiple off-licences	3,995	2,370	2.4
Symbol groups	6,360	4,331	4.4
Independents	54,933	12,615	12.8
Other impulse	3,418	4,724	4.7
Total coverage	82,783	98,721	100.0

Source: adapted from A.C. Nielsen and Advertising Association Marketing Pocket Book 2005, p. 82.

multiples within the food sector. The top 2 per cent of shops had 42 per cent of all commodity turnover; the top 5 per cent had 71 per cent; the top 10 per cent had 85 per cent and the top 20 per cent had 95 per cent (see Table 11.5).

Apart from organic growth, the trend towards concentration has been achieved by merger and acquisition activity together with collaboration agreements among the major retailers. For example, in the 1980s, Dixons, the electrical retailer, took over Currys and Asda linked with MFI and Allied Carpets. Sainsbury's and BHS entered an agreement to form Savacentre, selling both foodstuffs and consumer durables: BHS also linked with Mothercare, the baby and children's retailer, and Habitat, the designer houseware retailer.

In 1982 Woolworths was refloated as Kingfisher, which then acquired B&Q, the D-I-Y group, and Comet, the electrical wholesaler group, and Superdrug, the pharmaceutical retailer. Further expansion involved acquisition of the French D-I-Y groups Castorama and Brico Depôt. However, bringing together the diverse retail operations posed managerial problems, which led to some reconsideration of the benefits of large, dominant retail groups. Indeed, some degree of demerging took place as, in 2000, Kingfisher sold off Woolworths and other interests, including Comet, which had by then re-branded as Kesa. Meanwhile, Kingfisher is developing Asian sales, although expansion costs have led to a £2.5m loss in 2005 against a £1.6m gain the previous year.

Table 11.5 Concentration of turnover among the retail grocery trade in Great Britain, 2002

% of shops	Share of all commodity turnover
Top 2	41.7
Top 5	71.3
Top 10	85.3
Top 20	94.8

Source: adapted from A.C. Nielsen and Advertising Association Marketing Pocket Book 2005, p. 82.

Table 11.6 Grocery retailer market share in the UK, 2005 (%)

Retailer	Market share
Tesco	30.3
Asda	16.7
Sainsbury's	15.5
Morrisons	11.3
Somerfield	6.1
Others	20.1
Total	100.0

Sources: adapted from Rigby (2005b) and Thomson Data-stream: Goldman Sachs; SG Equity Research.

Other collaborative arrangements that were terminated, bringing more turmoil in the retail sector, included Asda's sale of MFI and Allied Carpets, Habitat's departure from the BHS and Mothercare group, which then became Storehouse and was taken over by Peter Green. In 2002 he added to his empire by acquiring the Arcadia Group, the UK's largest clothing retailer, with 2,000 outlets operating through eight brands: Burton, Dorothy Perkins, Evans, Miss Selfridge, Outfit, Topshop, Topman and Wallis, some of which have been expanding internationally.

As with general retailing, and discussed above, concentration occurred within the grocery industry. In 1994 Tesco acquired Wm Low, another food retailer with interests across northern England and Scotland. In 1999 the US-based MNC Wal-Mart bought Asda, in the wake of two loss-making acquisitions in Germany. In 2004 Morrisons took over Safeway, although it was obliged to sell some of the acquired outlets to meet competition regulations. By 2005 Tesco was UK leader with a 30 per cent market share (see Table 11.6) and, in general, food retailers have come to dominate among the UK retail multiples (Fernie *et al.*, 2003).

Price has become an important factor in store choice for many customers in the 2000s. By 2005 Tesco and Asda together accounted for about 47 per cent of supermarket spending and continued to pressure rivals with price-cutting campaigns. Tesco invested more than £300m (US$533) in price cuts from April 2004 to the end of 2005. Meanwhile Asda, with 17 per cent market share, invested even more with £361m (US$648m) in 2005 in its price-cutting fight to close the widening gap with its rival, Tesco. Asda took advantage of Wal-Mart's buying power to drive prices down for customers (Rigby, 2005a). The continued price cutting challenged all food retailers, especially Sainsbury's and Morrisons, ranked third and fourth respectively. Morrisons struggled to integrate its £3.35bn (US$6bn) acquisition of Safeway. Sainsbury's in a three-year programme to win back customers is spending £400m (US$718m) in cutting its prices in the three years to March 2008 (Rigby, 2005f).

It remains to be seen whether further consolidation in the market takes place. It is unlikely that the dominant grocery retailers such as Tesco will be allowed to take over much more of the market because of the critical concern of the Office of Fair Trading (OFT). Tesco, in particular, has raised concern by its purchase of convenience stores and large 'land banks' to allow future expansion.

Among European retailers UK grocery retailers are less dominant, with only Tesco among the top ten European retailers (see Table 11.7). In 2002 Tesco ranked third, behind French Carrefour, ranked top, and German Metro, ranked second. US Wal-Mart/Asda ranked twelfth and UK-based Sainsbury's ranked thirteenth, well behind the German and French retailers.

Table 11.7 Top twenty European retailers, ranked by turnover, 2003

Rank	Company	Home market	European turnover (€billion)	No. of European countries	% sales in Europe
1	Carrefour	France	61.2	13	87
2	Metro	Germany	52.6	23	99
3	Tesco	UK	40.7	8	92
4	Rewe	Germany	39.2	13	100
5	ITM	France	32.1	8	100
6	Edeka	Germany	31.3	5	100
7	Lidl & Schwarz	Germany	29.0	17	100
8	Auchan	France	27.3	8	95
9	Aldi	Germany	27.0	10	84
10	Spar	Netherlands	22.8	21	85
11	Leclerc	France	22.4	6	100
12	Wal-Mart	US	22.2	2	10
13	Sainsbury's	UK	20.8	1	100
14	Casino	France	19.0	1	83
15	Morrison/Safeway	UK	18.6	3	100
16	Tenglemann	Germany	15.4	12	58
17	Ahold	Netherlands	13.8	6	25
18	Migros	Switzerland	13.0	4	100
19	El Corte Inglés	Spain	12.0	2	100
20	Système U	France	11.4	1	100

Source: adapted from IGD Research and Advertising Association Marketing Pocket Book 2005, p. 179.

Note: currency conversion £1 = €1.4445.

Customer service

Customer demand has led to the need to provide extensive, convenient and free car parking close to retail outlets; this, in turn, has encouraged the development of out-of-town sites, to the detriment of traditional town-centre shopping. There have been suggestions that local authorities may charge for out-of-town car parking space to reduce car use and reverse the trend, encouraging shoppers back to their local shopping area. So far these proposals remain to be implemented. The advent of 'park and ride' car parking on the outskirts of urban areas is another method used to address the environmental issue and to encourage shoppers back to the city centres.

Customer demand has encouraged retailers to extend their hours of opening so that shops, especially food retailers, increasingly are opening from 8.00 a.m. to 10.00 p.m. seven days a week, some even offer twenty-four-hour opening. Sunday shopping has been common in Scotland since 1984 and, since deregulation of Sunday shop opening in England and

C
A
S
E

S
T
U
D
Y

CHARITY SHOPS

An exceptional business success in the UK has been the advent of charity shops that sell mainly second-hand donated goods, particularly second-hand clothing. The first fund-raising charity shop was established in 1947 by Oxfam in Oxford, following its appeal for aid to alleviate the post-war situation in Greece. The public donates more than 90 per cent of the goods sold in charity shops, although some shops sell goods that are bought in and sold for profit. However, a shop must sell wholly or mainly donated goods to qualify for rate relief. Traditionally, charity shops have been confined to unlet or unpopular shops.

Charity shops became especially apparent in the mid-1990s, when traditional high-street shopping suffered increased competition from out-of-town shopping sites which left many retail outlets empty, enabling charity shops to take prime trading locations. More and more, smaller retailers facing increasing pressure from supermarkets and multiple chains have become aggrieved at charity shops benefiting from substantial relief from business rates and value-added tax, according to lobby groups such as the Federation of Small Businesses, which complains its members face unfair competition. Furthermore, the rise of Internet shopping has exacerbated the situation.

In 2005, in the UK, there were about 6,500 charity shops, staffed by more than 100,000 volunteers. They have an annual turnover of more than £400m (US$718m) and raise more than £90m (US$162m) for their parent charities, according to the Association of Charity Shops (ASC). Most buyers and donors supporting charity shops are women, predominantly aged 45 or more, with a bias towards donors from A and B social classes. Although most supporters take their donations into charity shops, 43 per cent sometimes use door-to-door collections and 19 per cent use textile banks at collection points in recycling centres. ACS estimated that charity shops reuse or recyle more than 100,000 tonnes of textiles annually, 30 per cent of the UK recycled textiles volume (Bolger, 2005).

Oxfam is the largest charity retailer with 750 shops. In 2004 it made a profit of £21m (US$38m) on turnover of £70m (US$120m). The British Heart Foundation opened its five-hundredth shop in 2005, nearly four times its 128 outlets in 1995. It raises more than £9m (US$16m) to fight heart disease. Shelter, which campaigns against home-lessness, is rebranding its eighty-seven shops, which raise about £1m (US$1.8m) p.a. (Bolger, 2005).

As yet there is limited evidence of British-style charity shops developing in other international retail markets, but it could be envisaged in developed economies with a concern for recycling to aid charitable causes.

Source: adapted from Bolger (2005)

Wales in 1994, has been increasing throughout the rest of the UK. These extended opening hours have intensified the pressures on the management of the supply chain. In the UK, it is the large, out-of-town shopping centres that have benefited most from the extension of shopping hours, e.g. Lakeside in Essex, Meadowhall near Sheffield and the MetroCentre in Newcastle. For retailers that open, Sunday has become the second busiest day (after Saturday) typically achieving 30 per cent of Saturday sales (Healey and Baker Research, 1995, 1996).

DEVELOPMENTS IN INFORMATION TECHNOLOGY

As noted above, there is increasing concentration of ownership within the retail industry that has grown in size and complexity, in terms of both operations and marketing management. As retailers have expanded from small independents to larger multiple groups, so they have invested in IT to assess consumer demand, to control their operations and integrate them with those of the other intermediaries in the supply chain.

Operational performance

Retailers ensure their outlets are supplied with goods in various ways through the support of supply chain intermediaries (see p. 344). Many of the major retailers have their own networks of distribution centres that are used to support the retail outlets (details of which are beyond the scope of this chapter and should be examined within the remit of logistics). Such distribution centres are used as collection points for goods at which warehousing services may be undertaken. The goods are then transported and delivered to retail outlets as required. Logistics service may be provided by the retailer using internal resources or it may be subcontracted to third-party logistics services providers. Whatever way the goods are supplied to the retail outlet, the channel network requires to be closely integrated to enable the retail outlets to provide the goods for consumers to purchase as they require. This, in turn, necessitates the use of IT to monitor consumer demand and product supply within the channels of distribution. For retail operations, such assessments are made to maintain efficient stock control linked with customer-led stock ordering, including just-in-time (JIT) procedures, delivery schedules and operational control both within the supply chain and within the retail outlet itself, e.g. allocation of shelf space for products.

Consumer demand

In the 1990s much IT development focused on the introduction of bar coding and electronic eye readers to monitor the product movement within the supply chain to match consumer demand. At customer checkouts, sales are monitored using electronic point-of-sale (EPOS) systems which, in turn, are used to provide databases for operations and marketing management (see p. 360). Electronic fund transfer at point of sale (EFTPOS) is used for customers to pay for their purchases by a variety of methods, including Maestro direct to personal bank accounts, credit and charge cards. Many retailers offer their own in-house credit/charge cards such as M&S, Fraser's and Debenhams; as well as credit/charge cards managed by the banks, e.g. Visa, Access and MasterCard. Some retailers also accept credit cards such as American Express and Diners' Club.

Customer loyalty schemes

Smart cards using microchips with the capacity to store and process consumer consumption were pioneered by banks in France and Germany in the early 1980s to reduce fraud through their security features. In the 1990s retailers introduced their own smart cards alongside loyalty schemes to encourage customers to shop in their retail outlet, or chain, in preference to the competition. The schemes give regular and higher-spending customers bonus points, cash discounts and associated incentives which encourage their loyalty.

By 1997, in the UK, there were about 140 loyalty schemes operating, most of which were single company programmes. The food retailers Tesco, Asda, Sainsbury's and Safeway (taken over by Morrisons in 2004) linked with banks and building societies to offer customers participating in the loyalty schemes added financial services such as personal loans, life assurance and travel insurance. These schemes aimed to increase customer loyalty. They provided retailers with a database for monitoring customer demand to help managerial decision making within both the operational and marketing functions.

Other retailers and associations of retailers apart from food retailers introduced loyalty schemes. For example, in 1997 Shell started a smart-card loyalty scheme that linked a number of high-street retailers including Dixons, Currys, Victoria Wine and Vision Express with Hilton Hotels and Shell's own retail outlets. The consortium aimed to cover 70 per cent of consumers' weekly shopping, giving shoppers discounts worth about £50–£60 (US$90–108) p.a. However, as a reaction to necessary economies related to oil price-cutting competition, the Shell smart-card has been discontinued. Other examples of loyalty schemes include the British Airports Authority (BAA) scheme to encourage those passing through its airports to use the restaurants, shops, money exchange and car parking services. Airline loyalty schemes provide Air Miles bonuses to encourage customer usage.

In the UK, among the major food retailers, Tesco, in 1995, introduced its loyalty card, Clubcard, for use at its outlets as well as some of its associates. In 1996 Tesco, in partnership with the National Westminster Bank (now part of the RBS group), extended its loyalty scheme to include banking debit and savings facilities. By 1998, using the Clubcard database, Tesco was testing other approaches to shopping. In the early 2000s it formed a joint venture with a UK database management firm, Dunhumby, with Tesco owning 53 per cent. The objective is to develop the most innovative and effective use of the customer database to benefit Tesco's service provision. Customer standard shopping lists were drawn up to encourage customers to pre-order their shopping for collection at an agreed time, saving customers going around the shop. Since then an online ordering home delivery shopping system has been developed which is taking an increasing share of total sales for all the major food multiples. Indeed, Internet shopping for all goods and services has become increasingly important. Alongside this development, Tesco has introduced personal customer-serviced tills in its shops to provide quicker payment services in the conventional shopping process, and to reduce the number of conventional checkout operators over time.

In 1997 Safeway's loyalty ABC card scheme was introduced, linked with its 'Shop and Go' self-help shopping system. Customers collected bar code monitors as they entered the shop and used these to input the bar codes of their shopping as they gathered their purchases. Payments for the purchases were made at the end of the shopping visit with their charge cards using EFTPOS without the need to use conventional checkout services. The system enabled customers to monitor their buying while selecting their shopping and provided the retailer with an online customer sales database. Safeway had more than 4m ABC cardholders. However, the system proved costly to operate and after a few years was discontinued.

New methods of using IT continue to be tested to increase operational efficiency and market-demand awareness. For example, in 2005 Tesco announced plans to open a stand-alone warehouse at a cost of more than £10m (US$18m) dedicated to dealing with online grocery orders to cope with increased volumes of online shopping in the south-east of England and London. The move is a reversal of Tesco's previous approach of servicing Internet orders from its existing stores which it will continue for online shopping elsewhere in the UK. Tesco is delivering 170,000 orders a week and covers 97 per cent of the UK. Ocado, which is the UK's second largest online food retailer, is processing 36,000 orders a week and covers 40 per cent of the UK. Its founders have spent more than £200m (US$359m) with support from the John Lewis Partnership, owner of Waitrose. It is possible that Tesco will also build a distribution network to integrate its non-food and food and sell clothing online (Rigby, 2005e).

Sainsbury's brought in a similar customer loyalty scheme, Reward, which by 1998 had 10m cardholders. In 1998 Sainsbury's began to test customer reaction to interactive touch-screen kiosks within its supermarkets. The kiosks offered loyalty cardholders a personalized set of discounts (worth up to £25.50 (US$46) per visit) which could be redeemed together with loyalty points for purchases made. Customer behaviour related to the various discounts was monitored and used to gauge the success of Sainsbury's promotional activity. In the future these kiosks could provide suggested shopping lists prepared for customers based on their previous purchases as another service to encourage customer loyalty. This was the precursor of the current online Sainsbury.com house delivery service. Sainsbury's, like Tesco, has developed a home delivery service whereby customers order their groceries through the Internet and have them delivered for a fee or packed ready for collection at the store.

In 2002 Sainbury's extended its loyalty scheme to provide customers with increased convenience and benefits by launching the Nectar card loyalty scheme. This scheme, run by Loyalty Management UK (LMUK), enables points to be collected at more than one place rather than have the need for lots of cards for different shops. Nectar points can be redeemed for thousands of rewards ranging from free meals to days out, and from flights abroad to cinema tickets. Firms included in this alliance are Debenhams stores, BP petrol stations, Thresher and Winemark off-licences, Brewer's Fayre and Beefeater restaurants, EDF Energy,

Ford vehicles, Hertz vehicle hire, Magnet building supplies, TalkTalk mobile phones, Dolland & Aitchison opticians, American Express, ICI Dulux decorator centres; Brakes' food service and Ebookers cash-and-carry, for the trade also participate. There is also coverage of a range of e-stores using the Internet including Amazon.co.uk, eBay.co.uk, CDwow!, Dell, PC World, Comet, Dixons, More Th>n, B&Q and the motoring service groups AA and RAC, as well as Thomson travel. Within two months of the launch Nectar had 11m users spread across 8m households and was aiming to increase this to 12m.

In this way, retailers have used customer loyalty schemes to develop powerful customer sales databases which accurately reflect demand from their customers. Grocery retailers, in particular, have large market shares, so that their customer databases can provide a good monitor of national demand. Apart from using these databases for internal management, some grocery retailers are selling the customer sales data to the larger marketing research agencies, such as A.C. Nielsen, for use in retail sales monitoring in conjunction with retail audit panel assessment (see p. 134). This raises ethical concerns within the marketing research industry.

All these systems have used IT linkages to monitor customer purchasing behaviour to manage operational and marketing management more effectively. They demand high investment and place considerable power in the hands of those using them. Their use concentrates consumer knowledge among the leading retailers and service providers, increasing their dominance within the market.

Another development, mentioned above, that has had considerable influence on retailing has been the advances in the use of the Internet within the supply chain. The Internet is used in the search for goods and services from national, international, and even global, suppliers. While, at first, most products supplied through the Internet were books, CDs and records, e.g. Amazon.com, the product range has increased substantially so that an almost limitless range of products and services is now available with only limited geographical restraints. The speed with which consumers have adopted the practice of purchasing through the Internet suggests that, as home shopping (or office shopping) evolves, consumers are looking for greater flexibility in undertaking their shopping, posing challenges to conventional retailers. For example, the Ebay.com site for the US (or Ebay.co.uk for the UK) brings together sellers and purchasers in an auction environment without the need for conventional retailers or the other intermediaries in the supply chain.

According to the Interactive Media in Retail Group (IMRG) Internet sales account for 9 per cent of all UK retail spending. For 2005, overall, online shopping grew by 32 per cent to £19.2bn (US$34.4bn), with shoppers spending an average of £816 (US$1,464) p.a. Another study, published by European Interactive Advertising Association, estimated that the average UK online shopper spent £875 (US$1,570) in 2005, nearly double the average £452 (US$811) for the rest of Europe (Palmer, 2006). The growth of online shopping is related to the rapid take-up of broadband Internet lines, to shoppers becoming more comfortable with using the Internet for shopping and the easier use of increasingly sophisticated online stores. According to Point Topic, the broadband research company, the number of lines grew by about 60 per cent to 9.8m at the end of 2005, giving the UK the highest number of broadband lines in Western Europe. More than 66 per cent of homes have an Internet connection, according to Ofcom, the telecommunications regulator, and Point Topic estimates that more than 37 per cent of homes have broadband (Palmer, 2006).

UK Internet sales are more than double the traditional catalogue shopping, which accounts for about 5 per cent of retail sales. Increasingly, e-tailers are winning sales away from the traditional high street. For example, strong sales growth at Play.com, the online entertainment and electrical goods retailer and the UK arm of Amazon.com, had trading up 20 per cent in 2005 compared with the previous year, which was contrasting with falling sales at high-street music retailer HMV and the Ottakar's bookshop chain. Retailers with a combined Internet and high-street offering have performed better. John Lewis reported a 76 per cent year-on-year increase in sales in November and December 2005, helped by a 60 per cent increase in visits to the johnlewis.com website. The website took more than £100 m in sales over the year, boosted by sale of Apple's iPod music player. Argos reported a 37 per cent increase in Internet sales, contributing 6 per cent to overall revenue (Palmer, 2006).

Within the financial services sector, initially, home banking with telephone and television monitor linkage was envisaged. Yet this had a low take-up. Rather, direct telephone banking has been accepted by customers, which, in turn, has reduced the need for conventional bank branches, whose numbers have been reduced by most banks. Telephone and Internet online banking, working in conjunction with automated teller machines (ATMs), provide the benefits of usage flexibility (twenty-four hours a day) and the associated low costs. Lessons from the experience of the financial sector are being applied within other retail sectors. Increasingly, firms' websites are the initial sales window, reducing the need for conventional sales staff and shops in high-street locations.

As mentioned above, some retailers, such as M&S, have extended their charge card services to include other financial services previously offered only by the traditional banks, including mortgages, assurance and insurance. In 1997 Sainsbury's launched a fully licensed retail bank, Sainsbury's Bank, in a move to increase customer loyalty. Through a joint venture with the Bank of Scotland, Sainsbury's provided telephone banking services. It marketed Classic and Gold Visa credit cards as well as debit cards, savings and loan plans. The cards included incentive schemes linked with the Sainsbury's supermarket chain. However, as yet Sainbury's Bank performance has been disappointing, making a profit of £8m (US$14.4m) in 2004 against a three-year target of £90m (US$162m) and a loss of £5m (US$9m) in 2005 (Rigby, 2005d). Tesco, the leading UK food and FMCG retailer, also offers a wide range of financial services, including travel and house insurance. These ventures have posed a threat to traditional banking practices. The concerted retailer efforts, with the continued emphasis on price cutting, are achieving the desired customer loyalty and associated profits, taking custom from traditional banks and making the financial services market increasingly competitive.

In 2005 Tesco announced an interest in selling holiday travel much to the chagrin of conventional travel agents. It remains to be seen how successful that venture will be, but it is likely to introduce more price competition within the travel industry.

INTERNATIONAL EXPANSION OF THE RETAIL INDUSTRY

International expansion within the retail industry has been slower than for the manufacturing industry. From the UK it has been the consumer goods retailers rather than the food retailers that have expanded internationally (Alexander, 1997). M&S was one of the first retailers to expand internationally, starting within Belgium and France in the 1970s. It grew to have interests in over eighty countries covering North America, the Far East and continental Europe, including France, Spain and Germany. M&S's strategy was to take the UK operation to the international location, to accentuate the British element within its offering although making adjustments to suit local practices, e.g. introducing changing rooms in its Paris outlets prior to their introduction in the UK. Similarly, when Habitat, the designer household-ware retailer, expanded from the UK to France, it adapted its traditional UK approach to match local consumer tastes. However, in the late 1990s M&S experienced a severe downturn in performance and retrenched to the UK from most of its international locations, including France and Spain in Europe. Since then M&S has been under various take-over threats which, so far, it has been able to thwart. Other UK retailers have also had to retract their international expansion to the UK including Laura Ashley, the household and fashion clothes supplier, Thornton's chocolates and Boots the chemists, all operating in North America.

In the early 1990s some of the major UK food retailers began to expand to continental Europe. In 1992 Tesco bought Catteau, a small food retailer operating in northern France, but this was sold in 1998 to focus international expansion on CEE countries with underdeveloped retailing. From 1994 Tesco bought into retail groups in Poland, Hungary and the Czech and Slovak republics as well as opening its own superstores in Hungary. From 2000 it expanded its interests to the Far East, in particular to China. On the other hand, while Tesco expanded to CEE, Sainsbury's concentrated its expansion on the US, where it hoped to convince Americans that own-label products are a match for branded goods. But that expansion strategy was less successful so that Sainsbury's divested these interests in 2003. Interestingly, in 2005, Tesco announced its move to the US. It remains to be seen how successful this strategy will be.

Over this period, continental European retailers have directed their international expansion mostly across the continent and towards South America rather than to the UK. However, there has been some expansion to the UK. For example, Benetton, using franchising, expanded globally, including coverage of the UK. The Dutch C&A clothing group went to the UK as long ago as 1922, but latterly failed to cut a niche for itself between the higher-quality M&S and lower-priced Littlewood's and BHS multiples, so exited the UK a few years ago, although it continues with an international presence across Europe.

Among the European food retailers the Dutch Ahold expanded mainly to the US, from where it generates 40 per cent of its sales. It also operates across Europe and in 2005 announced a major acquisition programme in CEE. However, Ahold has encountered major financial problems that have obliged it to withdraw from many markets.

The German Aldi and Tenglemann have also expanded across Europe. Few of these continental European retailers have targeted the UK, where the strength of the leading grocery retailers would pose difficulties. Exceptionally, in the 1970s the French Carrefour, ranked top European retailer in 2003 (see Table 11.7) had a hypermarket in the UK in Wales but it retracted its UK expansion to favour expansion within continental Europe and South America and farther afield. By 1998 Carrefour had 369 hypermarkets in twenty countries, with its international operations contributing about half its profits (Hollinger, 1998). In 2005 Carrefour's overseas business continued to account for half its €90bn (£62bn) sales turnover, whereas Tesco's overseas sales provided a fifth (20.5 per cent) of its £37bn (US$66bn) turnover (Rigby, 2005c). In a move suggesting that grocery retailers have progressed in their operations from flag planting to a more mature approach of consolidation and concentration of international strategic interests, in 2005 Tesco and Carrefour agreed to exchange their assets in CEE and Taiwan. The move enabled the retailers to exit markets where they were weak in exchange for expansion in countries where they have stronger positions. The asset swap means that Tesco gained fifteen hypermarkets from Carrefour in Slovakia and the Czech Republic in exchange for six stores and two sites in Taiwan. Tesco paid Carrefour an additional €57.4m (£39.2m) to make up the difference in enterprise value between the retailers' respective assets (Rigby, 2005c).

During the 1980s and 1990s some continental European discounters, e.g. Germany's Aldi and Lidl and Denmark's Netto, expanded across Europe. Even in the US, where for years there was resistance to dealing with discounters, companies such as Sara Lee, P&G and Kimberly-Clark are starting to sell their most valued branded products on their shelves (Grant, 2005). Hard discounters are growing so fast and are used by so many shoppers across Europe that they cannot be ignored. The development is a recognition by US FMCG companies that the Wal-Mart retailing model, where branded products are sold alongside the retailer's own-label products, is growing fast in Europe. In Europe discounters have 40 per cent of retail sales in Germany, while in France and Spain they have 9 per cent and 10 per cent respectively. In Spain the Dia discount chain reported sales growth of 158 per cent from 1999 to 2003. In a study by Ronald Berger it was shown that the target audience of the discounters was so wide that it included shoppers who once might have shunned the discount stores (Grant, 2005). The study showed that the most successful brands in the period 2001–04 in Germany were the ones that had higher shares of sales in discount stores than rival brands. At the same time, discounters appreciate that selling branded products such as P&G's Pampers nappies/diapers is helping to attract customers. Lidl has been at the forefront of this trend in Germany, and has stocked products from P&G's rival, Unilever, for some time. Nevertheless, contrary to expectations, branded consumer goods companies currently appear able to resist any pressure from discounters for price cuts in their traditional retail outlets.

While the account above of the rapid development in the use of IT to improve operational and marketing effectiveness concentrated on the UK retail experience, similar developments have taken place internationally, although not necessarily at the same pace. For example, loyalty cards were introduced at the French Carrefour outlet in Castellon, Spain, only in September 2005, while they have been common in the UK for almost ten years, although general retail loyalty cards for petrol stations and airlines have been in use for some time in Spain. The high cost of IT investment necessary for introducing customer loyalty programmes may not be justified in all markets.

CONCLUSION

The nature of channels of distribution

Manufacturers and producers of goods and services use a variety of methods to move their products from the point of production to the consumer. They may go direct to the consumer or they may use the services of intermediaries to ensure that the products reach the consumer in the appropriate way to match demand. The intermediaries that are available along the value chain include sales agents, distributors, wholesalers and retailers and these may be used singly, or in conjunction with one another.

Developments among the intermediaries within the channels of distribution

During the 1990s pressures to achieve increased efficiency and control within the value chain led to considerable change among the intermediaries within the channels of distribution in terms of the nature of the services they provide. In the UK, while there was increased concentration on the larger grocery retailers, other retailers downsized to focus on key sectors. Change has continued into the twenty-first century at both national and global level. It is associated with the high investment in IT used to manage the operational and marketing activities of retailers as well as the activities of intermediaries within the supply chain. Retailer dominance is controlling manufacturer production and, increasingly, is used to manage customer demand.

There has been more and more pressure on the channel intermediaries, including sales agents, distributors and wholesalers. While sales agents continue to operate, especially within industrial markets and in association with international expansion, distributors and wholesalers have had to adapt their services, usually by extending their range of service provision. For example, some wholesalers have extended their services to include transport service provision over and above their traditional warehouse services; distributors have added component assembly to their product repair and service provision. Distributors are widening their customer base to service more than one customer, a move that leads to conflict with their original supplier.

The role of franchising within retailing

Franchising accounts for nearly one-third of retail sales. Its use enables retailers to expand with the minimum requirement of capital investment and encourages entrepreneurs wishing to set up new businesses to benefit from franchisors' marketing skills. While not without disadvantages, franchising does encourage expansion with fewer risks than in conventional new business enterprise.

Channel conflict management

Increasingly, the power within the supply chain is concentrated among the major retailers that are becoming ever more dominant. Conflict among the intermediaries arises as they fight to contribute to the process of moving goods through the supply chain to the ultimate consumer. While manufacturers might favour the conventional wholesaler to retailer route, yet retailers increasingly dominate the choice of intermediaries within the supply chain. The retailer can stipulate when, where and in what condition goods should be delivered to the retailer's distribution centre for despatch to the sales outlet. The retailer using the data gathered from its EPOS customer database determines the consumer demand in terms of the goods required, their quality and their price. The intermediaries within the supply are required to support the retailer to meet this consumer demand.

This dominance of retailers within the channels of distribution increasingly is critical in defining the nature of the marketing mix for the goods concerned. While the manufacturer appears to manage the marketing mix for the goods produced to match consumer demand, in practice it is the retailer that controls much of the decision making related to the marketing mix components. This poses questions concerning the control of the manufacturers' strategic management. Most certainly, increasingly retailers control the intermediaries within the channel of distribution and the nature of manufacturer production.

REVIEW QUESTIONS

1   Discuss the factors to be considered in setting up appropriate channels of distribution for a major food producer introducing a new brand of yoghurt.

2   How are the channels of distribution used for consumer goods likely to differ from those used for industrial products?

3   What can producers, sales agents, distributors and wholesalers do to counteract retailer dominance within the channels of distribution?

4   In what ways are retailing franchising arrangements beneficial to the consumer?

5   Evaluate how retailers have been influenced by the need for international expansion.

RECOMMENDED FURTHER READING

Akehurst, G. and Alexander, N. (eds) (1996) *The internationalisation of retailing*, London: Frank Cass.

Blythe, J. (1998) *Essentials of marketing*, London: Financial Times/Pittman, ch. 8, pp. 135–52.

Bromley, R.D.F. and Thomas, C.J. (eds) (1993) *Retail change*, London: UCL Press London.

Christopher, M. and Peck, H. (2003) *Marketing logistics*, 2nd edn, London: Butterworth Heinemann.

Corstjens, J. and Corstjens, M. (1995) *Store wars: the battle for mindspace and shelfspace*, Chichester: Wiley.

Davies, R.L. (1995) *Retail planning policies in Western Europe*, London: Routledge.

Fernie, J. and Sparks, L. (2004) *Logistics and retail management*, 2nd edn, London: Kogan Page.

Freathy, P. (2003) *The retailing book: principles and applications*, Harlow: Prentice Hall.

Guy, C. (1994) *The retail development process,* London: Routledge.

Hart, C. *et al.* (eds) (1997) *Cases in retailing,* Oxford: Blackwell.

Hoy, F. and Stanworth, J. (2003) *Franchising: an international perspective,* London and New York: Routledge.

Kahn, B.E. and McAlister, L. (1997) *Grocery revolution: the new focus on the consumer,* Reading, MA: Addison Wesley.

McGoldrick, P.J. (ed.) (1994) *Cases in retail marketing,* London: Pitman.

McGoldrick, P.J. (2002) *Retail marketing,* 2nd edn, Maidenhead: McGraw-Hill.

McGoldrick, P.J. and Davis, G. (eds) (1995) *International retailing,* London: Pitman.

Mendelsohn, M. (ed.) (1992) *Franchising in Europe,* London: Casell.

Miller, D., Jackson, P., Thrift, N. Holbrook, B. and Rowlands, M. (1998) *Shopping, place and identity,* London and New York: Routledge.

Newman, A.J. and Cullen, P. (2002) *Retailing: environment and operations,* London: Thomson.

Omar, O. (1999) *Retail marketing,* London: Pitman.

Spector, R. (2000*) Amazon.com: get big fast,* London: Random House.

Sternquist, B. (1998) *International retailing,* New York: Fairchild Press.

Sullivan, M. and Adcock, D. (2002) *Retailing marketing,* London: Thomson.

Varley, R. (2005) *Retail product management,* 2nd edn, Oxford: Routledge.

Varley, R. and Rafiq, M. (2002) *Retail management,* Basingstoke: Palgrave.

Walters, D. and Hanrahan, J. (2000) *Retail strategy: planning and control,* Basingstoke: Macmillan.

Wrigley, N. and Lowe, M. (2002) *Reading retail: a geographical perspective,* London: Arnold.

12 VIRTUAL MARKETING

LEARNING OBJECTIVES

On completion of this chapter you should be able to:

- understand the terminology used with respect to virtual marketing;

- appreciate the differences between the Internet and traditional media;

- consider the implications of the Internet for marketing theory and practice.

INTRODUCTION

Lamentably, discussion of the Internet is restricted in many marketing texts to a brief description of the role of email in direct marketing. Yet the Internet is so much more than this. As a new medium it constructs a new space and creates a new medium for exchange and for experience. The Internet may be described as a channel, but one where the poles are reversed and the consumer actively 'travels' to the seller's host site. The Internet is not just one channel but encompasses a range of media that are unique to it, in addition to subsuming other mainstream media such as newspapers and television. The Internet constructs new spaces in the Multi-User Domains (MUDs)[1] and websites which form a series of locations ranging from virtual communities such as 'TinyMud' to shopping malls and corporate sites. The Internet creates a new medium for exchange because novel constellations of buyers and sellers are brought together within the spaces contained within it. The Internet is complex. For example, it is possible for a virtual customer to wheel a virtual shopping trolley around a virtual store; to gain a 'feel' for the store through video; to select those items to purchase, place them in their virtual trolley, pay for the 'goods' and then leave. Everything is virtual, apart from the goods themselves which, hopefully, should arrive after a short period.

The Internet is more than any one of its constituent parts. Perhaps the most significant aspect to reflect upon is that it is in the early years of its development. It provides possibilities for novel forms of interaction and experience and that definitive judgements should not be made about it while it is in a rapid state of evolution. Having said that, there are several trends directly relevant to marketing which should be commented upon. The best way to study developments on the Internet is to use it. Consequently, this section has examples of sites that should be of interest. The only disadvantage of this is, of course, if the addresses of these sites change or if they should cease to exist, in which case you should know how to use a Web search engine.

THE INTERNET

The idea of a Wide Area Network (WAN) was first thought of in the 1960s with the earliest ancestor of the Internet (ARPANET) set up in 1969 in the US. The Internet comprises many physical computer networks in different countries, connected by telephone lines or satellite links. No one owns the Internet, nor does anyone pay for it. Instead all the participants pay for their part of the network, e.g. by way of paying for connection fees, telephone line charges and hardware set-up costs.

The Internet consists of the following. Probably email is its best known and most widely used feature, as it enables a speedy and efficient way to exchange text between two or more parties. Contemporary email systems allow files to be attached and transferred using File Transfer Protocol (FTP). Many files which are posted on the World Wide Web (the 'Web') are accessed and retrieved by browsers using FTP. Telnet allows users to log in to remote machines and run an interactive session. The Network File System (NFS) allows areas of disk on one machine to be accessed by another. To a user the remote disk appears to be a local one. Usenet News is a collection of computers which allow their users to exchange public messages on many different topics. Newsgroups are organized in a hierarchy of levels. The more useful levels for students would be those entitled 'soc', which refers to social and cultural discussions, and 'talk', which refers to high-traffic, noisy discussions. Most Usenet groups have a low signal-to-noise ratio, which in standard English means that there is considerable nonsense discussed on them. 'Flames', or insulting and angry diatribes against something or someone, are common, as is 'spamming', which is the multiple and inappropriate posting of messages to many newsgroups at the same time. Usenet messages are called articles and are grouped by topic into newsgroups. Discussions are organized into threads which refer to particular themes.

THE WORLD WIDE WEB

Many aspects of those systems briefly described above have been bundled into the Web, which is the first and current networked global implementation of a hypermedia Computer Mediated Environment (CME). The Web is both a text and a space. In one respect it can be viewed as a huge library or series of texts which are constructed using a special code known as HyperText Markup Language (HTML) using the Hypertext Transfer Protocol (HTTP). However, the Web may also be thought of as a linked chain of spaces or sites ranging from individual 'home' pages to organizational sites and online communities. The Web allows users of the medium to provide and interactively access hypermedia content and to communicate with each other.

Web penetration

This has changed markedly. Hoffman and Novak (1996) estimated that in 1996 around 30m people in the US aged 16 years and over had access to the Internet, which meant that 182.5m people did not, indicating that it was a minority activity in that country. More recent data shown in Figure 12.1 indicate that Internet use has increased dramatically since then in all 'developed' countries. Although there is a long way to go in the developing world, growing availability of WiFi 'hotspots' enables access to the 'wired' elite around the globe. As a marker of how indispensable it has become, one commentator is credited with saying that people would no sooner give up the Internet than give up their toilets (Hoffman and Novak, 2005).

The digital divide

The *digital divide* (Hoffman and Novak, 1999) is a term that has been coined to label the gulf that separates those who have ready access to Internet resources, and the competence to use them, from those who do not. There is a danger that because the Internet offers unique and often privileged access to a wide range of private and public resources this will further

Figure 12.1
Internet
penetration:
selected
countries

Source: Heriott-
Watt University
estimates.

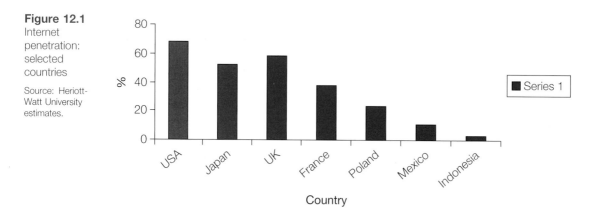

marginalize those who are already excluded. This includes the vast majority of those who live in what is known as the 'developing' world and includes the *quarte monde* constituted by the poor, the old, ethnic minorities and those who live in rural areas in 'developed' countries. If knowledge is power, then given that the Internet provides ready access to knowledge, those who are beyond its reach are further disempowered.

Value creation

Ideas change as to what constitutes value on the Web. In the 1990s a lot of effort was expended on the development of online 'malls'. At that time hardly anyone envisaged the reality. The Internet space is in a fluid and dynamic state. Because Internet spaces are being developed, huge companies must continue to deploy massive resources to fight battles on a number of fronts. Getting on to the Internet used to be a comparatively simple matter: you needed a PC to log on. Nowadays anything can be connected, from one's central heating boiler to the refrigerator, never mind mp3 players, phones, Blackberrys and televisions. At the same time battles are being fought over standards. The idea is that whoever sets the standard controls the market. Several decades ago Sony and Philips clashed in the battle over Betamax and VHS. Sony's Betamax was regarded as the better of the two systems but for various reasons VHS won the day – and a massive market. Another early example that demonstrates that what is better does not necessarily win out is that of the Apple MacIntosh, which lost the war, despite being much 'friendlier' to users than the IBM PC and its formidable Windows operating system. Below a few examples of value creation are discussed.

AUCTIONS

For the moment at least Ebay reigns supreme in the realm of virtual auctions. Until Ebay came along, despite the development of encryption, there were few who believed that consumers would risk spending more than $50 (£28) for an item on the Web. The rationale for this belief was that this was the sum that a person could accept losing without feeling too upset about it. Ebay identified and addressed a problem discussed by Williamson (1975) that is fundamental to the concepts of market and of organization. People prefer the freedom to do business in a market setting. The problem is that it is difficult, if not impossible, to establish a person's trustworthiness. In virtual space the problem is magnified, as a person can claim to be anyone they want to be. There are a few ways of addressing the issue of trust. One is to involve lawyers in drawing up expensive contracts. As these transaction costs reach a critical level it becomes more sensible to create an organization that subsumes some of the activities of the market. Through the development of Paypal, Ebay adapted an ancient practice to address the problem of trust in the electronic age. Paypal acts as a third party which holds the buyer's money on the seller's behalf (satisfying the seller) until the buyer has received the goods and has checked that they are satisfactory (which satisfies the buyer).

TELEPHONY

Just as Vodafone rose to challenge British Telecom in the early days of mobile telephony, Skype seemed to come from nowhere to challenge major telecommunications companies by enabling consumers easy access to VOIP (Voice Over Internet Protocol). This has forced other majors to offer packages to customers that enable them to switch to low-cost VOIP services when they are in the vicinity of WiFi 'hotspots', but to pay standard charges elsewhere. Additionally it allows them to charge premium rates for video downloads.

DIGITAL DOWNLOADS

Do you remember the Sony Walkman? Only a few years ago there were more Sony Walkmans around than there are mp3 players today. What happened? The 'Sony Memory Stick Walkman' was arguably the progenitor of today's mp3 players. Cunningham (2006), who bought one of them, argued that it was an excellent device that was years ahead of the arrival of the iPod. However, in Cunningham's view, Sony had an obsessive concern with controlling file transfer, which meant that he could not move the library of songs held on his PC on to another computer. By 2006 Apple's iTunes had gained 70 per cent of this rapidly expanding market. Through iTunes Apple does not simply offer music downloads but also provides tracks that are exclusive to its services from a number of top-selling artists. iTunes sells only in its own format, AAC, which is designed to be played on the iPod. The alternative WMA format offered by Microsoft can be played on devices from Creative, Rio, Dell and others. At the time of writing, Microsoft's MSN music offered more than a million songs (against the 2 million stocked by iTunes), and included some titles that could not be found on Apple's store. Unlike Apple, Microsoft acceded to artists' demands to sell only their complete albums and not individual songs. Other large brands include the now tamed Napster, MusicMatch Jukebox and Virgin Group, all of which offer music in WMA format. The more recent development of Windows' WMA system confronted Apple with a dilemma. It is debatable whether they should allow owners of iPods to access WMA files or should they 'tweak' new iPods to exclude them?

CONSUMER BEHAVIOUR ON THE WEB

Consumers engage in a variety of activities, some of which are shown below:

- *Research*: e.g. in researching the genealogy of their family history.
- *Work*: including remote tele-working.
- *Shopping*: surfing and gaining information about products.
- *Buying*: purchasing goods and services such as banking, travel and participating in auctions.
- *Instant chat*: Consumers have the ability to speak in real time to friends.
- *Catching up:* with current events such as reading sport, news, weather.
- *Games*: e.g. online chess and poker.

It should be emphasized at this point the way in which the Web encourages people to experience the dual roles of being a consumer and a producer. For example, a person may learn the rules of Ebay by watching an auction unfold. They may then participate by bidding for an item and eventually they buy their first item. Once they have signed up for Paypal they are ready to become virtual marketers themselves by offering goods for sale. One of us recently sold a car on Ebay and initially learned in this manner. The same holds for mp3 players like the iPod. A person initially buys an iPod to listen to music and to play videos. They then become aware that they can upload or 'podcast' their own blog (Web log), video footage or music to a site where it can be downloaded by millions of others.

Gender and Web use

In the early days of the Internet men used it more frequently than women. Over the last decade the number of women using the Web has increased to roughly the same proportion as men. However, the male 'geek' image has stuck and fuelled the stereotypical assumption that men and women use the Internet differently. This was explored in a study carried out by Hawfield and Lyons (1998).[2] The study investigated four common assumptions about women in relation to e-commerce, which were labelled 'conventional wisdom 1–4'.

1   The key to women is relationships.
2   Women are uncomfortable with technology.
3   Women love to shop.
4   Women are drawn to the Web by things like cosmetics and clothing.

The above correspond to what is taken to be the conventional stereotype of female behaviour. Hawfield and Lyons found that, with respect to the first claim, research suggests that there is no real difference between men and women with respect to seeking relationships or 'community' on the Web. While the 1998 GVU study found that overall this is true, it also found that more males than females reported feeling connected with professional and political groups on the Web, while more females reported feeling connected with religious

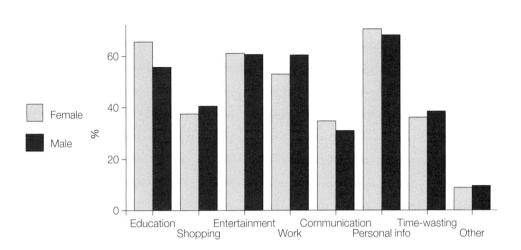

and support groups as well as families. Over 18 per cent of females reported feeling connected to groups associated with families by comparison with just under 15 per cent of males. While there is a difference between males and females on this score, there is considerable overlap.

Regarding the second conventional belief, that women are uncomfortable with technology, Hawfield and Lyons (1998) found that research suggests that it is the experience with technology that matters and that gender does not play a role.

In relation to Conventional Wisdom 3: Women love to shop, Hawfield and Lyons (1998) found that most women do not fit the 'love to shop' stereotype. This is backed by the GVU 1998 study, which, although it is dated, found that marginally more males than females reported using the Web for shopping purposes, which is shown in Figure 12.2.

Hawfield and Lyons (1998) found that some women reported experiencing benefits from the online shopping experience, including twenty-four-hour availability, access to purchase information and reduced sales pressure, which together made a more appealing alternative to the off-line equivalent. However, there was lack of enthusiasm for large commercial 'mall'-type sites, making it highly unlikely that women will be drawn to use the Web by the lure of cosmetics and clothing, although women do shop online, which is good news for retailers and advertisers. It was found that there is little evidence that women are interested primarily in retail categories like cosmetics and fragrances. Rather it was found that if women go online to search for information that helps in 'everyday' life, then sites that consolidate information on all aspects of women's lives come closest to what they search.

Experiences of Web use

Hoffman *et al.* (2004) divide Web use into four affective categories: Experiential, Rational, Overload and Entrapment. These will be discussed below.

EXPERIENTIAL

The experiential aspect of Web use highlights the manner in which this is a process of discovery that is positively engaging that brings people together. When surfing, people like to experience a sense of 'flow' (Hoffman *et al.*, 1996). In Chapter 3 Csikszentmihalyi (1977) discusses the extended self, describing flow as 'the holistic sensation that people experience when they act with total involvement'. Hoffman *et al.* borrow this term to describe the experience of surfing. In their explanation flow is:

> the state occurring during network navigation. It is:
>
> - characterised by a seamless sequence of responses facilitated by machine interactivity;
> - intrinsically enjoyable;
> - accompanied by a loss of self-consciousness;
> - self-reinforcing.

Flow has a seamless, drifting and almost dreamlike quality but one which is associated with a deep level of involvement. Hoffman *et al.* associate their explanation of flow as being in computer-mediated environments involving a high-involvement activity. The wake of a consumer's flow may be located in the clickstream, which is the record of the Uniform Resource Locators (URLs) and pages visited during the course of a Web session. Hoffman *et al.* proposed that flow has a number of positive marketing consequences, such as increased consumer learning, exploratory behaviour and positive affect (feeling). In a later study, Hoffman *et al.* (1998) explored the multidimensional aspects of the flow experience. Focused attention is a particular characteristic of high-involvement decision making and of the flow experience. The researchers found that focused attention was influenced by the degree of challenge, the importance of the search and the speed of interaction of the encounter. Speed of use was linked positively with the feeling of being in control, as was the consumer's skill in navigating the web. Both the feeling of being in control and the focused attention involved led to a feeling of playfulness and engendered a positive attitude. Skill and control are linked closely to flow and focused attention influences playfulness. The lessons for marketers from this study are that they should focus on the creation of environments which facilitate flow, which stimulate the creation of focused attention, which are fast, which enable feelings of control and provide a sense of challenge to the user or consumer. This, in turn, should lead to feelings of playfulness and of positive feelings or affect.

At a more general level commercial research indicates that the new generation will be even more committed to self-expression than Generation Y (anon., 2005a). Tweenies aged 8 to 12 are looking for ways to express their individuality in part by the products they choose. According to the report 55 per cent, an increase of 8 per cent over the previous year, are self-expressive, with their 'own way' of doing things, and are comfortable with, and cling to, their individuality. This is expressed in individualized ringtones on cellphones; instant messaging online in their own language and style.

RATIONAL

This builds on the ideas of freedom, empowerment and control that were described above. In this view the Internet provides powerful resources to enhance consumer rationality. For example, as discussed below, the Internet offers unrivalled opportunities for price comparison. Online consumers are thought to be highly involved and not as susceptible to advertising as they seek access to lots of sources of information about products and services. For example, for a major purchase such as a car, or mobile phone, most people will research the benefits and drawbacks of different models on the Internet prior to a visit to a showroom (anon., 2005b). Meanwhile new technology continues to erode the power of traditional media. For example, Digital Video Recorders (DVRs), Tivo and pop-up blockers enable consumers to determine their own viewing schedule and/or to skip advertising. However, there is another argument which suggests that consumers are not powerful when they use the Web. As discussed below under pricing, there is often little variation in prices offered on the Web. Additionally, increased industry concentration leads to reduced choice. Finally, as shown in the section on advertising below, Internet providers can track every aspect of the clickstream leading to purchase and can seek to control the behavioural setting in which consumption takes place.

From the point of view of business, consumers can seem to be unruly and even to be a threat to their business. For example, those who illegally use peer-to-peer networks in order to download copyright material are guilty technically of stealing. Consumers may file false identity information on sites. Ultimately they may form groups to boycott products.

OVERLOAD

Positive images of the experiential and rational consumer are counterbalanced by the negative experiential impact of overload. A feeling of frustration leading to overload is ever present in the following activities; ploughing unproductively through trivia; constantly being asked for passwords that are not remembered; removing spam from email; dealing with the difficulties imposed by spyware, cookies, remote diallers and viruses. Overload is increasing as workers seem to spend longer working at home without cutting back on work in the office (Nie and Erbring, 2000).

Researchers have noted the paradox that the Internet is used mainly for explicitly social reasons but can lead to a decline in social involvement and even to social isolation. People use the Internet to remain in contact with family and friends and to meet others through MUDs, chat rooms and via auction sites. However, Kraut *et al.* (1999) reported some initial findings from a longitudinal study which found that greater use of the Internet was associated with declines in participants' communication with others in the household, coupled with a reduction in the size of the social circle and increases in depression and loneliness. Nie and Erbring (2000) studied Internet use in the US. Their results support the findings of Kraut *et al.* (1999): a quarter of their respondents had reduced the amount of time spent with friends and family. In seeking to resolve the paradox mentioned above, it is suggested that people make shallower links with others online and are not nearly so likely to form long-term friendships.

ENTRAPMENT

There are those for whom the Internet has become an obsession and who feel trapped, enslaved and overwhelmed by it.

MARKETING AND THE INTERNET

In this section the implications of the Internet, and in particular the Web, are considered for marketing. In doing so the traditional approach is being followed, examining issues related to segmentation, targeting and positioning prior to a discussion of the marketing mix implications.

Segmentation, targeting and positioning

SRDS Lifestyle market analyst provides demographic and lifestyle segmentation analysis for the US.[3] A vast range of sites which are aimed at the particular requirements of different market segments have been developed. One such site is Senior.com[4] which targets the 'grey' market in the US.

Marketing mix: the product

Ultimately the Internet 'product' is literally the sum total of the experience (good or bad) which the user has derived from visiting a website. While the final product which is consumed is the users' experience of the site, a website is itself a form of product which can be targeted at a particular group of customers. It can be positioned to differentiate itself effectively from the competition by creating a source of sustainable competitive advantage.

Following Hoffman and Novak (1996) the optimum product will contribute most to the experience of 'flow', which was described earlier. A good site should be geared to fulfilling users' expectations and not what the producer thinks might be best for users. For example, it is becoming routine when buying books or CDs for site providers to show examples of other books or CDs in which the purchaser might be interested. Some purchasers will find this a valuable service; however, many others simply find it irritating. A good site will provide some means for users to attune the site and the service which it offers to their requirements.

Pricing issues

In the early days of its growth the development of the Internet seemed to signal bad times ahead for those who managed premium brands. They perceived the risk that years of expensive brand building would be put in jeopardy as buyers were led to focus more on price and less on the exclusivity and expensive aura with which they surrounded themselves. Traditionally, up-market brands have been available only from carefully selected retailers, e.g. leading department stores, fragrance houses and only those chemists with a genuine perfumery. Up-market brands have prevented price discounting by nurturing a more exclusive, premium image to support their relatively high prices. The development of the Internet allowing virtual organization seemed to signal a loss of control not only over distribution but also over pricing.

Not many years ago it was thought that shopping bots would enable customers to have more power over producers by reducing search costs to zero and providing them with the best prices. Shopping bots are software search agents that search thousands of websites for the best prices for commonly bought categories of goods, ranging from computer hardware and software to music, fragrances, books, gardening equipment and wine. The shopping agent, or bot, searches online stores for a desired product and returns a consolidated price list, usually with links to the sellers' sites. The idea behind shopbots makes economic common sense. If search costs are low then consumers will buy the cheapest available. If this is the case then Viaweb should have made a fortune through its shopbot Shopfind. Instead, by 2001 it was clear that the service was not making money and so Viaweb were forced to devise an alternative business model whereby Shopfind acts merely as a showcase for small to medium-sized companies. It is now hard to find any shopbots on the Web. So what went wrong?

For one thing companies began to develop blocking software in order to prevent bots from visiting their sites. Muhanna *et al.* (2005) argue from a supply point of view that intelligent agents such as shopbots enable suppliers to readily detect competitors' price reductions, using the same technology as consumers. As a consequence price competition between suppliers is perceived to be unsustainable. Say, for example, that a competitor reduces its price in order to pick up more trade. This initiative is picked up by the shopbot and is transmitted instantly to other competitors, who respond in kind. In a short time it becomes apparent to all that there is no incentive to reduce prices further. Another supply-side reason is that while a shopbot may signal those suppliers who offer the cheapest prices, the question of the trustworthiness of the supplier remains. The issue of trustworthiness is of prime importance on the Web, given the uncertainty as to identity on the Web and the risks associated with identity theft and entrusting one's financial details to others. Consequently it is thought that consumers are unlikely to do business with names with which they are unfamiliar.

From the demand side, a cognitive explanation might seek to explain this in terms of a consumer's attention and processing capacity. This differs from the rational economic explanation in that it suggests that consumers will not be too bothered by a difference in price if the difference is not noticeable. The classic economic argument is that a person should buy at the lowest price no matter what the difference is. However, Weber and Fechner coined the term 'Just Noticeable Difference' (JND) to illustrate their finding that the minimal perceptible difference is roughly proportional to the original intensity of the stimulus (Frank, 1990). The more intense the stimulus, the larger the difference has to be in absolute terms before we recognize it as being different. For example, if a bottle of Calvin Klein perfume costs US$50 (£28) in the shops, even though it is US$43 (£24) on the Web, the difference might not be perceived to be sufficiently different by a consumer to constitute a bargain.

ILLUSTRATION OF A 'SHOPBOT' SEARCH

Calvin Klein Obsession for Men Eau de Toilette 4 oz Fragrance Counter $43.00

Calvin Klein Obsession for Men spray 3.4 oz Scentiments $38.00

Obsession (Item No: OB15) EDT spray 4.0 oz. Empire Perfumes $43.95

Obsession C.Klein (Item No: MOBT40) EDT TST SP 4.0 oz Paris Fragrances $41.95

Calvin Klein Obsession Eau de Toilette Spray (No Box) 3.3 oz (100 ml) $42.95

Obsession EDT 4.0 oz Send-A-Scent $39.99

Obsession EDT Spray 4.0 oz Send-A-Scent $42.95

Obsession After Shave 4.0 oz Send-A-Scent $30.99

Obsession M EDT Spray 4.0 oz ScentStation $44.00

Calvin Klein Obsession Eau de Toilette Spray 4.0 oz. The Perfume Mart 45.00

Calvin Klein Obsession Cologne Spray 4 oz. FragranceNet $43.70

Rather a person might have a JND threshold of 20 per cent, which means that she will not think of this as a bargain until it is priced at around $40.

In practice, it is likely that a combination of factors is responsible for the failure of shopbots to catch on. Some time ago we asked Excite's Jango bot[5] to compare prices for Calvin Klein perfumes. The box shows what the shopbot came up with. The search yielded eleven sites, one of which had no address and included products offered by eight vendors. The products include Obsession for Men; Eau de Toilette Spray, After Shave and Cologne Spray. The products also differ by size, ranging from 3.3 oz to 4 oz. They are offered by a number of suppliers, most of whom are not instantly identifiable. Those price comparison sites that remain tend to focus on comparing major ongoing items of expenditure, e.g. heating, utilities, broadband, credit cards and loans (e.g. uswitch.com). However, customers have difficulties even when it comes to large differences in price for utilities. In 2005 there were large price differences in the offerings of UK energy providers but still a large number of customers did not switch.

Communications issues

Communications are central to any understanding of the Web. Below the differences between traditional and web-based communications are discussed. The ways that marketers seek to track the clickstream so as to target promotions are examined. Finally, the issues that marketers should attend to in promoting their products on the Web are considered.

DIFFERENCES BETWEEN TRADITIONAL AND VIRTUAL COMMUNICATIONS

One key question is what makes the Web different from conventional media? Hoffman and Novak (1996) point out that unlike the 'one to many' hypodermic model of communications discussed earlier, the Web is a many-to-many process. Consumers can interact with the medium, firms can provide content to the medium and, in the most radical departure from traditional marketing environments, consumers can provide commercially-oriented content to the medium. In this mediated model the primary relationships are not between sender and receiver but rather with the CME in which they interact. Often on entering the Web the user leaves a trail of 'clicks' as the individual follows his/her interest in moving from one site to another. This can take them in a 'journey' across countries. This journey is called by a number of names, among them 'surfing the Web' or 'following the clickstream'.

Authors have commented on the differences between traditional and virtual media. Some of the key differences are summarized in Table 12.1.

The typical communication process utilizing conventional media is the 'hypodermic needle' model which is described in Chapter 10. The sender–message–receiver model has been used to explain one-way mass communications involving one source and many receivers, using fixed media such as print or television advertising. This model assumes that the producer is active and the receiver is passive. The system is a mass-media delivery system whereby the majority of costs are incurred in booking media time. The aim of the mass communication is to 'tell and sell'; in other words, to make consumers aware of products and services and to persuade consumers to use them. Generally, it is only large companies which can afford the high costs of mass communications media to communicate effectively. Much mass-media communication is low-involvement communication. On the other hand, Internet communication often consists of two-way communication using email. While traditional communications are transported to the place of the sender through television and print media (hence their high cost of delivery), the Web user 'moves' to the source. Contrasting with the passive image of the television-viewing 'couch potato', the Web user is active.

A further difference between traditional media and Internet communications is with respect to costs. Primarily, the costs of traditional media are related to purchasing space on

Table 12.1 Differences between traditional and multimedia communications

Traditional	Multimedia
One-way communication	Two-way communication
Focus on fixed media	Focus on flow – the clickstream
Producer initiates	User initiates
Channel costs high	Bandwidth costs high
Appeals to customer self-image	Customer as part of community
'Tell/sell'	'Link/think'
Large companies	All sizes

the channel. Often the costs of booking space on television and print media are the most expensive component of advertising. By contrast it is bandwidth which carries the highest costs in Internet communications. The available band width is crucial to the notion of flow. Bandwidth is related to the capacity of the various channels to process information at a given time and place. Bandwidth is related to a number of factors, including the speed of the processor in the machine which is being used to access the Internet, the quality of the links between the user machine and the Internet Service Provider (ISP), the processing power of the service provider's network servers and of their international links. As bandwidth is fixed at any given point in time, the number of people using the Internet to transfer messages and files at any point in time will have a direct bearing on how long it takes to access files. For example, when accessing the Internet in the UK it is best to do so in the morning while most US users are asleep. By midday the time to access sites and files increases substantially as more US users log on to the Internet. The size of files is important. For a number of reasons the Web is ideally suited to the presentation of pictures and sound files rather than text. However, a picture takes a thousand times more data than a word and so as more and more sophisticated sites are created featuring video and sound file, the demands on the available bandwidth have grown.

SOME EXAMPLES: HARLEY-DAVIDSON AND MCDONALD'S6

A prime reason for people wishing to use the Web is to form links with other like-minded people. In the ninth GVU study (1998) 45 per cent of respondents stated such an aim. In addition to this 51 per cent of respondents had created their own websites. This latter figure supports the view that, once a person has paid the costs of connecting with an ISP, the costs and skills required to construct a site are not high. The implication of this is that someone with a small income can build a site which is just as impressive as that of a huge organization. Sometimes it is difficult to spot the identity of the core organization by browsing on the Web. For example, consider the following selection of sites that were found by carrying out a search for the cult US motorcycle manufacturers Harley-Davidson:

> Bob Dron Harley Davidson http://www.bobdron.com/
>
> North Texas HOG http://www.flash.net/~cmabrey/index.htm
>
> Wolverine Worldwidehttp://www.wolverineworldwide.com/brands/harley [lowbar]index.htm – manufacturers of Harley Davidson footwear.
>
> Ashfelt Angels magazine bi-monthly magazine for female Harley-Davidson owners http://www.asphaltangels.com/
>
> J&P Cycles. Claims to be America's largest dealer of parts and accessories for Harley-Davidson: http://www.j-pcycles.com/. Produces the *Motorcycle Dispatch* magazine devoted to Harley products.

The above list constitutes a small proportion of the actual sites which have been constructed. Many chapters of the Harley-Davidson Owners' Group (HOG) such as the North Texas chapter featured above, have created their own special websites. There are specialist sites and magazines for female Harley owners. Other sites have been established by distributors such as J&P Cycles, who also produce their own Harley magazine. From a traditional marketing communications point of view, the interesting point is that the actual Harley-Davidson Motorcycle site was not selected among the first fifty search choices. The implications are that the Web user is much more likely to discover discrepant messages concerned with the organization and its products than is the consumer of traditional marketing communications.

For example, consider McDonald's, the giant US hamburger chain. A search on the key word 'McDonald's' yielded a number of 'hits'. The first seven hits were analysed and are shown below:

1   Social Theory archives, June 1998 [at http://www.mailbase.ac.uk/
     lists-p-t/social-theory/1998–06/0123.html]

2   ETHOS News: McDonald's to introduce smartcard readers in 870 German
     restaurants [at http://www.tagish.co.uk/ethos/news/
     lit1/1010a.htm]

3   Crimes, Fires and Accidents, Gun Terror at McDonald's
     [at http://www.cwn.org.uk/999/9810/981014-mcdonalds.htm]

4   Reeve Analytical [at http://www.reeveltd.demon.co.uk/location.htm]

5   The Wonderful World of Jacinda Brunette

6   Social Theory archives, globalization and capital

7   East Berkshire Animal Aid

The above list is by no means extraordinary. Search engines such as Alta Visa will yield up hundreds of seemingly unrelated sites on a chosen topic. These sites contain a range of material.

1   First to be received was the post from the Mailbase (Usenet) Social Theory discussion group. Tom Scheff from Leeds Metropolitan University opens with the following. Tom Scheff says, 'An Australian policeman told me that McDonald's is the only company there that is NEVER vandalised.' 'Have you seen the size of Ronald McDonald's boots?'

2   ETHOS News is one of a growing number of news servers. This report concerns an agreement between McDonald's and Hewlett-Packard to install these into 870 German restaurants.

3   Report by *Coventry and Warwickshire News* 24 October 1998, which has the headline 'Gun terror at McDonald's' relating to an armed robbery at a local McDonald's in Coventry, England.

4   This is a company based in Glasgow, Scotland. The only reason reference is made to McDonald's is that it is featured in directions for those who wish to find Reeve: 'Turn right at McDonald's, Maryhill Road.'

5   The Wonderful World of Jacinda Brunette is a personal site which Jacinda has dedicated to her heroine, Celine Dion. The reference to McDonald's relates to the following: 'I work at McDonald's, and I think that everyone should see this website. It tells a lot about what's going on at McDonald's, the history of the company, and there are some games to play.'

6   This is a further message in the social theory thread featured in the first message. It is from Mark Cravalho in Brazil, who describes how McDonald's is perceived as offering good food in Brazil and is patronized by middle-class people because the food is regarded as being expensive. He then tells the following story: 'One incident that I found particularly interesting from a couple of years back. A pregnant woman found a beetle in her salad at McDonald's, and complained to the central management here (at the state level I believe). Their reaction was one of indignant outrage at her complaint. As I recall, they simply claimed that every care was taken. For as long as I followed the story in the paper, there was no attempt to even apologize to her let alone compensate her for the inconvenience. This seems pretty par for the course in these parts.'

7   This site is the home of East Berkshire Animal Aid in England. The page had last been updated in May 1997. McDonald's appears third on a highlighted list with the following text attached: 'McDonald's – We have produced a leaflet, 'McDonald's in their own words' which the text can be viewed here. The details in this leaflet were all taken from the McSpotlight pages, which document the libel case currently going on in the High Court in London. We recently picketed two local McDonald's including a Drive-Thru which had just opened, and handed out nearly 1000 leaflets in only a couple of hours.'

ANALYSIS

What can be learnt from the above jumbled pieces of information?

Judging from the way in which diverse groups from all over the world are juxtaposed – impersonal news services, McDonald's staff, academics and others 'chatting' to each other and a rural Animal Welfare group – it is curious that the site for McDonald's itself was not featured in the first seven hits! Message 1 illustrates what is meant in reality by the term 'low signal-to-noise ratio' for Usenet messages. In other words the message is trivial and could be regarded as being irritating by some.

The sites contain both positive and negative information from McDonald's point of view. On the positive side messages 1, 2 and 5 claim that McDonald's serves good food, is at the forefront of technology and at least one employee is also a fan of the company. Sites 1, 5 and 6 provide evidence for the idea that people use the Internet to achieve a sense of community. For example, Nos 1 and 6 link together two academics, one in England, the other in Brazil, while No. 5 is a site which a person has taken a great deal of time and care to construct in seeking to share her views with others. Site 3 provides a flavour of community as CWN is a local news site, while site 7 acts as a rallying point for local animal rights activists. The use of the Web for community building has been reported widely. In the ninth GVU Survey, 45 per cent of respondents stated that their purpose in using the Web was to become more connected with people like them and 51 per cent of the sample had created their own Web pages.

From McDonald's point of view sites 3, 6 and 7 raise negative and potentially damaging issues for the company. While the negative feelings in the content of the news report from site 3 may be associated with an external cause (armed robbers); the points made on sites 6 and 7 are potentially much more damaging. Site 7 contains a reference to the highly publicized 'McLibel' trial, which took place in 1997 and featured McDonald's lawsuit against two anarchists in London. As a result of this trial an anti-McDonald's website was constructed which is known as 'McSpotlight'. If one follows the clickstream to the McSpotlight[7] site, the following caption is displayed:

> McDonald's spends over \$2bn (£1.1m) a year broadcasting its glossy image to the world. This is a small space for alternatives to be heard.

In addition to this negative caption the McSpotlight site offers the following information:

- The 'McLibel' appeal begins in January 1999.
- The 'McLibel' video is to be shown at eighty venues around the world in 1999.
- Information about World Anti-McDonald's Day and other events.

The McSpotlight site is an anti-McDonald's site which has been constructed by those who are concerned to highlight information which may be potentially damaging or at least embarrassing to the company. The main difficulty for McDonald's is that it is not easy to deal with the allegations made on the McSpotlight site using the libel laws in any one country, as McSpotlight has three bases, one in the Netherlands and two 'mirror' sites in Australia and the US.

DISCUSSION

What can be said about these brief analyses of searches for Harley-Davidson and McDonald's?

- Web communications facilitate exchanges and a sense of community and solidarity among users.
- The identities of the companies themselves are obscured by a myriad of other groups and issues. For example, neither search yielded the official Harley-Davidson or McDonald's site. The only clue that either organization had a site was provided

Figure 12.3
Traditional
marketing
communications

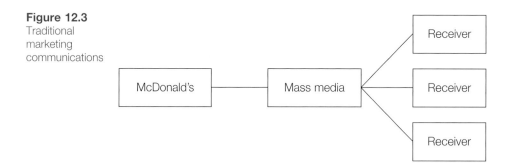

by Jacintha Brunette (site No. 5) who provided a link to the official McDonald's site. The proliferation of a large number of sites linked to the company makes the effective management of web communications difficult if not impossible for companies.

The above analysis highlights the differences between different forms of communication. Taking McDonald's as an example, Figure 12.3 summarizes the general flow of mass communications from McDonald's to its mass audience.

The pattern of communications follows the general S-M-R model which was discussed in Chapter 10. Here the sender (McDonald's and its advertising agency) encode messages which are then despatched through mass media, such as advertising, and are decoded by receivers. However, a model of Web-based communications based on the analysis which has just been conducted would look different. This is shown in Figure 12.4.

Figure 12.4 provides a partial view of the complexity of Internet communications. The key aspect is that people can behave in a number of roles with respect to the medium. A person can both provide media content and use the Web to access other sites. For example, the person who created the Jacinda Brunette site has produced the media content and may

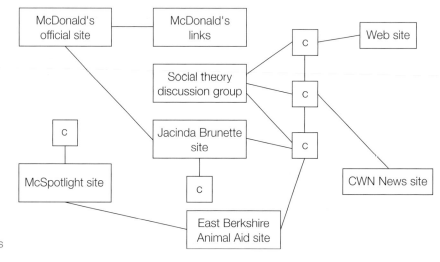

Figure 12.4
Internet-based
communications

participate in other Internet activities, by joining discussion groups such as Social Theory or through shopping, email or a number of other activities. Internet users are proactive and often communications are, but not necessarily, two way. A key difference between Web-based communications and traditional communications is that using the former the person interacts primarily with the environment itself.

The McDonald's 'McLibel' and 'McSpotlight' examples raise critical issues for marketers. As has been seen it is extremely difficult, if not impossible, for marketers to control the variety of information which is presented about their products, services and organizations in the marketing environment which is emerging. The implications are that marketers, and in particular brand managers, may begin to broaden their perceived primary role from a relatively narrow focus on advertising and sales promotion to one which emphasizes the creation of dialogue with others in seeking to influence public and media opinion.

TRACKING THE CLICKSTREAM

In contrast to traditional media online advertisers can use sophisticated technologies such as smart ad delivery and tracking on rich clickstream databases to develop individual models. Although online advertising has grown quickly, at around US$13bn (£7bn), this does not account for much of the US$250bn (£140bn) spent on advertising through traditional media. However, online banner advertising is of considerable importance to marketers, as it constitutes around 54 per cent of revenue. Online advertisers tend to use cost per thousand measurements in measuring consumer exposure to advertising. But advertisers want more than that to link exposure to actual response based on click through.

When a consumer clicks on a banner advertisement, a click-through is recorded in the server access log. Each time a consumer visits a website with an online advertisement an impression is recorded for the advertising sponsor. Research indicates that consumers rarely click on banner advertisements and, more worryingly for advertisers, that click-through rates have declined since the 1990s. Currently, less than three visitors out of every 1,000 click on a banner advertisement. With the importance of banner advertising, researchers have become interested in investigating the degree of 'wear-in' and 'wear-out' associated with it. Consumer responses to traditional communications follow an inverted U-shaped pattern. As it may take several exposures for a person to notice an advertisement, the communication must be repeated a number of times to enable it to 'wear-in'. After a threshold point has been reached 'wear-out' begins to take effect as each succeeding exposure reduces the probability that the advertisement will attract attention.

Researchers hypothesized that with Web banner advertising would be consistent with a 'wear-out' model. In other words because consumers are actively involved then it is likely that they will click on the advertisement the first time they see it and that this likelihood will be reduced thereafter. This is borne out by commercial studies of 'banner burnout' which show that the probability of a click is highest on the first banner advertisement exposure and then decreases, indicating that once consumers have attended to and recognized a banner ad they will ignore it. Despite these findings Chatterjee *et al.* (2003) thought that there might be differences between the majority of regular visitors to a website and those who visited it relatively infrequently. While the former group would notice the advertisement and then ignore it, the latter group could well fail to notice the advertisement for some time or might even forget that they had seen it on a previous occasion. If this were true then it would make sense for advertisers to construct different schedules of advertising for regular and more infrequent visitors to their sites. The study conducted by the authors confirmed that those who visit a site less frequently take some time to 'wear-in' to a banner advertisement.

OTHER ISSUES RELATING TO PROMOTION

Issues relevant to the topic of promotion include the use of email to promote products and the related issues of netiquette and spam and websites.

Netiquette and spam

During the early days of the Internet an informal but widely respected code of practice was developed which is known as 'netiquette'. Spam which involves the mass transmission of largely unwanted messages which usually are related to commercial activities was regarded as one of the worst violations of netiquette. One of the authors' worst experience of spam was a message which was received in 1998 entitled 'Investment Opportunities' and which was addressed to approximately 1,300 sites. The message was so large that it caused problems with the local mail server. When printed, the addresses covered twenty-eight pages while the content of the (unwanted) message took up less than one page.

Promoting websites

Once people have developed their website, often they think that they can sit back and wait for thousands of people to come and visit it. The Web does not work like that. For example, one of the authors created a site which deliberately was not publicized widely and has only been visited by fifty people. Once a site has been created and tested with a small sample of potential users, the next step is to promote it.

The site should be *highlighted on a list* revealed by a search engine such as Google, Lycos or Alta Vista. For this to happen those who operate the search engine should be notified of the site's existence. In addition, it is important that relevant key words are included on the welcome page as well as the site address on all traditional media such as letterheads and advertising. It helps if the domain name is similar to that with which users will be familiar. For example, it would be expected that McDonald's would be registered under the name 'McDonald's.com', which it is. Additionally, other users should be encouraged to provide links to the site. If a company is well known and well loved then fans will place links to corporate sites on their own pages (as in the case of Jacinda Brunette, the McDonald's employee). Potential users should be given a reason to visit the site. A key aspect of the 'flow' experience is that the visitor feels that the visit has been worth while. Depending

THE INTERNET COMPETING WITH TRADITIONAL CHANNELS: AMAZON.COM VERSUS BARNES & NOBLE

Jeffrey Bezos's Amazon.com is a textbook example of how to do things right in Web publishing. In 1994, being the first to start a Web-based bookselling service, Bezos chose a commodity ideally suited to the Web: a small-ticket item which could be identified easily and ordered and stocked by someone else with potentially high volumes. By 1995 Amazon.com could offer 2.5m titles and was selling around US$110m (£61m) books p.a.; two years later it had 1.5m customers and turned over its inventory forty-two times. By contrast the giant Barnes & Noble, the US's largest retail bookseller, with an annual turnover of US$3bn (£1.7bn), managed a stock turnover of only 2.1 in 1997. By the year 2000 the question was whether Amazon could fend off the challenge from Barnes & Noble, which was the world's largest bookseller.

At the time Barnes & Noble enjoyed a number of advantages over Amazon, most of them related to it owning a huge chain of stores. Amazon had limited capacity for storing stock whereas Barnes & Noble generated such volume in its own real-world stores that it could deal direct with publishers and stock a huge number of titles, enabling next-day or even same-day delivery to customers. Barnes & Noble wasted little time in developing its own Web-based operation, not least by copying aspects of the Amazon system. Barnes & Noble designed a web shopfront that was as inviting and useful as Amazon's, with easy-to-use subject indexes, online author events every day, book forums, book reviews and other features. In turn, Barnes & Noble made its own deals with heavily trafficked websites, including Yahoo (Amazon) and the *New York Times* Book Review. Barnes & Noble launched its site with 30 per cent discounts, forcing Amazon to match the cuts. As the war of attrition gathered pace it took its toll on Amazon's profits that were cut to a loss of over US$27m (£15m) in 1997.

In 1999 Amazon retaliated by suing Barnes & Noble for copying aspects of the Amazon system. It constructed a network of expensive distribution centres in seeking to match Barnes & Noble's responsiveness. Amazon took the competition to Barnes & Noble by announcing free delivery on a variety of products, an expensive gesture, amounting to $475m (£265m) in 2005. Furthermore, it launched Amazon Prime, which enabled consumers unlimited free delivery for US$79 (£44) p.a., another service that was very expensive.

As Amazon expanded outside its core books, music, DVD and video area it became clear that Amazon had ideas far beyond the confines of the book market. By 2006 Amazon activities included selling electronics, tools and kitchen equipment which reputedly accounted for 26 per cent of turnover as well as B-to-B services, including alliances with Toys 'R' Us and other merchants. By the end of 2005 international sales accounted for 45 per cent of Amazon's turnover. Overall turnover grew from US$6.9bn (£3.9bn) in 2004 to US$8.5bn (£4.7bn) in 2005. Amazon expanded into clothing and introduced an online auction site to compete with Ebay. Profitability was more variable, falling 39 per cent to US$399m (£222m) in 2005 against US$588m (£328m) in 2004. By contrast Barnes & Noble profits were US$419m (£234m) on a turnover of US$4.1 bn (£2.2 bn) in 2005.

Sources: adapted from Stross (1997), Jaffe (1998) and Willis (1998).

INTERNET ETHICS: THE DANISH CONSUMER OMBUDSMAN IDENTIFYING HIDDEN ADVERTISEMENTS ON THE NET[8]

In 2003 the office of the Danish Consumer Ombudsman conducted a survey of websites targeted towards children. The survey was conducted on 24 June and surveyed ninety-two websites to identify hidden advertising. In a report the previous year, the Ombudsman had suggested that the best way in which to address this issue was for children and adults to be taught to take an informed, objective and critical approach to advertisements. The report recommended a more long-term focus on media education, which should be given a permanent and legitimate place in school curricula. The 2003 report was much tougher. This time the Ombudsman recommended a ban on websites with a direct or indirect commercial message aimed at children and young people.

The survey found that most websites in Norway, Sweden and Denmark contained advertising in one form or another, regardless of which pages were surveyed. Finland was an exception, with only 23 per cent of the surveyed websites containing advertising. The products advertised most frequently were music, films and sweets, which concerned the investigators, as they can be bought by children from their pocket money, without involving their parents.

The survey scrutinized the websites of many familiar brands, including Coca-Cola, Disney, Lego, MSN/Orange, Krea and EuroToys. Investigators found that many of the largest producers and retailers' websites combined advertising and entertainment, using powerful tools such as live images, audio effects and interactivity to engage children directly by participating in the marketing games. For example, in some situations the child takes part in 'advergaming'; the situation where an advertisement is hidden within a game. The child plays with or against brand logos, or guides characters linked with products in search of adventure or helps the characters carry out specific tasks. The Ombudsman was concerned that this subtle mix of entertainment and advertising is beyond the comprehension of many young children. He felt that marketing should be designed so it is obvious to the target age group that marketing is involved.

The report scathingly noted that large companies exploit children loving to play games by providing free games and activities on their websites. Companies such as Disney and Lego are so well known that they do not even have to supply a logo for the brand to be recognized. These companies are accused of manipulating vulnerable children so as to turn them into loyal consumers who will wish for and buy the company's products, preferably whole series of them. The report noted that companies seek to incorporate the universe they have created on their websites into the daily lives of children in a systematic way: through educational materials, television commercials and documentary-style entertainment programmes. They imprint trade marks and logos even on very young children, according to the formula: 'The earlier you start, the better the impact of imprinting, so children will never forget it.'

Websites for mobile phone companies made use of more conventional advertising elements such as logos and product presentations. These sites had games and competitions as well. However, because the advertising element was identifiable, it was considered not hidden. These websites provided a perfect sales promotion tool for telecoms companies, by encouraging young people to visit and get the latest ring tones, new exciting logos, games, horoscopes and fresh jokes to send to friends. Researchers found that they could also send image messages, i.e. if their phone had an integrated camera. One website offered a test where young people could find out if they have picked the right girlfriend or boyfriend, or whether they were compatible with their 'true love'. All they had to do was to grab their mobile phone and follow the instructions on the site. The investigators argued that this type of marketing is even more effective than traditional sales promotion methods such as free gifts and prize competitions, forms of marketing that the Danish Marketing Practices Act prohibits if the gift or prize competition is conditional on a purchase.

The report concluded that companies exploit the natural gullibility and lack of experience of children and young people. Both types of website, (1) the Disney model and (2) those with obvious sales promotion, encourage them to buy things. They do not comply with the Nordic Consumer Ombudsmen's position statement on marketing directed at children and young people.

on user requirements the site could feature some form of interactive facility, or perhaps some text or music which can be downloaded.

Another approach is to *advertise on a highly trafficked site* such as a search engine or a heavily used news site.

The *interactive potential* of the Internet poses a major challenge for the assumptions embedded into 'one to many' forms of marketing communications such as advertising. Already this challenge has found a material basis with the proliferation of media, e.g. the growth of digital television networks offering hundreds of channels which is forming itself rapidly into a meta-network which, eventually, may be subsumed within the Internet. The resulting fragmentation of traditional media audiences together with the increased potential for interactivity has created a battle between marketing communicators for the ever precious attention of the consumer. Consumer attention is the gold dust of all marketing communications, as it forms the basis of consumer involvement and of consumer awareness, which is in turn the baseline of the hierarchy of effects. Marketers have been ingenious in devising new spaces for marketing communications.

Of course, the website itself is a prime promotional vehicle, as it can be used to *convey information* about the company and its products in an interesting and informative manner. However, this has its problems, as sites which attract vulnerable groups such as children may be acting against the public interest. The last two case studies at the end of this chapter, entitled 'Internet ethics: news from the Danish consumer ombudsman' and 'Walt Disney, waltzing into trouble?' introduce relevant pointers. As media fragment, advertisers are turning to other means to attract consumer attention. Routinely advertisements are being inserted into computer games formats. Another approach has been to sponsor communication on mobile phones and Personal Digital Assistant (PDAs). The way this works is that the user has the cost of using a phone, or PDA, subsidized in return for agreeing to listen to an advertisement while placing a phone call or sending a fax. Another approach would involve subscribers to 'pay per view' television agreeing to watch an advertisement and complete a brief questionnaire in return for subsidized viewing of the movie of their choice. According to Schrage *et al.* (1993) companies considered placing a fax machine into consumers' homes for free providing they fill in a product use questionnaire every month and agreed to receive a limited quantity of unsolicited commercial fax messages each week.

The Web allows marketers to combine promotions with education. Two important features of the Web are its potential for interactivity and its multimedia capability. Together these allow the development of useful educational sites.

CONCLUSION

This chapter reviews developments on the Internet and especially on the World Wide Web. Aspects of value creation on the Web, including auctions, telephony and digital downloads, have been discussed. Having read this chapter you should know more about consumer behaviour on the Web, especially about gender and Web use. You should be in a position to use the framework devised by Hoffman *et al.* (2004) in discussing four aspects of Web use, including experiential, rational, overload and entrapment. Finally, you should have an understanding of the implications of Web use for marketing practice. It is useful to appreciate the extent to which Web users act as rational agents who seek the lowest price. You should be aware of the differences between traditional communications and Web-based communications. You should be able to understand more about the extent to which the Internet really does empower the consumer.

REVIEW QUESTIONS

1 What are the key differences between traditional media and the Internet?
2 What is meant by 'flow'? Which factors can inhibit flow and how can it be enhanced?
3 What is the key consequence of Internet communications for marketers?
4 Describe how a website should be promoted.
5 How did Amazon.com establish an early lead in this area?
6 How has the pattern of competition faced by Amazon changed in recent years?
7 What is your view concerning the Consumer Ombudsman's report with respect to contact with children and young persons?
8 What are the future implications for marketing on the Internet if there are no prospects for the development of international consumer protection rules?
9 State your reasons as to whether you agree or disagree with the National Consumer Agency of Denmark's view of Web advertising to children?
10 Try to visit the official Walt Disney website. Do you agree or disagree with the National Consumer Agency of Denmark's view with respect to Walt Disney? You may wish to visit the Kellogg's (makers of cereal) site, as this was also found to have infringed the code.

11   In the light of the above, consider what would need to be put in place for the Internet to be effectively regulated.

12   Do you agree with the further regulation of the Internet and the Web?

RECOMMENDED FURTHER READING

Siegel, C. (2004) *Internet marketing: foundations and applications*, Boston MA, Houghton Mifflin.

13 MARKETING PLANNING AND IMPLEMENTATION

LEARNING OBJECTIVES

When you have completed this unit, you should:

- know the route through which planning for marketing should take place;

- understand the stages involved in planning;

- be aware of the advantages of planning;

- be attentive to the challenges posed by planning;

- appreciate the role of planning related to marketing in business.

INTRODUCTION

Marketing does not just happen. Products and services have to be developed in the most efficient manner to ensure that the goods or services reach the consumer in the right manner at the right place, time and price to create customer satisfaction and appropriate profit to the supplier. It is the planning required throughout the marketing process that will be discussed in this chapter.

The nature of planning

While it may be tempting for a young entrepreneur to rush off to market his/her brainchild new product or service, yet very soon hurdles will be encountered for which he/she is not prepared. The good idea will be unlikely to be successfully implemented, causing considerable loss of face, time and money through the venture. Although frustrating, it is better to sit down and plan out the process of getting the offering to market. However, as discussed in Chapter 2, good planning takes time and careful consideration to implement. Even established marketers who have products at various stages of the PLC find marketing planning challenging. Various academics have written useful texts which will provide further guidance to the process of developing and implementing effective marketing plans. The reader is referred to the work of McDonald (2002) and Cooper and Lane (1997) that discuss general marketing planning issues and to McDonald and Payne (1996) who extend the coverage to services marketing.

Business plan

The business plan is central to the planning process, often being the critical document that is needed to persuade others to support the venture. Business plans form a framework which outline the route to reach the business goals. Usually, business plans are made to cover a period of up to three, maybe even five years. Generally the detail is provided for year 1 of the operation, with more indicative expectations thereafter for years 2 and 3. Many business plans are prepared as part of the process of getting financing in the form of venture capital or loans from a bank, or equivalent institution. The firm's management will require the plan to ascertain that the proposals have been well considered and that projections of likely performance match expectations. The business plan will incorporate details of the proposed marketing plan (see Box 13.1) showing the direction that the marketing mix is expected to take. It will give estimates of customer demand in terms of market size, competitor activity, projected profit and loss together with the time scale, human resource and financial implications estimates. Supporting evidence in the form of test marketing findings may also be provided in the plan.

Generally, while the business plan is taken as the 'blueprint' for the venture to follow, it should not be a document that is written on tablets of stone. It should be prepared meticulously, using, as far as is practically possible, the most accurate market data available. Time spent at this early stage can avoid costly mistakes as the plan is put into practice.

<table>
<tr><td>

**B
O
X**

13.1

</td><td>

STRUCTURE AND CONTENTS OF A TYPICAL BUSINESS MARKETING PLAN

Business mission

Mission statement encompassing the whole operation, often following a general goal, e.g. to be 'market leader', 'the most ethically aware' or 'the most innovative supplier of goods and services' within a selected industry

Corporate objective

Covers the specifics of the business mission statement. Usually objectives are given in quantifiable terms, e.g. to achieve a given turnover, profit, market share or to increase on the previous year's performance; supporting qualitative objectives may be used, e.g. to raise product quality awareness among customers

Environmental audit

Market environment in which the firm operates in terms of Political (including legal), Economic, Social and Technological (PEST) issues

Marketing audit

Analysis competitor acivity, providing relative position of the organization within the market. It involves undertaking a SWOT analysis covering:

■　Firm's internal strengths and weaknesses;
■　Firm's external opportunities and threats.

Market analysis

Involves assessment of market size, trends and segments; regional and local market characteristics; seasonal variations in sales, etc.

Marketing objective and major strategies

Defines objectives in terms of forecasts of increased sales, customer awareness, channel coverage for the product or service, etc. Corporate strategies relate to the analyses of environmental and marketing audits discussed above

Marketing programmes and tactics

Implementation of marketing tactics to achieve the strategic objectives through the marketing mix, balancing product development, pricing, promotion and channels of distribution (place) decisions

</td></tr>
</table>

Market information analysis

Discovery of market gaps, new markets/segments, customer characteristics, product life-cycle positioning and targeting, etc. It incorporates developing the Marketing Information System (MIS), marketing research methodology and marketing research implementation including selection of marketing research agency, if appropriate

Marketing mix

Favoured combination of product, price, promotion and channels of distribution (place) approaches

Product

Assessment of product characteristics, range, features; sales trends, performance history and planned developments. Ascertaining competitive analysis and advantage

Pricing

Assessment of positioning strategy, customer-perceived values. Ascertaining competitive analysis and advantage

Promotion

Assessment of media advertising, direct mail, sales promotions, sponsorship, exhibitions, public relations, selling activity and measurement of communication effectiveness. Ascertaining competitive analysis and advantage

Place – channels of distribution

Assessment of channel strategy, channel selection, selling strategy, sales plan and sales force organization. Ascertaining competitive analysis and advantage

Resources

Constraints within which plan has to operate

Finance

Marketing budget, revenue and gross margin forecast, target marketing ratios and cash flow projection

Time

Scheduling of proposed marketing activities within the plan (often portrayed using a Gantt chart)

Human resource management

Personnel requirements for implementing the plan, including appropriate recruitment and training

ID	Task name	Start	Finish	Duration
1	Reduction of can production	01/06/2005	28/06/2005	4w
2	Recruitment of additional sales force	29/06/2005	10/06/2005	6.2w
3	Contact Philip Stark and Design team	11/08/2005	22/08/2005	1.6w
4	Training of sales force	23/08/2005	16/09/2005	3.8w
5	Contact and work with advertising agency	19/09/2005	31/10/2005	6.2w
6	Involve sales force to communicate image and reputation as market leader	01/11/2005	01/05/2008	130.6w
7	Increase price	01/12/2005	02/12/2005	4w
8	Incorporate design changes into campaign	05/12/2005	13/01/2006	6w
9	Change and improve bottle design	16/01/2006	02/02/2006	2.8w
10	Incorporate outdoor media advertising: posters and billboards in campaign	01/06/2005	28/06/2005	13.8w
11	Start communication campaign in Hotel bars and Restaurants conveying premium image with trained salesforce	03/02/2006	10/05/2006	13.8w
12	Change labelling and packaging	11/05/2006	30/06/2006	7.4w
13	Release of TV advertisement	03/07/2006	31/10/2006	17.4w
14	Increase price	01/11/2006	01/11/2006	.2w
15	Repeat action of outdoor media advertising	01/11/2006	30/01/2007	13w
16	Sponsoring of tournaments, exhibition and charity events	01/06/2005	01/05/2008	152.4w
17	Communicate image as market leader	01/06/2005	01/05/2008	152.4w
18	Use product placement in TV shows, films and soap operas	01/06/2005	01/05/2008	152.4w

Figure 13.1
An example of a Gantt chart used in marketing planning

However, ultimately, the plan acts as a guide which may have to be adjusted and revised over time to match the market conditions faced in its implementation. The business plan is a tool to help manage the venture through the various stages of its development.

SETTING OUT THE MISSION, AIMS AND OBJECTIVES

Initially, when starting the business, a mission statement should be determined to show where management wishes to strive to reach in due course. Usually, this statement is succinct, indicating an overall, even idealized, objective for the business. For example, it might be 'to become the leader in the mobile phone market' which in turn could be interpreted as being the provider of the most mobile phones in terms of sales and/or market share. It might also mean developing the most innovative mobile phones or of providing the 'best' customer service in the mobile phone market. 'Best' can be interpreted along a number of criteria such as in terms of new customers achieved, retained customers, customer satisfaction surveys, etc.

The aims, or objectives, of the business need to be defined as precisely as possible to match the requirements of the mission statement. They should follow the marketing strategy that has been determined, i.e. product differentiation, market differentiation, product development, cost focus or whatever other strategic direction that is favoured.

Market segmentation, targeting and positioning

At this stage it may be appropriate to undertake some form of market segmentation, targeting and positioning as discussed in Chapter 5. Segmentation, targeting and positioning can be directed towards the market in terms of what type of mobile phone to introduce, for what group of potential customers. Assuming the market could be divided into innovators and laggards in taking up the proposed product. If the latest technology was favoured it could be directed to younger, wealthier adults in their late 20s and early 30s who would be most likely to be innovators ready to consider the novel characteristics of the product. Alternatively, it could be found that there remains a sizable market of potential customers who are not particularly concerned to have the latest technological developments, the laggards, who would prefer the well tried, lower-cost phones. In this case, an older age group, perhaps, 45 years and above, might be targeted. Consideration could be made not only concerning the demographics of the selected market segment but also its geographical location. The more sophisticated and expensive phone could be targeted towards the markets in Germany, Hong Kong, Sweden and the UK, whereas the established phone might be directed towards less developed markets and economies. In this way, segmentation can take place on a number of criteria, but care should be taken that the process of segmentation does not become too burdensome as to be ineffective. Appropriate marketing positioning strategies will need to be put in place to enable the targeted customers to become aware of the product, or service offering. This will involve consideration of the marketing mix and the related nuances discussed in Chapters 7–10.

Marketing mix implications

With the increasing trend to outsource much of the internal operations care has to be taken that all concerned are aware of what is expected to be done. Usually a project brief is prepared and agreed by all the persons involved. While the practice of preparing briefs for contracts is commonplace for subcontracting, it is less common for internal arrangements. Sometimes the excuse is made that there is not time to prepare a comprehensive brief, or it may be felt that those involved know the project well enough not to have to formalize it through the preparation of a brief. This is a mistake. Time taken to clarify what is required of those involved in undertaking the work should help to avoid misinformation and will improve the end result. The better the understanding of the objectives of work the better will be the outcome of project.

TEST MARKETING

Test marketing (see Chapter 8) at the introductory stages of the PLC and even as the product is delivered during the development and mature stages can be helpful in management decision making. Test marketing can be undertaken using internal staff, in particular if it relates to testing in the industrial market. In this instance, internal staff are more likely to have the necessary expertise regarding the product technology and be better able to communicate with actual and potential customers. However, there is the risk that internal staff may be prone to bias in favour of introducing a product with which they have become very committed. In the case of new products entering the consumer market, it is more usual to have test marketing sub-contracted to a marketing agency. While costs may appear to be higher, the benefit is that the firm will not need to employ specialist staff on a permanent basis, but rather will use the services of the marketing research agency as, and when, necessary. There is the added advantage that the marketing research staff will be unbiased as to the outcome of the research findings.

RESEARCH BRIEF

Whatever the chosen situation, a marketing research brief should be drawn up for the project and agreed by all concerned. The objectives of the project have to be clearly defined. An indication of the resources to be used in terms of time, human resources and financial implications should be made and agreed in the final contract. Generally, the project brief is put out to tender and directed to appropriate marketing research agencies that, in turn, submit their proposals and budgets for consideration. Once the offerings have been examined, one will be selected to undertake the project and the formal contract drawn up and signed. Details as to who within the marketing research agency will undertake the research have to be agreed. In particular, the level of senior executive involvement in the project is likely to be critical to its successful completion. Usually the firm appoints a co-ordinator from within to liaise with the marketing research agency and monitor the progress of the project. In this way any problems that may arise can be dealt with appropriately and possible misunderstandings minimized.

The planning process for undertaking any marketing research should be considered carefully within the overall marketing plan.

PRODUCT

As discussed in Chapter 8, products and services can be introduced at various stages of the PLC. Those with the highest risk are those which are new to the market e.g. Furby (see the case study 'Feeding the Furby fad'), the cabbage patch doll, the Rubic cube and, recently, the delicate issue of introducing adult sex toys through UK traditional leading grocery and pharmacy retailers. Test marketing can be used to support marketing management decision making regarding specifics of product development.

PRICE

Chapter 9 considers the issues of pricing decision making. Careful monitoring through the MIS (see p. 115) can check pricing issues. Internal sales records can show the relationship between prices and sales achieved, providing an indication of the product's position in the PLC. Test marketing undertaken before introducing the product, and sometimes even at the more mature stages of the PLC, may be used to determine favourable pricing strategies. Pricing adjustments can be made in the light of changing conditions influencing consumer demand and competitor activity.

PROMOTION

As part of the marketing mix it is usual to undertake some form of promotional activity as discussed in Chapter 10. This is likely to include both 'above the line' paid-for advertising using the media and 'below the line', including sales promotion, sponsorship, personal selling and public relations (PR). Planning marketing communications campaigns is detailed at p. 308.

For test marketing, it is common practice for responsibility for consumer product advertising to be contracted out to advertising agencies (see pp. 322–326, especially p. 325). In the same way as for test marketing, a project brief has to be prepared and put out for tender to targeted advertising agencies. Once an advertising agency is selected, the final project brief is drawn up covering details of the project contract that has to be agreed by all parties concerned. In particular, the resource implications have to be formalized. As the project progresses it is useful to develop a detailed creative brief to provide a framework for the creative team to work. Figure 10.8 illustrates the topics that are likely to be covered in the creative brief including the reason for undertaking the advertising, the target market and consumer opinion. Issues such as approaches to branding messages may also be highlighted.

For industrial products and services it may not be necessary, or appropriate, to use advertising agencies at all. Rather, any promotional activity is likely to be undertaken within the firm, using internal staff who would have the necessary specialist technical expertise, e.g. sales engineers or even a dedicated advertising section operating within the marketing department. The firm's personnel can prepare and place advertisements directly in the technical press. Similarly, for trade exhibitions internal staff usually organize and develop display material for the event.

Whatever form the promotional communications take, it is likely to involve a relatively high share of the marketing budget, typically up to 6 per cent for FMCG. As such it is important that it should be planned carefully so as to make an effective contribution to the marketing effort, especially in terms of resource implications. As with contracting out test marketing to marketing research agencies, someone from within the firm should be appointed to liaise with the advertising agency. The agency will have its own account planner dedicated to monitoring the progress of the contract who should report to the firm's representative. In this way, understanding and trust between the various parties involved are increased and the contract is more likely to be completed to the satisfaction of all concerned.

PLACE: CHANNELS OF DISTRIBUTION

Decisions require to be made concerning the 'place' or choice of channels of distribution to be used to get the product or service to markets (see Chapter 11). These may take the form of the traditional options from the producer going direct to the end user to introducing various levels of intermediaries along the value chain. Increasingly, the role of the Internet for online shopping is adding another dimension to available channel choices. It may be used on its own or in conjunction with the traditional options between the producer, intermediaries such as wholesalers and jobbers, and retailers.

Plans should take into account that while a favoured channel route might be favoured, it may not be possible to gain access to the desired channels. The leading grocery retailers are unlikely to give shelf space to new products that they have not sanctioned. Rather, new products have to proceed through a laborious process to gain acceptance. Not only do the products have to be on the retailers' favoured product range list, new suppliers have to pass rigorous tests such as favourable test marketing evidence, competitive costing and adequate supply potential. Marketing plans should accommodate the considerable time that it can take to gain product acceptance from the retailers.

SERVICES

For services additional elements of the marketing mix should be considered, as follows:

People

The persons involved in providing the service make a critical contribution to the service experienced by the end user that will influence possible repeat business and word-of-mouth promotion. For example, while a reputable chef can produce a formidable dish, it requires to be served in the expected manner by a pleasant, courteous waiter or waitress. Should there be a lack of rapport with the waiter or waitress and the customer, no matter how well prepared the dish might be, the customer may fail to appreciate the supporting service and not return to the restaurant. Indeed, the customer may even openly criticize the service to other friends, thereby deterring their using the restaurant.

Processes

The operational processes whereby the service is provided influence the ultimate service experienced. Taking the example of the restaurant, numerous operations have to be undertaken to get the chef's dish to the customer's table. A menu has to be prepared. Food has to be bought from the market or wholesaler; it has to be cleaned and cooked; the dining room and tables have to be set; someone has to take the customer's order and to serve the meal. Drinks need to be ordered and served. The bill has to be made out and so on. All these procedures require to be undertaken efficiently, often by different persons, so that the customer can experience the appropriate service and end product.

The physical environment

The actual environment in which the service is provided also influences the service experienced. Referring to the example of the chef's dish and the restaurant, the ambience of the room in which the chef's meal is served will reflect on the way in which the customer will judge the quality of the dish. For example, if the restaurant is cold and draughty the customer is unlikely to enjoy the meal in the same way as if he/she were sitting cosy in front of a warm log fire. Smells may also influence customer reaction. Consequently, grocery retailers often introduce baking smells at the front entrance of a superstore to encourage customers to purchase more bakery products.

Resource implications

TIME

The marketing plan should show time markers as to when the various activities to get the product to market will take place. The most accurate estimates of time expectations should be made and some allowance for unforeseen occurrences should be allocated. It is most likely, especially for new products coming on to the market, that lead times to reach goals will be longer than initially expected. Problems of an unexpected nature may be encountered, e.g. excessive time to obtain necessary licences to operate, difficulty in obtaining suitable premises in the desirable locations or simply challenges in production, hiring suitable staff, etc.

It is usual to show the proposed time schedule on a Gantt chart (see Figure 13.1). Time is shown across the chart, with the various tasks listed below so that the timing and duration of the tasks can be given. In this way a clear view of what is to be done and when it should be undertaken can be made. Monitoring for any overriding (or shortfall) of these estimated times can warn management of possible problems to consider.

INTRODUCING STOATS PORRIDGE BARS

The UK snack food market is worth about £3.3bn (US$5.9bn) according to the British Sandwich Association (BSA) (Datamonitor, 2003: BSA, 2005); it is dominated by sandwich chains. At £204 (€291) a year, the British consumer spends the most on snacks in Europe, considerably ahead of Sweden and the Netherlands, in second place with £166 (and £165 respectively), followed by Germany with £162 and France with £146.

The average British commuter spends an average of over one hour travelling per day, giving time to eat and drink whilst on the go. Longer and more frequent journeys, changing working patterns and a rising number of missed meals have all contributed to the growth of on-the-move snacking. In 2004 Britons recorded the highest number of journeys per day, with an average of 6.4 journeys per person per day compared with the European average of 4.5 (Rebelo, 2006). Driving generates most of the on-the-move consumption and consumers are more likely to eat and drink on the move when the car journey includes a stop at a petrol station, where they have the opportunity for impulse purchases.

> Snacking is not seen as unhealthy but the product consumed determines one's attitude to the healthiness of the snacking occasion. Consumers desire healthy convenient products that provide guilt-free satisfaction. They are becoming more health-conscious and this influences product choice, but taste remains the number one influence.
>
> (Rebelo, 2006)

Consumers have become critical of their product quality and they are searching for alternative tasty, hot, on-the-move meals for which they will a pay a premium price. Increasingly, slow carbohydrate snacks have become popular, replacing high carbohydrate snacks as consumers try to avoid the 'quick boost' and subsequent 'post-food lull' that often happens after consumption of foods such as bread. Fast food outlets have reacted, e.g. in 2005 McDonald's introduced Quaker OatsSo Simple porridge to its breakfast menu in its UK outlets (Rebelo, 2006; www.nutraingredients.com 30 January 2006).

Porridge oat sales are worth £79m (US$142m) p.a., ranking second in breakfast foods and closing the gap with the nation's current favourite breakfast, Weetabix, according to the marketing research agency, TNS. Supermarkets confirm that oat-based breakfast cereal is selling well. Waitrose had a 70 per cent increase in sales of all porridge, with organic varieties up 40 per cent. Sainsbury's reported a 41 per cent increase in the year's porridge sales to 2005 with a 60 per cent increase in oat sales in the last six months of 2005 (Sawers, 2005).

According to the Milk Development Council (MDC), the farmer-funded body that promotes dairy products, sales of liquid milk to consumers rose over the two years to April 2005, from 4.45bn l for the year to April 2004 to 4.49bn l for the year to April 2005, an increase of 0.04bn l. The thirty-year decline in milk sales has been reversed with the help of the transformation of porridge. '[The rise is] down to an increase in the frequency of buying milk rather than people buying more during each shopping trip. The indications are the [the extra milk is] being used mainly in porridge, tea and coffee,' according to Liz Broadbent, director of market development of MDC (Harvey and Bolger, 2005).

Demand for organic products has increased substantially, with Britons spending more than £1bn (US$1.8bn) p.a. on them. Cereal suppliers have seen increased sales of organic porridge, with, for example, sales at Perwood Organic Cereal Company up by 25 per cent in the year to 2005. Its owner, Mark Houghton Browne, commented that 'We are at peak capacity at the moment and have had to take on extra staff to cope' (Hiscott, 2005). Large porridge manufacturers reported a similar picture. Jonathan Duffin, marketing controller for cereals at Jordans', commented that in 2005 sales of its Organic Porridge increased by 65 per cent compared with the previous year. Sales of its Conservation Grade Porridge increased even more, by 76 per cent. Ginny Mayall, an organic farmer who grows oats in Shropshire, considered it to be 'a hot crop'. Porridge, once seen as a winter warmer, has become a trendy, 'cool' product, especially among the young, thanks to the help of Heston Blumenthal, the celebrity chef and owner of the Fat Duck restaurant in Bray, Berkshire, famous for creating his much talked-about snail porridge (www.fatduck.co.uk).

Scots have long appreciated the benefits of oats. Native to Eurasia, oats are the seeds of cereals belonging to the *Avena* genus and have been grown in Scotland for centuries. They have a lower summer heat requirement and greater tolerance of rain than cereals such as wheat, rye or barley, so are well suited to the Scottish climate. In years gone by Scottish chieftains carried around small sacks of oatmeal when travelling by horseback and baked oatcakes on the back of their iron shields for sustenance. Currently a pack of emergency oatcakes in the pocket does the same job for the you-are-what-you-eat generation, proving that a good thing will stand the test of time. Increased concern regarding the nature and quality of food consumed, in the light of recent health scares and concern about pesticides, together with the promotion of diets, such as the Glycemic Index (GI), demanding 'pure' foods, has fuelled the move towards porridge eating.

Anthony Stone, a marketing and hospitality graduate from Strathclyde University, Glasgow, and young twenty-five-year old entrepreneur, is taking the development further by turning porridge into the latest take-away food through the newly established business, Stoats Porridge Bars. Aware of the nutritional appeal of oats, Stone is determined to change their dry and dull image, making them more fashionable. He was already a fan of porridge at breakfast time and, realizing that a small bowl of hot oats kept him going for hours, he began to snack on porridge throughout the day. He decided it was time to move on from hospitality management in Wales to return to Scotland to launch his own mobile porridge bars business (see Figure 13.2). Believing his idea to be an innovation that could encourage healthier eating habits among Scots, he gained support from the Scottish Executive and the Prince's Scottish Youth Business Trust (PSYBT), which provided him with start-up advice through a business pump-priming grant and loan.

Stoats porridge was branded to attract the dynamic, food-conscious, adventurous consumer wanting a change from hamburgers and sandwich fast food. With this in mind, Stone imported a state-of-the-art trailer from the US. 'I wanted the bar to be fresh and sexy, a new generation of healthy takeaway food. . . The van [I bought] is very modern [with stainless steel frontage] and has bar stools at the front – nothing like the common white burger van – and the porridge is served in environmentally friendly cardboard cups' (Beecroft, 2005).

Stone began trading in June 2005 at Leith market, Edinburgh. In place of the traditional splash of cream and sugar, or the sprinkle of salt, his porridge is offered with a range of exotic flavours to appeal to the youth market. While Stoats porridge is prepared traditionally, using a personal blend of natural Scottish porridge oats, there is a choice of toppings, including pear, peach and crushed almonds, Scotch whisky and honey, Cranachan with cream and raspberries, chunky marmalade and white chocolate and roasted hazelnuts. Stone commented that:

the Scots love their porridge, but recently it has started to appeal to people for its health benefits too. It's a great fuel on a cold day. We've taken a traditional Scottish product and presented it in a modern format. So far, the response has been brilliant. . . . We've already had a staggering amount of positive feedback and people even email us to suggest new toppings, so hopefully it'll be a Scottish success story.

(Beecroft, 2005)

Figure 13.2
Stoats Porridge
Bars' mobile
unit

Source: courtesy
of Stoats Porridge
Bars.

'The whole idea is proving very popular,' according to Stone.

Customers seem pleased to try something different. I was slightly worried at first that people might not want porridge outwith breakfast time, but we've found we often get a rush on about four o'clock when people get peckish but don't want to stop off at the burger van or chippy.

(Sawers, 2005)

Stone sells his porridge in small (8 oz), medium (12 oz) or large (16 oz) bowls, with a pot of basic salted porridge starting at £1.50 and a bowl of porridge with Scotch whisky and honey topping the price list at £3.20. Reacting to customer demand, he has started selling home-made porridge bars based on traditional flapjacks with a range of flavourings similar to those used in porridge. The apricot and hazelnut and white chocolate have been the most popular versions. Prices are £1 per bar or four bars for £3.50. He also sells hot home-made soup, which has proved popular.

From his experience so far, Stone has found that there is a ready-made summer market, concentrating on events and festivals. Not only has there been the development of loyal customers attending the weekend festivals but also there has been favourable support from tourists keen to explore this part of Scots heritage, even in hot weather.

> A lot of Americans are fans of porridge as it's a low GI food, too . . . I'm chuffed to see people moving on from the idea of porridge as prison food or something old-fashioned. They are realising that it is very Scottish, very tasty, very healthy and nowadays, very cool.
>
> (Sawers, 2005)

In the run-up to Christmas 2005 sales from a static pitch outside St James shopping centre, a major complex at the east of Prince's Street, Edinburgh, built up steadily as potential customers accepted the idea of a porridge snack. Customers ranged from local office workers who bought early morning breakfast to others who purchased late afternoon *en route* home and shoppers who were looking for a mid-morning/lunch snack. One surprise was getting a large order (£40 worth of porridge) for a Friday end-of-the-week office lunch.

Stone has secured a licence for an Edinburgh site in a popular student area. He is considering buying a second mobile unit and is investigating the idea of purchasing or leasing porridge café premises in the city centre. He has also gained a regular pitch at the weekly Saturday farmers' market in central Edinburgh. It remains to be seen where and in what format the future development of Stoats Porridge Bars will take place.

Business management issues

Mission statement

The vision for Stoats Porridge Bars is to provide organic porridge in a range of flavours from stylish mobile porridge bars in Scotland and across the UK to 'on the go' consumers. Stoats will support customer welfare by providing a healthy snack available throughout the day, which provides slow-release energy and assists in providing customers with a healthy and balanced diet (Stone, 2005).

Aims/objectives

The core organic porridge will be supported by the sale of Stoats organic oat blend, a range of porridge bars, merchandising, beverages and home-made soup. The objectives set in May 2005 are shown below.

Within six months (July 2005 to January 2006) of operation to:

- Test the viability of the Stoats Porridge Bars concept: (1) as a product, including verifying marketing mix elements, especially pricing and packaging; (2) suitability of the mobile trailer bar for product sales; (3) consider potential for a flagship shop in Edinburgh city centre.
- Develop branding of Stoats Porridge Bars through: (1) public relations; (2) a website; (3) merchandising.
- Determine the viability of expansion by setting up a second pitch with a second trailer unit.

Within twelve months of operation (July 2005 to June 2006) and subject to early results to:

- Investigate potential for Stoats premises as a 'flagship' shop in Edinburgh city centre, located in an area with high footfall rates, targeted at the 'healthy living' market. Possible site locations for consideration are Tollcross and South Bridge, Edinburgh.
- Invest in new trailers, costing between £12,500 to £15,000 each. Equipment and fittings such as sinks, burners, etc., would cost a further £5,000 (US$2,787).
- Consider the viabilty of expansion through franchising or licensing.

Within twenty-four months to have built up the brand to start further expansion through franchising of the Stoats Porridge Bars concept through:

- The potential for geographical expansion locally within Scotland to Glasgow and, perhaps, to Inverness, where there are plans to develop a café culture.
- The potential for other geographical expansion across the UK and internationally.

Practical experience
An initial test marketing trial began on 4 June 2005 at Leith market, Edinburgh. This was used to test customer reaction to the product together with proposed cooking methods. Effective operations started on 25 June 2005, again at the Leith market.

Test marketing findings
Festivals provide a receptive market and high 'footfall density' with associated porridge sales. Issues encountered that have to be considered:

- Most weekend music festivals involve camping in a remote location, e.g. a farm field. Customer demand for porridge products is related to weather, with inclement, cold wet conditions encouraging most sales, although sales are made when it is warm and sunny. Demand increases later on in the festival schedule when potential customers have used up their own food supplies.
- *Price competition*. Other food suppliers, primarily hamburger sellers, charge high prices for questionable quality, but hamburgers remain cheaper than porridge. In its favour, porridge is viewed as a novel, more healthy alternative.

- The challenge of matching porridge production with demand, which fluctuates according to the time of day, the weather and the musical performance.
- Many music festivals run for three or four days over twenty-four hours giving little lull in demand and necessitating long opening hours for the porridge bar.
- Transport and storing of sufficient stock.

Human resource management

With a business start up the critical issue is cash flow. While reasonable sales have been achieved as yet, they have not allowed for more than basic staff salaries. Consequently, friends' support has been sought for staffing in the short run. It was decided to employ a member of staff on a trial basis to service the Stoats Porridge Bar mobile unit placed in the pre-Christmas period at the St James Centre, Edinburgh. This trial was successful and has been extended to a more permanent arrangement as sales revenue more than matched overhead expenses, allowing profits to be made.

Product

The cost of raw materials for porridge making is relatively low. However, while fresh produce has been sought wherever possible, in keeping with the objective of satisfying targeted consumer lifestyle demands, it is more difficult to source and more expensive, with a shorter life than traditional oats. Moreover, as the raw material is bulky, storage problems occur, especially when transporting stock over considerable distances to weekend festivals.

Pricing

Pricing strategies have been developed using basic accounting cost-plus principles (raw material, transport, staffing, etc., together with a reasonable profit margin) as well as market segmentation and price positioning targeting:

- Daily commuters through permanent markets, etc.
- 'Foodies' through farmers' markets.
- Captive consumer through music festivals and events.

The daily commuter pricing is lower than that for the farmers' markets and festivals and events, which have associated higher costs and a more captive target market. Prices of competing products, e.g. hamburgers, crêpes and sandwiches, are monitored regularly to ensure the pricing of Stoats product range is in line with the competition, allowing for the higher efforts required to produce a quality product. Different price cards are displayed at the different venues. Little, if any, adverse comment has been made by customers regarding the pricing strategies used.

Promotion: publicity

Preparing the website (www.stoatsporridgebars.co.uk) proved challenging and has been critical in supporting public relations to develop the Stoats' brand. The site receives an average of 554 unique visitors per month in response to local press and specialist food journals, radio and television coverage (see Figure 13.3 and Table 13.1).

The website provides a source of extra income for online sales of pre-packed bags of porridge oats and merchandise, e.g. T-shirts. On occasion it has been used to test market reaction. Customers had been asking for 'Stoats Bars' in addition to porridge. It was decided to test a range of oat and fruit bars (popularly known a flapjacks) to complement the porridge offerings. Initially, apricot and sultana together with hazelnut and white chocolate-flavoured oat bars were tested. Favourable customer reaction has suggested that the test should be taken forward with the bars being added to the Stoats product line.

Table 13.1 Summary of Stoats Porridge Bars' website visitors, August to December 2005

| Month | Visitors | | | |
	Page load	Unique	First-time	Returning
December	1,068	384	351	33
November	1,705	616	564	52
October	1,402	502	470	32
September	1,525	646	605	41
August	1,415	622	588	34
Average	1,423	554	516	38
Total	7,115	2,770	2,578	192

Source: StatCounter.com (2 January 2006).

Note: for explanation of terms used see Figure 13.3.

Press

Visitors to the website increase notably in the days when articles on Stoats appear in the press, e.g. *Scotsman* and *Daily Mail* articles took 143 and 102 unique visits respectively. Further publicity in the local *Evening News* (Bradley, 2005), the *Strathspey and Badenoch Herald*, the *Daily Record* and even the national press in the *Times* have kept the website click rate at a high level for little up-front cost other than interview and photography time. A three-page article in 'You are what you eat', the monthly magazine supporting the Channel 4 television programme increased the breadth and depth of publicity coverage, providing potential for further promotion in the future.

Radio

Radio coverage has been obtained, with Stone speaking on Radio Scotland on 6 October 2005, covering preparations for the forthcoming Porridge-making Championships. Subsequently, mention of the Stoats Porridge Bars was made during a talk show on 7 October 2005

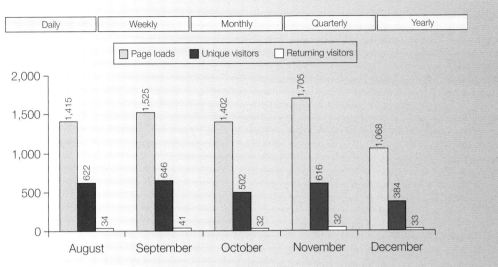

Figure 13.3
Summary of Stoats Porridge Bars' Website visitors, August to December 2005

Returning visitors: based purely on a cookie: if the person is returning to the webside for another visit an hour or more later.
First-time visitors: based purely on a cookie: if the person has no cookie then this is considered their first time at the website.
Unique visitor: based purely on a cookie: this is the total of returning visitors and first-time visitors – all the visitors. Page load:
the number of times the page has been visited

Source: StatCounter.com (2 January 2006).

which was repeated in November 2005 discussing *al fresco* food availability in Edinburgh during the lead-up to Christmas shopping, again increasing the profile of Stoats Porridge Bars and its website. BBC Newcastle covering the north of England audience has reported on the porridge venture. Stone had further live coverage on the Radio Scotland Fred McCauley show on 13 January 2006 when the benefits of eating porridge were promoted.

TV
On 11 January 2006 Stone was interviewed for 'Scotland today' Scottish television news regarding customer reaction to the new pitch for his mobile unit in the Edinburgh University location. He also had a five-minute slot on 25 January 2006 on the morning GMTV programme discussing the health advantages of eating porridge.

Merchandising
The Stoats porridge concept has intrigued the public at large and, in general, has drawn favourable opinion. Even if the persons concerned initially do not purchase the product, often they return at a later date or different venue to purchase the product. The brand image is one that meets favour because of its support for healthy and environmentally sound issues. There has been considerable interest in products other than the main-line product, especially in Stoats' own mix of porridge oats, together with the Stoats green-and-white logo T-shirts. These are available through the website.

C
A
S
E

S
T
U
D
Y

Table 13.2 Festivals and events attended, June 2005 to January 2006

2005	Event	Attendance (estimated)
25–6 June	Leith Market, Edinburgh	400
2–3 July	Leith Market, Edinburgh	400
9–10 July	Leith Market, Edinburgh	400
16–17 July	Leith Market, Edinburgh	400
22–3 July	Wickerman Festival, Galloway	8,500
12–13 Aug.	Belladrum Tartan Heart festival, Inverness	8,000
21–2 Aug.	Get Active Loch Lomond, at Lomond Shores	1,000
27–8 Aug.	Leith market, Edinburgh	400
3–4 Sept.	Scotland's Countryside festival, Glamis Castle, Angus	6,500
9–10 Sept.	Whisky Live, George Square, Glasgow	1,800
11 Sept.	'Grand day out', Countryside Alliance, Gosford House, Longniddry, East Lothian	1,250
16/17 Sept.	Festival, Knockindarich, Galloway	2,500
23/4 Sept.	Loopallu Music Festival, Ullapool	1,800
8 Oct.	Balerno farmers' market, Edinburgh (first Saturday of every month)	400
9 Oct.	Twelfth World Porridge Making Championships, Carrbridge	150
Nov./Dec.	St James's Centre (shopping centre), Edinburgh outside esplanade	Christmas shoppers and office workers: 2,000
Jan. 2006 onwards	George Square and the Meadows pitch (university area), Edinburgh	Up to 2,000
Jan. 2006 onwards	Edinburgh farmers' market (every Saturday)	Up to 1,500 general public
Feb. 2006 onwards	Loch Lomond Shores' farmers' market, Balloch (every other Sunday)	Up to 700 general public

Place: location

Music festivals provide good footfall trade together with concentrated demand. However, current resources can only cater for smaller festivals and events of up to 10,000 participants, e.g. Wickerman, Galloway and Belladrum Tartan Heart Festival, Inverness. The larger festivals, predominantly held in the south, demand larger operating capacity for Stoats.

Regarding obtaining Edinburgh city pitches for the trailer, some delay has been encountered in gaining licensing permission from the local authorities for trading at the proposed site locations. While environmental standards and checks related to health and safety of food distribution have been achieved, other issues related to possible community disturbance have been raised, necessitating further investigation. Planning applications can take more than six months to process. Even when the proposed site for the trailer location is on private land, gaining city licensing permission is time-consuming, although in this case having support from the landowner is beneficial. Applications can also be costly, incurring a fixed charge per application of £250 (US$315). Further complications relate to the duration of the licence. The more readily available licences are for twenty-eight days, but favoured demand is for at least six months, or even a year.

Venues

June onwards: Leith Market, Commercial Quay, Edinburgh (Saturday and Sunday weekends during the summer). The market moved to central Edinburgh in November 2005, providing much higher footfall levels. This venue was supplemented by attendance at festivals and events as shown in Table 13.2.

Applications to Planning Department for licence for pitches/stands

November to 31 December 2005 (twenty-eight days): St James Centre, Edinburgh. Application made beginning of October 2005 and received end of week 1, November 2005, to apply until June 2006. Stoats Porridge Bars operated mobile unit in the forecourt of the shopping centre.

November + (for seven months to June 2006): George Square/Meadows, Edinburgh. Application made at the beginning of June 2005. An objection was received from the local Traders' Community leading to deferment until 25 November 2005, when after further consideration a licence to trade was granted. In place of the expected six weeks to gain the permission there had been a delay of six months, preventing trade over that period.

Application for shop/café lease

October: Bridge Street, Edinburgh. In the light of other strategic moves, this proposal has been put on hold for the immediate future.

Task

Anthony Stone is required to report back at regular intervals to the Princes Trust regarding the progress of the Stoats Porridge Bars business. You, as Anthony Stone's personal assistant (and close friend), are asked to prepare a strategic marketing plan which will:

CASE STUDY

1   Indicate the progress made over the first six months of operating the business.
2   Outline future proposed developments for the next: (a) six months, (b) twelve months, (c) twenty-four months. Consideration should be made regarding strategic options and favoured direction to follow together with issues related to implementing the proposed marketing mix to achieve the desirable goals. The role of test marketing should in determining the marketing mix also be discussed.

Acknowledgements

The case has been developed in conjunction with Anthony G. Stone, founder of Stoats Porridge Bars, Edinburgh, who has discussed regularly the case from the incipient idea generation through to the implementation stages of the business.

Sources: Beecroft (2005), Breakfast Cereals Market Report (2004), British Sandwich Association (2004), Datamonitor (2004), Hiscott (2005), Sawers (2005), Stone (2005) (personal intimation, 2005).

HUMAN RESOURCES

Planning needs to take account of the recruiting and training staff necessary with the desirable expertise to be reliable and trustworthy to undertake the various activities highlighted in the plan. Estimates of the costs involved should be made, with allowances being made for possible absenteeism, holiday cover and so on. Again as with other planning estimates, care should be taken not to err on the too optimistic side by underestimating costs. It is preferable to be cautious, with some degree of overestimate concerning likely staffing costs allowing for any unforeseen situation.

FINANCE

The finance necessary for the implementation of the proposed plan has to be realistic, reflecting the needs of undertaking the various parts of the plan. Care has to be taken not to overstretch resources. Often a two-pronged approach to deciding on the specific budgets for the marketing plan has to be made. Consideration of the finance likely to be available will be reflected in the level of investment in the marketing mix components. Equally, if it is felt that to reach the desirable objectives of the plan in terms of given sales turnover, or market share, a given level of finance is necessary, then that should be sought if at all possible. Should it prove to be that the desirable level of finance is not readily available, serious consideration should be made as to whether or not to continue with the venture. Certainly it may prove necessary to revise the initial proposals in the plan to match the available resource. For example, it may be more appropriate to take a longer lead time to take the product or service to market, or to target a more local geographical customer base. It is critical that care is taken to ensure that the finance available matches the needs of the agreed marketing plan. Various enablers, including the banks, shareholders and other stakeholders, will influence decisions regarding the availability of finance to proceed.

It may be necessary, especially for a new product or service being introduced, to develop a contingency plan that considers various scenarios. In this case, it is even more critical to monitor closely the progress of implementing the plan and to be aware that, should conditions necessitate, modifications can be made to suit the conditions encountered in the market.

CONCLUSION

Effective planning is critically important for the successful implementation of marketing processes. Preparing a marketing plan involves careful consideration of the available market data and matching that to available resources to determine the most favoured marketing mix to put the proposed plan into practice. Financial resource plays a critical role determining the levels of investment available for the marketing mix, i.e. for product development, pricing strategies, promotion and place, or channels of distribution decisions. A degree of flexibility in the implementation of the proposed is desirable, although it is appreciated that the agreed marketing plan to be the framework for the scheduling. The plan should be a guide to be followed if at all possible, but market conditions or unforeseen circumstances may precipitate some modifications to be introduced. In this case, appropriate adjustments will have to be made to the original plan, and, once again, all parties involved should agree and understand the changes made.

RECOMMENDED FURTHER READING

Aaker, D.A. (1998) *Strategic market management*, 5th edn, Chichester: Wiley.

Anon. (2005a) 'Stirring times for world porridge', *Strathsprey and Badenoch Herald*, 5 October, p. 15.

Anon. (2005b) 'Porridge to go', *Times*, 7 October, p. 3.

Anon. (2005c) 'Doing porridge', *Herald and Post*, 17 November, p. 21.

Anon. (2005d) 'Porridge van will provide oat cuisine to cold shoppers', *Evening News*, 11 November, p. 18.

Anon. (2005e) 'Porridge stall in liqueur lure', *Evening News*, 12 December, p. 18.

Anon. (2005f) 'The best start to the day', *Food guide*, Christmas catalogue, Highland News Group, p. 42.

Anon. (2006a) 'Oat cuisine on the menu at porridge bar', *Evening News*, 13 January, p. 25.

Anon. (2006b) 'Wanderers who warm to the idea of oat cuisine', *Herald* (Going out), 23 February, p. 4.

Barrow, C., Burke, G., Molian, D. and Brown, R. (2005) *Enterprise development: the challenges of starting, growing and selling businesses*, London: Thomson.

Blackley, M. (2006) 'Oat cuisine set to bowl UK over', *Evening News,* 13 March, p. 10.

Bradley, J. (2005) 'Oat cuisine for breakfast? Get a spurtle on to porridge van', *Evening News*, 6 October, p. 3.

Chaston, I. and Mangles, T. (2002) *Small business marketing management*, Basingstoke: Palgrave.

Cohen, W.A. (1995) *The marketing plan,* New York: Wiley.

Cooper, A. (ed.) (1997) *How to plan advertising*, 2nd edn, London: Cassell.

Gray, L. (2006) 'Oat cuisine on menu as the first porridge bar opens', *Scotsman*, 10 January, p. 7.

Hiebing, R.G. and Cooper, S.W. (2003) *The successful marketing plan: a disciplined and comprehensive approach,* 3rd edn, New York: McGraw-Hill.

Hollensen, S. (2006) *Marketing planning: a global perspective*, Maidenhead, McGraw-Hill.

Hooley, G.J., Sanders, J.A. and Piercy, N.F. (1998) *Marketing strategy and competitive positioning,* 2nd edn, Harlow: Financial Times/Prentice Hall.

Hutton, G. (2005) *A bowl of porridge*, Glendaruel: Argyll Publishing.

Jain, S.C. (1981) *Marketing planning and strategy,* Cincinnati OH: South Western.

Johnson, G., Scholes, K. and Whittington, R. (2005) *Exploring corporate strategy: text and cases,* 7th edn, Harlow: Pearson.

Luck, D.J., Ferrell, O.C. and Lucas, G.H. (1989) *Marketing strategy and plans,* 3rd edn, Englewood Cliffs NJ: Prentice-Hall.

Lyons, W. (2006) 'The snack in a pot that leaves a sandwich looking limp', *Scotland on Sunday*, 15 January, p. 15.

MacLeod, J. (2006) 'Scotch beef is back on Europe's menus, sales of porridge oats are soaring', *Scottish Daily Mail*, 11 March, pp. 16–17.

Madeley, G. (2006) 'Cold comfort for those not getting their oats', *Daily Mail*, 16 January, p. 11.

Norris, C. (2005) 'Porridge to go', *You are as you eat*, November, p. 70–2.

Paley, N. (1999) *How to develop a strategic marketing plan: a step-by-step guide*, London: St Lucia Press.

Sawers, C. (2006) 'Oat cuisine is best served cold', *Scotsman*, 18 January, p. 22.

Siegel, L. (2006) 'What's worse: ready-meals or takeaways?' *Observer*, 19 March.

Tucker, J. and Storrar, K. (2006) 'Food for thought', *Skinny,* 7 March, p. 5.

Wiggins, J. (2005) 'Snack maker seeks fat rewards from slimming bars', *Financial Times,* 31 August, p. 19.

Wilson, R.M.S. and Gilligan, C. (1997) *Strategic marketing management*, 2nd edn, Oxford: Butterworth Heinemann.

Websites

www.fatduck.co.uk.

www.nutraingredients.com (30 January 2006).

www.stoatsporridgebars.co.uk.

NOTES

1 MARKETING: DEVELOPMENT AND SCOPE OF THE SUBJECT

1 A 'do-gooder' is an altruist, an unselfish person, although a connotation is that it has a derogatory tone.

2 Bauer and Greyser (1967) refer also to President Kennedy's attempt in 1963 to attempt to establish the right of consumers to be informed, to choose, to have safe products, to be heard (Office of the President, 1963). Consumer 'rights' referred to include the true interest cost of a loan; the true cost per standard unit of competing brands (unit pricing); the basic ingredients in a product (ingredient labelling); the nutritional quality of foods (nutritional labelling); the freshness of products (open-dating) and the price of gasoline (sign posting rather than pump posting). President Johnson also made a 'consumer message' in 1966 which raised interest in these affairs. Legislation in the late 1960s included major laws relating to consumer protection in the US: the Labeling Act (1966); the Child Protection Act (1966, amended 1969); the Traffic Safety Act (1966); the Flammable Fabrics Act (1967); the Wholesale Meat Act (1967), the Consumer Credit Protection Act (1968); the Wholesale Poultry Products Act (1968); the Radiation Control for Health and Safety Act.

3 In 1960, in the US, no state had a consumer affairs office; by 1970 thirty-three did and by 1973 all fifty did. In 1970 the ten most common complaints received were in respect of automobiles, advertising, appliances, credit, non-delivery of merchandise, home improvements, franchise dealers, warranties, guarantees and sales tactics. Source: Office for Consumer Affairs, State Consumer Action, Summary 71 (Washington DC) US Government Printing Office.

6 SEGMENTATION, TARGETING AND POSITIONING

1 For example, UK government reports usually refer to those of retirement age when referring to 'older' people (see Whiteford and Kennedy, 1995).

2 Care needs to be taken when interpreting statistics. For example, taking the proportion of pensioners by age group in the highest income quintile of the total UK population, this was estimated to be 9.5 per cent for 65–9 year olds; 6.1 per cent for 70–4 year olds; 4.5 per cent for those aged 75–9; 3.7 per cent for those aged 80–4 and 4.3 per cent for those aged 85 and over (Falkingham and Victor, 1991: table 4, p. 12).

3 VALS is now owned by SRI Social Values Business Consulting Intelligence (SRIC-BI).

7 BRANDING

1 Consider this against the average valuation of a UK company at around twice the net balance sheet assets.

10   PROMOTION

1   Felicity Lawrence, 'Should we swallow this?' *Guardian*, 8 February 2006, pp. 8–11.
2   Percentages should not be taken to be definitive, e.g. in Ch. 5 it is outlined that 1 per cent of older people in the UK and 15 per cent of older people in the US have to rely on incomes which are 40 per cent lower than the national average. This would lead to widely differing estimates of the number of potential 'laggards' in the grey market in each country.
3   The organization ensured that it had the ability to cope with a major upsurge in demand following its next major communications campaign in 1995.

12   VIRTUAL MARKETING

1   In order to visit some of these communities, the student may wish to visit a site such as 'Muddom' at this address: www.shef.ac.uk/uni/academic/I-M/is/studwork/groupe/home.html.
2   Cyber dialogue 'Customer relationships through digital media', Market Research study report, February 1998.
3   www.srds.com/lma[lowbar]sl.html, http://www.srds.com/.
4   www.senior.com/.
5   Source: http://jango.excite.com/xsh/query.dcg?cat=fragrance&svc=xsh&cobrand=xsh. When we last tried this site it was no longer operational.
6   This study was originally conducted in 2001. When we went back to redo it in 2006, a surprisingly similar pattern was found so it was decided not to change it.
7   www.McSpotlight.org/.
8   http://www.forbrug.dk/english/dco/speeches-and-articles/children-and-young-people/identifying-advertising-directed-at-children-and-young-people-2003/.

ANSWERS TO REVIEW QUESTIONS

1 MARKETING: DEVELOPMENT AND SCOPE

1 This depends on where one stands with reference to the debate surrounding the marketing concept. It can be argued that the marketing concept should be capable of relating to any and every activity. One view is that the sex industry is a commercial business much like any other. Some others might take Kotler's perspective and suggest that although the sex industry offers pleasing products, it does not act in the consumer's long-term welfare and so the marketing concept should not apply. A different interpretation might object not to the sexual nature of the business but to the role of organized crime and the ruthless exploitation of women, and even men.

2 A major focus of interest was in agricultural marketing, particularly on research into the role of intermediaries in different industries such as the dairy industry.

3 The Functional School focused on the 'how' of marketing, e.g. how are goods assembled, stored, rearranged, sorted and distributed? By contrast the Functionalist approach differs in that it develops a systems approach to marketing, whereby behaviour is seen to be systemic and goal-driven. These concepts form the basis of this text, which considers the organization to be a purposive organism that actively seeks to adapt to changes in the marketing environment.

4 The marketing concept is concerned with the idea that organizations can best serve their objectives by seeking to identify, understand and serve the needs of customers.

5 Kotler suggested that the reason for the consumer backlash was due to marketing managers misinterpreting the marketing concept by equating customer satisfaction with customer desire. He argued that managers mistakenly had catered to consumer desires, e.g. for products such as cigarettes, which while they were pleasing were also harmful to customers' long-run satisfaction. Kotler recommended that instead marketers should pay attention to ways of reformulating pleasing products such as tobacco so that they become more socially desirable.

6 Social marketing refers to Kotler's extension of the marketing concept into non-economic areas such as public services, the arts and religion. Societal marketing concerns the application of marketing principles to all organizational stakeholders.

7 The key elements of relationship marketing relate to reorienting marketing according to the interests of the consumer. Relationship marketing is concerned with treating people as individuals and not numbers and with closing the distance between the marketer and the customer. This is achieved by the mutual exchange and fulfilment of promises.

2 STRATEGIC MARKETING AND THE PLANNING PROCESS

1 A functionalist explanation would suggest that, for a firm to survive and to thrive, managers should ensure that it continually adapts to changing environmental conditions. Environmental scanning is essential to this process, as it provides the requisite information about changing environmental conditions which can then be treated as the basis of manaerial decision making and action.

2 PEST + C +C.

3 Globalization and fragmentation; increasing fascination with the body and time-space compression.

4 The key aspects of the marketing mix; the product, price, promotion and place (channels of distribution).

3 CONSUMER BUYER BEHAVIOUR

1 *Benefits*. It can be understood that the consumer is acting consciously, rationally and purposively in seeking to maximize SEU. On the other hand, this view downplays the social context within which choices are made. It makes the assumption that decisions are conscious and that consumers form systematic beliefs, attitudes and intentions on the basis of perfect information towards consumption objects. It can be concluded that such explanations tend to over-rationalize and to over-individualize consumer behaviour.

2 One major benefit of the Freudian approach is that it highlights unconscious and conflictual processes as part of its explanation of consumer behaviour. Freud's major contribution comes from his depiction of the struggle between biology and social forces which are mediated by the self. Additionally, Freud has supplied a rich vocabulary, including concepts such as *id, ego* and *superego* to enable which can provide a template for others who wish to explore the effects of consumer goods on consciousness. On the other hand, much of what Freud 'discovered' is not readily verifiable and there is evidence to suggest that some of his findings such as those which relate to female desire and 'wish fulfilment' are suspect.

3 Vance Packard's book *The Hidden Persuaders* attempts to explain why marketers resorted to the use of a 'depth' approach to marketing in the 1950s. What is the depth approach? The basic assumption is that a person's unconscious plays an important role in directing purchase activity and that as a result one should not pay too much attention to what people say. Packard argued that much traditional marketing research fails and cites a market study of women in Omaha to support this contention. Women between 23 and 35 years of age were asked if they would buy a three-legged stove for no more than $249. The number of those who said they would buy the stove bore no relation to the number that actually did buy it. On the basis of this example Packard argued that behaviour is not predictable and that one cannot assume that people know what they want.

Further questions

- **Do you think it was reasonable of Vance Packard to draw this conclusion?**
  Answer Yes, but there may be other explanations.

- **Can you think of any rational conscious reasons why the women might not have been able to provide an answer to this question?**
  Answer Yes, because they were not shown the stove itself; or perhaps they did not want a stove because they were happy with the one they already owned. Maybe the stove was not available in their local store or in the preferred colour; or perhaps they did not like the look of the salesperson; or perhaps their circumstances changed.

4   This is a difficult question as there are two studies which discuss inner-directed characters – Riesman and VALS. Riesman's inner-directed character emerged at a time of social mobility and so is not tied to the same sense of place that secured the identities of traditional characters. One key element of the inner-directed character is a form of psychological 'gyroscope' which is instilled in early childhood by parents and others. This is used to map out a life plan which keeps him. (At the time paid employment was usually available only for men.) The key element of the life plan of the inner directed character is work. It requires progress at work and saving for the future when he could retire. Related to the importance of the life plan, the inner-directed character held on to the value of deferred gratification; i.e. delaying enjoyment until another time. He was future-oriented and so the world of goods and consumption was marginal to his outlook and probably in his view was more part of the world of his wife, as consumption was something which was associated with 'women's work'. Where he did take an interest in consumption this would probably be conspicuous consumption which would seek to differentiate him from his peers.

The other-directed character is a product of the consumer society, who tends to be oriented in the present and towards instant gratification. Unlike the inner-directed character this person is acutely sensitive to the views of others and is concerned with keeping up appearances. The other-directed character is the modern consumer.

The inner-directed character discussed by VALS researchers is different in important respects to that described by Riesman. This character developed during the 1960s and early 1970s and is indicative of what is called the 'expressive' self.

5   Maslow disagreed fundamentally with Freud's view that biologically people are savage animals and that society civilizes them. Instead he poses a radically different view which suggests that even 'high' needs for belongingness and actualization can be partly biological. While a Freudian psychologist may place emphasis on training (from toilet training at the anal stage to other means for the exercise of societal restraint) Maslow's approach emphasizes nurturing and permissiveness. Maslow argued that society should focus on need gratification, not need inhibition, as that was the only way to ensure that the 'higher' needs could be satisfied and a more properly human personality attained.

6   Gender, family, social class, culture and consumption.

7 (a) See Figure 3.5 for the behaviourist explanation. This focuses on the behavioural setting and the reinforcement of response.

    (b) See Figure 3.11. The CIP process involved assumes a set of internal characteristics such as perception and attitude.

8 All the elements required to answer this question are awareness, interest desire and action (AIDA). Another way of expressing this is problem identification, information search, evaluation of alternatives, purchase, post-purchase evaluation.

9 Low-involvement consumers tend to be passive, to learn information at random, to buy first and evaluate later and to buy the brand least likely to give them problems. High-involvement consumers are highly involved and they tend to attach high *ego* value or badge value to the product. They are more likely to actively seek, and to systematically search for, information about the product and are likely to purchase that product which contributes most to their expected satisfaction.

4 INDUSTRIAL BUYER BEHAVIOUR

1 In order to explore this properly criteria on which to compare and contrast these options should be considered. For example, one might compare them on criteria such as the nature of demand; market demographics; complexity of the decision; number of people involved; roles played; complexity of the decision and nature of the decision process. The first difference relates to scale. B-to-B purchasing involves everything from jumbo jets to power stations to paper clips. B-to-B decision making relies on derived demand and not primary demand; business organizations are larger and more closely clustered; both consumer and B-to-B decisions can be complex. The nature of this complexity is different. Complexity is represented with respect to consumer markets with respect to the hierarchy of effects, whereby a person will follow the steps in the hierarchy of effects for complex decisions (unless it is a repeat purchase). Similarly, the notion of the 'new buy' with respect to the Buyclass represents a complex decision process. The more complex the decision-making process is in B-to-B behaviour the more people from the Buying Centre are involved. While both B-to-B and family purchases involve people playing roles B-to-B roles are often specifically defined, e.g. it is clear who has the responsibility for the budget. While some consumer purchasing decisions are complex, the overall level of complexity does not reach the same level to be found in most organizational purchases. As managers are directly accountable to others, B-to-B purchases tend to be more visible than consumer purchases in that specifications tend to be recorded and decisions noted; purchases tend to be better specified according to explicit criteria and to clearly follow a set process in B-to-B purchasing. Another difference is that with routine purchases in B-to-B behaviour the 'decision' to order is not made by a person but by a technology like MRP 2.

2 One difficulty with the traditional buying model is that organizational buying/ purchasing is not viewed as a value-adding function. Buying activity is perceived to

be a largely clerical operation with purchasing agents being evaluated on their negotiation skills. Typically, purchasing performance is measured by the levels of price discounts obtained from suppliers. This reward system tends to foster an adversarial climate between buyers and sellers because these goals are in direct competition.

3   Because it sensitizes those inside the organization and those who wish to market to it to the importance of the different roles played by different people. For example, while it would be appropriate for a company which was considering purchasing new technology to consult users it could be a major mistake for a vendor to confuse someone who was a user with a major decision maker.

4   Bringing together different partners with different systems, cultures and working patterns.

5   The appeal of extranets lies in their ability to provide cheaper, more effective and – most important – faster means of communicating with others.

6   Institutional.

7   It is certainly possible to fit this process within the brief model which was described in Figure 4.1. There was clear recognition and prioritization of need. Some form of specification was drawn up, a rigorous process of supplier selection was followed and a supplier was committed to. While the model does explain some aspects of the decision process, it is also useful to consider what it does not account for. Some major issues involved the difficulties for staff working at different hospitals with different priorities to work jointly in defining system objectives, criteria and relevant staff (who could be defined as users and influencers according to the Buying Centre model).

5   MARKETING RESEARCH

1   The four types of information gathering are: (a) *internal reporting*: covering the sources of information available from within the organization, e.g. company sales data; (b) *marketing intelligence*: being the sources of information available through networking to persons operating within a particular market, e.g. competitor information from trade seminars; (c) *marketing research*: desk and field research targeted at obtaining marketing information, e.g. defining market size, customer demand, competitor activity; (d) *analysis*: development of databases to help define market demand, e.g. potential and actual customer databases.

   Generally, information gathering types (a) and (b) will be undertaken by staff within the organization. Type (c) may involve internal staff but, more commonly, it will be subcontracted to marketing research agency staff to complete. Type (d), analysis, is most likely to be the responsibility of the organization's internal staff, although it may be that the marketing research agency staff will have some input into the analysis process, at least with regard to its own marketing research.

   All four types of data-gathering processes can be collecting data on a continuous or *ad hoc* basis but, ultimately, the MIS should be feeding continually and analysing market data which will be used for management decision making. Such data may be quantitative or qualitative in nature, or both. Marketing intelligence is likely to be the more qualitative in nature.

2 The general rule in determining marketing research methodology is to start by using exploratory research to investigate the issues associated with the market problem to be considered. For example, qualitative research might be used to examine consumer attitudes to the proposed new product or concept e.g. their opinion regarding the advertising for a new brand of yoghurt. In the initial stages of the marketing research a series of in-depth personal one-to-one interviews or focus group discussions might be undertaken to elicit attitudes towards the proposed advertising concept.

It is unlikely that qualitative research on its own would fully define consumer demand. Usually, it is preferable to determine, in quantitative terms, the demand for the product. Consequently the marketing research programme could progress to estimate the likely demand for the yoghurt using a particular advertising proposal. In this situation, test marketing could be undertaken within a selected commercial television region, say Granada in the north-west of England, and measures of sales achieved with the new product could be monitored using actual sales and consumer panel market share estimates. Should the results indicate unexpected findings, it may be advocated that further qualitative research is used to explain the situation. Once again, this could be in the form of either in-depth individual interviews or focus group discussions with the latter likely to be favoured.

In this way, both qualitative and quantitative research techniques could be used at different stages of the marketing research. It is likely that qualitative techniques would be used at the exploratory stages at the beginning and end of the study, while quantitative techniques would be used to quantify the demand that is confirmed through the qualitative methods.

3 In the UK, in 1997, nearly 60 per cent of the marketing research agency turnover used personal interviewing techniques of one form or another, suggesting that this is the favoured method of obtaining marketing research information. Postal survey techniques accounted for only 8 per cent of marketing research agencies turnover. The major drawback to using postal surveys is their low response rate, which is typically between 15 per cent and 20 per cent. The response rate can be increased with reminders and incentives, but it is unlikely to reach 50 per cent, unless the target population has a vested interest in the survey, e.g. members of a club on facility development. Postal surveys require a large contact sample to aggregate an adequate achieved sample size. It is likely that personal interviewing would be the preferred method of undertaking marketing research. Most certainly, if marketing research agency staff was completing the investigation, personal interviewing would be favoured. If, on the other hand, staff from within the organization were used to do the research, resource constraints might favour postal survey techniques. Often postal surveys are used as a first stage in the marketing research process to identify persons worthy of personal interview.

Personal interviewing has the advantage over postal questionnaire survey techniques of enabling more control over the survey process. It can enable the interviewer to manage the interviewee selection procedure, the actual interview process and may give additional information to that provided through postal questionnaire surveys. Personal interviewing in the form of face-to-face interviewing can ensure greater control over who responds to the interview; telephone interviewing gives less control but postal surveys provide little, if any, control regarding who completes them.

Usually personal interviewing provides a quicker response rate to the survey, especially in the case of telephone interviewing. Typically, postal surveys take three to six weeks to complete, and even then, postal returns can be received for several months after they have been sent out.

Personal interviewing is preferred for investigating complex behaviour which might necessitate prompt materials, as in the case of advertising effectiveness recall studies. It would be impractical to include the prompt materials with a postal survey questionnaire.

Examples of the use of personal interviewing techniques might be for assessing market demand, for assessing product preference and for opinion polling.

4 Continuous monitoring of market demand is becoming increasingly important in marketing research. Consumer panels provide a major source of information for tracking consumer demand over time. Consumer panels are made up of individuals, households or organizations whose behaviour, such as consumption, is monitored at regular intervals which may be undertaken daily, weekly, monthly or quarterly.

Consumer panels such as the TNS Superpanel can provide sales data for the major mass-consumer products in terms of type of sales, market share, brand, sales by region, type of retail outlet and link those data with the type of consumer purchasing the product, by socio-demographic profile. For example, the producer of a mass-consumer product such as chocolate bars, crisp chips or frozen peas could monitor the performance of the brand against that of competitors against the criteria of region, type of outlet and socio-demographic profile of the consumers.

This could be done at the beginning of a PLC when the new product might be introduced in one region at the test marketing stage and consumer panel data could indicate the likelihood of the new product's success. Subsequently it could be used to monitor the progress of the product as its sales grow during the 'roll-out' stage to achieve national market coverage when, again, the consumer panel data could monitor the product's success against the established competing products and brands. Once the product reached the mature stage of the PLC, consumer panel data could indicate how well the product was performing compared with competing products. These data could be used to monitor when the product reaches the decline stage of the PLC and should be replaced by other new products just being introduced.

Throughout, by monitoring the PLC, the consumer panel data can suggest when it would be appropriate to adapt the marketing mix to increase the product's success. For example, the consumer panel data can monitor the product's sales achieved against variations in the levels of promotional expenditure and within different regions. This information could help management to decide on the most advantageous level of expenditure at different stages of the PLC. If the sales/market share at the mature stage appears to fall, management could be encouraged to increase the spending on promotion to extend the PLC.

Similarly, at given stages of the PLC, the product itself might require to be adapted to meet changes in customer demand, or the channels of distribution may be changed. The data from the consumer panel provide monitoring of consumer demand, i.e. they add to the basic sales data that a firm might have by indicating the product's sales performance against its competition. This is much more powerful than the sales data alone and should justify the cost of purchasing the consumer panel data.

5   The marketing director could be advised that the effectiveness of the advertising expenditure should be monitored throughout the advertising campaign, i.e. before, during and after the advertising campaign, using both qualitative and quantitative marketing research techniques. Qualitative techniques might be used as a pre-stage, to pre-test the advertising campaign as it is developed, or diagnostically if the campaign does not appear to be achieving its objects in the quantitative tracking. These techniques could include in-depth focus interviewing, focus group discussions and/or projective recall techniques, particularly aided recall techniques.

Quantitative research could be used for advertising tracking to maintain awareness, impact, trial and use rates, and imagery. In this way the marketing director could track how the advertising had influenced consumer behaviour.

Quantitative methods could also measure the success of the advertising in terms of the sales achieved and how they compared with competing products. Actual sales as measured by the manufacturer could be used to monitor the success of the advertising. The manufacturer's sales data could be supplemented with data from consumer panels to measure the detergent sales performance against that of competing products or brands within the different UK television regions. The consumer panel data could be further analysed to determine any relationship between advertising expenditure and sales achieved by a commercial television region. Such sales data would have to be examined in conjunction with the image tracking data to help management to decide on the most appropriate marketing action to take.

6   SEGMENTATION, TARGETING AND POSITIONING

1   The market could be segmented according to organization size, location of buyers, type of industry, size of purchase and proposed use of the machines.

2   (a)   Rail travel: occasions used, e.g. weekends, peak periods; demographics, e.g. business commuter, students, pensioner and tourists.

(b)   Banks: benefits sought, geographic, demographic, benefits sought.

(c)   Ballpoint pens: benefits sought.

(d)   Package holidays: social class, lifestyle, demographics, purchase occasion, type of holiday, e.g. camping and outdoor activity.

3   First by defining more closely what is meant by 'grey'. Definition would need to be made concerning a more precise age band, perhaps 50–55. It may necessary to further refine the analysis to take account of income and/ or lifestyle criteria. Next there is a need to find out how satisfied the target group is with the products or services which currently exist. Probably, this will require both qualitative and quantitative marketing research which was covered in Chapter 5.

4   This would depend on which segment of the grey market that was being targeted. Those born before the baby boom tend to be cautious and suspicious of the hard sell and hype. They like to see good value for money and are more interested in a product's functionality than its 'badge value' or what it says about them to other people. This is a characteristic of those baby boomers who were born between 1945 and 1950.

One way of keeping up to date with trends in this market is by building a customer database. For example, Saga's insurance business is called Saga Services and is reputed to have a database of 4 million over-50s. This is a powerful resource, as it can be analysed by means of further criteria to yield up lists which can form the basis of targeted direct marketing communications.

Advertisers are finding it difficult to target the grey market. The last thing this group want to be labelled as is 'old'. Marketing's great dilemma when it comes to the 'grey' market is this difficulty of putting people into categories. How can a group be targeted when one of its prime distinguishing characteristics is that it resents being targeted? How can a group be sold to that prides itself particularly on being mature enough to see through marketing ploys and insists on getting what it wants?

A key question is whether grey spending power requires grey-specific products or more targeted advertising of mainstream products. Much depends on the product or service category. While *Seven Seas* and Sanatogen have taken the approach of creating health supplements targeted at over-50s, Levi's chose older models to emphasize the heritage and longevity of its brand. While this was not deliberately targeting greys, it will not have done Levi's any harm in that market.

Most answers opt for a relatively subtle approach. The trick is not to create or promote a product as a product for the older person. Rather the emphasis should be to appeal to maturer sentiments, e.g. emphasising comfort, safety and efficiency can replace sex, power and danger in car advertising.

5   A possible segmentation base could be the purchasing approach of the buyer. Many buyers will publish their purchasing criteria when issuing tenders.

6   *Undifferentiated*. It is difficult to find an example of this in the private sector. In the UK many public-sector organizations fall into this category, e.g. hospitals, police, schools and libraries. However, this is changing, e.g. schools have developed specialist programmes to cater to children with dyslexia and learning difficulties.

Differentiated: large car manufacturers.

Concentrated: specialist or niche operators can be found in any type of market. Luxury goods that target the top end of the market made by manufacturers such as Gucci, Rolex, Rolls-Royce Motors are obvious examples.

7   Quality; price; value; technical sophistication; size or duration; brand name or logo; other benefits or USPs.

8   Positioning is essential for many not-for-profit organizations as their environment is becoming increasingly competitive. Positioning has been used by many charities, such as Save the Children, Oxfam and Amnesty International, which have each used psychographic and demographic segmentation to appeal for donations. Other not-for-profit organizations that have used positioning in their marketing campaigns include the army and universities.

7   BRANDING

1   Self-congruity is the extent to which the brand values fit with those of the person. The brand values represent the 'personality' of the brand.

2   Briefly, CIP highlights the role played by attitudes as a precursor to behaviour and AIDA is a guide to marketers. It also highlights the persuasive role of advertising in building powerful brands. Behaviourists dispute points, arguing that there is insufficient evidence for the first. Second, they argue that advertising works after trial to provide reinforcement when satisfaction has been gained. Behaviourists pay much more attention to the context and situation in which brands are purchased and in particular to sources of informational and hedonic reinforcement.

3   The former would see nostalgia as being linked to personal identity and lived experience. Nostalgia is linked with the postmodern condition of feeling alone in the world. Consequently we identify strongly with those brands that we consumed at a time when we felt secure. B.F. Skinner would explain this as being the pain generated by a strong tendency to return to a previous state of affairs when return is impossible. When a person can no longer obtain reinforcement from that behavioural situation s/he may still try to attain it by buying the product associated with that experience.

4   The idea of a subculture is more bounded than that of community and community is more bounded than that of tribe.

5   It is suggested that reference groups be considered in relation to lived experience. Reference groups are explained within the context of lived experience and referent systems with respect to the mediation of experience.

6   Yes – so long as it has a property that can be leveraged.

7   The bank sought to achieve congruity by means of product development, the name of the brand and its advertising. The initial product was tailored to the express needs of the Opportunist in that it offered to save him or her time and money and also to reduce the hassle of unpleasant and expensive exchanges of correspondence with bank staff. Extensive research conducted into the name of the brand suggested that Vector had positive associations with the go-ahead, ambitious type of person the brand aimed to reach. Finally, advertising aimed to encourage the target group to believe that, although the manager was traditional, nevertheless he listened to them.

8 From the illustration it would appear that Midland Bank's personnel developed the bank's marketing and communications strategy in a manner which is consistent with a classic textbook approach. Yet there are crucial differences. (a) Branding was conceived of as the strategy: alternatives were not really considered. (b) A fundamental reformulation of strategy (the development of multi-service accounts) took place after the launch of Vector. (c) The 1991 decision by new chief executive Brian Pearse to shelve both Vector and Orchard 'which came as a surprise even to Midland marketing director, Kevin Gavaghan', smacks of political, not simply rational, motives.

Planning is far from a neutral, value-free and objective description of events. Rather it can act as a powerful normative force that can act to structure accounts in such a way that the eventual story emerges as a purposive, rational, linear sequence of events. This effectively masks, or at best glosses over, the dynamic tensions, complexity and contradictions that occur in everyday reality.

9 Carefully. Cult members believe that they are the true owners of the brand. The key is to give them a great product and the tools to use it. See also Wells (2001).

10 Generally, behaviourists focus on quantitative studies of brand loyalty. They tend to disregard the small but vocal minority that constitute the cult surrounding a brand in focusing on general buying patterns over time. Consequently they do not have much to say about this.

11 There is a danger in attributing too much of the change in French Connection's fortunes to the new image that was communicated through their advertising. Other factors were key, including store design, layout and merchandising, the design of the clothes and the quality of the clothes.

12 There is no doubt that advertising campaigns such as that devised by French Connection can arouse a great deal of interest and publicity. But how much of this trickles down to the bottom line? Such matters are discussed further in Chapter 10 on promotion and marketing communications.

13 Behaviourists would want to know more about the situational aspects of buyer behaviour and, in particular, the utilitarian and informational reinforcement patterns. For example, leaving the FCUK campaign aside, the overall shopping experience may have been improved as a result of the store refit, staff training and improved products. The more recent dip in sales may have been produced by a fall-off in product quality or because prices are thought to be too high.

8 PRODUCT

1 As consumers are becoming increasingly health conscious, this evidence may enhance the popularity of high fibre products, thereby prolonging the mature phase of the life cycle.

The following text applies to questions 8.2–5. 'In 1994 York Trailers decided to move back into the refrigerated semitrailer market following successful collaboration with a Danish company on the trailer design. "1994 is the right time to move back into the sector and we have made our plans accordingly," said York Managing Director, David Steel. "We have evaluated all the methods and materials in use in the UK and Europe.'"

2 Test marketing is used to ascertain the likelihood of success of a new product or concept. The new product is introduced to a small part of the total market which could be an area such as a television region, a particular town or a flagship shop. The product performance is tested under market conditions which as closely as possible match those of the total market. Essentially the manufacturer tests the new crisp product on a miniature version (or sample) of the total market. The success of the new product can be gauged in terms of sales or market share achieved and estimates can be made as to the likely sales that would be achieved for the total market.

However, test marketing does pose problems that have to be addressed. Test marketing can be expensive to undertake, with the costs not differing greatly from those that would be incurred by introducing the new product to national coverage. Test marketing may give competitors advance warning regarding the new product introduction and allow them to prepare a counter-attack against the new product.

It may be difficult to implement the ideal test market conditions. In theory, the test area, or town, should represent a sample of the total market, but few areas meet these conditions. It may be difficult to replicate precisely the marketing mix to be used nationally within the test area or town. The product may be manufactured in quantities that suit the test area, but major investment may be required to achieve the same volume per population for national coverage (as was the case for both Wispa and Spira chocolate bars). Pricing approaches and related channel discounts may well differ for the test area and for national coverage. The retail outlets that are prepared to participate in the test may demand higher inducements and rewards than would be expected if the product was marketed nationally. Regarding promotion activities, there may not be the equivalent promotional media in miniature in the test area. For example, the test area, or town, may not have a miniature version of the national press that would be used to target the desired consumer. It may be difficult to gain the appropriate channels of distribution; few major retailers want to encourage test marketing in their outlets.

While it is advisable that some form of test marketing should be undertaken prior to introducing the new crisp product to the national market, there are problems to overcome. It can be difficult and expensive to establish the favourable conditions for test marketing. Furthermore, competitors may try to negate the research findings by introducing atypical conditions within the test area, e.g. they may introduce sales activity over and above their normal level in order to distort the market conditions. Nevertheless, the large, successful mass-market producers such as Cadbury's do undertake test marketing in its various forms in an effort to reduce the risks of failure associated with NPD. This suggests that, despite the problems, some form of test marketing is advisable within the process of NPD.

9   PRICING

1   In general, it is assumed that if a product or service is price-elastic, a relatively small price decrease leads to a substantial rise in demand for it. A price increase results in a relatively large drop in demand for it. If the increased sales as a result of a price reduction produce a more profitable outcome than before the reduction was made, then the offering can be considered price-elastic. In the case of a price increase, if the product or service is perceived to have benefits that outweigh the price, e.g. Benecol, a margarine containing an ingredient that reduces cholesterol, and consumers have the kind of income to accommodate the increase, then the offering is price-inelastic.

Staple foods where no alternative exists, customized core products together with customized augmented products and services, are all classifications where the offerings within them are price-inelastic. Examples of inelastic products are Louis Vuitton travel goods, Mercedes cars and other luxury products and services. Elastic products are seen in train and bus fares, cigarettes and many varieties of food. In the vast majority of circumstances, standard goods are price-elastic.

If research is not feasible or profitable, e.g. with small companies, subjective estimation of customers' price sensitivity may be an answer. Adding services focusing on aspects that enlarge personal loyalty through personal contacts often results in inelastic behaviour. When there was an effective devaluation of the pound sterling by some 14 per cent some years ago, certain whisky manufacturers that passed the reduction on to US distributors on all whisky shipments lost out on profit. They forgot, or did not know, that with premium whiskies they were only putting more in the pocket of the distributor, who would not be passing on the benefit of the lower price to his (inelastic) customers. It would have been an acceptable pricing decision in the case of (elastic) immature whiskies for mixing with water or lemonade.

2   Costs represent the lower limits of price (the upper limit is what the market will bear). The desirability of knowing costs is deemed a necessary precondition for knowing whether a sale is profitable. Unfortunately, it is never possible to anticipate costs accurately. In large public works contracts and in contracts with government departments this problem is overcome by having cost-plus-a-fixed-fee or cost-plus-a-percentage-of-cost contracts. The weakness of this method is that sometimes cost overruns can take place and the buyer has to pay regardless unless limits on the eventual contract price are set. There are target-cost contracts which provide financial incentives to reduce costs below target.

If costs are divided into fixed and variable, it is possible to calculate break-even volume which shows the sales needed before the product moves into profit. The cost-based approach is simple but the costs themselves are historical and may be misleading in times of inflation. They do not take account of what is going on in the market place where consumers buy for different reasons like enhancing their egos. They are prepared to pay a premium price for this satisfaction. The relationship of price and perceived value is not considered by the cost-based approach. Sometimes it is reinforced by pricing for a target return on investment. While this will determine the feasibility of a proposed price, it does not take account of consumer behaviour which the demand-based and competition-based approaches that start with the buyer are more likely to do with a degree of accuracy.

That said, it is possible to be much more eclectic than consideration of the separate approaches might suggest. A cost-based approach can be modified to take cognizance of market conditions but may not produce the quality data that a demand-based approach can often give. A demand-based approach starting with an acceptable market price and working back through the retail and wholesale margins and the company's profit margin to a figure within which cost has to be met will depend on the accuracy of the likely costs for its effectiveness and the estimate of market take-up and capacity utilization.

3   In deciding whether or not to drop the free telephone service provided by the company's brand of computer software, certain factors will have to be taken into account. If the software is at a relatively early stage in its PLC and many users are unfamiliar with it, then there is a strong argument for its retention. The product and the service are complementary to one another. If the product is moving into the mature stage of the PLC, customers will be more price-sensitive than in earlier stages. They will possess more information about services and will perceive less risk. In other words, it is becoming a commodity. There may be glitches, and the creation of a website where frequently asked questions are given and updated may be sufficient guarantee to offset any worries the customer may have on that account. To meet the exceptional case, a back-up service that is paid for in full could be put in place. Just as there is a time for bundling products and services, so there is one for unbundling.

4   In deciding on the price and services to include as part of a new business-class air service, there are developments that have to be taken into consideration. Cost cutting by companies, in the rush to compete in the new global economy, has resulted in their cutting back on business-class travel on short-haul flights, e.g. within Europe, and insisting on 'no frills' flights for employees at all levels with low-cost companies like Easyjet and Ryanair. If it is assumed that this is a long-haul service, then it has to be made to be unique rather than just another airline competing for the cut-throat Far East or transatlantic business-class routes. It is known that service can be copied given time. A company should seek to build on the back of a service which it is the first to offer. For example, if the target market, based on marketing research, is businessmen on long-haul flights who have little interest in in-flight films or entertainment. But they may want to use their laptop computers throughout the flight or take advantage of the (nearly) global reach of Vodafone Air Touch to communicate by mobile phone with their colleagues or other persons. It is possible for IT to provide this without affecting the electronic equipment of the aircraft. Premium prices may be charged on these routes but only if by such means competitive advantage can be established to fill the aircraft. An additional service to attract US passengers might be to provide them with Internet access by mobile phone, not available in the US, connecting them to their company intranet systems.

10   PROMOTION

1 (a)   Background noise, accent, sucking sweets, gunfire, distraction thinking about something else.

   (b)   Eliminate background noise. Reduce the number of intermediaries. Build redundancy into the message by complicating it or by writing the message down.

2 (a)   A code: the alphabet is a conventional system from which combinations of signs may be constructed.

   (b)   A channel.

   (c)   A message: it is a unique combination of signs.

   (d)   Light can be a code (as it provides the basis for the combinations of flashes which make up Morse code). Light can be a signal (in the flashes that constitute Morse code). Light can be a channel (in that I can use a light to read a book);. Light can be a message. (If I leave a light in the window it means that my husband is out.)

   (e)   This refers to noise and redundancy. The crackly line is noise; the repetition of the message is redundancy

3 Figure 10.6 should be used as a template for this answer. Briefly, it should start with an analysis of the target market to investigate the codes and sub-codes and relevant referent systems used by the receiver group. This is to enable understanding of the denotations and connotations which people may bring to bear on the signifiers used in advertising or other advertisements. The analysis should be concerned to identify market segments within the target group, as these may form the basis for the development of a more targeted strategy. The analysis may also want to explore the social network of the addressee group and in particular to identify potential opinion leaders.

   Clearly stated objectives should be specified for the campaign which are measurable, accountable and achievable within a defined time period. Objectives may be stated in line with the AIDA model, although the potential difficulties with this model should be noted, in particular, with respect to the 'weak' theory of advertising effects. In considering the strategy, the marketing planner would address issues such as the mixture of 'push' and 'pull' to be used in the campaign. Next is considering the kinds of message to be constructed and a communications platform should be formed which can be used as the basis on which the message is created for the campaign. The platform creates the values, the sort of message to be constructed. The platform is important, as it communicates the 'tone of voice' and the appeal which is to be used in the campaign. The FCB grid could come in useful at this stage in that it advocates four possible strategies which might form the basis of a platform.

   Next the planner should consider the choice of contact mix: the blend of advertising, direct marketing, sales promotions, personal selling, sponsorship and publicity that is to be used in the campaign. The reach and frequency of different media should be determined. Once a detailed media plan has been drawn up, the planner should have a good idea of what the budget should be, if it is to be based on an objective and task approach. The planner should consider the response, particularly if potential customers are to be invited to write to, phone or email the company. A typical problem is where the level of response is underestimated.

The two final stages which should be attended to are follow-up and evaluation of the campaign.

4 The 'hypodermic' model is useful in that it helps to understand some key aspects of communication between information sources and addressees. The model helps to understand that communication is not straightforward but is always mediated through some channel. The channel is important as it helps shape the form of the message and the way in which it is coded. For example, television and newspapers are different channels: with television the medium is active and people are relatively passive, e.g. they cannot control the pace of television.

On the other hand, newspapers must be actively absorbed to understand their message. The channel can be a source of noise which interferes with or even drowns out the message. Noise may be the result of some physical disturbance on the channel itself, such as static or interference; or it can be present in the environment and compete with the message, e.g. the noise of a drill in the background while a lecturer is trying to speak. Or again noise could be the result of people whispering during a lecture. Noise can result from the inattention of the addressee: 'I may be having a daydream at the time the message is being broadcast.' The answer to noise is redundancy, either by repeating the message or making the code on which it is based more complex.

The concept of a code model also helps to understand that communication is not natural but cultural. Examples of codes are languages like the English language, Morse code and sign language. Often it is not sufficient to know the basic code that an addressee might use. The communicator must also strive to understand the sub-codes, e.g. dialects, that are employed. If the source and addressee do not share the same code then it is likely that miscommunication will take place.

The model is useful in helping marketers understand how complex the communications process is. It provides some clues as to how to achieve effective communications by:

■ identifying the relevant codes, sub-codes and referent systems;
■ trying to eliminate or reduce the effects of noise.

However, many authors suggest that too literal a use of the model can lead to a serious undervaluation of the power of the addressee to decode messages. The model does not account for the social basis of communications: the role of those in the addressee's social network such as opinion leaders. Marketers must be sensitive to the presence of opinion leaders and 'stars' in the network structure. Furthermore, the model assumes that the addressee is passive, a target for the communications campaign. Research has shown that addressees are creative and active in the way in which they can accept, reject or twist the message which is sent by the source. All this additional information suggests that it is only by means of a thorough understanding of the context in which the communication is being decoded that the communicator can hope to achieve effective communications.

In summary, the hypodermic model is useful but flawed. The principal lesson which the communicator can learn from this is to seek to gain a thorough knowledge of the addressee and of the social milieu in which s/he lives and to involve consumers in the design of the communications campaign.

5   Research should be carried out as part of an analysis of the key target group to determine what codes, sub-codes and referent systems are relevant to this group. The research will be qualitative, consisting of in-depth interviews or focus groups as we wish to learn the 'language' used by this group. For example, in researching for an anti-drug campaign aimed at 10–12 year old males marketers recruited several groups of children from this target population and hired a trained researcher to discuss drug taking with them. The researcher asked the children:

- what names they gave to different drugs;
- how the drugs were used;
- what age groups used them;
- key characteristics of users or non-users;
- people the children looked up to and respected and those whom they did not respect;
- what their fears were when they took drugs.

This information enabled marketers to gain knowledge of:

- The appropriate language to use in framing any communications, e.g. the correct words for using drugs.
- The fact that children did not 'sniff' glue, which was now regarded as being unfashionable; instead they 'buzzed' gas. These are the sub-codes used by the children.
- Information about referent systems, the contexts in which drugs are used and the sort of people who use them, deal in them and disapprove of them. Drug dealers were disliked by children, who felt that they exploited people while some celebrities such as football stars were regarded as anti-drugs and as 'cool'.
- Attitudes to the medium. The children did not like advertising, as they felt that it was another way for adults to tell them what to do. Even if they agreed with the message the knowledge might make them ignore it or even rebel against it.

This latter point meant that the advertisers tried their best to ensure that the communication did not look like advertising; the communications were not branded and the creative team went to considerable lengths to make the communications look as if they had been made by amateurs. The research helped in designing messages that were appropriate to the target group by using their language and referring to people who were known to be important, e.g. one execution depicted a drug dealer who cheated people.

The next stage of research was to test the actual advertisements for awareness, comprehension and understanding. Once more focus groups of children from the target group were shown different executions and were asked to tell a trained researcher what they thought of these. Following this research the final advertisements were selected.

Research is useful before a campaign is run by setting a baseline measurement. This quantitative study samples the entire population to ascertain the hierarchy of effects for drug use. It measured how many children were aware of the dangers of drug use, how many were interested in giving up drugs in addition to estimating numbers of children actually taking drugs. This research formed the basis for the tracking study which was carried out during the campaign and for several months after it. Tracking research measured recall and recognition of the campaign against competing communications (which could have been a source of noise), the number of children interested in giving up drugs and the numbers actually taking drugs.

A good answer to this question would indicate that different kinds of research are important at different points in the campaign. Both qualitative and quantitative research can be important before the campaign has started, for different reasons. Quantitative research can be useful in setting baseline statistics, qualitative research in finding out about codes, sub-codes and referent systems. Qualitative research becomes useful in pre-testing the communication, while quantitative research hand qualitative research are both of importance while the campaign is running and after it has been completed.

6   The objectives of the campaign, e.g. with respect to the hierarchy of effects, if it is to create awareness, interest, desire or action. For example, advertising and publicity are good at raising awareness and creating interest but not so good at stimulating action. On the other hand, personal selling although it is expensive often can result in a sale.

The characteristics of the product are important, e.g. if the product is an expensive industrial product then it is more likely that advertisements in the trade press and personal selling are used. If the product is a FMCG such as a soft drink then a mixture of mass advertising to raise awareness coupled with sales promotions to prompt initial purchase. It may form part of the 'pull' approach, while the firm may also 'push' the product through intermediaries by offering a range of incentives coupled with visits from the sales force to large suppliers. Direct marketing is more likely to be used for products that are relatively complex and high-involvement, e.g. financial services and cars. The relationship between the person and the product is important; e.g. for high-involvement products, television is not thought to be so effective, although it may form the basis of an emotional appeal, but press is.

Obviously, the resources available to the marketer are important. If the marketer has a limited budget this may curtail his/her ability to engage in advertising and he/she may have to rely on other below the line material such as brochures and leaflets.

7   The photo denotes Catherine Deneuve. The connotations of 'Catherine Deneuve' are that she is chic and sophisticated. The photo denotes Margot Hemingway. Margot Hemingway connotes assertiveness and being a 'tomboy'.

8   The denotation is the person, the US comedian; of course not everyone might think he is really funny. That would be to make a connotation. The connotations which the advertisers hoped would communicate the brand values were 'macho', 'tough', 'adventurous' and 'strong' and the advertising research indicated that these were the values with which the target audience associated the advertising.

9   Within an IMC campaign sponsorship will be used to support 'above the line' advertising in the media, such as television, press, cinema and radio. For a FMCG firm such as Kimberley-Clark this is likely to involve running an advertising campaign across the media and reinforcing the message using 'below the line' promotion such as sales promotion, sponsorship as well as public relations and personal selling (probably through merchandising). Sponsorship, such as that used with Madame Tussaud's, is a way of targeting population sectors (visitors to the waxwork attraction) to strengthen the advertising message for the IMC campaign. In this case, by sponsoring the Andrex puppy exhibit, Kimberley-Clark is endeavouring to attract favourable attention to the Andrex toilet paper brand among the visitors to the attraction. It is anticipated that such favourable attention will encourage visitors to remember the brand and increase purchases of Andrex toilet paper. At the point of sale the children might play on their parents to persuade them to purchase Andrex toilet paper in favour of another brand by recalling the 'cute puppy' seen at Madame Tussaud's.

10   The benefit of association of Madame Tussaud's with celebrity brands and for film companies is to encourage attraction visitors to become aware of and to favour the brands that are portrayed. For example, visitors will enjoy being able to feel associated with the waxwork of Madonna or David Beckham or with the Incredible Hulk. The visitors will promote awareness of the celebrity by word-of-mouth discussion with friends and family and raise the profile of the celebrity. The celebrities' brands and film companies are prepared to negotiate sponsorship deals to encourage awareness of their profiles among the public. Relatively the cost of sponsorship is much lower than equivalent expenditure on 'above the line' media. It can be more targeted, e.g. at the type of person that visits Madame Tussaud's, perhaps families with young teenagers. The message that is presented reinforces brand awareness, helping to bring together the components of the IMC campaign.

11   The potential value of a sponsorship agreement is ascertained in various ways. It is likely to relate to the 'passing traffic', the number and type of person passing by the exhibit and, as mentioned in the Madame Tussaud case, the time spent at the exhibit is considered. In effect, the 'rate card' takes into account the relative attractiveness of the exhibit taking into account competing attractions. Ultimately there is likely to be some negotiation between the sponsorship parties in deciding on the final agreement.

12   (a)   The target market for this advertisement consists of potential foster parents.

       (b)   It could be argued that there are two appeals. The attributes of the girl depicted in the advertisement are used to form an 'appealing' picture. The second appeal is financial.

       (c)   This publication charges £2,400 (US$4,306) for a full-page advertisement. The likely cost would have been around £600 (US$1,076).

(d) By comparison costs for a full-page advertisement in a national newspaper such as the *Daily Mirror* would be closer to £27,500 (US$49,335).

(e) The issue of 'social marketing' has aroused considerable debate among academics. Some question whether it is right for people to be treated as if they were products which can be bought and sold. However, many people use personal columns to advertise for new companions and so other academics suggest that the practice is acceptable.

11 PLACE: CHANNELS OF DISTRIBUTION

1 The producer should consider a number of issues, including the characteristics of the product, the market it is targeting, the size of the company itself and the structure of channels of distribution used for this type of yoghurt product. If the product is being distributed in a developed economy, say within Europe, estimates should be made regarding the likely demand for the product and its market share. Depending on whether the product is to be a specialist product, e.g. within the Häagen Dazs range or a standard yoghurt product, the alternative channels of distribution should be considered.

As this is a consumer product, the channels of distribution might be to use wholesalers and retailers. It is unlikely that the yoghurt producer would consider the use of agents. The product has a short life and will have to be moved between the producer and the consumer within forty-eight hours of production. Consequently it is unlikely that wholesalers, unless they owned the actual outlets, would be used. Rather the producer would attempt to move the products direct to the retailer, using the retailers' own regional distribution centre networks or by linking into a VMS, itself dominated by the targeted retailers.

It is likely that the producer already supplies the major retailers with other produce. It would be appropriate to use similar channels of distribution to those used for the other produce. Once again this suggests using the retailers' own regional distribution centre networks, their VMSs, or even any HMSs with which they might be involved.

The ideal solution would be to persuade the retailers to add this new product to the others that are already supplied by the manufacturer and to use the same channels of distribution. However, this can be difficult, especially in the UK, where the balance of power for yoghurt products is with the retailers because of the dominance of private label lines. The larger food retailers may be unwilling to support the introduction of another yoghurt product to increase competition against their own private lines and those other established brands. It could be difficult to gain acceptance for the new product from the established food retailers. It may be that it would be so difficult that national coverage using the major food retailers would not be possible and, consequently, the producer would be advised to concentrate on supplying the smaller, independent retailers. The volume of sales would be smaller than if distribution through the larger food retailers was achieved, but the profit margins on sales could be higher.

Clearly, it would be difficult to compete with the established yoghurt producers and the major retailers would pose a considerable challenge. It might be better to critically assess the viability of introducing the proposed new product into such a competitive market.

2 Consumer goods are targeted at the mass market, e.g. foodstuffs and domestic electrical equipment such as radios and washing machines. Industrial products, on the other hand, are targeted at organizational buyers representing industrial and commercial firms, e.g. fork lift trucks for warehouses, computers for commercial businesses, components for car producers and ships for leisure cruise firms.

The producer of the goods may use various routes (or intermediaries within the channel of distribution) to get the products to the end user. The choice of the route within the channel is considerable, as is shown in Figure 11.1.

Traditionally, producers of consumer goods have used more intermediaries than producers of industrial products, because they have a much larger number of consumers to reach. Usually the intermediaries within the distribution chain used for consumer products provide a range of services for the producer. They will store the products in warehouses until the consumer needs them. They will repackage the bulk consignments into quantities and volumes to suit consumer consumption. They will display the product in the appropriate manner in the right retail outlet, at the right time to suit the consumer. In order to provide these types of services, channels of distribution have evolved with a number of intermediaries taking on services within the value chain to ensure the products reach an end destination in the appropriate manner. Traditionally, for a consumer product, the services of any, or a combination of, agents, wholesalers and retailers might be used.

Latterly the roles of these intermediaries within the channels of distribution have become less clearly defined, leading to increasing overlap between them. The wholesaler role has been much reduced and in many situations it has been removed: the goods may move through the value chain without using the services of wholesalers. Agents may be used but, increasingly, their services are being subsumed within those of the retailers. VMSs and HMSs are evolving whereby one of the intermediaries within the channel of distribution links with, and may even own, other intermediaries within the chain. While, traditionally, consumer goods passed through a number of intermediaries to reach the consumer, it is becoming common for one of those intermediaries to dominate the other intermediaries, reducing the number of individual intermediaries involved.

With industrial products there is less need for the services of intermediaries within the channels of distribution. The number of customers is much smaller than in the consumer market: typically, it may be that no more than thirty or forty businesses and certainly not reaching the millions of potential customers in the consumer market. Usually, industrial producers have close links with their customers. The links can have been developed through liaison in research and development and through the personal networks that are encouraged in industrial markets. The channels of distribution will be shorter than those used within the consumer markets, although even those within the consumer markets are themselves becoming shorter. Industrial firms may use agents to initiate the contact with the customer. Generally, industrial producers do not use the services of wholesalers or retailers, although as their production has become more consumer market-oriented, they have begun to use the traditional consumer product channel system. For example, a building materials producer might supply house builders direct, using no intermediary at all, but the producer might also use the builders' merchants (wholesalers) and D-I-Y retailers to get the product to the general public consumer.

The traditional channels of distribution used for consumer goods are likely to be more extended than those used for industrial products, with the intermediaries for consumer goods providing a range of services including warehousing, repackaging and transport. However, the channels for the consumer market are becoming shorter and more similar to those used by the industrial producer.

There is considerable pressure to reduce the logistics costs within the channels of distribution for both industrial and consumer products. This is encouraging the reduction of stock movement and the associated costs of distribution of that stock along the value chain. While the channels and the intermediaries used differ for consumer and industrial goods, they are becoming more similar, although industrial products usually have the minimum of intermediaries between themselves and their customers.

Furthermore, suppliers may have so much of their business tied up with only a few dominant retailers that many consumer markets are becoming organizationally buyer behaviour-focused in terms of the relationships in the channel. Traditional consumer market channels of distribution have been restructuring towards direct distribution, with no intermediaries at all, providing similar channels to those used in industrial markets. It is forecast that direct distribution will be the most significant consumer channel of the future, making industrial and consumer channels of distribution all the more similar.

3   Increasingly, within mass consumer markets, retailers are dominating the channels of distribution. The retail industry is becoming more concentrated, with the surviving retailers increasing in size in terms of volume and market share, especially within the food retailing sector. These retailers have become involved in both VMSs and HMSs joining intermediaries within the supply chain. Usually these VMS and HMS arrangements have increased the influence of retailers within the channels of distribution, with the retailers controlling the services undertaken by the intermediaries.

Often, the intermediaries have little option but to accept their role within the VMSs and HMSs. If they are in this position, they must provide the required services, e.g. warehousing, stock management, repackaging and associated transport, at the standard specified by the retailer. In order to do so they are required to invest in the relevant IT and to have this integrated with all other members of the value chain, fully linking with the producer and retailer. Appropriate investment in IT is required. At the same time, the intermediaries must build up confidence between themselves and the producer and retailer so that there is understanding of their roles and trust between all concerned.

Alternatively, in place of working with the retailers, the intermediaries may decide to fight the increasing dominance of the retailers. In that case it could be appropriate for the intermediaries themselves to join forces against the retailers. For example, producers might consider linking among themselves, or more commonly, trying to make themselves more powerful within the channel. This could be achieved by increasing expenditure on marketing, e.g. by increasing promotional expenditure to heighten brand awareness and the associated consumer demand for the product. Brands such as Cadbury's, Heinz and Kellogg's have been successful in this way so that consumers demand retailers stock products within these brands. However, it is only the large companies that have the resources to develop such powerful brands.

Sales agents, distributors and wholesalers find it difficult to fight the dominance of retailers within the value chain. Ultimately they have to prove themselves to be cost-effective in providing their services and while that is the situation they will continue to be used. For example, in the fashion clothing industry it suits the large number of smaller retailers to continue to use wholesalers within the channel. They provide the appropriate service of storing stock and transporting it to the retail locations in the required volumes for the fashion boutiques. However, the larger clothing retailers do not need such services and may well undertake them within their own services, or subsume the services of a wholesaler that is included within an appropriate VMS. The survival of the intermediaries will depend on the relative dominance of all concerned within the channels of distribution and the efficiency of the service provided.

Other developments have been the advent of producers opening their own sales outlets, e.g. factory outlet centres, fashion designer shops and sports brands shops such as Nike, to control their distribution with manufacturer-integrated retailing. Usually such centres are located out of town and often on industrial estates. They have become popular with consumers. The Internet also provides opportunities to eliminate the traditional retailer-wholesaler intermediaries and is posing a considerable threat to traditional retailing.

4 Franchising arrangements have been beneficial to the supplier of the product or service concerned in acting as enablers to grow businesses at a faster rate than might have been the case if internal financial capital and human resources had been used. This has meant that consumers have benefited by having a larger number and range of retail outlets than would have been the situation if the franchisor (the originator of the product or service) had expanded using his/her own resources.

Furthermore, the franchise agreements involve providing products or services through systems that have a successful track record. The franchisee (who buys into the business agreement) starts a business that is likely to be successful, reducing the risk of failure and the start-up costs. This should result in the consumer having a wider range of goods and retail outlets available than might otherwise be the case.

Examples of retail franchise agreements include those for McDonald's and Benetton. McDonald's has been able to fund its global expansion through the use of franchising. Consumers have benefited by having an extensive network of outlets throughout the world which they can frequent and, at the same time, they can be assured of obtaining a standard product and service. With minor differences to match national culture and demand, the food and service in McDonald's outlets in Edinburgh will be the same as in Paris, Moscow or Washington, with the firm controlling the franchise maintaining overall control of the outlets. Consumers are guaranteed a particular type of product and level of service which gives them some assurance. Similarly, for Benetton, the clothing sold in its outlets throughout the world has a standard quality and portrays a particular brand image that is specific to Benetton clothes. Consumers benefit by knowing that, wherever they purchase Benetton clothes, those clothes will denote a particular image, i.e. that the wearer is young, environmentally aware, prepared to pay a higher than average price, and so on.

Retailing franchising arrangements are beneficial to the consumer that wants a global coverage of retail outlets and guarantee of product quality.

5   Generally, retailers have been less involved in international expansion than has been the situation for manufacturers. While manufacturers expanded to gain benefits including lower production costs and associated economies of scale, retailers have not found such international expansion so critical. While some retailers have expanded globally, these have not become as dominant as their counterparts, the MNCs, with manufacturing bases.

Traditionally, food retailers have remained within their own national boundaries and have not expanded internationally, e.g. the major food retailers in the UK, such as Tesco, Asda and Sainsbury's. It is only since the early 1990s that UK food retailers have begun to expand to continental Europe, targeting France, the Netherlands and Belgium. Usually expansion was undertaken by acquiring national chains and through collaborating in strategic alliances. More recently, European retailers have directed their international expansion towards CEE countries, especially to Hungary, the Czech Republic and Poland. Nevertheless, it is only in the 1990s that a few UK food retailers have considered it necessary to expand to continental Europe.

Similarly, within continental Europe, international expansion among food retailers was concentrated within the continental countries rather than across Europe. Some food retailers have also expanded to North America, e.g. Dutch Ahold, and to South America, e.g. French Carrefour.

Among the other retailers, international expansion has occurred to compensate for national markets not satisfying growth demands. Ikea, the furniture group, has most of its retail outlets outside its home base in Sweden. In the 1990s M&S from the UK undertook increasingly global coverage, with retail outlets across Europe, as well as in the Far Eastern markets, but since 2000 it has withdrawn from continental Europe. Other examples of international retailers include the Dutch C&A, the Italian, Benetton and the US Toys 'R' Us.

While European food retailers have been hesitant to expand across borders, the larger multiple retailers, especially clothing retailers, have found it appropriate to expand internationally. However, many such retailers have faced difficulties in this expansion, especially to North America, and have been obliged to retract. In particular, Body Shop, Laura Ashley and Boots the Chemist from the UK have found such expansion to be challenging.

Since the 1990s retailers have found it difficult to maintain their expansion targets to achieve desirable sales and profits. Consequently, within Europe at least, there has been considerable consolidation through merger and acquisition, especially within food retailing. While much of this consolidation has taken place within national boundaries, liberalization within the SEM has encouraged cross-border acquisition which has provided more potential for retailers to grow than the more traditional, but slower, organic growth. It is to be anticipated that more cross-border expansion will take place within Europe as the SEM becomes more harmonized.

Since the mid-1990s there has been a move for youth fashion clothes manufacturers to expand from their home country across Europe and beyond, e.g. Zara and Mango (Spain) and H&M (Sweden).

In conclusion, the international expansion of retailers has lagged behind that of manufacturers. Traditionally, most retailers have operated within their own national boundaries. As country markets are becoming more similar in terms of consumer demand and as opportunities for international expansion are showing more growth potential than domestic markets, international retailing is increasing. Nevertheless, such international expansion has not been without its difficulties. A number of retailers have tried to expand across borders, but been obliged to retract. It still poses many challenges to be implemented successfully.

12 VIRTUAL MARKETING

1   The key to the answer may be found at p. 381 and in Table 12.1. The differences may be summarized as:

-   ■   Traditional media focus on one-way communications; multimedia focus on two-way communications.
-   ■   Traditional media focus on fixed media; multimedia focus on the clickstream.
-   ■   The producer initiates with traditional media; with multimedia it is the user who initiates.
-   ■   Channel costs are high with fixed media; with multimedia high costs are associated with bandwidth.
-   ■   Traditional media focus on telling and selling; multimedia focus on linking and thinking.
-   ■   Usually traditional media are affordable only by large organizations; multimedia allows access to all sizes of organization.

2   Hoffman *et al.* (1996) define 'flow' as: 'the state occurring during network naviga-tion which is characterized by a seamless sequence of responses facilitated by machine interactivity, intrinsically enjoyable, is accompanied by a loss of self-consciousness and finally is self-reinforcing. Flow can be enhanced by ensuring the smoothness of the "trip"; minimizing waiting times and facilitating search by the use of clear navigation markers. Where content is provided this should be worthwhile and not merely hype.'

3   The key consequence of Internet communication for marketers is that it changes from 'one to many' (traditional mass communication) to 'many to many' (Internet communication). This has further important consequences. Increasingly it is becoming difficult, if not impossible, for organizations to control the flow of information about their activities which previously may have been concealed from others because they happened in remote parts of the world or because those concerned did not have access to the mass media. In the new and highly visible communications environment created by the Internet the organization is surrounded by a number of stakeholders, some of which may be campaigning against the organization and its activities. These stakeholders will have sites which are easily accessible to Internet users. A further implication is that organizations need to change their culture from one which seeks to gatekeep or protect information to one which welcomes visibility, openness and healthy debate and to persuade others that they are acting in the public interest. This new transparency of information should fuel concern to implement standards for corporate governance and to communicate effectively to employees and other stakeholders.

4   As explained in the text, a website does not promote itself but must be actively promoted to others by the use of conventional media such as stationery and traditional advertising vehicles, in addition to new Internet vehicles of communication.

5   Bezos was first into the market, having spotted the opportunity that the Web was ideally suited to small-ticket commercial items that were highly portable. Books also fitted the demographic of the average user of that time, who was of high social class and well educated. Better still for Bezos, commercial applications on the Web were in their infancy and Amazon stood out clearly from the competition. Consequently Amazon gained high recognition quickly, which was something that Barnes & Noble struggled to compete with when subsequently they started to trade online. On the other hand, Amazon had to invest in an expensive distribution network and to subsidize deliveries to its customers in order to compete effectively with Barnes & Noble.

6   This has changed as Amazon has entered the precincts of other kinds of business. The Amazon auction site competes with, and is reputedly no match for, Ebay; it also competes with large catalogue suppliers and with large electronics intermediaries and those in the kitchenware business.

7   This is up to you. Try to think of someone between the ages of 3 and 15 years old. What impact do you think that such advertising has on them?

8   Without regulation of some kind there is a danger of an 'anything goes' approach. This is a sensitive area where individual freedom must be traded off against societal good. However, it seems clear that some regulation is necessary.

REFERENCES

1 MARKETING: DEVELOPMENT AND SCOPE OF THE SUBJECT

Ames, C.B. (1970) 'Trappings vs. substance in industrial marketing', *Harvard Business Review*, July–August, pp. 41–52.

Bell, M.L. (1966) *Marketing concepts and strategy,* London: Macmillan.

Brown, S. (1995) *Postmodern marketing,* London: Routledge.

Brown, S. (1998) *Postmodern marketing II, Telling tales,* London: International Thomson Business Press.

Brownlie, D. and Saren, M. (1992) 'The four Ps of the marketing concept: prescriptive, polemical, permanent and problematical', *European Journal of Marketing*, 26 (4), pp. 34–47.

Carson, R.L. (1962) *Silent spring,* New York: Fawcett World Library.

Considine, S. (2004) '"Like a rolling stone" – the hit we almost missed', *New York Times*, 3 December, p. 29.

Davidson, H. (1975, 1987) *Offensive marketing: or how to make your competitors followers*, Harmondsworth: Penguin.

Drucker, P. F. (1955) 'The promise of automation: America's next twenty years' II, *Harper's*, 210 (1258), March, pp. 41–7.

Fine, S. H. (1981) *The marketing of ideas and social issues*, New York: Praeger.

Fournier, S., Dobscha, S. and Mick, D.G. (1998) 'Preventing the premature death of relationship marketing', *Harvard Business Review*, January–February, pp. 42–51.

Galbraith, J.K. (1967) *The new industrial state*, 2nd edn, London: Pelican.

Grönroos, C. (1996) 'From marketing mix to relationship marketing: towards a paradigm shift in marketing', keynote paper, MCB University Press: http://www.mcb.co.uk/.

Hayes, R. and Abernathy, W. (1980) 'Managing our way to economic decline', in N.L. Tushman and W.L. Moore (eds) *Readings in the management of innovation*, Mashfield MA: Pitman.

Hirschman, E.C. (1983) 'Aesthetics, ideologies and the limits of the marketing concept', *Journal of Marketing*, 47, pp. 45–55.

Hooley, G.J. and Lynch, J.E. (1985) 'Marketing lessons from the UK's high-flying companies', *Journal of Marketing Management*, 1 (1), pp. 65–74.

Kohli, A.K. and Jaworski, B.J. (1990) 'Market orientation: the construct, research propositions and managerial implications', *Journal of Marketing*, 54 (April), pp. 1–18.

Kotler, P. (1972a) 'A generic concept of marketing', *Journal of Marketing*, 36 (April), pp. 46–54.

Kotler, P. (1972b) 'What consumerism means for marketers', *Harvard Business Review*, May–June, pp. 48–57.

Kotler, P. (1991) *Marketing management*, Englewood Cliffs NJ: Prentice Hall.

Kotler, P. (2000) *Marketing management*, millennium edn, Harlow: Prentice Hall.

Kotler, P. and Levy, S.J. (1969) 'Broadening the concept of marketing', *Journal of Marketing*, 33 (January), pp. 10–15.

Laczniak, G.R., Lusch, R.F. and Murphy, P.R. (1979) 'Social marketing: its ethical dimensions', *Journal of Marketing*, 43 (spring), pp. 29–36.

Levitt, T. (1960) 'Marketing myopia', *Harvard Business Review*, July–August, pp. 45–57.

Levitt, T. (1962) *Innovation in marketing, new perspectives for profit and growth,* New York: McGraw-Hill.

McCracken, G. (1990) *Culture and consumption,* Bloomington IN and Indianapolis IN: Indiana University Press.

McKitterick, J.B. (1957) 'What is the marketing concept?' in F. Bass (ed), *The frontiers of marketing thought in action,* Chicago: American Marketing Association, pp. 71–82.

Marcuse, H. (1964) *One-dimensional man,* London: Routledge.

Narver, J.C. and Slater, S.F. (1990) 'The effect of a market orientation on business profitability', *Journal of Marketing,* 54 (October), pp. 20–35.

Packard, V. (1957) *The hidden persuaders,* London: Penguin.

Packard, V. (1960) *The waste makers,* London, Pelican.

Peppers, D., Rogers, M. and Dorf, B. (1999) 'Is your company ready for one-to-one marketing?' *Harvard Business Review,* January–February, pp. 151–60.

Ries, A. and Trout, J. (1981) *Positioning: the battle for your mind,* New York: McGraw-Hill.

Ries, A. and Trout, J. (1986) *Marketing warfare,* New York and St Louis MO: McGraw-Hill.

Sheth, J., Gardner, D.M. and Garrett, D.E. (1988) *Marketing theory: evolution and evaluation,* New York: Wiley.

2   STRATEGIC MARKETING AND THE PLANNING PROCESS

Anon. (1984) 'IBM PC's still bringing in the business', *PC Week,* 20 March, 1 (2), p. 54.

Anon. (1995) 'Apple seeks supreme appeal for Mac look and feel', *PC Week,* 30 January, 12 (4), p. 93 (1).

Anon. (1997) 'Apple shoots foot (abandoning clone strategy is a mistake)' *Company Business.*

Anon. (1998) 'Shouting from the billboards', *Forbes,* 23 February, 161 (4), p. S28 (1).

Anon. (2005) 'Coolest player in town', *Guardian* (Technology *Guardian*), 22 September, pp. 1–2.

Ansoff, I.H. (1969) *Business strategy,* London: Penguin.

Bauman, Z. (1995) *Life in fragments: essays in postmodern morality,* Cambridge MA: Blackwell.

Bell, M.L. (1966) *Marketing concepts and strategy,* London: Macmillan.

Consumers International (1998) 'Making the market safe and fair for Pacific consumers: food dumping in the Pacific: the case of mutton flaps', *SPCPP News Archive,* Consumers International, www.spepp.org.nz/archive/mutton.htm.

Day-Copeland, L. (1988) 'PC competitors are picking up market share at IBM's expense', *PC Week,* 17 October, 5 (42), p. 1, 50 (1).

Dixon, P. (1997) *Press Association,* 19 October.

Dunfee, T.W. and Warren, D.E. (2001) 'A normative analysis of doing business in China', *Journal of Business Ethics,* 32 (3), August.

Fukuyama, F. (1992) *The end of history and the last man,* London: Penguin.

Galbraith, J.K. (1992) *The culture of contentment,* London: Penguin.

Guo, G.X. (2001) *Guanxi in Chinese politics*: http://millercenter.virginia.edu/pubs/dissertation_chapters/2001/guo%20Chapter.pdf

Harvey, D. (1989) *The condition of postmodernity: an enquiry into the origins of cultural change,* London: Blackwell.

Henley Centre (1998) 'Consumer and leisure futures', *Henley Centre,* Issue 5 (28 September).

Hooley, G.J. and Lynch, J.E. (1985) 'Marketing lessons from the UK's high-flying companies', *Journal of Marketing Management,* 1 (1), pp. 65–74.

Ikeda, H. (1996) 'The first joint venture of brewing in China', *Institute of Brewing,* Asia-Pacific Section. Proceedings of the XXIV Convention, Singapore, 17 March, pp. 22–32.

Kahn, H. and Wiener, A.J. (1967) 'The next thirty-three years: a framework for speculation', *Daedalus*, (Boston MA: American Academy of Arts and Science), 96 (3), pp. 705–32.

Keegan, V. (1998) 'Not always the right company', *Guardian,* 9 November.

Kohli, A.K. and Jaworski, B.J. (1990) 'Market orientation: the construct, research propositions and managerial implications', *Journal of Marketing*, 54 (April), pp. 1–18.

Levitt, T. (1986) *The marketing imagination*, London and New York: Free Press.

Li, Y., Yin, X., Teng, J., Gu, G. and Dueker, K. (1996) 'An updated review of brewing and malting Industries in China', *Institute of Brewing*, Asia Pacific Section, Proceedings of XXIV Convention, Singapore, 17–24 March, pp. 11–6.

Luo, Y. (1997) 'Guanxi, principles, philosophies, and implications', *Human Systems Management*,16 (1).

McGuire, M. (1994) 'Mac gears up for second decade; set new standards for user interaction', *PC Week*, 17 January, 11 (2), p. 25 (2).

Mak, P. (1998) 'The challenges of marketing beer in the People's Republic of China, Glasgow: Heriot-Watt University, honours dissertation, School of Management, p. 49.

Miller, D. (1998) 'Coca-Cola: a black sweet drink from Trinidad' in *Material cultures: why some things matter*, London: UCL Press, pp. 169–89.

Morgenstern, D. (1996) 'Apple plots strategic shifts', *PC Week,* 8 July, 13 (27), p. 8 (1).

Narver, J.C. and Slater, S.F. (1990) 'The effect of a market orientation on business profitability', *Journal of Marketing*, 54 (October), pp. 20–35.

Paxton, A. (1994) 'The food miles report: the dangers of long-distance food transport', London: Sustainable Agriculture Food and Environment.

Plato Logic (2005) Chinese Beer Market www.platologic.co.uk/news.htm.

Robin, D.P. and Reidenbach, E. (1987) 'Social responsibility, ethics, and marketing strategy: closing the gap between concept and application', *Journal of Marketing*, 51 (January), pp. 44–58.

Schor, J.B. (1991) *Overworked American: the unexpected decline of leisure,* New York: Basic Books.

Sheldon, D. (1998) 'Retail distribution 1998', IGD Business Publication, Institute of Grocery Distribution, April, p. 252.

United Nations (2005) *Human Development Report*, 7 September, http://hdr.undp.org.

Vinzant, C. (1998) 'The iMac: fast like cheetah, cute like kitten', *Fortune*, 9 November, p. 46 (1).

Yeung, I.Y. and Tung, R.L. (1996) 'Achieving business success in Confucian societies: the importance of Guanxi (connections)', *Organizational Dynamics,* autumn, pp. 54–65.

Xin, K.R. and Pearce, J.L. (1996) 'Guanxi: connections as substitutes for formal institutional support', *Academy of Management Journal*, 39 (6), pp. 1641–58.

3 CONSUMER BUYING BEHAVIOUR

Assael, H. (1995) *Consumer behavior and marketing action*, 5th edn, Cincinnati: South Western, Figure 5.1, p. 153 and p. 156.

Azjen, I. (1991) 'The theory of planned behaviour', *Organization Behaviour and Human Decision Processes*, 50, pp. 179–211.

Baddeley, A.D. and Hitch, G. (1974) 'Working memory', in G.H. Bower (ed.) *The psychology of learning and motivation: advances in research and theory* VIII, New York: Academic Press, pp. 47–89.

Bandura, A. (1972) *Social learning theory*, Englewood Cliffs NJ: Prentice Hall.

Baudrillard, J. (1988) 'Consumer society' in M. Poster (ed.) *Jean Baudrillard: selected writings*, Cambridge: Cambridge University Press.

Belk, R. (1975) 'Situational variables and consumer behaviour', *Journal of Consumer Research*, December, pp. 157–164.

Belk, R. W. (1988) 'Possessions and the extended self', *Journal of Consumer Research*, 15 (September), pp. 139–68.

Bettman, J.R. Luce, M.F. and Payne, J.W. (1998) 'Constructive consumer choice processes', *Journal of Consumer Research*, 25 (3), pp. 187–218.

Buckley, K.W. (1982) 'The selling of a psychologist: John Broadus Watson and the application of behavioural techniques to advertising', *Journal of the History of the Behavioral Sciences*, 18, pp. 207–21.

Buckley, K.W. (1982) 'The selling of a psychologist: John Broadus Watson and the application of behavioral techniques to advertising', *Journal of the History of the Behavioral Sciences*, 18, pp. 207–21.

Coon, D.J. (1994) '"Not a creature of reason": the alleged impact of Watsonian behaviourism on advertising in the 1920s' in J.T. Todd and E.K. Morris (eds) *Modern perspectives on John B. Watson and classical behaviourism*, Contributions in Psychology, No. 24, London: Greenwood Press.

Cowan, N. (2001) 'A reconsideration of mental stage capacity', *Behavior and Brain Sciences*, 24 (1), pp. 87–185.

Cowan, N. (2005) *Working memory capacity*. New York: Psychology Press.

Craik, F. and Lockhart, R. (1972) 'Levels of processing: a framework for memory research', *Journal of Verbal Thinking and Verbal Behavior*, 11, pp. 671–84.

Csikszentmihalyi, Milahy and Rochberg-Halton, Eugene (1981) *The meaning of things: domestic symbols and the self*, 1995 edn, Cambridge: Cambridge University Press.

Darley, W.K. and Smith, R.E. (1995) 'Gender differences in information processing strategies: an empirical test of the selectivity model in advertising response', *Journal of Advertising*, 14 (1), pp. 41–56.

Dichter, E. (1960) *The strategy of desire*, London and New York: Boardman.

Dichter, E. (1964) *Handbook of consumer motivations: the psychology of the world of objects*, New York: McGraw-Hill.

Ehrenberg, A. (1972) *Repeat buying*, Amsterdam: North Holland.

Ehrenberg, A. and Goodhart, P. (2000) 'New brands: near-instant loyalty', *Journal of Marketing Management*, 16, pp. 607–17.

Ehrenberg, A.S.C. and Uncles, M.D. (1999) *Understanding Diriclet-type markets*, London: South Bank Business School.

Elias, N. (1939, 1994) *The civilizing process: the history of manners and state formation and civilization*, trans. Edmund Jephcott, Oxford: Blackwell.

Escalas, J.D. and Bettman, J.R. (2003) 'You are what you eat: the influence of reference groups on consumers' connections to brands', *Journal of Consumer Psychology*, 13 (3), pp. 339–348.

Eysenck, J. (1975) *Know your own personality,* London: Temple Smith.

Falk, P. (1997) 'The genealogy of advertising' in P. Sulkunen, J. Holmwood, H. Radner and G. Schulze (eds) *Constructing the new consumer society*, Basingstoke: Macmillan, pp. 81–108.

Fishbein, M. and Ajzen, I. (1975) *Belief, attitude, intention and behaviour,* Reading MA: Addison Wesley.

Fisher, R.J. and Dubé, L. (2005) 'Gender differences in responses to emotional advertising: a social desirability perspective', *Journal of Consumer Research*, 31 (4), pp. 850–58.

Foxall, G. (1990) *Consumer psychology in behavioural perspective*, London and New York: Routledge.

Foxall, G. (1996) *Consumers in context: the BPM research program*, London and New York: Routledge.

Foxall, G. (2005) *Understanding consumer choice*, London: Palgrave.

Freud, S. (1911) 'Formulations on the two principles of mental functioning' in A. Richards (ed.) *On metapsychology*, trans. James Strachey (1991), pp. 35–44.

Freud, S. (1914) 'On narcissism: an introduction' in A. Richards (ed.) *On metapsychology*, trans. James Strachey (1991), pp. 59–99.

Freud, S. (1923) 'The ego and the id', in Sigmund Freud, *On metapsychology* XI, ed. James Strachey, 1991 edn, pp. 350–66.

Freud, S. (1933) 'New introductory lectures on psychoanalysis', in *Standard edition* XXIII, ed. James Strachey, 1964 edn.

Fromm, E. (1978) *To have or to be?* London: Cape.

Fry, A. (1997) 'Reaching the pink pound', *Marketing*, 4 September, p. 23.

Gardner, B.B. (1959) 'The ABC of motivation research', *Business Topics*, 7 (autumn), pp. 35–41.

Goffman, E. (1961) *Asylums*, New York: Doubleday.

Johnson, M. (1991) 'LBS report debunks the effectiveness of promos', *Marketing*, p. 7.

Kapferer, J.N. and Laurent, G. (1985/6) 'Consumer involvement profiles: a new practical approach to consumer involvement', *Journal of Advertising Research*, 25 (6), pp. 48–56.

Katona, G. (1953) 'Rational behaviour and economic behaviour,' *Psychological Review*, September, pp. 307–18.

Keegan, V. (1998) 'Not always the right company', http://guardian.co.uk, 9 November.

Kotler, P. (1965) 'Behavioural models for analyzing buyers', *Journal of Marketing,* October, pp. 37–45.

Lastovicka, J. and Gardner, D. (1979) 'Components of involvement', in Maloney, J. and Silverman, B. (eds) *Attitude research plays for high stakes*. Chicago: American Marketing Association.

Leavitt, H.J. (1958) *Managerial psychology,* Chicago: University of Chicago Press.

Maslow, A.H. (1958, 1970) *Motivations and personality,* London: Harper & Row.

Mauss, M. (1966) *The gift: a study of exchange in archaic societies*, London: Routledge.

Meyers-Levy, J. (1986) 'Gender differences in information processing: a selectivity interpretation', in P. Cafferatat and A.M. Tybout (eds) *Cognitive and affective responses to advertising*, Lexington MA: Lexington Books.

Meyers-Levy, J. and Maheswaran, D. (1991) 'Exploring differences in males' and females' processing strategy', *Journal of Consumer Research*, 18 (June), pp. 63–70.

Miller, J. (1983) *States of mind: conversations with psychological investigators*, London: BBC/Random House.

Newell, A., Shaw, J.C. and Simon, H.A. (1958) 'Elements of a theory of human problem solving', *Psychological Review*, 65, pp. 151–66.

Newell, A. and Simon, H.A. (1972) *Human Problem Solving*, Englewood Cliffs NJ: Prentice Hall.

O'Donohoe, S. and Tynan, C. (1997) 'Beyond the semiotic straitjacket: everyday experiences of advertising involvement' in S. Brown and D. Turley (eds) *Consumer research: postcards from the edge,* London: Routledge.

Olsen, J.P. (1976) *Ambiguity and choice in organization*, Bergen, Norway: Universitetsforlaget.

Petty, R.E., Cacioppo, J.T. and Schumann, D. (1983) 'Central and peripheral routes to advertising effectiveness: the moderating role of involvement', *Journal of Consumer Research*, 10 (2), pp. 135–46.

Petty, R.E. and Cacioppo, J.T. (1986) 'The elaboration likelihood model of persuasion', *Advances in Experimental Social Psychology*, 19, pp. 123–205.

Petty, R.E., Unnava, R. and Strathman, A.J. (1991) 'Theories of attitude change' in T.S. Robertson and H.H. Kassarjian (eds) *Handbook of consumer behaviour*, Englewood Cliffs NJ: Prentice Hall, pp. 241–280.

Riesman, D., Glazer, N. and Denny, D. (1950) *The lonely crowd: a study of the changing American character*, New Haven CT: Yale University Press.

Samuel, N.S., Li, E. and McDonald, H. (1996) 'The purchasing behaviour of Shanghai buyers of processed food and beverage products: implications for research on retail management', *International Journal of Retail and Distribution Management*, 24 (4), pp. 20–29.

Simon, H.A. (1957) *Models of man*, New York: Wiley.

Skinner, B.F. (1938) *The behavior of organisms: an experimental analysis*, New York: Appleton Century Crofts.

Skinner, B.F. (1948) *Walden two*, New York: Macmillan.

Skinner, B.F. (1974) *About behaviorism*, New York: Knopf.

Skinner, B.F. (1989) *Beyond freedom and dignity*, New York: Knopf.

Strong, E. K. (1925) *The Psychology of Selling and Advertising*, New York: McGraw-Hill.

Tversky, A. and Kahneman, D. (1974) 'Judgement under uncertainty: heuristics and biases', *Science*, 185, pp. 1124–31.

Watson, J.B. (1931) *Behaviourism*, London: Kegan Paul.

Weinstein, A. (1998) *Handbook of market segmentation: strategic targeting for business and technology firms*, Haworth Series in Segmented. Targeted and Customized Markets, Binghampton NY: Howarth Press, exhibit 8.3, p. 139.

4 INDUSTRIAL BUYER BEHAVIOUR

Bahrami, H. (1992) 'The emerging flexible organization: perspectives from Silicon Valley', *California Management Review*, summer, pp. 33–52.

Bahrami, H. and Evans, S. (1987) 'Strategy in high-technology firms', *California Management Review*, fall, pp. 51–66.

Bird, J. (1997) 'Hospital's computer cost cure', *Management Today*, December, pp. 82–5.

Dwyer, E.R., Schurr, P. and Oh, S. (1987) 'Developing buyer–seller relationships', *Journal of Marketing*, 51 (April), pp. 11–27.

Gupta, M. and Zhender, D. (1994) 'Outsourcing and its impact on operations strategy', *Production and Inventory Management Journal*, 35 (3), pp. 70–6.

Hakansson, H. and Snehota, I. (eds) (1995) *Developing relationships in business networks,* New York: Routledge.

Howard, J.A. and Sheth, J.N. (1969) *The theory of buyer behavior,* New York: Wiley.

Johnston, W.J. and Bonoma, T.V. (1981) 'The buying center: structure and interaction patterns', *Journal of Marketing*, 45 (summer), pp. 143–56.

Lewin, J.E. and Johnston, W.J. (1996) 'The effects of organizational restructuring on industrial buying behavior: 1990 and beyond', *Journal of Business and Industrial Marketing,* 11 (6), pp. 93–118.

Marsh, P. (2005) 'Baxi looks to Europe for expansion', *Financial Times*, 4 May, p. 24.

Robinson, P.J., Faris, C.W. and Wind, Y. (1967) *Industrial buying and creative marketing,* Boston MA: Allyn & Bacon.

Sheth, J.N. (1973) 'A model of industrial buyer behavior', *Journal of Marketing*, 37 (October), pp. 50–6.

Webster, F.E. and Wind, Y. (1972) 'A general model for understanding organizational buying behavior', *Journal of Marketing*, 36 (April), pp. 12–9.

Wilson, E.J. (1994) 'Advances in business marketing and purchasing: mapping how industry buys', *International Journal of Purchasing and Materials Management*, 30 (4), pp. 54–6.

Wilson, E.J. (1996) 'Theory transitions in organizational buying behavior research', *Journal of Business and Industrial Marketing*, 11 (6), pp. 7–20.

Witte, E. (1972) 'Field research on complex decision processes', *International Studies of Management and Organization*, 2, pp. 156–82.

5 MARKETING RESEARCH

A.G. Barr (2003) Annual report and accounts, 2002.

A.G. Barr (2005) Annual report and accounts, 2004, www.agbarr.co.uk/agbarr/agb_inest.nsf.

American Marketing Association (1987) *Marketing definitions,* Chicago: AMA.

British Institute of Management (1962) *Definition of marketing research,* London: British Institute of Management.

Chaffin, J. and van Duyn, A. (2005) 'Nielsen focuses on getting the measure of TV ratings challenge', *Financial Times,* 18 November, p. 33.

Chisnall, P.M. (2005) *Marketing research,* 7th. edn, London: McGraw-Hill, p. 9.

Cravens, D.W. and Woodruff, R.B. (1986) *Marketing,* Reading MA: Addison-Wesley.

Delens, A.H.R. (1950) *Principles of market research,* St Albans and London: Crosby Lockwood Staples.

Donkin, R. (1997) 'No relish for cheese and pickle sandwich', *Financial Times,* 28 October in S. Wright *The Financial Times Marketing Casebook,* London: Pitman (1994), pp. 54–5.

ESOMAR (1997) 'Survey of world market research', Amsterdam: European Society for Opinion and Marketing Research (ESOMAR).

Greenbaum, T.L. (1998) *The handbook of focus group research,* 2nd edn, London: Sage.

Hart, N. and Stapleton, J. (1981) *Glossary of marketing terms,* 2nd edn, Oxford: Heinemann.

Honomichl, J. (2004) 'Honomichl global top 25', *Marketing News,* Chicago: American Marketing Association, August, pp. H3–H4.

Honomichl, J. (2005) 'Honomichl global top 25', *Marketing News,* Chicago: American Marketing Association, 15 August, pp. H3–H4.

JICNARS/RSL (1991) *The 1991 JICNARS/RSL marketing data book,* Harrow: Research Services.

Kotler, P. (1997) *Marketing management: analysis, planning, implementation and control,* 9th edn, Englewood Cliffs NJ: Prentice Hall.

Lehman, D.R. (1985) *Market research and analysis,* 2nd edn, Homewood IL: Irwin.

Mackenzie, Y. (2004) 'UK MR industry grows 2.8 per cent in 2003', *Research* (Market Research Society), May, p. 5.

Market Research Society (1989) *The members' handbook,* London: Market Research Society.

Market Research Society (1997) 'TV audience measurement', *Research,* London: Market Research Society.

Market Research Society (2005a) *Code of conduct,* London: Market Research Society.

Market Research Society (2005b) *The research buyer's guide 2005,* London: Market Research Society.

Market Research Society (2006) *The research buyer's guide 2006,* London: Market Research Society.

Parasuraman, A. (1991) *Marketing research,* 2nd edn, Reading MA: Addison Wesley.

Piercy, N. and Evans, M. (1983) *Managing marketing information,* Beckenham: Croom Helm.

Silverman, G. (2005) 'Why the boardroom believes in reality television', *Financial Times,* 1 March, p. 13.

Stone, M.A. (2005) 'Contribution of marketing research to strategic marketing in Russia', cameo case in P. Chisnall, *Marketing research,* 7th edn, London: McGraw-Hill, pp. 458–9.

Tarran, B. (2005) 'Aegis confirms interest of £1.5bn suitar', *Research,* 473 (October), p. 4.

Tull, D.S. and Hawkins, D.I. (1990) *Marketing research: meaning, measurement, and method,* 5th edn, New York: Macmillan.

USA Today (1989) 'Winging it at McDonald's', *USA Today,* 5/9, p. 1b.

Wentz, W.B. (1972) *Marketing research: management and methods,* New York: Harper & Row, ch. 1, p. 1.

Useful website
www.research-live.com

6 SEGMENTATION, TARGETING AND POSITIONING

Brassington, F. and Pettitt S. (1997) *Principles of marketing,* London: Financial Times Management, pp. 195–6.

Chisnall, P.M. (1995) *Consumer behaviour,* 3rd edn, New York: McGraw-Hill.

Erikson, E.H. (1965) *Childhood and society*, Harmondsworth: Penguin.

Falkingham, J. and Victor, C. (1991) 'The myth of the Woopie? Incomes, the elderly, and targeting welfare,' Discussion Paper WSP/ 55, Welfare State Programme, London: Suntory-Toyota International, Centre for Economics and Related Disciplines, London School of Economics.

Johnston, J. (2005) 'Church's hotel in Israel "taking cash away from HIV/Aids work in Africa", *Sunday Herald,* 1 May.

Kavanagh, M. (1995) 'Bright future for a grey sector', *Marketing*, 19 January, pp. 29–31.

Lansing, J.B. and Morgan, J.N. (1955) 'Consumer finances over the life cycle', *Consumer Behaviour*, 11, ed. L.H. Clark, New York: New York University Press.

Mitchell, A. (1990) 'Age of reason', *Marketing*, 22 March, pp. 29–31.

Whiteford, P. and Kennedy, S. (1995) *Incomes and living standards of older People,* Department of Social Security Research Report No. 34, London: HMSO.

7 BRANDING

Aaker, J. (1995) 'Measuring the human characteristics of a brand: a brand personality hierarchy', *Advances in Consumer Research*, 22, pp. 393–4.

Aaker, J.L. (1997) 'Dimensions of brand personality', *Journal of Marketing Research*, 34 (3), pp. 347–56.

Aaker, J.L. (1999), 'The malleable self: the role of self-expression in persuasion', *Journal of Marketing Research*, 36 (2), pp. 45–57.

Allen, D.E. and Olson, G. (1995) 'Conceptualizing and creating brand personality: a narrative theory and approach', *Advances in Consumer Research*, 22, pp. 392–93.

Anon. (2005) 'French Connection lists profits warning', *Guardian*, 9 December.

Anon. (2006) 'Kung-fu lesbian advertisement', *News Telegraph*, 16 February.

Belk, Russell W. (1988) 'Possessions and the extended self', *Journal of Consumer Research*, 15 (September), pp. 139–68.

Brady, D., Hof, R.D., Reinhardt, A., Ihlwan, M., Holmes, S. and Capell, K.K. (2004) 'The *Business Week*/Interbrand ranking of the world's most valuable brands shows the power of passionate consumers', *Business Week*, 9 August, i3895: 58.

Buzzell, R.D. and Gale, B. (1987) *The PIMS principles: linking strategy to performance*, New York: Free Press; London: Collier Macmillan.

Clark, E. (1988) *The want makers,* London: Hodder & Stoughton.

Cornelissen, J. and Harris, P. (2001) 'The corporate identity metaphor: perspectives, problems and prospects', *Journal of Marketing Management*, 17, pp. 49–71.

Csikszenmihalyi, Milahy and Rochberg-Halton, Eugene (1981, 1991) *The meaning of things: domestic symbols and the self*, Cambridge: Cambridge University Press.

Day, G.S. (1969), 'A two-dimensional concept of brand loyalty', *Journal of Advertising Research*, 21, pp. 30.

Dolich, I.J. (1969) 'Congruence relationship between self image and product brands', *Journal of Marketing Research*, 6 (1), pp. 80–4.

Doyle, P. (1998) *Marketing management and strategy*, Englewood Cliffs NJ: Prentice-Hall.

Ehrenberg, A. (2001) 'Marketing: romantic or realistic?' *Marketing Research*, summer, pp. 40–2.

Ehrenberg, A. and Goodhart, P. (2000) 'New brands: near-instant loyalty', *Journal of Marketing Management*, 16, pp. 607–617.

Ehrenberg, A.S.C. and Uncles, M.D. (1999) *Understanding Diriclet-type markets*, London: South Bank Business School.

Eliott, R. and Wattanasuwan, K. (1998) 'Brands as symbolic resources for the construction of identity', *International Journal of Advertising*, 17 (May), pp. 131–45.

Erikson, E.H. (1968) *Identity youth and crisis*, London: Faber.

Falk, P. (1997) 'The geneaology of advertising', in Sulkenen, P., Holmwood, J., Radner, H., Schulze, G. (eds) *Constructing the new consumer society*, Basingstoke: Macmillan, pp. 81–108.

Fournier, S. (1995) 'The brand as relationship partner: an alternative view of brand personality', *Advances in Consumer Research*, 22, p. 393.

Fournier, S. (1998) 'Consumers and their brands: developing relationship theory in consumer research', *Journal of Consumer Research*, 24 (4), pp. 343–73.

Foxall, G. (1996) *Consumers in Context: the BPM process*, International Thomson Business Press.

Foxall, G. (2005) *Understanding consumer choice*, London: Palgrave, table 7.4, p. 136.

Govers, P.C.M. and Schoormans, J.P.L. (2005) 'Product personality and its influence on consumer preference', *Journal of Consumer Marketing*, 22 (4).

Ha, C.L. (1988) 'The theory of reasoned action applied to brand loyalty', *Journal of Product and Brand Management*, 7 (1), pp. 51–61.

Hebdige, D. (1988) *Hiding in the light,* London and New York: Routledge.

Heider, F. (1958) *The psychology of interpersonal relations*, New York: Wiley.

Hirsh, E., Hedlund, S. and Schweizer, M. (2003) 'Reality is perception: the truth about car brands', *Strategy and Business*, 32.

Klein, N. (2000) *No logo*, London: Flamingo.

Landon, E.L. (1974), 'Self-concept, ideal self-concept, and consumer purchase intentions', *Journal of Consumer Research*, 1 (2), pp. 44–51.

Levitt, T. (1986) *The marketing imagination*, New York: Free Press.

Levy, S.J. (1959), 'Symbols for sale', *Harvard Business Review*, 37 (4), pp. 117–24.

McKay, G. (1996) *Senseless acts of beauty: cultures of resistance since the sixties*, London: Verso.

Maffesoli, M. (1996) *The time of the tribes the decline of individualism in mass society*, London: Sage.

Malhotra, N.K. (1988) 'Self-concept and product choice: an integrated perspective', *Journal of Economic Psychology*, 9 (1), pp. 1–28.

Mantoya, P. (2004) *The personal branding phenomenon,* www.PeterMantoya.com.

McAlexander, J.H. and Schouten, J. (2002) 'Building brand community', *Journal of Marketing,* 66, pp. 38-54.

Melander, C. (2005) 'Hog wild', *Williamette week online*, http://www.wweek.com/html/cbuzz 111297.html.

Muniz, A.M.J. and O'Guinn, T.C. (2001) 'Brand community', *Journal of Consumer Research,* 27 (4), pp. 412–432.

Newcomb, T.L. (1948) *Social psychology*, Hinsdale IL: Dryden Press.

Newcomb, T.M. (1947, 1952, 1958) 'Attitude development as a function of reference groups: the Bennington study' in Maccoby, E. Newcomb, T. and Hartley, E. (eds) *Readings in social psychology*, New York: Holt, Rinehart & Winston, pp. 265–75.

Petty, R.E., Cacioppo J. and Schumann, J. (1983) 'Central and peripheral routes to advertising effectiveness: the moderating role of involvement', *Journal of Consumer Research*, 10 (2), pp. 135–46.

Reynolds, F.D., Darden, W.R. and Martin, W.S. (1975), 'Developing an image of the store-loyal customer: a life style analysis to probe a neglected market', *Journal of Retailing*, 50 (4), pp. 73–84.

Rogers, C. (1980) *A way of being*, Boston MA: Houghton Mifflin.

Schouten, J.W. and McAlexander, J.H. (1995) 'Subcultures of consumption: an ethnography of new bikers', *Journal of Consumer Research,* 22 (1), pp. 62–74.

Sheth, J.N. (1968) 'A factor analytic model of brand loyalty', *Journal of Marketing Research*, 5, pp. 398.

Sirgy, M.J. (1982) 'Self-concept in consumer behavior: a critical review', *Journal of Consumer Research*, 9 (3), pp. 287–300.

Skinner, B.F. (1974) *About behaviourism*, New York: Knopf.

Wells, M. (2001) 'Cult brands: how companies manage loyal fans of their products', *Forbes*, 16 April, p. 198.

Williamson, J. (1978) Decoding advertisements: ideology and meaning in advertising, London and New York: Marion Boyars.

8 PRODUCT

Achembaum, A. (1974) 'Market testing: using the market place as a laboratory' in R. Ferber (ed.) *Handbook of Marketing Research*, Maidenhead: McGraw-Hill, pp. 4–32.

Advertising Association (2005) *Marketing Pocket Book 2005*, London: *Advertising Association*.

Bennett, P.D. (1988) *Marketing*, Maidenhead: McGraw-Hill.

Boyd, H., Westfall, R. and Stasch, S.F. (1989) *Marketing research,* 7th edn, Homewood IL and Boston MA: Irwin.

Brassington, F. and Pettitt, S. (1997) *Principles of marketing,* London: Pitman.

Cadbury (1991) 'Cadbury's and new product development', Birmingham: Cadbury.

Cadbury (2004) 'Cadbury: new product development', Birmingham: Cadbury.

Cadbury Schweppes (2005) 'Annual review and summary financial statement 2004', London: *Cadbury Schweppes,* p. 1.

Cannon, T. (1992) *Basic marketing*, 3rd edn, London: Cassell.

Czinkota, M. and Kotabe, M. (1990) 'Product development the Japanese way', *Journal of Business Strategy,* November–December, pp. 31–6.

Dibb, S., Simkin, L., Pride, W.M. and Ferrell, O.C. (1997) *Marketing concepts and strategies,* 3rd edn, Boston MA: Houghton Mifflin.

Dibb, S., Simkin, L., Pride, W.M. and Ferrell, O.C. (2001) *Marketing concepts and strategies,* 4th edn, Boston MA: Houghton Mifflin.

Doyle, P. (1994) *Marketing management and strategy,* 2nd edn, London: Prentice Hall.

Hill, E. and O'Sullivan, T. (1996) *Marketing,* London: Longman.

Hinde, S. (1995) 'Virgin moves from selling pop to PEPs', *Sunday Times,* 1 January.

Kotler, P. and Armstrong, G. (1996) *Principles of marketing,* 7th edn, Englewood Cliffs NJ: Prentice Hall.

Kotler, P. and Armstrong, G. (2001) *Principles of marketing,* 9th edn, Englewood Cliffs NJ: Prentice Hall, p. G-10.

Lancaster, G.A. and Massingham, L. (1999) *Essentials of Marketing*, London: McGraw-Hill.

Lancaster, G.A. and Massingham, L. (2001) *Essentials of Marketing*, 3rd edn, London: McGraw-Hill.

Market Research Society (2005) *The research buyer's guide, UK and Ireland, 2005*, London: Market Research Society.

Marsh, P. (2005a) 'Dumpy bottles for baby prove a world beater', *Financial Times*, 28 July, p. 25.

Marsh, V. (2005b) 'The merino makes a break from the flock for a life of luxury', *Financial Times*, 17 August, p. 11.

Nuttall, C. (2006) 'Smooth dinosaur senses way forward for robots', 6 February, p. 24.

Proctor, T. (1997) *Essentials of marketing research*, Harlow: Pearson FT Prentice Hall.

Rees, J. (1992) 'Getting hot ideas from customers', *Fortune,* 18 May, pp. 86–7.

Twiss, B. (1992) *Managing technological innovation*, 4th edn, London: Pitman, pp. 27–9.

Watson, J. (1998) 'Feeding the Furby frenzy', *Scotland on Sunday*, 20 November, p. 13.

Wilson, M.S. and Gilligan, C. (1997) *Strategic marketing management: planning, implementation and control*, 2nd edn, Oxford: Butterworth Heinemann.

9 PRICING

Bolger, A. (2005) 'Cashmere producers ready to take on Tesco's challenge', *Financial Times*, 24–5 December, p. 3.

Boxell, J. (2005) 'BAE forced into cut-price sale', *Financial Times*, 31 December, p. 15.

Dyer, G. (2005) 'Car-price war looms in China as Shanghai VW cuts prices', *Financial Times*, 10 August, p. 19.

Griffiths, J. (2005) 'Drivers face steep decline in value of cars', *Financial Times*, 9 April, p. 3.

Mackintosh, J. (2005) 'Rover dumped cars on dealers in final months', *Financial Times*, 25 April, p. 6.

McCall, J.B. and Warrington, M.B. (1989) *Marketing by agreement: a cross-cultural approach to business negotiation,* Chichester: Wiley.

Marsh, P. (2003) 'Dust is settling on the Dyson market clean-up', *Financial Times*, 12 December, p. 12.

Palmer, P. (2005) 'Bargain hunters stocking up', *Financial Times,* 26–7 November, p. 4.

10 PROMOTION

Anon. (1980) *Investors' Chronicle,* 8 August.

Anon. (1983) *Daily Express*, 3 August.

Anon. (1884) *Financial Times,* 10 March.

Anon. (1984) *Financial Times,* 13 April.

Bird, D. (1997) 'Image-conscious car makers take eyes off the road', *Marketing*, 20 March, p. 15.

Chaffee, S.H. (1986) 'Mass media and interpersonal channels: competitive, convergent or complementary?' in Gumpert, G. and Cathcart, R. (eds), *Inter media: interpersonal communication in a media world*, 3rd edn, New York: Oxford University Press.

Colley, R.H. (1961) *Defining advertising goals for measuring advertising results,* New York: Association of National Advertisers.

Davidson, M.P. (1992) *The consumerist manifesto: advertising in postmodern times,* London: Routledge.

Denny, N. (1995) 'Databases see dawn of glory', *Marketing*, 27 April, p. 9.

Duyn, van, A. (2005) 'Internet causes "fundamental shift in advertising"', *Financial Times*, 15 August, p. 21.

Eco, U. (1976) *A theory of semiotics,* Bloomington IN: Indiana University Press.

Eco, U. (1986) 'Towards a semiological guerilla warfare' in *Travels in hyperreality*, trans. William Weaver, London: Pan Books, ch. 4, pp. 135–50.

Ehrenberg, A. (2000) 'Repetitive advertising and the consumer', *Journal of Advertising Research*, December, pp. 39–48.

Ehrenberg, A. and Goodhart, P. (2000) 'New brands: near-instant loyalty', *Journal of Marketing Management*, 16, pp. 607–17.

Franzen, G. (1994) *Advertising effectiveness: findings from empirical research,* Henley on Thames: NTC Publications.

Gerson, V. (1998) 'Right on target', *Bank marketing*, 30 (3), pp. 24–9.

Jones, J.P. (1991) 'Over promise and under delivery', *Marketing and Research Today*, 19 November, pp. 195–203.

Katz, E. and Lazarsfield, P.F. (1955) *Personal influence,* Glencoe IL: Free Press.

Katz, E. (1957) 'The two-step flow of communication: an up-to-date report on an hypothesis', *Public Opinion Quarterly,* 21, pp. 61–78.

Katz, E. (1987) 'Communication research since Lazarsfield', *Public Opinion Quarterly*, 51, pp. S25–S45.

Kryzston, M. (1996) 'Are you really practicing marketing database? Four steps toward dynamic customer management', *Direct Marketing*, 58 (10), pp. 48–52.

Lavidge, R.J. and Steiner, G.A. (1961) 'A model for predictive measurement of advertising effectiveness', *Journal of Marketing*, October, p. 61.

MacMillan, G. (1996) 'Understanding dataculture', *Campaign*, 6 September, p. 42.

McDonald, C. (1992) *How advertising works*, London: Advertising Association in association with NTC Publications.

Monge, P.R. (1987) 'The network level of analysis' in C.R. Berger and S.H. Chaffee (eds), *Handbook of communication science,* Newbury Park CA: Sage.

Murphy, C. (2004) 'Madame Tussaud's seeks star partners', *Financial Times*, 5 August, p. 10.

Newman, K. (1994) *Marketing*, 26–7 October.

O'Donohoe, S. (1997) 'Raiding the postmodern pantry: advertising intertextuality and the young adult audience', *European Journal of Marketing*, 31 (3/4), pp. 234–54.

Richards, A. (1994) 'First Direct', *Marketing*, 27 October, p. 26.

Rogers, E.M. (1983) *Diffusion of Innovations,* New York: Free Press.

Rogers, E.M. and Kincaid, D.L. (1981) *Communication networks: towards a paradigm for research,* New York: Free Press.

Rogers, E.M. and Shoemaker, F.F. (1971) *Communication of innovation*, New York: Free Press.

Rogers, E.M. (1962) *Diffusion of innovations*, New York: Free Press.

Shimp, T.A. (1997) *Advertising, promotion, and supplemental aspects of integrated marketing communications*, 4th edn, Orlando FL: Dryden Press.

Silverman, G. (2005) 'Traditional pitches lose out', *Financial Times*, 19 April, p. 15.

Strong, E.K. (1925) *The psychology of selling,* New York: McGraw-Hill.

Wall, S.J. (1997) 'Creating strategists', *Training and Development*, 51 (5), pp. 75–9.

Widgery, R.A., Madhukar, G. and Nataraajan, R. (1997) 'The impact of employment status on married women's perceptions of advertising', *Journal of Advertising Research*, 37 (1), pp. 54–63.

Windahl, S., Signitzer, B. and Olson, J.T. (1992) *Using communication theory,* London: Sage.

Williamson, J. (1978) *Decoding advertisements,* New York: Marion Boyars.

11 PLACE: CHANNELS OF DISTRIBUTION

Advertising Association (1998) *Marketing Pocket Book*, London: Advertising Association.

Advertising Association (2005) *Marketing Pocket Book 2005*, London: Advertising Association.

Advertising Association (2005) *European Marketing Pocket Book 2005*, London: Advertising Association.

Alexander, N. (1997*) International retailing*, Oxford: Blackwell.

Blythman, J. (2004) *Shopped: the shocking power of British supermarkets*, London: Harper Perennial.

Bolger, A. (2005) 'Second-hand outlets a model for first-rate results', *Financial Times*, 29 June, p. 5.

Dibb, S., Simkin, L., Pride, W.M. and Ferrell, O.C. (1994) *Marketing: concepts and strategies,* 2nd edn, Boston MA: Houghton Mifflin.

Fernie, J., Fernie, S. and Moore, C. (2003) *Principles of retailing*, Oxford: Butterworth Heinemann.

Franchise Development Services (1995) *United Kingdom Franchise Directory,* Norwich: Franchise Development Services Ltd.

Grant, J. (2005) 'Feelings soften towards hard discounters', *Financial Times*, 29 August, p. 22.

Healey & Baker Research Services (1995) *Sunday trading*, London: Healey & Baker Research Services.

Healey & Baker Research Services (1996) *Sunday trading,* London: Healey & Baker Research Services.

Hollinger, P. (1998) 'Carrefour's revolutionary', *Financial Times*, 4 December, p. 13.

Johnston, R. and Lawrence, P.R. (1988) 'Beyond vertical integration: the rise of the value-adding partnerships', *Harvard Business Review*, July–August, pp. 94–101.

Kotler, P. (1997) *Marketing management: analysis, planning, implementation and control*, 9th edn, Englewood Cliffs NJ: Prentice Hall, ch. 18, pp. 529–61.

REFERENCES ▦ ▦ ▦ ■

Kotler, P. and Armstrong, G. (1997) *Marketing: an introduction*, 4th international edn, Englewood Cliffs NJ: Prentice Hall, ch. 11, pp. 351–90, and ch. 12, pp. 391–424.

Kotler, P. and Armstrong, G. (2001) *Principles of marketing*, 9th edn, Englewood Cliffs NJ: Prentice Hall, ch. 12, pp. 429–69 and ch. 13, pp. 471–507.

Kotler, P. Armstrong, G., Saunders, J. and Wong, V. (1999) *Principles of marketing: an introduction*, 2nd European edn, Englewood Ciffs NJ: Prentice Hall, ch. 21, pp. 900–7.

McCammon, B.C. (1970) 'Perspectives for distribution programming' in L.I. Bucklin (ed.) *Vertical Marketing Systems*, Glenview IL: Scott Forseman, p. 32.

Palmer, M. (2006) 'Online shopping sparkles for retailers', *Financial Times,* 20 January, pp. 1 and 3.

Pickard, J. (2005) 'Growing trend sees warehouses swell', *Financial Times*, 17 August, p. 25.

Rigby, E. (2005a) 'Price cuts fuel supermarket war', *Financial Times*, 4 April, p. 21.

Rigby, E. (2005b) 'Prosperous Tesco takes retailing to a new level', *Financial Times,* 21 September, p. 23.

Rigby, E. (2005c) 'Tesco and Carrefour confirm their store swap', *Financial Times,* 1–2 October, p. 16.

Rigby, E. (2005d) 'J. Sainsbury sees testing times ahead', *Financial Times*, 17 November, p. 21.

Rigby, E. (2005e) 'Tesco to open online grocery warehouse', *Financial Times*, 27 November, p. 22.

Rigby, E. (2005f) 'Asda pins future on price cutting', *Financial Times*, 14 December, p. 22.

Tassell, T. (2004) 'Affluence in effluent from Dyno-Rod sale', *Financial Times,* 2–3 October, p. M2.

Urbanski, A. (1988) 'The franchise option', *Sales and Marketing Management*, February, pp. 28–33.

Urry, M. (1990) 'Superstores where margin increases fuel profits growth', *Financial Times*, 2 September, p. 8.

12 VIRTUAL MARKETING

Anon. (2006) 'Peer to peer action forces drastic measures'. *Computer Weekly*, 68 (7 February).

Anon. (2005a) 'Roper Youth Report', *GfK NOP Consumer Trends*, New York, NOP.

Anon. (2005b) 'Crowned at last', *Economist*, 8 (2 April), pp. 6–15.

Chatterjee, P. Hoffma, D.L. and Novak, T.P. (2003) 'Modeling the clickstream: implications for Web-based advertising efforts,' *Marketing Science,* 22 (4), pp. 520–41.

Csikszentmihalyi, M. (1977) *Beyond boredom and anxiety*, 2nd edn, San Francisco: Jossey-Bass.

Cunningham, N. (2006) 'My advice to Sony: kick content business out of bed', *Financial Times*, letter page, 9 January, p. 16.

Frank, R.H. (1990) 'Rethinking rational choice', in R. Friedland and A.F. Robertson (eds.) *Beyond the marketplace: rethinking economy and society*, New York: Aldine de Gruyter, pp. 52–88.

Greene, J. (2004) 'Whistling a different iTune', *Business Week*, 8 November, issue 3907, p. 148.

Hawfield, K. and Lyons, E., http://ecommerce.vanderbilt.edu/research_studentprojects.htm.

Hoffman, D.L. and Novak, T.P. (2005) 'Consumer thinking style, task congruence, and performance: new measures of task-specific experiential and rational cognition', http://ecommerce.vanderbilt.edu/research_papers.htm.

Hoffman, D.L. (2005) 'Can we live without the Internet? Towards a model of internet indispensability', presented at Colloquium on Information Society and Technology, New York University, 22 April.

Hoffman, D.L. and Novak, T.P. (1996) 'Marketing in hypermedia computer-mediated environments: conceptual foundations,' *Journal of Marketing*, 60 (July), pp. 50–68.

Hoffman, D.L. and Novak, T.P. (1999) 'The evolution of the digital divide: examining the relationship of race to Internet access and usage over time', 18 May, Sloan Center for Retailing, Elab manuscripts, Venderbilt University.

Hoffman, D.L. and Novak, T.P. (2003) 'A conceptual framework for considering Web-based business models and potential revenue streams', Sloan Centre for Internet Retailing, Vanderbilt University, December.

Hoffman, D.L., Kalsbeek, W.D. and Novak, T.P. (1996) *Internet and web use in the United States: baselines for commercial development*, www2000.ogsm.vanderbilt.edu/papers/internet [lowbar]demos[lowbar]july9[lowbar]1996.html.

Hoffman, D.L., Novak, T.P. and Venkatesh, A. (2004) 'Has the Internet become indispensable?' *Communications of the ACM*, 47 (7), pp. 37–42.

Hoffman, D.L., Novak, T.P. and Yung, Y.F. (1998) *Measuring the flow construct in online environments: a structural modeling approach*, May. Project 2000.

Jaffe, T. (1998) 'Early birds: them that have, git. Look who cleaned up in Amazon.com', *Forbes*, 161 (9), pp. 47–51.

Kraut, R., Lundmark, V., Patterson, M., Kiesler, S., Mukopadhyay, T. and Scherlis, W. (1999) 'Internet paradox: a social technology that reduces social involvement and psychological well-being?' *American Psychologist*, 53 (9), pp. 1017–31.

Muhanna, W., Campbell, C. and Ray, G. (2005) 'Search and collusion in electronic markets', *Management Science*, 51 (3), pp. 497–507.

Nie, N.H. and Erbring, L. (2000) 'Internet and society: a preliminary report', Stanford Institute for the Quantitative Study of Society (SIQSS), 17 February.

Schrage, M., Peppers, D., Rogers, M. and Shapiro, R.D. (1993) 'Is Advertising finally Dead?' http://advertising.utexas.edu/research/papers/index.asp.

Stross, R.E. (1997) 'Why Barnes & Noble may crush Amazon', *Fortune*, 136 (6), pp. 248–50.

Williamson, O.E. 1975. *Markets and hierarchies: analysis and antitrust implications*, New York: Free Press.

Willis, C. (1998) 'Does Amazon.com really matter?' *Forbes*, 161 (7), pp. 55–9.

13 MARKETING PLANNING AND IMPLEMENTATION

Beecroft, J. (2005) 'Oat-meals on wheels', *Daily Mail*, 22 August, p. 18.

British Sandwich Association (BSA) (2005) Sandwich facts and figures to make your mouth water', 1/5: www.sandwich.org.uk.

Cooper, J. and Lane, P. (1997) *Practical marketing planning*, Basingstoke: Macmillan.

Datamonitor (2003) 'Bakery and cereals in the UK to 2006', 1/1: DMCM0327.

Datamonitor (2006) 'Bakery and cereals in the UK to 2006', 1/1: DMCM0327.

Harvey, F. and Bolger, A. (2005) 'Milk sales boosted by popularity of porridge', *Financial Times*, 20 May, p. 5.

Hiscott, G. (2005) 'So who's been eating our (organic) porridge?' *Daily Express*, 26 August, p. 3.

McDonald, M. (2002) *Marketing plans: how to prepare them: how to use them,* 5th edn, Oxford: Butterworth Heinemann.

McDonald, M. and Payne, A. (1996) *Marketing planning for services,* Oxford: Butterworth Heinemann.

Rebelo, D. (2006) 'NPD focus for convenience snacks', Datamonitor and www.nutraingredients. com (30 January 2006).

Sawers, C. (2005) 'Porridge is the new fast food', *Scotsman*, 17 August, p. 37.

Stone, A. (2005) 'Stoats Porridge Bars' business plan', (unpublished) (personal intimation).

INDEX

Note: page numbers in italic denote references to illustrations/tables.